CW00672944

THE DAMNED BALKANS

– a refugee road trip

(*humanitarne mućke*)

PROKLETIJE, LONDON

ISBN: 978-1-5272-1045-5

Cover: Battle of Stubica, by Krsto Hegedušić, 1939[1]

Showing the widest extent of medieval Croatia (925), Bosnia (1390), and Serbia (1355).

FOREWORD

I had been a career policeman in Durham and got the taste for travelling when I went on a secondment to Hong Kong in 1977. I joined the newly set up Independent Commission Against Corruption & worked there for 7 years. While representing Hong Kong on a cricket tour in Bangladesh I saw abject poverty for the first time in my life & I think that planted the seed which almost a decade later set me on the road of a second career as an Aid Worker.

It was at the end of 1992 the Balkans, Bosnia & Herzegovina (BiH) and Croatia in particular, became a very important part of my life, when I started to work with a small British Charity called Feed the Children (FTC) which was based in Reading. Initially working close to the Dalmatia Coast from a base in Split, it only took one trip to the central Bosnian town of Vitez, to realise that was where the greater need was. We went to Vitez because that was the base of "The Cheshires" the first British Regiment to be sent to BiH as Peace Keepers. With their charismatic Colonel, Bob Stewart (now an MP) they gave the FTC team fantastic support, and protection in their camp when necessary.

Unlike many preceding emergencies, man-made or natural, this was in Europe. Zagreb, the capital of Croatia was only 2 hours by air from London. To get aid to Split by road was easily achieved – getting it to the most needy in BiH was however a very different story! The pre-war roads were either closed because of fighting or bridges had been blown up. Country tracks, similar to those rally driver face in the Welsh or Scottish hills, became the main access routes into and through BiH. What had been a 3-4 hour journey pre-war often needed an overnight stop to get from Split to Vitez.

Being a policeman was a great help in many aspects of my aid work life, seeing people in very difficult situations & working to help them. However, nothing could have prepared me for the scenes I witnessed both during the war with people of all ages in desperate need, and years later when seeing mass graves being excavated while working on the Missing Persons issue.

I was the father figure of the FTC team, as most of the men & women who joined were decades younger than me. John Farebrother was one of the young men who joined the team, intent on helping his European neighbours in their time of great need. Most of the team, including myself, had not been in a war zone before, or witnessed people existing in such dreadful and degrading circumstances.

The weather in the winter was savagely cold, temperatures of -15C to -20C every year, snow & ice making the roads extremely dangerous. In summer it would get to +35C or higher, yet the team worked relentlessly to get the aid through.

All wars are terrible, bringing death & injury, destruction and great sadness, with most often the civilian population suffering the greatest hardship - as we are seeing in Syria now. One of the saddest conflicts in BiH was when Muslim fought Muslim in the far North-west, the so called UN Safe Haven of Bihac.

Followers of local businessman, Fikret Abdić, backed by the Croatian Serbs, fought against the Bosnian Muslim army (Armija BiH). Abdić's army was forced out of BiH territory, across the border into the surrounding part of Croatia that was held by Croatian Serbs. Some 30,000 displaced people took shelter there, half in a war destroyed town called Turanj, and the other half in a twin sited disused chicken farm at Batnoga. The conditions in both locations were truly awful and the FTC team took many truckloads of emergency aid during the time the refugees were there.

Some months later they returned to the town of Velika Kladuša, within the Bihać pocket only to become refugees again in late summer 1995. This time however it was not their allies the Croatian Serbs, who controlled the area they fled to. The Croatian Serbs had been defeated by the Croatian Government Forces and there wasn't great sympathy for the Abdić followers, as they had sided with the Croatian army's enemies.

They "made camp" in a valley with very few houses but became a small town known as Kuplensko Camp. There were some tents but shelters were made from all manner of things, crudely made bricks, wooden pallets, corrugated iron sheets, cardboard & plastic sheets nailed to wooden plans. With winter approaching UNHCR did not want NGO's like FTC to assist the refugees, saying they could not stay there during the winter. But stay they did along with John Farebrother & other members of the FTC team. The aid trucks that had made so many trips to Turanj & Batnoga delivered their aid to Kuplensko.

Along the valley John & the team organised a number of delivery points, each with a designated number of beneficiaries. With a donation from another NGO candle making machines, with the necessary wax crystals were delivered by FTC, so the people had some light as there was no electricity. John is an excellent linguist and not only learned the language but was frequently taken to be a local by people who did not know him. He still has many friends among the local people he met during his time in Kuplensko.

Kuplensko was a desperately sad place and an awful sight to see the plight of so many European people living in conditions that many animals wouldn't survive in. As a former sportsman I found it terribly sad to see so many young men with one or both legs missing, many because their legs had been blown off by a land mine or anti-personnel mine. However, others had their legs amputated because there weren't the medical facilities to treat serious injuries without the risk of infection setting in.

Being an aid worker during such times and in such conditions certainly wasn't easy for John and his colleagues. Quite naturally it was very upsetting to see people, particularly babies, children, women & old people suffering in such a way. However, to a man and woman, the people who made up the FTC teams still talk about it as one of, if not the most amazing and rewarding period of their lives.

I call it the aid worker's "fix" – seeing people in awful conditions with great needs and the efforts of you & your team mates make life easier for them. The smiles, or indeed sometimes, the tears of gratitude are what it's all about.

John Farebrother knows that feeling better than most, as he endured the shocking conditions along with the refugees and, 20 years on still remembers it as if it were yesterday. If it were tomorrow, I know he would do the same again.

Gordon Bacon OBE (Former Country Director of FTC BiH)

13 February 2016

PREGOVOR

Ako pitate mene, biti izbjeglica je osjećaj gorkog beznađa, slatke volje za životom i naivne nade u čudo. Shvatiti ih u potpunosti mogu samu rijetki oni koji su kroz to iskustvo prošli. I, naravno, John Farebrother.

Tjeran nekim urođenim nagonom da nesebično pomogne nemoćnima dok bježe od progona i smrti, blagoslovljen dobrotom na humanoj misiji, on je postao svjedokom krutih i krvavih vremena, kao zalutali prolaznik kroz tuđe tragedije koje su nekako postale i njegove. U malim izbjegličkim sobama i šatorima, napućenim izbjegličkim kampovima, u paklu ljudskih tragedija i smrti, John je uvijek dočekivan osmijehom, kao prijatelj.

U ljeto 1995, kad sam kao poraženi i razoružani vojnik bio stjeran u žicu, izolovan i bez prava, iscrpljen od neizvjesnosti, i umoran od straha da me bar ne ubiju pred očima mojih roditelja, John je žrtvovao svoj život, da bi spasio moj. Njegova dijela čvst su dokaz da ljudskost i čojstvo itekako postoje.

Upoznali smo se pred kraj Bosanskog rata u proljeće 1995. Šta je Johna dovelo do našeg rata a šta mene da sa 19 godina ratujem u ratu kojeg baš i nisam razumio je duga priča, ali pod tim nesretnim okolnostima smo se sreli. Baš kao i mnoge druge stvari u ratu, uključujući i smrt i trenutke kad smo je varali, naše upoznavanje je bila puka slučajnost.

U to vrijeme služio sam u 2. jurišnoj brigadi Narodne Odbrane, pubunjeničke vojske Autonomne pokrajine Zapadna Bosna. Tih godina sam bio u opasnom društvu. Moj komadant je bio bivši legionar, Milorad Ulemek Legija, koji danas služi 40 godina robije kao organizator ubistva Predsjednika vlade Srbije, Zorana Đinđića. John je tek došao u Veliku Kladušu, gradić u ratu zahvaćenoj sjeverozapadnoj Bosni, radeći za humanitarnu agenciju "Feed the Children". Upoznali su nas zajednički prijatelji jednom prilikom kada sam došao na jednodnevni odmor sa fronte.

Nekoliko mjeseci kasnije, početkom augusta 1995, viđam John-a drugi put. Tada dolazi do totalnog sloma moje vojske, i po drugi put, desetine hiljada stanovnika Cazinske Krajine bježi pred naletom Armije BiH, protiv kojih smo ratovali. Duga kolona civila i naoružatih vojnika među kojima sam bio ja, prelazi u Hrvatsku i zaustavlja se nekih 20-tak kilometara od granice sa Bosnom. Tu nastaje izbjeglički kamp "Kupljensko", jedan od bezbroj izbjegličkih kampova u svijetu za koji niko nije želio da zna.

Humitarna katastrofa u kampu iz dana u dan postajala je sve veća. Izbjeglicama nije pružena adekvatna primarna pomoć a njihovo izgladnjivanje i iscrpljivanje nije bilo slučajno, već metoda stvaranje pritiska da se vrate svojim kućama, koje su tada bile pod kontrolom neprijateljske vojske. Kršeći pravila ratovanja propisanim Ženevskom konvencijom, Povelju Ujedinjenih Nacija i Opštu deklaraciju o pravima čovjeka, Hrvatska vojska i policija bi ulazila noću u kamp, odvajala muškarce od njihovih porodica, te ih predavala režimu koji ih je progonio.

Kao i svi drugi oko mene, ja sam nervozno brojao dane kad će i na mene doći red. U strahu sam išao spavati, u strahu sam se budio. I onda jednog dana dok sam kroz kamp šetao sa prijateljom koji me i upoznao sa njim, vidjeo sam opet Johna. Taj dan nikada neću zaboraviti. Spavao je u prašnjavoj bijeloj Tojoti parkiranoj ispod debelog hrastovog drveta koji mu je pravio hlad tog vrućeg augusta. Kada smo ga kucanjem po prljavom staklu probudili, ludo sretni što ga

vidimo, pitamo ga od kud on tu, jer smo znali da je tada bio stacioniran u srednoj Bosni. Johnov odgovor na to pitanje je promenio, a možda i spasio naše živote:
"Došao sam da vas spasim", rekao je u polusnu, sretan što nas je našao žive.
U to vrijeme pobjeći iz kampa je bio nezamislivo. Hrvatska vojska i policija je stegla obruč oko kampa i nekoliko pokušaja da se pobjegne završilo je krvavo. Sa namjerom da pošalju jasnu poruku ostalima, oni koji su uhvaćeni u pokušaju bijega su bili tučeni, nekima je čak bilo pucano u noge i ruke, a onda su ih deportovali nazad u Bosnu, na milost i nemilost onih od kojih su pobjegli.
Šta smo mi naumili je bio velik rizik, ali za nas petoricu nije bilo dvojbe. Bili smo očajni. Johnov plan je bio da sjedemo sa njim u auto, i da nas on samo izveze van kampa. Međutim, na ulazu i izlazu iz kampa bila su postavljena tri kontolna punkta puna vojnika kroz koje je trebalo proći, a da nas ne zaustave. Njegova ideja je bila toliko luda i opasna, da nam se je odmah svidjela. Nije bilo drugo nego da se počastimo rakijom, a nje je uvijek bilo za posebne trenutke. Na kraju, ostao je tu samo jedan sitan detalj koji nismo u potpunosti razumjeli.
"Johne, šta će biti ako nas vojska zaustavi na jednom od ta tri punkta", pitali smo ga očekujući odgovor koji će nas uvjeriti da se radi o dobro smišljenom planu koji ima neku šansu da uspije.
John nas prvo gledao u tišini, nazdravio čašicom rakije i rekao "Pa, onda smo svi najebali".
Po onoj paklenoj vrućini od 35 stepeni, vojnicima pod punom ratnom opremom se nije ustajalo iz hlada da zaustave prašnjavu Toyotu "Feed the Children-a". Nakon tri i pol godine, za nas je rat bio gotov.
John je nakon bivše Jugoslavije svjedočio ratovima i prirodnim katastrofama, patnjama izbjeglica i raseljenih ljudi, u zeljama bivšeg Sovjetskog Saveza, Afrike, srednje Amerike te juzno-istočne Azije. Njegova bogata iskustva daju mu neupitnu kvalifikaciju da pristupi tematici izbjeglica i raseljenih osoba, kroz svoja posmatranja iz prve ruke, ali takođe da skrene pažnju na žalosnu činjenicu da su izbjeglice i raseljene osobe nevine žrtve, ne samo pomahnitalih autorativnih i totalitarnih režima, geo-politike Zapada, već i neadkvatnosti institucija zaduženih za pružanje pomoći i zaštite.
Danas smo svjedoci najvećeg broja izbjeglica i raseljenih ikad. Trenutno, oko 70 miliona osoba je prisiljeno živjeti od svojih kuća, a među njima je oko 25 miliona izbjeglica. Oko 10 miliona prognanih danas luta svijetom a da nema države, i samim time im je osporeno pravo na osnovnu zaštitu koju država pruža, obrazovanje, zdravstvo, sloboda kretanja.... Na žalost, situacija postaje sve gora ako uzmemo u obzir da je 35 hiljada ljudi svakog dana prisiljeno da napusti svoje domove zbog oružanih sukoba ili straha od progona.
Današnja tragedija izbjeglica i raseljenih osoba se razlikuje od prijašnjih jer je njihova borba za preživljavanje, potraga za sigurnim domom i nastojanja da svojoj djeci obezbjede sretno djetinstvo, praćena neviđenom medijskom kampanjom i dizanjem popularnosti desničarskih fanatika u Evropi. Čak i u Americi, koja je direktno odgovorna za milione izbjeglica, na njih se gleda kao prijetnja nacionalnim interesima i sigurnosti, te čak potencionalnim teroristima. Činjenice uvjerljivo pokazuju da je strah od izbjeglica neosnovan. Od tragedije koja se desila 11. septembra 2001, u Ameriku je došlo skoro milion izbjeglica i do sad, niko od tih izbjeglica nije uhapšen na osnovu aktivosti vezanim za terorizam.

Mi, građani bogatog i bahatog Zapada, dopustili smo svojim demokratski izabranim vođama da se upuštaju u svoje kriminalne geo-političke avanture, kako i kada hoće, bez obzira na štetu, bez straha od odgovornosti. Posljedice su smrt, razaranje i neviđena ljudska tragedija. Broj mrtvih, ranjenih, izbjeglica i raseljnih je samo običan broj, statistika.

Prije nego što neko kaže da nemamo nikakvu obavezu prema tim ljudima, tim brojevima, podsjetimo se na neke činjenice. Nije istina da smo oslobođeni odgovornosti vezanom za tragediju koja je zadesila Afganistan, Irak, Libiju, Siriju ili Jemen. Direktno ili indirektno, mi smo te zemlje uništili. Nije istina da Islamska država i zločini počinjeni od njenih militanata nema povezanost sa rušenjem režima u Iraku i Siriji. Nije istina da zemlje zapadne Evrope i Amerika, nemaju direktnu odgovornost za stvaranje regionalne nestabilnosti u Arapskim zemljama. Nije istina da nam je savjest čista.

Istina je da su naše ruke krvave. Itekako! Istina je da smo laži o našoj nevinosti toliko puta ponovili da sad u njih čvrsto vjerujemo. Istina je da fanatici Islamske države ratuju sa najmodernijim oružjem Američke vojske. Istina je da se financiraju prodajom nafte Turskoj i Izrealu. Istina je da se škole i bolnice u Jemenu ruše avinioma i projektilima kupljenih od Zapada. Istina je da su islamski militanti u Libiji naoružati od Zapada da bi svrgnuli Gadafija, a danas se oružjem snabdjeva Al Kaida u Siriji. Istina je da smo ostavili nevine izbjeglice na milost i nemilost organiziranih kriminalaca koji ih dnevno šalju sa brodovima ka Evropi, uzimajući im svu životnu ušteđevinu za taj put koji mnogi ne preživljavaju. Istina je da puštamo te izbjeglice da se guše u dubokom Sredozemnom moru kad im se prevrne brod. Istina je da ćemo to činiti i dalje.

Migracija izbjeglica je medjunarodni problem i obaveza je svih zemalja, njihovih političkih i socijalnih institucija, da tim ljudima obezbjedi pravo na život. Danas kad smo bogatiji nego ikad prije, kad možemo pomoći daleko više, mi gledamo izbjeglice kako umiru od gladi, izlječivih bolesti, u tamnim vodama sredozemlja. Gledamo i kažemo, to nije naš problem.

U potpunisti sam svjestan koliko sam sretan jer je moja izbjeglička priča imala sretan kraj. Nisam jedini kojeg je John spasio, niti je John jedini koji je spašavao. Ja sam jedna od rijetkih izbjeglica koja je prebačena u sigurne zemlje i kojoj je ponuđena šansa da krene ispočetka. Po zvaničkim statistikama UNHCR-a, manje od 1% izbjeglica biva prebačena u sigurne zemlje. Zar mi ne možemo bolje? Zar mi ne želimo bolje? Šta je sa milionima izbjeglica zbijenih u mega izbjegličke kampove u Libanonu, Jordanu ili Turskoj? Uslovi u tim kampovima su toliko loši da sve veći broj ljudi se vraća u ratom zahvaćenu Siriju, u taj pakao na zemlji. Mi im međutim ne želimo pomoći.

Johnova knjiga, u kojoj on nesebično dijeli svoja bogata životna iskustva, šalje veoma jasnu i jednostavnu poruku. Izbjeglice su obični ljudi koji u najmračnijim trenucima svojih života nisu zaboravili na humor, na ljudskost, da se bore za svoja prava, za šansu za život. Izbjeglice slave rođendane, ljube se i žene, kriju se kada plaču, imaju ambicije, žele postati neko i nešto. Ova knjiga će sa pravom zasramiti mnoge, pa će se možda pitati zašto nisu učinili više kad je izbjeglicama iz Bosne trebala pomoć. Međutim, zaboravite Bosnu i pružite pomoć onima kojima je to potrebno danas.

Pomoć je potrebna hitno. Postoje i oni koji tvrde da je trenutni institucionalni okvir adekvatan da se bavi problemima izbjeglica. Nije! Uzimajući u obzir da skoro i nema kontinenta sa kojeg izbjeglice ne dolaze, da nema godine u *kojoj ne dolazi do novog vala izbjeglica, mi i dalje svakoj novoj izbjegličkoj krizi pristupamo kao ad hoc nesreći. Ovo mora da se mijenja. Naš stav prema izbjeglicama i njihovim problemima mora da se mijenja. Ništa bolnije ne postoji, od onog trenutka kad pakujete u mali kofer svoj život i napuštate svoju kuću, i krećete na put bez povratka znajući da više nemate dom. Izbjeglice plačući napuštaju svoje domove ne zato što to žele, već što moraju. Umjesto da se pred njima stidimo, mi se izbjeglica bojimo.*

Priča mojih prijatelja i mene je imala sretan kraj. Danas, više od 20 godine od tih događanja, Samir je kao diplomirani magistar politologije uspješan savjetnik u Danskoj, Nero i Seki su izgradili karijere u Americi, Denis je poslije završenog fakulteta postao državni službenik u Engleskoj. Nakon završenog fakulteta i magisterija, ja sam izgradio karijeru u financijskom sektoru u Londonu. Baš kao izbjeglice koji se danas upućuju na opasan put i brodovima stižu u Evropu, mi smo samo obični ljudi koji su prošli kroz neobičnu tregediju. Uspjeli smo da napravimo neke normalne živote, mada su ožiljci od trauma zarezani duboko u nama.

Dok čitate Johnovu knjigu pitajte se zašto naša priča sa sretnim završetkom, od prije 20 godina, je i dalje ostala rijetkost. Ili, zašto skoro 99% izbjeglica nikad ne biva raseljena u mirne zemlje, već su prisiljeni da godinama, u nekim slučajevima i decenijama, žive u izbjegličkim kampovima ovisni o tuđoj milostinji i uskraćeni osnovnih ljudskih prava. Upitajte se kako možeti pomoći.

Dragan Karajić

3 September 2016

For David Haines

"Our country isn't like any other, nor are our people like any other. It's a wretched, miserable country. Did you ever notice the names of our villages? Tell them, Osman!"
"Zloselo, Blatište, Crni Vir, Paljevina, Glogovac, Gladuš, Vukojebine, Vučjak, Vukovije, Vukovstvo, Trnjak, Kukavica, Smrdljak, Zmijanje, Jadovica...[i]"
"There you go! Nothing but distress, poverty, hunger, and misfortune. And as for the people, it makes me sick just talking about them. And why is it like that? I don't know. Maybe we were born evil, marked by God. Or maybe because we're constantly hounded by misfortune, we're afraid of loud laughter, afraid we'll anger the evil spirits who are always circling us. Is it any wonder then that we twist, hide, lie, and think only of today and of ourselves, and only find pleasure in the misfortune of others? We have no pride, no courage. They beat us, and we are grateful."
"You shouldn't look at everything so negatively, Šehaga."

Meša Selimović, The Tower

"No-one is allowed to beat you."

Slobodan Milošević, Field of Blackbirds speech (Kosovo, 24 April 1987)

"The young foreigner was carried away by his blood and a feeling of total happiness and unrestrained vindication. Boundless visions flashed before him. This was it! He had always felt and insisted that this stricken, bleak and neglected country was in fact rich and abundant. Now one of its hidden beauties was being revealed to him."

Ivo Andrić, The Travnik Chronicles

"They're just a bunch of seedy, squalid bastards like me: little men, drunkards, queers, hen-pecked husbands, civil servants playing cowboys and Indians to brighten their rotten little lives."

John Le Carré, The Spy who came in from the Cold

"History appears to show clearly that nationalism as an idea is stronger than communism as an idea."[2]

Zbigniew Brzezinsky (Jimmy Carter's national security advisor), August 1978

---

[i] Evil Village, Bog, Black Whirlpool, Arson, Hawthorne, Glutton, Back of Beyond, Wolfhound, Wily, Canny, Bramble Patch, Coward, Stench, Vipers Nest, Woe.

CONTENTS

LOCAL ABBREVIATIONS

ABiH - Bosnian (mainly Muslim) army
DNZ – Bosnian Muslim rebel party
HDZ – Croat nationalist party
HV – Croatian army
HVO – Bosnian Croat militia
JNA – Yugoslav National Army
KM – Bosnian currency
KN – Croatian currency
KPJ – Yugoslav Communist Party
LCK – Bosnian Red Cross
NDH – WWII Croatia, Bosnia and Srem (Vojvodina)
NOZB – Bosnian Muslim rebel militia
RTS – Serbian broadcasting corporation
RTVBiH – Bosnian broadcasting corporation
SDA – Bosnian Muslim nationalist party
SDS – Bosnian and Croatian Serb nationalist party
SPS – successor to KPJ in Serbia and Montenegro
SVK – Croatian Serb militia
UÇK – Kosovo Albanian militia
VJ – successor to JNA in Serbia and Montenegro
VRS – Bosnian Serb militia

PREFACE

Refugees are the product of a failure by national and international power structures to protect society.

At the end of 2015, there were over 65 million forcibly displaced people worldwide, the highest level since WWII, and practically equivalent to the UK's population. Since before the turn of the century, there has been a steady trickle of people entering Europe from the Middle East and Africa. Many are economic migrants, seeking their fortune, or at least a living, as young people everywhere have done throughout history. Others are refugees, fleeing violence and death and seeking a safe haven. Because it is largely illegal and therefore by necessity underground, an industry has grown up around this migration, with criminals taking control of and organising popular routes, transporting human cargo from A to B on clandestine paths for a fee. Such routes are fraught with danger.

In 2007, Turkey's land border with Greece became a major crossing point for illegal migrants into the EU. In 2012, the EU's border protection agency, Frontex, upgraded border controls there, and in 2015, Bulgaria erected a fence on its border with Turkey, to block the migrant flow that had spilled over onto its territory as a result.

Since the foreign intervention in Libya in 2011, and the subsequent failure of that state, illegal departures from there have become possible, and indeed commonplace. To compound this state of affairs, the many African economic migrants who previously headed to Libya to seek a better life, now look further afield, to Europe. A new illegal migration route was established from Libya to the Italian island of Lampedusa, 113 km from Tunisia and 205 km from Sicily. In October 2013, the deaths of over 350 migrants in a shipwreck led the Italian government to set up a major naval search and rescue operation, Operation Mare Nostrum. In 2014, Frontex took over responsibility for search and rescue in the Mediterranean with Operation Triton. Meanwhile, other migration routes were established via Malta and the Spanish enclaves of Ceuta and Melilla in Morocco. It is thought that over 3,500 people died attempting to cross the Mediterranean in 2015. The tragic tally for 2016 will be even higher.

The ongoing war in Syria (a country that itself previously hosted refugees from countries such as Iraq, Palestine and Lebanon) has generated over 3 million refugees since 2011, overwhelming the capacity of neighbouring Turkey and Lebanon to absorb them. In the first half of 2015, a new migration route was established, by sea from Turkey to the Greek islands. It is thought that in 2015, over 1,200,000 people entered the EU by sea, the majority by this new route, from which traffickers are said to have earned up to EUR 6 billion. Once in Greece, the refugees make their way to the mainland, and then head north into the Balkans ("wooded mountains" in Turkish), hoping to reach Germany or other west European countries[3]. This is the largest refugee crisis since WWII.

But it is not the first refugee crisis in the Balkans. The last one was 20 years ago, during the Yugoslav Wars. Today's refugees are not only treading the same paths and resting their heads under the same skies, but having escaped from the threat of immediate violence are facing the same challenges and traversing the same trials, in the same hope of reaching a place of safety and stability where they can live with dignity as human beings. Shorn of possessions and rights, they carry with them *a spark of humanity, in search of a place where it can once again be fanned into the eternal flame of civilisation. Refugees come from a multitude of different and varied origins, but once they set out on their odyssey they become one people, an untouchable mass of humanity with one God and one nationality, a shadow nationality that it is their stated aim to shed. They are also one nation over time, a nation with a long and distinguished pedigree, living a recurring nightmare, whether they are the Kindertransport children or the Boat People.*

"…Idu naprijed i samo dalje
Niko se nazad ne okreće
Imaju nadu, Bog im je šalje
Cilj im je sunce zaloazeće

Djeca, žene, starci razne boje
Različitih vjerskih ubjeđenja
Bježe, ostavljajući domove svoje
Ne rekoše im ni doviđenja…"[ii4]

Refugees have no rights and no voice. This is the inside story of one part of that earlier crisis.

---

[1] Maclean, 1980:20-91
[2] Dizdarević, 2000:428
[3] Wikipedia
[4] Hirkić, 1998:363

[ii] "…*They move on, ever onwards*
No-one turning to look back
A grim hope, God will provide,
Towards the horizon they trek

All ages races and faiths,
Men and women in adversity,
Fleeing and leaving their homes
Without saying goodbye…"

PROLOGUE
PATRIA O MUERTE

"What's the difference between Sarajevo and Auschwitz?
At least the gas wasn't cut off in Auschwitz".[i][1]

---

[i] Told by Adis, a colleague, in Konjic, 1994. As Ivo Andrić observed, see below: "In Bosnia, there is more spirit and more jokes than a foreigner would imagine looking at the country through a train window. But the jokes are often rough and harsh: they are cheerless, if that can be said of a joke, and hard on the person who is the butt of the joke, while revealing that the joker is himself no better off". And as they say in the Balkans, "*U šali pa upali*" ("there's many a true word spoken in jest").

Showing the de facto *independent Montenegro.*

"Our shadow will roam the tyrant's capital, stalk the corridors of power, and strike fear into his heart – *patria o muerte!*"[2]

So spoke Gavrilo Princip, the 19-year-old Bosnian Serb who assassinated the heir to the throne of the Austro-Hungarian Empire, Archduke Franz Ferdinand, and his wife, Sofia, in Sarajevo on St. Vitus's Day, 28 June 1914. Gavrilo was born to a poor family in the Bosnian Borders and had moved to Sarajevo to study, after wandering as far as Belgrade[3]. A plaque inscribed with the words he uttered at his trial, "*Mi smo voljeli svoj narod*" ("we loved our people"), marks the spot, on the wall of a museum dedicated to the event by the north end of Latin Bridge. 28 June is also the anniversary of the battle of Kosovo, Serbia's Hastings, when the army of the Serbian Tsar Lazar was defeated by the Turkish Sultan Murad I, in 1389 (although unlike at Hastings, both rulers were killed in the battle). The diplomatic spat between Vienna and Belgrade resulting from the assassination quickly escalated into the cataclysm known as WWI, as Austria accused the Serbian government of being behind the attack. However, the Serbian government had warned the Archduke that his visit would inflame passions that might have uncontrollable consequences[4]. Furthermore, Gavrilo was one of a group of six friends, five Serbs and one Muslim, all determined to kill the tyrant, who were armed and deployed by Milan Ciganović ("MacGypsy"), an associate of the secret organisation the Black Hand, that answered to no-one. Ciganović, who had been a *Četnik* (see below) irregular in the Balkan Wars, was a Bosnian Serb living in Belgrade, working for the Serbian railways but allegedly a Serbian security service agent[5]. The Black Hand was dedicated to promoting a Balkan Slav state, and had assassinated the previous King of Serbia, Aleksandar I Obrenović (along with his much-hated wife, and the prime minister) in 1903, as well as attempting to assassinate the Emperor Franz Josef in Sarajevo in 1911[6]. Hedging their bets, the group organised several assassination attempts that fateful day. The first real attempt was by Nedeljko Čabrinović, but the bomb he threw at the imperial car bounced off, wounding an Austrian officer. The car accelerated and as a result, Gavrilo was unable to take his own shot. The other attempts also failed or were non-starters. Finally, and as if that wasn't enough, the lead car in the convoy deviated from the planned route, as a result of which the Archduke's driver stopped at the junction by the bridge, unsure whether to follow or stick to the itinerary: the Archduke's wife had decided she wanted to visit in hospital the officer wounded in Čabrinović's attempt, but no-one had informed the first driver. This hesitation was fatal, as Gavrilo literally walked into them from a bar where he had been consoling himself for his earlier failure, and opened fire[7]. While most of the conspirators were rapidly captured at the scene or elsewhere in Bosnia, the authorities in Belgrade subsequently refused to extradite Ciganović and others who sought refuge in Serbia. On 28 and 29 June, the Austrian police, on the orders of the Habsburg governor, organised an anti-Serb riot in Sarajevo, in which two people were killed and much property destroyed or looted. This was followed by smaller riots in Zagreb and Dubrovnik[8].

The Archduke's visit was intended to stamp his authority as the new strongman of the Empire, and to show he would take a hard line with the troublesome Balkans. He had set up a shadow government within the Habsburg state in anticipation of his elderly uncle's impending demise, and the week before he had been visited by the German Kaiser, who discussed with him plans to remake Europe, which included an offensive war against Serbia[9]. In his arrogance the Archduke had not bothered to arrange his visit via the official civilian channels, but turned up in Sarajevo, after inspecting manoeuvres on the Serbian border, with his own close protection. This meant that the Sarajevo authorities were unable to make proper arrangements for his security; indeed, the Sarajevo garrison was away on the manoeuvres he had insisted upon.

Thirty-six years previously, in 1878, the Congress of Berlin of the Great Powers and four Balkan states, hosted by German Chancellor Bismarck, who once said the "whole Balkans [were] not worth the bones of a single Pomeranian squaddie", had been convened to revise the Treaty of San Stefano of earlier that year (San Stefano is on the Greek island of Corfu, while Pomerania was part of defunct Prussia, the engine of Hitler's war machine, which is now the Russian enclave of Kaliningrad and Gdansk in Poland, in whose shipyards the Solidarity union was born[ii10]). This was a peace treaty between Turkey and Russia, further to a war that developed out of a crisis provoked by peasants' revolts in Bosnia and Bulgaria, preceded by an attempt by Serbia and Montenegro to seize Bosnia and Herzegovina respectively[11], and had created an independent, much enlarged Greater Bulgaria, and made Bosnia autonomous. Now it was decided to recognise the already autonomous Serbia, Romania and Montenegro as independent states (but not Bulgaria, which became a reduced autonomous region), and that Austria-Hungary should occupy Bosnia as a protectorate, as the unrest there, aggravated by Serbia's new status, meant that Turkey was no longer in a position to administer it (the province was anyway now largely cut off from the rest of the Ottoman Empire). The European powers thus took away from Russia the slice of the Balkan cake it had carved from Turkey, isolated and contained Balkan independence to those states that *de facto* already had it (Greece had been independent since 1832), and imposed a further term of colonial rule on Bosnia (and Bulgaria): the two ailing oriental powers and the various native peoples were informed in no uncertain terms that there was a new dispensation in the Balkans[iii]. Local Muslim and Serb forces, who, while harbouring different ambitions for Bosnia, were united in their dismay at seeing the *de facto* independence they thought they had just won snatched away from them, mounted unsuccessful attempts to prevent the Austrian takeover. The view in Serbia was that Bosnia was rightfully theirs and should become part of their fledgling state, while the local Muslim lords had long yearned for independence from Istanbul and its constant interference in their affairs[12]. In 1882, the first King of Serbia reached a secret agreement with Austria not to sponsor Serb nationalism in Bosnia, but this policy was dropped in 1903[13]. Meanwhile, Croatia and Slovenia were already Austro-Hungarian realms of centuries-old standing, with the exception of the Dalmatian coast, which had been dominated by Venice, and Dubrovnik, the pearl of the Adriatic, which had been an independent city state under the name Ragusa, until the demise of both cities in the Napoleonic Wars of 1803-1815 and their subsequent annexation by the Habsburgs[14]. The early Kingdom of Croatia had been conquered by Hungary in 1102, and spent much of the next 800 years playing off Hungary and Austria against each other, seeking to maximise its autonomy within the common

---

[ii] The quote is from an address to the German parliament two years earlier, debating the crisis in which other powers were becoming embroiled in the Balkans. However, more famous is Bismarck's speech to the Prussian budget committee after he became PM in 1862, when he convinced them of the need to invest in "*Blut und Eisen*" ("blood and iron"). Bismarck was sacked by the third and last Kaiser in 1890.
[iii] The same year, the Sultan ceded Cyprus to the British in return for guarantees the island would be used to prevent Russian expansion.

Habsburg state, and prevent total absorption by Hungary[15]. Vojvodina was captured from the Turks in the late seventeenth and early eighteenth centuries.

Russia's defeat by and loss of the strategic warm-water Port Arthur to Japan in 1905, after the Baltic Fleet spent seven months sailing around the world only to be sunk in the Yellow Sea (and after Japanese artillery had sunk the Russian Pacific Fleet at anchor, as well as two major defeats on land inflicted by the Japanese army), only the second time a European power had been defeated by a non-European power (Ethiopia, aided by Russian military advisors, had successfully repelled an Italian invasion in 1896, killing 4,000 and capturing 2,000 of the 11,000 would-be imperialists[16]), sent shockwaves through the Balkans, as did the first Russian revolution of later that year. The same year, Serbia formed a customs union with Bulgaria and started to buy arms from France, rather than Austria. The Habsburgs responded by imposing an economic blockade on Serbia's only export, pork, in what became known as the "pig war"[17]. Belgrade was only further enraged when Vienna went on to annex Bosnia in 1908 (although the annexation was never ratified by the Austrian or Hungarian parliaments[18]). In the Balkan Wars of 1912-1913, when Serbia and Montenegro, Bulgaria, Greece and Romania fought to establish their borders after banishing the Ottomans, Serbia gained Kosovo and part of newly-liberated Macedonia (Montenegro gained western Kosovo and half of Sandžak, doubling its territory), and Albania became an independent kingdom[19]. Gavrilo had tried to join up in the Balkan Wars, but as a result of his deprived childhood, he failed the fitness test[20].

In the subsequent hostilities, the Slovenes and Croats fought as part of the Austrian army (as did the Albanians after the Austrian occupation of Kosovo in 1915[21]), hoping to gain more autonomy, if not independence after the war. This was the first conflict between Serbs and Croats[22]. The youngest sergeant major in the army was a young Croat called Josip Broz, who was badly wounded and captured by the Russians in the Carpathians. After the October revolution in 1917, he joined the Red Army, fighting in the Russian Civil War[23]. In 1937 he returned to the Balkans to head the banned Yugoslav Communist Party (KPJ)[24], and later made a name for himself in Bosnia as the leader of the resistance during WWII, under the nickname "Tito" ("you do that"), with the support from 1943 onwards of British military advisors and the RAF[25]. He had previously used that and other pseudonyms in false documents when travelling illegally around Europe as a communist activist, especially during the Spanish Civil War of 1936-1939.

Whether Gavrilo Princip was manipulated by forces he didn't understand, or whether he grasped the underlying issues only too clearly with the incisive instinct of youth, the fact that the thunderbolt that shattered the old imperial order in central and eastern Europe (and the Middle East) was wielded by a teenager, makes him as much a representative of the lost generation as Alain-Fournier.

The Corfu Declaration of 20 July 1917 signed by the Croatian and Serbian leaders Ante Trumbić and Nikola Pašić, known as the Yugoslav Magna Carta, advocated the creation from the ruins of the moribund Habsburg Empire and victorious Serbia of a single state for the South Slavic peoples: the Kingdom of the Serbs, Croats and Slovenes, to be led by the Serbian royal family, the Karađorđevićes (the rivals of the Obrenović dynasty since Serbia's first successes in the struggle for independence, in the early 19th century[26]). This was a compromise between the initial Serbian position of a Greater Serbia built on the spoils of victory (the Serbian position was weakened by the withdrawal of Russian support as a result of the revolution) and the desire of the "Yugoslav committee" (made up of Croats, Slovenes and Serbs from within Austria-Hungary) for equal standing in the new state (without having any occupied territory to bring to the table, and concerned they might lose the Adriatic coast to Italy[27]). A few months before the end of the war, when there was no longer any doubt about the outcome, the Slovenes formed a council with the purpose of uniting the South Slavs within a sovereign state, and on 29 October 1918, the Croatian parliament agreed to join the new state. The Kingdom was proclaimed on 1 December 1918, comprising the former Austro-Hungarian territories of Bosnia, Croatia, Slovenia and Vojvodina together with Serbia, Montenegro and Macedonia (and Kosovo), and participated in the Paris Peace Conference of 1919, gaining international recognition of its borders[28]. The new country's closest ally was France[29].

From as early as 1921, there was disagreement over the new constitution, which the Croats considered to be too centralised and giving too much power to Serbia, while the Bosnian Muslims were concerned to preserve Bosnia's autonomous identity within the country[30]. In 1929, a year after the Croat leader, the HSS MP, anti-Communist and pro-Habsburg Stjepan Radić, a personal friend of the Serb King, was shot in parliament by a Montenegrin *Četnik* MP, King Aleksandar I Karađorđević abrogated the constitution and changed the name of the country to Yugoslavia ("South Slav Land" - which by definition excluded the non-Slav Albanians) in an attempt to defuse the endless disputes that had led to 25 changes of government in 10 years[31]. He was assassinated in Marseille on 9 October 1934 while on a state visit, by an assassin sent by Mussolini from Ante Pavelić's Croat *Ustaše* ("rebel militia") in exile in Italy (operating in collaboration with Macedonian nationalists), hoping to provoke another war in the Balkans[32] (the assassin was actually a Bulgarian, who had previously been a *Četnik* in Macedonia, before joining the *Ustaše* in Italy). Two months earlier, the Austrian Chancellor, Dolfuss, had been assassinated in an attempted *coup* inspired by Hitler[33].

Tito died on 4 May 1980. During WWII, his Partisans not only held out against and ultimately defeated superior German and Italian forces (up to 30 divisions) and *Ustaše* largely without the aid of the Red Army (the Soviets arrived at the Yugoslav border in September 1944, to participate in the battle for Belgrade, the last major action in WWII Yugoslavia)[iv34], but also fought a successful rearguard action against Draže Mihailović's *Četniks* (Serb nationalists seeking to restore the Serbian monarchy in exile in London, where it remains to this day; originally they were Serb militia fighting the Turks in the 19th century), who saw the Communists as a greater threat than the German occupier they purported to be fighting. Hitler had invaded Yugoslavia in April 1941 when the government that had signed a pact with him (in the Archduke's former palace in Vienna) effectively placing the Yugoslav economy at the service of the Third Reich, as had Romania and Bulgaria, was overthrown by popular outrage, and the new pro-British government led by the new 17-year old King Petar II Karađorđević refused to do so[35]. The country was broken up, and Croatia and Bosnia were combined to create the Independent State of Croatia (NDH), an Italian satellite, while Dalmatia went directly to Italy, and Serbia and Montenegro were occupied by Germany and Italy respectively. Slovenia was annexed to the Reich, Macedonia went to Bulgaria, and Kosovo was annexed to

---

[iv] According to Lord Owen, the real number was nearer six divisions, and the Red Army occupied a third of the country by the end of 1944.

Albania (itself occupied by Italy, as was Greece). In May 1945, tens of thousands of *Ustaše* attempted to surrender to the British at Bleiburg in Austria, but were sent back[36]. At least one million Yugoslavs were killed in the war, the majority by other Yugoslavs[37]. In August 1945, women were given the vote in Yugoslavia. On 29 November, Tito, having won a majority in the first post-war elections, established the FNRJ (changed in 1963 to SFRJ)[v], a federation of six republics with two autonomous regions, Kosovo and Vojvodina, both in Serbia, as opposed to the previous centralised kingdom, but with the KPJ as a powerful centralising force[38]. He was prime minister from 1944-1963, president from 1953 and life president from 1974 until his death[39]. Fiercely independent Tito's relationship with the West quickly soured after the war (he had initially wanted the new Yugoslavia to include occupied Trieste, but Churchill insisted he return the border city to Italy after a 40-day occupation[40]), while in 1948 Stalin excommunicated him from the Eastern Bloc.

Five years after the war, the last peasants' revolt in Europe took place in the Bosnian and Croatian Borders.

Tito's was the largest state funeral ever recorded. It was attended by, among others, four kings, 31 presidents, and 22 prime ministers, including Margaret Thatcher, Leonid Brežnev, Walter Mondale (US vice president) and Yasser Arafat[41]. Three years later, rationing was introduced for petrol, electricity, sugar, and flour in Yugoslavia for the first time since the early 1950s[42].

In 1981 there were major student demonstrations in Kosovo, calling first for an improvement in students' living conditions, and finally for independence from Serbia, which led to thousands being jailed[43]. On 28 March 1989, a constitutional amendment engineered in Kosovo by Slobodan Milošević, a career KPJ official and the rising star of Serbian politics after his off-the-cuff address to Serbs in Kosovo two years earlier, effectively put an end to the autonomous region's home rule. On 7 September, Albanian members of the dissolved provincial assembly proclaimed the constitution of a republic of Kosovo[44].

Slovenia and Croatia, the two majority-Catholic republics, both declared independence on 25 June 1991. Belgrade deployed 2,000 Yugoslav National Army (JNA) troops, mainly conscripts, to Slovenia to back up federal police and customs officers. The Slovenian TA resisted, and Belgrade deployed the air force. After one week, the Slovenians requested a ceasefire and a truce, and the JNA withdrew. Within six months Slovenia had received international recognition as a sovereign state[45].

Meanwhile, Croatia, with its significant Serb minority (12% of the population, who wanted to remain part of Yugoslavia), watched and waited to see how Belgrade and the international community would react. At first there were only local skirmishes between the Croat police and Serb militia. The first major fighting took place in Vukovar in Slavonia (northern Croatia) in August 1991, when the Croats dismissed the local assembly, and the JNA overtly supported the Serb militia against them. The same month there was a general mobilisation in Croatia. On 19 December 1991, German Chancellor Helmut Kohl recognised Croatian independence, and the Croatian Serb political entity, the Serb Borders republic, was proclaimed, with its capital in Knin[46]. By the end of 1991, Serb militia and the JNA controlled over 30% of Croatian territory, almost cutting the country in three. On 15 January 1992, two days behind the Vatican, at German insistence and over the objections of France and

---

[v] Federal People's Republic of Yugoslavia and Socialist Federal Republic of Yugoslavia.

the UK, Croatia was recognised by the EU (at that time the EC), but not by the US[47], and a tentative ceasefire was agreed. Under pressure from the US, four UN protected areas (Sectors North, East, South and West) were created, covering the Croatian Serb areas, and supported by the deployment of UN peacekeepers[48]. The JNA withdrew officially in May 1992 (mainly to Bosnia), but left much of its hardware in the hands of the local Serbs (SVK). The warring parties now turned their attention to Bosnia[49].

While the war raged in Croatia, the Bosnians had looked on. However, tensions spilling over from Croatia only aggravated the existing internal and external pressures on the country. Franjo Tuđman, the Croatian leader (a historian, former Partisan, and the JNA's youngest general in 1958), stated he considered part of Bosnia to be Croatia, while Milošević wanted the whole of Bosnia to remain within Yugoslavia. Meanwhile, the Muslim leader, Alija Izetbegović (a lawyer, and the only national leader not to have previously been a KPJ official, while Milošević, the son of a Montenegrin priest, was the only one who hadn't served time in prison), initially opposed to the breakup of Yugoslavia, sought to retain Bosnian integrity and sovereignty, and later sought international recognition for Bosnia as a means to do so[50]. The Bosnian Serbs (32% of the population) proclaimed their own entity, Republika Srpska, on 9 January 1992, with its capital in Bosnia's second largest city, Banja Luka in the north (it was later transferred to Pale, a ski resort on the outskirts of Sarajevo), and held a referendum among Bosnian Serbs on whether they should stay within Yugoslavia (the majority were in favour). Shortly thereafter, after a referendum on independence held at the insistence of the EU and boycotted by the Serbs produced the expected result, in March 1992 Serb militia set up barricades in Sarajevo and the fighting started. Once again, the JNA sided with the local Serbs. Bosnia was recognised as a sovereign state by the EU and the USA on 6 April (the US simultaneously recognised Croatia and Slovenia), and the siege of Sarajevo began[51]. Irregulars from Serbia and Croatia joined in, as did regular troops, and they were later joined by Arab and Iranian as well as western and former Eastern Bloc fighters. Initially, the Croats and Muslims were allies (Tuđman and Izetbegović signed a military alliance in June 1992, thereby legitimising the presence of Croatian troops (HV) in Bosnia[52]), with the objective of ensuring Bosnia did not remain in Yugoslavia, and expelling the JNA. By June 1992, the JNA had withdrawn, transferring much of its hardware to the Bosnian Serbs, and destroying facilities they could not move to Serbia (secret transfers in the meantime ensured that 85% of JNA personnel in Bosnia were Bosnian Serbs, which meant they could legitimately stay and reinvent themselves as the VRS[53]). On 18 November 1991, the Bosnian Croats (17% of the population) had proclaimed their own political entity, Herzeg-Bosna, with its capital in West Mostar, and in the spring of 1993, the Croats (HVO) turned on their erstwhile Muslim allies (ABiH), with Mostar the scene of the heaviest fighting between them. The objectives of the warring parties were now to conquer and ethnically cleanse territory from the other ethnic/religious groups, and the Muslims (44% of the population), with no big brother to help them, were losing on both fronts. In September 1993, after the breakdown of peace talks on HMS Invincible in the Adriatric, the town of Velika Kladuša in the Bosnian Borders was declared the autonomous region of West Bosnia, and another front line emerged, this time between the Muslims[54].

In 1991, a referendum on independence in Macedonia, boycotted by the Albanian minority (21%), decided in favour. The country, surrounded by four hostile neighbours, gained international recognition in April 1993. UN peacekeepers deployed to Macedonia in December 1992 in a preventive capacity, where they stayed until 1999[55].

In June 1996, Albanian (82% of the population[56]) militia (UÇK) started a campaign of bombings and shootings of Serb police and officials in Kosovo. The political crisis and resulting collapse of the army in neighbouring Albania in the spring of 1997 allowed large quantities of looted weapons to be smuggled into Kosovo[57]. In May 1998, the JNA (now the VJ) and the police launched a crackdown on areas under the control of the UÇK.

---

[1] Andrić, 1967:185-186
[2] Blic
[3] West, 1942:352
[4] West, 1942:344
[5] West, 1942:366
[6] West, 1942:358-360
[7] West, 1942:346-349
[8] West, 1942:372
[9] West, 1942:340
[10] Brown, 1991:37; Owen, 1995:17
[11] Malcolm, 1994:132-134
[12] Crnobrnja, 1994:23
[13] Crnobrnja, 1994:32
[14] West, 1942:331-350
[15] Crnobrnja, 1994:25
[16] Pakenham, 1991:484
[17] West, 1942:469, 573
[18] West, 1942:377
[19] Baker, 2015:13
[20] West, 1942:357
[21] Malcolm, 1998:260
[22] Crnobrnja, 1994:49
[23] Maclean, 1949:310
[24] Crnobrnja, 1994:62
[25] Maclean, 1949:305-356
[26] Maclean, 1949:284-285
[27] Baker, 2015:15
[28] Crnobrnja, 1994:46-48
[29] Crnobrnja, 1994:62
[30] Malcolm, 1994:164
[31] West, 1942:597-598; Malcolm, 1998:283
[32] Baker, 2015:17; West, 1942:14-18; Crnobrnja, 1994:60
[33] West, 1942:1112
[34] Crnobrnja, 1994:67; Maclean, 1949:504-514; Owen, 1995:6, 9
[35] Crnobrnja, 1994:62
[36] Baker, 2015:19
[37] Malcolm, 1994:174
[38] Baker, 2015:18; Crnobrnja, 1994:70
[39] Trkulja & Božić, 2008:189
[40] Crnobrnja, 1994:63-68
[41] Crnobrnja, 1994:81
[42] Crnobrnja, 1994:84
[43] Judah, 2002:39-40
[44] Malcolm, 1998:344-347
[45] Crnobrnja, 1994:161-164
[46] Crnobrnja, 1994:137
[47] Silber & Little, 1995:219-222
[48] Crnobrnja, 1994:207-208

[49] Crnobrnja, 1994:165-172
[50] Crnobrnja, 1994:7; Owen, 1995:40
[51] Silber & Little, 1995:252
[52] Malcolm, 1994:240
[53] Silber & Little, 1995:240
[54] Silber & Little, 1995:339
[55] Baker, 2015:27; Crnobrnja, 1994: 84-85, 243
[56] Judah, 2002:44
[57] Malcolm, 1998:354-355

PART 1
THE BADLANDS

"One day Mujo went fishing. He caught a golden fish.
The fish said to him, 'Let me go Mujo, and I'll grant you one wish.'
'Alright', said Mujo, and pulled a map of Bosnia out of his pocket. 'Put this back the
way it was before it imploded – prosperity, security, brotherhood and unity.'
'That's a bit of a tall order, I'm afraid, Mujo', said the fish. 'Isn't there anything
more feasible you would like?'
'Yes', said Mujo. 'My wife's fucking ugly; can you turn her into Miss World?'
'No problem', said the fish. 'Call your wife.'
'Fata!' called Mujo, and Fata came running up from the house.
The fish took one look at Fata and said, 'Let me see that map again!'"[i]

---

[i] Told by a hospital doctor in Kakanj, 1994. The F-word is heard not infrequently in the Balkans.

Showing the front lines, the UN protected areas and UNPROFOR routes.

The Croatian Borders were unworldly in August 1995, as I drove north along the equivalent to a B road in the UK, until 2005 the main artery between western Europe and the Croatian coast. The rugged, timeless hills were still as indifferent and unfeeling, the thousand shades of green of the foliage no less verdant, the sun still as hot as on previous drives. But the adrenalin of driving through a countryside at war now had a harsher edge tinged with sorrow, and fear of the unknown, as I made my way through the evidence of a major human tragedy. At the picturesque Austro-Hungarian market town of Slunj, with its ruined Habsburg *tvrđava* ("fortress") and Franciscan *samostan* ("monastery"), where a fast-flowing stream divides into multiple rivulets to cascade down rocks in a series of miniature waterfalls, driving as it descends a clutch of strategically perched 18th century wooden *vodenice* ("watermills") before merging with the powerful river Korana as it levels out from its steep-sided gorge, a section of the bridge bearing the *magistrala* ("main road") had been blown out by the retreating SVK, and I would have to take a detour on partly unfamiliar roads.

I had left Croatia's second-largest city, the port of Split that morning, heading north-west along the picturesque coast road, with to my left the unbelievably clear waters of the Adriatic, that allow the observer to see right to the bottom, such that boats appear to be floating in the air, and to my right the sun-baked grey Dalmatian (from *dele*, the Albanian word for "sheep"[1]) cliffs with their sparse, thirsty vegetation. A lovely start to what promised to be a long and difficult day. Driving for just over an hour from Trogir, our base near Split airport and a UNESCO world heritage site on its own little island, whose walls were destroyed by the Saracens in the 12th century and never rebuilt, and formerly the residence of Marshal Marmont, Napoleon's governor of Dalmatia[2], I passed Primosten and approached Šibenik with its UNESCO listed 15th century cathedral, smaller but even more magnificent than the monolithic 12th century cathedral further up the coast in Zadar, the home town of former Spurs player Luka Modrić, who I worked for several times when he first moved to the UK (Zadar was the seat of Habsburg rule in Dalmatia in the 19th century, and became a refuge for Montenegrin malcontents, who the Austrians eagerly welcomed. It is said that they supplied the assassins who killed Prince Danilo of Montenegro in 1860, and Prince Mihailo Obrenović of Serbia in 1868[3]). Just before Šibenik proper, there is a turning to the right onto a steep country road almost completely shrouded in tall, thick foliage, which suddenly deadens the noise from the busy coastal highway, and leaving the coast behind leads up swiftly into the hinterland of the Dinaric Alps, a sea-change with its noticeably different microclimate, in particular the abundance of grass and other vegetation. The busy traffic all but disappeared, which was nothing new. The fuel shortages in SDS territory had meant that previously, only military and police vehicles were on the roads on the other side of the front line, and there was little reason for anyone else to be driving in the vicinity on this side. It was noticeably cooler in the hinterland, and subject to heavy snow in winter, but still hot enough at this time of year. A few kilometres after reaching the high plain and passing several seemingly lifeless hamlets, was the former front line between the HDZ and the SDS, set among rolling meadows.

The HV *punkt* ("checkpoint") had been a simple rope barrier, usually manned by just two *vojnici* ("soldiers"). Having checked our credentials, they would let us through. A few hundred meters further on, and out of sight of the HV, was the SVK front line. They always had a dozen TMRP-6 anti-tank mines placed on the road, and again upon production of the right credentials, one of the half a dozen or so soldiers would push a couple of them aside with a broom to let us through. I was always slightly nervous driving close to those evil contraptions, with their sensor sticking up in the air like a malevolent insect's antenna. Anti-tank mines are generally set to go off when subjected to a pressure of around 250 kg (these ones required 150 kg), whereas anti-personnel mines can be set at as little as 20 kg or less (the PMA3 mines popular in the Balkans could be set at 3-15 kg of pressure). In Kosovo in 1998, a police car hit an anti-tank mine and was thrown completely off the road, with the three police officers inside all killed. I saw the car a few days later, and it was literally a twisted piece of wreckage. A few days after that an NGO vehicle hit an anti-personnel mine which blew its wheel off, causing it to leave the road. The only person inside not wearing a seatbelt was thrown out of a window of the Toyota Landcruiser and into a tree, dying instantly. Now, there was no sign of the SVK or their mines. The first time I had crossed into SDS territory six months earlier I had been quite apprehensive. After spending the best part of a year in Muslim and Croat-controlled territory, constantly living and working in the threatening shadow of the unseen Serbs, existing as it were at their violent pleasure, I had, quite unconsciously and involuntarily, formed the impression that they were the worst of the lot, and their territory the heart of darkness. It was therefore quite an anti-climax when I first approached them from no-man's land, to find them to be quite normal, and the same as everyone else; the only difference seemed to be that they wore *panciri* ("flak jackets") and *šlemovi* ("helmets"), while their enemies only had fatigues. Today, I was just as apprehensive, if not more so, in their absence.

Just after the front line, and in what had been Sector South, was the village of Drniš, which never seemed to me to be very welcoming, either before or since. Driving on for another hour or so I reached the market town of Knin, the former capital of the Serb Borders republic. There was considerable visible war damage, and the enormous Croatian flag commissioned specially for the occasion by president Tuđman (20 x 5 m) waving over the fortress could be seen well before the town itself. Knin had been a comparatively bustling town, and even now, there was some civilian activity, although most of the people on the streets were wearing HV uniforms. I noticed they had already started to replace the Cyrillic road signs[ii4]. Just over 20 km north-east of Knin, across the border in Bosnia, is the village of Obljaj, the birthplace of Gavrilo Princip. But my road from Knin continued north-west. Once when heading south along the same road, we had come across a funeral procession about 5 km north of Knin. We respectfully pulled off the road, removed our headgear, and switched off our radios and engines. As the mourners slowly walked past us, one said in English, "It's easy for you." In my best Serbian accent, I replied, "*Nije uvek lako*" ("Not always").

[ii] Serbian is written in Cyrillic, while Croatian is written in Latin script. Bosnian uses both. The Cyrillic alphabet was invented in the 9th century by St. Cyril, a Greek missionary, and his brother, Methodius, using Latin, Greek and Hebrew letters, to translate the Bible for the first time into a Slavic language, Bulgarian, which had no writing of its own. This translation formed the basis for the litany of the Slavic Orthodox churches which is still used today, thus establishing an indissoluble link between the alphabet and cultural identity; by contrast, the Catholic Slavic peoples adopted the alphabet of their church.

At that time *humanitarci* ("aid workers") enjoyed a certain appreciation and protected status, and were usually only in danger if they found themselves in the wrong place at the wrong time. The biggest killer of aid workers was (and still is) traffic accidents. I once rolled a vehicle while driving one morning between Šibenik and Split: there had just been a light shower, the sun was just starting to emerge through the dissipating clouds, and there must have still been a thin layer of oil on the *kolnik* ("roadway"), because as I followed the curve of an uphill bend around to the left, the vehicle suddenly slid sideways in the same direction and before I knew it, trying to correct the skid, I went into the vertical rock face on the left-hand side of the road. The impact bounced the vehicle back over onto the right-hand side of the road and turned it on its side, where it came to a rest, spinning around to end up facing the right way, and fortunately not plunging over the drop down towards the sea below. My window was open, and I swiftly leapt out as soon as I was stationary. It was lucky there was nothing coming from the other direction, or behind me, because otherwise there could have been a collision. I couldn't get the radio to work to call in, but fortunately an UNPROFOR[iii][5] vehicle stopped and the peacekeepers, two Ukrainians, let me use their satphone. Soon afterwards the *murija* ("police") stopped as well, and had a look; and instead of breathalysing me, they offered me a beer! They conveniently had a crate in their vehicle, and had a cold one themselves while they were inspecting the *prometna nesreća* ("RTA"; it was later explained to me that they were probably at the end of a *treća smjena*, "night shift"). My vehicle was a write-off, with the front of the chassis bent upwards. My colleague Kiwi, a former fireman from New Zealand, came from the office in Split to collect me, and I had a check-up including a neck scan at the British UNPROFOR base near the airport, who gave me a clean bill of health. Things are very different now with aid worker security, as the recent murders in Syria have shown. The roots of this unwelcome change are to be found in the humanitarian response to the NATO invasion of Kosovo, where the less professional NGOs found themselves in bed with one of the belligerent parties. Ironically, this situation came about because the international community was caught unprepared for the exodus of refugees from Kosovo resulting from its own intervention, and NATO had to do the UN refugee agency (UNHCR)'s job for it and provide shelter[6][iv]. Kosovo was also the direct precursor to regime change in Iraq (US secretary of state Madeleine Albright, who was mistaken for a cleaner by the UÇK delegation at the Paris peace talks in 1999, see below, later said, "Getting rid of Milošević was my highest personal priority [...] we had the power to do it and we ought to be willing to apply it"[7]). This carrot and stick approach to foreign policy, where aid agencies and the armed forces are two sides of the same coin, the left and right hand of state policy, was the brainchild of Tony Blair, and was further pursued in other theatres, to the general detriment of aid workers' safety everywhere. Between 2004 and 2014, annual aid worker deaths in attacks rose from 56 to 121 (with kidnappings up from 23 to 120)[8]. As Sir Michael Rose, UNPROFOR commander January 1994 - January 1995, said,

---

[iii] UN peacekeeping mission in Bosnia and Croatia; from 31 March 1995 onwards the mission in Croatia was known as UNCRO, after Tuđman threatened to not renew its mandate. At that time, there were 39,000 peacekeepers on the ground. UNPROFOR suffered 167 fatalities during the war.
[iv] Professional armies are good at large-scale logistics; but aid work is about delivering the last mile. That is what aid workers are good at.

"The clear lesson of Somalia and Bosnia is that to confuse the strategic goals of war-fighting and peace-keeping will risk the success of the mission and also the very lives of the peace-keepers and aid workers themselves"[9].

This mission-creep was also a significant factor in the failure of the UN "safe areas" doctrine, which Izetbegović described in April 1994 as the "most unsafe places in the world"[v][10].

Driving for over another hour through a deserted Van Gogh landscape, I passed the villages of Gračac and then Udbina, with its *vojni aerodrom* ("airbase"), from where Bihać was bombed in November 1994 as part of *Pauk* ("Operation Spider", see below), in the region known as Lika (the SDS's other military airbase was in Banja Luka). The road running north from Udbina is dead straight for 3.5 km, and doubles as a second runway, which was not damaged by NATO's retaliatory air strike after the Bihać bombing (the first such operation in NATO's history)[11]. The UN had declared Bosnian airspace a no-fly zone in October 1992, and this was policed from March 1993 by NATO with the consent of the Russians[12] (it later came to light that the policing of the no-fly zone was prone to recurrent blind spots, that were open to abuse by anyone in the know, i.e. the US[13]). Udbina was the scene of an important victory by the Turks against the Habsburgs in 1493. Just further on, with the Bosnian border and the former Bihać pocket (now called the Una-Sana canton[vi]) drawing closer to my right, I stopped at a roadside bar/restaurant that, surprisingly, happened to be open, for a bite to eat and some coffee. The trestle tables and benches outside were full of HV squaddies, in visibly triumphant but not particularly friendly mood. I sat by myself, and when the waitress eventually noticed me, ordered something. With so many thoughts racing through my head I was not in the mood for conversation, nor did anyone approach me, although my Toyota Landcruiser drew several hostile glances. The waitress was not very friendly either. I had experienced the same sullen, passive xenophobia on earlier occasions in Herzegovina (southern Bosnia), where Tito once said that only snakes and *Ustaše* grow (my boss, Reinhard, was not amused one afternoon in Herzegovina when, after we had stopped for a coffee in the village of Ljubuški, the waitress, a pouting, ignorant creature, decided to put on some very loud neo-Nazi rap for our edification).

After I had finished, I continued on my way, passing through the village of Korenica. In less than an hour I reached the spectacular UNESCO world heritage site of the Plitvice national park, a series of 16 pastel-coloured lakes cascading one into the next, set in thick forest that extends east to the Bosnian border, and linked by a network of colour-coded paths worthy of Dodd's Wood in Cumbria in the English Borders; but a visit was not on my agenda that day. A few months previously, we had spent a day visiting the lakes, on a day out organised by two Dutch officers from the Slunj UNPROFOR base, for which we all chipped in. The tourist centre with its imposing stuffed brown bear was closed due to the war, but the upside was that there

[v] According to Owen, "The 'safe area' mandate was a totally inconsistent one: for the areas to be safe they had to be demilitarised, then defined, and then defended by the UN. As it was, in the absence of consent and cooperation it was impossible to fulfil the mandate, and Serb attacks into and Muslim attacks out of 'safe areas' continued".

[vi] Under the Dayton constitution, Bosnia consists of two entities, of which the Federation of Bosnia and Herzegovina is comprised of 10 cantons (five Muslim, three Croat and two "mixed"), subdivided into 79 *općine* ("districts"), while Republika Srpska ("Serb republic": the local name for the Bosnian Serb entity is usually used in English in order to avoid confusion with the Republic of Serbia) is divided directly into 64 *opštine* ("districts").

were no other tourists and we had the whole place almost to ourselves. Almost to ourselves, as we ran into a group of SDS special forces training in the forest, who were as surprised at the encounter as we were (I didn't notice which mutation of the JNA they were, SVK, VRS, or even VJ). Nowadays it costs twenty quid to get in. The two Dutchmen had even chartered a pleasure barge, although due to rumours of mines in the water we couldn't go that far out. But it was exhilarating to dive from the vessel's roof into the freezing waters, hoping not to detonate anything. The food and drink flowed freely, and an excellent time was had by all. Or rather, almost all, as when we were back on dry land I heard someone vomiting behind the latrine block. Concerned, I waited to see what was happening, and was both surprised and relieved to see the captain of the vessel emerge after a few minutes, visibly the worse for his *rakija*. Relieved to be back on *kopno* ("*terra firma*"). My first experience of *rakija* had been in our communal house near Split the previous year. One very hot summer's night, unable to sleep, I recalled having noticed a plastic bottle of clear liquid in the fridge. "Just the job", I thought, "a nice draught of cold water from the fridge, *aferim* ['good thinking'] by someone to have put it there". I proceeded to the kitchen, opened the fridge, and upending the bottle, took a long, deep swig. Suddenly I understood what a diesel engine must feel when flooded with petrol, for it was not water, but *rakija*. I coughed and choked with tears running down my face as the fiery liquid sputtered out of my nose and mouth. For Fitzroy Maclean, the SAS officer parachuted into Yugoslavia in August 1943 to assess whether the UK should continue to support the royalist *Četniks*, or change horses and back the Partisans, after a short time "it seemed to us the most natural thing in the world to gulp raw spirits at breakfast"[14]. He quickly came to the conclusion that the UK should drop the ineffectual, collaborationist *Četniks*, and provide "all-out assistance" to the Partisans with their "total war" against the enemy. This conclusion was reported to Churchill, and swiftly acted upon[vii][15].

The Toyota Landcruisers beloved of the aid community, with their no-nonsense interior and double fuel filters fitted with a manual pump (fuel quality can be very poor in some countries), are excellent work tools, sturdy, reliable, and well suited for off-road conditions. Their only drawback is that most models are not compliant with EU emission standards, although that is rarely high on the list of priorities in the field during an emergency response. For that reason, some agencies have switched over to Nissan Patrols, that purport to be cleaner, but which I personally find unreliable, because of an incident in Mozambique during the flood response of 2000 when the strut holding the driver's side lower ball joint failed, disabling the vehicle. Fortunately, we were driving slowly down a sandy track at the time (heavy rainfall in south-east Africa at the end of 1999 and in February 2000 resulted in major *inundações* ("floods") in low-lying Mozambique, which were worsened when the Kariba dam in Zimbabwe upstream on the river Zambezi was opened that month; the situation was further aggravated when cyclone Eline made landfall at the port of Beira the same month, driving flood waters back up the river Save. 700 people were killed, up to 500,000 made homeless, and *machambas* ("agricultural land") and *gado* ("livestock") were devastated). However, although they can be driven on the road with an ordinary driving licence, Landcruisers are

---

[vii] Churchill also masterminded the disastrous Dardanelles campaign against Turkey in February 1915, to encourage Bulgaria and Greece to enter the war, relieve the Russians in the Caucasus, and ultimately capture Istanbul. The campaign was abandoned at the end of the year, after the defeat of Serbia, with over 50,000 dead on each side, many of them Irish, Indians and ANZACs from the other side of the world.

quite different to handle than a car and present a number of challenges. The more professional NGOs make sure their people go through proper training before being let loose in one, which includes off-road use and basic care and maintenance. But it is one thing to receive training, and quite another to have enough driving experience to be a competent driver. For that reason, local drivers are usually employed, not only because they have the knowledge and understand the local driving conditions, but also because in the event of an accident they are less likely to become a focus for local rage. Ironically, this means that international staff have even less opportunity to gain experience driving the vehicles. The former Yugoslavia was an exception to the local driver rule because it was generally not possible for local staff to cross from one territory to another. When I was working in Kosovo in 1998, two French *infirmières* ("nurses") took a Landcruiser out one evening in Priština, to have a modest night on the town. I had told them they had to be back at 9 pm, but as the deadline approached, there was no sign of them. I was quite tired and wanted to go to bed, but sat up waiting for them. Just after 9 pm the phone rang: they had a puncture and didn't know how to deal with it. Out I went, drove down into the town centre, and changed their wheel, theoretically at risk at that late hour. The two angels had already received training on how to change a wheel, among other things, and that was the last time they were allowed the use of a vehicle by themselves. A Hungarian MSF nurse was nearly the death of me in Sierra Leone in 2015. This problematic state of affairs is compounded when armoured vehicles are deployed to a theatre. Armoured Landcruisers can weigh up to 5 tons (as opposed to 1 ton for a "soft skin"), and have a much higher centre of gravity, and yet sitting in the driving seat and going straight with your foot down feels almost the same as in a bog-standard version. But a sharp turn can easily cause the vehicle to roll, and the heavy armour means it can be very difficult if not impossible to get out in an accident. Reversing an armoured Landcruiser out of a cargo plane on two narrow ramps 5 m above the ground is not a task to be undertaken lightly, especially in the rain, as the weight means you have to get it right first time, low ratio and brakes notwithstanding. In Afghanistan in 2005, a civil servant, who had also received thorough training, managed to crash an armoured Landcruiser inside Kandahar airbase, which was a blanket 10 mph zone. He reversed into a parked truck while doing a three-point turn on his way to a free lunch, and smashed the back window. As they say in the Balkans, *"Vuk dlaka mijenja a ćud nikad"* ("you can't make a silk purse out of a pig's ear"). Because of the specialist nature of the vehicle, a custom-made armoured replacement window had to be ordered and delivered from Europe at great expense, and DFID's vehicle specialist, Stuart, had to fly out to Kandahar from the UK to fit it. Ironically and tragically, in 2004 a British ICRC (see below) delegate, Derek Tooke, who was a very experienced field logistician, was killed in Eritrea when driving across what was normally a dried-up river bed, and was swept away by a powerful flash flood[viii]. In 1996 in Chechnya we used local drivers, but they were unable to cross from Ingushetia (to the west of Chechnya; the Ingush are a Chechen tribe, and the two peoples are known collectively as *Vajnah*, "our people") into the neighbouring republic of Alania/North Ossetia (further west again). After a brief, little-reported but very violent war in the disputed Prigorodnij district in 1992, the Russian army had set up a buffer zone between the two republics. The main crossing point between the two was a roundabout that the squaddies had turned into a strong

---

[viii] Eritrea seceded from Ethiopia in 1993, and the two countries were at war between 1998-2000 over border disputes that persist to this day.

point with a tank in the middle, and an abundance of razor wire. When we had to travel from one side to the other, we would change drivers just before the roundabout. A Russian driver who worked for us, an old boy called Jurij, was generally used at the exchange point, as he could move freely from one side to the other, not being from any of the local ethnic groups (although we never took him to Chechnya). He once asked me what I thought of the state of the *doroga* ("road"), and when I made a non-committal response, observed, "In your country this road would be a disgrace, but here it's deemed one of the best" (he had obviously never been to the UK). The first time I crossed the fortified roundabout, I noticed a *bomž* ("tramp"), who came up to my window and asked me for a cigarette (Russian cigarettes, *papirosi*, only have a short section containing tobacco at the end, and the middle is hollow; the tobacco is also liable to fall out if it is not handled expertly. I preferred to stick to Marlboro). I gave him one, and then he asked for some *toplivo* ("fuel"). Looking at him again, I noticed that under the dirt his face was quite young, and then I realised he was armed, and that his dirty, ragged attire was actually a uniform. He was one of the peacekeepers. Life for *sročniki* ("conscripts") in the Russian army is not easy. It was said that the Russian peacekeepers in the former Yugoslavia brought a mobile brothel with them, although I never saw it myself. Brothels were introduced into Bosnia by the Habsburgs, a novelty that did not survive their term of office, at least overtly. Officials were paid danger money in Bosnia as if they were deployed to a war zone, and needed something to spend their money on[16]. In West Timor in 1999, we had a local driver whose real name was Hitler (I checked his ID card). Someone had told him that "*Heil*" means "How are you?", and that "*Sieg Heil*" means "I'm well", which led to some bizarre exchanges of greetings when arriving at the office in the morning (it was later explained to me that Hitler was a popular Christian name in Indonesia at the height of the Cold War, as the *Führer* was regarded as a scourge of communism)[ix]. His favourite driving music was a tape of *We wish you a merry Christmas* with a manic acid beat, that seemed to just go on and on forever. Perhaps he thought the *orang barat* ("western man", as opposed to *orang utan*, "forest man") would appreciate it.

Continuing north for another 20 km, crossing into what had been Sector North and Kordun, and through the village of Rakovica, I would reach Slunj. Sector North was the scene of the worst genocide in the former Yugoslavia in WWII (2,700 people were killed here in August 1941 alone, almost exclusively civilians)[x17]. Slunj

---

[ix] Similarly, soon after I arrived in Croatia, I was told by a Bosnian refugee, from Bužim, that "*Crkni*" ("drop dead") was a greeting. Fortunately, someone corrected my use of the insult before I had the chance to get into hot water.

[x] Unlike in post-WWII (West) Germany, there were no attempts in Yugoslavia to confront and process the atrocities of the recent past: Tito swept everything under the carpet of his policy of "*bratstvo i jedinstvo*" ("brotherhood and unity") once he had secured his victory. Legija, see below, whose father was a former Partisan and *vojno lice* ("career JNA officer") from Petrova Gora, wrote in respect of 1992, "We who live here know only too well that here across the Drina there isn't a family or home who didn't lose someone in the last war; and that the surviving members of those families, somewhere in the depths of their souls, secretly cherished a desire for revenge. The surviving children listened, as I did, to the stories told by their elders of the atrocities they had suffered in these parts. They listened to how people who had until the day before been their neighbours went to war, and slaughtered them like the cruellest of enemies. And now the beast has reawoken in the hearts and souls of a new generation cast headlong into war, killing and destruction. I cannot say that any of the three peoples who lived in these parts was not exposed in the hatred incarnate to suffering, persecution and loss. But, unfortunately, we Serbs have always suffered the most in everything, in particular in the recent past. We have been slaughtered and killed by all and sundry,

was never conquered by the Turks, and during WWII was an important *Ustaše* administrative centre[18].

Located in the most westerly of Milošević's realms, and thus at the very end of the tenuous supply chain from Belgrade[xi], Slunj had previously had a truly Wild West feel[19]. One afternoon, while waiting fastidiously at a red light to turn left onto the main road, I was accosted by a middle-aged officer the worse for drink who had just emerged from a popular watering hole located at the junction (off limits to us after one visit convinced my predecessor, Steve, that the bar games, which included Russian roulette, were as bad if not worse for our health than the alcohol and tobacco smoke in there). Noticing my aid vehicle, he tried to engage me in conversation and impress on me the rightness of his cause. My non-committal responses did not meet with his approval, and as I finally drove away he called that I should watch out, or I would have my throat cut. The bar is now boarded up, and apparently for sale by the two brothers who own it. Steve used to wear an Australian bush hat, with a rim that could be buttoned up on either side. On one side he had a rash of SVK, VRS and NOZB badges, and on the other HV, HVO and ABiH badges. He would adjust his headgear according to where he happened to be at any one time, and was generally greeted with approval at checkpoints.

Steve had befriended, or perhaps it is more accurate to say, had been befriended by the late Mario, a former university lecturer who spoke English of sorts, and who now wandered around in a state of permanent intoxication, armed to the teeth with side arm, knives and grenades, with wild eyes and a biblical beard. I was introduced to him one afternoon near the Orthodox church in Slunj, and he assured me they would "never forget the Hitler time" (the 18th century Orthodox church in Slunj was converted into a Catholic church during WWII, before being burnt down. It was restored in 1967, but has been closed since the war, although it recently underwent restoration works. There is also a Catholic church that was burnt down during the Yugoslav Wars[xii], but has now been fully restored[20]). He came round to our house that evening, while we were entertaining a French colleague. Working our way through a bottle of *rakija* with him we listened to his anecdotes, on occasion challenging his blinkered perspective on the war ("There is no tradition of Islamic fundamentalism in Bosnia", "The Bosnian Muslims are not seeking to establish a caliphate"[21]), while endeavouring to keep him in a positive frame of mind, and trying to judge when it would be diplomatic to suggest we call it a night. On a previous occasion, I had heard, Steve had gone to the khazi in the morning to find Mario unconscious in the bath, clutching a *ručna bomba* ("grenade"). Mario recounted how

---

[even] our 'liberators'. And now, after so many years, we are again heading for an encounter with the beast that rages mercilessly in these parts".

[xi] Nikola, see below, told me that after Operation Storm, see below, he was surprised to see how empty the shops in the Serb Borders republic were, which went some way towards explaining the SVK's low morale. Our *gazda* ("landlord") would ask us to purchase items for him whenever we travelled to HDZ territory. Arkan, see below, in a motivational speech to a ragged band of SVK squaddies standing wretchedly to attention before Operation Storm, said "Don't tell me you're tired after four years. Because you're not tired. What if the war lasts 40 years?"

[xii] The official name for the war in Croatia is "*domovinski rat*" ("war of independence"). In Bosnia it is referred to officially as the "*agresija protiv Republike BiH*" ("aggression against Bosnia"), and in Serbia the two acts of the war are the "*rat u bivšoj SFRJ*" ("war in the former Yugoslavia") and "*albanski terorizam/NATO agresija*" ("Albanian terrorism/NATO aggression") respectively, although across the board, most people simply refer to it as the "*rat*" ("war"). The Albanians call it "*lufta e Kosovës*" ("the Kosovo war"), while for the Romanies, "*O maripe či anel khanikaske lačipe*" ("war is hell").

he had recently been in Bosnia, when he had come across two Albanians in a forest. It being the duty of all Serbs to kill Albanians wherever they find them, he promptly did so. The last we saw of our Gallic colleague was him leaving town at high speed at dawn, like Napoleon on his return from Moscow.

During this period there was a spate of robberies of international organisations in the Croatian Borders - but not us, perhaps because we got on well with the local bobby, Miloš, himself a *raseljeno lice* ("IDP", internally displaced person, as opposed to an *izbjeglica*, "refugee", who finds him or herself in a different country), from Ogulin, near Karlovac, downstream from Slunj. His wife was a Croat, and they had a young boy, and a pit bull pup he was training to be a fighter. He could also come up with an excellent rendition of Pink Floyd's *Wish You Were Here* on guitar, complete with vocals. At the beginning of the war, his Croat colleagues came round to his house and tried to arrest him (after Tuđman's HDZ won an absolute majority in the Croatian elections in 1990 and he became the country's first elected president, he acted to change the composition of the police force, in which, as in the JNA, Serbs were over-represented, by sacking Serbs and replacing them with Croat rookies[xiii22]). It was rumoured that the SVK had a special workshop dedicated to respraying stolen Toyota Landcruisers from white to military green[xiv23]. One Sunday, after spending an afternoon by the river near Velika Kladuša with the beautiful Seka and her *raja* ("group of friends"[xv24]), we were given a lift back to the town by an admirer of hers, a Serb captain, in his military green Landcruiser. I commented on the nice paintwork, and he just grunted. I couldn't tell where he was from, and so asked him. He replied that he was from Yugoslavia, and was fighting to restore his country. The EU monitors were particularly *baksuz* ("unlucky"), hard hit by the robberies. A new team was robbed in their home in Slunj the same evening they arrived, and they lost not only their vehicles and all their work equipment, but also their personal items, including toothbrushes and underwear. Someone gave them a lift to Zagreb, and a replacement team was sent. This team had even less luck, and were held up on the main road from Karlovac before even reaching their new base. They had to walk back to the front line near Karlovac and seek refuge from UNPROFOR. They were not replaced. More tragic was a subsequent incident in Knin on June 11, when the minibus carrying UN staff back to their homes from the local UNPROFOR base after work was held up by two masked and armed men. The Kenyan peacekeeper in the bus went for his weapon, and was shot dead. The Kenyans were on edge for some time after that, as Gary (see below) discovered one day when he attempted to drive his truck into the UNPROFOR base with his usual nonchalance, and was dragged roughly from his cab. In an unconnected case, there was a rumour that there was a serial killer at work in the Croatian Borders, but the *milicija* ("police") did not have the resources to investigate anything not directly related to the war effort.

It was a popular pastime for local squaddies to try to intimidate aid workers, especially when they encountered them on the road and an interaction was

---

[xiii] According to Nikola, the Slunj, Cazin and Velika Kladuša police chiefs had always been Serbs, despite the fact that Serbs were a minority in all three places: Serbs were used to being "*Bog i batina*" ("having the whip hand") throughout Yugoslavia.

[xiv] Legija describes in his memoirs how his men "blagged" him a UN Nissan Patrol at this time, to replace his cramped Lada Niva; but this time they sprayed it black.

[xv] During the Turkish period, the word *raja* ("herd") was used to refer to subject peoples, in particular Christians, who were governed by different fiscal and other regulations under the Ottoman *apartheid* system.

unavoidable. Once in the centre of Split, a uniformed skinhead (on foot) had given me a one-finger salute and invited me to step outside my vehicle. Another day, Kiwi and I were driving to Topusko, east of Petrova Gora, when a military green Landcruiser coming towards us from the opposite direction suddenly veered onto our side of the road. It kept coming towards us, on a collision course. Kiwi, who was at the wheel (or "aiming", as he put it), kept his nerve and just kept driving straight. As they approached I could see there were two local squaddies sitting in the vehicle. At the very last moment, Kiwi swerved sharply to the right and then straightened up again, and at the same time the Serbs executed the same manoeuvre, so that the two vehicles missed each other by a hair's breadth. They were probably expecting us to stop and let them walk all over us. If so, they picked the wrong aid workers. As they say in the Balkans, "*Udri jače!*" ("better luck next time"). Another afternoon in Slunj, on foot this time, I was told by a squaddie that he was going to force-feed me a phosphorous grenade, which he conveniently had clipped to his flak jacket. I remonstrated with him that, as I was a civilian, and an aid worker, that would not be the done thing. I could not help thinking that it would have been more constructive for him to threaten the HV. He was in the company of a middle-aged officer, who said and did nothing, and appeared to be waiting for him to finish before going about their business, as would an adult with a favoured but naughty child. More generally, most men in uniform had been civilians with families, jobs and ordinary lives until the outbreak of the war just a few years previously, and lamented the breakdown in law and order that the war had brought. It was generally the younger ones who were potentially trouble. This trend reaches its extreme logical conclusion with *bakadogo* ("child soldiers") in Africa, who are truly terrifying.

On the evening of 28 May, we heard that a helicopter had been shot down nearby, between Slunj and Batnoga, with 2 million deutschmarks in cash on board (800 thousand pounds at the time, in the *de facto* and default currency of the former Yugoslavia). The Bosnian foreign minister, Ljubijankić, a former ally of Veladžić (see below), was also on board. No-one survived[xvi][25]. In the latter part of the war, the 5th Corps of the ABiH in Bihać, known as the "*sila nebeska*" ("celestial force"), spent DM 46 million buying munitions and food from the SVK/VRS, even as Milošević's Operation Spider sought to ensure the victory of the rebel NOZB in the Bihać pocket. The cash was delivered as required from Sarajevo to Bihać by helicopter (usually via Zagreb, to shorten the flights over SDS territory), and a large part of it ultimately ended up in Arkan's pocket. The 5th Corps General Dudaković's logistics coordinator would travel to Glina ("clay"), in Banija in SDS territory to the north-east of the enclave, to conclude the deals. Money changed hands and the goods were delivered, on the nail. As Legija ("legion"), a former foreign legionnaire with links to the Zemun Clan in his native Belgrade, the most powerful mafia organisation in the Balkans, dominating the drugs trade, described it:

"They couldn't provide the 5th Corps with everything they needed by helicopter from Croatia, because of the bulk and volume required, but from time to time they provided them with serious quantities of cash. DM, of

---

[xvi] According to Babo (the leader of the rebel Muslims), a close friend of Veladžić's who was also supposed to be in the helicopter that day, was persuaded not to travel, and an UNPROFOR investigation established that last-minute changes to the flight plan and the cargo were leaked to the SVK from Bihać. It is said that the minister was investigating a major passport fraud ring. No helicopters had been shot down on the Bihać run before.

course. And then with those marks they bought everything they needed from the Serbs who had them surrounded. Thus it transpired that we were keeping our own enemy alive"[26].

Meanwhile, the VRS's chief of staff, General Milovanović, who refused to accept orders from a "policeman" (i.e. Stanišić, see below) and was therefore kept outside the Operation Spider inner circle, couldn't understand how the besieged 5th Corps seemed to have an endless supply of *mine* ("mortars"). Finally, in the spring of 1995, he telephoned Dudaković and asked him. "I buy them from your Serbs" was the reply[27]. But consorting with the enemy wasn't restricted to the high command. At all levels, munitions and commodities, especially cigarettes, were traded for cash or favours, including attacks staged at agreed times for the purpose of influencing the decisions of superiors, such as forestalling transfer from what was seen as an easy posting[28]. It was not unknown for the 5th Corps to capture a hill from the NOZB by agreement in the morning, on the understanding that the NOZB would then recapture it that afternoon in order to be paid a cash bonus by Babo, to be shared with the enemy. In early 1994, there was a thrice-weekly corridor between the NOZB and the 5th Corps front line, to allow commerce[29]. Retail prices for necessities fluctuated wildly from place to place and over time during the war, depending on the extent to which a place was cut off from legitimate civilian supply routes at any given time. By way of example, the price of a sack of flour (50 kg) reached DM 1,000 in Velika Kladuša at its highest point during this period, and a litre of oil, DM 50. A calf could be bought for a carton of cigarettes. Kiwi and I debated whether we should join the treasure hunt, but on reflection decided that the characters we might run into chasing around the countryside in the dark would probably be worse for our health than the 30 Marlboro we were each getting through every day (one of the golden rules of NGO safety is anyway to avoid travelling at night). It was said the village in question was literally covered in cash. Legija let his two young NOZB bodyguards keep as much as they could stuff into their uniforms, 67 grand[30]. There were regular helicopter runs from Zagreb into Ćoralići near Bihać during this period (officially, over 90 between June 1994 and August 1995), carrying arms and cash. Previously, in December 1994, Izetbegović's private helicopter, a Mi-8 MTV-I, had crashed at Zagreb airport filled with ammunition and explosives destined for the Bihać pocket, resulting in a large explosion and killing the *posada* ("crew")[31]. Shortly thereafter, I saw a Gazelle (built under licence in Mostar under the name Soko ("hawk") SA 341H) helicopter parked one day on flat ground on the way out of Velika Kladuša, on the road south towards Cazin. The only person near it was an armed guard, who looked very alert and much more professional than the common run of squaddies, which was enough by itself to ensure that no-one came near the helicopter. No-one was able to tell me what it was all about, and I judged it imprudent to go and ask. It was parked across the road from what was until very recently the best pizza restaurant in Velika Kladuša, Hamm (named after the German town of the same name where the owner used to live), and which at the time was one of the Bosnian Red Cross (LCK) distribution points (I was later told by an old boy, Mile, that an Italian plane was shot down in the same place during WWII. Once it had been spotted flying low over the town, anyone and everyone with a firearm started taking pot-shots at it, to enthusiastic if erroneous cries of "*Švabo! Švabo!*" ("Kraut"). The pilot was handed over to the Partisans). Every time I have a pizza there now, I remember one day unloading a truck of flour and other staples through the *pendžer* ("window"). I never did discover what or who the helicopter was transporting that day, or even who it belonged to, but there were a lot of things happening behind the scenes at that time that we only heard rumours of. One evening, having a beer in Slunj, Kiwi and I fell in with some local lads, one of whom was nicknamed "Kladuša", because he said he was from there. The very next day, when I arrived in the eponymous town for work, I ran into a group of SVK soldiers, and one of them was Kladuša. They were waiting to be transported to the front, and he didn't seem happy at all, so I gave him a packet of Marlboro to cheer him up. *Sevap* ("good deed for the day"). Officially, there were no Serb troops in Velika Kladuša. On another occasion in Slunj, one Sunday afternoon, we fell in with another group of lads who were amusing themselves down by the river with a tyre hanging by a rope from a tree, seeing who could swing the farthest out over the water before letting go while drinking a bottle of beer. We gave them a good run for their money. After a while, a middle-aged *Četnik* in battledress and sporting a pistol appeared, who they all addressed as "Brada" ("beard"), on account of his physiognomy. He was keen to engage us foreigners in conversation, and I noticed that he appeared to have a Serbian accent. And indeed, when I asked him, he confirmed that he was from Serbia. Officially Serbia was not at war[32].

Just outside Slunj, across the bridge and just before the junction towards Velika Kladuša and Bosnia, was another pizza restaurant, Viktorija, which was much quieter than the bar in the town. We used to go there for a hot meal and a cold beer some evenings, depending on whether the owner, Stanko, had managed to get hold of any supplies. He used to enjoy talking to us foreigners, and the two pretty waitresses were an additional draw. The building is a burnt-out shell to this day, with the inscription *Viktorija* still just visible on the wall above the completely overgrown grounds. One evening, I arrived home late and on foot. It was a pitch black night, and in our street I couldn't see my hand in front of my face, and the silence, with no vehicles passing in the distance to cast ripples on the dead pool of the night air, was absolute. I had to rely on memory to negotiate my way down our hill. As I neared our house, I was suddenly challenged with "*Ko ide?*" ("who goes there?"). I stopped and said nothing, hoping I could get away with playing dumb. The challenge was repeated with a threat to shoot. "It's me", I said this time. "Alright", said our landlord, Milorad, who was in the SVK *vojna policija* ("military police"), "go inside" (I once played Postman Pat with his sister in Zagreb – she had travelled from Serbia via Hungary).

North-west of Slunj, driving straight on past the bridge, the road winds its way onwards for 45 minutes towards Karlovac, passing through the quaint village of Tušilović (formerly the home of a former Partisan and Serb minister in the Croatian government, Stanko "Ćanica" Opačić who, together with two of his brethren, fell from grace in 1950, alleged to have had links to the *Cazinska Buna*, the 1950 Peasants' Revolt[33]), with its roadside restaurant/bar named after *Oluja* ("Operation Storm"). Karlovac is only one hour's drive from the capital of Croatia, to the north. On the southern outskirts of Karlovac, at Turanj, was the front line between the SVK and the HV, separated by an UNPROFOR base. On the other side, the main road leading from Turanj to Karlovac town centre was closed to local traffic (Karlovac, named after its founder, Archduke Charles II, famous for its four rivers - the Mrežnica, Korana, Kupa and Dobra - and for centuries, like its counterpart Banja

Luka, "baths of St. Luke", a centre of gravity of the Borders[xvii], is now increasingly becoming a ghost town[34]). There is now a war memorial at Turanj, with various pieces of artillery and armour on display. For a time, the base was manned by a Jordanian unit, and according to Kiwi, the SVK would fire a mortar into the camp at the same time every day. The Jordanians were then replaced by a British unit, who promptly fired back the first time a mortar landed. The SVK repeated, and were again answered in kind. After a third pot-shot, the local mortars fell silent, and never tried their luck again. I had already learned that some peacekeepers are more equal than others, and that in the Yugoslav Wars, the only contingents consistently ready to stick their necks out and go the extra mile to enforce their mission as they saw it, were the British and the French[35]. It is no coincidence that those two countries have the largest defence budgets in the EU. They were also the two largest contributors to UNPROFOR[xviii][36]. If only they had been in charge of the Srebrenica "safe area"… Some peacekeepers from other countries I came across appeared to be simple civil servants in green. For peacekeepers from developing countries, a UN barracks is a place of luxury, where soldiers have their own beds, regular square meals, and proper hygiene facilities. By saving up their UN *per diems* (which I have it on reliable authority British soldiers did not receive, it being retained by HMG), peacekeepers from countries such as Malaysia could buy a house in their home country at the end of their mission. Indeed, some countries manage to make a profit, and even cover a chunk of their defence budgets with UN peacekeeper reimbursements. For example, in 2003 Bangladesh and Ghana were reimbursed USD 54.8 and 12.7 million

---

[xvii] For Christians living under Ottoman rule in the Borders, Karlovac had the mythical status of America, or Belgrade. After WWII, Karlovac and Banja Luka became the capitals of neighbouring provinces, and until the Yugoslav Wars they were both important economic centres and university towns. The best restaurant in Karlovac is now Tiffany's Pizza.

[xviii] The US did not contribute troops to UNPROFOR; in 1992, US defence secretary and future vice president Dick Cheney said, "If we had 200,000 US troops on the ground in Bosnia, I'm not sure what I would tell them to do". However, I came across US "peacekeepers" in Haiti after the 2010 *trambleman* ("earthquake"), and found them to be very heavy-handed, even though they were only fulfilling what was effectively a police role in what was definitely not a war zone (albeit racked by violent organised crime, which was only aggravated when the walls of the country's high-security prison were knocked down by the earthquake). A colleague and I, Chris, both obviously European, and civilians, found ourselves cornered by two Humvees gorging with US squaddies armed to the teeth when we remonstrated with two US MPs for arresting two local blokes, who had just dug us a fresh pit as a depository for the biodegradable bags that held the contents of the latrine in our camp in the airport grounds. I had paid them the agreed price of USD 50 each for what was a few hours' work, and had also given them a receipt. But locals were not allowed into the airport, which meant they were stopped and searched, and when the cash was found on them, it was concluded they must have stolen it – their receipts notwithstanding. I attempted to appeal to the MPs' human side - after all, it was only two blokes trying to earn a living in a ruined country where 200,000 people or more had just been killed – but to no avail. The atmosphere started to get very tense, and I thought we were going to be arrested as well, or even taken out: people have gone to Guantánamo for less (at least we wouldn't have far to go: the US enclave, a natural harbour inaccessible from the interior and let by Cuba under a perpetual lease in 1903, is just across the water from Haiti). But reason finally prevailed, and the MPs said they would release the two locals (although we never saw them again). The reader may already have concluded that this incident can be put down to racism – but the two MPs, one of them a woman, were themselves both black (Haiti, unlike its Spanish-speaking neighbour, the Dominican Republic, with which it shares the island of Hispaniola, is almost exclusively inhabited by the descendants of slaves transported by the French from Senegal. It was one of the first countries in the Americas to become independent, in 1804, the result of the only successful slave rebellion in modern history, led by Toussaint l'Ouverture, the "Black Spartacus", who died in prison in France after scuppering Napoleon's American dream, but is now the poorest country in the Americas, with the highest prevalence of HIV/AIDS. Although nominally a Catholic country, the most prevalent religion is voodoo). The MPs appeared unable to distinguish between Port-au-Prince and Baghdad. But they certainly had no difficulties distinguishing between Americans and Strangers.

respectively for deploying peacekeepers to UN missions, while the estimated "troop costs" item of their respective defence budgets was USD 23.5 and 2.1 million[37]. None of this creates an environment that encourages exceptional soldiering, as recent events in the Democratic Republic of the Congo have shown, to mention but one example. On 6 June 2014, Pakistani peacekeepers failed to intervene to stop an attack that resulted in the deaths of at least 30 civilians, 9 km away from their base in Mutarule, in South Kivu in the eastern DRC, even though they were aware of what was going on[38]. As if that wasn't enough, there has been a string of rape and other sex abuse scandals, including child prostitution, involving UN peacekeepers deployed to conflicts from the Balkans via Africa to the Caribbean and beyond[39]. And after the Haiti earthquake in 2010, UN peacekeepers brought cholera to the country for the first time in 150 years. The resulting epidemic spread beyond Haiti's borders and has killed 9,000 people[40].

Turning instead off the main road at the sharp right-hand junction past the Slunj bridge is a *poligon* ("firing range"), which during the war also housed a cake factory, run by our landlady's brother (the range, the largest in Yugoslavia, was created in the early 1960s, and formed a barrier disrupting the Serb communities in Lika and Kordun, the future Sectors North and South, that had until then been contiguous. This was interpreted by many as a sign of trouble to come, and led to an increase in migration to Srem, see below. Major manoeuvres were held between Bihać and Karlovac in 1971[41]). Continuing, country roads lead to Velika Kladuša and Bosnia through the small town of Cetingrad, before the war a predominantly Croat community surrounded by Serb villages. There is a short cut from Cetingrad to Velika Kladuša by a back road (only 7 km), but it was closed during the war and remains closed to all but local traffic today (resident within 5 km). Because of its ethnic/religious make-up and its strategic position, the town was largely destroyed at the beginning of the war. It fell on 27 November 1991, 11 days after Slunj, and the local HV withdrew to Bosnia, with most of the civilian population, 2,500 people. Previously, an annual agricultural show was held there to celebrate St. Joseph's day, 19 March. During the war, many Serbs from the Bihać pocket took refuge there, among them some of the teachers from Velika Kladuša, as the whole county teaching staff had been replaced by Serbs and Montenegrins in 1950 in the aftermath of the Peasants' Revolt (the local teachers were seconded to posts elsewhere in Bosnia). It was also the site of the main cemetery for the Catholic minority from the Bihać pocket. The position of Croat refugees and IDPs in the Bihać pocket became precarious once the war started in Bosnia, and as a vulnerable minority they became scapegoats and the targets for abuse, labelled *Četniks*. When the HDZ-SDA war started, this label changed to *Ustaše*. In the summer of 1994, Steve, Kiwi, our boss Gordon, and another colleague, Canbat (a former Canadian peacekeeper) had heard sporadic *pucnjava* ("shooting") while driving through Cetingrad. They accelerated, and too late saw a wire with flagging stretched across the road near the cemetery. Whether it was a *mina* ("IED"), or an *otmica* ("kidnapping"), they never found out, as in the event fortunately nothing happened and no-one appeared as they skidded through the *žica* ("wire"). Having come to an uneventful stop, they put their foot down and left Cetingrad behind them. Cetingrad was captured by the Turks from the bishop of Zagreb in 1584, four years before the Spanish Armada, and during WWII was an *Ustaše* stronghold[42]. 142 Serb civilians were killed in Cetingrad in 1941[43]. The main local agglomeration, Vojnić, a quiet market town, can be reached by this roundabout shorter route, or by continuing along the main road from Slunj towards Karlovac and turning right at the village of Krnjak. Just east of Vojnić is the mountain range of Petrova Gora ("Peter's mountain"), which was the location of the Partisans' first central hospital in the second half of 1942, hidden in a series of tunnels, and never discovered by the enemy. It was also the Partisan HQ for Croatia, and became a symbol of resistance to the *Ustaše* at the beginning of the war in 1941[44]. The road then continues south from Vojnić towards Velika Kladuša. On the road north out of Vojnić, just on the outskirts of the town, is a timber yard, outside which our truck drivers (usually Gary, John and Diane, all Scots; I later came across John in Cyprus during one of Israel's incursions into Lebanon[xix][45], in 2006, and in Haiti, after the 2010 earthquake) used to park their Scanias overnight on the two-day drive from Split into the Bihać pocket. The alternative was to park in the UNPROFOR compound in Slunj, but that made the run into Velika Kladuša and Cazin, and then back to Split the next day, a longer drive. But at least then we could offer them some hospitality. Another consideration was the charge levied by the Polish peacekeepers for truck stop services, if not bread and breakfast, which was payable not in hard currency, but consisted of consuming an inordinate amount of vodka with the duty squaddies, something that tended to have a deleterious effect on one's driving skills the next morning. At one such session I was told the story of Katin forest, where Stalin massacred the Polish officer corps (over 4,000 men) after invading eastern Poland in collusion with Hitler in 1939 (ironically, the Soviet Union later sat on the Nuremberg Tribunal that tried the remaining Nazi leaders in 1946 for "planning and waging an aggressive war", as well as the newly-developed offences of war crimes and crimes against humanity[xx][46]. After Hitler and Stalin had carved up Poland between them, tens of thousands of Poles made their way to France to carry on the fight, and after France's capitulation in June 1940, to the UK. 145 Polish airmen fought in the battle of Britain, and 29 of them were killed defending our country in its hour of greatest need since 1588[xxi]). Now the timber yard has recently started working again. Driving south from Vojnić, or north from Cetingrad, then east, the countryside opens out into a plain, a brief respite from the hills, and leads to the hamlet of Maljevac (*malj* means "mallet"), the *GP* ("border crossing"). Immediately beyond the border the hills resume, with a steep slope leading straight up into the town of Velika Kladuša. The first time I crossed the border, I noticed someone's ominous addition in English to the sign greeting the traveller: "Welcome to hell". Today, this is the border of the EU, and has bog-standard EU infrastructure, centred around a large roofed area for passport control and customs inspections, with numerous uniformed *službenici* ("officials") looking busy, or merely loafing about.

[xix] Since the end of Lebanon's civil war, which lasted from 1975 until 1990, there have been regular clashes between the Hezbollah ("party of God") movement in Lebanon, supported by Iran and Syria, and Israeli forces. In 2006, Israel invaded southern Lebanon, and on 30 July, 16 children were killed in an Israeli air strike. Tony Blair said the war crime was "absolutely tragic", but refused to call for a ceasefire. Because Beirut airport had been disabled by the Israeli air force, aid flown in from the UK had to be transferred to RORO ("roll on roll off") ferry in Cyprus. This process was greatly facilitated by the fact that the head of customs at Larnaca port and airport was the same bloke, Kostas, who would travel between the two on a scooter. Since the one-month war there have also been repeated incidents between the Lebanese and Israeli armed forces. Blair was Middle East peace envoy between 2007 and 2015.
[xx] One of the guards at the Nuremberg Tribunal, an English Romany, lost his cool and bayonetted a SS prisoner who insisted on giving the Nazi salute when ordered into the courtroom. No Romany witnesses were called to give evidence at the trials, despite the fact that it is thought that up to 500,000 Romanies perished in the *Porrajmos* or *Uštavipe*, Hitler's Holocaust.
[xxi] The French capitulation was signed in exactly the same place, in a forest in northern France, and in the same railway carriage, which was brought out of retirement in a museum for the occasion, as the armistice that put an end to WWI (the subsequent Treaty of Versailles was signed exactly five years after the Sarajevo assassination).

Now the Croatian authorities are hoping to further expand the facilities using the fabled "European funds", as the crossing is subject to long *gužva* ("traffic jams") on bank holiday weekends (as with the other recent adherents to the EU, the lack of absorption capacity, i.e. the arcane bureaucratic knowledge of how to turn on the EU tap, has meant that much of the EU cash spent in Croatia has thus far found its way into the pockets of contractors from the more established member states). Twenty years ago, it was the border between the SDS and alternatively the SDA and the DNZ, and was manned on the Croatian side by two old Serb boys, and on the Bosnian side by two teenage Muslims. It was once also the border between Austria-Hungary and Turkey. I saw one of these two after the war walking down the street in Velika Kladuša in civvies, and asked him if he remembered me. He looked over his shoulder to make sure no-one was listening and said he did. I enquired after his friend, and he told me he was in Germany, and that he hoped to join him soon. Our trucks were escorted from Maljevac to our *skladište* ("warehouse") in Polje ("field") and then on to the front line on the road south to Cazin (and back) by Riki, a local *murjak* ("copper"). We used to fill his tank with fuel for his trouble. Some people might call that *korupcija* ("bribery"); we called it engaging with the real economy in wartime. Riki's family lived right beside the Maljevac border crossing and owned contiguous land on both sides of the border, but after the war started (and even after it ended), they were no longer allowed free access to their land in Croatia.

My destination was the village of Kuplensko[xxii], 3 km south of Vojnić. However, the route described above was closed to me because of the tactical partial demolition of the Slunj bridge, and I had to take an extensive detour through Bosnia, a route I had never taken before. Turning right onto a single-track country road halfway through the Plitvice national park, I slowly and carefully drove 10 km uphill through Ličko Petrovo Selo ("Lika Peter's village") to the Bosnian border. Until very recently this crossing had been a front line, and closed to most traffic. After crossing the border at an isolated, windswept post set high up in the hills on bare rocks, which took so long that I fell asleep at the wheel waiting for the Bosnian official to check my *pasoš* ("passport"), even though I was his only customer, I headed through the village of Izačić south-east on the road to Bihać, passing more horses and carts on my way than cars. Izačić was a favoured entry point for HV *diverzanti* ("special forces") into the Bihać pocket during the war, among others. After 10 km, I reached Bihać with its fortress, captured by the Turks from the Habsburgs in 1592, and recaptured in 1878 after resistance by the local Muslims was crushed in two weeks[47]. It was also Tito's headquarters in the second half of 1942, up until the Axis fourth offensive, and the scene of the first *AVNOJ* ("resistance") conference on 26 November that year, which established the KPJ as being the heart and soul of the resistance, with the slogan, "*Smrt fašizmu – sloboda narodu!*" ("death to fascism – freedom to the people!")[48] (Bihać was finally liberated by the Partisans on 28 March 1945, after three months of intense fighting from the Plitvice lakes, followed by Slunj on 14 April and Karlovac on 8 May, VE Day[xxiii][49]). Just before the town centre, I turned sharply north and drove the 15 km to Cazin, our new base after Operation

---

[xxii] "Kuplensko" was the Serb name for the village, while in Croatian it became "Kupljensko". But the name "Kuplensko" was most commonly used by the refugees at that time, despite the fact that Bosnian phonology favours Croatian, and it is used throughout this book.
[xxiii] The Soviet VE Day, *Denj Pobedi*, 9 May, was celebrated in the former Yugoslavia. The Nazis capitulated to the Allies in Riems on 8 May, but Stalin insisted on a capitulation in Berlin, which took place the following day.

Storm, where I met up with Kiwi. Cazin, like Slunj was an *Ustaše* administrative centre in WWII[50]. I was now back on familiar ground. It being quite late in the day, I decided to spend the night there, get a briefing on the latest developments, and continue my journey in the morning. The next day, I drove the 35 km north across the old front line through Pećigrad to Velika Kladuša, and from there crossed the border back into Croatia at Maljevac.

As I progressed, the interconnecting country roads, transporting the traveller through expanses of the primeval European forest where medieval beasts still lurk, in the company of more ancient spirits, were as humped and winding as any in Cumbria. Between the swathes of deciduous foliage on my route were orchards and fields of irregular shapes and sizes, some flat, some bent absurdly over a hillside, as if to defy the very idea of agricultural health and safety. The few deserted settlements I had to drive through were as menacing, if not more so, than the wilderness, as they not only concealed potential dangers, but also exuded less, rather than more life. Yet the sun was shining, and the pleasant heat on my arm resting on the open window sill belied the prospect of evil deeds. There were no vehicles or people visible anywhere. The day before, I had noticed houses with white *čaršafi* ("sheets") hung outside on the washing lines, and front doors that had been left open, and I saw more of them now. I realised later that it was an attempt to discourage the HV from demolishing them, by making it clear there was no resistance within (as the Nobel-prize winning Yugoslav writer Ivo Andrić[xxiv] wrote in respect of 1878: "All gates should be open when an army approaches, because they shoot at houses they find closed"[51]). It had clearly worked in some cases, at least. I also learned later that the order for the population to clear out had come from the top as soon as the HV offensive started (or even before), and was swiftly executed[xxv][52]. Most people had already prepared their two or so evacuation bags containing documents, photographs, clothes and some food. Our landlady, Vesna, a Croat, had shown me hers, and she had even included eggs suspended in flour to prevent them breaking. Her father, Ivica, later told me that he was so stressed driving to Belgrade via Bosnia after Operation Storm that he didn't eat or drink a thing for 24 hours. When he finally reached relative safety, he devoured a loaf of bread and two litres of water in one sitting. Those Catholics who had remained in the Serb Borders republic during the war were faced with a quandary: sit it out and wait for the HV, at the risk of being branded an *izdajnik* ("traitor"), or flee with the Serbs, and risk being arrested as a *špijun* ("spy"). Would-be refugees were screened as they boarded buses, and anyone suspected of being a Croat might be asked a culturally-specific question, such as the identity of their *krsna slava* ("family saint and feast day"), in an attempt to catch them out.

In contrast to this human desolation, the animals had reclaimed the preserve of man's hegemony – the roads. I came across and startled a huge *krmača* ("sow") sun-bathing on the tarmac. Horses, sheep, and cows wandered at will from one property to another, where fences and gates allowed. Some of the cows had bloated udders,

---

[xxiv] A Catholic from Travnik, who was detained in the crackdown following the Sarajevo assassination. He was the Yugoslav ambassador to Germany from 1939 until the outbreak of war in 1941, and wrote some of his most important works living in Belgrade during WWII. He won the Nobel prize in 1961, and donated the prize money to public libraries in Bosnia.

[xxv] According to Legija, "The Serb Borders forces, after a single day, instead of organising a defence, were only interested in getting away, if not fleeing". He compares them unfavourably to the 5th Corps, and indeed to the Partisans, and points out that Tuđman met with Milošević in Geneva just three days before Operation Storm.

and were clearly in need of being milked. It was a curious liberation, even a revolution, sweeping aside the old order and its artificial divisions of ownership. In earlier months I had got used to nature's partial repossession caused by the fuel shortages, in the shape of an eagle that slowly took off from the tarmac when I approached on the road winding down from Krnjak to the village of Kolarić, on my morning commute from Slunj to Velika Kladuša. But that was merely a foretaste of this. It was truly Orwellian, and on a grand scale. Yet it didn't last long. The increased amount of traffic led to an increase in the number of dead animals on the road; and the following month, when the VRS were pushed back from Bosanski Petrovac (where Fitzroy Maclean parachuted into on his second trip to Yugoslavia, in early 1944, before travelling on horseback and by train to Tito's new headquarters in Drvar; and also the site of his second improvised airstrip, in the spring of that year, from where 2,000 wounded Partisans were flown by the Allies to Italy for medical care[53]: an old C47 Dakota, somewhat battered now, can still be seen on display there) 30 km south-east of Bihać, I saw other "liberated" livestock being herded *en masse* towards Cazin by civilians and squaddies (the two often interchangeable in the Yugoslav Wars) by a variety of modes of transport, including two live sheep tied to the roof of a Yugo ("south wind") beetle (it is not unusual to see even more fantastic sights when driving along the main north-south coast road in Mozambique, from a flock of goats perched on top of an artic-load of timber, to a live cow strapped to the roof of a car). Discipline in what was still a war zone was non-existent, at least for secular offences[54]. According to Zuhdija "Hope" Miljković, a graduate of the Belgrade JNA academy and a veteran of both sides in the intra-Muslim war, described by him in exhaustive detail in his memoirs, *Circle of Death*, on 17 September the Bužim brigade, described by Legija as "the most problematic and notorious" of the 5th Corps, killed some of their comrades from the Krupa brigade outside Bosanska Krupa for spit-roasting a liberated pig[55]. This is a recurrent feature of war's wide wastes, where man and beast alike are freed from the trammels of civilisation. In 1997, I was invited to the execution by pistol to the head of two teenage squaddies in the small town of Baraka ("blessing") in South Kivu in the DRC, for shooting a beer-seller when she refused them credit. The background to the murder was that the new Rwandan-backed authorities after the overthrow of the dictator and CIA man Mobutu wanted to put an end to the days when the army lived off the poor, taking what they wanted by force, and as a first step to doing so introduced pay for the army. The very first pay packet the *askari* ("soldiers") had ever received resulted in *pombe* ("beer") prices doubling, as supplies dried up in the sudden spike in consumption. Afterwards, the general feeling in the town was that justice had been done[xxvi]. The end of the colonial period in Africa, from the 1950s onwards, saw the dark continent plunged into the Cold War, with the two northern belligerents seeking to place their stooges in positions of absolute power at key strategic points (the most repressive regimes and the most violent and tragic conflicts resulting from this policy were in those countries rich in mineral resources, such as the DRC and Angola). In particular, the Portuguese Colonial Wars of the 1960s and

---

[xxvi] The mayor of Baraka was the spitting image of *rahmetli* ("the late") Muhamed Ali – perhaps a souvenir of the 1974 Rumble in the Jungle. I had the occasion to visit him in his office one morning, and as we discussed official business I noticed a huge, black spider, motionless on the wall behind him. The place stunk of *mapopo* ("bats"): there must have been a colony of them in the space between the roof and the ceiling of the single-storey building. That afternoon I had to go back to follow something up with him, and was surprised to see that the formidable *mdudu* ("beastie"), almost too big to be an arachnid, hadn't moved an inch. *Akuna shida* ("no problem").

1970s (Portugal was the first European power to have a presence in Africa, and the last to leave) were succeeded by a proxy war fought between Cuba and South Africa in Angola and Mozambique, which in the case of oil and diamonds-rich Angola, descended into a gang war that outlived the Cold War by over a decade, until 2002[xxvii]. A local colleague, Paolo, was killed in an attempted *roubo de carro* ("car-jacking") in Luanda just after the war ended. Now, the reason I had been living in Slunj and not Velika Kladuša was because while there were many empty houses in Slunj, the majority of the Croat inhabitants having left for Karlovac in November 1991 (20,000 people from the town and surrounding villages, among them Nikola, who spent the rest of the war fighting to get his town back, with multiple missions behind enemy lines and in Bosnia) after losing 350 men in a three-month blockade, Velika Kladuša was full of IDPs from the outlying villages and further afield (up to 70,000, of which 15,000 from Cazin[56]), and so renting a house there would have meant putting a family out into the street, quite apart from the problem of tracking down the lawful owner (in Nazranj, the capital of Ingushetia, we became embroiled in a dispute between the businessman with whom we had concluded a lease agreement for our *sklad* ("warehouse"), and a third party who claimed to be the real owner. The putative *hozjain/hakim* ("landlord") told me when I met with him to discuss the imbroglio that he was in the middle of organising a *jadernij udar* ("nuclear strike") on Vladikavkaz, the capital of North Ossetia). Many IDPs from Slunj were unable to travel directly to Karlovac, and instead made their way to Cazin, from where they were able to pass via Herzegovina back into Croatia. Some of the empty houses in Slunj were occupied by newcomers from the outlying villages, for security reasons among other things (before the war started, some Serbs had taken to spending the night on the JNA range for the same reason).

In June 1990, Tuđman's new government, elected with 42% of votes on a pledge to deliver Croatian statehood (but under the proportional representation rules

[xxvii] The former Warsaw Pact puppet, Dos Santos, a statue of whom with raised fist in Luanda donated by North Korea is said to have originally been a statue of Kim Il Sung with a recast head, also outlived the Cold War by doing an about-face and outsmarting his erstwhile rival and champion of western values, Jonas Savimbi, who ultimately died of starvation in the bush after being abandoned as an anachronism by his former patrons. The atmosphere in Luanda after the death of Savimbi, who had cast a long and very dark shadow over much of Angola for more than 30 years, was electric, and I was put in mind of what the atmosphere must have been like in Germany after the death of Hitler. One day in Luanda I had cause to read the CV of one of the local members of staff, Abel, and was surprised to see that his previous work experience included a five-year period as a slave in the vast territory controlled by Savimbi's UNITA, now plagued by untold land mines. The final bell tolled for Savimbi when a hunting rifle that had been presented to him by South African president P.W. Botha was captured from a camp he had hastily abandoned, after his last, desperate offensive on an electricity substation that supplied the vast slums of Luanda. Dos Santos remains in power to this day, presiding over one of the poorest countries in the world while simultaneously being one of the richest men in Brazil; during the war, he controlled Angola's oil and gas fields, and was one of the US' largest suppliers of the black gold, communist credentials notwithstanding, while Savimbi controlled Angola's diamonds. Cut off from the rest of the country, Luanda was a bubble, and an extremely expensive one, dependent on exports from Portugal and Brazil (at least as far as residents with a western lifestyle were concerned: by way of example, I found restaurants to be at least five times more expensive than in South Africa, while African groceries such as fresh tropical fruit and vegetables, even though delivered from outside the city, could be obtained for far more realistic prices). The last I heard, this situation has changed little since the war. But even during the war, with so much money in circulation, Luanda held out the promise of success for some: I was surprised one day to meet a young man from Portugal who told me he had just moved there, looking for work. At the other end of the scale, Paolo, a former captain in the Angolan army, told me that basic training was not considered tough enough to prepare new recruits to face UNITA unless at least one out of every intake didn't make it. Over 500,000 people were killed during the war.

introduced by the KPJ, gaining a two-thirds parliamentary majority), produced a draft new *ustav* ("constitution") which made no mention of the Serbs ("Croatia is the homeland of the Croats")[xxviii][57]. This was to be a Central European, Catholic state, bound by historical and cultural ties to Germany and Italy, and as far removed from their oriental Orthodox and Muslim neighbours as possible. The JNA started withdrawing arms from TA units in Croatia and Slovenia after the election of their respective new governments (as it had done in Kosovo in the late 1980s)[58]. Meanwhile, the SDS party, founded in February and led from October by dentist Milan Babić, the mayor of Knin and later prime minister, in tandem with Milan Martić, the Knin police chief and later president of the Serb Borders republic (described by Legija as a "half-educated traffic policeman"[59]), had set up an association of Serb district councils, which soon had a handful of adherents, including Vojnić. Before the war, Serbs were a majority in 13 of the 100 districts in Croatia[60] (Croatia is now organised into 20 *županije*, "counties", plus the city of Zagreb). These 13 districts, largely underdeveloped (the question of "neglect of Serb areas in Croatia" was a bone of contention within the Croatian government from immediately after WWII onwards[61]), corresponded roughly to the former Austro-Hungarian Military Frontier, which was administered directly from Vienna and not subject to the autonomous Croatian parliament in Zagreb until it was demilitarised in the 1870s[62]. This division within Croatia was also one of the tactics by which the Habsburgs sought to facilitate their rule[63]. Orthodox refugees fleeing the Ottomans were settled here and given certain privileges, such as home rule, in return for defending the border against the Turks from 1527 onwards[64]. Whereas 6% of men were under arms throughout Austria-Hungary, in the Croatian Borders this proportion was 60%, and the population had the status of soldiers, as opposed to serfs[65]. Ironically, the original Orthodox settlers are said to have been largely Vlachs, a pastoral Romanian-speaking minority, and the same people who were resettled by the Turks in the Bosnian Borders in the same period, and especially after 1699, when the current border was more or less established[xxix][66], in order to perform the same function as their brethren on the other side of the frontier, in return for similar privileges. They had come mainly from Herzegovina, as well as from elsewhere in Bosnia, where they had originally been settled from the Belgrade and Smederevo regions of Serbia to repopulate areas devastated by war, plague and other disasters. Over time they were subsumed into the Serb identity[67]. Much has been made of this historical detail by some Croatian historians, who argue among other things that Serbs should go back to Romania[68]. Following the same logic, the whole Balkans should revert to Albania[xxx]. Today, the word *Vlah* is a derogatory term for Serbs and

---

[xxviii] The constitution now states in its recitals, "The Republic of Croatia is hereby established as the nation state of the Croat people and as the state of the following ethnic minorities", followed by a long list which includes Serbs (as well as Jews, Muslims, Romanies, Albanians and "others").

[xxix] Yugoslavia's internal administrative boundaries were set by Milovan Đilas, see below, during WWII, and according to Owen, were "often arbitrary and driven by political expediency [...] and never intended to be international borders". Đilas had originally considered making the Croatian Borders an autonomous region. In 1972 and in 1986, Slovenia and Macedonia blocked resolutions recognising the existing borders as permanent and immutable. In 1978 Tito said, "We have never had, nor do we have, any territorial claims in respect of any of our neighbours". Despite this, any discussion on redrawing the borders to facilitate a peaceful settlement was rejected by the international community at the beginning of the Yugoslav crisis.

[xxx] The question of the origins of the inhabitants of various territories is an extremely controversial subject in the Balkans, and a variety of weird and wonderful pedigrees going back to antiquity are claimed by extremists of all stripes in an attempt to lend legitimacy to their present-day territorial ambitions.

Croats in particular, and Christians in general, while Muslims are sometimes referred to, equally contemptuously, as *Turci* ("Turks"). The Military Frontier was not restricted to the Croatian Borders, but extended through Vojvodina as far as Transylvania in Romania[69] (the most celebrated commander of the Military Frontier was *Ban* ("lord") Josip Jelačić, count of Bužim, born near Novi Sad ("new garden") in Vojvodina, who held the post from 1848 until his death in 1859. In 1835, he had led a campaign against the Ottomans in Velika Kladuša. His greatest achievement was to shake off Hungarian domination of Croatia within the Habsburg state, albeit temporarily, and there is a statue of him mounted on horseback brandishing a sabre in the direction of Budapest in the main square in Zagreb, which is also named after him. After the Hungarian revolution of 1848, which abolished serfdom, he invaded Hungary in order to restore Habsburg rule. The revolution was crushed in 1849 when the Russians came to the rescue, only for Hungarian sovereignty over Croatia to be re-established in 1867. Jelačić's statue was removed by the communist authorities in 1947, but restored in 1990)[70]. With the coming of peace to the Military Frontier with the Svištov peace agreement of 1791, there was a migration of Serbs (and some Croats) into former Ottoman lands in Croatia, and after the occupation of Bosnia in 1878, across the border into the future Bihać pocket, where the population density was lower and agricultural land more freely available. Crnaja ("black country") was one such settlement[71]. *Milom i silom* ("by hook and by crook"), more district councils were added to the SDS's association, and in July 1990, 49 years since the Serb uprising against the *Ustaše* (see below), it convened a Serb assembly, announcing it would hold a referendum on sovereignty the following month (which the government in Zagreb declared would be illegal). In September, they declared their own autonomous region, the Serb Borders[72]. The same month, Martić informed his superiors in Belgrade that his men would not wear the new Croatian police uniform with its controversial revisionist symbols from WWII (for example, the Croatian *šahovnica* ("chessboard") coat of arms is the fascist NDH coat of arms reversed). There was a stand-off with a delegation from Zagreb that resulted in a climb-down by the latter, and the federal government in Belgrade warned Zagreb not to use force to impose its will on Knin (the federal president at the time was Serbia's Borisav Jović, and Milošević gave Martić to understand that he enjoyed their full support). On 17 August, the *policija* ("police") attempted to take Knin by force, but withdrew when JNA jets forced their helicopters to return to Zagreb. Meanwhile, the SDS declared a state of war, and the local militia revealed itself to be well-armed, thanks to the JNA[73]. The HDZ, outgunned, started to smuggle in arms from abroad. In February 1991, the SDS movement reached Pakrac in the north. Federal vice president and future president of Croatia Stipe Mesić and the head of the KOS, General Aleksandar Vasiljević, both appeared on the scene. The police retook the town, and the JNA was mobilised to keep the two sides apart. This was the first fighting in Croatia[74]. On 16 March, after a referendum, the assembly declared that the autonomous region was part of Serbia[75]. The next clash was in Korenica in Plitvice on 31 March, in which one Serb and one Croat were killed. The JNA deployed again to separate the sides, but the police refused to withdraw, and the militia blocked the roads and the railway with logs cut from the forest. In Slavonia in the north-east, Serb and Croat militia began to set up barricades in villages. A small group of senior HDZ officials, including Gojko Šušak, a Canadian pizza millionaire who bankrolled Tuđman's election, and later Tuđman's *oficir bez veze* ("liaison officer") with the Bosnian HDZ (i.e. "governor" of Bosnia), as well as Croatian defence minister 1991-1998[xxxi][76], fired a RPG at a Serb village, Borovo Selo ("pine village"), near Vukovar ("city of wolves"), and on 2 May, a busload of policemen, acting on their own initiative, attempted to take the village, but were ambushed by the Unit (see below), resulting in 12 fatalities. This led to major demonstrations in Croatia, and once again, the JNA deployed. The government of Serbia accused Zagreb of preparing for war[77]. Tuđman formed a national guard from police reserves, and the JNA deployed, via Bosnia, to the majority Serb areas of Croatia. Over half a million people had already had to leave their homes and move to areas where they belonged to the ethnic/religious majority[78]. The next flashpoint was the Croat village of Kijevo, 10 km south-east of Knin. The SDS ordered the police to leave, but they refused. The new JNA commander on the ground was Colonel Ratko Mladić, a Bosnian (when he was arrested by the SAS in Lazarevo in Serbia in May 2011 for extradition to The Hague war crimes tribunal, ICTY, established by the UN security council in 1993, he said, "It's a fair cop"; and on the first day of his trial, a year later, he made a throat-cutting gesture to the angry public gallery, who included women from Srebrenica[xxxii]). On 26 August, after a 12-hour JNA artillery bombardment, which flattened it, the militia attacked the village. At this time, the siege of Vukovar, and with it the real war, began. The population of Vukovar had been 44% Croat and 38% Serb (the remainder were Yugoslavs and ethnic minorities, such as Hungarians, Slovaks, Poles and Muslims)[79]. There were defections by Croat JNA officers, and large scale desertion by non-Serb *vojni obveznici* ("conscripts"), who were quickly replaced by local *dobrovoljci* ("volunteers")[80]. One such defector, Albanian Tom Berisha, became a general in the HV, and went on to command the UÇK in Kosovo in 1998[81]. Only majority-Orthodox Serbia and Montenegro ("black mountain", the smallest Yugoslav republic, named after Black Ivo, a medieval Serb chieftain[82]) continued to provide conscripts and funding for the JNA[83]. Fighting erupted all along the confrontation line between the SDS and HDZ-controlled councils, with the SDS militia providing infantry supported by JNA hardware. Those JNA *kasarne* ("barracks") in Croatia outside SDS areas found themselves besieged, and the squaddies were generally only allowed to leave after surrendering all their hardware[84]. Vukovar fell on 18 November, after 15,000 people had been killed. Slunj had been occupied two days previously, allowing the SDS to secure a road link between Knin and Glina. The same month, Milošević, president of Serbia since 1989 but *de facto* ruler of Yugoslavia (and officially federal president from 1997 until 2000, after the expiry of the maximum of two terms in his former post; and after Dayton, the international community's *de facto* interlocutor for all matters of war and peace in the Balkans[85]), agreed to the deployment of UN peacekeepers along the confrontation line, which had the effect of freezing the belligerent parties' positions and consolidating their gains, a partition he aspired to convert into a new international border (federal president Mesić had requested peacekeepers in September)[86].

[xxxi] Tetin, see below, told me that in 1992 he was present at a meeting in Sarajevo at which Izetbegović offered Šušak "unlimited funds" to procure munitions for the ABiH. After Izetbegović had left the room, Šušak ridiculed the offer.
[xxxii] Like Milošević, see below, Mladić, described as a "disgusting man" by Colonel Bob Stewart, UNPROFOR commander 1992-1993, was no stranger to personal tragedy: his daughter committed suicide at Belgrade university in 1994, where she was studying medicine.

Now, four years later, some houses had signs of fire and other damage, or graffiti, such as "Bad Blue Boys" (Dinamo Zagreb football firm) and "*HOS*" (Croat paramilitary unit, who recently erected a controversial memorial to their fallen comrades in Jasenovac, see below[87]). There were also swastikas and *U* signs in evidence. Down a side road I spotted a defunct Sherman tank[xxxiii][88] with "We are *Četniks*" sprayed in Cyrillic on the side. I noticed at a crossroads that one house was entirely missing.

I had stopped there once before, when I stupidly volunteered to help an incompetent colleague who had suffered a puncture. As she had no idea what to do, she took my vehicle back to base in Slunj while I remained to clear up for her. I found out later that she never did alert Kiwi as to where I was (I had been unable to reach him on the HF radio at the time). This and other experiences taught me that one of the greatest hazards to aid workers is an unreliable colleague. Two years later at a checkpoint in Bukavu in the DRC, a colleague thought it would be amusing to leap over the barrier. The Rwandan soldiers, from one of the few professional armies in Africa, Paul Kagame's FPR, were not amused, and ordering him at gunpoint to lie down on the grass beside the road, confiscated his shoes. After half an hour they let him (and everyone else) go, but he didn't get his shoes back. He had endangered not only himself but the whole team. On another occasion, I was in the rear vehicle in a convoy of three heading south from Slunj. My two colleagues up ahead were chatting away merrily in French on the VHF radio, when one of them suddenly said, "By the way John, we've just run someone off the road". I slowed down, and coming round the next, narrow bend, I saw a local civilian vehicle parked at an odd angle on the edge of the road, and just about to pull away in my direction. However, when he saw me, the driver, a man of my age, got out, blocking the road. I was forced to stop. He was dressed in civvies, and not visibly armed, but as he walked towards me I could see he was shaking with anger. I greeted him in my friendliest manner, but he didn't reciprocate. Instead, he let me know in clear, controlled and no uncertain terms, without swearing, what he thought about overpaid foreigners driving recklessly around his country ("You're not worth two rolls of sheep shite"). There was nothing I could do but apologise on behalf of my colleagues (who had not stopped), and remind him that I wasn't the culprit. After he had got this off his chest, he got back into his car and we both went our separate ways. As I continued my journey, I pondered how it was that, in an environment where safety is supposed to be the paramount consideration, I had become bound to these two beauties as if fitted with a ball and chain. I learned later that it had been insisted upon by an institutional donor, the EU, who wanted to fund more than one NGO working in this part of the country. The fact that there was a reason why only one NGO had managed to set up a

---

[xxxiii] Named after American Civil War hero General William Sherman, who wrote in 1866, "We must act with vindictive earnestness against the Sioux, even to their extermination, men, women and children", after a unit of 81 US squaddies were wiped out near Fort Phil Kearney in Wyoming. The Sioux, originally from Minnesota, were the only Indian nation to defeat the US and obtain a peace treaty in their favour, in 1868 (although the US reneged on the treaty in 1877 when gold was discovered in the Paha Sapa/Black Hills, in Dakota and Wyoming, which were described 100 years later as the "largest operating gold mine in the western hemisphere"; in 1980, the US supreme court ruled that their land, described by the flamboyant "General" George Custer, who led the incursion, as "beautiful parks and valleys", had been taken from the Sioux illegally. Custer, known by the Sioux as Pehin Hanska, "Long Hair", had attained the rank of major-general during the Civil War of 1861-1865, but at the time of his death at the battle of Peji Sluta/Little Bighorn in 1876, he was a lieutenant-colonel). In 2016, president Obama blocked a project to build an oil pipeline running past the Sioux reservation in Dakota and threatening its water sources after stand-offs between demonstrators and police.

programme here seemed to have escaped them. Now, I discovered too late that the tools in my colleague's kit were incomplete. As I pondered what to do, I heard sporadic shooting in the distance. It was a lovely late summer's afternoon, and I realised that standing as I was beside a conspicuous white vehicle in the middle of a magnificent wide valley, traversed by ominously dark, ever-lengthening shadows cast on the lush green by clouds rolling majestically overhead, made me an obvious target for anyone who fancied taking a pot-shot at a foreigner. I decided to walk to the nearest house, about 20 yards away, as anyone who saw me from afar talking to locals would assume I was one too.

But who would I find inside the house? A gang of bloodthirsty *Četniks*? An equally desperate *domaćica* ("housewife")? Or an IED? The door opened at my knock and call to reveal a *seljak* ("crofter") in his forties, who kindly and rapidly fixed my predicament with his own tools. He then invited me inside for the obligatory few shots of *rakija* (home-made), accompanied by a plate of *meza* (dried meats, cheese and pickles, also home-made) served up equally rapidly by his wife. He was a Serb and she was a Croat. They had no children. When it was polite to do so, I suggested I should be on my way, as I had to be back at base by dark. Outside he asked if I could get him some *gorivo* ("fuel"). As he had done me a favour, I agreed. "90 litres?" he enquired. "*Mre* ['alright']", I said, "as a one-off", and he loaded a drum into the back of the vehicle. I never did work out where a drum with such an irregular capacity could have come from.

The next morning, on my way to work, I refuelled at the Polish UNPROFOR base in Slunj. The soldier on duty was used to me and so filled my tank as usual. However, once he had finished, I indicated there was another job this morning. He spoke no English or Serbian/Croatian, and I speak no Polish, but I tried to explain to him that the drum in the back needed to be filled as well (I did not grow up speaking the local language, but when I first went to work as a volunteer in the Yugoslav Wars, I took with me a book called *How to Speak Serbo-Croat*, which greatly facilitated my cultural learnings of the Balkans). He raised an eyebrow inquiringly, and I nodded, to which he proceeded to fill it. I then signed his book as usual and was on my way. Arriving at the house, I stopped and my new friend heroically wrestled the 90 litres to the ground single-handedly. He asked me to stop by again on my way back from work that evening. When I did so, he plied me with bottles of *rakija* and plates of *meza* to take away, and proposed we set up business together: I could supply fuel from UNPROFOR, he would sell it, and we would share the proceeds fifty-fifty. I regretfully declined, as my role as an aid worker precluded me from profiting from the war, but thanked him again for his generosity. Back at base, Kiwi and I did not go hungry that night. In war zones, the first component of the precept "eat, drink and be merry" is often forced to take a back seat to its two comrades. At least our landlord kept us well stocked with *rakija* (home-made, the only one worth drinking, as the stuff sold in the shops is generally factory made and vile, producing devastating *mamurluk*, "hangovers").

Now the house was gone, although the outbuildings were still there. I could see no rubble at a swift glance in passing, and was at a loss as to what had happened. I was reluctant to enter the premises or even stop for fear of IEDs, or ghosts, and so continued on my way through the familiar landscape, now suddenly so devoid of the familiar signs of life. A few days later, I encountered a checkpoint outside the house and so was forced to stop. The three HV military policemen were so drunk on *rakija*, at 9 am, that at first I didn't notice and took them to be sober. I tried in a friendly manner to turn the conversation to the fate of the house and its occupants, but that only provoked an offensive and aggressive response, such that I drove on my way. We are merely cheated of our lives by *bekrije* ("drunkards").

A few km further along, a *hambar* ("barn") that had served as a workshop for SVK armour was still there, but the mechanics weren't. One day I had been slowed down on my way to work while they road-tested a tank they were working on. Many of the houses in this part of Croatia are deserted to this day, especially those further away from the main road. Some more isolated villages are completely abandoned, and incursions by wolves have been steadily increasing since the war. The Croatian authorities initially wanted to seize all abandoned land and property after the war, but had to be seen to respect the rule of law when applying to join the EU. The whole area has since been designated a *"posebne državne skrbi"* ("special state assistance") area in the government's efforts to comply with the Copenhagen criteria (economic and political criteria for accession to the EU, including respect for and protection of minorities), but despite this most of the previous occupants have chosen not to return, either selling up (where a buyer could be found) or completely abandoning their former homes (the majority of the Serb houses in Crnaja in neighbouring Bosnia were sold off by 2006[89]). On more than one occasion, I have translated probate documents for Serb refugees living in the UK, as they attempt to dispose of their families' former homes in Croatia. Nor have the majority of Croats who left at the beginning of the war returned, mainly due to the lack of employment and other prospects, and there is a continual exodus of young people to Zagreb, the coast, or abroad. Today only 7,000 people (88% Croats and 11% Serbs) live in and around Slunj, an increase on the 4,000 during the SDS time, but only a fraction of the pre-war population (which was 64% Croats, 30% Serbs and 3% Muslims; in 1931, the last census before WWII, it had been 53% Serbs and 47% Croats[90]). Every year there are fewer children attending the Slunj secondary school, and there is now talk of teachers being made redundant. Serbs seeking to return to Croatia after the war had to first apply for citizenship, a catch-22 situation made all the more complicated as the government of Serbia would not let them leave[91]. Since the war, as many Croats have left the country as the Serbs who were ethnically cleansed in Operation Storm.

Then there was a surprise: most mornings, a boy in a field near the road had waved to us on our way to work, described by Steve as the "shepherd boy". I had assumed he would also be long gone now, but there he was still. Intrigued, I stopped for the first time and called him over. He seemed surprised and even afraid, but he came closer. I asked him whether he recognised me, and went on to inquire into his story. He was a Croat, and his family had stayed. Curiouser and curiouser.

At the beginning of July 1995, the war in Yugoslavia took a dramatic U-turn. Since 1991 (and 1992 in Bosnia), the SDS had held their dominant positions practically unchanged, bordered to the north, west and south by the HDZ (in September 1993, the HV had attempted to capture the Medak pocket, a bulge of SDS territory protruding north west from Sector South into the suburbs of the town of Gospić, but after initial successes on the ground, the HV withdrew after fierce fighting with the SVK and a clash with Canadian UNPROFOR; and in May 1995, the SDS lost Sector West, a bulge of territory approaching the Hungarian border in Slavonia and cutting the Zagreb-Belgrade motorway, previously known as the "Brotherhood and Unity" road, between Okučani and Novska), and in the centre, almost splitting their territory in two, like a split cleaved into a block of firewood by an axe, that has not quite cut right through to the chopping block underneath, by the

HDZ-SDA Federation (after the initial onslaught, there were various lesser changes to the map on the more volatile Bosnian front, see below; meanwhile, the conflict between the Bosnian Croats and Muslims ended nominally with the Washington agreement that created the Federation of Bosnia and Herzegovina in March 1994[92]). At its narrowest point, the Brčko corridor in north-east Bosnia, north of Tuzla ("salt mine") and on the border along the Sava river, the SDS territory secured in October 1992 was only 5 km wide[93], and subject to fire from the HV in the north and the ABiH to the south (although an unofficial arrangement was reached between the VRS and the HV, whereby the HV would allow traffic to pass along the Brčko corridor, in return for undisturbed use of the river crossing at Orašje, 30 km upstream[94]). This allowed the HDZ and the SDA a potential stranglehold on all supplies to the SDS territories to the west. Before the war, most of the majority Serb district councils in Bosnia had been in the west of the country[95] (many Serbs were resettled from the east to the west of Bosnia during WWI, to prevent any attempts at unification with Serbia[96]). Now their territory had included five Muslim enclaves: Bihać, Goražde, Sarajevo, Srebrenica, and Žepa, plus the quasi-enclave of Tuzla, all with their populations swollen to several times their original size by the flow of IDPs from the surrounding territory, and dependent for survival on humanitarian aid: the first Médecins Sans Frontières team to gain access to Srebrenica, in March 1993, reported that dozens of people were dying from starvation and lack of medical attention every day[97] (there had previously been another enclave, Maglaj, created by joint VRS and HVO action in mid-1993, but the siege was lifted under pressure from British UNPROFOR in March 1994)[98]. For the SDS, all of this meant extremely long and necessarily porous front lines (over 2,000 km; according to Nikola, "you could practically walk from Karlovac to Knin without being challenged"). I was working in the largest enclave, the Bihać pocket.

Between 1991 and 1995, over half the Croatian Serbs left the country, disillusioned with their own leaders and distrustful of Tuđman (as many Croats left the HDZ territory over the same period), while some Croats started to return to Sector West in 1993[99]. On 9 December 1994, the UN general assembly voted to label the Serb Borders republic "occupied territory" within Croatia, which meant that any attempt to integrate it into the rump Yugoslavia (Serbia and Montenegro) would be illegal[100]. Meanwhile, on 2 December, the SDS and the HDZ had signed an economic agreement, which covered water and electricity supply, and opened the Zagreb-Belgrade motorway to traffic from both sides, with crossing points into Sector West at Novska and Okučani, near Nova Gradiška and just across the border from Gradiška in Bosnia[101]. No sooner was the ink dry on the economic agreement than the "Z-4 plan", which would effectively relegate the SDS to the status of a local authority subordinate to Zagreb, was drawn up by the US, Russia, the EU and ICFY[xxxiv]. Milošević, having seen the writing on the wall, and whose priority was to have the UN sanctions lifted for his own political survival (the real economy in the rump Yugoslavia contracted by more than 50% in 1993, and by a further third in 1995, while GDP shrank from USD 18.38 to 9.53 billion and GDP per capita from USD 1,766 to 908 between 1991 and 1993; or, by another measure, GDP per capita in Serbia fell by USD 900 over the war[102]), supported both the economic agreement and the Z-4 plan[103]. The Z-4 plan was signed by Tuđman in January, and the US ambassador took it to Knin in February, where the SDS, with the threat of the withdrawal of peacekeepers from Croatia in April hanging over them, refused to

---

[xxxiv] International Conference on the Former Yugoslavia, co-chaired by Lord Owen.

consider it[104]. On 14-15 April, at a meeting in Sanski Most ("Sana bridge") in Bosnia, the Bosnian and Croatian SDS leaderships decided to start moves towards political and military unification, further sidelining Milošević (see below), even as the HV was capturing territory from Livno in south-west Bosnia, ostensibly in support of the HVO in the Bihać pocket, bringing them ever closer to Knin[105] (Livno was described in 1943 by Fitzroy Maclean as a "*notorious Ustaše* stronghold", even when it was temporarily in Partisan hands[106]). In March and April 1995, the HV positioned men and equipment at strategic points around Sector West, and also on the neighbouring border with Bosnia. A series of incidents at the checkpoints on the motorway gave the HDZ the excuse they needed, and on 1 May the HV launched *Blijesak* ("Operation Flash"), an all-out attack on Sector West. The SDS fired five Orkan rockets at Zagreb in retaliation, resulting in five deaths[107]. Four days later the local SVK surrendered, and within a month less than 1,500 people of the Serb population of 14,000 remained, the rest having crossed the single bridge over the river Sava south into Bosnia, most of them on the first day[xxxv108].

Meanwhile, in March 1995, Izetbegović's SDA launched a series of major offensives in central Bosnia, in the vicinity of Tuzla, Zenica ("pupil") and Travnik (*trava* means "grass"), the capital of Bosnia from the 1690s until the demise of Ottoman rule, in breach of the cessation of hostilities agreement brokered by Jimmy Carter on 31 December 1994, and Radovan Karadžić, the Bosnian SDS leader, who had predicted in the Bosnian parliament in October 1991, just before the SDS walked out, that "the Muslim people could disappear", issued "Directive 7" to the VRS to execute a final solution to the eastern enclaves[109]. This was not the first ceasefire breached by the SDA: indeed, in the absence of equivalent military capacity, one of Izetbegović's consistent strategies since the start of the war had been to prolong his people's agony in the hope of provoking a decisive international response which would enable his objective of a sovereign unitary Bosnian state[110]. Izetbegović wrote in his *Islamic Declaration* (see below) that

> "Anyone who means our community well, should not spare it exertions, danger and disaster, but should do everything he can to ensure it exercises all its power, puts all its capacities to the test, and takes risks [...] the Islamic renaissance is [...] a state of practical, living idealism in which ordinary people become capable of extraordinary acts of courage and sacrifice"[111].

He said he regarded the various peace plans on offer at different times as rewarding ethnic cleansing and destroying the viability of a multi-ethnic Bosnian state, refused

---

[xxxv] Legija said in respect of Operation Flash, "To be honest, I wasn't surprised. After the Maslenica bridge that the Croats had managed to take in a surprise attack two years earlier, I knew it was just a matter of time before they would take West Slavonia in the same way [...] That piece of territory was the running sore of the Borders. It cut the motorway at Okučani and irritated the Croats as much as they had been irritated by the fact that they did not have free access across the Maslenica bridge at Zadar and Biograd [see below] Our military and political leaders clearly failed to understand basic tactics and strategy in this war [...] The *Ujke* ['Croats'] are clever, they do everything methodically. They go quiet, then they strike and take territory that has been carefully identified in advance. Then they dig in and go quiet again. That's the way they played it with Orašje, Maslenica and the Medak pocket. They work methodically, unlike our people, who don't seem to have any master plan in this war". The operation was presented by Tuđman as a simple police operation to reopen the motorway. It was followed by a parade in Zagreb on 30 May.

to enter into any negotiations with Babo[xxxvi], and in April 1995, he summoned the military commanders of Srebrenica to Tuzla and banned them from returning, stating that the international community was responsible for the "safe area"[112]. Likewise, the SDS and the HDZ (the latter at least until the Washington agreement that created the Federation, the first piece in the US' master plan to end the war, and which it was hoped would also reduce the likelihood of Bosnia drifting into Islamic extremism; it also provided for the creation of a devolved single state consisting of the Federation and Croatia[xxxvii]) used their stranglehold on the supply of aid - and utilities - to the enclaves to blackmail the international community, letting through just enough to keep the life support machine ticking over[113]. However, the Bihać pocket also had strategic importance for Tuđman, because as long as it subsisted it tied up SVK forces and prevented them forming a united front with the VRS, only one hour south of Zagreb. Listening to the BBC world service on our vehicle HF radios, we heard when Srebrenica fell on 11 July, to be followed two weeks later by Žepa. We feared that we were next. The sounds of mass vehicle movements at night and incessant heavy *granatiranje* ("shelling", outgoing, towards Cazin) only confirmed our worst fears. I was put in mind of the opening lines of Meša Selimović's powerful novel about PTSD, *Silences*[xxxviii]:

> "For three days the guns thundered, drawing nearer, and on the third day the shells started to land everywhere around us. I didn't know exactly where, because sound is distorted in the cave, everything is unclear which makes it even more terrible than outside: the all-encompassing roar, the darkness that had become a part of us, the rasping pointless whisper by which we revealed our fear, the helplessness binding us to this damp hole. Delirious, not distinguishing clearly things or people or dimensions or sense, I plunged into a nightmare panic which in the brief instants of consciousness crept into my fevered blood and filled me with an expectation of unknown horrors. It wasn't fear of the proximity of the enemy, or of death waiting at the entrance to the cave blocked with rocks, but something inexpressibly more terrible: it was as if the world had died, and the last man, alone, was going mad in the face of his fate"[114].

"It's not right, indiscriminate shelling", our neighbour commented to me. We could only imagine the fate of the overrun enclaves even as we listened to the preparations for the next. Then suddenly, the HV's Operation Storm offensive put an end to the Serb Borders republic, with the green light from the US[115] (and preceded by training by a US private military contractor, in breach of the UN arms embargo; the US also turned a blind eye to arms smuggling into Bosnia and Croatia from Iran, on which Tuđman spent USD 1.4 billion, 10% of GNP, in 1994 alone[116]). At the end of June, the US had decided that the "endgame strategy" to the war had to be "bombing the

---

[xxxvi] According to the EU monitors, in early 1994, "Abdić was [...] quite willing to negotiate with anyone, but Sarajevo had no intention of doing business with him [...] Izetbegović had long since abandoned any intention of negotiating with Fikret Abdić ever again".

[xxxvii] According to Owen, "in the longer term it may well prove to be that the Washington Accords have the effect that many feared of legitimising a greater Croatia".

[xxxviii] Muslim Partisan from Tuzla, whose brother was summarily executed for theft during WWII, despite his intercessions.

Serbs into compromise"[xxxix][117]. On 22 July, Tuđman made a pact with Izetbegović to defend Bihać (thus allowing him access to the enclave[118]), and on 28 July, the HV pushing northwards in south-west Bosnia occupied Bosansko Grahovo, just across the border from Knin. The SVK mobilised 50,000 men, but 7,000 of them were bogged down by the 5th Corps. The HV had over 100,000 men deployed strategically to allow them to strike anywhere in Sectors North and/or South. Tuđman wanted Babo on board, but Babo decided he wasn't for turning, as he didn't trust Tuđman's other Muslim ally, Izetbegović, a decision that would have drastic and far-reaching consequences for the people of West Bosnia, and for him personally[119]. On 1 August, the Bosnian and Croatian SDS called for immediate intervention from Belgrade, but the response was not encouraging: Milošević was practically bankrupt, with hyperinflation in Yugoslavia in excess of that of Weimar Germany[120]. He could not afford another major JNA adventure, as the QE that had underwritten previous campaigns had reached its limits, and anyway the outcome was far from certain. The Croatian and Bosnian Serbs were abandoned to their fate[xl][121]. Meanwhile, the NOZB were making progress against the 5th Corps, closing in on Cazin. On 3 August, Babić announced he would accept the Z-4 plan. The next day, the HV, ostensibly to relieve Bihać, attacked Sectors South and North simultaneously, while the 5th Corps attacked Sector North from the east. By the end of the day, 90% of the Croatian Borders were in the hands of the HV. The vast majority of the territory extending along Croatia's border with Bosnia from the coastal hinterland near Split to within an hour's drive of Zagreb, and then east to Novska in Slavonia, was practically emptied of civilians in a matter of hours, with most of the remaining Croatian Serb population, 200,000 people, now heading east in cars, vans, tractors, horse-drawn carts or on foot along the main Zagreb-Belgrade motorway through Slavonia into Vojvodina, completely clogging both carriageways, or across the long border into Bosnia, to build a new life there or subsequently be granted refugee status abroad. Among them was Goga, Kiwi's assistant, who lived with her parents on their farm near Vrginmost, east of Petrova Gora (before the war she had lived in Karlovac). Many of the Croatian Serbs now live in the UK, while there is a community of Borders Serbs in Srem in Vojvodina which goes back to WWII[122]. Danish UNPROFOR were used as human shields by the HV, and there were several incidents of shelling of refugees trapped near Glina, and even an air strike on a column of refugees. Five VRS planes were scrambled, but two of them were shot down. A ceasefire was agreed on 8 August, allowing unhindered access to Bosnia for disarmed Serbs[123]. Only Sector East, a strip of land along the north-eastern border with Serbia, remained of the Serb Borders republic. The satirical Croatian newspaper *Feral Tribune* led the next day with the headline "Serbia is where the Serbs are", a parody of Milošević's rhetoric that "Serbia is wherever there are Serbs" (and in Serbia, the historic defeat was only mentioned in the 18th minute of the evening news[124]). As if by an ironic twist of fate,

---

[xxxix] According to Owen, "The first air strikes choosing targets not directly related to attacks that had been undertaken took place when NATO jets bombed the Bosnian Serb ammunition dump near Pale on 25 May 1995. A far better judged use of air strikes was the action taken on 30 August to enforce the Sarajevo exclusion zone. When targets were bombed as far afield as Banja Luka, relating to Serb air defences, and bridges bombed around Foča, air power was also sending a political message to the Bosnian Serbs".

[xl] According to Owen, "The fact that neither Belgrade nor Pale came to the aid of the Croatian Serbs was a sign that the direct and indirect dialogue that Tuđman had maintained with both Milošević and Karadžić paid off for the Croats. Zagreb and Belgrade had been heading for a regional solution for some time, making deals on the ground to change the map in the former Yugoslavia to order their own relationship, with scant regard for the international community".

but probably for much more cynical reasons, only a few weeks previously, on St. Vitus's Day, 28 June, Slunj had been the scene of a military parade, a miniature version of the Red Square parades in Moscow, that we had watched for a time from the balcony of the Polish UNPROFOR base, before withdrawing when we realised we might be captured on film and used for propaganda purposes (Legija referred to the parade as a "charade"[125]). The HV only suffered 200 casualties in Operation Storm, which was led by former foreign legionnaire Ante Gotovina, who Tuđman had quickly promoted to general at the start of the war (he was convicted of war crimes by the ICTY in 2011 after being arrested in Tenerife in 2005, but was acquitted on appeal in 2012)[xli][126].

Meanwhile, the NOZB in Velika Kladuša, in the north of the Bihać pocket, suddenly saw their imminent victory turn to defeat, as their SVK ally to the north and west disappeared into thin air and the 5th Corps attacked the town, to the very public delight of the Bangladeshi peacekeepers based there[xlii] (according to Mirvet, see below, Tuđman had wanted the HV to create a buffer zone between the NOZB and the 5th Corps, but things moved too fast)[127]. As if obeying the law that nature abhors a vacuum, on 7 August a large part of the swollen population of Velika Kladuša, together with their defeated army (and 800 *ranjenici*, "wounded"), spontaneously left Bosnia and embarked on an exodus north-west into the newly-liberated, but as yet unclaimed provinces of Croatia. Around 150 people were taken prisoner by the 5th Corps and didn't make it across the border[128]. As the column of cars, tractors, horses and carts and pedestrians passed through deserted villages and hamlets on their trek into the unknown, mothers with children in particular would stop to rest in abandoned houses, helping themselves to whatever happened to be in the kitchen, and even cooking meals, or at least making coffee. The more enterprising started looting. They continued for 25 km until around 3 pm they were stopped by the HV at

---

[xli] According to the HV: "In vain, the commanders of the enemy paramilitaries tried to motivate their men to offer decisive resistance, but it was clear that they would not succeed. It was a clash of the armies of two completely different civilisations, a collision between a modern, western European army, trained and motivated to perfection, and an undisciplined, paramilitary TA, a mass of hardened criminals who saw in flight the only way out of a doomed continuation of the struggle [...] The Serb minority in Croatia, an instrument in the hands of Slobodan Milošević's Greater Serbia policy, paid the highest price for the war they had brought about themselves". Legija commented that, "While the black market with the other side was booming and bars were springing up by the side of the road, in which *Serbia to Tokyo* was sung enthusiastically to the accompaniment of a genocide of lambs and suckling pigs, on the other side they were quietly putting together a serious army". The SVK failed to notice how the HV were stealthily surrounding them in Bosnia. As the Croatian writer Miroslav Krleža, who died in 1981, wrote, "God preserve us from Serbian heroism and Croatian civilisation". Nikola is of the view that the HV could have conquered the Serb Borders in 1993, but that the political conditions were not right. Adis recently heard the announcement at Belgrade airport: "*Franjo Tuđman zatvoren zbog oluje*" ("Zagreb airport closed due to storm", but also "Franjo Tuđman locked up because of Operation Storm"). Tuđman also has a bridge named after him in Dubrovnik.

[xlii] The Bangladeshis engaged in a sustained session of celebratory shooting to show their approval of the 5th Corps' victory (on the occasion of the 5th Corps' previous occupation of the town, on 21 August 1994, they had officially congratulated the 5th Corps commander). Some time later, I had occasion to visit the Bangladeshi peacekeepers with my young *šegrt* ("apprentice"), Kami. The officer we met with started the meeting by asking her if she was a virgin. Before I could react, Kami let him know in no uncertain terms that it was none of his business. The meeting didn't last much longer than that. Babo had had very good relations with the previous incumbents of the UNPROFOR base in Velika Kladuša, the French, who arrived in 1992. Agrokomerc immediately granted them premises in Polje, see below, and embarked on a major conversion project which included 25 km of roadways for their use. Contracts were signed for other infrastructure projects in Velika Kladuša, including a centre for orphans from besieged Sarajevo, but the climate changed once Izetbegović got wind of the cooperation projects, and the French withdrew from the joint venture soon afterwards.

the village of Kuplensko. Many of the refugees thought they would only be there for a short time before continuing (no-one knew where), but the HV were dismayed to find such a large, foreign population at large in their new territories, and tried to turn them back (an advance party of refugees had encountered the HV at Vojnić, where a film crew were hoping to obtain dramatic footage of the capture of the town, only to find it completely abandoned apart from the refugees. This group continued on to Turanj). The 30,000 men, women and children then promptly took up residence in the village, which had previously had a population of 96, most of whom had left, apart from half a dozen pensioners, unwilling or unable to start a new life in Serbia or Bosnia.

Three years later, when working in Kosovo, I discovered that the halls of residence of Priština University were full of young refugees from Croatia. On their arrival in Serbia they had been directed south, to boost the local Serb population and act as *topovsko meso* ("cannon fodder"), in pursuance of the 1986 programme to prevent the emigration from and encourage the return of Serbs and Montenegrins to Kosovo[129] (older and wiser refugees simply refused to go to Kosovo, sometimes by force; indeed, one busload of refugees forced their driver to return to Belgrade at gunpoint when they learnt of their destination[130]). In total, 16,000 refugees from Croatia ended up in Kosovo[131]. Besides Priština, some of them were also housed in Srbica/Skenderaj in the Drenica valley (see below)[132]. The NATO invasion the following year obliged the youngsters to flee yet again – a classic case of out of the frying pan, into the fire. Meanwhile, refugees in Serbia, in particular those of military age, were generally blamed for losing the war in Croatia, and even regarded as traitors. For some extremists in Serbia, the refugees were not even real Serbs at all, but Orthodox Gypsies. Some defeated soldiers were arrested in refugee centres in Serbia and beasted by the secretive *Jedinica* ("unit") in Arkan's stronghold in Erdut in Sector East, held in kennels and made to bark, with a *metak* ("bullet") in the leg for anyone who refused.

The Unit, for want of an official name, was set up in April 1991 by a Serbian golf coach and retired *plaćenik* ("mercenary") living in Australia known as Captain Dragan, with the objective of knocking the SVK into shape from the drunken rabble they were, at the instruction of Jovica Stanišić, the head of the Serbian security service (and the CIA's man in Belgrade from 1992-2000; in 2002, he was handed over to the ICTY[133]), after the SDS militia's failure to dislodge the Croatian police from Plitvice (the once powerful and professional Yugoslav security service soon fell prey to its new paymasters in the different republics, while continuing to exert an insidious, unaccountable influence in all areas of public life. According to Babo, there was a smooth transition between the KOS (military intelligence) and the new democracies' security services, i.e., the same individuals continued to operate, merely changing hats. They were also suspected, as early as 1980, of acting outside their mandate, failing to report faithfully to the federal presidency, and even spying on it, even as the quality of their work declined. The Bosnian security service, the AID, went so far as to assist the FBI in a sting against the Yugoslav consul general in Chicago, who in 1989 was tried for - and acquitted of - money laundering, while Izetbegović ordered them to bug Babo's office in the presidency as early as August 1993. The UDBA was officially dissolved in 1991, having anyway been superseded by the AID and other successor agencies[134]). The Unit answered, unofficially, only to Milošević. Its first deployment was to Borovo Selo in May, where it successfully mobilised the local villagers and ambushed the police. In June it was deployed to the

Croatian Borders in support of the Lika Corps (Sector South) and the Kordun and Banija Corps (Sector North), who were effectively autonomous, and also acted independently of each other (according to Legija, the commander of the Lika Corps ran a large black market operation with the 5th Corps, which he was reluctant to see disrupted by Operation Spider)[135]. After Glina was taken, in July, the Unit adopted the red beret, and was reconstituted with the primary objective of controlling the Croatian SDS[136]. Meanwhile, the notorious Arkan, another of Milošević's *opričnina*[xliii], and his "tigers" formed another wing of the Unit in eastern Slavonia (later Sector East) and he became the overall commander. Wanted by Interpol for among other things killing two Swedish police officers, he was the biggest fish in the pool of football hooligans (Red Star Belgrade's *Delije*, "folk heroes", whose slogan "Serbia to Tokyo", coined when they won the European Cup in 1991, thereby qualifying for the Intercontinental Cup in Japan, quickly spread and took on wider pan-Slavic connotations) used by the UDBA for "black ops", which mainly meant silencing over-vociferous members of the Yugoslav diaspora abroad[137]. In return, a blind eye was turned to their other activities when on deployment. He had been arrested in October 1990 in Croatia with a car-full of *oružje* ("weapons"), and after six months in custody he was sentenced to five years' *robija* ("imprisonment"). Curiously, he was then released on bail pending appeal (allegedly in return for using his connections to procure Tuđman 12 articulated lorries of weapons; the KOS were also anxious to spring him in case he blew anyone's cover[138]). It was said he maintained "prison discipline" over his men, with corporal punishment, and never took prisoners[139]. The Unit's first action under Arkan's command was in Osijek in June 1991, Croatia's third largest city, on the river Drava, a tributary of the Danube, which did not have a Serb majority. It was shelled for days by the JNA and the Unit entered the town, but Milošević finally decided not to take it, and the JNA withdrew. As a result, it did not form part of Sector East, remaining on the front line[140]. In 1992, the leader of a notorious HDZ paramilitary unit, Branimir Glavaš, was appointed mayor of Osijek (after a successful career in politics, in 2009 he was convicted of war crimes and sentenced to 10 years' imprisonment, but his conviction was overturned in 2015)[141]. Before the war, Osijek was one of Croatia's industrial centres, and is now much diminished (in 2013, the major food concern IPK Osijek ceased trading after 52 years. In the 1970s it had contributed to the success of Agrokomerc, see below[142]). After the fall of Vukovar, the Unit carried out the cleansing operations there[143]. When death stalked the land in Bosnia the following spring, the Unit was active in Banja Luka in March, and played a key role in the ethnic cleansing of Zvornik and the strategic crossroads of Bijeljina in north-eastern Bosnia in April (to secure the land link between Serbia and western Bosnia, with its denser Serb population, and beyond to the Croatian Borders), and didn't miss out on Srebrenica in 1995[144]. There was method in their madness, and the Unit jump-started the war in Bosnia by sweeping away the vestiges of law and order with a campaign of terror that echoed and reverberated throughout the country like the 2004 tsunami passing through the Indian Ocean, now travelling silently along in the depths, now erupting violently onto dry land. Babo led a presidential commission to Bijeljina to investigate alleged atrocities there, but said the local Muslims were too afraid to meet with them[145]. At a checkpoint on the way there he was ordered at gunpoint to lie on

---

[xliii] Ivan the Terrible's knights of the round table, a hand-picked gang of ruthless peasants who helped him secure and keep absolute power, temporal and spiritual, in very turbulent times, with Russia surrounded to the east, west and south by predatory enemies without, and riven by aristocratic ambitions within.

the ground, but refused to do so, and demanded to speak to whoever was in charge. Eventually Arkan appeared, and told the commission to come back the next day, which they did (safe in his ivory tower in Sarajevo, Izetbegović only declared a state of war two months later, in June 1992[xliv][146]). Striking west and south from Bijeljina, by the end of April the Unit had expelled 95% of the population of Zvornik, Foča and Višegrad in eastern Bosnia[147] (the people of Višegrad later returned, to their cost, see below). This had been preceded by hysterical media claims of an imminent takeover by Muslim fundamentalists and impending WWII-style genocide by a Croat-Muslim axis of evil, and the proclamation by Karadžić's SDS party of three (later six) autonomous Serb regions in Bosnia, loyal to Yugoslavia. In August 1991, the last federal prime minister, Ante Marković, a Catholic from Konjic ("little horse") in Herzegovina, who had ordered the JNA deployment to Slovenia before condemning its use of force, released a recording of a telephone conversation between Milošević and Karadžić, in which the former was giving the latter details of his next shipment of arms[148]. In September 1991, Karadžić called for the JNA to deploy to protect the Serb areas (the largest around Banja Luka in north-west Bosnia; then around Bijeljina in the north-east; south-eastern Herzegovina including Trebinje; and Romanija, the mountains between Sarajevo, Žepa and Goražde, and including Pale)[149]. There were JNA air strikes against Kupres, Doboj and Tuzla[150]. Arkan's attacks on towns, which he generally did not bother to coordinate with the military authorities, and dictated to the civilian authorities (as did the military authorities[151]), were accompanied by a fleet of artics, which then transported his loot back to Belgrade, where giant car-boot sales were held (although Legija, who has never been charged with war crimes, insists that he never allowed his own men to loot private property, or indeed to abuse prisoners[152]). One high-level meeting between the Unit and the MOD in Serbia in May 1999, during the NATO bombing, literally descended into a fight, with a general having a pistol shoved into his ribs by Legija[153]. Having an *avtomat* ("gun") shoved into your ribs is a painful experience in and of itself, as I learned in Chechnya. After the withdrawal of the JNA from Bosnia, General Mladić, the new VRS commander, appointed by Milošević in May 1992, pulled rank and insisted over Karadžić's objections that the high-profile loose cannon Arkan likewise withdraw, to which Stanišić agreed (the same month, Karadžić set out to the Republika Srpska parliament his plan to create an unbroken and economically viable territory linking Serbia to the Croatian Borders, by "separating" Serbs from Muslims and Croats[154]). Arkan, born in Slovenia, where his father, a former Partisan and career JNA officer from Belgrade, had been based, became a Kosovo MP, but the Unit continued to operate in Bosnia in support of the VRS, and Arkan reappeared there briefly in 1994 for Operation Spider. He didn't stay long, because he "didn't like Muslims, and they didn't like him". He was fragged in 2000 by his own *dželati* ("murderers") and left his widow, the singer Ceca, whose head he once famously shaved for alleged infidelity, a fortune in very dirty money. At the height of Operation Spider, theirs had been the celebrity

---

[xliv] Throughout the spring of 1992, Babo travelled to hotspots in different parts of the country, attempting to calm feelings run wild and find local solutions to problems. Another place he visited was the oil refinery in Bosanski Brod, at the invitation of its director, because it had been threatened with destruction by shelling. The other members of the presidency made far fewer or no field visits during this period, and Izetbegović never ventured out into the countryside. Babo soon acquired a reputation as a troubleshooter, and was sent on several occasions by both Izetbegović and Tuđman to negotiate with the SDS on the ground to resolve various tricky situations. This was later used against him as evidence that he had been a *Četnik* all along.

wedding - and marriage - of the century in Serbian pop culture[155]. Meanwhile, in March 1993, after the HV seized the Maslenica ("pastry pie", a popular Balkan speciality) gorge near Zadar, the Unit had deployed under Captain Dragan to seize the small town of Škabrnja, cutting the main road south from Zadar (Swedish Manchester United footballer Zlatan Ibrahimović's mother is from Škabrnja, while his father is from Bijeljina). In the second half of 1994, Legija was deployed to command the Unit's largest, and most profitable, venture, Operation Spider, with the objective of restoring Babo to Bosnia after the 5th Corps occupied Velika Kladuša in August of that year. He described it as "the battle they couldn't afford to lose". By this time, the Unit was significantly increased in terms of hardware and men, and the headquarters for the operation were in Petrova Gora. Legija was able to mobilise both the SVK and the VRS, as well as deploying VJ units. I met him briefly in June 1995 when the town of Vrnograč, east of Velika Kladuša, had been liberated by the NOZB, and he seemed more interested in practising his squaddie French with the NGO girls than anything else. One of them described him afterwards as a "professional killer" (although he said himself that he "didn't really like killing, it's dirty work"[156]). There was significant damage to the town, which the UNHCR delegate added to by driving *rikverc* ("reverse") into one of the few *bandere* ("lampposts") still functioning. There was also a wide trail of blood leading down the steps from the hospital main entrance. Apart from us, there didn't seem to be a single soul anywhere. In the final months of the war, as the VRS started to lose territory, Arkan deployed to boost their morale, but was again sent packing by Mladić. After the war, the Unit withdrew to Serbia, and in 1996 officially became part of the Serbian security service under Legija's leadership. Its resources were increased even more, making it the envy of the police, and indeed the VJ. In October 1998, Milošević lost confidence in Stanišić and replaced him with Radovan Marković, a confidant of his ghastly wife's (the Miloševićes were childhood sweethearts, and she was a Partisan lovechild, her father a Partisan commander[xlv]; but her mother, Vera, known as Mira, whose cousin Zdenka was Tito's secretary and mistress in his cave in Drvar, see below, before becoming his fourth wife, was later executed for treason after being arrested and then released by the *Gestapo*. After Zdenka, described by Fitzroy Maclean as a "strange, pale, fanatical little creature", died of TB in 1946, her parents adopted the future Mrs Milošević and were given a country house by Tito. She now lives with her playboy son in splendid exile in Russia, wanted at home for fraud and conspiracy to murder, the latter in connection with the Unit's subsequent activities[xlvi][157]). In 1998, the Unit deployed to Kosovo, and during the NATO bombing, it came to dominate public life in Serbia, with a series of assassinations in the political, business and media worlds[158]. In a supreme irony, Milošević was finally overthrown by the mob in Belgrade on 5 October 2000, for refusing to recognise the

---

[xlv] In November 1988, Milošević's father-in-law, a highly respected former revolutionary, Partisan and KPJ official, who was in poor health, visited federal president Dizdarević and warned him that his son-in-law was a "dangerous man"; that he was afraid he would destroy Serbia, and with it the whole country; that he should be stopped before it was too late; and that he – and his daughter - were driven by an ambition for which they were ready to play the most extreme nationalist card. Dizdarević asked whether there were any forces within Serbia that could stop him, as external interference would only make things worse, but Marković replied that Milošević had already seized all the reins of power within Serbia, and had removed or was removing anyone who was not loyal to him. The Miloševićes cut off all further contacts with Marković, who died in 1992, just as his worst fears were realised.

[xlvi] Marković's grandson, Marko, is a sad, lost figure, unable to live up to the achievements of his parents. After dodging his national service, he used their patronage to fund a lifestyle of fast cars, failed business ventures, and night clubs.

results of the September presidential elections (future prime minister Zoran Đinđić had obtained an agreement from Legija not to fire on protestors). Meanwhile, Legija deployed with the Unit to deal with another Albanian insurgency in southern Serbia, further raising his profile and popularity in Belgrade. After Đinđić came to power, he arrested Radovan Marković (no relative of the former federal prime minister), but the Unit was now so powerful and established at the heart of the state machinery that it could not be disbanded, even as it continued to provide cover for the Zemun Clan's criminal activities (Zemun, once a Hungarian border town, was the scene of the *Wehrmacht*'s last stand in the battle for Belgrade in October 1944: after crossing the city's last remaining bridge, the Old Sava Bridge, they attempted to blow it up, but the detonators for the pre-positioned explosives had been removed by a local retired teacher, who had performed exactly the same feat during the Balkan War of 1912. As a result, they were pursued and destroyed by the Red Army and the Partisans[159]). Milošević, abandoned by his allies because of the catastrophic failure of the Kosovo war, not least the "very high-level" and serious economic damage caused by the NATO air strikes (described by Legija as sending the country "back to the eighteenth century"), was arrested by the Unit for extradition to the ICTY on 1 April 2001, and three months later, on St. Vitus's Day, and over the opposition of president Vojislav Koštunica, who called it "unconstitutional", he was extradited[160]. The Godfather was dead, devoured by his own children like a Russian *vor v zakone* ("crime lord"). The arrest was brought about largely as a result of Đinđić's efforts to reform Serbia and re-establish the rule of law (and gain favour with the US), and was executed after a 36-hour standoff, allegedly staged by the Unit for effect. The Unit's highest profile (and last) act was the assassination of Đinđić himself on 12 March 2003. Legija was facing trial for the attempted assassination of opposition leader Vuk Drašković in 1999, and in November 2001, the Unit blocked a major artery in Belgrade during rush hour, demanding the resignation of the interior minister. The minister duly resigned, and his successor dropped the case against Legija and released Zemun Clan members from custody. However, Đinđić was determined to break the Unit, and when a new gangland incident provided him with the case and the witness he needed, Legija decided his only option was a full stop. The public outrage was such that the government proclaimed a *vanredno stanje* ("state of emergency") and the police were finally able to arrest the Unit's main players, including Legija, and they were all sentenced to long prison terms[161]. But Milošević, like Rasputin, refused to die[xlvii], even as Tony Blair continued his miraculous pilgrim's progress in search of bigger beasts to bag.

Meanwhile, a campaign of NATO air strikes with the blessing of the US after the second infamous market bombing in Sarajevo on 28 August 1995[xlviii], combined with ABiH, HV and HVO ground offensives against the VRS, meant that the SDS were now being rolled back in Bosnia as well, a process that culminated in the Dayton peace accords of 14 December, preceded on 10 October by a country-wide ceasefire, that only took effect on the 15th[162] (the US had been periodically airing

---

[xlvii] The Siberian mystic, who by seducing the last Tsar's wife became *de facto* ruler of Russia in 1909, was ultimately poisoned, shot three times, and when he escaped, clubbed to death by his enemies, before being thrown into the river Malaja Nevka in St. Petersburg, where he drowned attempting to claw his way out through the ice, in 1916.

[xlviii] There was disagreement among UNPROFOR experts on whether the mortar shell in question, which killed 37 people, had actually been fired by the VRS. NATO concluded that it had, and that it had bounced off a roof before landing in Sarajevo's Markale market.

Izetbegović's proposed policy of "lift and strike" – lift the arms embargo against the ABiH and use air strikes against the VRS – since May 1993, but had always deferred to EU leadership in the conflict; meanwhile, the Bosnian SDS had been threatened by the UN with military action because of the shelling of Sarajevo as early as 26 June 1992[163]). Previously, the VRS, like the SVK, had been able to rely on superior hardware, while the ABiH had had to learn soldiering the hard way (for example, the VRS' SOPs to the south of Bihać in early 1994 were to fire back ten shells for every shell fired at them by the 5th Corps, ceasefire or not)[164]. Kulen Vakuf, Bosanska Krupa, Bosanski Petrovac, and Ključ ("key") in western Bosnia were occupied by the 5th Corps in September in Operation Sana 95, while the 7th Corps from Travnik occupied Donji Vakuf and the HV occupied Jajce in central Bosnia, and Gotovina reached the outskirts of Banja Luka[165] (according to Hope, after Operation Storm the 5th Corps could have walked into Prijedor and Banja Luka, and could have reached the Drina, the river marking the border between Bosnia and Serbia, in two weeks, rolling up the SDS and HDZ entities in Bosnia; but for reasons that have not been explained, Dudaković delayed the offensive for a month, until 13 September. Hope also claims that only ten percent of the 5th Corps' forces were deployed on Operation Sana 95, and that most of the rest of them were busy looting or shooting pigs in the liberated territories. Curiously, as soon as the Muslims started to gain territory, the war ended, and they had to give much of it back[xlix][166]). In October, after a counter-attack led by the Unit from Sanski Most held up the 5th Corps advance, Sanski Most was finally captured by the 5th Corps, and the HV took Mrkonjić-Grad[167] (Mrkonjić-Grad was the first place in Yugoslavia visited by Fitzroy Maclean, in August 1943, from where he travelled in a captured *Wehrmacht* truck to Jajce for his first meeting with Tito. It is named after Petar Mrkonjić, whose real name was King Petar I Karađorđević[168]). SDS territory in Bosnia was reduced from approximately 70% to 45% of the country. Thus, tough new US negotiator Richard Holbrooke succeeded in bringing about peace where Lords Carrington and Owen had failed[169]. Meanwhile, the US stopped short of allowing Tuđman to capitalise on his gains on the ground by annexing those parts of Bosnia dear to his heart: in March 1991, Tuđman had proposed to Milošević (and allegedly obtained his agreement to) the expansion of Croatia to comprise the territory of the *banovina* ("province") of Croatia, formed in 1939 by agreement of the then Serbian and Croatian leaders, Cvetković and Maček, as an autonomous Croat entity within the Kingdom of Yugoslavia in an effort to appease the Croatian nationalists, and including, in addition to Croatia, Bosnia from Livno up to Travnik and then down to Neum on the coast by way of Stolac, and the Sava basin including Gradačac and Brčko; and most of Srem, in the south-west of Vojvodina in Serbia, including Zemun and Šid, the border crossing now being used by the refugees from the Middle East to pass from Serbia into Croatia (Šid was shelled briefly in November 1991, in retaliation for JNA artillery fire originating from there)[170]. Izetbegović once said that choosing between Milošević and Tuđman was like choosing between leukaemia and a brain tumour[171]. Who was which, he didn't say, but from 1991 onwards, there were constant contacts between Zagreb and Belgrade on the creation of Greater Croatia and Greater Serbia out of Bosnia[172] (on 6 May 1995, Tuđman drew Lord Ashdown a map on a napkin of how Bosnia could be

---

[xlix] Lord Owen disagrees with this, and states that by October, Tuđman had pulled the handbrake on the HV/HVO, and the VRS had strong defensive positions.

divided between Croatia and Serbia[173])[1]. But who was the bitch? Tuđman ultimately outplayed Milošević with the Americans, using Izetbegović as his trump card, while the joker in the pack, Babo, was discarded. Under the peace agreement, the SDS got 49% of the territory, and the HDZ-SDA Federation 51% (with the exclusion of Brčko, see below), as per the original contact group peace plan (itself a rehash of the Vance-Owen plan of January 1993), albeit with a slightly different map[li][174].

I had been working for a British NGO, Feed the Children, in the Bosnian Borders for several months, after transferring from the more accessible war zone in central Bosnia. FTC had been the first NGO to deliver aid to Bihać, in December 1993. I was running a distribution programme to the most vulnerable families in the NOZB-controlled territory, working closely with the LCK and using their distribution network on the ground. Once a month we would receive an aid convoy from Split on the coast, which would then be distributed from our secondary warehouse in Polje. We had similar programmes in Cazin and the Croatian Borders, and this arrangement greatly facilitated our access to the Bihać pocket. The LCK was mainly supported by an outstanding team from the International Committee of the Red Cross, whose mandate under the Geneva Conventions includes, in addition to emergency medicine and relief, prevention (mainly the dissemination of international humanitarian law, such as respect for the protective emblem) and control: the protection of civilians (in particular IDPs, as refugees nominally fall under the mandate of UNHCR) with protection and assistance programmes, the protection of detainees with visits to POWs and civilians deprived of their liberty in order to prevent violations of IHL and restore family links, and more widely, the restoration of family links by means of Red Cross messages sent via its central tracing agency (and sometimes by issuing travel documents to allow repatriation and family reunification, or facilitate the movement of individuals granted asylum)[175]. Their neutrality, and professionalism, generally allow them to gain the confidence of all sides in a conflict, and their discretion and prestige lend them weight when seeking to influence the practices of the warring parties on the ground. On 19 May 1992, a rocket had destroyed an ICRC convoy heading to Sarajevo hospital, killing one delegate and wounding two other passengers, and on 17 January 1994, a bomb blew up an ICRC Landcruiser parked outside their residence in Banja Luka[176]. After the fall of Sector West, the SVK prevented UNHCR trucks from crossing their territory, as UNHCR had failed to mount an adequate response to the resulting refugee crisis in Banja Luka[177], and Babo would not allow them to proceed to Cazin. As a result, a convoy of ODA Bedfords (now known as DFID, the UK government's international aid department, who did UNHCR's trucking for them) were stuck in the UNPROFOR compound in Velika Kladuša for a few weeks. To make matters worse, the DFID truck drivers had a fall-out with the small number of British soldiers based

---

[1] According to Owen, "To both presidents the Bosnia-Herzegovina border was largely theoretical and in political terms did not exist". He also said that while "Milošević [...] is a total pragmatist, Tuđman is an opportunist", and Izetbegović was a "perplexing personality".

[li] A plan put forward by the contact group of the US, UK, France, Germany, and Russia to create a Bosnian state composed of two entities, 49% of territory for the Serbs and 51% for the Muslim-Croat Federation (its predecessor, the Vance-Owen plan, had offered the Serbs 43%, but was rejected by Karadžić, to Milošević's dismay; Izetbegović had tentatively accepted it after initially holding out for a better deal). Izetbegović agreed to the contact group plan and map in June 1994, as did Milošević in July, but Karadžić rejected it in August. Izetbegović then changed his mind and rejected it; he had only accepted it because he knew the Serbs would reject it. He refused Babo's offer to continue talks with Karadžić in his stead.

there, and as a result they were banned from their exclusive (and the only) bar in the compound (there was no shortage of pubs in the town, 1 km away, but their security rules precluded them from going there). Their trucks had names, such as Big Ted and Little Ted. Little Ted was subsequently blown off Mount Igman on the run into Sarajevo by a VRS anti-tank weapon. The restriction (and indeed the bans) did not apply to us, however, and our trucks continued to roll into Cazin. At a meeting on 22 June, UNHCR accused us of bribing Babo, which was not only absurd but also completely unfounded, and indeed part of the problem was UNHCR's own inimitable negotiation style, which seemed to consist of shouting at locals, in bad English. They also accused ICRC of failing to carry out proper relief activities in the north of the enclave, which ICRC refuted by referring them to their monthly distribution reports, which were shared with the local authorities and publicly available (as were ours; between 6 January and 15 May, a total of 3,000 tons of aid were delivered to the enclave, of which 800 tons to Velika Kladuša and 2,200 tons south to Cazin and beyond[178]). I was now returning to the field from an ill-timed holiday in France, which meant I had missed all the action.

As I approached Kuplensko, that until then had only been yet another flat, winding valley about 5 km long on my way to work, thickly wooded on either side and containing corn fields and orchards interspersed with houses, I began to see signs of human life, beginning with an army checkpoint. The HV military police seemed cheerful enough, perhaps due to the infectious Bosnian good humour, or merely glad the fighting was over, for them at least. I wondered how many of my friends and colleagues I would find there, and more ominously, how many I wouldn't.

THE SITUATION IN YUGOSLAVIA AND THE BOSNIAN/CROATIAN BORDERS BEFORE THE PEASANTS' REVOLT: SOCIAL, ECONOMIC AND POLITICAL CONTEXT WITHIN YUGOSLAVIA IN THE EARLY POST-WAR PERIOD - A BASIS FOR SOCIAL UNREST IN THE COUNTRYSIDE

The Second World War did not bring about any significant changes to the social structure of the population of Yugoslavia. Despite massive human losses, which were proportionally highest in the countryside, Yugoslavia continued after the war to be a predominantly rural country, with over three quarters of the population engaged in crop and livestock production. On the eve of the war, agriculture had provided over 50% of the country's national income, and in the first post-war years its share in Yugoslavia's total production only increased, as the non-agricultural economic infrastructure had suffered even more devastation in the war, such that in 1945 agricultural production was the main, and by far the most important source of general economic growth. Even before the war, Yugoslavia was regarded within Europe as an agriculturally backward country, for various reasons, in particular for its agricultural density and limited use of technology, and during the war itself Yugoslav agriculture suffered huge losses. Apart from the countless number of farms burned down and destroyed, with many villages simply wiped from the face of the earth, and agricultural land either neglected completely or poorly cultivated, it is estimated that 56% of the agricultural inventory was destroyed, 20.7% of houses destroyed or damaged, 24.2% of orchards destroyed, with the number of horses falling by 60%, sheep by 63.2%, cattle by 55.6%, and pigs by 58.7%. Livestock was exhausted, emaciated and sickly[lii]. It must also be borne in mind that these overall statistical indicators for the whole country do not show the fact that certain areas and regions suffered far more.

The greatest losses were, of course, human, and again these were greatest in the countryside. The new government was therefore all the more indebted to the peasants, forming as they did the social basis of the successful struggle for national liberation and social revolution, and in 1945 the government should absolutely have looked after their strategic interests. In concrete terms, this should above all have taken the form of an attempt to satisfy the peasants' age-old hunger for land, by taking it away from the large landowners and distributing it among the peasant farmers. As early as August 1945, at the third session of AVNOJ (the Yugoslav resistance), also known as the first People's Transitional Assembly, a Federal Land Reform and Resettlement Act was passed, the new government's most significant political measure in 1945. The main purpose of the act was to remedy, via land reform together with "Vojvodina" resettlement[liii][179] or inter-republic resettlement, and intra-republic resettlement, the social injustice felt by the peasants in the "old" Yugoslavia, which had also been the main platform of the KPJ in agricultural and rural affairs almost without interruption since its founding in 1919.

Due to the specific conditions of historical rural development in the various parts of Yugoslavia, and in particular due to the decisive role played by the peasants

---

[lii] Tetin tells me that today there is visibly less livestock in the fields than there used to be before the 1990s. A local man who became a millionaire in the US after the war recently returned, with plans to revive animal husbandry, using western methods.

[liii] To replace 350,000 ethnic Germans and Hungarians expelled at the end of WWII. The Habsburgs had settled Germans along the Danube in Vojvodina and Slavonia, and in Hungary, after capturing them from the Turks.

in the war and the revolution, the KPJ, in 1945 not even thinking of land nationalisation (which may well have been an option at that time in Yugoslavia's social development, given the general tendency to copy Soviet experience), aspired through land reform and resettlement to achieve a redistribution of land into private peasant ownership, which would then lead to the formation of a peasant class made up mainly of small and medium-sized farmers. These "small and medium-sized farmers", that is farmers with between 2 and 10 ha of land, would then be or become the main political ally of the working class, upon whom was conferred the lead role in the construction of socialism. It was considered that these "worker-peasants", unlike the "*kulaks*", or wealthier peasants, sometimes with little more than 10 ha of land, would in time engage fully in the effort to build a complete socialist society, and in particular in the "socialist transformation" of agriculture and rural affairs, which slogan was actually a euphemism for gradual collectivisation on a voluntary basis. From the very start, the most important role in this process in Yugoslav rural affairs policy, both in theory and practice, was assigned to peasant workers' associations (SRZs), a *kolkhoz*-type[liv] of rural association. Since their formation at the end of 1945, and in particular from the beginning of 1946 onwards, these associations received material support and political patronage from the government, that is, the ruling political elite. The results of the distribution of land via land reform and resettlement, mainly completed by the end of 1948, differed widely from the original idea and stated principle of transferring arable and other agricultural land into mainly private peasant ownership. Of the total of 1,647,305 ha land acquired under land reform, not even half ended up in private peasant hands, as prospective landowners received 405,582 ha, internal resettlers 90,655 ha, and external resettlers 213,526 ha, in other words in total just over 700,000 ha, while most of the land went to state agricultural estates (354,799 ha), peasant workers' associations (37,158 ha), and various state institutions (41,655 ha), or was classified as forest (401,395) or not distributed at all (101,995 ha).

One of the new government's most significant political measures as regards the peasantry must be the passing of the Agricultural Debts Forgiveness Act, also in 1945. Under this act, with its heavily ideological themes, the debts which peasants in the "old" Yugoslavia had perceived as an oppressive burden and interminable problem, were effectively written off or significantly reduced. It was widely known that before the war the government had failed, despite several attempts, to solve the problem of peasant debts, the debt crisis, which of course only served to alienate the peasantry, among other things. With its land reform and resettlement, and the forgiveness of pre-war peasant debts, as well as several other statutory measures (in particular as concerns the socialist effort) also favourable to the peasants' economic interests, the new government sought, immediately after liberation, to reconstruct rural infrastructure by strictly centralised policies implemented on the ground by its local officers. It organised the reconstruction of village houses, roads, various types of farm buildings and, which may have been most important at that time, directed support from relatively better-off areas to those which had suffered the most during the war. Of course, two years of post-war reconstruction, despite significant outside aid, in particular from UNRRA[lv], were not enough to restore pre-war basic production conditions. That would have been impossible, not only due to the scale of the destruction wrought by the war, but also because agricultural production, by its

---

[liv] Soviet collective farm.
[lv] UN Relief and Rehabilitation Administration.

60

very nature, and in particular livestock production, requires a long period for regeneration. As it was the peasants, forming as they did the overwhelming majority of the population, who had to bear the brunt not only of the material difficulties but also of the reconstruction efforts, it is no surprise that some sporadic dissatisfaction was expressed, in particular in those "rebel" areas which had also suffered the most in the war, with peasants regarding themselves as marginalised, and the like. This was particularly the case in those rural areas where in addition to the general difficulties (for example, obtaining the building materials required for house reconstruction) certain specific local problems also existed, such as arbitrary or clearly improper acts by the local representatives of the authorities. It must be borne in mind that the "rural infrastructure reconstruction" process was itself causing considerable dissatisfaction among the peasants. In Slunj county there was no shortage of all these problems.

Another relevant issue is that of the political status of the peasants in the new state. It was impossible for the KPJ, which had emerged from the war with enormous moral and political capital and which was not ready to share its leading social position with anyone, whether in 1945 or later, to align its strategic economic and political interests with those of the peasants. The KPJ, despite being the party of the working class, and furthermore modelling itself to a large extent on Soviet (Stalin's) socialist solutions for social development, was a political force which, although it sought and had the best long-term intentions, could not have an objective attitude towards the peasantry or even towards agriculture. Such a state of affairs can only have been disadvantageous for Yugoslavia in 1945, being as it was a predominantly peasant country in terms of its social structure, economic characteristics, traditions and culture. Although the peasants' second-class role was not expressly determined as such in 1945, its presence even then on the political scene can be observed by careful analysis. Under both the charter of the Yugoslav Popular Front[lvi][180] of 1945 and the constitution of the Federal People's Republic of Yugoslavia of 1946, the peasants were effectively denied the right to political representation as is the due of the working class as the "officially" most progressive section of society. This fact was of enormous, if not critical importance, not only for agriculture and the peasants but for society as a whole, and not just in the first post-war years but for Yugoslavia's entire post-war development. Even in the first years after the war, every means was deployed to remove from the political scene any forces and individuals who, like Draglojub Jovanović[lvii] for example, might advance the interests of the peasants from a "bourgeois" or "middle-class" position.

The first national five-year plan, adopted in the spring of 1947, did not herald any fundamental new concept of Yugoslav economic development. Modelled on the Soviet Union, the plan's overall direction was towards basic industrialisation, and it provided for four times more investment in industry than in agriculture. While this had been the course of development since liberation, it is the implementation of the plan after the brief period of "reconstruction" that really reveals Yugoslavia's social and economic long-term direction at that time. From 1947 onwards in particular, the peasants experienced first-hand the fundamentals of the country's economic policy, with significant increases in the "compulsory" or "administrative" agricultural produce quotas. The government, in order to successfully meet food requirements in

---

[lvi] According to George Orwell, the "'popular front' is a temporary alliance that fascism [...] forces upon the bourgeois and the worker".
[lvii] Serb dissident in post-WWII Yugoslavia.

conditions of significantly increased demand as a result of the process of forced industrialisation, gradually exercised ever greater, but in Yugoslav terms until 1949 not significantly greater pressure on individual farmers, including pressure on them to join the peasant workers' associations.

The *kolkhoz*-type associations were supposed to perform a double function. Firstly, they were to gradually attract the peasantry into collective ownership, then considered to be the right socialist economic model, and secondly, they would allow effective economic development planning, which was fundamentally infeasible with splintered land ownership. While the process of mass organisation of peasant workers' associations was not subject to government compulsory measures until the end of 1948 (with the exception of the destruction of the local peasants' associations in Vojvodina, with its specific conditions), this type of forced collectivisation in rural areas was nevertheless controlled. Significant changes occurred in this area at the beginning of 1949, coinciding with the political strategy adopted at the second plenary of the KPJ executive.

The new direction in rural affairs policy was undoubtedly linked to external pressure from the Cominform[lviii][181] countries and accusations made by the Soviet Union and other Cominform member countries against the KPJ executive and about Yugoslavia generally from the first half of 1948 onwards. Yugoslav rural affairs policy was accused of allowing the "growth of capitalist elements in rural areas" and the KPJ was denounced as a *"kulak* party". These accusations were rejected at the fifth congress of the KPJ in June 1949, and Yugoslav rural affairs policy remained practically unchanged, although contemporary documents show that within the party itself there were efforts to push the peasant workers' associations as the highest form of farming association. At the conference, Edvard Kardelj[lix][182] argued decisively against those within the party advocating a swift collectivisation of land on the Soviet model, describing it as "completely erroneous" and "self-destructive" as it failed to take account of the existence, or not, of the requisite suitable conditions, as did Boris Kidrič[lx], who gave a detailed exposition of the material difference between the peasants' historical rights to land and the role of the peasants in the 1917 Russian revolution and the 1941-1945 Yugoslav revolution.

However, the general party line on rural affairs and the peasants did "relax" only six months later. While the documents of the second plenary of the KPJ executive, which has many times been described as decisive in this area, do not show that the party leadership, especially Kardelj and his then main ideologue on land affairs, materially changed their view, the fact is that immediately after the plenary, the main focus of which was the "socialist transformation" of rural affairs and the countryside, practice took a radically different direction. In the plenary at the end of January 1949, the KPJ executive, clearly acting in response to the continued pressure from the Cominform on Yugoslavia, which was becoming ever greater and taking on ever more varied forms, as well as in response to the realisation being expressed even more loudly within the party, no doubt as a result of that pressure, that more

---

[lviii] The Cominform (1947-1956; earlier, from 1919-1943, the Comintern) was the international communist organisation. According to George Orwell, in the 1930s "The whole of Comintern policy is now subordinated to the defence of the USSR".

[lix] Slovene and leading liberal post-WWII KPJ official and economist, and number two in the government after the war. Fitzroy Maclean described him in 1940 as "looking like a provincial schoolmaster, which, as it happened, was what he was. He, I found, was the theoretician of the party, the expert Marxist dialectician."

[lx] Also a Slovene, in charge of the Yugoslav economy from 1946 until 1953.

rapid class differentiation, "dekulakisation", was needed in the countryside, in other words, more rapid strengthening of the socialist (i.e. state and association) sector in rural affairs, adopted to that end the well-known resolution under which it was deemed "necessary and possible to approach the creation of peasant workers' associations more swiftly and with greater boldness".

Forced collectivisation therefore had, perhaps predominantly, purely pragmatic goals besides the professions of ideological orthodoxy in the relationship with Stalin and inside the country. The country's difficult economic situation, isolated and under blockade as it was from the East, and with its relations with the West not yet developed and still characterised by fear, meant it was forced to rely almost exclusively on its own resources, which meant none other than agriculture and the peasants. With no deviation from the general strategic direction of economic growth, that is to say accelerated industrialisation of the country, and with expenditure on the army and defence increased several fold due to the real threat of an invasion from the East, there was no doubt about the financial implications: agriculture, the countryside and the peasants had to produce more.

The authorities set about implementation of the plenary directive on the ground with a will and without delay. Within a period of two months, from the beginning of February until the end of March 1949, more SRZs were established in Croatia, Macedonia, Bosnia and Herzegovina and Montenegro than had appeared in any of those republics between 1945 and 1949. In Serbia and Slovenia, the new SRZs represented almost 100% of the total. By the end of 1949 the number of SRZs had grown enormously, from 1,318 at the end of 1948 to 6,625 or, according to another source, 6,978 at the end of 1949. Admittedly, many of those SRZs throughout Yugoslavia only existed on paper, but once they were set up they aspired to proper organisational structure and development into real associations. This led to many serious problems on the ground. The KPJ executive's rural affairs committee informed Marshall Tito's office as early as 21 April 1949 of many individual cases of improper acts on the ground, in particular concerning breaches of the principle of voluntarism: "throughout the whole country peasants are being pressurised into joining the workers' associations". In order to force peasants to join the SRZs, local officials would increase the taxes and compulsory cereal and meat quotas of individual rich and average-income peasants beyond the prescribed amounts, which the farms concerned could not produce. Simultaneously, their property would be subjected to consolidation, putting rich and average-income peasants in an "impossible position". The price for this development in relationships in the countryside was of course high in social, economic and political terms. The bill was paid first and foremost by the peasants and agriculture as an industrial sector, but subsequently by society as a whole.

In addition to the difficulties of land collectivisation, which were particularly acute in 1949, the administrative compulsory quotas of agricultural products were seen as an even greater burden. From 1948 onwards "indexed price purchases" were introduced parallel to the compulsory quotas, under which the peasants were offered somewhat more favourable opportunities to purchase non-agricultural products. However, these products were either not available or were only available in insufficient quantities or in an unsatisfactory range. Despite this new, and not particularly successful type of quota policy, the fact remains that compulsory quotas continued to dominate and the free market in agricultural products continued to be blocked. This situation frequently forced peasants to buy a quantity of cereals or meat in order to be able to hand them over to the administrative quota officers.

It was these compulsory quotas of agricultural products which constituted the greatest burden for the peasants in the first post-war period, right up to 1951 or 1952, when this most hated of measures was finally abolished. Each year, the government reset what and how much the peasants had to provide in the form of the "compulsory quota", in consideration for their equivalent value in vouchers as a means of making purchases. These vouchers were generally provided instead of money as payment for the goods, and could in theory be used to buy industrial and other goods which the peasants needed for their everyday lives and agricultural production in the peasant workers' associations and association shops. The assessment of the quota per individual peasant was as a rule set impossibly high in almost all villages, with peasants having to provide more than they actually had. Furthermore, in order to meet their own targets for agricultural produce, local officials, party members, state security agents and policemen used all possible means on the ground to collect the quotas. Many party documents from those years show that the party leadership was made aware of many improper acts related to the collection of quotas on the ground. For example, in 1949 a resolution was passed in the cabinet's October session whereby the decree for cereal quotas for the 1949-1950 financial year was to "state clearly that the quota is only to be collected for land set apart for sowing by the government. The decree is to detail all appellate authorities…".

Under the government provisions, peasants were fined, their property partially or fully confiscated, and they were sentenced to periods of several months or even years of prison or "community service" in the mines, forests, or construction. In addition to the householder, the head of the family, who was the "official" convict, the whole family would be proscribed and mistreated by the local strongmen for failing to meet the household's quotas. In rural families the psychological pressure was so great that people actually dreamt that their stores of cereal in the attic were growing during the night, i.e. the fear and dread of the consequences of not having enough cereal for the quota affected peasants' and their families' mental wellbeing. Only a few courageous and belligerent peasants dared to protest, as for example did a peasant from Bijeljina in eastern Bosnia, who led a cow to the ward council and in his rage suggested the local official mate with it in order to produce the required quantity of livestock for the quota. He may have later had cause to regret doing so, although he was probably provoked by some unpleasant act of the authorities in his village.

Extremely rough treatment by officials was in fact a regular feature of the campaigns to obtain the assessed quota amounts in local areas. Peasants were frequently abused and even tortured in order to force them to provide the quota set for them. This general phenomenon is confirmed by numerous examples, and more are and will come to light with new historical literature on the period. The head of the party and state himself was well aware of what was happening on the ground in connection with the quotas. Logically, the problems were most prevalent in Vojvodina, the country's breadbasket, as is set out, for example, in Jovan Veselinov's[lxi] presentation at the third plenary:

> "Around 1000 confiscations have been carried out in Vojvodina, of which 160 'total' confiscations as they are called there. Total confiscations, whereby we take everything, were applied where people were unable to meet their obligations. It was nothing more than a dekulakisation policy. For example,

[lxi] Minister of land reform in post-WWII Yugoslavia.

someone claimed to have 140 metres, when he was supposed to provide 220, which meant he was short by 80 metres. We therefore applied the measure and carried out a total confiscation, even though we knew he really didn't have the full amount. We did it in order to meet our target, because we were pulling out all the stops to meet the white cereals target. I think that's why we resorted to such methods, but we had no choice. There were other mistakes as well, our people were losing their tempers, slapping people and pulling their moustaches[lxii]. (Comrade Tito: 'Some people need more than a pistol shoved in their mouth'). All kinds of things were happening. We even arrested members of county party agencies. But otherwise we think we wouldn't have been able to meet the target. Maybe not so many confiscations were needed. But under the decree we couldn't meet the target and we had to break the rules".

The top party leaders, who toured the whole country as part of "training teams", all expressed similar observations on the situation in the countryside, in particular as regards the tyranny visited on the peasants, while still mercilessly criticising them as being *"kulaks"*. Nevertheless, the torture of the peasants because of the quota system stayed in the minds of the officials. For example, Vida Tomšić[lxiii], who in 1950 visited Istria, Bosnia and Herzegovina and Macedonia with a training team, recalls that the "soles of peasants' feet were burned" for failing to fulfil the quotas. Some peasants were even killed. Data were presented at the end of 1949 at the third plenary of the KPJ executive mentioned above, during the discussion which followed Kidrič's paper *Current Tasks in the Struggle to Implement the Five-Year Plan*. Tito broached the dreadful matter by asking for an explanation from the comrades from Croatia. This led Vladimir Bakarić[lxiv] to state that "there was resistance in Slavonia during the collection of the quotas and around 50 people died in the fighting", adding that this had occurred because of the six Croatian territories, Slavonia had to provide 60% of the total quotas planned for Croatia. He also explained the "mistakes" which had led to that tragic event in 1949. It must be borne in mind that the recorded events are only the tip of the iceberg, such that the real tragic results of implementation of the quota policy in the Yugoslav countryside must have been far greater.

Apart from the difficulties with the SRZs and the quotas, the "labour mobilisation" programme was already causing serious resistance from the peasants, in particular from 1947 onwards, i.e. from the introduction of the five-year plan. Under this programme, peasants had to leave their homes and farming for a set period of time and take part in forestry work, mining, heavy industry and other types of work, with human resources "targets" set centrally and "assessed" per district and locality by government officials. This "labour service" did not only have a negative effect on agricultural production, which was sometimes interrupted at the height of seasonal work with peasants being co-opted away from agriculture due to poor planning by the authorities, as Kidrič, the chairman of the planning committee, expressly noted at the third plenary of the KPJ executive at the end of 1949. The

---

[lxii] A serious insult for a veteran.
[lxiii] Slovene KPJ activist and Partisan, imprisoned in Italy during WWII, and women's activist and federal KPJ official after the war.
[lxiv] Croat Partisan, first prime minister of post-war Croatia (1945-1953), leader of the Croatian KPJ 1948-1969, and later served two terms as federal deputy PM.

labour mobilisation also resulted in highly politicised situations on the ground leading to bad blood between the peasants themselves, as in the case of Omer Mujagić in Kladuša county in 1949 (see below). In the absence of concrete empirical research, it is difficult to determine the scale and gravity of the problem in individual parts of Yugoslavia as regards labour mobilisation. In Bosnia and Herzegovina for example, the problems were so serious that at the end of 1949, Đuro Pucar[lxv] suggested that the best thing to do in the circumstances would be "to pass a decree on forced labour, which would make it easier to get peasants to work in the mines for a period", as the shortage of "volunteers" in Bosnia meant that "the police were being used to round up the requisite number of people". To Tito's observation that he thought it must still be possible to use activists and propaganda to get people to volunteer for the work, Pucar replied that slogans about volunteering no longer had any effect. Without going into details that will be discussed further below, Bakarević's remark that in Croatia the use of labour mobilisation in the form of volunteer "front" brigades and teams of oxen for forestry work was "the most serious political problem in the countryside, even more serious than the quotas", indicates how grave the situation was.

Within the very short period of less than five years since the end of the war, Yugoslav society and in particular the peasants had been exposed to many major changes and new phenomena in economic, political and social relations. The peasants' life was becoming harder from year to year, their obligations increasing, and their rights to social decision-making reduced in practice. The peasants' burden, from the imposed hated quotas, labour mobilisation, SRZs, tax and other circumstances, culminated in 1949 and 1950. The party's moral capital in the eyes and hearts of the peasants had not only collapsed, but the peasants had begun to see it and the government as the enemy. The peasants' discontent was fanned by foreign propaganda, from both the East and the West, attempting to promote their own interests.

The interests of the East and the West were of course diametrically opposed in the context of the Cold War. In 1949 and the first months of 1950, in particular leading up to the outbreak of the Korean War, Yugoslavia was the focus of this crossfire. As of February 1949 the West, still harbouring its long-term strategic aspirations to see Yugoslavia return to the capitalist path of development, embarked on a new political course, called "keeping Tito afloat". The policy was to help Tito stay in place faced with the formidable political, economic and military pressure applied to Yugoslavia by Stalin, especially from 1949 onwards, with his blockade by Cominform countries in an attempt to overcome Tito's resistance and subject Yugoslavia to his hegemony and domination. In the first months of 1950, the country was facing its greatest threat of external aggression, an invasion from the East. Tension on the borders with Hungary, Romania, Bulgaria and Albania grew in 1950, and April saw the highest number of border incidents ever, 89.

All these internal and external elements mixed and combined and the result was the Peasants' Revolt in 1950 in the traditionally bellicose Borders – the former Turkish borders on the Bosnian side of the river Korana and the former Austro-Hungarian Military Frontier on the Croatian side[183].

Vera Kržišnik-Bukić, Cazinska Buna 1950 (footnotes omitted)

[lxv] President of Bosnia from 1946-1953.

[1] Malcolm, 1994:2
[2] West, 1942:171-183
[3] West, 1942:1050-1051
[4] Crnobrnja, 1994:16
[5] O'Shea, 1998:178-179
[6] Judah, 2002:252
[7] BBC, 2003:part 4
[8] Humanitarian Outcomes
[9] O'Shea, 1998:44
[10] Silber & Little, 1995:368; Owen, 1995:355
[11] O'Shea, 1998:107-109
[12] Silber & Little, 1995:288, 345-346
[13] O'Shea, 1998:158
[14] Maclean, 1949:362
[15] Maclean, 1949:337,402
[16] West, 1942:443
[17] Trkulja & Božić, 2008:96; Crnobrnja, 1994:69, 209; Ulemek, 2016:34-35
[18] Trkulja & Božić, 2008:39
[19] B92 & Vreme Film, 2006:II
[20] Trkulja & Božić, 2008:234
[21] Malcolm, 1994:219
[22] Crnobrnja, 1994:96; Silber & Little, 1995:105
[23] Ulemek, 2016:253-257
[24] Malcolm, 1994:49
[25] Abdić, 2016:329; Ulemek, 2016:316
[26] Ulemek, 2016:375
[27] B92 & Vreme Film, 2006:II
[28] Miljković, 2014:32-33
[29] O'Shea, 1998:66
[30] Ulemek, 2016:318
[31] O'Shea, 1998:156
[32] Ulemek, 2016:132
[33] Kržišnik-Bukić, 1991:266
[34] Trkulja & Božić, 2008:39-40
[35] Roberts, 2014:300-303; Crnobrnja, 1994:218
[36] Silber & Little, 1995:288
[37] Sandler & Hartley, 2007:750
[38] Human Rights Watch
[39] Aljazeera America
[40] Guardian
[41] Trkulja & Božić, 2008:194; Ulemek, 2016:428; Kržišnik-Bukić, 1991:xiii
[42] Trkulja & Božić, 2008:35
[43] Trkulja & Božić, 2008:81
[44] Trkulja & Božić, 2008:76, 100
[45] Guardian
[46] Kenrick & Puxon: 1996:140-142
[47] Trkulja & Božić, 2008:47
[48] Maclean, 1980:184, 66
[49] Trkulja & Božić, 2008:128-131
[50] Trkulja & Božić, 2008:88
[51] Andrić, 1967:138
[52] Ulemek, 2016:478, 486
[53] Maclean, 1949:415-442
[54] Miljković, 2014:363
[55] Miljković, 2014:374; Ulemek, 2016:48
[56] Stević, 1995:25, 62
[57] Silber & Little, 1995:89; Baker, 2015:42; Crnobrnja, 1994:259; Zakon.hr
[58] Crnobrnja, 1994:152; Judah, 2002:61
[59] Ulemek, 2016:13
[60] Crnobrnja, 1994:25
[61] Kržišnik-Bukić, 1991:266

[62] Crnobrnja, 1994:26
[63] West, 1942:97
[64] Silber & Little, 1995:100
[65] Trkulja & Božić, 2008:39, 45
[66] Baker, 2015:10; Owen, 1995:33-34; Dizdarević, 2000:164
[67] Malcolm, 1994:70-81
[68] Tolj, 1996:214
[69] Baker, 2015:10
[70] Tolj, 1996:187-191
[71] Trkulja & Božić, 2008:45-47, 55
[72] Baker, 2015:49
[73] Silber & Little, 1995:104-111
[74] Crnobrnja, 1994:157
[75] Silber & Little, 1995:139
[76] Freshpress
[77] Silber & Little, 1995:146-160
[78] Crnobrnja, 1994:171
[79] Crnobrnja, 1994:25
[80] Silber & Little, 1995:195
[81] Judah, 2002:114
[82] West, 1942:056
[83] Crnobrnja, 1994:169
[84] Silber & Little, 1995:186-193
[85] Buckley & Cummings, 2001:18
[86] Silber & Little, 1995:207-208; Crnobrnja, 1994:205
[87] Balkaninsight
[88] Ambrose, 1975:8, 247, 374-384, 395; Brown, 1991:368
[89] Trkulja & Božić, 2008:224
[90] Trkulja & Božić, 2008:78, 222
[91] Wikileaks
[92] Crnobrnja, 1994:174-188
[93] Crnobrnja, 1994:181
[94] Ulemek,2016:37
[95] Crnobrnja, 1994:23
[96] Malcolm, 1994:158
[97] Médecins Sans Frontières, 2015:67
[98] Independent
[99] Silber & Little, 1995:385 ; Crnobrnja, 1994:210
[100] O'Shea, 1998:122
[101] O'Shea, 1998:121
[102] International Relations and Security Network; International Journal of Peace Studies; Hirkić, 1998:308
[103] O'Shea, 1998:129
[104] O'Shea, 1998:151-152; Owen, 1995:314-315
[105] O'Shea, 1998:192
[106] Maclean, 1949:351
[107] Tolj, 1996:100
[108] O'Shea, 1998:201-211; Ulemek,2016:26-27, 368-369
[109] O'Shea, 1998:184; Guardian; Baker, 2015:61
[110] Crnobrnja, 1994:178, 184; Abdić, 2016:250
[111] Bastabalkana, 20, 22
[112] Silber & Little, 1995:307,336-339, 378-379; O'Shea, 1998:66-67; Guardian
[113] O'Shea, 1998:140; Owen, 1995:353
[114] Selimović, 2006:5
[115] O'Shea, 1998:xiii
[116] O'Shea, 1998:40, 150
[117] O'Shea, 1998:214; Owen, 1995:355
[118] Baker, 2015:76
[119] IndexHR
[120] Silber & Little, 1995:386
[121] Silber & Little, 1995:388; Owen, 1995:353
[122] Kržišnik-Bukić, 1991:555

[123] O'Shea, 1998:217-228
[124] Ulemek, 2013:254
[125] Ulemek, 2016:429
[126] Tolj, 1996:101-103; Ulemek, 2016:370
[127] Stević, 1995:57; Abdić, 2016:104-105
[128] O'Shea, 1998:229
[129] Dizdarević, 2000:338
[130] Malcolm, 1998:353
[131] Judah, 2002:130
[132] Judah, 2002:162
[133] Los Angeles Times
[134] Dizdarević, 2000:282; Abdić, 2016:142, 458
[135] O'Shea, 1998:28; Ulemek, 2016:376
[136] Silber & Little, 1995:191
[137] Crnobrnja, 1994:170; Silber & Little, 1995:91; Malcolm, 1994:226
[138] Freshpress
[139] B92 & Vreme Film, 2006:I
[140] Silber & Little, 1995:205-206
[141] Crnobrnja, 1994:170
[142] Abdić, 2016:420
[143] Malcolm, 1994:236
[144] Crnobrnja, 1994:181; Silber & Little, 1995:247
[145] Silber & Little, 1995:248
[146] Abdić, 2016:92, 95, 136-142
[147] Malcolm, 1994:236-237
[148] Baker, 2015:51; Silber & Little, 1995:177; Malcolm, 1994:224-225
[149] Malcolm, 1994:227
[150] Malcolm, 1994:238
[151] O'Shea, 1998:48
[152] Ulemek, 2013:180, 221
[153] Ulemek, 2013:11
[154] Baker, 2015:63
[155] Baker, 2015:119
[156] Ulemek, 2016:103
[157] Maclean, 1949:328; O'Shea, 1998:174; Independent
[158] Judah, 2002:238
[159] West, 1942:497; Maclean, 1949:511-512
[160] Ulemek, 2013:7; Baker, 2015:83-84; Buckley & Cummings, 2001:276
[161] B92 & Vreme Film, 2006:II-III; Baker, 2015:86-87
[162] O'Shea, 1998:234; Baker, 2015:67; Miljković, 2014:435
[163] Silber & Little, 1995:280, 318; Crnobrnja, 1994:138, 182, 190
[164] Miljković, 2014:27; O'Shea, 1998:68
[165] Miljković, 2014:352
[166] Miljković, 2014:345; Owen, 1995:339
[167] Miljković, 2014:430
[168] Maclean, 1949:305-307; Trkulja & Božić, 2008:38
[169] Judah, 2002:122; O'Shea, 1998:53
[170] Silber & Little, 1995:143,196; Crnobrnja, 1994:61
[171] Malcolm, 1994:228; Owen, 1995:38, 74, 348
[172] Silber & Little, 1995:341
[173] O'Shea, 1998:234-236
[174] O'Shea, 1998:51-54; Silber & Little, 1995:306, 378; Owen, 1995:102, 121
[175] Kolb, 2014:189-192
[176] Médecins Sans Frontières, 2015:41 ; Owen, 1995:249
[177] O'Shea, 1998:217
[178] Stević, 1995:61
[179] Judah, 2002:45; West, 1942:262
[180] Orwell, 1962:56
[181] Orwell, 1962:56
[182] Maclean, 1949:326; Kržišnik-Bukić, 1991:220
[183] Kržišnik-Bukić, 1991:3-14

PART 2
THE INFERNAL VALLEY

"Mujo and Huso spent years working as zidari *['brickies'] in Germany*[i1]*, saving among other things for their retirement. Finally, the time came, and they set off back to Bosnia to enjoy their well-earned rest. However, tragedy unexpectedly struck, and they were taken out by an artic on the* autobahn *near Munich.*

They appeared before God, who said, 'I'm afraid I can't let you two grešnici *['sinners'] into* dženet *['heaven']. However, as you weren't any worse during your lives than can be expected from Bosnians, I'm prepared to make a special case, and a low-security, lenient* džehenem *['hell'] has been prepared especially for you. What's more, you get a choice.'*

'What's the choice?' asked Mujo.

'You can choose between the German hell or the Bosnian hell', replied God.

'What's the difference?' asked Huso.

'It's just like life on earth', replied God. 'Except that in the German hell you have to eat a spoonful of shit every day, and in the Bosnian hell it's a shovelful.'

'I'll go for the German hell', said Mujo. 'Forsprung dirh tehnik.'

'Not for me', said Huso. 'I've had enough of Dojčland *to last me an eternity. I'll take the Bosnian hell.'*

And with a final 'Auf Viderzehn, prijatelju', *it came to pass.*

Some time later, they met up again. After exchanging greetings, they enquired about how each was faring in his new environment. 'The German hell isn't so bad, except that every morning when I wake up there's a German devil standing there with a spoon of shit, and I have to eat it before I do anything else' Mujo said. 'I'm starting to get tired of it. But at least I'm better off than you, with that shovelful.'

'Fakat ['actually'] it's not so bad', replied Huso. 'Every morning when I wake up, either there's no shovel or no shit, or the devil hasn't turned up for work!'"[ii]

---

[i] Unlike citizens of other communist countries, Yugoslavs were allowed to travel and work abroad, including in the West. This not only reduced unemployment, but also produced much sought-after hard currency in the form of remittances. The red Yugoslav passport was welcomed at the borders of most western countries; but nowadays, Balkan passports tend to set off red warning lights when presented to customs officials in the West. One day after the war, at a London crown court, an (allegedly) Croatian Romany whose pregnant wife, the *optuženica* ("defendant"), was in *phanglipe* ("custody") and facing a *lišenje slobode* ("custodial sentence"), asked me whether I had a red passport. I replied that I did (a British passport), whereupon he pulled a £50 note (also red) from his wallet and said, "This is my passport". As they say in the Balkans, *"Kasno se jebenom kajati – ma rov so čordili e zumi le jekh kotor khos e skafidi"* ("there's no point crying over spilt *varenka* ['milk']"). On another occasion, a Romany suspect, born in 1996, assured me that both her parents had been killed in the war in Bosnia. When I pointed out to her that the war had ended in 1995, she said, "Not for us it didn't".

[ii] Told at a funeral in Nottingham, 2007. *Prijatelj* means "friend".

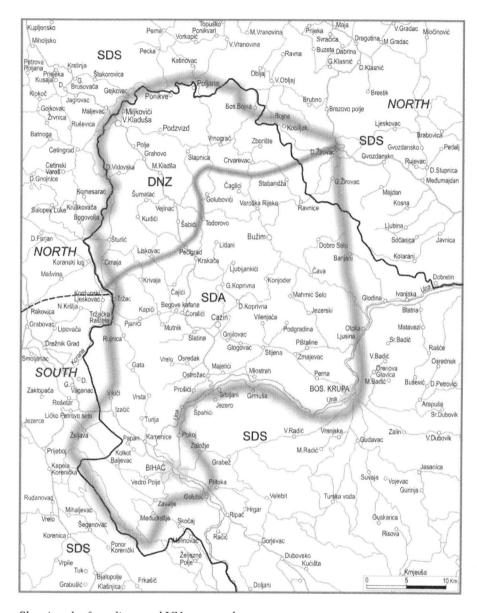

Showing the front lines and UN protected areas.

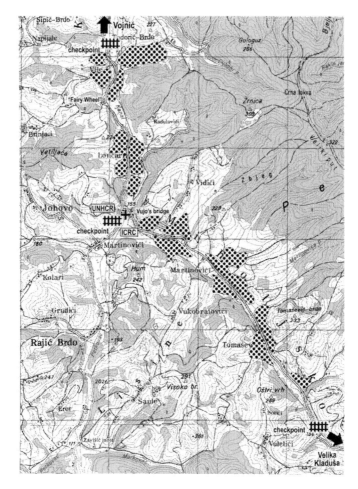

Showing the main infrastructure and population areas.

Good people of this world
Hear my poem's entreaty
Help us over here
Remember your own family

Must our little children
In these days of winter cold
Trample in the mud
Barefoot, naked, starved?

O what is your heart
Of ice or of stone
Can the whole world really
Just watch this misery unfold?

Do you really think, people
That it isn't a great sin?
Give back to our children
Give their smile back to them

Why do you keep silent and watch
Our troubles and our sorrow?
Remember your own children
Remember the time is now

Is it our children's fault
That they're homeless and uncovered?
Remember your own home
And ours, made of brushwood

Remember your villas
Remember your central heating
Remember our houses
With roofs of plastic sheeting

Remember your food
What you have for lunch and supper
Must our children in Kuplensko
Really toil and suffer?

And wonder what for breakfast
Their mothers will provide?
Remember our children
Remember now is the time

Now I ask you gentlemen
And beg you all and each

Where will our little children
Warm their little feet?

While you sit in your houses
Watching news on your TV
Ask yourselves good people
What will our children eat?

Maybe there will be a response
To my rhymed entreaty
Can this really be happening to us
At the end of the twentieth century?

The whole world is just watching
Do you know that that's a sin?
Only you can give
Our children's smile back to them[2].

Sead "Tetin" Kajtazović, Paklena Dolina

I exchanged a few brief words with the military police at the entrance to the village-cum-camp and was allowed to drive in. Today, Kuplensko is less than two hours' drive from Zagreb, with its cafes, shops, trams, *velesajam* ("trade fair") and cathedral, but 20 years ago it might as well have been two light years away. In striking contrast to my experiences earlier that morning and the previous day, now there was human activity everywhere. The narrow road was full of throngs of men, women and children clad in a variety of colourful traditional and western garb walking purposely in the execution of some task, or strolling leisurely in groups chatting and laughing, or engaged in the construction of shelters on both sides of the road (one of which was the bottom of the U-shaped valley, effectively a marsh traversed by a stream, now called the Kupljenčica, while the other was an irregular rising slope; halfway through the camp, the road crossed to the other side of the steam). Some of them were wearing Pink Floyd "Mission Bell" T-shirts, as we had previously received a large stock of unsold tour merchandise, which had been distributed to the most needy in our operations in Bosnia and Croatia. Some of the women were wearing *dimije* (traditional baggy women's trousers that look like a skirt, but narrow at the ankle) and *marame* (head scarves). I saw one team of men cutting steps into the embankment to facilitate access to their newly-constructed shelter overlooking the road on one side, while on the other a shanty town had sprung up on the edge of the road itself. The construction materials were a mixture of plastic sheeting, wood and nondescript items salvaged from somewhere in the village, or brought with them. In addition to household items, all the artefacts of the Balkan farmyard, such as *ćumez* ("chicken run") and *dižva* ("milk pail"), were appropriated and assigned more substantive and vital functions. Later, refugees cannibalised houses in the outlying villages for construction materials[3]. My senses, until now starved of any except visual stimuli, were suddenly assailed by a concentrated, if not distilled essence of the sounds and smells of Bosnian country life. Witty, earthy idioms, formidable oaths, and strains of *turbofolk* music combined with fresh farmyard fragrances to deliver a triple whammy. From time to time I also caught the mouth-watering scent of roasting meat. I noticed pro-Babo graffiti sprayed on some houses, which can still be seen today[iii], and there was the occasional defiant rallying call of "*Živio Babo!*" ("long live Babo!"), echoed by its refrain "*Živio!*". There was a tangible atmosphere of industry, and as well of reunions of family and friends, as the vagaries of war had meant that many of these people had been separated from each other for extended periods of time over the past three years. Others were newly separated from family members, and had no news of how or even where they were. I had been struck before by how hardy and steeped in country lore these people were, and now I was struck by their sheer resourcefulness: used to physical work outside in all weathers, they were almost completely self-sufficient, and accustomed to wresting a living from a hostile environment by the sweat of their brow: *Ko radi taj se ne boji gladi* ("if you want something done right do it yourself"). They expected little or nothing from the authorities or anyone else, and only wanted to be left in peace. A few days later, while down in the centre of the valley, I noticed a washing machine drum suspended over a minor branch of the stream, with some electrical wires leading away from it to a small shelter made of pallets. Intrigued, I investigated, to discover that it was functioning as a dynamo, and had been rigged up by the householder to provide light for his family. I later discovered his wasn't the only one. In Chechnya two years later I was introduced to an IDP family who were living in an abandoned railway carriage, with no hygiene facilities. While I sympathised with their plight, I couldn't help thinking the head of the household, a young man, could have shown some more initiative (other *bežencaš*, "IDPs", were housed in conditions that can only be described as grim, especially in winter). In late October, people living in the flood plain or on the road were moved to a more suitable location in the camp[4].

Travelling north-west from Maljevac along the country roads towards Vojnić, though the hamlets of Donja Brusovača and Krstinja, the 5 km stretch of road between Miholjsko and Kuplensko is reached after about 30 minutes. The valley is subject to strong south winds that blow up the valley only to bounce around from the surrounding hills until they run out of steam, and cold winds blowing straight down from the hills[5]. Continuing along the road after Kuplensko, a right turn at the T-junction leads to Vojnić 3 km away. Midway through the stretch that was the camp, at the road bridge known as Vujo's bridge, which separates Miholjsko to the south from Kuplensko to the north, another country road leads through the hamlet of Dunjak south towards Cetingrad (this access road was only used by the police). The gap between the two roads immediately south of the junction was spanned by a small bridge crossing the stream, that has since been demolished. The whole 5 km came to be known as Kuplensko.

In defeat, there was a tangible sense of relief that the war was over, at least for now, and that communities had been reunited, at least partly. I discovered that the delicious scents of roasting meat wafting on the *hava* ("air") emanated from the newly liberated livestock, as the people made the most of the summer's day and the bounty that had fallen into their laps in their misfortune. The villagers' stocks of *rakija* were quickly discovered and widely appreciated. I met one of the original villagers one day, a pensioner called Ilija, who was not happy that his livestock had

---

[iii] Also visible today sprayed on a ruined wall, just legible above the delinquent undergrowth, is the observation, "*Vratit ćemo se kad nam dođe pamet*" ("we'll come back when we come to our senses").

been plundered, but seemed pleased at least to have the company and the safety in numbers. The days of plenty, however, were not to last long. Nor was everyone happy even then: towards one end of the camp, 500 m from the northern exit, a deserted *kafić* ("pub") with a natural *česma* ("spring"), known as *"Vilin Točak"* ("Fairy Wheel"), was being used as a makeshift hospital for the 80 seriously wounded[6], with support from ICRC. Other wounded men were languishing in a trailer[7]. MSF subsequently took over their care, and the most serious cases were ultimately, after extensive and frustrating negotiations with the HDZ, transferred to their civilian care. On 15 November, ICRC took the unusual step of issuing a press release, expressing its alarm that "life-threatening cases are not allowed to be transferred to the hospital in Karlovac and that the few that did reach the hospital were refused treatment"[8].

I had to drive very slowly to avoid hitting anyone. I was scanning the pedestrians as I advanced, hoping to recognise someone I knew. Suddenly I heard my name called, and turning round, saw Seka waving to me. I knew her from the LCK in Velika Kladuša, where she was responsible for a public kitchen that we supported, where the poorest families could at least get one square meal a day. Unusually, although she was Bosnian, she had been born in Kosovo, where her Slovene father had been working. I stopped and we talked. She was well, she said, except that she was *hasta* ("sick") with an ear infection, and was living in a bedroom with her sister's extended family, 10 people who ranged from a baby (Haris) to his grandmother. As they say in the Balkans, *"Kad čeljad nije bijesna kuća nije tijesna"* ("bricks and mortar make a house but the laughter of children makes a home"). On the morning of the exodus she had woken up about 7 to find the town in turmoil. After her morning coffee, she joined the human river heading for Maljevac. Her sister, Jadra, had mislaid the bag she had taken with nappies and other items for Haris, and had gone back, to find the streets deserted. After leaving the house again empty handed (someone had loaded the bag onto a trailer), she had had to run to Maljevac with bullets whistling past her ears. She was reunited with the bag later on. Seka seemed cheered up to see me, and I was glad too. She was trying to get a permit to travel to the hospital in Karlovac to get her ear looked at, which would also allow her to visit her other sister, who lived in Karlovac, and who she hadn't seen for two years. An ambulance that had arrived with the refugees transporting the wounded and was subsequently based in the camp would drive out-patients to the hospital most mornings at 8, where they were generally not made welcome, even though their medical expenses were being covered[9].

As I drove on, I saw my former teenage foreman Denis still in his uniform, and he saw me at the same time and gave that curious Bosnian wave, a gesture that seems to say "damn it" in a positive way. I stopped and got out, and we went to see his family, who were living in the corner of an attic. I learnt that all my former local team had got out in one piece. The fact that all men over the age of 18 were under arms had meant that our local team, recruited the year before by Steve during the refugee crisis in Turanj (see below), all had to be under that age. When our first convoy arrived in Turanj, they came forward and volunteered to help unload the trucks, and were later rewarded by being given jobs. This also meant that one by one as they reached majority themselves, they had to join up. Dragan was the first to go, followed by Denis, Šeki and Elvir. I tried to obtain an exemption for them, but Ramo (see below) refused to contemplate it (I had found the authorities in Konjic to be more accommodating, at least until they wanted to launch an offensive, see below).

They were replaced by Adis and Dževad. I visited Adis's home once, and there was a shell crater about a metre in diameter in one of the external walls, penetrating right through, and making that room unusable as anything other than a shed. Samir was saved by Operation Storm, which took place before his eighteenth birthday. Ironically, the basic training centre, *"Pobjednici"* ("the victors"), in which Legija took a personal interest (even though officially he was never there) was just across the road from our warehouse, so we kept seeing them before they were deployed to the front. Dragan told me that Legija said to the recruits he wouldn't want anything to happen to any of them, and so he would give them the training they needed to be able to go to the front with confidence (three of the recruit intake ended up wounded)[iv][10]. I was put in mind of my grandfather, Grattan, who was killed at a similar age in WWI. I wonder whether anyone showed him any acts of kindness in his most difficult moments. T.E. Lawrence wrote after WWI: "We stammered that we had worked for a new heaven and a new earth, and they thanked us kindly and made their peace"[11]. Denis later told me that, after the rout of the NOZB, young and fit as he was, he was surprised to be overtaken in his efforts to get away from the 5th Corps by a much older squaddie who, in addition to his weapon and personal kit, was carrying a stove loaded onto his back! Later, Denis's family upgraded to a family *šator* ("tent"), and we became neighbours.

The day before, driving through Velika Kladuša, I had been surprised to see that, far from being empty, the town was full of people. But they were different people, and I hardly knew a soul. I used to run into people I knew all the time when walking about. Now almost everyone I knew was in Kuplensko (or was not venturing out of doors). Many of the new inhabitants of the town were locals who had been IDPs in Cazin during the conflict, while others were people from the outlying villages who for one reason or another preferred to live in the town, perhaps for security reasons, or because there were more opportunities there.

I later started to receive complaints from Split that we were not returning the pallets that came to us in our aid convoys. I had to explain that they were being put to extremely good use, providing shelter for whole families. Later we were able to provide family-size tents, which were very much appreciated. Those refugees better versed in *građevina* ("construction work") were able to convert their makeshift dwellings into comfortable homes-from-home that would be the envy of Butlins. One refugee, Baći, who I met 20 years later working as a builder in London, used an abandoned tent to build an external shell for the tent he was living in with his family, providing excellent insulation. He also built a fully-fledged *šporet* ("range") from bricks and metal sheet salvaged from an isolated house on a hill that was cannibalised by the refugees. Some of the tents were even put to commercial use, while one was consecrated as a mosque. One became a cinema, entrance DM 1, which premiered with *Pulp Fiction* on 27 September, subtitled in Croatian, and before its official release date. Seka and I took Mirsad, Denis's elder brother, and his

---

[iv] Legija himself wrote, "I suggested to [the NOZB] that we organise solid, accelerated training for the recruits, so that if any of them should later be killed on the threshold of manhood, at least it would be known that they hadn't gone gentle. Hard, but that's the way it was. We were unable to give them proper training, because there simply weren't the conditions, but we managed to improvise something [...] Their whole training lasted 45 days. No more time was available [...] As busy as I was with other matters at the time, I always made the time to see how the youngsters, sucked up by fate into this murderous war, were progressing with their training".

wife Sanela to see it. Mirvet used to buy films for the cinemas in Croatia via a NGO driver. The film *Streetfighter*, in which Jean-Claude van Damme plays a tough UN peacekeeper, was widely heckled and ridiculed by local film buffs (Legija later commented that Sylvester Stallone would have met his match in the Balkans[12]). Another cinema, Cobra, started to show erotic films after 7 pm[13]. The houses of the village had been filled with people first, very quickly. It is traditional in the Balkans to build houses floor by floor over time, occupying the completed ones and adding others when finances permit, in the hope that the younger generation will ultimately move in and not flee the nest. This means that houses in the country tend to be large, with each floor a more or less stand-alone residence, and the total number of rooms quite large. Now the sheer number of refugees meant that extended families of 10 or more were occupying a single room, so that there could be 30 or more people per floor, all sharing a bathroom. Some people ended up living in cars or trailers, while later others lived in containers brought in by aid agencies[14]. There was one tragic event on 19 March 1996 when a trailer caught fire at night, and two children were killed, one at the scene, and the other two days later in hospital in Karlovac. Apparently their mother fell asleep and left a candle burning near a *kanta* ("jerrycan") of fuel. There were no emergency services to call in Kuplensko. Tetin (see below) and five other refugees were arrested trying to help. The camp committee (see below) wrote a protest to UNHCR, asking for those police officers who had abused refugees verbally or physically to be identified[15]. Tetin and another two were returned to the camp the next day, when UNHCR were still unaware of the incident[16]. The rest of the unhappy family were transferred to Gašinci on 6 May, for resettlement abroad[17].

As the supplies of fresh food and drink, and firewood ran out, things started to get more difficult, especially as summer turned to autumn and then winter. However, the local home-brewing tradition thrived, with the distillers resorting to any vegetable matter, and more, for their raw materials. I heard a rumour that someone had succeeded in making *rakija* out of washing powder, and was assured it took effect "*brže nego rengen*" ("faster than an X-ray"). The once thick woodland on both sides of the valley began to thin rapidly, until the police banned the practice and started to arrest anyone found up on the slopes. Ten people were arrested chopping wood on 27 November[18]. As for food, the people were forced to rely on humanitarian aid. The more enterprising refugees started to smuggle goods in from outside, and sell them at improvised stalls. By December, there would be a dozen refugees making their way to Velika Kladuša every night, and the fluctuation in prices the following morning was an indicator of what they had brought back[19]. On 25 February, four *šverceri* ("smugglers)" were caught returning to the camp; one of them was wounded by the police[20]. There was improvised everything in the camp, from *šišanje* ("barbers": men's haircut DM 4, shave DM 2; credit was available, to be paid on return to Bosnia[21]), to *šusteri* ("cobblers") to *krčme* ("bars"), where you could imbibe Croatian *konjak* ("brandy") or even enjoy a cold beer while having your eardrums pounded by such *turbofolk* classics as *Wolves across the Drina*, *HVO Brigade*, *Nowt Against Split*, *Gypsy Blonde*, or the once iconic and now ironic *Whose Country is This?*[v] Most bars closed in the evening, but some stayed open until late,

---

[v] The song went:
"Whose country is this? Babo's! Babo's!
What army is this? The NOZB!"

and *tučnjave* ("fights") were not uncommon, some with serious consequences. Alcohol combined with the general stress and uncertainty, arms, and sometimes unresolved issues going back to the war were a potent mix[22]. On the evening of 6 November, after a brawl at one of bars, 50 inmates were arrested and taken to Vojnić police station, while on 7 November, 32 "criminals" were removed and handed over to the Bosnian police[23]. Further to this incident, MSF wrote to Tuđman's special advisor on humanitarian issues, the late Slobodan Lang, on 10 November, calling it a "clear violation of the principle of non-refoulement of the 1951 Geneva Convention relating to the status of refugees". In the letter, MSF also urged the Croatian authorities to immediately stop forced movements or repatriations; recognise the Bosnian refugees as such; allow the refugees freedom of movement; ensure adequate protection for the refugees in and outside the camp, to prevent a further deterioration of the security situation in the camp that could result in a violent confrontation between the security forces and the refugees; and to allow the necessary preparations for winter[24]. Dr Lang responded by visiting the camp with a loudspeaker and haranguing the refugees. A rowdy evening on 23 December was reported to the police as a fight, and the revellers were all arrested and taken to Vojnić. Fortunately, they managed to convince the custody sergeant that it was a mistake and they were allowed back[25]. Some people managed to set up telephone links, either with satellite phones or landlines (these were the days before mobile phones were readily available), and would charge for phone calls back to Bosnia. This was one of the most profitable activities in the camp, and the owner could earn over DM 1,000 a day. In early November, cigarettes started to be sold individually[26], and the price was twice that outside the camp. On 2 December, two packets of Drina could be bought for DM 3.50, while a litre of cooking oil cost the same[27]. On 15 October, sugar had cost DM 4 per kilo[28]. Meanwhile, in Bosnia, the average monthly pay at that time was DM 46, while the average consumer basket for a four-member family was DM 357[29]. In November, average pay was DM 50, and consumption DM 220, at a time when Croatian riot police deployed to the Bihać pocket could be paid USD 60 per day[30]. From September onwards, whenever the decision was taken to slaughter one of the few remaining heads of livestock its new owner had prudently decided to keep alive and look after, the word would go round the camp that there was going to be fresh meat. On 2 September, it cost DM 1 per kg, and some visitors from outside would even go shopping in the camp and take meat home with them[31] (I later encountered a similar practice in rural Mozambique, with the uniform price dependent solely on weight, such that gristle cost the same as filet). Those with the means would turn up at the appointed time and place, and the butcher would carve off cuts to order. Initially there was some confusion and a few errors when slaughtering pigs, as the Muslim butchers did not have experience with that animal, and the fatal knife blow only made it squeal. Alen (see below) made several unsuccessful attempts to slaughter a pig with a sharpened breadknife, until a more skilled and better equipped refugee stepped in and did the job for him. On Christmas Eve, a Kuplensko schnitzel cost DM 7[32]. The news of mad cow disease in the UK was followed avidly on the radio by this farming community, and became a hot topic

---

During the siege of Sarajevo, Adis told me that a Serb radio station once received a telephone request to play the patriotic song *Hold Your Head Up Serb!* When asked who the song should be dedicated to, the caller replied it was for the Muslim snipers. A popular 5th Corps song from this time was
"*Mudžahedin*, Turkish son
Fighting heart and soul, til Bosnia's won".
As Zahid, see below, commented to me, "*Šta će mi turski sin?*" ("do me a favour'").

of debate[33]. I heard one woman say, "Thank God we're here!" Some people succeeded in setting up meat smoking houses, and started to make *pastrma* (*"biltong"*). Some took to livestock rustling from the outlying villages, and in October an elderly Serb woman was killed when she interrupted the rustlers at work in her barn[34]. Because of this, on 20 October, all the butchers in the camp were arrested by the riot police and taken to Vojnić[35]. As a foreigner, I had freedom of movement, and would often go shopping in nearby Vojnić, where Croat refugees displaced from Banja Luka in northern Bosnia by Serb refugees in the aftermath of the fall of Sector West, were being resettled. People traffickers, working with the police and the Croatian mafia, could get a refugee abroad from between DM 3,000-10,000, and a *putovnica* ("Croatian passport") could be obtained for DM 6,000 (half up front)[36]. On 23 January, the UN police (IPTF, whose mandate was to investigate any reports of breaches of the human rights of returnees and report them to the local police[37]) visited the camp and enquired about people trafficking links to Switzerland and the Baltic states[38]. The oldest profession in the *dunjaluk* ("world") made a discrete appearance in the form of women visiting the house that served as a police barracks at the north end of the camp[39]; I heard it had been more overt in the previous refugee crisis. Another, possibly even older profession, espionage, was present everywhere, in the camp and back in Bosnia, as it was throughout the former Yugoslavia. Everything anyone said or did was reported to someone somewhere and had a tendency to be used against them[40] (at the beginning of the refugee crisis, I would be regularly asked by people I knew, and others, to deliver letters to their families in Velika Kladuša. I referred most requests to the LCK, where they could complete and submit a Red Cross *haber* ("message"), but in the face of persistent requests I agreed to deliver some. However, returning to Bosnia on one such day, I was told at the border in Maljevac to exit my vehicle because it had to be searched. Two very severe middle-aged women in ABiH uniform, one of them a platinum *plavuša* ("blond") with a chain-smoker's husky tones, honed in immediately on my bag on the back seat where I had placed the letters. Despite my protests, Blondie extracted the letters, opened and read them, and then confiscated them, informing me that I would be jailed for espionage. I was then allowed to continue on my way).

Despite the straightened circumstances, the Balkan tradition of hospitality did not die, but rather flourished; indeed, it was an essential part of the community's social cohesion and individuals' mental wellbeing in the face of so many physical stresses. The Balkan *domaćin* ("householder") will always go out of his way to make his guests feel at home, and offer them something to eat or drink, even in the most straightened of circumstances. Anything placed on the table is at the disposal of the guest, who will be encouraged with *"Prijatno"* or *"Bujrum"* (*"bon appetit"*) to partake, and more will be added until he or she says, *"Ne mogu više"* or *"Čaljom"* ("I've eaten my fill"; although there is a limit to this hospitality: *"Svakog gosta tri dana dosta"*, "absence makes the heart grow fonder"). In Konjic one day in 1994, a pensioner offered me a pear, the only piece of food visible in his house. I saw a similar tradition in Chechnya. It is customary in the Balkans for visitors to be served coffee in *fildžani* (small cups, traditionally without handles), from a *đezva* (a lidless coffee pot with a wide bottom and long handle), with the foam meticulously tea-spooned in first. This is often accompanied by various home-made cakes, circumstances permitting (especially *rahat lokum* ("Turkish delight") and *čupavac* ("hairy pie"), or a simple *loma* ("sugar lump")), much smoking, and *rakija*. It is also customary for the women to roast the raw coffee beans themselves, before grinding them in picturesque, cylindrical coffee mills, an activity that appears to be without end. The year before in East Mostar, I had been offered a coffee grinder said to have been made from a *granata* ("shell"). When I enquired which side the shell had come from, the market trader only shrugged his shoulders with a grin, which might have meant, "Does it matter?", or that could have meant, "You've got me, it isn't really from a shell!". In any case, there was certainly no shortage of raw materials for him to work from. The coffee, *kahva*[vi], is a powerful brew, drunk black, with a lot of sugar, and not to be consumed to excess, as I learnt to my cost. It is also a communal activity, and the ritual setting for much lively debate and discussion (by contrast, the same central, communal role is played in Chechnya by tea: not Earl Grey, but a sweet lemon tea, drunk in glasses, and without milk. Another difference is that in the Caucasus, and Central Asia, communal activities tend to be segregated by sex, or at least, where there is mixed company, interactions are discretely but religiously controlled). One lady, Hasiba, who had two small boys, and was also a prime mover in the LCK, was extremely hospitable, and would not only entertain a dozen or so of us with dinner on a regular basis, but would also do the washing for some men who found themselves without their spouses in the camp. On 6 March, when an Irish delegation from the EU visited the camp to see the conditions for themselves, she organised a splendid reception for them with cake and drinks in the LCK tent, including home-made *halva* ("fudge")[41]. I wonder whether any of the delegates suspected how much effort had gone into it. I certainly tried to impress it on them.

As time went on, to cut down the time spent commuting from Cazin, I moved into the camp, into a tent on the small bridge which doubled as Mirvet's storeroom, beside the LCK and ICRC office tents on one side, Mirvet's office on the other, and opposite the late Zahid, Denis's father. Most aid workers were now living in Vojnić; I was the only one actually living in the camp. I had a bed made of pallets in my tent, and installed two candle-making machines delivered from Split, where two local lads, Alen and Dajo, would spend the day churning out candles that were then distributed throughout the camp, the only source of light for many. Kami's boyfriend Enes told me that it was considered bad form to light a cigarette from a candle, as according to the superstition, that meant one more soldier would die. He returned to Bosnia in the New Year to be with Kami, determined to show his face in post-war Velika Kladuša, come what may. Alen invited me to a birthday dinner one evening, and treated us royally. Around 20 of us sat *al fresco* at covered tables to feast on roast beef and potatoes with beer, followed up by cake with lashings of *rakija*. Who would have thought we were refugees, the lowest of the low in Croatia, unwanted and unwashed? (in January I registered as a refugee with UNHCR, under the pseudonym Jovo Autonomašević ("Jonty MacSeparatist"). One of the ICRC delegates also registered, as Justin Krstević ("MacCross"). The official from Zagreb was surprised to hear I was born in the UK, and asked me why I was still there. I told her I wouldn't miss it for the world. Her surprise was only compounded when she heard Seka's surname and place of birth). Alen was a family man with two girls back in Bosnia, and homesickness got the better of him soon afterwards. When the war started he was still doing his JNA national service in Dalmatia, and he just managed to get home before the borders closed (national service was generally served in a

---

[vi] If you ask for *kahva* anywhere in Croatia (or *kafa*, drunk in Serbia), you're likely to get the Spanish archer: in Croatia, they only drink *kava*. I observed a similar coffee ritual in Ethiopia, although there the *džebena* (black glazed earthenware coffee pot) has a spout, and a tall neck with a wooden stopper; the coffee itself has a bitterer taste than in the Balkans, and does not produce so much foam.

republic other than the conscript's own. There was a similar system in the Soviet Union, as I was told by a colleague in Tajikistan who had done his service in Murmansk, on the Arctic coast: his sergeant major was a Chechen, who relentlessly beasted the Russian and Ukrainian conscripts, but went easier on the *čurki*, those from Muslim republics. The first time I went to Turkmenistan, I was surprised to see that there appeared to be squaddies everywhere. But it was only after a while that I noticed that none of them were armed, and that they were all engaged in menial, physical tasks, such as digging out ditches. The government was resorting to extended national service – two years – to kill two birds with one stone: reduce unemployment and avoid spending money on public works. I would be surprised if there weren't also large sums of money being made on the backs of the poor wretches; but theirs wouldn't be the first MOD to usurp civilian activities to supplement its budget). Alen was a dog whisperer, and I once witnessed him subdue within five minutes, using nothing more than a raised forefinger, a crazed *Ustaše* attack dog who answered to the name of Adolf.

One night, I was awakened by the sound of muffled scrabbling near my door. I quietly rose to my feet, and waited. Sure enough, a form slowly edged his way into my tent, under the canvas near the door. When he was halfway in, I challenged him. Feigning mistake, he said, "Where's Bato?" at which I ordered him to leave. Swearing, he did so. Fortunately, Seka had not noticed anything. That was a sobering reminder that not everyone in the camp regarded me with appreciative eyes, but that some wanted more – my wallet, which they supposed must be full. I tried to remember his face so I could track him down the next day, but it was no use in the dark.

My neighbour, Zahid, a *kamiondžija* ("truck driver"), went out of his way to show me the ropes of refugee living. He had rigged up an implement that allowed him to scrape the snow off his tent roof in the morning, which he encouraged me to use. I was a guest of his family's hospitality on more than one occasion, and he was not an unknown guest in my humble abode either. His brother was Fikret "Babo"[vii][42] Abdić, the leader of the rebel Muslims, the boss of the food concern Agrokomerc,

---

[vii] "*Babo*" means "dad". The nickname was given to him in the early days of Agrokomerc, when he was employing more and more young people in the Bosnian and Croatian Borders, for many of whom it was the first time anyone in the family had had a proper job. For the workers, and indeed the whole region, he was a second father, providing the means to sustain the life generated by their primary progenitor. By contrast, his arch-rival Izetbegović was known as "*Did Alija*" ("grandad"). Izetbegović was originally a construction foreman, who managed to reinvent himself as a lawyer. It was said in Velika Kladuša that Izetbegović slept in a bank vault in Sarajevo on a pile of money. The schism between the two dates from the SDA conference in November 1990, after the first Bosnian elections, during which, according to Babo, Izetbegović established a personality cult and absolute power within the party, accompanied by a series of assassinations in Sarajevo. He later wrote, "A string of situations that Alija served up to me convinced me that there was not only a lack of trust between us, but that on the contrary, our differences were so profound that any cooperation was doomed in advance to failure. What Alija was advocating was unacceptable to me. While I wanted and sought Bosnia as a well-organised state, he created a Bosnia in which he would have the leadership function of president, without any care as to how the state would actually work. He endeavoured to make it an Islamic state, that he would rule at all levels of government and with an obedient party machine that would carry out his orders, a state that would be his private property, a feudal estate in which he could do whatever he wanted, however he thought best. We were and are two different worlds. It was clear that Alija was carrying on a silent but brutal and decisive battle against me with all his resources, that he wanted by all means to isolate me from the other members of the presidency and other people within the SDA, to gradually turn me into an enemy who he would soon accuse of cooperation with the *Četniks* and of treason, and ultimately of war crimes". A pair of twin boys born in the camp in July were give the names Fikret and Alija. A report from 2000 by the ombudsman, see below, cites a refusal by the registrar in Velika Kladuša to allow a child to be called Fikret.

and a benefactor to the region since the 1970s, and so Zahid was a potential target for forced return to Velika Kladuša (under the Yugoslav economic system known as *samoupravljanje* ("self-management", sometimes described as "self-mismanagement"), corporations were either *javna preduzeća* ("public corporations") or *društvena preduzeća* ("cooperatives"), owned publicly, but not centrally, and with no titular owner: effectively everyone's and no-one's. The state was ready to underwrite losses, as long as a business was delivering on its political function, i.e. contributing to social stability. All imports/exports were controlled by a quota system[43]). Zahid had also been in charge of the Velika Kladuša TA. Despite all the pressures he must have been under, for himself and his family, he was always cheerful, and he seemed to spend an inordinate part of his time helping other people out with their multiple difficulties. One of the nicest blokes I've ever met. In late 1991, before the war started in Bosnia, he had given shelter in his house for a month to a Croat JNA pilot from Zagreb. After borrowing a Bosnian *lična karta* ("ID card") from someone who resembled the pilot, he drove him to Brčko in north-east Bosnia, from where he was able to cross the border into HDZ territory (Dragan told me that at that time, they used to watch the war across the border from their terrace in the evening, with a cup of *kahva*. It was clear to most people in Bosnia then, incredulous as they might have been when Slovenia left the federation (or not – the Slovenes were always "different", i.e. more Teutonically staid, and prosperous, as well as speaking a different, albeit related, language), that it was now only a matter of time before the war spilled over into their republic too). Tragically, Zahid's younger son, Denis's brother Fikret, died without warning from leukaemia at the age of 16. He used to help me out most days in Kuplensko, and was always cheerful. He told me his ambition was to be a truck driver.

Babo, a local boy made good from the village of Donja Vidovska near Velika Kladuša, won the first free, multi-party Bosnian elections in November 1990, standing as a SDA candidate (with the support of 45% of voters, while Izetbegović received 38%: as the Muslims constituted 44% of the population, this suggests that not only Muslims, but also many Serbs and Croats voted for him[44]), but did not take up the post of president, as the Sarajevo political clique decided that party leader Izetbegović should have that honour, and sidelined him, much to the surprise of Lord Owen[viii][45]. In May 1992, Babo is said to have attempted to remove Izetbegović when the latter was kidnapped by the JNA at Sarajevo airport after flying in from talks in Lisbon (with his daughter in tow; the talks had been arranged by the EU, who had

---

[viii] The election was not for an individual president, but for seven members of a joint representative presidency. Babo enjoyed the support of 1.05 million of the total 2.34 million votes cast (voters could choose as many candidates as they liked on the ballot sheet). Such governance mechanisms were used across the board in the former Yugoslavia, in business as well as in politics. Under the constitution, the presidency's mandate could be extended in time of war, and according to Babo, that was one of the reasons why Izetbegović "failed to act to bring about a peaceful resolution to the conflict in Bosnia and avoid war". Izetbegović also repeatedly invoked the same provision to prevent his 12-month mandate rotating to another member of the presidency. Babo explained to Lord Owen in December 1992 that the president was elected from among the members of the presidency by parliament, and that Izetbegović had reached an agreement with Milošević whereby the Serb MPs would vote for him. Nevertheless, there was only one vote in favour and no abstentions; votes against were not invited. Owen urged Babo to remain within the presidency, as otherwise he would lose his influence, and be portrayed as a "Serb pawn". In 2012, after his release from prison, Babo stated that it would not have been possible to run Bosnia and Agrokomerc at the same time. He was not originally interested in politics, but as the most popular and charismatic figure in Bosnia, was approached by various parties, and eventually agreed to join the SDA, who promised to invest in Agrokomerc by way of damages and disband the UDBA/AID who had wrecked it, see below.

"guaranteed" Izetbegović he would be able to return to Sarajevo without any difficulties), and Babo appeared from nowhere in the Sarajevo television studio. The alleged *coup* was foiled when Izetbegović's deputy, Ejup Ganić, who also happened to be there, convened an emergency meeting of the presidency and blocked attempts to appoint a new acting president. However, according to Babo, the real story is much simpler: he had just travelled back to Sarajevo from Vienna, via Ljubljana, Zagreb, Rijeka and Split, and in Sarajevo, UNPROFOR directed him to the TV station rather than the presidency because of heavy shelling. He had been able to pass through checkpoints unhindered because the shelling meant the soldiers were taking cover (the same day, the JNA attempted unsuccessfully to cut Sarajevo in half with two armoured columns, although they gained control of the borough of Grbavica and cut off the suburb of Dobrinja, a partition that lasted until the end of the war). There was a quorum of the presidency present, and it would have been quite logical for them to elect an acting president (Izetbegović was exchanged the next day for the JNA commander in Bosnia, Mladić's predecessor, who was trapped inside his barracks, in a bungled exchange that cost the lives of six JNA men. The original idea had been for the JNA to completely withdraw with their weapons and equipment from the Sarajevo JNA barracks, escorted by Canadian UNPROFOR, in exchange for the president, travelling in an UNPROFOR APC with the general, but the local TA, hoping to loot some kit to improve the woefully inadequate state of their *tehnika* ("materiel"), opened fire once Izetbegović was clear, and most of the column returned to the barracks). Four days later, Babo was authorised by the presidency to negotiate the completion of the JNA's withdrawal from Sarajevo, under the auspices of UNPROFOR[46]. Increasing tensions between Velika Kladuša and Sarajevo on the (mis)handling of peace negotiations, and Izetbegović's strategy of attempting to force international military intervention, led to Velika Kladuša being proclaimed an autonomous region in September 1993[47]. The final straw was Izetbegović's rejection of the joint action plan, proposed by the US, France, Spain and Russia after the demise of the Vance-Owen plan in early May[48] (UN human rights rapporteur Tadeusz Mazowiecki, see below, reported that the Vance-Owen plan incited the Bosnian HDZ to go to war against the Muslims because its proposed map, generous to the HDZ, encouraged the idea of a Greater Croatia at their expense, especially in those proposed provinces that it had left "TBC"[ix49]). In July, after a disagreement on talks in Geneva, boycotted by Izetbegović after an initial appearance, as he and Ganić refused to entertain any talks that included partition, but attended by Babo, who was accompanied by Lord Owen, Babo wrote an open letter to Izetbegović and the other members of the presidency decrying Izetbegović's refusal to contemplate any kind of deal and his autocratic management of the presidency (according to commentators, but denied by Babo, the mediators, Owen and Stoltenberg, encouraged him to challenge Izetbegović for the Muslim leadership[x50]). Along with the *Islamic Declaration*, and the *Memorandum on the position of Serbia in Yugoslavia* (see below), Babo's open letter is one of the most important documents of the war:

[ix] According to Owen, the opposite was true: under the peace plan, Karadžić would have had to relinquish 39% of the territory held by the VRS, and the failure of the US to back the plan only sent Tuđman the message that ethnic cleansing paid off.

[x] Lord Owen was the EU's negotiator, and Thorvald Stoltenberg replaced Cyrus Vance as the special representative of the UN secretary general. Stoltenberg junior is now NATO secretary general.

"Dear Mr Izetbegović and members of the Presidency,

"I am writing to you all at a time of high drama and tragedy for Bosnia and Herzegovina, its citizens and peoples, and in particular for the Muslims, who are facing total disaster and annihilation. The situation in the territory under our control is, as I hope you are aware, becoming ever more critical from day to day, and as if daily fatalities from bullets and shells were not enough, we are now threatened with mass epidemics of hepatitis, the plague, and typhus, as well as starvation and thirst. The approaching cold will only bring additional distress. Goražde is surrounded, as is Žepa, and it is only a matter of days before the last resident of Srebrenica is evacuated. Trnovo and Rogoj have fallen. There is practically nothing standing between the Serb forces and Sarajevo. Food and medicines are becoming an increasingly serious problem for almost a million people in the Tuzla region, while fighting in central Bosnia between Muslims and Croats has dispelled the last rays of optimism. The residents of our capital are exposed to daily torment and death, and have run out of strength and morale. Just at the time when the problems in our country are compounding, it appears that the international community is getting ready to wash its hands of us, such as we are. The news that the peace negotiators Lord Owen and T. Stoltenberg are going to propose to the UN that it withdraw from Bosnia and Herzegovina if the situation here continues to deteriorate, is disastrous and a final wake-up call[xi][51]. We have run out of time, too many people have already been killed and slaughtered, the majority Muslims, such that any continuation of the killing and the bloody war could result in us disappearing entirely. I am afraid that tomorrow it could already be too late for our country of Bosnia and Herzegovina, and above all for us Muslims.

"While you have failed to keep your word that there would not be another Foča, never mind the terrible slaughter from the last war, now, Izetbegović, you must do everything you can to put a stop to this ordeal. You and I carry the greatest responsibility and are under the greatest obligation, you as president and I as the person who received the most votes and in whom the voters placed most trust, to urgently put a stop to this bloody tragedy of the Muslims, as well as of the other peoples. In parallel with talks on a constitutional solution, we must, with the active participation of the co-presidents, run the country in those territories we still hold. In order to do so, I propose the following action points.

"Firstly and without delay, we must do everything we can in order to normalise our relations with the Croats, because that is a basic precondition for a global peace. Otherwise we will be unable to ensure a minimum functioning of the government institutions in our territories, and it is clear that such a chaotic and anarchic situation will only lead to total collapse. By way of illustration, I have set out the need in the Bihać region to establish a proper chain of command between the Presidency, the command of the Bosnian armed forces, and the command of the various corps. Without such a chain of command, we cannot reliably guarantee that our order to stop the fighting

[xi] UNHCR had suspended its operations in Bosnia, such as they were, because of ongoing difficulties with access in February 1993, and threatened to withdraw from the country entirely. In May 1993, and again in July 1994, Lord Owen advocated withdrawing the UN from Bosnia entirely and proceeding with "lift and strike" to impose first the Vance-Owen plan, and then the contact group plan.

between the Croats and the Muslims will be carried out. The Presidency has agreed to this, and in order to ensure sustainable principles of command, we agreed to carry out, within 10 days, an analysis of the military, political, and economic, or at least the humanitarian situation. This analysis was supposed to be examined at the next meeting of the Presidency. But it was not. The failure to establish the said chain of command within the Bihać region has led to a deterioration of relations between the army and the police, and the order will come to provoke a conflict between them somewhere in Bihać. We are not taking account, as we should, of the need for the state to function to the extent possible where it still exists.

"If we are to emerge from this dead end, we must, and above all you, Izetbegović, must, because you exercise total control and influence over the state media in Bosnia and Herzegovina, immediately advocate an end to further media campaigns against talks and the negotiation process. I hope you share the view of the majority of well-informed citizens of Bosnia and Herzegovina, and the wider international community, that there will be no military intervention. We have to tell our people this openly via the state media, RTVBiH [Bosnian broadcasting corporation], *Oslobođenje*[xii52], and *Večernja Novina*, rather than continuing to stubbornly propagate the view that our position as victim will materially influence the international community's commitment to solving the Bosnian crisis. The international community has consistently respected all adopted resolutions, and pedantically adhered to the powers granted it by its mandate. None of the competent international politicians has been categorical in terms of military intervention, unlike our minister Silajdžić and the monopolised state media which so zealously supports him. By propagating such inadmissible illusions, the whole media has, completely uncritically and with no sense of reality, cultivated false hopes among the public, who living in the dark without electricity, have been afflicted by blindness as the last batteries run out. The initial euphoric announcements of military intervention have been replaced by even more euphoric announcements of a lifting of the arms embargo for the Muslims. How can such an editorial policy, which denies the exhausted public a basic

---

[xii] *Oslobođenje*, founded in Sarajevo in 1943, means "liberation". However, it might be better interpreted as "freedom is slavery", for as Izetbegović wrote, "...all freedom must be first and foremost spiritual freedom. The independence of a people who have not first obtained this spiritual freedom, will quickly be reduced to a national anthem and flag, both of which are insignificant for real independence [...] There is no Islamic order without independence and freedom, and vice versa: there can be no independence and freedom without Islam". Izetbegović also wrote that "The education of the people, in particular the media, television and film, should be in the hands of people whose Islamic moral and intellectual authority is unquestioned". While the quality of *Oslobođenje*'s journalism throughout the war was superior to that of the rabid tabloid press, such as *Ljiljan* ("lily", but also "fleur-de-lys"), it was unashamedly pro-government (i.e., SDA): the adjective "Serb" was invariably accompanied by the noun "aggressor" or "*Četnik*", and anything relating to the ABiH was "heroic" (the newspaper is now said to be pro-SDP). For example, the front page of 3 October 1993 headlined with "Open Treason", the title of an interview with Izetbegović condemning Babo, which also starts on the first page. There is then an anti-Babo article, and an article justifying the rejection of the Geneva peace "packet". This is followed by the leader for an interview with UNPROFOR inside, cast in equally tendentious terms, and finally a report on a major earthquake in India. That year, *Oslobođenje* was awarded the EU's Saharov Prize: its main achievement was to continue printing throughout the 1,425 day-long siege of Sarajevo (apart from one day), operating from the bomb shelter in the basement of its destroyed premises, 50 m from the VRS lines, with Serbs and Croats on its staff as well as Muslims. Apologists for *Oslobođenje* - for the most part journalists themselves - point out that the newspaper did the best it could in the circumstances, caught between a rock and a hard place: between Izetbegović and everyone else.

level of information on the real state of affairs, be allowed? Everyone is well aware, Izetbegović, that you have placed your minions and political allies in all positions of responsibility in the state media. In such a space of usurped media monopoly, the old rule of hearing both sides is never respected, but rather, any disagreement with your policy results in the persons concerned being declared the enemy and traitors to Muslim interests.

"I ask myself on what basis you consider yourself the embodiment and personification of the interests of the Muslims? Now that we are seeing bloody fighting between Muslims and Croats in central Bosnia, I have to remind you that after one of your military emissaries rejected the possibility of the HVO relieving Sarajevo in June of last year, a propaganda war started against all Croats. Step by step, natural allies with a common interest are being turned into enemies. Wasn't one confirmed enemy enough for the Muslims, that you had to create another? The media has turned every Croat soldier into an *Ustaša*, and the logical conclusion of such a generalisation is that every Muslim soldier becomes a *Mudža*. Thus we are moving further and further away from the heart of the problem and the essence of the war, which is increasingly becoming a religious and ethnic conflict. As a result, the initial interest of some of the international community for energetic action to end the fighting is turning into indifference, a waiting game to see what happens next. And if energetic steps are not taken, what happens next will be tragedy.

"Therefore, Izetbegović, because I say again, the state media are under your absolute control, you must prevent any further media campaigns against talks and the negotiation process. When I insisted on this myself at the Presidency meetings in Geneva and Sarajevo, I became the victim of an even greater campaign in the state media. Efforts to discredit me on RTVBiH, and in *Oslobođenje* and *Večernja Novina*, in Sarajevo, began immediately after the first multi-party elections, and reached their culmination when I attended the peace talks in Geneva. The Presidency is aware that I am the greatest victim of my electoral triumph in the first multi-party elections, about which I have written and spoken at length. My very presence at the Geneva talks was proclaimed by the Sarajevo media as treason, and they didn't have the decency to publish any of my statements, or even talk to me. I experienced an almost identical situation six years ago when the Agrokomerc affair broke, and the very same people in the state media first declared me a counter-revolutionary and a criminal, only to praise and exalt me to unheard-of heights when things started to move in my favour. Now, Izetbegović, under your supervision, the editorial policy of the state media has turned a blind eye to the basic tenets of the profession. Rather than affirm the talks in Geneva as the act of all the members of the Presidency, as collective head of state, after ten months, the state media maliciously interpreted it as an attempted coup by Abdić.

"At this dramatic time for our country and its people, the head of state must work at full capacity, at full steam. Thus, the Presidency is not only Izetbegović and Ganić, but also the other members. After a full fifteen months of this tragic war, tragic above all for the Muslims, you Izetbegović, as well as Ganić and Silajdžić, have failed to bring about any good. I won't say it wasn't for want of trying, but it's obvious that you haven't achieved anything. With this policy you have only harmed yourselves, which unfortunately means the vast majority of Muslims. You have also recently led the Muslims into doubt and disbelief by supporting the election of the provisional deputy mufti of Bosnia, Mustafa Cerić, and establishing a parallel Islamic Board in Bosnia and Herzegovina. Once again, the state media began to obsequiously favour the new institutions of the Islamic Board and created a space for daily addresses by Cerić. Are you aware how much anger this unprecedented *coup*, once again led by you, Izetbegović, has attracted from the Islamic world? Do you think that such an unconstitutional act, violating the independence of a religious community, which is also protected by international law, will be tolerated by the international community? Once again, using the tried and tested method, the media campaign allowed the presence of only one side, while the other, in this case Selimoski, was given no opportunity to be heard[xiii]. At the Presidency meeting in Sarajevo, I was the only one to speak against this violent act in the Islamic Board, and I raised a series of questions to which I have still not received an answer, either from you, Izetbegović, or from the other members of the Presidency.

"This media unitarism took on disastrous proportions at the time of the Geneva talks, which I am sure was no coincidence. It has to be explained to the people of Bosnia and Herzegovina that there will not be a military intervention, or a lifting of the embargo, and that at this moment we are unfortunately not in a position to defeat the superior enemy militarily. The only alternative is negotiation, and for that reason you have a responsibility, above all to the Muslims, to do everything within your power to create via the state media in Bosnia and Herzegovina a favourable atmosphere for talks. Instead of taking such a position, the Sarajevo media mercilessly loose poisoned barbs against me, personally. With the assistance of some of the SDA party leadership, and people who disagree with me in the Presidency, as well as your personal efforts in the media, imputations are made against me. First I am accused of being in favour of a partition of Bosnia and Herzegovina, which is not the case, and then a meeting with Karadžić is fabricated, which is also not the case. The only thing that is the case is that you, Izetbegović, have met with both Karadžić and Milošević, and that in Lisbon you consented to a partition of Bosnia and Herzegovina, the very things of which I am now perfidiously accused[xiv53].

"I am now only insisting on talks, on a negotiation process, to put an end to this bloodshed, of everyone's blood, but above all ours, the Muslims. This is the last opportunity for the Muslim representatives to unite in the interest of the Muslims. Any further polarisation and antagonistic rivalry will only lead to further defeatism, decapitation, and more victims. That is why we must, via the Bosnian media, inform our people of all the options at play for the future political order of Bosnia and Herzegovina, regardless of which options we may favour as individuals.

"No Presidency, or negotiating body, may suspend the will of the people, who in any case must give their final consent to the future state model of Bosnia

---

[xiii] The pro-Yugoslav incumbent Jakup Selimoski was ousted in April 1993 in a *coup* staged by Izetbegović. His replacement, Cerić, was previously the imam of the Zagreb mosque, and went on to become the grand mufti of Bosnia, a post he held until 2012.

[xiv] In Lisbon, on the eve of the referendum that would lead to international recognition of Bosnia as an independent state, the three Bosnian leaders agreed to recognise Bosnia's existing borders, and to the formation of ethnic/religious territorial units within the country. Izetbegović changed his mind upon his return to Sarajevo.

and Herzegovina. But we must do our utmost to prepare them for that historic act. It is the state media who must take this task upon themselves, with our help, but through the prism of the real situation in which we find ourselves. Comprehensively and in good time, but above all objectively and realistically, our people and the citizens of Bosnia and Herzegovina must become fully acquainted with both the federal and confederal options, as well as with the possibility of a protectorate. Our task in all of this is to engage all our strength, capacity and potential for the option which is best for us. At the same time, we must prepare ourselves and our people for the less than optimum variations and options. That is the reality we should have faced before the war broke out in Bosnia and Herzegovina.

"I am sure that, at the end of the day, you are aware of the deadly danger of disregarding and denying the right of the Presidency as collective head of state to negotiate, and of your persistent efforts to appropriate for yourself and a few like-minded politicians the mantle of the legality of decision-making, and that you are finally ready to give up such a sterile policy. By affirming the Presidency as the legal collective representative body of the state, and taking your place in the real position of 'first among equals', we can allow the peace process to move forward and establish a pluralism of views, rather than the monopoly of decision-making by two or three individuals. With our country of Bosnia and Herzegovina in its current state, we cannot afford the luxury of allowing the politically imprudent whims of any individual to push the people into further disaster, even if he is president. Before our state is still-born, and the Muslims placed in reservations and condemned to slow extinction, we must turn the situation to our advantage, and finally become mature partners equal to the challenge of the historic fracture which we face"[54].

Instead of a public response, as Babo expected, there was a deafening silence from Sarajevo, and he was quietly expelled from the presidency[xv][55]. Meanwhile, talks continued in Geneva (according to Owen, "Abdić, who came to most sessions with Izetbegović, showed himself to be an excellent negotiator, flexible but never deserting Izetbegović's position in front of us"), and despite a "breakthrough" with the "union of three republics" proposal at the end of July, at the end of September, after the talks had moved to HMS Invincible, Izetbegović rejected the map, which gave the SDS 53% of territory (and might have opened the door to secession of the occupied SDS and HDZ territory to Serbia and Croatia respectively, leaving an unviable homeland for the Muslims). Parallel talks on a ceasefire between all three

---

[xv] According to Owen, "The collective Presidency in Bosnia-Herzegovina, elected in 1990, consisted of seven people, but by 1992 was exercising less and less of the collective power given to it under the constitution. Its cohesion was not helped by the fact that Fikret Abdić, the Muslim leader in Bihać, who had polled more votes than Alija Izetbegović in the Presidency elections, never came from Bihać to Sarajevo for meetings of the Presidency [...] But by the end of 1992 it was becoming clear to all that [...] all power had gone to a small group of Muslim Ministers appointed by President Izetbegović and their nominee as Vice-President, Ejup Ganić. The collective Presidency as a democratic body with meaningful representation from the three constituent nations was by the autumn of 1993 no longer a reality. The real decisions were made elsewhere. We were in effect dealing with a Muslim government for a predominantly Muslim population". An internal SDA analysis of Babo's open letter states that, "In his letter, Fikret Abdić sets out views on the war that coincide with those of the aggressor". Babo was expelled from the presidency by a parliamentary vote held without a quorum on 29 September 1993 (two days after the proclamation of the autonomous region), allegedly because he had been expelled from the SDA the week before and had been dismissed from Agrokomerc – but with no mention of an attempted *coup*.

sides were scuppered when the SVK shelled the Maslenica bridge in August and Izetbegović refused to meet with the Bosnian HDZ, even as Babo acted as a consultant to Tuđman on the talks at his lair on the island of Brijuni (despite the fact that as early as autumn 1992, Izetbegović had appointed one of his cronies the "exclusive" liaison with the Croats; meanwhile, Izetbegović and Tuđman signed an inchoate cessation of hostilities agreement on 14 September)[xvi56]. The intra-Muslim war started at the beginning of October. In early 1994, the US encouraged Babo to enter into talks with Izetbegović's prime minister, Haris Silajdžić, and to recognise the Federation, and in April 1994, Babo sent the Sarajevo government, via UNPROFOR, a white paper proposing the incorporation of the autonomous region into the Federation as a canton with special status to be agreed; but when asked about it during the 1994 refugee crisis, Silajdžić denied ever having seen or heard of the document[57]. Nor did the international community make any effort to use this proposal as a platform for building peace. Velika Kladuša was proclaimed the republic of West Bosnia shortly before Operation Storm. To mark the event, two fatted oxen were slaughtered and spit roasted at the town's hotel, the *Konak* ("night's rest", but also "residence"), owned by Agrokomerc, with a plate of meat each for a large number of guests sat eagerly at trestle tables, of which I was one (*"kao mačka kad ugleda slaninu"*). I tried to do an Oliver Twist, but to no avail, as there was only enough for around 300 people. Babo was granted *azil* ("asylum") in Croatia by Tuđman at the end of the war. On 4 April 1996, after the Dayton peace accords had been signed but before the first elections since 1990, the AID tried to assassinate him near his office in Rijeka ("river") in Croatia, but they were arrested before acting (the hit squad were graduates of an Iranian training camp near Fojnica, which had been raided by IFOR two months earlier, and four of the five ended up in prison in Croatia). There had been several prior attempts on his life during the war[58]. Babo was subsequently (after Tuđman's death in 1999) convicted of war crimes by a Croatian court (Karlovac district court) and sentenced to 20 years' imprisonment (15 on appeal) in what he described as a rigged political trial, and he served 11 years in a Croatian prison (in Rijeka), even though the alleged offences took place in Bosnia and the alleged victims were all Bosnian (121 civilians and three POWs[59]). Despite the fact that the Karlovac district court was not competent to hear war crimes cases (this obstacle was lifted to facilitate the appearance of 40 prosecution witnesses from the Una-Sana canton, 14 of whom had the same address – the 5th Corps barracks in Bihać[xvii]), the matter was tried there, on the case prepared by the Bihać prosecutor, without any investigation. Contrary to practice in war crimes trials, he was not granted legal aid, as the media described him as the "richest Muslim in Bosnia". No medical evidence was submitted to substantiate the injuries allegedly suffered by the victims. After the initial hearing, Babo concluded that the judge was biased against him and, changing tactics from his marathon defence in the Agrokomerc affair trial (270 days, conducting his own defence with the support of a pro bono legal team, see below), he decided not to submit a defence in the first instance proceedings. But in the hearing on his appeal to the supreme court, in which he challenged his conviction, and not the sentence, he was not allowed to call any of the 280 witnesses

---

[xvi] According to Owen, "The Muslims had clearly chosen to continue with the war, believing that sanctions would soften up the Serbs and, on the advice of their military commanders, that they could defeat the Croats in central Bosnia".

[xvii] Helsinki Watch reported in 2001 that the brother of a prosecution witness who, as a hostile witness, gave evidence in Babo's favour, was assaulted in Bihać, and that potential witnesses were coached and/or intimidated by the AID.

he proposed[60]. War crimes are defined, further to the Nuremberg principles and the Geneva Conventions, as "grave violations of international humanitarian law" (in an armed conflict)[xviii][61] The HDZ was also said to be fond of spit-roasting oxen, as it went on a decade-long looting spree of the Croatian economy after the triumph of Operation Storm[62]. To the victor the spoils[63]. The first genuinely non-HDZ president was Ivo Josipović, from 2010-2015 (his predecessor, Mesić (HNS), 2000-2010, had been HDZ secretary general until a rift with Tuđman in 1994, and was also formerly prime minister of Croatia, in 1990, as well as the last president of Yugoslavia), and the current president is HDZ, while the first non-HDZ prime minister was Ivica Račan (SDP, former KPJ) in 2000, who was followed from 2003-2011 by more HDZ. Whether Babo was manipulated by the big boys in the Yugoslav Wars, or whether he really could have brought about peace and turned conflict into prosperity, history is written by the victors. What is certain is that this much-maligned community, branded alternatively "misguided"[xix] and "traitors", have never had the opportunity to present their side of the story[64][xx].

Another brother, Hasan, committed suicide in 1989 as a result of the Agrokomerc affair. Babo took over and built up the poultry business Agrokomerc in the 1970s using money from the Yugoslav regional development fund, as the Bosnian Borders were the poorest part of Yugoslavia[65]. The fund was created in 1965, designed to support economic and infrastructure projects in underdeveloped areas of the country, with the long-term and ultimately unsuccessful aim of reducing the sharp disparities between different parts of the country (in 1981, the Yugoslav average *per capita* income was 89,466 dinars, while in Slovenia it was 160,905 and in Kosovo only 29,684 dinars)[66]. The development of Agrokomerc was facilitated by Yugoslavia's leading Muslim clan, the powerful Pozderac brothers, Hakija and Hamdija, from Cazin, who were close to Tito due to services rendered during WWII (their other brother, Sakib, was a JNA general). Their uncle, Nurija, before WWII a local MP, and the first prominent Muslim politician to join the KPJ, in 1941, was appointed vice president of the resistance at the first resistance conference in Bihać[67][xxi], but was killed in 1943 near the river Sutjeska in eastern Herzegovina during the Axis fifth offensive. He was instrumental in delaying the impact of the *Ustaše* state terror against Serbs in the future Bihać pocket in July and August 1941[68]. Babo's father, Hašim, who was a people's representative at the Mrkonjić-Grad KPJ conference in 1943, was close to Nurija. The share allocated to Bosnia of a

---

[xviii] As opposed to crimes against humanity, which are certain acts, including rape, "deliberately committed as part of a widespread or systematic attack directed against any civilian population", whether in war or peacetime.

[xix] According to the EU monitors.

[xx] Foreign commentators have tended to pass over the phenomenon of Babo and the intra-Muslim war as a minor sideshow, an anomaly distracting from the main, bigger picture. But in fact, understanding the conflict in the Bihać pocket is the key to understanding the Yugoslav Wars. It was not a spontaneous, inevitable tribal conflict, but the logical result of a deliberate policy by entirely unscrupulous criminals to impose "divide and rule" on their own people. Like Srebrenica, it was a manifestation of the introspective death spiral set in motion in a different time and place, by people who move in different spheres. As in the Spanish Civil War, see below, the belligerents had analogous aims, and a common enemy: the Yugoslav people.

[xxi] The other prominent Muslim politician at the time was Raif Dizdarević, from Fojnica in central Bosnia, the first Muslim president of Bosnia, from 1978-1982, and president of Yugoslavia after Hamdija's resignation, from 1988-1989. His whole family were Partisans: one brother was killed by the *Ustaše*, and another by the *Četniks*. He was also speaker of the federal parliament 1982-1983 and Yugoslav foreign minister 1984-1988. His brother Nijaz was also a high flyer in the Yugoslav foreign ministry. After the Yugoslav Wars, Raif became a political adviser to the SDA.

DM 1 billion credit provided in 1973 by German Chancellor Willy Brandt by way of war reparations after a secret meeting with Tito at his favourite villa on the island of Brijuni, was originally earmarked for investment in the Banja Luka region, but the Pozderaces successfully diverted it to the Bosnian Borders[69], much to the chagrin of then Bosnian KPJ president Milan Uzelac (Brijuni, near Pula in Istria, later became Tuđman's favourite residence, and it was rumoured he also used to wear Tito's suits[xxii70]). Hamdija, the most senior Muslim Communist, whose career took off after the fall of Ranković (see below), was the head of the committee for institutional reform, and he played a key role in bringing about the recognition of Muslims as a constituent people in the 1974 constitution, according them the same status as Serbs and Croats (and Slovenes, Macedonians and Montenegrins – although Montenegrins are often identified as Serbs; Albanians and others had the status of ethnic minorities)[71]. The constitution also significantly expanded the powers of the two autonomous regions, effectively giving them home rule, at the same time as abolishing earlier economic reforms that had fuelled calls for more autonomy in Croatia[72xxiii]. Hamdija had previously been president of Bosnia, and in 1987 he was vice president of Yugoslavia on the nine-member rotating federal presidency (the 6 republics, the 2 autonomous regions and until 1988 the KPJ) that ruled after Tito's death, and was in line to become president (the collective mechanism had been in place since 1974, but Tito as life president was the real seat of power). Hamdija had a decentralisation agenda that was widely supported by the Slovenian and Croatian Communists, but was also seen as a threat to Serbia's dominant position. As one of the few remaining old guards, Hamdija was also well connected with the pro-Yugoslav (communist) faction in the JNA, who were uncomfortable with the rise in nationalist sentiment after Tito's death (in addition to being the guarantor of all matters of defence, the JNA was an executive agency of the KPJ[73]). After 1979, questions began to be raised in the Bosnian KPJ about Agrokomerc's continued access to federal development funds, as meanwhile the Bosnian Borders had ceased to be the least developed region in the country thanks to the extensive road-building, electrification and running water programmes driven by Babo. But this did not dampen his appetite for further expansion. Hamdija's connections allowed Agrokomerc to expand its business with the JNA, and it became an integral part of the JNA national defence system (with major contracts to feed the standing army and conscripts doing their national service, although it didn't have a monopoly, and at the time of the Agrokomerc affair this represented less than 1% of turnover), a key component of which was located in Bihać, with an airfield built into a mountain that cost between USD 1.2-2.5 billion to build, and was destroyed by the JNA when they withdrew from Bosnia in 1992[74]. By 1987, Agrokomerc employed 13,000 people, most of them in the Borders, as well as attracting *majstori* ("skilled labour") from all

---

[xxii] By contrast, according to Owen, Milošević had "no affection for the trappings of power: he live[d] modestly", unlike his wife, said to be the driving force of their political partnership, who was an unashamed WAG.

[xxiii] This constitution followed a crackdown on liberalisation, first in Croatia, then to a lesser extent in Serbia and Slovenia, which had been preceded and enabled by the reforms of 1965, see below. The economic success of the late 1950s and early 1960s was slowing, liberalisation began to threaten the hegemony of the KPJ, and the Soviet Union had invaded Czechoslovakia in 1968. While the 1974 constitution further decentralised the administration of the country, it recentralised control of the economy, which only made it more inefficient. This wasn't helped by the 1974 "oil shock", when the price of oil quadrupled. It has been argued that the 1974 constitution effectively made the country dysfunctional, and that it would have been wiser to allow economic and political liberalisation to run its course.

over Yugoslavia (not to mention foreign consultants), and was one of the 30 largest businesses in the country, with its products sold in 22 countries, and a USD 34 million joint venture industrial zone in Rijeka, Croatia's largest *luka* ("port"), a Panamex (deep water) port known in Italian as Fiume[75] (Rijeka was seized in September 1919 by 2,000 Italian irregulars led by Mussolini's predecessor as fascist leader, who wanted it restored to Italy, and after a brief period as a free city, it was annexed by Italy in 1922. I once drove a truckload of flour the 400 km from Rijeka to Split, and it was as if the narrow, winding coast road was endless; the journey seemed to last all day, as indeed it did). Agrokomerc had a fleet of 700 trucks, and more reefers (refrigerated trucks) than all other Yugoslav businesses put together[76]. The success of Agrokomerc only added to the Pozderaces' prestige. However, by that time Milošević had the support of a number of high-ranking generals (such as former federal defence minister and former president of Serbia Nikola Ljubičić[77]) as he sought to promote the pro-Serb faction within the JNA (the JNA had anyway been dominated by Serbs since its creation out of the victorious, mainly Serb Partisans towards the end of WWII, but its ideology and loyalty were to Tito and the Yugoslav state; however, during the 1980s, all the former Partisans in the JNA top brass retired, and at the same time its ethnic/religious composition became increasingly Serb, largely a result of recruitment practices over previous decades. By 1991, all the generals in the general staff but one were Serbs[78]). In addition, the JNA's doctrine was built on the premise of an external threat, and it struggled to respond adequately to a crisis threatening it from within[xxiv][79]. Meanwhile, the KOS answered to no-one[xxv][80]. Milošević was also seeking to place his own people on the rotating presidency in order to gain a controlling majority, as well as to thwart any attempts at constitutional reform that might dilute Belgrade's central influence. In order to achieve this, the Pozderac clan, among others, had to be destroyed. In late 1987, Babo was detained for allegedly issuing USD 360 million (the figure of USD 500 million is also commonly cited) in unbacked promissory notes (the biggest financial scandal in Yugoslav history, even though it was common practice: the Bihać Bank had given Babo its stamp so that he could endorse his own promissory notes, effectively a licence to print money), and Hamdija was implicated in the affair, not least because Hakija was on the board of Agrokomerc (he was found by the court to be the corporation's controlling mind)[81]. Uzelac also allegedly recorded him discussing the practice with Babo in the toilet during a break at a KPJ conference. According to Babo, the 17 promissory notes at issue were not unbacked, and their total value was only ten percent of the book value of Agrokomerc (although cashflow problems might have left a shortfall of up to USD 200 million). He was tried for sedition under art. 14 Criminal Code (by undermining the country's system of payments, potentially facing the death penalty[xxvi]), but was ultimately only convicted of a minor white-collar offence, technically not attracting a custodial

---

[xxiv] This disorientation also affected operational matters, as Legija observed: "I was not one of those JNA officers who failed to understand that different rules now applied as concerns leadership, and that it was pointless trying to be a knight in shining armour. Such officers objected to a soldier having an earring or failing to fall in, for example, or for standing with his hands in his pockets while an officer delivered an 'important' briefing".

[xxv] At the beginning of the war in Croatia, the KOS launched Operation Labrador, a secret campaign to use acts of terror to discredit Tuđman's government. After two bombings of Jewish cemeteries, the operation was uncovered when the HV captured the JNA headquarters in Zagreb in September 1991; most of the KOS agents escaped to Serbia.

[xxvi] Yugoslavia had a USD 500 million line of credit with the International Bank for Reconstruction and Development, and it was feared that exposure from the promissory notes could compromise this.

sentence, and his sentence subject to appeal of 4½ years imprisonment never became absolute. He was released pending appeal at the end of the trial, in October 1989, having spent two years on remand (the next year, the judgment subject to appeal lapsed. The case was reopened in 2004, and the investigation concluded that the total losses caused by Babo and the other defendants were the equivalent of only KM 48.60)[xxvii][82]. When Babo was finally told he was "free to go" by the court, he travelled straight back to work in the Agrokomerc offices in Velika Kladuša, where 5,000 busloads of his supporters from all over Yugoslavia and abroad cheered him[83]. The fallout of the affair was not only the end of the Pozderac brothers in public life, but also meant that the cash tap was turned off for Agrokomerc[84]. Hamdija resigned under pressure from the Serbian media, with the campaign against him led by Uzelac at the instruction of federal prime minister Mikulić (he was also promised that Babo and Hakija would be released if he resigned), and died of a stroke – or was killed[85] - in hospital in Sarajevo shortly afterwards, in 1987, while Hakija, a MP and the holder of various federal posts, was jailed for counter-revolutionary activities. At his trial in Bihać, described by locals as the trial of the Bosnian Borders, he said, "We Borderers know how to wait"[86] (he was released from prison a month after the trial, and died in obscurity in Belgrade in 1994. Izetbegović held the brothers directly responsible for the five years he spent in prison in the 1980s, see below, while in 1990, the two sons of one of the ringleaders of the 1950 Peasants' Revolt, Milan Božić, accused Hakija of having staged the revolt in order to get rid of their father and the other Bosnian ringleader, Ale Čović, who he allegedly saw as a challenge to his authority[87]). Hamdija was replaced by Dizdarević, another Muslim, in order to conceal the hand of Belgrade in the affair, which effectively marginalised the Bosnian Muslims as a force in Yugoslav politics. The shockwaves from the Agrokomerc affair not only discredited the KPJ, with unprecedented media coverage (for what was intended to be a show trial, but which backfired), but also created a void in Bosnia's political, business and media elite, which was swiftly occupied by outsiders and upstarts peddling the nationalist narrative as their ticket to legitimacy (although Babo came out of it a celebrity, having faced down the UDBA: during the trial he said, "I don't fear the truncheon. I don't fear the dungeon. And I don't fear the death penalty". Both Dizdarević and Mikulić, the heads of state and government respectively, attended the trial, although in his memoirs, Dizdarević makes no mention of either Agrokomerc or Babo, and only mentions Izetbegović once)[88]. More widely, Bosnia was conspicuous by its absence in federal affairs during this period, when it could and should have contributed to solving Yugoslavia's problems, and Dizdarević has been accused of sacrificing the interests and influence of the Bosnian Muslims for his own political ambitions[89]. Hasan, who had been heavily involved in the rapid socio-economic development and urbanisation of Velika Kladuša, was broken by the systematic destruction and theft of Agrokomerc property under the auspices of the Sarajevo regime during the affair. After his release, Babo returned to the helm of Agrokomerc to find 12,000 workers unemployed, the poultry dead, and the business looted and effectively shut down (liabilities of USD 530 million were borne equally by creditors and the state; according to Babo, the financial damage caused by the trial was far greater than the alleged loss it was supposed to remedy)[90]. But he used his contacts in Croatia and Serbia to build it back into a success, re-employing 8,000 of the workers. In 1990 he requested USD 200 million from the

---

[xxvii] According to one conspiracy theory, Babo was a Trojan horse, released by Milošević as a sleeper, to be activated and destroy Bosnia from within once the war started.

UN's food and agriculture programme for Yugoslavia[91]. In 1992, he also started the process of transforming Agrokomerc from a public corporation into a public limited company under Marković's new Privatisation Act (see below)[xxviii], holding the positions of chairman of the board and managing director (Babo was dismissed as the boss of Agrokomerc by the Velika Kladuša district council in August 1992, although he only found out later; and he was reinstated in December after a large protest demonstration in the town centre[92]). During this turbulent period in Yugoslav politics, when a worsening economic situation fuelled the centrifugal nationalist forces that threatened to tear the country apart, despite the determination of the JNA, increasingly isolated and diminished at the centre as the guardian of KPJ ideology and a centralised Yugoslavia, to hold it together[93], Izetbegović was jailed for five years (1983-1988) for conspiracy to commit treason. The main prosecution evidence against him was his *Islamic Declaration*, written, according to the judgment, in 1974, which advocated an Islamic renaissance as an alternative to communism and capitalism, with the ultimate aspiration to an Islamic state stretching from Morocco to Indonesia[94]. This was part of a wider crackdown on Muslim intellectuals, supported by Hamdija. Thus two alternative approaches to Islam in politics were discredited, and the Bosnian Muslims marginalised, even as the central communist ideology of the Tito era was pushed into the background. But both made a comeback in the war. Izetbegović founded the SDA in 1990, bankrolled by a disillusioned former Partisan from Foča living in exile in Switzerland, Adil Zulfikarpašić, who had assisted Izetbegović's family while he was in prison (the SDA's original plan was for Zulfikarpašić to become president of Bosnia, and Izetbegović president of the SDA)[95]. But aware that their true programme, with its regressive, Walter Mitty objectives, had only limited appeal, the SDA leadership decided they needed Bosnia's most successful businessman on board in order to ensure electoral victory (they were also concerned he might stand against them: he originally considered joining Marković's reform party, see below, but finally decided to join the Muslim party because it was the Borders Muslims who had born the brunt of the recent upheaval. The subsequent SDA rally in Velika Kladuša, two months before the elections, was the largest gathering of Bosnian Muslims in history, 400,000; a later rally in Sarajevo only attracted a tenth of that number[96]). Once they had power, Babo was excluded from all decision-making mechanisms and sidelined with the economy portfolio, before withdrawing to the Borders (this also suited the HDZ and the SDS, because it provided ammunition for their inflammatory anti-Muslim rhetoric; meanwhile, Zulfikarpašić had left the party, disillusioned with Alija's nationalism, and Izetbegović became the absolute leader, uniting the positions of head of party and state[97]). In this respect, Babo was indeed a Trojan horse, albeit unwittingly, and perhaps naively: his primary objective was to rebuild Agrokomerc and create prosperity, and he failed to realise how ruthless and dangerous Izetbegović was[98]. In July 1991, just as the conflict shifted from Slovenia to Croatia, Izetbegović, who when he died in 2003 left behind him up to four widows, applied for membership of the Organisation of Islamic States[99] (he had written in the *Islamic Declaration* that "Pakistan is our great hope, beset by trials"[100xxix]).

[xxviii] Agrokomerc was incorporated as a plc in 1992, with 53% private share capital, and 47% public; shares were issued to workers in accordance with their seniority. According to Babo, a great injustice was committed, because there were only 7,380 shareholders, and the majority of the workers who had built Agrokomerc were excluded. He also argues that it was a cooperative rather than a public corporation.
[xxix] Bangladesh seceded from Pakistan in 1971 in a short war that resulted in over three million deaths, apparently before the *Islamic Declaration* was written (although various putative dates exist as to its

In 1986, a memorandum by a group of Serbian intellectuals *On the position of Serbia in Yugoslavia*, a list of nationalist grievances calling for the constitution to be redrawn, was leaked[101]. Particular gripes were the bureaucratic hobbling of Serbia in both internal and federal affairs by the vetoes enjoyed by its two autonomous regions, which placed the largest republic at a disadvantage to the others, and the fact that the largest Yugoslav nation was also the only one without a republic of its own[102] (unlike the other main ethnic/religious groups, except to a lesser extent the Croats, the Serb population was not conveniently contained within one Yugoslav republic, but was spread over three - or four if Montenegro is included - and the two autonomous regions[103]). The federal development fund was another bone of contention challenged by the memorandum, with the four recipients (Bosnia, Kosovo, Macedonia and Montenegro) siding with the three donors (Slovenia, Croatia and Vojvodina) to oppose any reduction in Serbia's contributions: the memorandum cited an "anti-Serb coalition" within Yugoslavia[104] (arguments between the northern and southern Yugoslav entities about contributions to the fund started immediately after the death of Tito; for the Bosnian leadership, it was a key guarantor of equality within the federation[105]). The memorandum also expressed alarm about the position of Serbs in Croatia, and claimed the Serbs were undergoing "genocide" in Kosovo[106] (Serbs had been leaving the second-poorest region of Yugoslavia, with its underlying conflict between the authorities in Belgrade and the Albanian population, for decades - as had, to a lesser degree, Croats and Serbs from Bosnia - despite attempts to attract colonists from elsewhere in Yugoslavia and from the Serb diaspora abroad post-WWI onwards. Not only were economic prospects far better in Serbia proper (and, counter-intuitively, land cheaper), but the inter-ethnic tensions in the autonomous region were a cause of uncertainty[107]. In 1961, Serbs and Montenegrins had represented 28% of the population, but 30 years later they were only 11% (in the 1890s, they are estimated as having been approximately 30%, dropping to around 21% in 1912, when Kosovo was incorporated into Serbia and Montenegro[108]). Albanians had also been leaving due to discrimination and oppression, mainly for Bosnia, although in smaller numbers. In 1937, the historian Vaso Čubrilović, the youngest of Gavrilo Princip's group of assassins in 1914, who had been sentenced to 16 years' imprisonment, proposed expelling all the Kosovo Albanians to Turkey, and an agreement was reached with Ankara to that end[109]). The memorandum, which effectively called for a Greater Serbia at the expense of Yugoslavia, came to be known as the "obituary of Yugoslavia", and served as a blueprint for the actions of the Serbian leadership[110]. Milošević never publicly condemned it (although he once said in private that it was "...black nationalism [...] proposing the destruction of Yugoslavia. It means eliminating our country's existing order, a process of destruction which none of the Yugoslav peoples could survive"[111]). The communist insider, who stated at a rally in Belgrade in 1987 that "Serbia must be united or there will be no Serbia", gained *de facto* control of Serbia in 1987, Vojvodina and Montenegro in 1988, and Kosovo in 1989 by manipulating the bureaucratic power structures and co-opting or destroying key individuals, all the while appealing directly to the mob with a series of intimidating mass "rallies for truth" (likened by Dizdarević to Mao's cultural revolution, and indeed also called Milošević's "anti-bureaucratic revolution", with its promise to restructure the dysfunctional state bureaucracy[112]) and hysterical media coverage designed to harness popular

---

genesis, from the early 1960s until 1974, and it was never published). The war was preceded by the worst tropical cyclone on record, Bhola, which killed up to 500,000 people, and led to widespread civil unrest.

discontent and fuel nationalist sentiment[113]. After spontaneously playing to and winning over the mob in Kosovo with his vague but convincing promise to champion the cause of downtrodden Serbs, Milošević took control of Serbia at a party conference in 1987, where he politically assassinated the president of Serbia, his friend from their student days, *kum* ("best man") and patron, Ivan Stambolić[xxx][114] (the nephew of a former prime minister, and who had been instrumental in Milošević's promotion in 1986 from the position of chairman of the Belgrade party office to president of the Serbian KPJ, in what was seen and welcomed as a move to bring new blood into the higher echelons of power. He was kidnapped by the Unit and assassinated for real in 2000[115]). By the same act, the moderate tendency in the Serbian KPJ lost out to the nationalists[116]. Stambolić was replaced by one of Milošević's closest partners at the time, Petar Gračanin, a former Partisan and general who would be president of Serbia until 1989, and federal interior minister in Marković's government until 1991[117]. Milošević then embarked on a tour of Serbia to whip up popular support for his pro-Serb platform (as did the relics of Tsar Lazar), and he placed his people in all positions of power in Serbia, including in the media and major businesses. In July 1988, defending the rallies for truth, he called for equality for Serbia within Yugoslavia at a meeting of the federal KPJ executive held further to the first such rally to be organised outside Kosovo, in Novi Sad a few days earlier[118] (he later said he was opposed to the rallies, just as he was opposed to inflation, bread queues and rape in Kosovo[xxxi][119]). A few days later, the federal presidency held a meeting with the Serbian leadership in an attempt to put out the nationalist forest fire before it spread beyond Serbia, but the mass rallies continued, with increasingly overt jingoistic slogans, in towns and cities throughout Serbia, fuelled by the media and directed by Milošević[120]. One such slogan which became popular among Serbs affected by the nationalist fever throughout Yugoslavia was "*Samo sloga Srbina spasava*" ("only solidarity saves Serbs": the Serbian coat of arms features a cross with four symbols that resemble the Cyrillic letter S). For the first time, the word "war" was spoken, when the media frenzy was described as a "verbal civil war"[121]. In September, there was an attempt to organise a rally in Jajce in Bosnia; and it was discovered that there was a plan for a hand grenade to be thrown into the Partisan mass, which would then provide the impetus for further rallies in Bosnia. The Bosnian authorities prevented the rally taking place[122].

In 1987, the Slovenes blocked the adoption of the federal budget, demanding more control of foreign currency at republic level[123], and for the first time since 1945, in 1988 the country started the new year without a budget. Inflation reached 167%, Yugoslavia was the only country in Europe whose economy was shrinking, and 270,000 workers went on strike, raising serious concerns about the potential for public disorder. There were even more *štrajkovi* ("strikes") the next year, and the country was compared to Poland, where the Solidarity union brought about semi-free elections in 1989 after a decade of industrial action. But in the Balkans, it was *s konja na magarca* ("out of the frying pan, into the fire"). At the end of 1988, when the collective federal presidency looked back over the year, it was noted that

---

[xxx] Both Milošević's separated parents, his priest father and communist mother, committed suicide, when he was 11 and 21 respectively.

[xxxi] The rabid anti-Albanian propaganda of the time included the assertion that there was an epidemic of rapes of Serb women in Kosovo. In fact, an analysis of the statistics in 1990 showed that rape was less common in Kosovo (0.96 cases per 10,000 men) than in Serbia proper (2.43 cases), and that in Kosovo rapes by Albanian males of Serb females had the lowest reported incidence (only 31 cases between 1982 and 1989), whereas in 71% of cases the rapist and victim were from the same ethnic background.

inflation was 250%, 10% of national income was going on servicing debts, no budget could be adopted for the following year, the JNA was insolvent, the very existence of the federal government was being questioned, and images of the "rallies for truth" broadcast around the world had seriously damaged the country's international reputation[124]. The federal government (with a Bosnian prime minister, Mikulić), attacked from all sides and in open conflict with Slovenia and Croatia, resigned at the end of the year, the first time this had happened since WWII. Mikulić was replaced by Marković[125]. At this time Croatia was paralysed by strikes, and there was talk of a general strike there[126].

With the end of the Cold War and the reduction in a perceived external threat, the JNA began to focus its attention on the domestic enemy, which in 1989 was deemed in Serb circles to be the flourishing "anti-revolutionary" activities in Slovenia and Kosovo. While there had been unrest in Kosovo since 1981, in the latter half of the decade there was a rise in anti-JNA and anti-KPJ popular sentiment in Slovenia, which was manifest in (and fuelled by) the local media. The JNA, the main pillar of the establishment, felt under attack in progressive Slovenia, and the defensive response that this provoked may have contributed to its failure to see the threat of Serb nationalism it was facing from within, even as the conflict between Belgrade and the two autonomous regions was being reported in increasingly inflammatory language in the press (as were the differences between Belgrade and Zagreb)[127]. The JNA was also in favour of a more centralised federal government (in 1988, the JNA learnt that NATO was of the view that there were divisions within the JNA, and that it could no longer guarantee Yugoslavia's independence. The federal defence minister, Veljko Kadijević[xxxii], wanted to operate in an undeclared state of emergency, in order to prevent the "opposition" taking over the country; he also considered that, with the current constitutional arrangement, Yugoslavia was practically without a head of state. However, federal president Dizdarević insisted on a "democratic way out of the crisis"[128]). The Slovenes reopened the debate on decentralisation to counter the growing Serb nationalism, while the Croats, still wary after the crackdown on the "Croatian spring" in 1971, when they had called for national self-affirmation after achieving more economic independence in the 1960s (in particular calling for money earned in Croatia to be retained there rather than being transferred to Belgrade), initially kept quiet, but were inclined towards the Slovenian position[129]. In 1987, the Slovene nationalist press published articles calling for a return to Catholic traditions, and arguing that Slovenes would be better off outside Yugoslavia (this was regarded by the KPJ and the JNA as a response to the Serbian memorandum)[130]. There was also criticism of the privileged lifestyles of JNA generals, and of arms sales to Ethiopia during the famine[131]. In turn, these media reports, tolerated by the Slovenian KPJ, led to irritation with Slovenia in the rest of the county, as did the impression that Slovenia was profiting from the economic crisis. In 1988, the Slovenian leadership met with the federal presidency in an attempt to iron out their differences. They complained that they were being portrayed nationally as a destabilising factor, like Kosovo, and accused the federal leadership of being opposed to democratic progress and of being "counter-revolutionary"[132]. The same year, the JNA increased its strength in Slovenia, for the security of its staff and facilities, and the JNA commander in Slovenia visited the

---

[xxxii] The general was minister of defence from 1988-1992, when he retired. In 1992, he was charged by the Bjelovar public prosecutor with war crimes in Vukovar. He was contacted by the ICTY in 2001, and fled to Russia where he was granted asylum.

Slovenian interior minister. This was interpreted in Slovenia as an attempted *coup*, and described in the local media, citing classified documents leaked by the Slovenian leadership, as the "night of the long knives"[xxxiii], the worst slur on the JNA since WWII. There were no prosecutions for libel in Slovenia as a result[133]. The hostility against the JNA in Slovenia, coupled with Milošević's careful cultivation of the mainly Serb officer corps, meant that it was involuntarily drawn into the conflict[134]. In May, a popular Slovene youth leader was arrested in possession of the leaked documents, and handed over with two newspaper editors to the JNA military police, which predictably caused a media frenzy. The interviews were carried out by Vasiljević. Thus the Slovenian authorities were also able to channel the public's frustrations with the deteriorating economic situation to their own ends, and like Milošević, they manipulated the federal agencies to provide fuel for anti-Yugoslav sentiment in the local media, as well as paralysing them with endless bureaucratic requests. The JNA began to be seen as an occupying force, and the rest of the country as an exploiter, and major demonstrations began to be held in different Slovenian towns[xxxiv]. Federal president Dizdarević accused the Slovenian leadership of abusing their position as the most developed Yugoslav republic to try to obtain favourable treatment, and of harbouring separatist ambitions[135]. Towards the end of November, the president of Slovenia, on a trip to the US, aired Yugoslavia's dirty washing to foreign journalists. This was picked up by the Yugoslav media, and only further inflamed feelings, especially in Serbia. The president of Serbia published an open letter, criticising not only Slovenia, but also the federal president[136]. In early 1989, during the general strike in Kosovo (see below), a demonstration of "solidarity with Kosovo" was held in Slovenia. When it was televised, another media frenzy erupted in Serbia, and Milošević's well-oiled mass mobilisation machine (which also included the trade unions in major businesses) kicked into action. The aggravating factors of the JNA's heavy-handed approach to constitutional matters in Slovenia, the blazing nationalist forest fire in Serbia, and suspicion between the Slovenian and federal leaderships, all meant that the differences of opinion on how to deal with the crisis proved fatal[137]. Later that year, the Slovenian KPJ changed its name and held the first free elections in the former Yugoslavia, resulting in a coalition government that had campaigned for a referendum on independence, with the former KPJ leader, Kučan, the new president[138]. Milošević threatened to hold a mass rally in Ljubljana in support of the KPJ and the JNA, with Serbs bused in from Kosovo and elsewhere; but the Croatian government said it would not allow them passage through Croatia. It has been argued that while Tuđman countered Milošević by applying the same methods, Kučan countered him by applying the same logic[139]. Small as it was, Slovenia became an unwelcome counterweight to Milošević's policies and domination, and further to his strategy of a Greater Serbia ("Yugoslavia cannot exist without Serbia, but Serbia can exist without Yugoslavia"), he decided not to stop them leaving the federation[140]. A western portrayal of the Yugoslav crisis in the late 1980s was of two alternative scenarios for Yugoslavia: the Slovene path (modern, civilised and democratic) or the Serbian path (Balkan, nationalist and

---

[xxxiii] A violent purge of the Nazi party carried out by Hitler in 1934.

[xxxiv] After the military trial had started, the Slovenian leader, Milan Kučan, gave a speech in Slovenian at a meeting of the KPJ executive in Belgrade, lamenting the fact that the trial in Slovenia was being conducted in Serbo-Croat (although there had been an option at the beginning of the trial for proceedings to be held in Slovenian), and claiming that it undermined Slovenia's sovereignty and identity as a nation. He was backed by Milošević, who expressed his "shame" at this turn of events.

conservative)[141]. In 1990, Milošević started a trade war with Slovenia[142]. Dizdarević put the split down to a failure to communicate[143].

In 1987, as Bosnia imploded with the Agrokomerc affair, the Yugoslav security service learned that NATO considered the country had entered an acute crisis that could explode at any moment into a Lebanon-like civil war, and that the country's defence capabilities were degraded and would not be able to withstand a Soviet invasion (Yugoslavia was seen as the only communist country in Europe whose further development was uncertain, with the exceptions of Albania and Romania; it was also noted that the republics were acting like sovereign states, while the collective federal authorities were paralysed, which could lead to a power vacuum that would be filled either from outside, or by an internal authoritarian factor[144]); meanwhile, Bulgaria and Hungary held military exercises near the border in order to preclude any attempts by NATO to use Yugoslavia as an offensive springboard. It was also learned that the US and Soviet military attaches in Belgrade were sharing intelligence. The EU began to put pressure on Yugoslavia to improve the state of minority rights[145], even as nationalist circles in Slovenia and Serbia touted the propaganda that Yugoslavia was "sliding east" and should abandon its non-aligned path in favour of the EU. These were the first cracks in Yugoslavia's foreign policy, until then the last pillar of Tito's legacy that still had universal credibility[146]. In 1988, 40 years after Tito's split with Stalin, and the year before the Soviet Union withdrew from Afghanistan, new Soviet leader Mihail Gorbačev paid a five-day visit to Belgrade, and in his speech to the federal parliament and the subsequent joint declaration largely buried the hatchet[xxxv][147]. The same year, the federal presidency noted "a growth of nationalist activities calling for ethnic rallying and inciting an increase in racism" as well as "calls for ethnic homogeneity"[148]. *Siladžije* ("bullies") and *degenerici* ("perverts") crawled out of the woodwork, thinking their day had dawned, as indeed it had. In October of that year, president Dizdarević addressed the nation on television, the first time this had been done since Tito's day, appealing to all leaders to do their duty, and warning that otherwise the crisis could lead to a state of emergency. This address resulted in many messages of support, but also criticism in Serbia and Slovenia. The presidency was nevertheless determined to deal with the crisis by "democratic means". This was followed by the broadcast of a heated debate at a federal KPJ session between Milošević and the federal KPJ president, Croat Stipe Šuvar (who Milošević called a "psychopath"), which served once again to derail attempts by the bureaucratic federal agencies that led Yugoslavia to solve the crisis, and resulted in a virulent hate campaign against Šuvar[149]. During 1988, there was a media war between Croatia and Serbia, and it was all the government of Croatia could do to prevent the flames of nationalism taking hold there[150]. The Croatian communist leadership still hoped an accommodation was possible with the Serbs, namely more autonomy for the Serbs within Croatia in return for more autonomy for Croatia within Yugoslavia, but they were later eclipsed

---

[xxxv] Soviet leader Nikita Hruščev, known among other things for his enigmatic phrase, "We'll show you Kuzjka's mother", and for periodically breaking into Ukrainian when delivering speeches, much to the chagrin of interpreters, complained on Brijuni in 1956 that Yugoslavia was like the only soldier in a heroic platoon who refused to march in step. Spanish Civil War veteran Koča Popović retorted, "Perhaps their commander is no good". According to Fitzroy Maclean, Popović "was one of the outstanding figures of the Partisan movement. I have seldom met anyone who gave a more vivid impression of mental and physical activity [...] Though barely 30, he had the same tense, strained look as all the Partisan leaders, a look which comes from long months of physical and mental stress. But in his case the life he had led seemed to have fined him down rather than worn him out".

by Tuđman's nationalist rhetoric[151]. At the end of that year, the federal president noted that the country was facing its worst crisis since WWII, ordinary people's dissatisfaction with the economy was being misappropriated and channelled into mass rallies, *Ustaše* and *Četniks* were now showing themselves openly, and a climate of fear had been created, affecting both individuals and institutions[152].

Meanwhile, Tuđman, a dissident with impeccable pedigree (he was sacked from his KPJ post for nationalism in 1967, and was jailed in the 1960s and the 1970s), but whose Partisan record entitled him to certain privileges, such as retaining his passport, took advantage of the prevailing mood to voice Croatian nationalist ideas that had been taboo for over 20 years (and some that had been taboo since 1945[xxxvi][153]). He founded the HDZ in 1989, and embarked on a fund-raising tour of the diaspora. The party quickly became a mass movement with the slogan "The thousand-year-long dream of independence", a revival of the *Maspok* ("national movement") crushed in 1971, which had led to 20 years of silence from the Croats. When he was inaugurated as president on Palm Sunday the following year, Tuđman was hailed as Jesus entering the new Jerusalem, Zagreb[154]. As Croatia and Slovenia sought a more decentralised Yugoslavia, and Serbia and Montenegro consolidated power in Belgrade, Bosnia (and Macedonia) found themselves treading the shaky middle ground through no-man's land, even as the two diametrically and uncompromisingly opposed camps sought to entice them into their respective folds. In October 1990, a joint Slovenian-Croatian proposal for further decentralising constitutional reform was blocked by federal president Jović[155].

At the end of this period, in December 1989, the year of the velvet revolutions throughout most of eastern Europe, the month after the Berlin wall was torn down, and the month when Milošević secured his legitimacy as leader of the Serbs with a landslide victory in early presidential elections in Serbia (opposition parties were not legal)[156], the revolution in Romania put an end to the brutal communist dictatorship there, and the liberated Romanian people were welcomed out of the cold into the fold of European democracies[xxxvii]. However, it later transpired that the revolution had been staged, and that apart from the dictator Ceaușescu and his wife, who were shot, the same individuals continued to run the establishment, trading under a different ideology[xxxviii] (in 1979, Ceaușescu GCB, a violent petty thief, kept Tito waiting in the

---

[xxxvi] NDH interior and justice minister 1941-1943 Andrija Artuković had said, "No mercy. We know that Greater Croatia can only survive if we uproot and exterminate in the cradle everything that is Serb". After WWII he fled to the US via Éire/Ireland, but was extradited to Yugoslavia in 1986 where he died in 1988, sentenced to death but too ill to be executed.

[xxxvii] There were calls for autonomy from Moscow in the Caucasus and the Baltic states in the late 1980s, aggravated by the Černobilj disaster in Ukraine of 1986, which practically bankrupted the Soviet government. Free elections were held in Poland in June 1989; a new constitution was agreed in Hungary in September 1989; in December 1989, the East German communist party was dissolved; communist rule ended peacefully in Czechoslovakia the same month, and the country's constituent parts divorced amicably in 1993; also in December 1989, the Bulgarian government announced free elections would be held; and free elections were held in Albania in 1991.

[xxxviii] In the former Soviet Central Asian republics, dominated by Russia since the early 1800s, the local communist presidents simply changed the names of their parties and remained in power in their respective republics after independence, with practically no attempt to cast a democratic gloss on the new constitutional order. Ten years ago, I was told by the head of logistics of the Turkmen Red Crescent, an Uzbek, that the country's late dictator, Turkmenbaši, whose father was killed in action in WWII, once sent a commission of enquiry to the Caucasus to establish exactly where the great man (a *rjadovoj*, "private") had met his end. After the site of the tragic event had been carefully and scientifically identified, the ground on which the sacred blood had been spilt was dug up and transported to Central Asia, where it was placed in the national hero's extravagant tomb. I asked my interlocutor why they didn't send a commission of enquiry to Germany to identify the culprits of the heinous *voennoe prestuplenie* ("war crime"), and then

winter wind at Bucharest airport during his last state visit abroad[157]. His illiterate wife had a PhD in chemistry). This same image of a conflict between regressive, cold war communist forces and ordinary, downtrodden people seeking the liberty that was rightfully theirs was also superimposed by the western media on the Yugoslav conflict two years later, with the Serbs who dominated the police and army cast in the former role, as the villains, and the Slovenes, Croats, and Muslims in the latter. The image of Dinamo Zagreb's captain kicking a Serbian riot policeman, in full Warsaw Pact repressive garb, during a match between Dinamo Zagreb and Red Star Belgrade on 13 May 1990, stopped due to fighting between fans, was iconic of this (in late 1995, Kiwi was invited to a football match in Cazin, a revival of the classic Borders derby between Cazin *Krajina* and Velika Kladuša *Krajišnik* ("Borderer"), which literally descended into a fight – not between the fans, but on the pitch, and had to be called off. Apparently it happens all the time, even today)[158]. Indeed, in the run-up to the war, sections of the Croatian media accused the Serbs of harbouring (and deploying) former members of the Romanian security service, the notorious *Securitate*[159]. But yet again, this simplistic portrayal of the conflict was erroneous: while Milošević was happy to make use of the communist state machinery, in particular the police and military, all the new leaders displayed residual authoritarian instincts despite their democratic credentials (and almost all of them had learnt their trade in the KPJ)[160]. Meanwhile, on 27 June 1991, after the JNA deployed to retake control of the federal borders in Slovenia after its declaration of independence, the Slovenian TA shot down an unarmed JNA helicopter on its way to resupply a barracks, killing the pilot and mechanic on board, the first official casualties of the war (ironically, the pilot was himself a Slovene, only the first of many "friendly fire" casualties in what was anyway a civil war). Yet the Slovenes, broadcasting images of the Soviet invasion of Czechoslovakia, skilfully portrayed themselves as the victims, and the JNA as the aggressor. At the same time, the political leadership in Belgrade, such as it was, distanced itself from the JNA. Once the fighting started in Slovenia, a 19-year-old Bosnian JNA conscript, Bahrudin, from near Tuzla, was interviewed by the Yugoslav television news in action in a forest. When asked whether he knew what was going on, he said, "Apparently they want to secede, and apparently we are stopping them". He said that four conscripts had been killed already, and all they wanted to do was return to their barracks in Karlovac. He also took the opportunity to ask the *novinar* ("journalist") interviewing him to appeal to everyone to put a stop to what was happening. His appeal fell on deaf ears (he ultimately survived the war,

---

deploy *specnaz* ("special forces") to take them out. "There's no such thing as Turkmen special forces", he replied. Another of the great leader's brainwaves was to demolish traditional crofting communities' housing and replace it with high-rise buildings delivered by a Turkish construction company (as part of a general trend in Central Asia to sever links with Russia, which previously provided everything). Unfortunately, the new buildings were substandard and unfit for habitation, with the result that the residents, who had once been poor but self-sufficient, were now destitute, having lost not only their homes but also their land. Similarly, the government of Tajikistan contracted an Iranian construction company to build a road tunnel in the mountains linking the north-west to the rest of the country, on the main road into Uzbekistan, with which relations are strained. Water has been running through the tunnel since the day it opened, and driving through the poorly-ventilated, dank subterranean catacomb is like embarking on a wall of death. To make matters worse, the stability of the structure is regularly compromised by the seismic activities of a Chinese gold-mining corporation, which holds a monopoly on the industry. In the harsh winter of 2008, there was a *ČP* ("emergency") when the dam powering the country's largest *ges* ("hydroelectric power station"), the Nurek, froze, further straining the country's inadequate grid at a time when the need for heating was greatest. Tajikistan is particularly prone to *navodnenija* ("floods") and other *stihijnie bedstvija* ("natural disasters"). In Belarus, an unknown former Communist party official won the first democratic elections in 1994, and has been in power ever since.

but was killed in a RTA between Zadar and Rijeka in 1998)[161]. Foreign governments were quick to condemn the JNA deployment to Slovenia, with the German foreign minister stating it had "run amok", which was echoed by the UK, Italy and the US[162]. The idea that the Serbs were to blame for everything was here to stay. General Radislav Krstić, the logistics coordinator of the VRS at Srebrenica, who served part of his 35-year sentence for aiding and abetting genocide (which he denies) in the UK, told me that what affected him the most was being treated like a criminal by the British. He had been brought up in the Partisan tradition of camaraderie with the British army, but was arrested by the SAS while driving in eastern Bosnia in 1998, before being delivered to the ICTY. After his conviction, he was attacked one morning in his cell in Yorkshire by an Albanian prisoner with two accomplices, one a convert to Islam, who attempted to cut his throat with an improvised knife[xxxix]. They were prosecuted for attempted murder, but convicted of assault at Leeds crown court, in 2011. The Albanian "avenger" was already serving a life sentence for raping and murdering a schoolgirl in Reading in 2005. Genocide is defined by the Convention on the Prevention and Punishment of Genocide, which came into force in 1950 and was ratified by Yugoslavia in June of that year (one month after the Peasants' Revolt), as

"acts committed with intent to destroy, in whole or in part, a national, ethnic, racial or religious group, as such
(a) killing members of the group;
(b) causing serious bodily or mental harm to members of the group;
(c) deliberately inflicting on the group conditions of life calculated to bring about its physical destruction in whole or in part;
(d) imposing measures intended to prevent births within the group;
(e) forcibly transferring children of the group to another group"[163].

Slovenia's exit from Yugoslavia was the moment everyone's bluff was called, the hamstrung central government blinked (there was no head of state, as Milošević had blocked the rotating presidency passing to Croatia's Mesić, before magnanimously backing down at the EU's request), and the JNA was humiliated (having deployed for a purely police mission rather than an invasion, they were defeated by the local TA after Milošević blocked further intervention[xl])[164]. The Slovenes, ahead, walked away from the table to cash in their chips, and the stakes were suddenly raised dramatically for the remaining players. What until then had been brinkmanship, was now an impending collision. The game changed from poker to Russian roulette. First blood had been drawn, and there was no way back. For the EU, it was a triumph of diplomacy[165].

Looking back on the 1980s in 2000, Dizdarević, the president of Bosnia at the time of Tito's death, wrote:

[xxxix] Whereas in the recent past, prison populations in the UK used to divide along regional lines, with the Cockneys, the Scousers, the Jocks etc. flocking together, nowadays the most potent force behind bars is radical Islam, with gangs of the faithful actively recruiting and converting disaffected and disadvantaged youngsters. Organisations like the Jehovah's Witnesses, with their magic book bearing God's signature, employ the same tactics in universities. As they say in the Balkans, "*O bidžanglo si phral le bengesko*" ("the devil makes work for naive hands").
[xl] The initial deployment was arranged by the MOD with the green light from PM Marković in the absence of a commander-in-chief, and so was technically illegal. Kadijević then advocated a "massive attack" to restore control over Slovenia within 24 hours.

"That was the flaw in our efforts at the time: we failed to understand, or perhaps we underestimated, the need in a new period of Yugoslav history for new and deeper concepts for the development of society and the system; new, bold breakthroughs into new processes and new solutions; to see and make use of what was new in global developments and changes. Unfortunately, a spirit of practical pragmatism dominated social affairs"[xli][166].

By allowing the Slovenes to leave, Milošević strengthened the case for allowing the Serbs to decide on their own destiny, i.e. to remain in a single state. He also isolated the Croats, who would have to face him alone. The remaining pro-Yugoslav generals, weakened by the Slovenian fiasco, and including KOS chief Vasiljević, were purged from the JNA in May 1992, after Arkan had been feted as an example of patriotism and military prowess by Milošević and his media at the end of 1991[167]. At the same time, the JNA was reconstituted as the VJ[xlii][168].

Even during the war, Agrokomerc continued to trade with Zagreb and Belgrade (from November 1993 onwards; and in April 1994, after a two-year forced closure, the Agrokomerc production lines were restarted. Meanwhile, work on repairing and upgrading Agrokomerc's facilities carried on right up until Operation Storm[169]), arranging corridors with all sides except Sarajevo until May 1994, when the US told Tuđman to stop undermining the SDA regime and by extension the shaky Federation, and in return promised him assistance in the war in Croatia[170] (the US had been instrumental in the creation of the Federation, and from as early as August 1993 onwards brought pressure to bear on Tuđman to call off his 30,000 HV soldiers fighting the ABiH in Bosnia, or be faced with the same sanctions as Milošević[171]). It is said that these corridors had allowed Tuđman to sell oil and other essential goods to Milošević, who had been placed under unprecedented UN sanctions at the beginning of the war in Bosnia at US insistence and with the support of Russia[172] (UN security council resolution 757 of 30 May 1992 condemned the Yugoslav authorities for failing to stop the fighting in Bosnia, and placed the rump state under sanctions, while resolution 713 had placed an arms embargo on the whole of the former Yugoslavia on 25 September 1991; the sanctions were suspended the day after the Dayton peace accords were signed in 1995, but Yugoslavia was not allowed to return to the World Bank and the IMF due to ongoing unrest in Kosovo[173]). They also allowed *struja* ("electricity") to be supplied into the pocket. The Unit controlled, and taxed, all commercial convoys passing through the corridors[xliii][174]. From the summer of 1994 onwards, with the tacit approval of the US, large quantities of illegal arms and equipment were regularly flown by Iranian aircraft into Pula in Istria on the north-west Croatian coast, before being trucked to

---

[xli] Or in the words of former Yugoslav EU bureaucrat Mihailo Crnobrnja, "Yugoslavia did away with itself because it was unable to generate the internal momentum for democratic change at the right time".
However, Mirvet and many others in the former Yugoslavia are today of the view that their country was eliminated as a potential rival to the EU: there was no room in the world order for a loose cannon challenging the hegemony of the great powers.
[xlii] According to Owen, in August 1993 Mladić became the *de facto* head of the VJ, and was thus able to defy Milošević.
[xliii] According to Babo, these corridors were arranged with UNHCR, who in 1992 Agrokomerc provided with 12 artics painted white for the transport of aid into Bosnia (escorted by French UNPROFOR), as UNHCR did not have the necessary transport. Babo successfully sued the Croatian newspaper *Globus* because of an article that accused him of selling fuel to the Serbs. Meanwhile, the SDA refused to enter into negotiations with the SDS on anything, including humanitarian access.

the HVO and ABiH in Bosnia. Another route for the same freight was by air-drop from Cyprus into Tuzla in north-east Bosnia, flown by retired US air force pilots[175]. Meanwhile, Serbia continued to receive supplies by road and river from Greece, Russia and Ukraine. Milošević had the largest stocks of JNA hardware anyway, and had bought 14,000 tons of weaponry from the Middle East just before the sanctions were imposed[176]. Babo also arranged safe passage across SDS territory for busloads of Croats who had taken refuge in Velika Kladuša from the Croatian Borders, Bihać or northern Bosnia and who wished to make a new start in Croatia, but tickets were not free of charge: DM 4,000 per person, including children, plus DM 100 per bag (this has often been cited as an example of how Babo was not averse to squeezing money out of the most vulnerable, but as Mirvet explained to me, there were many palms to be greased between Velika Kladuša and Karlovac, and the bus drivers themselves would only get behind the wheel for a small fortune for what was a trip with no security guarantees: on 3 October 1991, before the war started in Bosnia, a column of 30 civilian workers returning abroad with their families from a visit to Velika Kladuša and Cazin had been deliberately taken out by the SVK at Batnoga, on their way to Karlovac)[xliv][177]. A Catholic priest, now living in Cetingrad, arranged one convoy free of charge with French UNPROFOR in March 1994. A total of 11,000 Croat refugees and IDPs passed through Velika Kladuša. Residents who needed to travel outside the enclave temporarily, to draw their pension in Slovenia, for example, could do so if they paid a cash deposit of DM 2,000; but some subsequently found that the deposit was not reimbursed after their third such trip. In April 1994, three buses a day were making the run to Karlovac; according to Hope, when the Croats ran out, 5th Corps deserters smuggled across the front line at night by UNPROFOR took their place[178]. At this critical time there was a *policijski čas* ("curfew") from 4 pm to 8 am; anyone caught outside during that time was liable to *hapšenje* ("arrest"). Beatings were not uncommon during detention, and some women had their heads shaved. Neighbours of the prison in Grupex, a construction materials business around the back of Hamm, that recently almost went bust (after being run by the SDA since the war, according to Babo as a vehicle to misappropriate Agrokomerc assets, in particular land with planning permission[179]), and where Legija had an office, were treated to a variety of weird and wonderful cries during the night. One guard was heard to say, *"Nema ništa bez batina!"* ("this is the only language we Bosnians understand"). LCK staff and others with the right connections (such as Mirvet) could obtain a *propusnica* ("pass") allowing movement after curfew. However, people were much more fearful of falling into the hands of Legija's military police, who sometimes patrolled. Nevertheless, in practice it was not Legija's MPs, who did their work professionally (and sometimes even bought groceries for locals they had befriended), but rather certain locals suddenly finding themselves in a position of physical power over their fellow-citizens, and hoping to curry favour with the Serbs, who were the worst abusers. The most notorious nick was the dispensary in the hospital, where prisoners were interviewed, and which was also the HQ of Babo's police and the NOZB[180]. Legija's MPs were much more concerned with breaches of discipline by the squaddies, in particular theft and looting by the SVK and paramilitary units, such as the "Scorpions" (one such

---

[xliv] According to Legija, the Ukrainian pilots on the Zagreb – Ćoralići helicopter run were paid USD 20,000 per month. When I was working in Angola, we had to pay the UN over a thousand dollars per truck to transport our aid from the capital to Uige, a government enclave in the north of the country, bordering the DRC.

incident led to friendly fire casualties and then a not-so-friendly standoff between the Unit and the SVK during the battle to retake Velika Kladuša, see below. On another occasion, Legija stuck a knife in a SVK squaddie's leg for stealing a tractor from a Muslim, and warned that if anyone else did anything like that, he would personally cut their hand off)[181]. One tactic used to avoid being mobilised in the street was to go out only in the company of a small child, as the military authorities, reluctant to be landed with responsibility for the child, would leave its guardian alone. For men from minorities in particular, the prospect of being mobilised was not a welcome one. Today, Agrokomerc's installations in the Bosnian and Croatian Borders stand empty, unused for 20 years, at a time when unemployment in Bosnia has never been higher.

No-man's land in this forgotten corner of the war, and indeed forgotten corner of Europe, was for much of the time centred around the area stretching from Šturlić and Liskovac (*liska* means "moorhen") in the west (the epicentre in Cazin county of the 1950 Peasant's Revolt), where the road running south along the border to Bihać forks off towards Cazin; through Pećigrad on the main road from Velika Kladuša to Cazin; and north-east to Vrnograč near Bosanska Bojna, from where the road leads south to Bosanska Krupa and also forks off towards Cazin, after Bužim. Following the main road from Maljevac (Victims of Fascism Street) down to the *čaršija* ("town centre") of Velika Kladuša, past the Orthodox church on the left, closed since before the war (and the only Orthodox church in the former Bihać pocket not damaged or destroyed[xlv][182]), turning right at the mosque at the top of Mujo Hrnjica park, nowadays frequented by *bradonje* ("men with beards"), past the Agrokomerc *robna kuća* ("supermarket") and the park and then turning left at the bottom (the road to the right leads to the *stari grad* ("castle") on the hill overlooking the town, once Babo's office, and continues to the border, and the short cut to Cetingrad), the road negotiates several bends and slopes (including a half constructed bridge which one aid worker mistook for the real thing one night after several beers in 1996, writing off his Toyota Landcruiser, but fortunately emerging unscathed himself), before traversing the village of Polje, the site of Agrokomerc's main facilities, which also housed the UNPROFOR base and our warehouse (rent free). The entrance was guarded by two old boys with bolt-action rifles. I later learned that the more fierce-looking of the two, Muhamed, had, in his youth, been a UN peacekeeper in Syria and Lebanon. It also turned out that he was Kami's father. One day, before Operation Storm, when I was working in the warehouse, I was distracted by a strange and wonderful sound coming from outside. Downing what I was busy with, I went outside to investigate. From the neighbouring godown, used by Agrokomerc, wafted an incredibly powerful and evocative multi-harmony chant, like Highland precenting. While one voice delivered the text in a slow, deliberate melody, conjuring up the age-old sorrows of separation from home and loved ones, the others produced constant and seemingly unending supporting harmonies, like the background notes of the *gajda* ("pipes", not to be confused with *gajba*, "crate"). It was a *sevdalinka* ("Bosnian serenade"). Entranced, I listened for a while, and then advanced to learn more. Unwittingly, I thereby broke the spell, for as I entered the warehouse to discover a team of women doing physical work, simultaneously they

---

[xlv] The Catholic church in Bosanska Krupa was also destroyed during the war, but was rebuilt with donations from local Muslims, and re-opened in 2009. The Orthodox church there was damaged but never destroyed.

saw me and broke off in laughter from their wonderful distraction. One of them was called Šeherzada. In this part of the country during the war, women did most of the physical work, as most men over 18 were fighting. The *viljuškar* ("fork-lift") driver appeared to have a dispensation, and was often to be seen racing around with female workers perched on his conveyance. Sometimes there were also gangs of POWs doing physical work such as scything the grass around the Agrokomerc facilities. I was uneasy the first time I saw them, before I realised that it was actually a perk. Most POWs in the war were cooped up 24 hours a day in unsuitable premises, a mass of desperate humanity with little or sometimes no hygienic facilities. Babo had a prison camp at Drmeljevo, a poultry hangar on the outskirts of Velika Kladuša, 250 m from the border, which opened on 8 June 1994 (it also served as an accommodation centre for IDPs, from the summer of 1993 onwards, i.e. before the proclamation of the autonomous region, and as a filtration centre for POWs, to distinguish 5th Corps hardliners from those who were prepared to join the NOZB) and through which 1,500 prisoners passed, for periods ranging from a few hours or days to several weeks or in some cases months, and sometimes more than once (one of them later called Babo's state an "Orwellian chicken farm")[183]. Prisoners were also used for digging trenches (it is illegal under IHL to use prisoner labour in dangerous places or in connection with the operations of war[184]). Women prisoners were sometimes used for menial council activities, such as sweeping the roads. After nine days, ICRC gained access to the camp, registered the prisoners, and provided basic items (food, bedding and clothing). As is their practice, ICRC also followed up on their visit with a confidential report to the authorities detailing improvements to be made to the conditions of detention in order to safeguard the prisoners' physical and mental wellbeing[185]. There was another camp in the north of the enclave, in a former chicken farm at Dubrave near Ponikve, also a wartime cemetery, where other POWs and suspected 5th Corps sympathisers were detained, under the usual grim conditions[186]. Having a relative in the 5th Corps was enough to qualify for detention[187]. It is also frequently claimed that local "intellectuals" (i.e. anyone with higher education, but especially professionals, although the majority of educated people in the district were from elsewhere in Yugoslavia, who had moved there to work for Agrokomerc or one of the other local businesses it engendered[xlvi]) were more likely to find themselves imprisoned, for their political convictions (i.e., pro-SDA). At any one time, an average of 400 people were in some place of detention[188]. According to Mirvet, 10% of the population of Velika Kladuša held dissident views, and national security considerations required a crackdown on potential troublemakers, while according to the DNZ, "breaches of IHL were under control"[189]. UN human rights committee special rapporteur and former Polish PM the late Tadeusz Mazowiecki[xlvii][190] was particularly critical of Babo's treatment of

---

[xlvi] According to Babo, Izetbegović sought to banish the sophisticated urban elite that Velika Kladuša had begun to attract and foster, and revert the whole region to the Ottoman days of serfs terrorised by the tyranny of lame priests.

[xlvii] He was instrumental in the discussions that led to the creation of the first independent trade union in eastern Europe in 1980, and oversaw the transition from communist rule as prime minister of Poland from 1989-1990. He resigned from the UN over what he called the organisation's "hypocrisy" in respect of Srebrenica and Žepa the day after the press conference on his visit to West Bosnia. He also visited the 5th Corps barracks in Bihać where Tetin was being held, but they were not allowed to speak to him unsupervised, and so were unable to inform him of the 30 Serb POWs who had been moved into a separate room just before he arrived, as they habitually were every time there was an international visit. Mazowiecki appears to have taken particular umbrage at Drmeljevo because it was a "civilian detention camp", as he described it in his subsequent report, which was used as evidence in Babo's trial, and that

prisoners. After visiting Drmeljevo, where he was allowed to speak to prisoners in private, he held a press conference on 26 June. However, when Babo called him live on Velkaton, his radio station in Velika Kladuša, and challenged him to present his report, he declined[191]. Babo accused him of working for the SDA[192]. He also wrote to Babo in a letter dated 28 July 1994 that conditions of detention were in breach of IHL; that people were being held illegally; that some prisoners were subjected to violence; that the practice of forced labour was contrary to IHL; and in conclusion, he urged him to release all political prisoners[193]. According to Hope, NOZB prisoners received the same rations as the soldiers did, such as they were[194]. At least the soldiers had opportunities to loot to supplement their meagre diet, if only stealing onions from people's gardens, as Denis told me he did. On another occasion, I happened to go around the back of our warehouse, where there was more commercial infrastructure, and ran into Ibrahim Đedović, the NOZB chief of police, originally from near Tuzla, who told me sharply that he would arrest me if he caught me trespassing again. He had graduated from the JNA academy in Belgrade before the war, and in 1991 offered his services to Izetbegović, who wasn't interested. He was then recruited by Babo[195]. His signature it was on my *odobrenje* ("visa") for Babo's republic (no visa was required for SDA territory; although just after the war I was asked to produce my visa by an aggressive young 5th Corps squaddie when I was crossing the border at Maljevac in a bus. I decided against producing my NOZB freedom of the city, and merely let him know that as a British citizen I didn't need a visa[xlviii]). From Polje the road continues through Mala Kladuša (just south-west of Mala Kladuša, towards Johovica, the village of Gornja Vidovska was the epicentre of the Peasants' Revolt in Kladuša county), with its outdoor swimming pool, built by Agrokomerc and supplied by a spring, but now in disrepair, twisting its way through a succession of hamlets with an abundance of *džamije* ("mosques") and *mezarluci* ("graveyards"), flanked on either side now by irregular steep, menacing humped and sharp features, almost Picasso-like in their deformity, bearing meadows of dull vegetation and woodland, where it seems as though the surface of the earth itself has been tormented by a primeval, supernatural conflict, now by the flat valley floor, through Pećigrad with its six abandoned chicken hangars, and over a series of hills up to the heights of Skokovi. As Andrić noted, "There's room under the ground for everyone here"[196]. Babo had an array of hundreds of poultry farms throughout the Borders, ranging from micro installations run by individual families, to larger facilities such as at Batnoga and Pećigrad, to the largest chicken farm in Europe in

---

while the NOZB had 300 civilian detainees (and 150 POWs), the 5th Corps only had two (and 450 POWs). Was that because the 5th Corps were more tolerant of dissidents, or simply because Dudaković (and Izetbegović) managed to pull the wool over his eyes? Tetin certainly didn't appreciate the distinction, which appeared to legitimise and sanitise his own captivity, and nor did he appreciate the use of the highly charged word "camp" ("*logor*"), with its WWII connotations. He also points out that as the 5th Corps regarded them as "unlawful combatants", they were all civilians, and as such, deprived of the protected status of POW, were subject to criminal prosecution for acts of war. Zlatan, who was also detained in Bihać, told me that one day when they were being marched to the front to dig trenches, they crossed the path of a group of 5th Corps squaddies returning from the front. Suddenly, one of them lunged at Zlatan with a large knife; but he was pulled out of the way by a fellow POW, nicknamed "54", because he was said to be the youngest of 54 children. Mazowiecki did however note that "it is obvious that a significant number of alleged 'POWs' on both sides have never engaged in any military operation; they are simply men of military age. They have been held under very difficult conditions and are being used for forced labour at the confrontation lines". Helsinki Watch wrote in a 1994 report that "Access to detention camps was denied by all parties to the conflict". Mazowiecki died in 2013.

xlviii The extensive network of bus routes linking Velika Kladuša with Croatia and central Bosnia, which was restored immediately after the war, vanished over a decade ago, starved of public funding.

Bosanska Bojna, supplied with corn from Vojvodina (this model of rural development was intended to prevent urbanisation, among other things)[197]. In winter, both here and across the Korana in the Croatian Borders, the leafless trees grasp for the oppressive white sky like spiteful fingers, clutching angrily from the desolate earth as if to poke out the eye of God. Driving south on this road one day after the war, when the rain was so heavy it was as if the carpet of clouds was being hosed down with a pressure washer, I passed two girls pushing a wheelbarrow. Even though they were already soaked to the skin, I had to stop, and loaded their wheelbarrow, which contained a sack of potatoes, into the back of the Landcruiser (most agencies have a ban on giving lifts to civilians, even unarmed, not least because it can invalidate the insurance. Nevertheless, I once gave a pregnant hitchhiker a lift from Kakanj to Zenica hospital, where she was due to give birth; but Stefan, a German colleague, was robbed at gunpoint by two hitchhikers he picked up on the way to Tuzla). The girls belonged to a family of four teenage sisters living alone, their father having been killed in the war, and their mother by a landmine only a few weeks previously. After about 5 km, they asked me to let them out, as their house was just up a side road. I wanted to drive them right up to their house, but they were very insistent that I should not do so, and in the end I relented and let them out at the junction. I imagine they were afraid the aid vehicle might attract unwelcome attention. The road then descends from Skokovi with more of the same evocative, mournful landscape, steeped in frightening feudal madness, past the right turn to Ćoralići, where the Danish UNPROFOR base was located, before traversing a series of smaller rises to reach the next town, Cazin, in the centre of the enclave, 35 km and about an hour away from Polje. It took longer during the war, with a long waiting period at the checkpoint at one end of no man's land before a hair-raising cannonball run to the other, as the local squaddies were liable to take pot-shots at aid vehicles; armoured vehicles were a magnet for target practice. At the 5th Corps checkpoint, names had to be verified on a list before entry was granted (staff movements had to be reported in advance to the authorities on both sides of the intra-Muslim conflict). On the main road, the dynamic and active front line was generally anywhere between Mala Kladuša and Ćoralići, in 1995 reaching Cazin, and twice overwhelming Velika Kladuša. This meant that families frequently found themselves separated by the front line. It was not unusual for family members to attempt to cross the front line at night in order to be reunited, sometimes only to find that it had moved and they were on the wrong side again. No-man's land was indicated by a triangular warning road sign featuring a skull and crossbones and reading *"Ratna Zona! Zabranjen prolaz!"* ("war zone! no entry!"). The first time I saw it I wondered idly whether they had already had a stock of them before the war started. Then I realised they actually must have: JNA military doctrine was based on the WWII experience, i.e. occupation by a larger enemy, followed by a long and difficult but ultimately successful guerrilla war. Post-WWII, the most likely enemy was seen as the Soviet Union. In practice this meant that, in addition to Yugoslavia having the largest standing army in eastern Europe at federal level after the Red Army (over half a million men: approximately 3% of the population were trained and active military personnel; by way of comparison, the UK's current armed forces, atrophied by decades of budget cuts, are a fraction of that), and a well-funded defence industry, each republic had its own fully equipped and trained, decentralised TA units (located within district councils, and even major businesses), capable of mounting an independent guerrilla campaign[198] (theoretically independent of the JNA, although in 1990 federal president Jović, Dizdarević's successor but one, was able to disarm the Slovenian and Croatian TAs, and at the end of 1991, Izetbegović signed an order handing all the Bosnian TA's hardware over to the JNA![199]). Bosnia with its mountains was the backbone of this doctrine, and became the location for armaments and other strategic industry, cut off from markets, skilled manpower, and even roads[200]. The Bosnian TA was also the largest and most developed[201]. As Fitzroy Maclean wrote, "Everything in Yugoslavia favoured the guerrilla"[202]. Tragically, this set-up only hastened the violent demise of the country, because district councils could decide which side they were on and come out fighting against their neighbours. As if that wasn't enough, children received weapons training in secondary school, with live *streljivo* ("ammunition"; in early 1980, when Tito was on his deathbed, and the country was practically in a state of emergency, it was assessed that in the event of an invasion, the Warsaw Pact would be able to deploy up to 50 divisions, one million men. It was also considered likely that in such an event, NATO would invade from Greece and Italy, in order to prevent Yugoslavia being absorbed by the Warsaw Pact[203]).

Before the war, over 250,000 people lived in what became the Bihać pocket, an area the size of the Isle of Wight, the majority Muslims (81%), with Serb (12%) and Croat (3%) minorities (and 2% Yugoslavs), surrounded on all sides by majority Serb communities, in Croatia to the north, north-east, west, and south-west, and in Bosnia to the south and east. The Serb minority was concentrated mainly in Bosanska Krupa and Bihać, and the Croat minority in Bihać (in 1931, the last census before WWII, the population had been 66% Muslims, 29% Serbs and 4% Croats. The area was liberated by the Partisans in April 1945[204]. According to the 2013 census, the proportions are now 91% Muslims, 1% Serbs and 2% Croats, with a total population of 209,000). Besides Agrokomerc, the local economy consisted of textile, construction, timber, transport, metal, graphics and medical supplies industries, as well as agriculture. There were two colleges in Bihać (which now also has a *faks*, "university")[205]. In 1527, after the fall of Lika, Jajce and Banja Luka to the Turks (the territory north of a line extending from Bihać north-east as far as Doboj had not been part of medieval Bosnia, but formed part of Hungarian Croatia; conversely, half of Montenegro, and a slice of south-west Serbia had belonged to Bosnia, as had Lika and much of the coast[206]), the Croatian authorities set up the Bihać *kapetanija* defensive system of fortified towns to prevent them making further territorial gains. Knin had been captured in 1522. However, the *kapetanija* was gradually overrun, losing Đakovo in 1537, Pakrac in 1543, the whole Una valley between Jasenovac (*jasen* means "European ash") and Bosanska Otoka (near Krupa) in 1556, Bužim and Cazin in 1575, Bosanska Bojna and Velika Kladuša in 1577, and Bihać in 1592 (the Una flows north from its source just inside Croatia in Lika, 5 km west of Drvar, up along the border before cutting north-east through Bihać and Krupa to rejoin the border to the east of the enclave, near Dvor, and then constitutes the border before flowing into the Sava at Jasenovac. The name Una-Sana is thus a misnomer, as strictly speaking it only describes territory to the south and east of the Bihać pocket. According to Mirvet, this exclusion of Velika Kladuša and Cazin is not by chance. There is also a railway line, now unused, running through the Una valley from Knin in Sector South to Bosanski Novi in Sector West, and linking the region to Split, Zagreb and Belgrade). Karlovac was established in 1579 as a new line of defence against Ottoman expansion, and the Turks were stopped at Sisak in 1593, with Croatia reduced to a rump, serving as a buffer for the Habsburgs[207]. According to T.E. Lawrence, the Turkish yoke was "a slow death. Their goods were stripped from them; and their spirits shrivelled in the numbing breath of military government. Turkish rule was gendarme rule, and Turkish political theory as crude as its practice"[208]. Many of the villages in the Bihać pocket were abandoned after the Turkish conquest. Selimović describes an analogous incident during WWII in his novel *Mist and Moonlight*:

> "The village was emptied, the Germans were coming, there was no need to inquire, even the deaf would have heard, she saw the last of them hurrying towards the hills, they were driving the livestock off, in the hope that it wouldn't be caught in the expanse, no-one was thinking about their homes or their crops, a flood was coming and anything that survived would be pure luck. The people were fleeing its boom, and only those who had had enough of life or believed in fate remained"[209].

These abandoned villages were only resettled in the mid-17th century, by Muslims and Vlachs from the interior. However, the largest influx of Muslims into the Bosnian Borders was from Lika after it was recaptured by the Habsburgs in 1699[210]. By the beginning of 1993, the population of the enclave had swelled to 300,000, with 50,000 men fit for military service. Nikola happened to visit Velika Kladuša in early 1992, and was surprised to see that even before the war started in Bosnia, the crisis was such that cigarettes were being sold by street vendors in batches of five. The war started here on 21 April 1992, when Bosanska Krupa in the south-east was attacked by the VRS from across the river Una. The first military fatality was Sead Ćehić, from Barake ("portacabins") near Velika Kladuša. But not everyone waited for the war to start before making preparations. Gun-running from Croatia was rife for months beforehand, and not only by the main players; and a "silent war" started in Banja Luka and parts of the Borders as early as mid-1991[211]. In Velika Kladuša, they remembered not only 1941, but also 1950 and 1987. Bosanska Krupa remained a front line town for three years, with the right bank of the Una occupied by the VRS, and suffered extensive damage as a result. In July of 1991, the SDS leaders of the town had set up their own parallel council, and local Serbs (and strangers) began sporting paramilitary and police uniforms, and weapons, as well as *Četnik* regalia (shaggy caps, long hair and beards[xlix]). Zuhra, see below, told me that at this time one of her former teachers stopped her and a group of friends at gunpoint at a checkpoint and demanded to see their identity documents, even though he knew them personally. Her younger brother was later killed by the VRS. The Muslims either fled the attack or were detained. However, the well-armed SDS were unable to complete their conquest and take the left bank of the town, despite heavy shelling. At the end of April, Babo convened a meeting of the local HDZ, SDA and SDS in Bihać, the last such meeting, which concluded with a local peace agreement[212]. He then travelled to Vienna, where he signed blank cheques in the sum of DM 61 million to allow Agrokomerc Vienna[l] to function as a logistics centre for the Una-

---

[xlix] By contrast, *Ustaše* tended to be skinheads, while the *Mudžahedin* appeared to be a cross between the two – skinheads with beards. The UÇK started life as grizzly as any *Četniks*, but once they started receiving US support, they cleaned up their image (if nothing else), and a three-line whip ensured they appeared in the western media as clean-shaven, smart, earnest young men.

[l] In January 1993, an anonymous tipoff was conveyed to the Austrian police to the effect that the company (Agrokomerc Vienna was a separate legal entity) was involved in gun-running and the sale of humanitarian aid. Supporting documents were supplied to the Austrian foreign office (indicating that the source of the tipoff was the Bosnian embassy). After an eight-year investigation, the Austrian police concluded there was no evidence of wrongdoing, and the investigation was closed; but by then, the damage to the company's reputation with its international partners had already been done, and Agrokomerc Vienna was practically insolvent.

Sana operational group, the future 5th Corps[213]. In May, the Sarajevo government ordered the creation of a new Bihać regional assembly parallel to the existing elected local authorities, to be run by the SDA in the person of Mirsad Veladžić from Bužim (Veladžić, a former Agrokomerc mechanic who was promoted to head of the works council under the UDBA/AID's administration of the business during the Agrokomerc affair, was related to Izetbegović's inner circle by marriage, and after the 1990 elections he consolidated the fundamentalism for which Bužim was known during WWII, when it was an *Ustaše* hotbed, making it the most fundamentalist community in the Bihać pocket; he it was who founded the SDA in Velika Kladuša[li][214]. An earlier request for the creation of a regional assembly in Tuzla had been refused by the presidency because there was no legal basis for such a constitutional arrangement, until relevant legislation was adopted in August 1993[215]). In July, Babo informed Izetbegović that he was moving his office from Sarajevo to Velika Kladuša, to facilitate his development of Agrokomerc as the main mechanism for the supply of the civilian population and the armed forces (in his own words, to "create a little Switzerland in West Bosnia", as it had all the necessary advantages[216]). In September, he asked Izetbegović to set up a dedicated defence budget, and to provide Agrokomerc with DM 4 million to cover funds already disbursed to support the ABiH in the Bihać pocket, including pay and direct support to casualties and their families, which had averted a potential munity. But Izetbegović preferred to operate slush funds, disbursed via the SDA, and reneged on his election promise to invest in Agrokomerc. Babo also informed Izetbegović that the local civilian administration and armed forces were in a state of chaos, with no clear hierarchy of decision-making and reporting processes or chains of command, and proposed a new structure with clearly defined roles and responsibilities[217]. Meanwhile, a unit from the operational group took the regional commander prisoner in Ćoralići[218]. On 29 September, the regional assembly established the 5th Corps of the ABiH, under the command of Ramiz Dreković, a former JNA NCO from Sandžak ("province" in Turkish), Serbia's mainly Muslim province, wanted in Croatia for war crimes committed in Mostar in 1992, and suddenly a general. According to Hope, the Sandžak mafia's real loyalty was to Milošević, and Dreković was imposed on Izetbegović. This appointment, and more widely the arbitrary command structures, meant there were serious divisions and dissatisfaction within the 5th Corps from the very beginning[219]. The ABiH chief of staff, Rasim Delić, sentenced by the ICTY to three years' imprisonment for war crimes in 2008, visited Bihać from Sarajevo as part of a nationwide tour, and "couldn't believe" how poorly equipped the 5th Corps was, "worse than anywhere else in the country"[220]. There was also a HVO brigade in the Zavalje hills, south-west of Bihać, near the former high-tech military airport, which changed hands several times during the war. In these hills is the hamlet of Vučjak ("wolfhound"). Meanwhile, Velika Kladuša in the north of the pocket had become a thriving black market, for foodstuffs, arms and fuel[221].

[li] In 1996, while working with a team of monitors during the election campaign, we were looking for a particular candidate in a village near Bužim. Unable to find him, I decided to ask an old man I saw leaning on a farm gate if he knew where he lived. "Good afternoon", I greeted him. "No it isn't" he replied. "Here we say *salaam alejkum*" (when looking for another candidate, an imam, on the outskirts of Cazin, we had no trouble locating his house this time, but the only person we found there was one of his *hanume* ("wives"), chopping wood with an axe in the backyard; he was, she said, in the pub). At least one POW in Bužim prison was killed by being beaten with breeze blocks, for a DM 100 bet. The culprit was later appointed chief of police in Velika Kladuša.

Nekom rat a nekom brat ("every cloud has a silver lining"). Andrić describes the phenomenon during WWI in his short story *The Wedding*:

"Before the war, Huso had sold chickens and eggs, awaiting peasants at the entrance to the town and carrying his whole business in a basket on his back [...] When war was declared, there was a general alarm in this town on the border, some citizens were mobilised while others were arrested, crowds of IDPs rubbed shoulders with military transports, and the arrival of supplies and fantastic news only added to the general chaos [...] In all that confusion, the authorities formed a militia of idlers and drunken youths, mostly Gypsies. Then the town was treated to the sight of Huso Chicken, riding like a man possessed through the town on a wild horse, with a rifle on his back [...] For a while [after the front had moved away] he stayed on in the militia, patrolling the surrounding villages with the army, who were mostly foreigners and unfamiliar with the country, searching for hidden wheat and weapons. Travelling from one village to the next, he started to buy up sheep- and goatskins from the few remaining women and pensioners. They sold them to him cheaply, more as a bribe than a commodity. When the civilian police force was re-established and the militia disbanded, Huso continued his business, and with a speed that is only possible in wartime, he became rich, while the other traders disappeared or barely subsisted. His whole appearance and bearing changed: his unaccustomed feet were clad in new shoes; around his waist he wore a wide, brightly-coloured belt from Istanbul; around his neck hung a silver chain and a black ribbon, one bearing a watch and the other a large cloth purse from which he paid peasants and workers for goods and transport [...] Now no-one called him Huso Chicken, but according to his stamp and firm: Husein Huskić. His workers and anyone who needed his services called him Sir [...] From time to time, thanks to his connections and in return for skins, he would procure a cart of potatoes or jam, and distribute it to the poor [...] In such periods of transition, all relations are dislocated. Suddenly no-one knows any more what is allowed and what isn't. In such times, everything is possible, and even a chicken vendor can become a powerful authority"[222].

Bullets became an unofficial alternative currency in the Bihać pocket, value DM 1[223] (the new Bosnian dinars were not available in the Bihać pocket until October 1992, two months after the unbacked currency was launched elsewhere in the country, and only after Babo officially replaced the old Yugoslav dinars with the deutschmark to prevent hyperinflation[224]. When I first travelled to central Bosnia, the only local banknote available was the ten-dinar note, and all of them had "10,000,000" stamped on their face; their value, where used, was a *cener* ("DM 10"), but the deutschmark was the real currency[lii][225]). Bananas could be bought from French peacekeepers,

---

[lii] The Croatian currency introduced in 1994, the *kuna* ("marten"), was a medieval currency that had made a brief reappearance during the NDH. I once fuelled up at a petrol station near Konjic, and paid as usual in DM. The vendor opened a drawer containing a jumble of currencies, mainly dinars, DM, Austrian shillings, Slovenian *tolars* and *kune*, but also a ten-pound note, and put together my change the best he could. The Bosnian currency, the *konvertibilna marka* ("convertible DM", value half a euro), was introduced in the Federation and Republika Srpska in 1998, originally in the form of a voucher, and now as a banknote in its own right. On another occasion when I pulled up at a fuel station near Cazin, the

stationed there before the Bangladeshis, for DM 6 a piece (the Bangladeshis replaced them in April 1994, and were deployed with only half their equipment and one rifle between four, a state of affairs that took six months to rectify[226]). Some French peacekeepers were happy to exchange expensive equipment, even generators, for authentic Bosnian *trava* ("weed"). Even dead Serbs became a tradeable commodity at one stage[227]. Croatian ID cards were also in demand, as they facilitated passage out of Bosnia (Croats found that by selling their ID card they could buy a Bosnian one and still have change. Babo was happy to issue Bosnian ID cards with Muslim names to Croat refugees before the war started in Bosnia). In October, Babo again asked Izetbegović for funds, as Agrokomerc was being exhausted supporting the 5th Corps, despite the backing of its subsidiaries in Austria, Croatia and Slovenia. He was told funds would be provided if he accepted foreign fighters into the 5th Corps, which he refused to do. He was asked to travel to Sarajevo to attend presidency meetings, but refused, as the crisis in the Bihać pocket was so acute, and communication was possible via satphone (not to mention the dangers of travel in wartime Bosnia)[228]. The local SDS received reinforcements from elsewhere in Bosnia, and from Croatia, and started their offensive against Bihać in the south-west, the largest town in the enclave, on 1 December 1992, while the HVO were attacked directly from Croatia. The HVO and the 5th Corps held out, and a state of siege developed. Local elections were held, which Veladžić lost, but that didn't stop him staying in power. Babo called upon Izetbegović to dissolve the "illegal and illegitimate" parallel power structure of the regional assembly, but as was the case with the numerous other reports and initiatives he had sent to Sarajevo since moving his office to Velika Kladuša, the response was a deafening silence (Babo believes that his departure from Sarajevo was, as far as Izetbegović was concerned, the end of their relationship, but also a relief, because Izetbegović was now able to exercise total domination over the presidency, the remaining members of which were much more passive, if not compliant[liii])[229]. Meanwhile, the local economy ground to a standstill, and apart from intermittent power from the grids under SDS control, electricity depended on one small (and unreliable) hydroelectric power station on the Una north of Bihać, the "Una Kostela". Medical services soon suffered, and food became scarcer. Velika Kladuša became a magnet for IDPs from elsewhere within the pocket[230]. Those with a heightened survival instinct quickly realised that the real money was to be made by those holding power within the military/civilian power structures, trading not only in commodities, but also in intelligence and territory[231]. The northern border between Bosnia and Croatia is marked for 18 km east of Velika Kladuša, as far as Katinovac, by the river Glina, which eventually flows into the Kupa ("cup", but also "tile"), and this presented many ideal spots for the illicit movement of goods and people[232]. In January 1993, the Bosnian magazine *Slobodna Bosna* reported a crime wave in the Bihać pocket, involving everyone from

---

attendant greeted me with, "*Jebeš li šta?*" ("are you getting your oats?"). On yet another occasion, in Herzeg-Bosna, a bus deliberately blocked me head on as I pulled in to the pumps at a fuel station, and I had to reverse my truck out to let him through. Cliff Richard he wasn't. This initiative of Babo's resulted in an indictment for sedition from the Bihać prosecutor, which was dropped when Izetbegović adopted the same measure a few months later.

[liii] A report by the ombudsman from 2001 stated that in the Federation "there is still no proper division between the legislature, the executive and the judiciary". Mirvet recently asked the ombudsman why so few cases were successful in the courts, and was told it was because of a lack of evidence: certain public records are systematically transferred from Velika Kladuša to Bihać, and from there to Sarajevo, and are never seen again. Thus Babo's time in the Bosnian presidency could soon be expunged from the public record, and only his conviction for war crimes will remain.

individual members of the public to senior figures in the civil and military authorities, including the police (in August of that year, an information was laid against Veladžić and 30 others for theft of public reserves to the value of DM 960,000)[233]. In March 1993, as conditions became ever more chaotic (and as the HV achieved their first major victory, in Maslenica gorge), Babo floated the idea of implementing the proposals of the Vance-Owen plan (which had been eagerly accepted by the HDZ, rejected and then accepted under pressure by Izetbegović, because he knew the SDS would not sign it, and ultimately rejected by Karadžić, against the wishes of Milošević; Babo was sure he could win Karadžić over, but Izetbegović refused to let him try[234]). The plan was effectively the predecessor of Dayton, and provided for the country to be divided into "provinces": not only was it the only realistic option on the international table, but the war meant that the centralised state was anyway not functioning as a political or economic entity. Babo's initial idea was to name the province/canton after the WWII Bihać republic (see below), but he decided against this as it sounded too secessionist, which was not the aim[235]. The desperate position of the Bihać pocket was brought home to the leadership when the SVK captured Bosanska Bojna, near the border in the far north-east of the enclave. At dawn on 27 April, 11 days after the HVO's Ahmići massacre in central Bosnia (see below), VJ units from the Novi Sad and Niš Corps, in Serbia, masquerading as SVK, together with the Unit and local VRS, over 2,000 men with 20 tanks and artillery, overran the 5th Corps lines. Yet according to Hope, the 5th Corps had known the details of this offensive in advance, and also in advance, the Kladuša brigade, under instruction from the 5th Corps high command, had secretly prepared detailed maps of all their strong points and minefields, redeployed the "Scorpions"[liv] special forces unit away from the front, and removed mines to allow the SVK tanks through, before withdrawing itself. Only one undermanned battalion led by Hope insisted on remaining, and they successfully held up the *dušman* ("enemy") in Bojna[236]. The objective of the offensive, which was preceded by a football match between the SVK and Danish UNPROFOR[237], was to overrun Velika Kladuša, before advancing on Cazin to attack Bihać from the north (according to the EU monitors, the objective was to force the 5th Corps to divert men from the southern front[238]). A counterattack was launched by the lone battalion, supported by volunteers from Velika Kladuša and a battalion from Bosanska Otoka, and the SVK offensive was halted at Bojna. The Kladuša brigade redeployed there after a week[239] (in 1950, after the Peasants' Revolt, two local KPJ officials had attempted to set up a *Četnik* organisation in Bojna[240]; now a fundamentalist community has taken up residence there). According to Hope, Dudaković wanted to sacrifice Velika Kladuša in order to draw the SVK into a trap near Bihać, where they would be overstretched and could be destroyed. Ill feeling in Cazin, Bužim, and in particular Bihać with its (relatively) urban population towards Velika Kladuša, that had only been fuelled by the prosperity created by Agrokomerc, was nothing new[241]. The declaration of Bihać as a safe area the same month did little to reassure the Muslims (especially as its actual extent was undefined, and it did not appear to cover the whole Bihać pocket, such that Velika Kladuša was left exposed to the SVK on the northern border: in

---

[liv] Not the *Četnik* paramilitary unit of the same name. According to Legija, there was a whole menagerie of paramilitary units roving the countryside during the war: tigers, panthers, wolves, grey wolves, mad dogs, cobras, doves, larks, etc. HV paramilitary units had names such as the Apostles. Most of them were made up of weekend warriors, tourists from Belgrade (or Zagreb) looking for the chance to commit serious crimes with impunity, and according to Legija, were more trouble than they were worth.

November, the UN confirmed that the "safe area" was restricted to Bihać town[242]). On 20 July, four pro-Babo police officers were assassinated in an ambush in Bihać organised by the 5th Corps. Not only were the police divided along political lines, but Veladžić, the regional executive, was also seeking to challenge Babo's hegemony over the local economy[243]. Babo complained to Izetbegović about Veladžić's antics as early as August 1992, but Alija only feigned surprise[244]. The 5th Corps was increasingly being used by the SDA as a tool of repression of the civilian population within the enclave, and when the Owen-Stoltenberg barrel organ finally wheezed its last in August, Babo decided to take things into his own hands[lv245]. On 5 September, Agrokomerc stopped supporting the 5th Corps with logistics and supplies[246], and on 7 September, Babo launched an "initiative" for the formation of an autonomous region with the objective of ending the war, a model that could be rolled out elsewhere in the country, starting with Tuzla. The initiative, accompanied by rallies and a media campaign, received support throughout the enclave, especially from the police and the 5th Corps soldiers on the front line (according to the DNZ, it was signed by over 65% of residents on the electoral roll, 50,000 people, although it is alleged that not everyone signed voluntarily; meanwhile, the 5th Corps military police took a dim view, and prevented people collecting signatures[247]). At this time, the HV attempted to seize the Medak pocket, which resulted in at least 100 civilian deaths among local Serbs. The initiative was adopted unanimously at an extraordinary session of the regional assembly held on 13 September, and a new regional government was formed, made up of people from Bihać and Cazin, but mainly from Velika Kladuša[lvi]. There were heated debates in the enclave, including a fight in the Old Mosque in Cazin that had to be broken up by the military police. Babo publicly attacked the 5th Corps high command, and the mutual suspicion and distrust within the officer corps reached new heights, spilling over into the rank and file, while those who had been excluded from the existing power structure saw the opportunity for a new lease of life, on one side or the other[248]. According to Hope, Babo bought the 5th Corps from Dreković for DM 150,000. On 27 September, in the Velika Kladuša cinema, with 10,000 people outside, Babo proclaimed the enclave an autonomous region and the pocket was immediately polarised, with two competing local authorities, in Velika Kladuša and in Bihać[lvii249]. Izetbegović ordered the 5th Corps to

---

[lv] In January 1993, Bosnian deputy PM Turajlić was shot dead by the VRS in Sarajevo while sitting in an UNPROFOR vehicle, and Zgibniew Brzezinsky wrote in the *Washington Post* that the "negotiators [...] basic concept of dealing with thugs is to talk endlessly while assuring the aggressors that their use of force will not be matched by a counterforce". The response from Vance was "hogwash". Owen concludes his memoirs of the Yugoslav Wars: "The role of the negotiator is a complex one, and there can be no specific rules [...] The negotiator is a lightning conductor for governments. But a negotiator has to be able to move between the parties [...] The balance to be struck in international diplomacy between waiting for the ideal and settling for the achievable is never an easy one to find. Certainly I made mistakes, both of omission and of commission, during my tenure as Co-Chairman [...] As for the ICFY, I believe the record will show that we were the most consistent protectors of the interests of the Bosnian Muslim citizens". I was once on a beach that was struck by lightning, in Antigua in the Caribbean. It caused a great deal of consternation, and I felt the power of its boom through the sand where I was lying about 100 m away, but no harm was done. I was there looking for suitable premises for a regional warehouse. When someone is struck by lightning in the Balkans, they are half buried in a shallow trench to ensure any residual electricity leaves the body – despite the fact that 19th century pioneer of electricity Nikola Tesla was a Croatian Serb. His image it was on the Serb Borders republic dinars I first saw in Slunj. I once tried to pay for a beer with them in Cazin, but was told they weren't legal tender.

[lvi] Although according to the EU monitors, the opposite is the case, i.e. the initiative was not adopted.

[lvii] According to Owen: "Now Abdić, sensing Izetbegović was vulnerable to criticism from those who wanted peace, particularly the Bihać Muslim community, began to force the pace over local autonomy in that region. It looked as if there could develop a military confrontation between himself and those loyal to

close down the autonomous region, by force if necessary[250]. Babo founded a new party, the DNZ. After first blood drawn by the 5th Corps firing on civilians failed to have the desired effect, a high-level delegation including Rasim Delić, and the now grand mufti of Bosnia, Mustafa Cerić, flew in from Sarajevo for talks on 6 October, but failed to obtain the support of the civilian authorities in Bihać for the use of force, while Babo refused to meet them (or, according to Babo, they did not attempt to speak to him). Izetbegović then decided to play his *lil* ("tarot card"), and Cerić accused Babo of treason on Bihać radio[251]. On 12 October Babo formed the NOZB from the 5th Corps Kladuša brigade and the TA in Velika Kladuša (as well as a general mobilisation there, and an appeal to 5th Corps soldiers in Cazin to defect), under the command of a major. Those who didn't want to – or couldn't - be on board defected across the front line when and where they could[252]. While the new NOZB was soon well supplied, with arms from Tuđman and munitions from Milošević (all paid for, although ostensibly free of charge), its officer corps was mainly made up of Agrokomerc workers, with little or no military training other than their national service, and special forces units were relied upon for offensives[253]. This lack of a military structure would appear to give the lie to accusation that Babo had been preparing an armed uprising since the start of the war, or even earlier, and he had to seek assistance from outside. The VJ set up an intelligence office above the police station in Velika Kladuša[254]. The following month, Babo signed non-aggression pacts with the Bosnian HDZ (on 21 October in Zagreb), the Bosnian SDS (the following day in Belgrade under Milošević's auspices, based on the Owen-Stoltenberg plan, partition into a union of three republics within Bosnia, rejected by Izetbegović in September[255]), and the Croatian SDS (on the 28th)[256]. Babo has been much condemned for even holding meetings with the leaders of the Serbs (and the Croats), but he points out that he was flown to each of them by the UN, not least because he didn't have a passport (during his visit to Belgrade, he also visited Hakija Pozderac, who told him that Muslims shouldn't be fighting each other[257]). At the same time, he submitted four separate written proposals to the Bihać assembly on a peaceful resolution, none of which received a reply (meanwhile, on 30 October, 18 people including six policemen were killed in a shootout in Sarajevo between the SDA and their rivals in the Bosnian mafia, as Izetbegović set off on a belated tour of

---

him in Velika Kladuša, and General Dudaković, the able commander of the Bosnian 5th Corps with barracks in Cazin and Bihać. Izetbegović said of Abdić on Sarajevo television [via a poor interpreter, which may, perversely, have lent the message an obscure credibility among foreign listeners captivated by the fantasy of ancient Balkan nation states]: 'Muslims have finally succeeded in becoming state-building and constitutional people. Abdić is trying to pull us for at least fifty years back just to become a head of state. He is cleaving us to tribes, he is trying to feudalise us, he is giving our territories to Serbs and Croats'. The two men worked surprisingly effectively together at the end of July and early August in Geneva over the Invincible package; now the Izetbegović-Abdić relationship was sulphurous. We had urged Abdić to stay in the collective Presidency and warned him that his influence would go if he broke away, that he would be depicted by the world's press as a pawn of the Serbs while within the Presidency his influence was legitimate and benefited from his realism. Tragically, he was tempted by Milošević and Tuđman to break out on his own". According to the EU monitors: "The root causes of Abdić's declaration of autonomy lie in local factors. For many years the Bihać region has regarded itself as having a separate identity. But Abdić's action is motivated by an intense personal rivalry towards Izetbegović and deep-seated disagreements over the Bosnian Presidency's attitude towards the peace process [...] Abdić claims he has 80% of popular support but 50% is a more accurate estimate. Sympathy for him is balanced by concern for his methods [...] Abdić will remain a potent political force for as long as Izetbegović continues to encourage Muslim Bosnians that the war must continue. An early rapprochement between Abdić and Izetbegović may prove elusive and the present uneasy stand-off between Bihać and Velika Kladuša will therefore continue".

SDA territory in an attempt to drum up support for his suicidal *džihad*, "holy war", like Tsar Lazar 600 years before him. *Nema ništa bez rata* ("war is peace")[lviii258]. This split was a new fault line that shattered communities and families, and another bloody twist to the war, with brothers and even fathers and sons finding themselves on opposing sides of an active front line that claimed another 3,000 lives. The decision on what side to join was based for some on local loyalties; some thought the war with the Serbs was not inevitable and a peace could be reached, while others thought that any breach in national unity was treason; yet others simply did not want to leave their homes and joined the side holding power where they lived, while many were driven by the prospect of personal gain. Some saw in Babo the only alternative to Izetbegović's all-or-nothing policy. Sitting on the fence was not an option. For some, as in WWII, opportunities for *pljačka* ("looting") were a powerful motive[259]. Many people ended up changing sides, often more than once, especially after being captured (defecting was for many seen as preferable to being a POW). As George Orwell observed, "People forget that a soldier anywhere near the front line is usually too hungry, or frightened, or cold, or, above all, too tired to bother about the political origins of the war"[260].

The first clash was on 2 October in Skokovi. According to Hope, this happened when a group of civilians marching south to occupy the council and 5th Corps HQ in Cazin, and escorted by UNPROFOR, were stopped by 5th Corps supporters, while according to the award-winning *Oslobođenje*, under the headline "Abdić's police fire on civilians",

> "around ten thousand citizens of Bihać, Cazin, Bosanska Krupa, Bosanska Otoka and Bužim set off from a rally in support of BiH and the ABiH in Cazin towards Velika Kladuša to express their dissatisfaction with the formation of the so-called autonomous region of 'West Bosnia'" and were halted at a barricade in Skokovi by a "hail of bullets from heavy weapons"[261].

One person was taken to hospital in Bihać and died the next day. The following day, the DNZ's founding rally was held in Polje, and the 5th Corps military police started a crackdown on Babo's supporters[lix262]. They stopped buses, and tried to prevent people attending. Despite this, at least 20,000 people turned up. According to Hope, the first armed clash was on 4 October, near the school at Johovica, north of Šturlić, when a group of pro-Babo military police opened automatic fire on the 5th Corps, who had been sent to disperse a crowd that had gathered and were blocking the road to prevent Dudaković travelling to Velika Kladuša. In the resulting firefight, three 5th Corps soldiers were killed. But according to Tetin, the 5th Corps hardliners fired first that day, not only at Babo's supporters in the 5th Corps who had gone over to the crowd of civilians, but also at the VRS, from a M53/59 Praga mobile anti-aircraft gun (obsolete against modern aircraft, but devastating for other purposes[263]) that was

---

[lviii] Babo said that Izetbegović was a very poor public speaker, and that whenever they were both to address the same event, Alija would ask him to speak last, so that people wouldn't get up and walk out when he took the floor.

[lix] On the same day, 3 October 1993, 18 American soldiers were killed in Mogadishu in a failed unilateral humanitarian intervention, as dramatised in the 2001 film *Black Hawk Down*. Somalia became independent from Italy and the UK in 1960, but the government was overthrown in a *coup* in 1969. The military dictatorship was itself overthrown in 1991 by a coalition of clans, and Somaliland seceded. Since then, Somalia has effectively been without a government. Over 250,000 Somalis live in the Dadaab refugee camp in northern Kenya, which opened in 1992. The country is now facing starvation.

malfunctioning and rotating by itself. The VRS were not slow to respond. It had been leaked from within the 5th Corps that Dudaković was deploying with 1,200 men and a tank from the front to Johovica, and when word reached the people at the rally, some of them travelled to Johovica to stop him, while others travelled to Skokovi to block a march on Velika Kladuša from Bužim. The police set up barricades in Pećigrad and Skokovi, and the 5th Corps tried to disarm them in Skokovi, which resulted in another firefight. Some 5th Corps soldiers dressed in civvies then attempted to drive through the barricade, but were detained[264]. According to Sutko (see below), they travelled unarmed to Johovica with the objective of reaching a peaceful resolution, and when the 5th Corps opened fire, two brigades refused to obey orders and defected to protect the civilians. According to Mirvet, a woman and a child were killed at Johovica. He had travelled there with a truckload of food and drink for the protestors, who had spent the whole night there, and saw that, although most of the 5th Corps squaddies were in jovial mood, drinking with the civilians, Dudaković had a unit in full battle dress out of sight behind a wall. The 5th Corps started playing loud martial music, and when this was countered by a civilian blasting out *turbofolk* from a truck, it was fired upon. Until then, the event had had the character of a *teferič* (combined picnic, *dernek* ("beano") and voluntary work). Meanwhile, Babo called Izetbegović and invited him to travel to Polje, if necessary with UNPROFOR protection, to discuss the blockade of the enclave, but he refused. According to Babo, Dudaković could not have authorised such drastic action on his own, and the order must have come from higher up, namely from Izetbegović[265]. On the same day, "patriots" broke into and partly destroyed Velkaton's facilities in Velika Kladuša[266]. There was also an attack on the police station there, and one person was killed. According to Hope, the 5th Corps' commander masterminded this first bloodshed, acting on orders from extremists in Bihać, together with Babo's representatives, in a pub in Begove Kafane just outside Ćoralići (Begove Kafane was also the main headquarters of the Peasants' Revolt in 1950[267]). It had to be a fight to the death. As elsewhere in the country, the war quickly acquired a dynamic of its own, and slipped from the control of the civilian authorities. The full extent of the dark forces that were concentrated and took their pound of flesh that day in the hamlet of Johovica remains shrouded in mystery; but both Milošević and Tuđman stood to benefit from the Muslims being divided and ultimately destroying each other, while Izetbegović was determined to stamp out any dissent; as for Babo, his motives at that time of shifting tectonic plates, high stakes and innocent blood remain obscured by rumour and propaganda, but it appears that the only option left open to him was total war[lx268]. More fundamentally, Babo faced the same existential question as Hamlet, not only in terms of his career as a businessman and a politician, but as the *ataman*[lxi] of his people. The usurpation of their democratic rights, compounding the violent theft of their livelihoods six years earlier, called out for justice and demanded action. Nor can Babo's brother's death in 1987 be ignored, even as his people came out of their homes to bear on their frail shoulders the destiny of their

---

[lx] Babo wrote that, "Even today I'm convinced that at least the intra-Muslim war could and should have been avoided. Alija's determination not to talk to people who didn't think like him was such that there was very little space for any kind of dialogue, but it did create fertile ground for conflict and war". He also stresses the significance of the fact that the initial shooting was not restricted to Johovica, in Velika Kladuša district, but also occurred in Skokovi, in Cazin district, i.e. the violent suppression of popular dissent was not an isolated incident.
[lxi] Cossack chieftain appointed by popular acclamation.

day, as their fathers and grandfathers had done. According to former Yugoslav chess grandmaster Dr Kržišnik-Bukić,

> "The separatism of this area cannot be explained merely by the political ambitions of the undisputed leader of part of the Bosnian Borders, possibly Europe's last feudal lord. The event can only be understood if looked at in its wider, philosophical-anthropological, non-ethnic/religious perspective. If due account is taken of the underlying historical and geographical conditions, the deeply-rooted traditional patriarchal mentality of the population and their security interests, then the genesis of Fikret 'Babo' Abdić's ideological and political concept can be understood; indeed, the concept can even be defended and advocated. It was forged in the crucible of the relationship between the immediate and the long-term interests of the Bosnian Borders. In such cases, there is always a dilemma which cannot be answered unequivocally in advance. What is certain is that in the prevailing interlinked conditions, any real expectations were extremely difficult to conceive of"[269].

More pragmatically, ABiH chief of staff Halilović, originally from Sandžak, acquitted by the ICTY of war crimes in 2005[lxii], wrote that

> "As soon as he left [Sarajevo], he made contact with the Serbs. Abdić attempted to organise an autonomous region politically. His autonomous region had less powers than the cantons do today, and so Alija should not have made it a problem. Perhaps he should have talked about it[lxiii]. Abdić didn't create an army, but he wanted to reshape the Borders politically. We tried to stop that, because Tuzla had also sought autonomous status [...] The danger existed that Bosnia would fall apart politically and that what we had defended with arms would unravel. We tried to convince Abdić of this. Duraković [not Dudaković, but the 5th Corps deputy chief of staff] then attacked Abdić's group, and then the soldiers who supported him got involved [...] Fikret was attacked and started to defend himself, but he defended himself in the wrong way, by making contact with our enemies. He wasn't ready militarily and he only wanted to take political control of the region"[270].

According to Hope, Milošević and Tuđman's plan A was for Babo to achieve victory in the enclave, which would allow them to reconstitute it to suit their interests, while their plan B was for the enclave to be dominated by the Sandžak mafia who controlled the 5th Corps and the AID, which would allow them to achieve the same result. In both outcomes, the local Muslims would be the losers. For the SDS, the Muslims were an immediate thorn in the side, tying up large numbers of men, and

---

[lxii] Halilović, who fell foul of Izetbegović by publicly disagreeing with him, wrote in his memoirs that "I had the good fortune to be tried by professionals, who refused to take things for granted and insisted on examining all the evidence presented from all angles. And once the 'security service' submissions had been examined from all angles, they were treated for what they were: rubbish. I can only imagine what would have happened if the ICTY had accepted at face value the service's 'evidence' that I was in contact with criminals, encouraged them to revolt and organised a *coup* with them just to get the top job in the ABiH, and that, aware of their reputation, I took them to Herzegovina and later covered up their crimes".
[lxiii] According to Babo, Izetbegović's intolerance, and refusal to negotiate or compromise with anyone, was one of the causes of the outbreak of the war in Bosnia.

obstructing communications between Croatia and Serbia, while for the HDZ, they were a historical aberration going back to 1592, that needed to be corrected. In any case, as Dr Kržišnik-Bukić observed in her seminal work on the Peasants' Revolt (described in an anonymous phone call during its preparation as the "Satanic Verses"[271]), "The peasantry is a tried and tested, rewarding experimental medium that absorbs any failures. It is the cheapest possible sacrifice in any political machinations" (and as Legija wrote, "in war, human lives are, unfortunately, the cheapest")[272]. Soon afterwards, Dreković was sacked, according to Hope for gambling away the 5th Corps budget playing poker in another pub (while according to Babo, it was because he was not robust enough in his opposition to the autonomous region)[273]. He was replaced by his deputy, Atif Dudaković, previously a JNA major, and a defector from Mladić's artillery unit in Knin who had seen action in Zadar. Dudaković had originally considered joining Babo, but couldn't resist the glory of high command offered him by Izetbegović[274]. Curiously, there were several highly qualified locals with experience of senior JNA rank, but they were all passed over. Dudaković was born near Gradiška, north of Banja Luka and outside the enclave, which appears to have been a requirement of the job: Izetbegović didn't trust the locals, and needed his own pit bull on the ground. As in the NOZB, there were those in the 5th Corps who quickly realised that not only personal security but also wealth and power were to be found in the civilian and military power structures; but instead of "*Živio Babo!*", this time the password to the alternative reality above the law was "*Allahu ekber!*"[275] ("God is supreme"; describing the situation in the Borders on the eve of the Peasants' Revolt, Milan Božić's son Stevo said: "The police and other people in the authorities had everything. Guns, meat and *rakija* went together, while ordinary people were dying of hunger"[276]). Hope said he always preferred to be on the front line rather than in the hornets' nest of HQ, among other things because it was safer: anyone who stood out for any reason, either for learning too much, or just being good at their job, was liable to be terminated. In 2006, video footage surfaced that appears to show Dudaković ordering the execution of two NOZB POWs in 1994 (according to Tetin, Dudaković once opened fire with a tank on a group of NOZB POWs, killing six of them, and in 2010, he laid an information against him at the ICTY office in Sarajevo)[277]. Videos of executions at Srebrenica surfaced at the same time. Dudaković was now forced to commit troops along a new front line at the same time as facing increased shelling of Bihać and Bosanska Krupa by the VRS[278].

On 15 October, the NOZB occupied Cazin for one day, but was unable to win over the Cazin brigade, and was pushed back by the Bihać brigade. The NOZB occupied Crnaja, between Šturlić and Liskovac, in December (the population had been 93% Muslim and 7% Serb in 1991: most of the Serbs left at the end of 1991 and the beginning of 1992, to Vojvodina, Vukovar or Slunj. Their houses were not burnt down)[279]. On 26 and 27 December 1993, NOZB special forces unsuccessfully attempted to assassinate Veladžić[280]. According to Hope, on 11 January, Vojislav Šešelj's *Četnik* paramilitaries (see below) arrived to assist the NOZB, but they were more interested in raping Muslim women, even the wives of NOZB soldiers, than fighting. Babo wanted to recruit their best Serb officers, but they weren't interested (Babo maintained a strict separation of his forces from SDS forces on the ground)[281]. On 13 January, talks started on a ceasefire, and on 29 January Izetbegović offered the NOZB an amnesty, valid until 10 February[282]. The amnesty was rejected, although the ceasefire held until 16 February and was used by both sides to regroup, and by the 5th Corps to increase actions against the VRS in the south and the east (the first

Sarajevo market bombing happened at this time, see below)[283]. Babo wanted an exchange of prisoners before any talks, while Dudaković wanted control of all military structures before starting any political negotiations. Babo proposed holding a referendum in the pocket on whether it should be run as an autonomous region or under the previous regional assembly model, and a white paper to that end was delivered to the assembly in Bihać, UNPROFOR, UNHCR and the EU monitors[284]. On 6 February, a pro-5th Corps rally was held in the Velika Kladuša town centre: it attracted a lot of hostility, and the 400 participants dispersed when it looked like there would be bloodshed. Some of them were later arrested. The same day, the VRS renewed their offensive all along the Una on both sides of Bihać, with the objectives of pushing the 5th Corps back over the river in the north, capturing the Kostela power station, and cutting the town off from Cazin[285]. On 16 February, the NOZB launched an offensive and pushed the front line south[286]. Meanwhile, having failed to achieve their initial objectives, the VRS started heavy shelling of the south of the pocket, with the objective of pinning the 5th Corps down along the Una, in order to allow the NOZB a free hand in the north (it was later reported that Mladić was organising a combined assault on the pocket from all sides[287]). On 17 February, 1,000 people sought refuge at the French UNPROFOR base in Ćoralići, but were turned away[288]. On 24 February, Babo signed a peace agreement in Belgrade with Karadžić and Martić, again under Milošević's auspices[289], while continuing to meet regularly with Tuđman in Zagreb as a representative of the Bosnian presidency. On 7 March, the VRS destroyed the Bihać post office, the local communications hub, with tank fire, killing three people[290]. On 31 March, Dudaković agreed to a ceasefire with the VRS, which would allow him to concentrate his efforts on the north. The ceasefire only lasted two days[291]. In March, the NOZB had a series of successes pushing towards Cazin from the north-west, according to Hope to the general relief of the rural population there. Meanwhile, neither side was winning on the 5th Corps' front with the VRS, despite fierce fighting and heavy losses on both sides. On 13 April, the NOZB launched another offensive, supported by SVK and VRS artillery, which ground to a halt 1 km south of Todorovo[292]. Having failed to break through the 5th Corps' lines, the NOZB and SVK started to rely on artillery[293]. There was a series of unsuccessful NOZB attacks that month. Despite superior firepower, the NOZB did not have the necessary officer corps, and units acted independently of each other[294]. Hope later said that Babo was good at everything except waging war. Meanwhile, in the 5th Corps, the Bužim brigade, with its links to fundamentalism, was particularly jealous of its independence[295]. On 18 April, the Agrokomerc production lines were restarted in Polje, the HVO held a parade in Bihać, and Milovanović stated that the VRS' priority was now the Sava basin in the north east of the country[296]. On 20 April, there was a demonstration in Bihać against the UN's handling of the situation around Goražde (see below)[297]. On 8 May, Tuđman agreed under US pressure to stop supporting Babo. The next day, the NOZB attacked the 5th Corps in the west, in an attempt to cut the road from Cazin[298]. At this time, Babo announced that his armed forces and police were part of the Federation[299]. There was another NOZB offensive at the beginning of June, again unsuccessful. Babo then imposed a blockade on the southern part of the enclave. There were restrictions on UNHCR convoys, who were also "taxed" by the VSK, but FTC's trucks kept running, untaxed[300]. On 2 June, the 5th Corps took the initiative for the first time by attacking Liskovac, and the following day attacked Pećigrad[301]. That month, a Sudanese *Mudža* was flown in to assist the 5th Corps with training, and set himself up in Bužim[302]. There were as many as 300 Islamic foreign fighters active in the enclave at the height of the war, most of them in the Bužim brigade's *Hamze* and *Gazije* ("war heroes") units, the successors to the *Handžar Divizija* established by the regional assembly in 1992, of which Babo warned Izetbegović in vain (the *Mudžahedin* were usually smuggled in via Croatia, disguised as aid workers. As late as 2006, Dudaković expressly denied there were any foreign fighters in the 5th Corps)[303]. On 10 June, after a week of heavy rain, the NOZB occupied territory around Pećigrad and Skokovi, but lost it as well as territory around Todorovo in a counterattack[304]. Two HV Mi-8 helicopters, disguised with the Red Cross protected emblem[lxiv], started nightly runs flying munitions into Ćoralići from Croatia for the 5th Corps, and it was rumoured that Iranian aircraft were flying in men and equipment from central Bosnia[305]. At the end of June, the 5th Corps cut Pećigrad off from Velika Kladuša, when a NOZB brigade disobeyed orders and withdrew[306]. The 5th Corps offensive began to run out of steam, and Operation Liberty 94 was devised, whereby the NOZB would occupy territory behind 5th Corps lines by striking from Croatia, preparing the way for an assault on Bihać from the north. The plan was approved by Martić, and Polish UNPROFOR paid no notice to NOZB trucks driving through Izačić in early July[307]. However, 5th Corps intelligence did notice. Dudaković devised a counter-operation, an elaborate hoax with the objective of arresting or assassinating Babo: Operation Tiger Liberty 94. A group of senior officers, including the commander of the Bihać brigade, Hamdo "Tiger" Abdić (no relation), crossed the front line, managed to arrange a meeting with Babo, and convinced him they had defected. They set up headquarters near Izačić, controlling the border crossing into Croatia, and received supplies from Babo via the SVK. The following day, 6 July, there was a series of explosions in Bihać, and the local radio reported there had been a *coup*, and that Dudaković had surrendered to the VRS. Other local radio stations, in particular Velkaton, spread the news further, and by the end of the day, the *coup* was declared a success. Now it was expected that Babo would travel to Izačić to take part in the celebrations, at which point he would be detained or shot. But ever cautious of security, he never arrived. When the plot started to unravel on 9 July, a SVK liaison officer was shot trying to make his exit, as was Babo's senior security officer[308]. This was a major blow for Babo[309]. By mid-July, his funds were starting to run low, and the NOZB no longer had the material advantage[310]. But he tells the story rather differently: Tiger's brother, Hakija, defected from the 5th Corps, and in a meeting with Zahid, a friend of his, reported that 100 men were ready to follow him, and more importantly, that he thought it would be possible to negotiate a peace settlement with Tiger. A meeting was arranged with Tiger in Velika Kladuša, where he travelled under truce via SVK territory, and where his request for DM 40 grand in cash as a sign of goodwill was granted, but the outcome was not satisfactory. Nevertheless, peace talks were arranged in Izačić, where the NOZB delegation, unaware of the staged attack in Bihać, the purpose of which was to justify what followed, were captured on the orders of Dudaković, and three of the five, including the SVK liaison officer, were brutally executed. The other two were badly beaten, and then beasted in Dudaković's presence, which included perching naked with arms extended on the bonnet of a jeep as it drove around Bihać. Video of this stunt appeared on the internet in 2006[311]. The 5th Corps was determined to destroy the very idea of an autonomous region by exclusively military means[312]. A three-stage

---

[lxiv] The Red Cross is not a religious symbol, but is the Swiss flag reversed. It (and the Red Crescent, adopted as a concession to the Ottomans in 1877 during the Crimean War) confers protection with legal force in IHL, and its use is strictly controlled.

operation, also called Operation Liberty 94, was devised: the first stage was to take Pećigrad; the second stage was to liberate all the territory south of Pećigrad; and the final stage would be to occupy Velika Kladuša[313]. At the same time, the 5th Corps were to hold defensive positions against the VRS[314]. The fall of Pećigrad was preceded by a general mobilisation in Velika Kladuša, including *komunalci* ("public utilities staff"), and a withdrawal of tanks to Velika Kladuša[315]. On 29 July, Pećigrad was surrounded by the 5th Corps, and 1,000 NOZB men dug in (one brigade managed to escape west and withdraw via SVK territory to Velika Kladuša, accompanied by .7,000 civilians)[316]. The next day, the besiegers turned off the water supply to the town[317]. On the night of 30/31 July, there was a failed attempt at a breakout towards Velika Kladuša[318]. Dudaković held talks with the besieged "separatists", and on 4 August, 972 men surrendered, and were taken to the 5th Corps barracks in Bihać (among them were Tetin and Hope)[319]. The next day, they had to perform a march past in the Bihać football stadium in front of the local military and civilian dignitaries, and the mob. They saluted the Bosnian flag, but refused to salute Dudaković, even when they were made to do a lap of honour and given a second chance to do so[320]. Meanwhile, on 9 August, the 5th Corps had gained control of the whole Cazin district, and the NOZB began to organise the defence of Velika Kladuša[321]. On 12 August, Babo organised a press conference via satphone in Zagreb, and proposed a Mostar-type settlement, with the whole pocket a EU protectorate (Mostar was administered by the EU from June 1994 onwards). Peace talks hosted by UNPROFOR on 14 and 17 August failed[322]. The second stage of Operation Liberty 94 was concluded on 18 August[323]. On 19 August, the 5th Corps launched an all-out attack and overran the NOZB lines. After an attempt at more talks on 20 August failed, on 21 August the 5th Corps entered Velika Kladuša, and Babo flew out by helicopter[324]. The NOZB withdrew to the Croatian Borders, with cover from SVK artillery, to whom they had to surrender their weapons[325]. The "First Autonomy" was over.

NOZB POWs were drafted into the 5th Corps, mainly into the new Kladuša brigade, but many of them preferred to desert to the Croatian Borders, where most of the civilian population had gone[326]. Anyone suspected of harbouring sympathies for Babo was dealt with swiftly and ruthlessly[327]. The Kladuša brigade was viewed with suspicion and hostility by the officer corps, and was consistently deployed to the heaviest fighting (by 19 March, of 338 men who had joined the brigade since 16 November, only 47 were still fit for duty)[328]. Meanwhile, the black market with the SVK continued, and wholesalers would turn up with tractors from Cazin and Bužim at the border crossing at Čikin Most, near Katinovac, to load up with goods for retail. High-value military hardware was also available, such as Russian Strela-2 ("arrow") rockets, for DM 20,000 or near offer[329]. On 1 September, there was a major SVK attack from Bosanska Bojna towards Bužim, which was pushed back. However, it later transpired that the objective of this attack was to tie down the 5th Corps in support of the VRS's Operation Beech 94. On 9 September, two Orkan rockets were fired into Velika Kladuša from VRS territory[330], and on 12 September, the VRS attacked towards Bužim from the south and pushed back the 5th Corps. But the 5th Corps successfully counterattacked by encircling the VRS and attacking their rear. The VRS were routed and suffered heavy losses: Mladić was wounded and barely escaped with his life, abandoning his personal vehicle[331]. At the beginning of October, the SVK started shelling Velika Kladuša[332]. On 27 October, the 5th Corps launched a two-pronged attack to the south and east outside the pocket, a technical breach of the "safe areas" doctrine, as the Russians pointed out to the UN security council, and reached the outskirts of Bosanska Krupa, while the HVO reached as far south as Kulen Vakuf, parallel to Udbina. Meanwhile, in central Bosnia, at this time the HV retook Kupres, southwest of Bugojno, from the VRS, who had captured it in 1992[333]. However, the 5th Corps lines were now overstretched, and on 4 November the HVO withdrew from Kulen Vakuf, and the next week the 5th Corps was back within the limits of the pocket, having also lost the bridge in Bosanska Krupa[334]. Meanwhile, on the morning of 16 November, Operation Spider started with two attacks by the NOZB supported by the SVK and VRS, preceded by heavy shelling (the NOZB had been rearmed, but not with their own weapons, which had been sold, a few days previously[335]). Legija's two initial objectives were Velika Kladuša and Vrnograč, but after heavy fighting on the first day, he decided to concentrate on taking Velika Kladuša[336]. On 18 November, napalm and cluster bombs were dropped on Bihać (the napalm failed to ignite), and the next day a VRS plane crashed into a block of flats in Cazin[337]. This was followed by NATO air strikes against the airfield in Udbina, and against VRS missile sites near Bosanska Otoka and Dvor after a VRS radar system locked onto two British Harriers near Bihać (they destroyed it). The VRS responded by taking peacekeepers hostage in central Bosnia[338]. In the west, the NOZB pushed through Bugar ("Bulgarian", whose Serb population was cleansed by the *Ustaše* in 1941[339]), 10 km west of Cazin and near the Croatian border, north of Izačić, towards Cazin. In the north, Velika Kladuša was attacked simultaneously from Cetingrad and Maljevac, while the road to Vrnograč was attacked at various points as far as Bosanska Bojna to prevent reinforcements being sent from there[340]. Maljevac held, while from Cetingrad the NOZB advanced as far as Polje. Heavy fighting continued on the main road into the town beyond the Maljevac border crossing, exposed to fire from the castle. The 5th Corps retreated to Vrnograč and Todorovo, while continuing to hold Trnovi, the Velika Kladuša suburb east of the town centre, and north of Polje[341]. The HVO had been defeated at the border crossing from Cetingrad[342], and had to be supported by the 5th Corps around Zavalje. On 19 November, the Unit attacked from Katinovac, supported by helicopters. By the end of the 22nd, the NOZB held the territory west of the main road from Velika Kladuša to Pećigrad, while fighting continued in the town[343]. On the 24th, the NOZB pushed south-west of Cazin, and by early December, there was street fighting in Bihać[344]. The VRS came within 500 m of Bihać hospital (the pocket's main health facility, which was seriously damaged in a fire in 2013), and Babo told me that Ganić called him and asked him to intercede with Milošević to prevent a bloodbath in the town. Babo flew to Belgrade by helicopter, along the river Sava, and as a result of his advocacy, Mladić's special forces units were replaced by the regular VRS, and the offensive against Bihać sputtered out. SVK and VRS forces were then summoned south to deal with the HV, who were threatening Bosansko Grahovo, across the border from Knin[345]. After weeks of fierce deadlock, on 17 December the 5th Corps withdrew from Velika Kladuša, preceded by a large part of the civilian population[346] (Legija's initial objective had been to take Velika Kladuša within a week, and Cazin within three[347]).

The previous civilian population returned from SDS territory in time for New Year, and what became known as the "Second Autonomy" began. Rather than push south down the main road towards Bihać, Legija's next strategic objective was Vrnograč, which would mean a direct confrontation with the Bužim brigade[348]. On Christmas Eve the NOZB, supported by the Unit and VJ paratroopers, launched a major assault, accompanied by SVK shelling of Cazin and Ćoralići[349]. On 31 December, Izetbegović (and Rasim Delić), Karadžić (and Mladić) and Krešimir

Zubak (Mate Boban's successor as president of Herzeg-Bosna, see below, and president of the Federation, and Tihomir Blaškić, HVO commander, sentenced to nine years by the ICTY in 2000) signed Jimmy Carter's cessation of hostilities agreement[lxv]. Babo had also indicated he would be on board[350]. The 5th Corps attacked the VRS near Bihać hospital in breach of the agreement on 13 January, and in January and February, the NOZB gradually gained territory around Velika Kladuša[351]. The day after international women's day, the HVO commander in the enclave, General Šantić, disappeared, allegedly at Dudaković's orders. With Vrnograč coming under pressure, Dudaković carried out a surprise diversionary strike into Lika, breaking through a part of the front that had been quiet for more than a year, near the former Bihać military airport, before withdrawing when Legija reluctantly diverted forces there to protect Slunj[352]. According to Hope, in fighting on 21-22 February there was an incident when the NOZB disarmed and then released captured 5th Corps soldiers, telling them to run for it: if the Unit coming up behind got hold of them, they would be executed[353]. In early March, the 5th Corps attempted to break through enemy lines into Velika Kladuša. The action failed, as the NOZB were now stronger than they had been before, with a new professional commander, Colonel Kobac ("sparrowhalk", a former football referee) from the Unit, and had Legija's direct support[354]. On 6 March, a new military alliance with the blessing of the US and Germany was announced in Zagreb, with the HV, the HVO and the ABiH to operate under a joint command[355]. From April onwards, the SVK and VRS wanted to focus their efforts on the approaching threat of the HV from Livno in the south, but they were overruled by Legija and told that Operation Spider was the priority, and that Bihać had to be captured first[356]. On 6 April, the 5th Corps in the north of the pocket withdrew to better defensive lines[357]. On 14 April, the NOZB attacked towards Pećigrad and Vrnograč[358]. At a Croatian-Bosnian SDS summit in Sanski Most, Mladić was instructed to push for final victory in the absence of a political solution, "as supreme commander of the Serb forces" (Karadžić had earlier allegedly attempted to have him replaced)[359]. There were further NOZB attacks that month, preceded by heavy shelling. By this time the NOZB held the north-west corner of the enclave[360]. In May, after Operation Flash, the 5th Corps pushed the VRS back in the south-east and the east of the enclave, and consolidated their hold on the west bank of the Una (on 6 May, the VRS shelling of Sarajevo restarted, with eight deaths near the entrance to the tunnel, see below, after a five-month lull. There was also increased fighting between the HVO and the VRS in the Sava basin, and on 25 May, 71 people were killed by shelling in Tuzla, just as Mladić started his second offensive against Goražde)[361]. Kiwi travelled to Krupa at this time and told me that some of the houses on the right bank, that had been converted into billets and cover, were full of filth and shit. According to Andrić, "All armies in the world create such infrastructure for their own exclusive objectives and immediate needs; and afterwards, looked at in the perspective of civvy street and the requirements of peacetime, they appear absurd and irrational"[362] (and as George Orwell observed in Spain, "every room that was not in use had been turned into a latrine – a frightful shambles of smashed furniture and excrement")[363]. Munitions and basic commodities

---

[lxv] The former US president, who had a successful track record of peace negotiations, averting a civil war in Haiti in 1994, was invited to become involved in the Balkans in a surprise move by Karadžić. The notion that the since-convicted war criminal was able to initiate a window for peace, while Izetbegović consistently found excuses for walking away from talks, flies in the face of received wisdom. Attempts to extend the agreement were scuppered by the ICTY's announcement in April that it was investigating Karadžić and Mladić for war crimes.

were running short in the enclave, and the helicopter runs from Croatia had stopped[364]. On 20 June, the NOZB finally took Vrnograč, preceded by shelling from Bosanska Bojna and Katinovac[365]. Legija considered that he had broken the back of the 5th Corps. His next objective was Cazin, to confine Dudaković to Bihać. This was followed up by an attack towards Bužim (which gave the 5th Corps the impression that Legija's objective was to take the town and destroy its notorious brigade before proceeding to Bosanska Krupa)[366]. The 5th Corps started moving reserves and hardware there, as if preparing for the decisive battle of the enclave[367]. In the largest single action of Operation Spider, the NOZB started a push south from Velika Kladuša and Vrnograč in July, preceded by heavy shelling, and missiles, even as Delić toured the ABiH front lines in central Bosnia in preparation for the upcoming US-backed offensive[368]. On 13 July, two days after the fall of Srebrenica, the NOZB and SVK pushed through from Slunj towards Johovica, on the road to Šturlić. In the east, held up on the road to Bužim, they focused their push against Pećigrad[369]. On 19 July, the SVK and VRS launched a major attack, Operations Sword 95 and Shield 95, with the objective of taking Cazin and then Bihać. There was major shelling from Slunj, including SAM-6 missiles, and the NOZB/SVK overran Johovica. Simultaneously there was an attack towards Bužim by the VRS, but it ran out of steam due to lack of fuel. The next day, the NOZB overran Šturlić and Tržac (and Crnaja), with heavy losses, and turned towards Cazin (Tržac was the scene of an important victory by the Turks in 1578[370]). On the 22nd, they continued towards Begove Kafane and captured Liskovac, to the north-west of Cazin. The same day, Izetbegović signed the Split agreement with Tuđman, which gave the HV the green light to operate in the Bihać pocket[371]. Legija was now 6 km from Cazin, closing in from three sides. But Babo took the decision to halt the offensive (according to Legija, this was because they had overstretched themselves, and only had enough men to hold a defensive line; but Babo says the real reason was to avoid a bloodbath in Cazin)[372]. The 5th Corps transferred men from Bužim to defend Cazin, and the Bužim brigade carried out a diversionary attack towards Drvar in the south, threatening to link up with the 7th Corps in central Bosnia. The Unit was forced to deploy via Dvor and Bosanska Krupa to counter this[373]. The "safe area" of Žepa fell on 25 July. The next day, the Republic of West Bosnia was declared. Looking ahead, Babo proposed the creation of a decentralised Bosnian state for a transitional period, with the final decision on its constitution to be taken at a later date. He predicted that Agrokomerc would quickly be able to return to full production capacity as soon as the conflict ended, with West Bosnia a free trade zone[374]. Meanwhile, the shelling of Cazin continued into August, but the 5th Corps held their positions. With the Cazin front in deadlock, another attack was launched towards Bužim[375]. On 3 August, the day before Operation Storm, Martić requested a meeting with Dudaković, which was refused[376].

Legija travelled to Velika Kladuša from near Bužim on the morning of Operation Storm to find out what was happening, as HV artillery could be heard in the distance and his comms were dead, and discovered utter chaos. After arranging trucks for his men, he ran into Babo in his deserted office in Grupex, who advised him to leave while he still could, as it was "all over". He drove to the Operation Spider HQ in Petrova Gora, only to find it abandoned, and so returned to Kladuša, from where he left with his men via Dvor, taking the time to escort refugees from Glina[377]. On 5 August, the 5th Corps launched a partly successful counter-attack. The Bihać brigade linked up with the HV in Rakovica in Croatia (after initially clashing with them), and over the next two days, the SVK was driven out of the enclave. A vast amount of hardware was captured. The 5th Corps took part in joint operations with the HV in Croatia, and also pushed north-east to Dvor on the border to block the SVK withdrawal (the SVK's only escape routes from Croatia were via Bosansko Grahovo and Dvor)[378]. It is alleged that nine disabled Serbs and their carer, a Croat woman, were killed by HV troops in the school in Dvor on 8 August, as portrayed in the 2016 Danish film *Massacre at Dvor*, which is banned in Croatia. On 2 March 2016, the Croatian newspaper *Večernji List* blamed the 5th Corps for the atrocity, and Danish UNPROFOR for failing to stop it[379]. General Izet Nanić, the Bužim brigade commander, and also the best man of the NOZB's 2IC, had been killed just west of Dvor three days previously, and the killings were said to be revenge for that[lxvi][380] (the Croatian government now plans to build a nuclear waste storage site in Dvor, to the militant dismay of local communities on both sides of the border). The 5th Corps then turned their attention to Velika Kladuša. While former draft-dodgers volunteered for the final scene of the intra-Muslim war with its promise of rich pickings, 5th Corps forces in Croatia attempted to encircle the NOZB, but the column of refugees encountered the HV first[381]. The first units to enter Velika Kladuša on 8 August spread disinformation about summary executions by the *Mudžahedin*, with the objective of encouraging even more civilians to leave[382]. Eleven people were killed in the town over the next few days, and there was looting of business premises and private homes[383] (the stock in our warehouse was not looted, but the truck parked inside was cannibalised – not by the 5th Corps, but by a French NGO we had allowed to share our warehouse and who needed a new battery for their own *bagnole* ("conveyance"), a former Securicor *kombi* ("van") they called a *voiture blindée* ("armoured vehicle"). As they say in the Balkans, "*Ko će kome nego svoj svome/Šaj aves amal e džuklesko*" ("keep your friends close")[384]. After this we moved our warehousing to Cazin to better respond to the new reality). A unit was formed of 5th Corps squaddies under the auspices of extremists to prevent the return of the NOZB to Velika Kladuša, even as real fighting continued to the south and east of the enclave, in Operation Sana 95[385]. Former NOZB soldiers now in the 5th Corps found themselves constantly deployed to the most dangerous positions of this operation, without a break[386].

Throughout the SDA-HDZ war (and indeed afterwards), the local HVO maintained a strategic, if sometimes strained, alliance with the 5th Corps and, despite the fact that the local commander, General Šantić, initially voiced support for Babo only to later disappear (and the fact that the "joint statement" signed in October 1993 by Babo and Mate Boban, leader of the Bosnian HDZ, provided for the HVO in the Bihać pocket to come under the NOZB, even as the Sarajevo HVO was "assimilated" into the ABiH the following month[387]), observed studious neutrality in respect of the intra-Muslim conflict, as Tuđman hedged his bets[lxvii][388]. Tuđman finally signed the

---

[lxvi] The popular front-line general, a former JNA lieutenant, was killed in circumstances that have not been fully explained, in an area where according to Babo there were no Serbs (the official version is that he was shot in the neck in close-quarters fighting with a group of fleeing VRS squaddies who ran into him and his bodyguards). According to Hope, Nanić's success in the field made him a threat to Dudaković, while Babo speculates that he might have found out too much about the 5th Corps' dark side, and was "fragged". The fall of Vrnograč had also resulted in a major row between Nanić and Dudaković. Legija, who while evacuating was told the news by the SVK, who claimed the credit, said, "While Nanić was the enemy, he was a serious opponent and worthy of respect. Whatever else, he fought all those years in unequal conditions for his home and his ideas, and gave his life for them, and that deserves respect".

[lxvii] The controversial and obnoxious commander of the HVO in the enclave, a former corporal and a friend and former business partner of Tuđman's and answering only to him (he was originally infiltrated into the enclave on foot via Izačić by HV special forces operating behind SVK lines, but was often to be

Split agreement with Izetbegović two weeks before Operation Storm. After the war, the Croatian consulate in Bihać would approve anyone's application for a *domovnica* ("Croatian certificate of nationality") for DM 500, no *krsni list* ("baptismal certificate") required (see below). Enes got one (in 1998, Babo obtained 700 work permits for Bosnian Agrokomerc workers deployed to Croatia). On the back of the certificate of nationality, which was transferrable to the holder's children, a Croatian passport could be obtained. As a result, a large proportion of the population in the former enclave looked to Zagreb rather than Sarajevo as their natural economic and political patron, which formed and continues to be part of the HDZ's long-term strategy for Bosnia (Zagreb is anyway only 106 km from Velika Kladuša, while Sarajevo is 364 km away, a six-hour drive on country roads). It also meant that Tuđman had more voters, and party activists do not hesitate to cold-call numbers in neighbouring Bosnia at election time in Croatia, canvassing among Croatian certificate of nationality and passport holders. In addition, many people from the former enclave now live and work in Croatia, or have become economic migrants further afield, such as in Austria and Germany, thanks to their Croatian documents (the procedure was far slower and more convoluted for refugees who had already found their way to Croatia during the war). Twenty years later, with Croatia in the EU, this secular strategic move is still facilitating the exodus of young people from the former enclave, for many of whom a job in MacDonalds in Germany is a giant leap forward, while skilled workers will never look back, further impoverishing the local economy and any prospects it might have of a renaissance. The low natality in the countries of destination means there is no shortage of demand for cheap labour[lxviii]. The local population increases significantly on holidays, as does the amount of cash in circulation, as the "foreigners" come home to celebrate, a cause of major traffic jams at the border crossing points.

Ramo Hirkić, in his own words the economy minister in Babo's government, although he was described to me as Babo's prime minister (before the war he was

---

found in Zagreb or Mostar, and indeed Velika Kladuša) disappeared on 9 March 1995 in Bihać, allegedly at the orders of Dudaković. In February 1994, he had come out in support of Babo on Croatian and Bosnian television. The day before his disappearance, international women's day, a reception had been held in the hotel Sedra in Bihać. According to Hope, Dudaković publicly accused Šantić of incompetence, and threatened to take the local HVO under his personal command. A fight broke out, and Šantić left. His car was found the next day halfway to Cazin full of bullet holes and blood. An internal 5th Corps report concluded he had been killed in an ambush by Tiger, who had been at the reception. According to Tetin, Tiger struck Šantić on the head with an ashtray during the reception, and Dudaković ordered him to "put Šantić to bed". He had allegedly already paid the SVK to allow him to secretly withdraw the HVO from the enclave to Zagreb. According to the EU monitors, he was arrested by the 5th Corps military police when he left the hotel the next morning, amid much shooting (which Dudaković never heard): he had rubbed too many people up the wrong way, and got his just deserts (he was also accused by the mayor of Bihać of having personally executed two Serb POWs). Body parts were later found in a barrel filled with petrol, oil and *razređivač* ("thinners"), buried near Bihać, but it was not possible to extract a DNA sample for identification. It is said he had a variety of shady business interests, which may be what was really behind his demise.

[lxviii] I recently interpreted for a shoplifting suspect from Rijeka in a London police station. When asked why he had walked out of a well-known supermarket chain store without paying for a basket of food, the *osumnjičeni* ("suspect"), in his mid-thirties, replied that he hadn't eaten for three days. He had a job, but was unable to work because he didn't have a bank account for his wages to be paid into; and he couldn't open a bank account because he didn't have a fixed address (until recently, his wages had been paid into a colleague's account, but the colleague had moved on). He said he targeted the supermarket because "they can afford it", unlike a corner shop family business. He was *neosuđivan* ("without form"), nor was he a *drogiraš* ("substance abuser"), and he had come to the UK to earn money to pay his mother's mortgage, who was facing foreclosure in Croatia. At least he got a square meal while he was in *pritvor* ("custody").

marketing manager in Velika Kladuša's second largest employer, Saniteks), when challenged in Kuplensko with the accusation that they had fought against the Serbs and the Croats, and then against each other, replied, "The truth is that we didn't want to fight against either the Serbs or the Croats, and the intra-Muslim war was imposed on us"[389]. Ramo was the chairman of the camp committee that was swiftly established once the *muhadžiri* ("refugees") had settled in.

After these tumultuous events, time stood still in Kuplensko. To paraphrase Andrić,

> "It was still hot summer weather. Everything was as ever in the [camp]. Some people left, while others arrived unnoticed to take their place. Individuals were secondary and unimportant: the [camp] lived for itself, with myriad changes and yet always the same [...] Life in the [camp] never really changed. But time changes, and with it the image of life each of us sees. It began to get dark earlier. The thought of autumn and winter, of long nights and cold, wet days, was a cause of dread [...] life was always the same, but it was like a narrow and increasingly poorly-lit corridor which one knows is an inch or two narrower every day even if it doesn't change perceptibly. This brought on short-lived but irresistible panic attacks among the inmates, affecting even the strongest, if only for a moment"[390].

As the people started to get used to their new lifestyle in the camp, provided for their immediate needs, and the shadow of war receded, so enforced idleness began to pose a problem. For a time, there was a craze for horse-and-cart racing along the narrow, pedestrian-filled road. It was amusing to see them pound along like Ben Hur, until one day a small child was run over. The sport ended then. But the idleness also released the creative forces of some refugees, and Tetin produced a remarkable opus of poetry. To my eternal regret I lost some priceless originals in a moment of carelessness. He was a giant crofter, who had been one of the most successful NOZB field commanders, and had also been Babo's personal bodyguard. In October 1993, he held off a whole brigade for several days from Muratovo Brdo, a height near Skokovi, with a handful of men, and only withdrew when the enemy deployed a tank. *Rakija* was the only anaesthetic available for emergency operations, including amputations. Tetin was captured after the surrender of Pećigrad. When ordered to give up his possessions, he informed his captors that his *sahat* ("watch") remained his, and that he expected it back in due course. He wears it to this day. He ultimately escaped from the 5th Corps, only to end up in a *minjsko polje* ("minefield"), where he received 40 shrapnel wounds. He was extracted by the VRS (with 20 *Kalašnjikovs* aimed at him, and after they had established he was from the NOZB), who gave him treatment in a field hospital, before exchanging him for 40 litres of fuel. His younger brother went missing in action in November 1994 in Bugar, and it was only in 2007 that his remains were identified in a mass grave near Cazin with five other corpses, victims of the 5th Corps. Tetin was highly intelligent and witty, with the prodigious memory of self-educated country people. He was a natural leader, and always found himself at the centre of any debate, or indeed any happening, attracting others who were convinced by his common-sense, well-informed rural rhetoric (and aware of his reputation as a *borac*, "fighter"), and who would be ready to throw in their lot with him if necessary. As usual in Bosnian debate, humour was never far away, even in the worst of times. One day he suggested the refugees set up a *rakija* party, with a manifesto pledge not to allow a single plum to go to waste. Like many refugees, his only clothes were the uniform he had been wearing at the time of Operation Storm, supplemented later from humanitarian aid. He shared a living room in a house with another refugee (there was more space available once people started to go back home, and people moving out of a room on their departure from the camp would "sell" it to someone else[391]), and he had a wife and daughter waiting for him in Bosnia. She had been born in Croatia during the war, but due to the sudden change in sovereignty, the new authorities had refused to issue her a birth certificate, so that legally she did not exist. He had not even seen her yet. Kuplensko even had its own folly, a crow's nest of a tree house overlooking Fairy Wheel and built in October[392]. A retired electrician with a large white beard, Pandža, lashed together living saplings and trunks to create four pillars, between which three levels sheltered by plastic sheeting were linked by hand-crafted ladders leading to the vantage point, decorated with symbols of peace. It took him 68 days to complete, which was also his age. Pandža had served 27 months' community service in Breza mine (see below) in his youth for tagging along in the 1950 Peasants' Revolt, when he had been a KPJ youth activist (volunteers for the mine received a full loaf of bread per day, while prisoners on lighter work only got ¼ loaf). He said of the revolt, "The main objective was to get some corn and secure foodstuffs"[393]. He reminded me of Uncle Albert in *Only Fools and Horses* (Peckham's finest, known in the former Yugoslavia as *Mućke*). Both Pandža's sons had been killed in the war, one in action and the other in the earlier refugee emergency. His daughter had also died from a beating after her husband was killed. He had 16 grandchildren[394]. Such stories were not rare in Bosnia. As he was keen to tell anyone who would listen, things were never better than in Yugoslavia[395]. I've heard it said by many former Yugoslavs that in the old days, you could leave your house unattended for days on end without bothering to lock it, and it would never be robbed. The "house of peace" as he called it was demolished by the Croatian police for health and safety reasons in the new year.

For the children like Šejla,

"I still believed that this was a bad dream and that I just needed to wake up from it [...] This was a nightmare for all of us, but at the same time it was the safest place to be [...] No-one knew what to think of this place and how long we would have to stay there, but at least our lives were not in danger, and we had no bullets above our heads. The second day at the camp was so overwhelming. This entire nightmare turned into real life – my life [...] To me this was just another day – as long as I was with my mother. I could tell that my mom had deep thoughts about this whole situation, and we had no words where my father was or if he was alive [...] The days went on; I had my brother and my cousins there, and I had also made friends with other kids [...] For us kids, this was not as overwhelming as it was for our parents because we didn't know how to worry or what to really worry about [...] We had no idea how long we would have to stay there, and since the winter was headed our way, people panicked a little [...] By the fourth week, the UN brought in some sponges for us to sleep on, and by just passing those out they created a fight among the refugees. Every person wanted one or more for their family, but there were not enough to give to each person [...] This was a small place where many people settled in, and everything that was happening was right in front of our eyes [...] just getting drinking water for us was a disaster [...] There was a time when the women, including my mother, would stay in line for many hours and come to the point to get water and the tanker would be empty. Not to lose the line for the next day, my mom – among others – would spend the night there so that the next morning, she would be among the first ones to get clean drinking water. Days went by, and there was not much to do – just having our day to night pass safely and praying for this to be over with […] One of the names that my grandma gave the leaders matched the list. We went down to the organisation's office to see if we could recognise any of them. For sure, one of them was my uncle […] Another month passed by. Our days were usually about the same. At this point, we still had no idea when we were going back home […] My mother panicked because for the longest time, we hadn't heard of my father, but we never lost our hope […] we went to the organisation's office to see the list; there must have been hundreds of women and children waiting to see the list as well. My mom was patient but nervous […] When we came closer to the list, my father's name was glowing in front of our eyes. Not only was my dad's name on their list but also my other uncle was on the list as well. My mom was relieved at the time, and so was my grandmother. Their prayers had been answered. For all the troubles we had all gone through, at least my mom still had a husband, I had a father, and my dear grandmother had all her children alive […] I only know that we were good people who wouldn't harm anyone. We prayed to God to just protect all of us. We had to live in fear for almost two months until we heard that it was safe to go back home"[396].

Meanwhile, the HDZ were not letting anyone leave the camp. They had set up checkpoints at the two main entrances, and the one side entrance, but did not actually enter on foot as a matter of course. Tudman refused to recognise the refugees as such, and a UN report for January described the Croatian police's control of the camp as "prison-like"[397].

I really marvel at myself, I'm amazed
How I manage to live at all these days
The humanitarian aid I receive
I eat most of it by the end of the eve

Once a week the aid is distributed
And the whole camp is amok with it.
The food causes many anxieties
Because they only get two fishes.

Let's say last Thursday for example
When the trucks came to the camp.
Bringing aid for us refugees
It's not easy to live these days.

Family member two fish per head
No-one here's satisfied
No mention of beans, a kilo of sugar
And half a kilo of milk powder.

My food is always dry and arid
In the morning half a kilo of bread
For lunch I eat the two fish alone
Only supper isn't dry as a bone

How could it be dry, my supper
When I only eat water and sugar
The next day a kilo of milk I eat
My stomach till next Thursday must wait

What can I tell you now in my poem
Here it's a real famine
My stomach doesn't have any peace
Because there's no flour or taties

And I'm really starting to look weak
I'm hungry five days a week
So the only exception is Thursday
And also, perhaps, on Friday

Fish on Thursday milk on Friday
And next Thursday is far away
It seems that that's to be my fate
Saturday and Sunday sit and wait

I've wasted away just bones and skin
Monday and Tuesday we're a-fasting

And the whole wide world just watching
Even Wednesday is no exception

Dear God what is happening here
When no-one will decide our future
Can one kilo of flour out be eeked
To last all of four weeks?

Really with such little flour
It's not at all easy in our camp-*logor*.
Even though Ramazan's far away
Here we're fasting every day.

We haven't got food, there's no electricity
The people are wretched and prone to obscenity
Does the world really want this disgrace
When they give so little to help?[398]

Sead "Tetin" Kajtazović, Paklena Dolina

The police were not letting anyone leave to wander Croatia at will. The population were unwilling, in some cases unable, to go back to Bosnia, as feelings were still running very high, and reprisals were a real possibility. Indeed, some who did decide to go back were severely beaten or even killed. Nor did they wish to remain in Kuplensko, where life was becoming increasingly difficult. Likewise, the police were reluctant to allow visitors to Kuplensko, although some friends and relatives of the refugees did succeed in paying visits, in many cases the first time they had seen each other for several years. The amount of items visitors were able to bring into the camp was minimal[lxix].

ICRC was the first international organisation in the camp, three days after the refugees themselves, after difficult negotiations with the Croatian authorities[399]. As some of their local team were among the refugees, they were able to quickly set up

---

[lxix] Nikola visited his father-in-law in the camp at this time, and despite the fact that he had briefly experienced refugee living himself in Bosnia, he told me that he was shocked by the deprivation that he saw in Kuplensko. Twenty years later, I was reminded of the camp by a street in Freetown in Sierra Leone. DFID's warehouse was separated from the main road by a 100 m stretch of single-lane track. Off to one side of the track was a cement factory, and on the other side of the main road was the city dump, which appeared to be in a perpetual state of low-level combustion, only adding to the pernicious cement dust that filled the air at all times. In this brief corner of no-man's land, a whole community had found a place to call home. Along both sides of the track, wooden dwellings, that could not have been more than 2 m deep, and were only about 4 m wide, were ranged, and the track itself was the stage for the whole spectrum of community and family life. Every time a vehicle traversed it, which was several times a day (and often HGVs), children, fires, cooking utensils, and household furniture were picked up and moved aside, to be immediately returned once the temporary inconvenience had passed. It was certainly one of the most wretched streets in the world. But it was not a scene of misery: laughter and human intercourse were to be heard at all times during the day. Members of such communities achieve self-realisation in the fulfilment of their role within the group, while in our world, we strive to attain individual rewards. Who is getting the best of it? The poor, who find shared satisfaction within themselves, regardless of material deprivation, or the rich, who exchange awareness of something greater than themselves for individual luxuries?

office and start working. For the first two weeks, the authorities did not allow aid into the camp (freedom of access for the aid community was granted on 17 August[400]). There was a shortage of everything: water, food, hygienic items, clothing and bedding. Some items could be salvaged from the abandoned houses, but consumables did not last long. Nevertheless, the people already had experience of refugee living, and had known what to bring with them (although not many people anticipated the need to bring winter clothes and footwear[401]; FTC later brought children's winter gear to the camp). However, useful items were not all that was found in the houses: in some there were corpses, pensioners who had apparently committed suicide rather than face the HV (over 500 pensioners were killed by the HV during Operation Storm[402]). The Croatian authorities were keen to remove the refugees from the still active war zone, without international involvement[403]. The day after the exodus, on 8 August, the political leaders of the refugees had signed an agreement in Zagreb with the Bosnian and Croatian authorities, allowing everyone unconditional (and immediate) return to their place of previous residence, with their personal security, civil rights and property guaranteed; NOZB soldiers would be offered the opportunity to join the ABiH or the HV, or to hand in their weapons and be treated as civilians. The agreement was signed by Bosiljko Mišetić (Croatian deputy prime minister), Zubak, and Babo, among others. However, it was not subsequently ratified by the government in Sarajevo. On 12 August, the Croatian and Bosnian authorities, again including the Croatian deputy PM, turned up with 120 *specijalci* ("riot police") and a unit of ABiH military police to enforce the agreement. The refugees were given four hours to organise themselves. Men of fighting age would be separated and treated as POWs, and exchanged for prisoners from Žepa being held in Serbia (Žepa had fallen 18 days earlier, and many of the men had fled to Serbia before then, after the fall of Srebrenica. In Serbia, 800 of them were detained by the VJ and held in custody as illegal immigrants in Šljivovica, near Čajetina, and Mitrovo Polje, near Aleksandrovac, until 1996. In 2008, they sued the government of Serbia for their mistreatment there, and in 2015, two of them were awarded damages by a county court in Belgrade[404]). Four chartered buses arrived to start taking people back. In the resulting tension, a 5th Corps squaddie who had entered the camp was injured in a fight and taken to hospital in Karlovac. The refugees refused to go, and the stand-off continued until the evening, when the bailiffs were finally stood down. Two ICRC trucks were then allowed to enter the camp with water tanks and medical supplies, and hygiene parcels were distributed to the refugees[405]. The buses left empty, but continued to return over the next few days just in case, this time without the heavy mob in evidence. There were several EU monitor vehicles in sporadic evidence over the next few days as well, and a permanent, albeit clandestine, ICRC presence in the camp, in constant radio contact with their head office in Zagreb from a Landcruiser hidden in a barn. ICRC and the EU monitors were then asked to leave the area, but Mike and Justin from ICRC stayed, under cover[406]. The visible presence, or otherwise, of international agencies was a barometer for the refugees of the likelihood of the impending use of force against them. On 16 August, a policeman let it be known there would be another attempted forced return that day. In the event, the order to proceed was not given by Zagreb, and in the late afternoon ICRC entered the camp overtly, with MSF[407]. ICRC was widely credited with having averted a major incident. At the end of September, the Croatian authorities told the US embassy they planned to repatriate all the refugees within two weeks if no agreement was reached by then, because they did not want them to spend the winter there. They claimed they already had the authority to remove all armed men, and asked the US to put pressure on the Bosnian authorities to provide security guarantees for the refugees, to be supported by international police. The Americans urged them not to use force. The Croatian authorities also noted they did not want to see a fundamentalist regime on their border[408].

Previously, the difficult access to Velika Kladuša had meant that only a small number of aid agencies were active there; in fact, it was only ICRC and FTC, as well as a nominal presence from UNHCR, and later on some French NGOs, who among other things tried to supply destitute families with unpalatable "high-energy biscuits" rather than real food. Now, however, with the Croatian Borders cleansed and cleared of the Serb Borders republic, the whole flying aid circus started to arrive. The good, the bad and the ugly, for, as George Orwell observed in Spain, "war attracts riff-raff"[lxx][409]. The first international agency coordination meeting was chaired by UNHCR on 30 August, with a high-level delegation from Zagreb, and the camp committee established the future pattern of their systematic participation by attending. In this way, the refugees insisted from the very beginning on having a voice in the determination of their fate. However, the extent to which that voice would be heard beyond the UNHCR tent up on a bank overlooking the bridge would be a different matter. Direct participation by refugees in the work of the international organisations and government bodies that rule over them is unheard of: they are usually the last to learn of fateful decisions that affect them directly. Some organisations that had grown up working in Africa had brought neo-colonial attitudes with them to the Balkans, and were not used to being held to account by their mušterije ("customers").

ICRC stopped bringing in relief goods into the camp on 6 September, as other organisations had meanwhile taken up this task, allowing ICRC to concentrate on its core mandate. Meanwhile, water and sanitation, shelter, and protection were still sources of major concern[410]. UNHCR had not yet got its act together, and ICRC were bringing in a 15,000 litre water tanker from Vojnić six times a day, which was used to fill static water tanks fitted with taps, where women could fill buckets for domestic use (to be carried sometimes several hundred meters). UNHCR later

---

[lxx] During the response to the Haiti earthquake in 2010, John Travolta flew the Scientologists in in his private plane. They set up operations and accommodation in a large yellow marquee next to our camp on the airfield, near the runway. Their joyful chants, added to the round-the-clock cargo flights 100 m away and the endemic burrow-dwelling, man-eating mygales ("spiders") didn't make sleeping any easier (someone later discovered that pouring water into a burrow caused the resident to rapidly emerge a few moments later). Water for our camp was kindly provided most days by the airport fire engine, in exchange for fuel. The operation of filling our storage tanks always resulted in a certain amount of standing water, and on one such occasion, I was surprised, amused and then alarmed in short order to see first one and then the rest of the firemen suddenly start jumping up and down, flailing their arms. Uncertain what was happening, I started looking around wildly, and when I saw the source of the drama, a giant tarantula perched on one of the firemen's backsides, I started jumping myself. It had been driven out of its shelter by the water and had run up the fireman's leg, and his frantic efforts to dislodge it caused fear of its companions to spread like wildfire, infecting everyone nearby. Matt Damon also flew in to Port-au-Prince, and gave a press conference on the runway apron, before returning back where he had come from. I also saw Sean Penn waiting in the queue for the UN plane to Santo Domingo, accompanied by a lone CP with a pistol in the back of his trousers. It was good to see so many tough guys rolling up their sleeves and getting stuck in when the chips were down. Less amusing were some American NGOs whose activities consisted of rescuing "orphans" for adoption in the US, without permission from the authorities, proper attempts to find their families, or even proper records of who had been taken where.

brought additional tankers. The first MSF delegation to visit the camp assessed the watsan (water and sanitation) situation, and within a matter of days had set up a more permanent and extensive system of water bowsers and taps near Fairy Wheel, with an area where women could wash their families' clothes (no easy task later on in the freezing winter), as well as a water purification system to treat the water from the stream. It was pumped into a 30,000 litre "onion" tank (also known as an "Oxfam tank": MSF and Oxfam are the leading authorities on emergency watsan) placed high up on a hill. Aluminium sulphate was then added to cause flocculation (the particles in the water are attracted to each other, and becoming heavier, sink; ferric chloride can also be used, and is generally more widely available, but tends to give the water a brownish colour that consumers can mistake for contamination). Once the water is clear, chlorine can be added to destroy any bacteria, in particular e-coli (if the chlorine is added to murky water, then the particles absorb it and it does not act). A swimming pool tester is used to determine how much chlorine is required, and once it has been well mixed into the water and has had time to act, the water is suitable for drinking. However, the main source of water in Kuplensko remained the tanker. I was impressed by the speed with which MSF were able to deliver such a professional piece of work. I later used the same equipment myself in Mozambique and West Timor. But by late September, the sheer amount of pollution combined with heavy rains meant the stream was no longer a viable source of water, even for *veš* ("washing")[411]. MSF built an extension to the water distribution system near the bridge in January[412]. On 27 May, when the camp population was greatly reduced, MSF announced the water would be turned off between 12 and 2 pm every day, as it was being wasted[413].

Seka told me she had been told she had to pay the Croatian doctor working for MSF DM 10 to get a permit to go to the hospital in Karlovac to have her ear seen to. I accompanied her to Fairy Wheel, and sat in silence while the young *liječnik* ("doctor") explained the system. It was only when I spoke up that he realised I was a foreigner. His assistant, a refugee, previously employed in the hospital in Velika Kladuša, made a swift exit and, thinking on his feet, denounced the practice of taking *bakšiš* ("bribes") to the MSF foreign staff, thus casting himself in the role of *pokajnik* ("whistle-blower") rather than accomplice, which is what he was. When I was later working for MSF in Kosovo, I learnt that this incident had caused a scandal within the organisation. However, despite MSF's efforts, the local medical staff involved in the corruption were not struck off. The *hajvan-hećim* ("quack") wasn't the only *šalabajzer* ("wide boy") making money out of the refugees (corruption in the provision of medical services is a widespread, deeply-rooted problem in Bosnia to this day, with many medical professionals expecting a "present" from their patients, and patients afraid they will not receive adequate - or any - care if they turn up without one). Meanwhile, Seka got her permit (free of charge), and was able to have her ear treated, and visit her elder sister to boot.

A doctor who was one of the refugees, Dr Vesna, set up a separate clinic with the support of other NGOs, especially Médecins du Monde and the Norwegian Refugee Council, to deal mainly with children's and women's health. She had done a similar thing in the previous refugee crisis. Refugee living was particularly difficult for pregnant women, of whom there were over 130 at the height of the refugees' iliad. Expectant mothers could apply to be transported to Karlovac hospital to give birth. The first four births were on 15 August – conceived during the previous refugee crisis[414]. After three days in the maternity ward, it was back to roughing it in Kuplensko. On 26 April, there was a second birth in the camp itself, at Fairy

Wheel[415]. In May it was calculated that there was an average of 15 births per month[416]. There were also weddings in Kuplensko, three in the first month alone[417]. On 13 September, Dr Vesna organised a measles vaccination for all children up to the age of five[418]. The same day, three cases of shigella (bloody diarrhoea) were confirmed. The hygiene problems were compounded by heavy rain, and there were fears of serious and widespread health problems to come[419]. On 20 September, after three days of rain, the centre of the valley flooded. That was bad news for everyone, as it meant a lot of latrines not only became inaccessible but were emptied of their contents, and Dr Vesna's clinic was under an inch of water. MSF quickly added proper flood defences to her tent, in the form of ditches and raised earthworks. There was further flooding just before Christmas, as a result of a temporary thaw. This also knocked out many people's dynamos[420]. The same thing happened, less dramatically, on 21 February[421]. Some people had managed to get hold of generators, but getting fuel was a problem in itself. On a good day a generator could be filled for DM 10[422]. The worst flood was 27 December, after heavy sleet, and exposed the measures taken after the September flood as being inadequate[423]. Meanwhile, MSF quickly brought the shigella under control and extended the health facilities at Fairy Wheel; but there was an increase in respiratory infections[424]. The health of the refugees was said to be "stabilised" by mid-October[425]. On 10 November, a flu vaccination for the over-65s was launched[426]. On 23 January, the EU brought in two containers for use as paediatric facilities, but the police made them take them back out[427]. They were finally set up in the first week of February[428]. That month, a gynaecologist starting visiting twice a week[429]. One day an ambulance from the UK turned up in the camp, with a load of medical aid. I persuaded them to donate a lot of it Dr Vesna; the rest went to Fairy Wheel. At the end of October, MSF reported that patients returning from the hospital were being refused entry into the camp, and were being referred to Velika Kladuša[430]. Some patients complained of verbal abuse in the hospital. This situation was resolved, or at least improved, on 8 November[431]. The final agreement on transferring the seriously wounded to hospital was signed by UNHCR, the EU and MSF on 9 January, but that was just the first step: the first four wounded were transferred the next week[432]. Other cases, those with fixators, were supposed to be taken to Karlovac hospital in mid-February, but some minor operations ended up being carried out in the camp[433]. On 13 March, MSF and Handicap International held a meeting with 238 registered wounded and others who required prosthetics, but there was no solution for them as yet[434]. However, not all the cases fell within the categories defined by the EU's budget, and MSF had to look for additional financing for some of the cases[435]. On 26 April, the committee made a video of the most seriously wounded, featuring a MSF doctor, with the objective of encouraging donors to take on their care[436]. It was sent out of the camp for copying and distribution via a visitor from the diaspora the next day[437]. Prosthetics were supplied on 8 May, and this was followed up with visits from a specialist to help the beneficiaries adjust to and properly use them[438]. In July there were still 72 wounded in the camp, of whom 44 required operations[439]. On 24 July, three of the most seriously wounded, accompanied by others from Karlovac hospital, were finally taken to a sanatorium[440]. The EU paid the refugees' healthcare bill from Karlovac hospital, and were surprised when an audit of the services billed revealed surnames that were not from West Bosnia. It would appear that the EU were being charged for services to other patients as well[441]. Their budget expired in May[442]. There were also 20 diabetic patients without insulin in the camp[443]. I saw the World Health Organisation at the camp once, but the only impact they seem to have had was to block the entrance to Fairy Wheel by parking their vehicle in the middle of the busy access road, and leaving it there.

While there was basic provision for physical health, there was very little attention given to problems of mental health. Yet there were certainly people in the camp displaying worrying symptoms and engaging in disturbing conduct. There was one character in particular, who appeared to have only one working eye, and who I would see laughing and talking to himself in his ragged uniform and wellies, pointing out imaginary things. Then there was Šejla. She was an army groupie from Liskovac, who followed the troops and stayed with them on the front line. Alen described an incident to me once when, Rambo-like, she got hold of a *mitraljez* ("machine gun"). She was attractive in her own kind of way, or at least had an animal sensuality, and drew cat calls and lewd comments wherever she went, to which she responded in kind, in good measure, and with obvious enjoyment. She enjoyed a sort of tragic celebrity status, yet it was clear to me she was not a full shilling. I later heard she died in Cazin. Her place has now been taken by "Asfaltina" ("kerb-crawler"), who carries on a roaring trade with visitors from the diaspora to Pećigrad. On 6 October, a doctor from a Croatian NGO working in mental health visited the camp from Zagreb. It was established there were 20 potential beneficiaries of his services in the camp[444]. Depression started to become widespread among men in the camp in December[445].

Mirvet, a refugee known as the "Director", was the humanitarian aid coordinator for the camp in the first few months. Working with the LCK and ICRC, he quickly set up a system of ten *kvartovi* ("distribution points", literally "quarters") throughout the camp. Previously, he had been the production manager at Agrokomerc in Velika Kladuša, where he was our contact for matters concerning our warehouse, and was known for being a gourmet. He was highly qualified in his field, having studied in Zagreb, and was as ready with witty banter as any of his countrymen. His motto was "All's fair in love, war and business". Mirvet spent six months as a political prisoner of the 5th Corps, and was refused compassionate parole to attend his mother's funeral. He was convicted of sedition at Bihać district court (he had been looking after an Agrokomerc warehouse), and Veladžić told him he could attend the funeral if he applied for a pardon. He was released in a prisoner exchange, having lost 25 kg (he told me that underfeeding prisoners was a deliberate strategy to keep them docile – well-fed men are more likely to plan and attempt escapes). The distribution of tasks among the international agencies, nominally under the supervision of UNHCR, but actually organised by Mirvet, was as follows: Equilibre and Solidarités looked after the distributions of aid, MSF took care of the water and sanitation, general health and the wounded, as well as human rights, MDM did paediatrics with Dr Vesna, Caritas brought firewood and supported the schools with Baja (see below), ICRC concentrated on their core mandate of protection and restoring family links once the other organisations had taken up the relay on other tasks, and FTC, with its flexibility, able to source a variety of goods from the UK at a few days' notice (trucked over by another John, English this time, among others), filled in gaps as and when they appeared. Edinburgh Direct Aid delivered toys and clothes on 21 July[446]. Mirvet later worked for another NGO, IRC, whose main activity was building infrastructure in the camp. In that role he also organised rubbish collection and disposal and vermin control throughout the camp. On 13 September, ICRC had arranged access to a tip in Vojnić and a dustcart that would pass regularly through the camp[447]. Meanwhile, a dump was dug on one of the hills overlooking the camp, and with the help of two tractors and around 30 individual *smećari* ("rubbish collectors") and an *izvoditelj deratizacije* ("rat-catcher"), constantly patrolling the camp, the acute rubbish and vermin problems reported by Canbat in Turanj in 1994, were not repeated (see below)[448]. On 7 February, the police allowed rat poison to be brought into the camp[449]. Mirvet had played a similar role for ICRC during the refugee crisis in Batnoga, when he was Družan's predecessor as head of the LCK (see below). He also built a series of proper pit latrines in November, that didn't run into the stream when it rained[450]. At the end of January, IRC complained that some people were dumping weapons in the rubbish, and that refugees were not leaving the *ćenife* ("khazis") in a fit state[451]. This is a common problem in refugee camps, where there is little or no ownership of the infrastructure by the community, due among other things to their transitory nature. I found a similar problem working with refugees from Tim-Tim (East Timor), as well as in Guinea. At home, the Timorese lived in isolated villages in the bush, in sufficiently small numbers that calls of nature could be adequately responded to in the open air. However, when they suddenly found themselves concentrated in large numbers in refugee camps in the west of the island, a different approach was required. Working with the local *departemen pekerjaan umum* ("public works department"), who were responsible for the camps, we constructed a series of pit latrines (all at a distance of at least 150 m from the wells to avoid any contamination of the ground water; we were also trucking water in, *à la* Kuplensko), and carried out awareness-raising campaigns to alert the refugees to the need to use them religiously (the public works department had originally built a series of latrines themselves, but they very quickly proved to be ineffectual, because they had failed to take account of their neighbours' hygiene practices: the refugees used corn cobs to wipe their arses, and the discarded cobs blocked up the angled inlets to the latrines in a matter of hours. The only thing for it was to bulldoze the lot). Some micro-communities within the Timorese camps ended up putting padlocks on "their" latrines, which at least ensured they were properly maintained. In Kuplensko, it was also Mirvet I had to thank for my bed and the lockable wooden door with frame on my tent. Alas, that did not make it burglar-proof, as it was simple enough to cut through the canvas with a *skalper* ("Stanley knife") at the back, as I noticed one morning. On 19 October, Mirvet obtained the agreement of UNHCR to a more efficient organisation of the distribution of aid, with ration cards, and a central warehouse in Vojnić from where goods would be drawn down[452]. The refugees working at the distribution points were familiar with the people living there, and could produce reliable statistics of various population categories, such as babies, under-fives, pregnant women, the disabled, and the elderly, which could then be used to plan the distribution of aid. The main deliveries to the camp were now on Thursdays, with exceptional items delivered on other days. Despite this, UNHCR continued to work with people outside Mirvet's organisation, and on 28 October there was an incident at one of the distribution points when things got out of hand while a truck was being unloaded, and there was some looting[453]. This also led to problems in the distribution of wood in December. The UNHCR representative blamed the refugees for this at the coordination meeting on 13 December, which caused an immediate uproar. Mirvet was involved throughout this time in the committee's occasional talks in Velika Kladuša and Vojnić aimed at bringing about the conditions to allow a safe return of refugees. I was taken aback one day to see him in the back of a Croatian police *marica* ("black Maria", although it was actually white) at the border at Maljevac. I thought he had been snatched, and tried to intervene, but he winked and assured me that everything was under control.

In November, some NGOs set up makeshift primary and then junior schools in tents, at the initiative of Baja, the head of the junior school in Velika Kladuša. Unfortunately, the school complex was located on the top of a hill with no path (there was no room anywhere else), so that in no time the hillside was a mud bath, and children and parents alike were covered in mud each day. As if the women didn't already have enough on their plate. One day, ICRC received a visit from their head office in Zagreb. The local team leader, Mike, made a point of taking them up the hill and down again, and getting them covered in mud, so that they would have a proper understanding of how difficult everyday life was for the refugees. There were 20 teachers among the refugees in October[454]. A first consignment of school books was delivered by Caritas on 31 October, and daily snacks were provided by the Jesuits[455] (the Jesuits first came to Bosnia with the Habsburgs, joining their Franciscan and Dominican brethren, who have a much longer history in the country[lxxi][456]). Correspondence with schools in Italy, France and Croatia resulted in donations of equipment and gifts[457]. By June, the children had successfully completed a full school year, with an average mark of 4.15 (83 %), and with the teachers doing everything they could to carry on as normal[458]. At the end of the school year, the children were issued certificates that were recognised in Bosnia[459]. School children were given satchels and presents sent by families abroad just after Christmas[460].

One day I spotted and flagged down a Transit van with UK *tablice* ("number plates") near the north entrance to the camp. As it stopped, out jumped a *fratar* ("Catholic priest") complete with habit and sandals, and started to remove boxes from the back of his van, which he immediately thrust into the hands of whoever happened to be nearest, while crying in English, "What a lovely camp!". I talked to his lay companion, who told me they had decided to bring aid over from the UK, and were told once they arrived in Croatia that this was the nearest refugee camp. I tried to explain that it was better to plan who would be the most appropriate beneficiaries of aid, rather than dishing it out at random, but as it was such a small quantity I left it at that. I introduced him to Mirsad, who was working as my assistant, and we spent the next hour or so showing them round, mainly to help them understand the situation, so they would not feel an anti-climax after their odyssey. On another occasion, a representative of Mother Theresa – or, according to some refugees, the venerable mystic herself - visited the camp, and asked whether she could leave a bag at the LCK tent while she had a look around (Mother Theresa, from Macedonia, was fluent in Serbian/Croatian). Her request was graciously granted, and she went on her way; but it was soon noticed that the half-open bag was bulging with chocolates. Some of the young Red Cross volunteers, including Smajo (see below), found themselves unable to resist temptation, and before anyone knew it, all the chocolate had been devoured, and there were chocolate wrappers all over the workplace. When the elderly saint returned to the tent, she was so angry when she saw what had happened, that she stormed out of the camp, never to return. Meanwhile, and ignorant of this development, Tetin was asked by the ICRC local team to show her round the camp. She gave him three bags, with the instruction (Tetin thought) to distribute the contents to the needy. Tetin made the necessary arrangements, and they set off on a tour of the camp. When they returned, Tetin was surprised when she asked for her bags prior to her departure: it transpired that only one of the bags contained alms distribution, while the other two contained her personal items, in

---

[lxxi] According to George Orwell, there is a saying that "night and the Jesuits always return".

particular coffee, and candles that she was taking to the shrine at Međugorje ("between the mountains", see below). Tetin attempted to reassemble the items, but the coffee was being drunk, the clothing worn, and the candles were providing light. Half an hour later, Tetin was summoned to the radio in the ICRC tent, where he spoke to the *redovnica* ("nun"), who was by then in Karlovac. She apologised for losing her temper over the misunderstanding, and wished the refugees all the best.

One day, UNHCR Croatian local staff driving through the camp spent an extended period of time exchanging derogatory and offensive observations over the VHF radio on the refugees, in particular the women, whose protection was their mandate. The remarks were broadcast to all the aid community vehicles, individual aid workers, and the ICRC office, and were heard by anyone who was within their earshot. Complaints were made to UNHCR, but no apology was forthcoming. While superficially polite to NGOs (yet unable to deliver much), the head of the UNHCR office in the camp, like several UNHCR staff I have met, seemed to regard refugees as a necessary evil, who should be seen but not heard. Indeed, she once stated in a public meeting that she "hate[d] these people"[lxxii]. I had met her briefly earlier one day when Kiwi and I were looking for warehouse space in Topusko. Fortunately, the protection officer appointed on 31 January, Tom, was much more willing to engage with the refugees and listen to their problems, and made efforts to find real solutions, albeit within the limits of his institutional framework[461]. Ironically, three years later, he was attacked and injured by a crowd of refugees on the border between East and West Timor. The radio communications used by aid agencies operate on HF (high frequency – most suitable for distances over 80 km, and used in vehicles and base offices; the signal is transmitted in a series of bounds between the earth's surface and

---

[lxxii] Perhaps the most patronising remark I have heard in respect of refugees was overheard one Sunday afternoon in 1997 at the best restaurant (and hotel) in Bukavu, the *Orchid Noir* ("Black Orchid"). One among a group of UNHCR international staff sitting at a table on the terrace overlooking Lake Kivu said, "We all know that refugees never cry". Just the previous week, I had visited a rural clinic with a local engineer, Adrian, to assess what improvement work, if any, could be carried out on the building. As we inspected the mud-brick, corrugated iron-roofed premises, we passed an unconscious malarial teenage girl with a drip in her arm; her family were waiting in the lobby for news. After we had completed one circuit of the building, we went back into the main area, only to discover that a blanket had been drawn over the girl's head. "Dead", my colleague said to me in English, to avoid being overheard by the family. Without thinking, I said something appropriate in French, and thereby unwittingly notified the family that their daughter and sister had passed away. The consequent scene of grief would have convinced anyone that refugees and the poor are no strangers to genuine expressions of emotion, when they have the luxury of a time and place where they can stop and deal with their loss. As one of MSF's top logisticians, Christophe Delaude, commented to me once, "to reach old age in Africa you need to be very tough AND very lucky". UNHCR's other topic of conversation in Bukavu was who had managed to bag the most luxurious colonial residence with their housing allowance. Mere mortals could let a single-room breeze block dwelling in the town for USD 10 per month, while the outside of the entrance porch to a bank or similar commercial premises, partly sheltered from the elements and providing a solid foundation and supporting wall for a temporary extension (to be removed during business hours), could be had for a single dollar per month. As they say in the Balkans, "*Sit gladnog ne razumije*" ("let them eat cake"). Bukavu was hit by a magnitude 5.8 *séisme* ("earthquake") in 2008, which was followed by a number of aftershocks. One occurred in the middle of the night, and caused me to leave the hotel building (not the *Orchid Noir*) in great haste; standing outside, I remembered that when I was trying to get to sleep earlier that night, I had been struck by an overwhelming sensation of impending doom, a black feeling of despair that I have never experienced before or since. They do say *wanyama* ("animals") are earthquake sensitive. For the rest of the deployment, I slept in a tent in the hotel grounds, only venturing inside to use the bathroom. When I finally checked out, the hotel manager assured me I would have the "*feu vert*" ("green light") the next time I visited his establishment, part of which was slipping into the lake at a 30° angle. I have heard tell that there is a vast amount of methane at the bottom of Lake Kivu, which the periodic seismic activity may one day cause to rise to the surface in a ginormous belch, and which if ignited, would cause an apocalyptic explosion. It would certainly pen and ink.

the ionosphere, and can theoretically be used to communicate with someone on the other side of the world. Blind spots typically occur at certain times of day and night, caused by the terrain and celestial conditions, and so a range of frequencies are used in any particular location, set in advance for different times of day by trial and error; a "ground wave" also permits communication up to 60 km, but there can be a black hole at distances of between 60 and 80 km, as I discovered when we responded to a refugee influx in Forecariah in southern Guinea, see below) and VHF (very high frequency – for distances up to 20 km depending on the terrain, although much wider networks can be set up by using "repeaters" placed at strategic high points, that retransmit the message; the signal is transmitted in a straight line, and VHF is used in handsets, vehicles and base offices. UHF, ultra high frequency, is also sometimes used, although it is only good for far shorter distances than VHF, but has the advantage of not being blocked out by electronic counter measures, that cast a telecoms-free zone around a vehicle to preclude the use of remote-controlled IEDs).

On 26 September the EU arrived to great fanfare[462]. Their convoy was preceded by an attractive young Spanish lady, who insisted on walking through the camp ahead of her trucks as if she was Lady Godiva with her kit on, or perhaps Isabella of Castille inspecting the Moors after the *reconquista*. In her train was an ancient general, with a chest-load of medals. I refrained from asking him whether he had bought them as a job lot at a jumble sale (however, despite his incongruous appearance, he turned out to be a good bloke, and one day he even gave Ramo his shoes when he noticed Ramo's weren't waterproof). I wonder whether the refugees ever suspected how many important people they had managed to mobilise by their presence, or indeed what all of these people would have been doing if they had not had the excuse of the refugees to go on a day trip to the field, so close to their offices in Zagreb. They distributed their aid and left after meeting various local dignitaries, most of them foreign themselves. Shortly thereafter, we received a visit in our Cazin office from a team of three young Spaniards from the EU office in Zagreb. The conversation moved to the recent Serb exodus. "What a shame", the team leader commented with a grin. We threw them out of the office for their insolence. We were later informed we had been awarded EU medals, if only we would go to their office in Zagreb to collect them. I never bothered. I was recently sent David Cameron's ebola medal for spending at least three weeks in West Africa during the ebola crisis, even though it was only the medical staff who put their lives in danger during that operation. As the going rate on Ebay is less than one pound, I think I'll keep it with my breaststroke and cycling proficiency certificates. I had a far tougher time of it working for MSF during a cholera outbreak in the port of Quelimane in Mozambique in 1998. The logistics team converted an *armazém* ("warehouse") into a functioning cholera camp within 24 hours, divided into three sections: observation, treatment and recovery (with a morgue in a shed outside the back for the *óbitos*, those who didn't make it), separated from each other by fencing (wood and plastic sheeting) and checkpoints with an obligatory and rigorously applied cholera solution footbath and hand wash. Even smoking a cigarette after having been in contact with the disease can be sufficient for transmission, if the strictest hygiene, underpinned by generous amounts of chlorine solution, is not observed. Members of the local team, equipped with large spray canisters carried on their backs, were positioned at all crossing points between the different zones, and enthusiastically policed this protocol. The only treatment for this diarrhoeal disease is IV-administered oral rehydration salts to the unconscious patients, laid out on makeshift beds with a hole in the middle and a bucket underneath. If they are still alive on day three, they are over the worst. The complex plumbing of the treatment centre, which had to contain the infectious water-borne disease (although the obsessive application of chlorine meant the chances of it surviving were much diminished), was aggravated by the fact that the water table was only 30 cm deep, which meant that all the watsan installations, particularly the latrines and showers, had to be constructed off the ground, above than the drainage repositories into which they ran. A system of tanks, *bombas* ("pumps"), and *camiões-cisterna* ("tanker trucks"), some procured locally and some flown in from Europe, one set for water, the other for diarrhoea (and all clearly and suitably labelled, and with their separate teams; the *equipa da merda* ("shit squad") was paid a bonus for what was essentially the same work, albeit with a more noxious subject matter), was used to ensure the camp, which was later deemed by the Mozambican MOH to have been extremely successful in terms of morbidity and mortality rates, functioned (I was told by the medics that during a cholera epidemic, between 1-10% of the population fall sick, and likewise, of those, between 1-10% die, all depending on the quality of the response and the preventive measures taken. Meanwhile, ebola kicks in within three weeks of infection, and kills within ten days, with a mortality rate of 50% or higher, depending on the care received). The diarrhoea, rendered harmless, was dumped into a specially-prepared tank off-site (where, having been sterilised, it would not decompose as is the normal run of things, a problem in itself), while the waste water, also disinfected, was fed in the humid, tropical country into various evaporation traps (one of which included several palm trees that thirstily guzzled it up, leaving the harmless residue in the soil, itself contained). One of my tasks was to remove solid objects dumped into the diarrhoea tanks to stop the pumps from getting blocked up (cholera diarrhoea, due to its unusual appearance, is known as "rice water"). A major problem I had was family members bringing their sick relatives *latas* ("cans") of Coke, which found their way into the latrine system, and had to be located and removed with the aid of a stick. It didn't take long to get used to the sights, sounds and smells of the sick and dying, but it was nevertheless always nice to see someone who had turned up at death's door and been unconscious for a day or two, quickly recover on the third day, and graduate to the recovery zone, where you could at least have a conversation with them. An American colleague, Dr Brian, had to revive one of the patients in recovery who slipped back into unconsciousness, with an adrenalin injection stabbed directly into the heart. We hired an *empresa de segurança privada* ("private security firm") to hold back the mass of worried family members trying to push their way in – for their own good as well as everyone else's. I had occasion to reprimand several times one of the guards who kept entering the camp to see a relative of his; and sure enough, one morning I came to work to find him stretched out on a bed with a drip in his arm, still in his uniform. "I told you so", I said. Fortunately, he made a quick recovery, and on the third day he wanted to go straight back to work, without even going home to rest or get changed! In another incident, a local who had made a particular nuisance of himself attempting to force his way into the camp one day, and who had been detained by the security guards, was found dead the next morning outside the premises. The security firm was adamant he had died of cholera, and as far as I am aware there was no police investigation to establish the real facts, despite our protests. The whole operation lasted about three months; then the disease had already worked its way through the community and continued north up the East African coast, as had MSF, always trying to keep one step ahead. We all went out for a meal and a drink in a local restaurant/bar/disco to celebrate the conclusion of the operation. I was surprised during the meal to suddenly see a lot of Europeans flood in; and I was even more surprised when I heard them all speaking Russian. They were merchant sailors from a Russian ship that had docked in the port for a few days (relations between Mozambique and Russia go back to the Cold War, and I had already met a Russian girl who lived in the town, married to a local; I was also surprised to discover that one of the local *emfermeiras* ("nurses") at the cholera camp spoke fluent German, having studied in East Germany. There was a Cuban doctor among the local MOH team as well). After the meal, we let our hair down a bit, and having avoided the cholera, were struck with Saturday night fever. At a certain point, I'm not sure how, a fight broke about between the MSF logisticians and the Russian sailors. Needless to say, we won. This kind of field emergency healthcare, providing effective care fast in locations that have little or no facilities, is MSF's speciality. By contrast, unlike MSF, who also had previous experience working with ebola, and the Red Cross, with its core medical competence, some of the NGOs responsible for managing the ebola treatment centres in Salone (Sierra Leone) had no institutional medical experience at all. And yet the institutional funding was there for almost any Travelling Wilburys outfit ready to give it a go. Rather than emulate the streamlined, tried and tested MSF model, capable of hitting the ground running, they attempted to recreate the NHS in the African bush, an unwieldy, top-heavy endeavour which was ultimately far less efficient in terms of resources, time, and most tragically, lives. As they say in the Balkans, "*Za pare sve - O lovo mangel inkaldo le barrestar*" ("where there's muck there's brass")[463]. Meanwhile, the WHO failed to recognise the seriousness of the ebola outbreak in Guinea, Sierra Leone and Liberia, and assume its leadership role in the international crisis, despite being urged to do so by MSF as early as March 2014 (WHO finally declared an "international public health emergency" in August). The total death count from this, the worst ever outbreak of the disease, declared over in March 2016, was more than 11,000 (including 500 health workers), but it could have been far lower if the UN had acted in a timely and professional manner[464]. The director of WHO continues in her post, which she has held since 2006.

UNHCR and then the EU financed a daily delivery of fresh bread from Karlovac to the "bakers" in the camp, where all refugees could pick up a morning loaf free of charge, which provided a welcome staple (bread is eaten far more in the Balkans than in the UK, and features in every meal). The actual baker in Karlovac charged 2 kg flour for 700g of bread[465].

From the end of August onwards, the EU organised a daily free bus run back to Bosnia, for anyone who had had enough and was ready to take their chances back home. UNHCR took this over from November[466]. From the end of January, it was three times per week[467]. Upon entering the bus, the traveller's status changed from "refugee" to "returnee"[468]. Cigarette smugglers started to use it, travelling to Velika Kladuša as if they were returning, and then changing their minds and coming back with as many fags as they could carry[469]. The drivers would charge them DM 600 each[470]. Some people also returned as they had come, in horse-drawn vehicles or tractors (not always their own – the police confiscated some trying to return on 7 December[471]) loaded down with their meagre possessions (sometimes augmented by loot and humanitarian aid), and fellow travellers, as well as the surviving livestock they had appropriated[472]. Once, when leaving the camp in a van, a policeman at the southern checkpoint asked me where I was going. When I told him I was on my way to Velika Kladuša, he roused a dozen or so people squatting in silence at the side of the road (mainly women and children, and some elderly men), and encouraged them to jump in the back of my vehicle. I got out and asked him what he was doing, and he replied they wanted to go back to Bosnia. Uneasy, I asked the group of passengers why they were going back. Silence. I then asked them who their leader was, which again elicited no response. Most of them weren't even looking at me, absorbed in their own thoughts and worries, conserving their strength. Their faces looked tired and drawn, but not fearful. I then asked them, more forcefully, whether they were going back voluntarily. A woman spoke up, as if surprised at my insistence, and said that yes, they all wanted to go back, and had been promised transport. I then asked whether they had paid anyone for transport, or had been told they would have to pay. The policeman, still there, confirmed that no-one had paid a thing. Suspecting that he had already charged them a fee, I reiterated that if I was to give them a lift, it was completely free of charge, and that I could take no responsibility for their fate upon arrival in Bosnia. After some more cajoling there were a few grudging assents, and we left. Upon arrival in Velika Kladuša, having been waved through the border, they all jumped out and went straight into the *sud* ("court building") to register, while a 5th Corps squaddie on guard outside accosted me very *nekulturno* ("rudely"), I imagine in the hope of getting a bribe. He didn't care that I was a foreigner, but neither did I care that he had an AK47, and continued about my business. When I returned to Kuplensko later that day, I was, unusually, held up at the checkpoint, even though mine was the only vehicle; I heard the same policeman, obviously the *šef* ("boss"), tell his colleagues to search my vehicle, but they were more preoccupied with someone who was apparently hiding in the cornfield by the side of the road, for I heard one of them shout: "*Izađi iz kukuruza!*" ("come out of the corn"). After a while, when despite the boss's insistent instructions I saw they were paying me no attention, I just drove forward, and the barrier was moved aside to let me pass.

It was as if the great international institutions were competing with each other to demonstrate who could be the most inconsiderate to ordinary members of the public. Earlier, before Operation Storm, I one day received a message from Split that a French NGO was organising a visit by French schoolchildren to Velika Kladuša, and that I was to act as a liaison between the local schools, UNHCR and the EU. It was immediately clear to me that that no school would ever allow its pupils to go on a trip abroad to a war zone, across two front lines and back again, and that the trip would never happen. I met Baja and told her as much. Nevertheless, she had been assured it was going ahead, and my efforts at communication with UNHCR and the EU produced the same answer. On the day in question, the whole school came out, refreshments had been prepared (at great effort and expense given the circumstances), and the children had painted pictures to give to their foreign visitors. Unsurprisingly, the phantom French schoolchildren failed to appear. Nor was there any message from any quarter letting us know the event had been cancelled. I stayed around for an hour or so to cheer the children up in their disappointment, and got one of the paintings for my trouble. It is now on my mother's wall in Cumbria (a retired teacher herself). The next time I managed to get hold of the UNHCR representative, I asked why no-one had alerted the school that the trip was not going ahead, and was told that it was the EU's responsibility to communicate that kind of information. Not satisfied, the next time I was in Zagreb I visited the EU office and collared Klaus, the contact person for the trip. He put the blame squarely on the shoulders of UNHCR, who had someone on the ground and should have communicated it. Even then, none of them saw fit to apologise. This complete lack of consideration is one of the most despicable acts I have ever witnessed. Such top-down organisations can never have a truly humanitarian agenda, because individuals are only incidental to their true purposes, which are by definition political. By contrast, organisations such as ICRC and MSF grew out of specific humanitarian needs identified on the ground. The Red

Cross was created by Swiss businessman Henri Dunant to provide medical care for battlefield wounded after the battle of Solferino in Italy in 1859[lxxiii][473], while MSF was formed when some ICRC staff decided there was a further need to testify to what they were seeing on the ground during the Biafra war of 1967-1970 (during which HMG's international procurement agents acquired on behalf of the Nigerian government "much" of the arms it used in the civil war against its breakaway southern province, in which up to three million people died[lxxiv][474]). Dunant died in poverty in 1910. Meanwhile, the EU and the UN with their byzantine procedures and structures have, according to Crnobrnja, a "natural tendency to compromise"[475], something which is anathema to MSF and ICRC. It is common, in large emergency responses, to find only a few agencies, almost always among them the Red Cross and MSF, working on the front line of the emergency, where the danger is greatest and the need for a professional response most acute. As one moves away from the epicentre, the number of agencies present, and the number of people they deploy, increase exponentially. In Kosovo, MSF lent ICRC, the only other agency operating regularly in the field, medical supplies as they were facing temporary import problems, while in West Timor, ICRC's warehouse manager, Richard, kindly lent me a submersible pump to clean wells that were being used by the refugees from the East. I later worked with Richard for the British Red Cross in London, in the legendary Mike Goodhand's team. During the emergency caused by hurricane Katrina in 2005, Mike and another logistician, yet another John, deployed to the US and lent the American Red Cross invaluable assistance on the ground, managing the movement, reception and distribution of aid from throughout the country within Louisiana[lxxv][476]. Nearly 2,000 people were killed by Katrina, and over a million were displaced.

In October and November, Bangladeshi UNPROFOR troops being redeployed from the Bihać pocket would pass through the camp early in the mornings[477]. As they passed, the more adventurous refugees would try to blag *lopate* ("shovels") and other *alati* ("implements") that were attached to the outside of their vehicles[478]. The Organisation for Security and Cooperation in Europe visited the camp on 15 December[479] (OSCE, whose headquarters are located in the magnificent Hofburg in Vienna, from whose balcony in 1938 Hitler informed the adulating mob in Heroes Square that he had annexed their country (and his)[lxxvi], and next door to the Spanish Riding School with its rural fragrance, would be responsible for monitoring the elections, local, cantonal, parliamentary and presidential, the following September. OSCE also had an office in Nazranj, and one of their staff, a Scandinavian, was in the habit of stepping outside his office for a smoke at 5.30 pm most days. One evening in early 1997 he was quietly contemplating his day – or his night – with a fag on the quiet street when a handful of *Kalaš* rounds, fired from the end of the road, slammed into the wall behind him. I understand he abandoned his vice after that).

[lxxiii] During the battle of Solferino, in which France and Sardinia fought against Austria, out of almost 40,000 casualties, there was only one civilian death. The situation is very different today, and civilians bear the brunt of modern warfare, making up 90% of casualties.

[lxxiv] A Nigerian peacekeeper told me in Slunj that during their civil war, squaddies were given a pair of wellies and told "God help you" before going into action.

[lxxv] Louisiana was bought by Napoleon from Spain in 1800, but sold to the US three years later after the loss of Haiti and its vast sugar-cane revenues.

[lxxvi] In 1938, *Time* featured Hitler as their man of the year; in 2014, the "Ebola fighters" were their persons of the year. No comment.

On Sunday 25 February, a weapons amnesty was organised by the committee under the auspices of UNHCR and NATO, in order to allow a reduction in the number of firearms in the camp. The refugees had been asking for this since October. The weapons were not only a hazard in their own right, but were also an excuse for heavy-handed tactics by the police, not to mention propaganda by the local media directed against the refugees. Among the hardware brought by the refugees when they arrived was a mini T34 ex-WWII *belaj-bager* ("tank"), rammed into a ditch by the side of the road, and which was used by the Croatian authorities for propaganda purposes, regularly appearing in the media. It was never removed. Meanwhile, much of the original armaments brought to the camp had already gone back to Bosnia with returnees, or been sold to the police, while many people retained concealed sidearms for their own security[480]. One of the fears had been that the Croatian police would use the amnesty as an excuse for another raid, and for that reason the committee insisted UNHCR take the lead, at least officially[481]. The refugees were informed of the amnesty by written notices posted throughout the camp two days in advance, and on the day in question the police were not allowed to enter the camp between 12 and 2 pm[482]. Someone dumped a rocket launcher in a latrine rather than hand it in. The day before, the local radio in Bosnia had broadcast information contradicting the purpose of the action, citing UNHCR, which discouraged many people from taking part[483]. It also reported that the refugees would be returning in a week, which for some may have been a reason to retain their weapons[484]. In total, three bayonets, one home-made pistol, two detonators and one magazine were handed in during the amnesty[485].

In September, a human rights lawyer from the London School of Economics, Curtis F. Doebbler, spent two weeks in the camp. Dr Doebbler, who still works as an international human rights lawyer, based in Washington DC, was invited to visit Kuplensko by MSF. He subsequently wrote a letter to Tuđman's chief humanitarian, Dr Lang, who had been a regular fixture in the Croatian authorities' dealings with the refugees, reminding him that under international obligations to which Croatia was party, the primary responsibility for ensuring the welfare of the refugees was with the Croatian government, and that the government could ask UNHCR for assistance if it was unable to do so itself. He stated that, regardless of efforts to arrange a voluntary return, the dire conditions demanded immediate action, all the more so in view of the impending advent of winter, and recommended rehousing the refugees in permanent accommodation as a matter of urgency[486]. He also recommended the refugees push UNHCR to give them information about their situation and help them resolve it, and to increase its capacity to process applications for resettlement (at the time limited to 20 per day)[487]. His report, CC'd to Ramo, stated among other things that, "UNHCR has not devoted much attention to the refugees' immediate humanitarian needs and there has been no serious attempt to ensure Croatia respects its obligations under the Refugee Convention"[488]. It also concluded that the agreement signed on 8 August was not valid in international law (even though it was drawn up by four *advokati*, "lawyers", including a PhD) because: it was signed under duress; Babo had no international recognition; he had no authority to sign on behalf of people who had fled the Bihać pocket; and the agreement breached the human rights of the refugees. Dr Doebbler had also been told by the head of police in Velika Kladuša that it would not be possible to prevent revenge attacks against returning refugees[489]. Many refugees started writing to the government in Zagreb asking to be granted refugee status[490].

The international media took an intermittent interest in the camp, as so many other things were happening at the same time, not just elsewhere in the Balkans, but also in the Caucasus, Central Asia and the Great Lakes region of Africa. On 30 September, German and US media visited the camp[491]. There was a report on Kuplensko on German television in October[492]. Finnish journalists visited on 26 October[493]. Dutch television was there on 27 November[494]. CNN visited Fairy Wheel on 13 December[495]. Reporting by the Croatian media on the refugees generally served the cause of the Croatian authorities, who wanted the refugees gone[496]. The propaganda circulating about the refugees to justify their forced return included the claim that they were sheltering several thousand Četniks amongst them[497]. The Croatian evening news first reported on the refugees on 21 August, while the first long report (five minutes) on Croatian television was on 16 October, perhaps due to criticism expressed to Tuđman's humanitarians by Emma Bonino, the EU's humanitarian commissioner, who had recently visited the camp[498]. At the end of 1998, she visited Kosovo, and later supported NATO's bombing campaign. On 24 October, Sarajevo radio reported that 400 armed rebels who were preventing the return of refugees were being disarmed[499]. In October and November, many refugees' attention was captured by the reporting on the radio and in the newspapers of the peace talks in Dayton, Ohio[500]. The news that NATO was replacing the UN in Bosnia was met with approval on 12 December[501]. *Muštuluk* ("glad tidings"). On 6 November, the Croatian newspaper *Vjesnik* reported that the refugees had started to return home, that 175 had gone the preceding Friday with the UNHCR bus, but that their leaders in the camp were physically preventing others from leaving[502]. Meanwhile, the refugees were portrayed by the local media, citing the police, as dangerous criminals, apostates, and even *majmuni* ("apes"; I once heard it said in Chechnya that non-Muslims, not being the sons of Adam, were equivalent to *obezjani*, "apes")[503]. The same hostile line was taken by the Bosnian local radio in Velika Kladuša, that had replaced Velkaton, and who referred to them as "renegades"[504]. *Oslobođenje* reported on 8 November that the riot police had been deployed to prevent smuggling, people trafficking, livestock rustling, gangland killings, prostitution, kidnapping, illegal logging and robbery[505]. But there were some real criminals in the camp: in the early hours of 21 September there was a double murder, when an attempt to extort DM 10,000 from a couple went wrong. The murderer escaped, but was detained by the police later that day. He had extorted DM 5,000 from the same couple in the last refugee crisis, in Turanj, but the other refugees had beaten him up and forced him to return the money[506]. *Oslobođenje* also reported that the Bosnian ministry of justice had applied for Babo to be extradited from Croatia, where he was allegedly under house arrest[507]. On 26 November, Croatian television reported on a ministerial visit to the camp the previous day, a balanced report that met with the general approval of the refugees[508]. On 8 December, *Večernji List* reported there were still 15,000 refugees in the camp, including 500 wanted for war crimes. On the same day, the Croatian television and radio Free Europe also reported on the refugees[509]. Croatian television also reported there were 800 firearms in the camp[510]. On 23 December, the Bosnian local radio reported that "Separatists should be ashamed to show their faces in Velika Kladuša"[511]. The importance of the local media in shaping attitudes and informing decisions both within the camp and in the former enclave, and fanning fear and hatred, should not be underestimated. One day a member of the FTC local team in Cazin, Arijana, visited the camp with Kiwi, because she had a cousin there. I was surprised at how scared she was, even in our company: she seemed terrified of exiting the vehicle to have a conversation with her cousin by the side of the road, despite our promises to keep her under close observation. That brought home to me how powerful the media was in driving the way the population at home in Bosnia saw the refugees.

Over time, the number of visitors increased (they had to leave the camp by 8 pm unless they had a special permit to spend the night), and on Sunday 27 August there were 250 registered visits at the northern entrance alone, most of them by people who were already living abroad, either in Croatia or Slovenia, or even further afield (the south entrance was mainly used by traffic coming from, or going to Bosnia)[512]. There were attempts to organise the West Bosnian diaspora to provide assistance and lobby for a just solution to the crisis[513]. The diaspora from Slovenia sent several trucks of aid, including potatoes, onions and beans, Balkan staples[514]. On some days no visits were allowed, and at the beginning of October they were banned, at least officially[515]. They were reactivated on 28 January[516].

After a few weeks it was rumoured that there was a death list of 400 individuals with prices on their heads, and people started disappearing from the camp[517]. It was said that the Croatian police were seizing and transporting certain people back to Bosnia, to claim the bounty: DM 200 for an ordinary refugee, and a higher price for certain individuals[518]. It was certainly the case that anyone who stepped out of line, such as by chopping wood in the forest, or who happened to find themselves alone at the edge of the camp, was liable to be arrested, and was usually not seen again in the camp, if at all. On 28 September, 17 people were arrested chopping wood, but were later released after intervention by the UN police[519]. In an earlier wood-chopping incident, a policeman from Varaždin, in the far north of Croatia and far from any war zone, had commented, "*Dosta što se Hrvatska podkrada od 1918 godine*" ("they've been pilfering from Croatia since 1918")[520]. On 1 October, four women were arrested digging up potatoes near the camp, and were taken in handcuffs to Vojnić *SUP* ("nick")[521]. It was also rumoured that the 5th Corps were driving into the camp, pretending to be visitors, and then seizing people and driving off with them[522]. On 21 August, 21 refugees were caught in Turanj and returned to Velika Kladuša[523]. MSF published an open letter calling on the Croatian authorities to halt forced repatriation from Kuplensko[524]. In September there was a series of incidents where detained refugees were deliberately shot in the hand[525]. On 11 September, a delegation of refugees visited the police station in Vojnić to propose an agreement on policing the camp which would reduce insecurity[526].

On 17 October, the civilian police who had been in charge of the camp until then were replaced by the riot police, who immediately set about reinforcing the isolation of the camp. Such relationships as had been established with the police were now over, for better and for worse. This was immediately perceived as a bad sign by the refugees, but UNHCR and the EU monitors regarded it as the successful result of their lobbying, as it would improve security within the camp[527]. The price of cigarettes went up immediately, and the cost of an illegal transfer to Zagreb doubled, from DM 1,000 to 2,000[528]. All incoming vehicles, including aid trucks, were now subject to thorough searches. As of 8 November, the riot police had an APC, in which they sometimes cruised through the camp[529]. The day before, the riot police had dragged someone out of his car in view of aid workers and removed him from the camp. UNHCR explained they had no power to do anything other than protest and report this, which they had done[530].

The Croatian authorities did not want the camp there, and were putting pressure on UNHCR to facilitate this, as well as putting pressure on the refugees to give up and go home. On 13 November, the Croatian police decided they wanted to set up checkpoints inside the camp, to "prevent illegal activity". One of the activities they said they wanted to combat was tax fraud, as the stallholders and other entrepreneurs were not paying any taxes. The more professional NGOs, led by ICRC, were vehemently opposed to this plan. As MSF pointed out, there was no tax office in the camp, and as the refugees were not allowed to leave, they had no opportunity to pay taxes even if they wanted to, and besides, the refugees had already asked the authorities to allow lawful commerce in the camp, to put an end to the smuggling. UNHCR, who regarded the issue a mere question of "detail" of police organisation, approved the plan, and soon barbed wire barricades divided the camp into four, manned by officers in flak jackets and helmets, generally hostilely disposed towards the "*ratni zločinci*" ("war criminals")[531]. There was an immediate increase in the number of refugees being transported back to Bosnia. On the evening of 19 November, 15 APCs entered the camp, but the much anticipated use of force did not materialise (possibly due to Mirvet's intervention – together with an international colleague he provided the US embassy in Zagreb with real-time information on the APCs' manoeuvres, via their vehicle HF)[532]. After the riot police relaxed the rules on visits in mid-November, there was another wave of returns – after meeting their nearest and dearest, some refugees decided to throw in the towel[533]. On 28 January, a refugee was arrested very roughly early in the morning for no apparent reason and removed, the first such case for a while[534]. He reappeared the next day, apparently none the worse for his ordeal[535]. On 15 February, the Croatian police conducted an exercise with dogs in the neighbouring valley. The news quickly spread through the camp, and was the cause of not inconsiderable alarm. Ramo raised the issue with UNHCR and ICRC, and the explanation that eventually arrived from the police was that the bodies of two smugglers had been found there, and that they were strengthening resources to combat such activities[536]. After another series of restrictions, there were a number of visits on 23 March, and thereafter visits were only allowed on weekends[537]. It wasn't unknown for visitors to move into the camp, thereby bringing about the fabled "family reunification"[538]. In July, one unit of riot police, from Zagreb, disguised themselves as smugglers by donning civvies and carrying rucksacks. They then went walkabout in the hills around the camp, and were able to get close to groups of smugglers before calling in support and arresting them. The smugglers were then deported to Bosnia, via Vojnić[539].

One day, Mirsad and I unwittingly strayed beyond what were considered the acceptable bounds of the camp at the south end, to the side of the road where there was no physical *rampa* ("barrier"), and where Babo's wife, Fazila, lived. We were accosted very aggressively by a Croatian civilian policeman. He started shouting at Mirsad, asking him whether he didn't know he wasn't allowed out of the camp, that he wasn't a Croatian citizen, and that he was liable to arrest and return to Bosnia. Mirsad responded calmly that he had not been aware we had crossed the boundary, and that we had no intention of leaving the camp. Fearing the situation could escalate, I also intervened in a calm manner, but that seemed to only make things worse. The policeman got so worked up and enraged, and his manner was so threatening that you would have thought he had caught us red-handed desecrating Zagreb cathedral (finished in 1217, and described by Rebecca West, the English writer who toured Yugoslavia for two months in the first half of 1939, as one of the few fine buildings in the city, a "Gothic cathedral [...] that has been forced to wear an ugly nineteenth-century overcoat"[540]). We continued to respond in a calm, deferential yet insistent manner, and slowly moved back towards the camp. Eventually, like a fierce farm dog guarding the entrance to his master's property against any and all passers, he grew tired, and having established his supremacy, returned to his vigil on the road.

But it wasn't all bad with the Croatian police. I saw at least one instance, and heard of several others, of civilian police officers, shocked by the level of deprivation in the camp, bringing in groceries they had bought with their own money, and giving them to families they had befriended. The relief arriving every day at 6 am would often bring sweets and give them out to the children[lxxvii541]. Typically, each time a new contingent arrived (they were each units from different parts of the country, one contingent from Vinkovci for example, the next from Zagreb, and then Lika-Senj), they would be very hostile, having had it drummed into them that the refugees were the worst of criminals. There would be a peak in arrests after every change, and 9 people were arrested on 9 January[542]. However, as time went by, the police would quickly see the refugees weren't so bad, and relations would improve. I wondered one day whether the people who had worked in Auschwitz had realised they were participating in the most monstrous enterprise of the twentieth century, or whether they just kept their heads down and made the best of a bad job in wartime, hoping things would improve, and blinded by the prevailing propaganda from calling a spade a spade[lxxviii543] (the whole range of human interactions is possible beyond, and in spite of, imposed labels such as "perpetrator/victim" or "enemy", that are supposed to divide people and cast them into set roles. I was once interpreting for a Croatian Serb who was being prosecuted for drink driving at a London magistrates court, and who it transpired had during the war been a guard at a prison camp. I was surprised to say the least when, among the character witnesses who came to give evidence that he was teetotal, I learned that one was not only a Muslim, but had also been one of his prisoners during the war! Their friendship dated back to then. But that didn't stop him being found guilty; indeed, because he had insisted he was teetotal, he was denied the option of attending counselling, which would have allowed a reduction in the term of the ban to which he was sentenced). In December, I started hearing the camp referred to by inmates as a "*konclogor*" ("concentration camp")[lxxix544]. I was sceptical at first, because I knew far worse things had happened over the previous five years. But now I take a different view: a civilian population was deliberately deprived of their basic rights, in breach of international law, with the purpose of pressurising them into accepting a

---

[lxxvii] This appears to have been a widespread practice, for according to Legija, "Every morning, before I got dressed, the first two things I would check [in my pockets] were my fags and my sweets. I never eat sweets, I used to give them to children". The first time I went to Kakanj, our truck was greeted by three youngsters by the side of the road, who after waving to us, shouted, "Hey you! Fuck you! *Daj bonbon!* ['give use some sweets']".

[lxxviii] As George Orwell wrote, "One of the most horrible features of war is that all the war-propaganda, all the screaming and lies and hatred, comes invariably from people who are not fighting".

[lxxix] The term "concentration camp" was borrowed by Lord Kitchener in South Africa in 1900 from the Spanish policy of *reconcentración* in Cuba (to deal with a rebellion which was to lead to the "splendid little" Spanish-American war of 1898, and the loss of the last remnants of the Spanish Empire in the Caribbean and the Pacific), as part of his strategy to bring about an end to the Boer War (1899-1902) by interning the Afrikaners' *vroumense en kinders* ("women and children") and burning their *plase en voorrade* ("farms and food"). The mortality rate in the overcrowded, poorly-supplied camps was found by a government commission in 1901 to be 34%. The Dutch word *boer* means "farmer". Kitchener, who "want[ed] you", was killed in 1916 when the ship on which he was travelling to Russia to arrange military aid to the Tsar, struck a mine off the Orkneys.

regime they had fled from, at the end of the twentieth century in Europe, and the international community was doing nothing! The Croatian government refused to recognise them and provide them with basic security; kept them cold and hungry and denied them basic medical care; obstructed the work of aid agencies; sealed the camp off and prevented visits or the receipt of letters, money and other essentials; directly caused the deaths of several refugees as well as deliberately wounding others who were searching for the means of survival; deported refugees by force; seized private property; and committed multiple cases of verbal and other minor abuse[545]. Some refugees are more equal than others[546]. Why was the international community so swift to accept the propaganda that they were traitors? The EU monitors called Babo's project a "political experiment", that after Operation Storm was "well and truly dead"[547]. *Svakom loncu moraju biti poklopac* ("there's many a slip between cup and lip"). Was it because in a war with officially three sides, another one was just too much to get one's head around? Or because the idea that one ethnic/religious group could have more than one voice went against the "ancient hatreds" mantra that had been peddled by western leaders? Or because Izetbegović, who appears to have considered Babo a greater threat than Karadžić, had been so skilfully portrayed to the world as a kindly old man, a victim rather than a perpetrator, and the incarnation of Sarajevo and its suffering?[548] A clear-cut case of the emperor's new clothes – but who was Sinbad the Sailor? One reason must undoubtedly have been the paucity of primary sources of intelligence. Despite the unprecedented scale of the international deployment to the Balkans, and in particular the number of experts drifting on the wind, the vast majority of opinion-makers and decision-takers were dependent for their raw intelligence on a very restricted number of local intermediaries, who were thus able to feed their propaganda to their international interlocutors, confident that it would be universally diffused and accepted as the regurgitated Gospel. It is certainly true that the Muslims were the underdogs until the final phase of the war, which encouraged and enabled certain apologists for Izetbegović, as the only face of the Muslims to the outside world. Whatever the answer, Izetbegović, who aspired to a unity of faith and the law, of the religious community and the state[549], succeeded in imposing a single narrative of the war. The international community was happy to accept as the legitimate representatives of the Yugoslav people the *vojvode* ("warlords") who had come to power by creating artificial crises, but ignored the sidelining of the only Bosnian politician to ever win over a million votes in an election, and was thus complicit in his political assassination, not to mention the wider war (the much-maligned David Owen appears to have been the only international figure to have paid much attention to Babo, and held a meeting with him in the UNPROFOR base in Polje in December 1992[lxxx][550]). Babo demonstrated

---

[lxxx] Lord Owen writes: "I left in a UN convoy to drive to Velika Kladuša to stay with the French battalion […] That night I met for the first time the leader of the Bihać Muslims, Fikret Abdić. Though later often described as a businessman and rebel Muslim leader, he was in fact a member of the collective Presidency which was the governing body of Bosnia-Herzegovina; popular as a secular Muslim, he had polled the largest number of votes. The snag was that Abdić preferred to stay during the war in the Bihać region […] he was forthright, confident and different from the Sarajevan Muslims. He was in favour of negotiating and compromising with Croats and Serbs to achieve a settlement, and scathing about those Muslims who wanted to block any such settlement. In many ways it was easier for him to adopt this approach than Izetbegović, for he had a regional constituency who for centuries had traded with Croats and Serbs in and around Bihać […] At this stage Abdić was semi-detached from the Sarajevo government and had no time for Izetbegović's attitudes, believing that he was perpetuating the war, and made this unequivocally clear. I urged him to attend Presidency meetings in Sarajevo more often and to use his influence there". Izetbegović accused Owen of being pro-Serb.

that consensus is possible in the Balkans, but his position that peace should come first, regardless of the model adopted, was discredited and portrayed as evidence of treason. On 28 February 2006, the Croatian weekly *Nacional* published a list of 1,700 former KOS agents in Croatia, which included Izetbegović (but not Babo, who can count the charge of being a KOS agent as just one of the many accusations frequently levelled against him): Izetbegović was apparently recruited while he was in prison in the 1980s[551]. As they say in the Balkans, "*Ničija nije do zore gorila*" ("you can't fool all the people all the time"); but as George Orwell said in *1984* (the year Milošević became head of the Belgrade KPJ[552]), "Who controls the past, controls the future; who controls the present, controls the past"[lxxxi][553]. The international community was also complicit in Auschwitz (the Allies acknowledged Hitler's policy of extermination in December 1942, and discussed Nazi death camps in April 1943, but no action was undertaken to disrupt their operation. ICRC also failed to publicly condemn the death camps, concerned that its access to POWs would be compromised if it did so. This is now acknowledged as having been a tragic error[554]).

In September, 200 Feds (federation police, i.e. joint SDA-HDZ, from central Bosnia) were deployed to Velika Kladuša and Cazin, to increase security and reduce tension, as the refugees had more confidence in people from elsewhere in the country, in fact in anyone except the 5th Corps. At the end of November, a tripartite Turkish-Croatian-Bosnian police force (100 Feds, 50 Croats and 50 Turks) was set up in the former enclave, based on a model that had apparently proved effective in Mostar, ostensibly to serve as guarantor for the safety of returnees[555], although I didn't see much evidence of them on the ground. Nor was their mandate communicated to the refugees in Kuplensko[556] (it was only investigative, not executive[557]). Refugees said that anyway 200 of them couldn't provide lasting security anywhere[558]. The Turks drove through Kuplensko on their arrival on 5 December; some thought they were three months too late, while others were concerned they would regard them as Kurds; still others thought they would feel an affinity with Izetbegović's politics. Some people didn't think much of their presence at all[559]. The three commanders of the new police visited the camp on 15 December, together with a delegation from the three governments. Their position was that there would be no resettlement abroad, and that the only options were to return or stay in the camp[560]. It was said the Croatian riot police would guard the houses of "at-risk" individuals in Bosnia 24 hours a day[561]. The tripartite police came back on 6 January, and again on the 16th[562] (and on 7 February, when they reported a drop in the number of incidents in the former enclave[563]), and the Bosnian local radio later reported they had told the refugees the best thing for them was to go home. As Ramo commented, everyone seemed to know what was best for the refugees; but the real problem wasn't in Kuplensko, it was in the former enclave, and it wasn't a police problem, but a political one, as the local authorities were behind the crimes visited on returning refugees[564]. The tripartite police's mandate was for six months, and they left on 5 July[565]. I had previously, in 1994, encountered the West European Police on the road between Konjic and Mostar, composed of a Muslim, a Croat and a German (he was one of 200 EU police officers deployed to Mostar under the Washington Agreement). The German was very polite and seemed to be doing all the work, and

---

[lxxxi] In May 1937, Burmese-born George Orwell was shot through the neck while fighting in Spain, and was told he would never speak again. Was Izetbegović one of his "obscure martyrs to [poly]gamy"?

asked me to humour them and go along with the charade, while the Muslim appeared to be just standing there swearing, and the Croat was nowhere to be seen.

Many of the political leaders from Velika Kladuša, as well as the NOZB high command, found themselves among the refugee population. While they had quickly formed a camp committee, and made sure they were visible in all dealings with the aid community, their official authority was largely eclipsed by events and was effectively confined to the ongoing political negotiations on the future of the camp and its inmates. They had had more authority during the previous refugee crisis, so much so that they had been able, under pressure from Legija, to impose a general mobilisation for the recapture of Velika Kladuša. Nevertheless, they retained a moral authority, and by November Ramo was generally recognised by the international community as the legitimate leader of the refugees in the camp, and the more professional organisations went out of their way to keep him informed[566]. While in the previous refugee crisis the local authorities had been accused of controlling the refugees, this time the international community eventually came to rely on the organisation and management of the committee, as it was reliable and efficient[567].

In September, the committee produced an action plan for implementation of the agreement signed in August, which was sent to all and sundry and formed the basis of all their efforts at negotiation. There was no response from any quarter. In Kuplensko, the ten distribution points were used as a basis for forming a series of *mjesne zajednice* ("ward committees"), on the same model as existed in Bosnia before the war (and which were effectively a tool of KPJ control at grassroots level). On 11 September, a public meeting was held in an attempt to create some order in the camp[568]. At the same time, the proceedings of the weekly coordination meetings were followed carefully by a wide section of the population, and here the politicians' experience and skills came into their own: they mounted an uncompromising defence of the interests of the refugee population with (and against) the international community and the Bosnian and Croatian authorities. In the previous refugee crisis, their relationship with UNHCR had been described by the EU monitors as "hostile"[569]. On 6 October, the committee wrote a letter to UNHCR asking for better coordination, and an improvement in security in the camp[570]. At the coordination meeting of 25 October, Ramo accused UNHCR of a litany of failings, and said that the only thing that worked in the camp was the daily bread run[571] (the only time the bread was late, other than on public holidays when a double ration was delivered the day before, was on 18 July, when due to complications the bakers had to get extra bread delivered from Zagreb and it arrived at 11.30 am. There may also have been another reason for this hiccup, see below[572]). UNHCR were keen to find a solution that would see the refugees return as soon as possible[573]. The leaders, including the *efendija* ("imam"), were of the view on 9 November that UNHR was "working against us", and that once the tripartite police was established, they would all be sent back. According to reports from the ground, the security situation was deteriorating for returnees in the enclave[574]. On 14 November, the 100th day in the camp, the committee submitted a report to UNHCR, setting out the priority needs and calling for a political solution. They also asked UNHCR to identify the "war criminals" that the Bosnian local radio reported were hiding among the refugees, and were allegedly an excuse for the Croatian authorities' failure to allow basic welfare[575].

On 29 September, a meeting with the authorities was organised in Velika Kladuša at the request of the committee, to discuss implementation of the agreement. The delegation from the camp, which included Mirvet and Ramo, was driven by

UNHCR, and entry into Velika Kladuša was not without its problems. Eventually the Feds were summoned and escorted them into the town (and back again afterwards). Both sides were politely uncompromising: the local authorities insisted everyone come back before discussing further issues, while the refugees wanted a series of guarantees concerning their immediate and long-term future which were not forthcoming. A list of 70 people who had been returned by force was submitted, with a request to establish their fate; apparently, many of them had been detained despite assurances of an amnesty[576]. Among them was Čauš, another well-known NOZB figure and natural athlete. Throughout this period, both here in the camp, and in Velika Kladuša and Cazin, there was a constant coming and going of people trying to establish where their loved ones were. Some had become refugees and were resident somewhere in the camp, others had gone further afield, others had stayed at home or later returned home, while still others had disappeared during hostilities.

The committee's weekly meeting on 27 November was attended by a large number of refugees: they were informed that the conditions for return requested by the committee had not yet been provided by the authorities in Velika Kladuša, such that the recommendation was to wait, but that the decision of those who had decided to go back should be respected[577]. On Saturday 9 December, the committee decided to organise a demonstration outside UNHCR the following Monday. The riot police were informed on the Sunday[578]. The demonstration was to be strictly peaceful, and anyone planning to return on Monday was asked to do so earlier or later, so that there would be no returns that day[579]. The demonstration took place at 12.30, and was attended by 5-6,000 refugees as well as Croatian journalists and most of the aid agencies operating in the camp. The police were there in force, but there were no incidents. Placards carried slogans such as, *"Hoćemo razgovore"* ("we want to talk"), *"Dok je nas biće i Zapadna Bosna"* ("we are West Bosnia")[lxxxii], *"Mi mladi tražimo što hitnije rješavanje našeg statusa"* ("we young people want an urgent resolution to our status"), *"Sve je džabe kad nema Babe"* ("Babo or bust"). There were several addresses by the refugee leaders, including a letter from Babo[580]. The following day the Croatian newspaper *Vjesnik* reported the demonstration under the headline, "Fear and distrust hinder return", and stated that 400-600 refugees were now returning every day[581]. On 14 December, a rally was held, attended by 4-5,000 refugees, and there were calls for a visit by Babo and the US ambassador on Christmas Day, when the next rally would be held (the police were informed on 21 December, and weren't happy that they would have to work on Christmas Day[582]). The same day, the Dayton peace agreement was signed in Paris by the three warlords[583]. The committee now had a further legal basis for insisting on proper security conditions for their return. On 19 December, it was announced that 100 refugees would hold a 48-hour hunger strike, in the international community's tents, as of 21 December, with the objective of raising awareness of their demands[584]. If there was no response, then further and wider, possibly unlimited hunger strikes would follow[585] (hunger strikes had also been arranged during the previous refugee crisis)[586]. On 22 December it was decided to continue the strike until Christmas Day[587]. Two foreign journalists visited the strikers on 23 December, while UNHCR were conspicuous by their absence during the whole period of the strike[588].

Meanwhile, the committee was in sporadic contact with Babo, who was in Rijeka, and by November were urging him to take a view and communicate it to the

---

[lxxxii] Was Kuplensko the 144th district of Bosnia?

refugees[589]. The position appeared to be that Babo was waiting for the next elections, when he would be able to obtain new legitimacy[590]. Soon after the exodus, posters of Babo with the slogan "*Ja sam opet tu!*" ("I'm still here") had started to appear in the camp. When I had first started working in Velika Kladuša, there had been posters of him with the slogan "*Ja sam tu!*" ("I'm here"), which I was told dated from the previous refugee crisis. On 28 November, a 30-minute address by Babo was recorded over the telephone and played to the refugees. He started by reiterating that the same peace agreement could have been reached in 1993, but that Izetbegović had rejected it, and that as a result they had been forced to go their own way. He then enjoined on them that West Bosnia wasn't finished, and that they would have final victory at the ballot box (even though Izetbegović was attempting to disqualify him from standing by charging him with war crimes, a bar under Dayton). He also accused UNHCR of being politicised and acting in contravention of its mandate by bringing pressure to bear on Tuđman on behalf of Izetbegović, in the guise of warning him not to do anything to undermine the Federation; in particular, he stated that Izetbegović was not happy Babo was one of the signatories to the August agreement. Babo had been given a mandate by the Bosnian people in the 1990 elections, but power had been usurped by Izetbegović *et al* who in five years had led the country to ruin, in sharp contrast to his own success in 36 years of business. He stated that now Izetbegović was capable of anything, including placing them in a concentration camp in an attempt to destroy them, and was manipulating the international community in order to discredit and disqualify the people's true choice. He accused Izetbegović of autocracy and branding anyone who disagreed with him a traitor, and of resorting to JNA tactics and using the media to defame him, in particular when Babo was representing the presidency at peace talks in Geneva in 1993. He said the real issue wasn't about providing security so that refugees could go back to destroyed houses and unemployment, but rather about regaining the freedom to determine their own destiny. He said the Bihać pocket was now under the control of the mafia, in the persons of Izetbegović and Dudaković, and that Dayton opened an opportunity for them to restore the political project that Izetbegović had sought to destroy by force. He said Izetbegović was establishing himself as a military dictator, using the Serb threat as a smokescreen to block demobilisation. In conclusion, he stated that return had to be on their terms[591]. In their reactions to the address the refugees were divided: some were inspired to hold out, while others decided it was time to go back in the absence of any concrete plan. However, fears of insecurity were still founded[592]. The committee set about canvassing the refugees for membership of the DNZ[593]. Within a week they had nearly 9,000 paid-up members[594].

In the words of another child, Amela:

"My home is Kumarica. It was quite built up, but now it's destroyed, because there was a lot of fighting there during the war. A lot of houses ended up with no roof or furniture, and some of them were burned down. I was first a refugee in Turanj, and went back with my family in 1995. We were in a house in Velika Kladuša, and after a time we returned home. We rebuilt our village, Kumarica. I lived there until 7 August 1995. Now I'm a refugee again with my family in Kuplensko. All my close relatives are refugees too. My best friends Alma, Aida, Edita and others stayed in Kladuša. I really miss them. My friend Mirela came here with me. We did English together, and later we were in year three together. Mirela went home with my cousins on 15 March.

161

I have a brother and a sister. Here I live in a small room in the attic. We've been here for nine months. I'm in year three of junior school. I completed years one and two in Podzvizd [a suburb of Velika Kladuša, east of Trnovi], with distinction. I don't have a lot of friends here. I want to go home, to live in peace and freedom again. And to continue at my school. I would like to meet my friends again one day and my teacher Biserka who taught me in years one and two. I would like Ahmet to teach me again, he was my teacher in year three in the refugee camp. I would like to live with my relatives again and see my aunt again, who went to live in Canada a long time ago"[595].

BOSNIAN RED CROSS

In the tent of the Red Cross
On the bridge, sixth quarter
Every service is offered by us
To each and every visitor

A personal message is read
Other favours are offered
Coffee is often served
And blank messages proffered

Družan is the director
Of the Bosnian Red Cross
There isn't a bigger fool
From Skopje to Trieste

And it's like this every day
Many people call by
You'd have to look far and wide
For a fool bigger than Smaj'

In the camp I'm all alone
And make coffee just for me
Am I a fool as well
No comment for now from me

Let's put aside for now
Those dilemmas and pains
Let's move on and see
All the main problems

For instance the fire won't burn
Because there isn't any tinder
And always shouting to be heard
Smajo Seka and Minja

Today I'm on duty
Tomorrow you, maybe
In the tent of the Red Cross
It seems we're all crazy

Then when I go in
And stand beside the wall
Read my fortune in the beans
Crazy Aida calls

Fadila sitting at the table
Always writing some stuff

What they've written on the door
Ćamila has to wipe off

Then I have a look at her
On her face a strange expression
Smajo gives her a new name
It's not Fadila but kitten

Husmira just keeps still
She's too quiet somehow
Another one changes her name
And that's our Mediha

Zlatan sitting to the side
To be precise on his right cheek
Mediha isn't Mediha
Now she's cheeky chick

Then Račinović Ajša
That's my weaker side
She's always keeping quiet
And smiling on the side

If it isn't like this
Then may God deal me a blow
There's still Rurić and Velić
And with them Kudić Zumro

I totally forgot
Družan's godmother was there
Peaceful peaceful engaging
Feđinca Purić Džemila

But there's one more problem
Curić still isn't there
We've got a special case here
That Omanović Eka

She's strange really strange
Just yawns and keeps quiet
With Mirvet she plays poker
Always something on the side

Sweet attractive cheerful
Suddenly lost in painful thought
She's thinking again of
Holland and Orčev Port

She's troubled by a problem
She's hiding it here

I know it's difficult for her
And she often sheds a tear

I know that problem of hers
Time has told it to me
But she is soon going to
Solve her difficulties

Irfo and Hasiba at the side
They're cheered up by a fuss
They call us every night
And come round to see us

And that's the way it goes
In the tent of the Red Cross
There isn't a bigger madhouse
From here to Trieste[596].

Sead "Tetin" Kajtazović, Paklena Dolina

Družan, the head of the LCK, was always around during the day. Previously, he had held the same post in Velika Kladuša, and I had worked closely with him. He had organised a system of 12 (later increased to 18) distribution points throughout the territory controlled by the NOZB, and we would carry out monthly distributions to beneficiaries at each of the points, based on criteria and statistics agreed together. Družan had the use of a truck and a fuel allowance from the council for his work, and I had a truck for local distributions as well (we would also top the LCK truck up from time to time. The driver, Did Šakan, died shortly after the war). Some of the villages were extremely isolated, practically cut off even in peacetime, with no proper roads. I attended one of the distributions outside the town, in the village of Ponikve to the north of the enclave, with a barite mine and close to the border (usually I was refused access to territory outside the town, other than when travelling to Cazin). Mining and forestry were and are Bosnia's main sources of potential wealth, and like Central Asia, it also has major fresh water resources (the economic crisis that erupted after the death of Tito most affected those parts of Yugoslavia whose economies were based on raw materials and energy production, while those republics where the raw materials were processed into finished products benefited from consumer inflation that reached 40% by the end of 1980; the same year, the government of Slovenia attempted to persuade the Bosnian authorities to accept the role of service economy, a supplier of raw materials, energy and cheap labour to the more sophisticated Slovenian economy, and organise their affairs accordingly[597]). It was only 5 km or so to Ponikve, but the roads were so bad it took the best part of an hour to get there. Everything went off without a hitch – the list of beneficiaries had been agreed in advance, and everyone knew what they were entitled to receive. On the way back to the town, we came across a group of squaddies at what appeared to be a RV. They were milling around a civilian truck, looking very irregular, with few proper uniforms and a variety of weapons. Sometimes only a white ribbon tied to the shoulder served to distinguish the NOZB from the 5th Corps[598]. Uniforms were often home-made, cut from tent fabric[599]. Their units had picturesque names such as

Popeye, Metalci ("metalheads"), and Šejla. Painted on the *cerada* ("tarpaulin") on the side of their truck was a giant, grotesque picture of Rambo (I didn't ask whether it was from Rambo 3, when he joins the *Mudžahedin*). They appeared to be a ragged band, but both they and the 5th Corps had a fierce reputation with the Serbs (in total in the intra-Muslim war, more 5th Corps soldiers were killed fighting the NOZB (1,700) than fighting the VRS and SVK (1,300))[600]. Legija described them as a "motley crew", adding: "In many ways we actually looked more like Partisans from WWII, than a modern army from the end of the millennium"[601]. Družan's team consisted mainly of very pleasant young women, a unit of Amazons with a sacred trust that they executed diligently, day in day out. Legija would make a point of dropping in to enquire after their welfare whenever he was in Velika Kladuša. One weekend Družan invited me to a LCK *teferič*, which was an experience not to be forgotten. Družan was now living in a hut he had built for his wife and boy from plasterboard, among other materials. He had worked closely with Mirvet in setting up the similar system of 10 distribution points along the road at the beginning of the refugee crisis. Because there was no warehouse space in the camp, we had to unload our trucks directly at the distribution points. To facilitate this, we asked the team in Split to load them in such a way that the goods could be brought off in 10 equal parts. This inevitably led to some difficulties, with the result that not every distribution point received an equitable share, and consequently nor did every beneficiary. The variety of goods provided, which could not always be conveniently broken down in advance, meant that the staff at the distribution points sometimes had to make decisions on the spot about how to distribute goods, which led to some complaints, accusations of unfairness, and inevitably corruption. This only made a potentially explosive situation worse[602]. Point 7, the most problematic, was discontinued in February, ostensibly due to the reduced number of refugees[603]. Družan had a splinter of *geler* ("shrapnel") in one eye, and was no longer eligible for military service. He had been wounded after walking for miles waist-deep in the snow in a flanking manoeuvre by the NOZB into the Bihać pocket from Plitvice via Izačić in December 1993 (made possible by the grant of freedom of movement by the SVK, a tactic successfully used to a lesser extent the previous month to advance on Šturlić from Johovica[604]). He was a born organiser and leader, which is just what the local Red Cross needed.

We would gather in the LCK tent in the evenings to make merry. There were never fewer than a dozen of us, and we had some legendary sessions. We would play charades, tell stories, and many of the other activities that have sustained communities for millennia, and which have now been supplanted by technology and isolation. Tetin was a dab hand at *gatanje/drabaripe* ("reading fortunes"), either by casting the *grah* ("beans"; uncooked, and cast onto a cloth: the best possible forecast, a full house, is indicated by simply covering the beans up with the cloth, any explanation being inadequate and superfluous), or reading the *talog od kafe/boštiji kafake* ("dregs in the bottom of a coffee cup"). Good, clean fun. The candle-lit, dark tent was more than illuminated by the hopes and dreams of the young spirits who gathered within.

Sometimes the ICRC staff would join us, especially Justin. Eddie, a rocker who spoke excellent American English, was not only a key member of the ICRC local team but also doubled as the interpreter at the interagency coordination meetings at UNHCR. Mirvet was also a regular feature. His brother, Irfo, was a rock guitarist who had fought on four sides before ending up in Kuplensko. Such was the devastating logic of the Yugoslav Wars. Their other brother had been killed in the 5th Corps. One of the songs Irfo used to sing was one of Tetin's poems set to music:

> *"Deseto čudo ovog je rata*
> *Da puca brat na svoga brata*
> *Ne pamti niko to od davnina*
> *Da puca otac na svoga sina*
>
> *Imamo devet mi svjetskih čuda*
> *Deseto kod nas desi se sad*
> *Umjesto sreće i lijepih ruža*
> *Želimo bijedu nesreću i glad*
>
> *Razmisli malo ti rođeni oče*
> *Da li da pucaš kad sina vidiš*
> *Kako ćeš sutra mu gledati u oči*
> *Zar nećeš pred njim da se stidiš"*[lxxxiii]

Smajo, the youngest of the crowd, from Skokovi, who had been too young for military service during the war, was also the life and soul of the party. His job was to leisurely cycle through the camp with a megaphone, announcing the names of people who had a Red Cross message ready for collection. He had been Seka's assistant in Velika Kladuša before Operation Storm. When his family returned to Bosnia from Kuplensko, he remained behind, as a precautionary measure, which was just as well, because his whole family were attacked and severely beaten in their own home. When he heard the news he drank himself into a pitiful stupor, to much consolation and reassurance from the rest of us. That night, trying to re-enter the tent from a vomiting session outside, he got stuck under the pallets that formed the floor of the LCK tent and had to be hauled out.

Not among the refugees was Timka, who having experienced refugee life in Turanj, decided to give it a miss this time. Timka and Seka had been inseparable, a blonde-brunette double act, and together they were the LCK's ambassadors to the outside world. Never mind that neither of them spoke English, their very presence had an articulate and convincing rhetoric all of its own, backed up by hand-written monthly distribution reports. Timka was originally from Pjanići, but happened to be in Velika Kladuša when the intra-Muslim war started, and stayed there until

---

[lxxxiii] "The eighth wonder of this war
Is when brother shoots at brother
Something unheard of in history
Sons shot at by their father

Seven world wonders there are
The eighth one is right here
But instead of a bed of roses
Our lot is hunger, woe and fear

Think for a moment father
When you see your son before you fire
How will you look him in the eye
Tomorrow he'll call you a liar".

Operation Storm, steadfastly refusing to take a view on who was right in the fratricidal conflict.

On Christmas Day, Jamie from FTC (another Scot, who also spoke the lingo) turned up dressed as Father Christmas and handed out *pokloni* ("presents") to children, which was very much appreciated. He was a former *unproforac* ("peacekeeper"), and had been taken hostage by the VRS in Goražde the year before. ICRC brought their local team a giant Toblerone, so large that the individuals slabs were said to weigh 1-2 kg. Midnight on Christmas Eve was marked by a session of shooting and detonations by the patriotically religious police. Some of the shooting was into the refugees' tents, which caused some deaths; the tents in question were later inspected by the UN police. UNHCR were not open on Christmas Day, nor was there a bread delivery that day[605]. Deliveries of other aid over the festive period were also reduced[606]. Another rally was held on Christmas Day, attended by 4-5,000 refugees. It began with a show of *folklor* ("country dancing") and singing, followed by speeches. A large Christmas tree was set up on the bridge, decorated with slogans and messages. Bosnian prime minister Silajdžić briefly visited the periphery of the camp, just long enough to be filmed, and allegedly promised to come back on 4 January[607]. He turned up again on 6 January, and advised refugees to return home, saying the security situation was in hand. The visit was reported on the local radio, who added that there was a problem with returnees bringing back weapons with them, especially to Cazin[608].

However, New Year is the main annual celebration in the former Yugoslavia, and New Year's Eve 1995/1996 was an especially intense and emotional festival in Kuplensko, as people were reminded all the more of how they were cut off from those they loved and would have loved to be with that night of all nights. They were also reminded that the previous year, they had just returned home triumphant from a refugee crisis, determined to never let it happen again[609]. Nevertheless, an effort was made by some aid agencies, despite the police, to provide the means to eat, drink and make merry in due and proper form, such that the winter of discontent was not entirely bleak. For a time at least, people could put out of their minds the "cold, the hunger, the fear, uncertainty, lack of prospects and general stress", as Ramo put it[610]. And the war was officially over! Pandža dressed up as Father Christmas and gave children presents (as the population were mostly Muslims, Christmas had not been celebrated in the camp, other than by the riot police, who were not paragons of good will to all men, and aid workers). The first IFOR (post-Dayton peacekeepers) column on its way to West Bosnia passed through the camp on New Year's Day[611]. There was a rally at 2 pm by the bridge, attended by 2,000 refugees in the sleet, with *a capella* music and country dancing. The head of the riot police contingent was among the speakers, and briefly wished everyone all the best for 1996[612]. The real celebrations kicked off in the evening. Timka visited from Velika Kladuša, courtesy of ICRC. In the middle of the festivities, someone said that Tetin was lying outside in the snow. In our high spirits, we roused ourselves and went out to get him. There he was, blind drunk, lying on his back despairing in the snow. We managed to get him back on his feet and back inside, where we returned to our vice with a will. It was that evening that I learnt the word *ringišpil* ("big wheel"), used to describe the stage of inebriation when the world starts to spin around the drinker. As is traditional, and right, there was some shooting into the air to mark the occasion, although it was subdued for fear of provoking a response from the police (at the same moment, there was uncontrolled shooting into the air in a mass public victory celebration in Cazin; of the many rounds fired up into the skies, one came back to earth and struck a child on the head, killing her instantly). Outside, the valley partly lit by the few generator-driven spotlights, I felt like I was walking through a Christmas card. There was a thick layer of snow everywhere, that had accumulated over several days, and now everything was still. There was no biting wind as there tends to be in the north of England, and it was as if the earth, the trees and the sky had conspired to suspend for a kind moment a fragile bubble of warmth for the fleeting benefit of man. The crunch of our feet in the snow only reinforced this magical, festive image, and the intoxication raised our spirits up to the black heavens. All the joys of life can be condensed into such instants, undergoing a mystical transformation and multiplication of intensity. It is not in longevity or material possessions that we should seek satisfaction.

The main Muslim festival, Bajram (*Eid al Fitr*), which follows on from the month of fasting, Ramazan[lxxxiv], was celebrated in subdued and emotional manner in the camp on 20 February (in the former Yugoslavia there were not only two Christmases - Catholic on 25 December and Orthodox on 7 January – but also the main Muslim festival, held every 12 lunar months, and so occurring earlier each year. However, Easter is more important than Christmas in the Balkans). "Happy Bajram" is expressed using the Turkish formula, "*Bajram šerif mubarek olsun*". It is usual at Bajram to visit family graves, which was not possible this year (although Muslims at home in Bosnia were allowed to visit their relatives' graves located in SDS territory, with an IFOR escort). Bajram is usually celebrated with roast lamb and *baklava* (a very sweet, many-layered pastry), part of which has to be distributed to the poor. It is also a day for giving *sadake* ("alms")[613][lxxxv]. It is customary to leave the *kapija* ("gates") to one's home open, indicating to anyone passing by that they are welcome to come in and partake of God's bounty. I later noticed the same tradition in Chechnya, where I bought a lamb which Adam, one of our drivers, skilfully transformed into *šašliki* ("kebabs"). There were two services for 400 believers in the makeshift mosque in Kuplensko, and most people watched the proceedings from Sarajevo on the few televisions available[614]. A rally was held the next day, with an address by the imam, followed by Ramo, and attended by 1,000 refugees[615]. A letter with season's greetings was written to the grand mufti of Croatia, Šefko Omerbašić[616]. The second part of the festival, Second Bajram (*Eid al Adha*), was held on 28 April, with a rally attended by 1,500 refugees[617]. The graves of those buried in the camp, to the right of the road in Kuplensko, were visited[618]. This time, a letter with season's greetings was written to the grand mufti of once-

---

[lxxxiv] The ninth month of the Islamic calendar. Fasting is between dawn and dusk, the official times of which are communicated by the religious authorities. During daylight hours, nothing must pass the believer's lips, including cigarette smoke, and even water. Officially, alcohol (and sex) is forbidden during the whole month, and the three-day festivities that follow (as an infidel, I was granted a dispensation). An Algerian ICRC engineer in Timor, who had previously worked in Chechnya, once told me that he had found it very difficult fasting one Ramazan while working during the dry season in Sudan, although fasting is not obligatory during emergencies. In the Balkans, believers usually get up very early to have a large breakfast before dawn, and then break their fast in a communal ritual at dusk, *iftar*. Like *Korizma* ("Lent"), not everyone commits to keep the fast.

[lxxxv] Once in Turkmenistan, when travelling incognito by minibus-taxi through the semi-desert from the capital Ašhabat to the town of Mari, once a logistics base for ICRC operations into Afghanistan, I was surprised when the driver suddenly swerved right over to the other side of the road and stopped. Leaning across, he wound down the passenger window, and with a few words I didn't catch, thrust a handful of banknotes into the hand of an elderly man in a wheelchair on the pavement. At first I assumed they were related, but when I saw the old man make the Muslim gesture of thanks to providence (the hand travelling down the beard), I realised the driver had just given alms.

Byzantine Macedonia, Jakup Selimoski[619] (no letter was sent to Cerić in Sarajevo, Izetbegović's grand inquisitor[lxxxvi620]).

On 8 March, international women's day, an important holiday in former communist countries and celebrated religiously in the former Yugoslavia, was marked in style. 2,000 refugees gathered to enjoy a show of music, dance, singing and comedy, supported by the NGO Marie Stopes[621].

The Islamic New Year was celebrated on 19 May, in much improved weather, with speeches[622]. The committee informed the refugees that they had been assured the camp would not be closed by force, and that humanitarian aid would continue until the last refugee had left[623].

On 18 April, the two-year anniversary of the relaunch of Agrokomerc, a shaky and ultimately unsuccessful first step towards turning swords into ploughshares, was celebrated with speeches, dance, song, and a karate performance[624]. On 29 June 1996, a sunny day, a sports day was held in the camp, attended by 3,000 refugees, to celebrate the registration of the DNZ for the elections[625]. After the main events, which included football, 1,000, 2,000 and 4,000 metres, 100 metre sprint, standing jump and shot put, paralympics, horse racing and a comic donkey race, as well as junior events, darts and table tennis, accompanied by music, singing and speeches, Babo was on the phone and addressed the people. He was optimistic of victory, having qualified for the elections against all the odds. He lamented that thus far he had not had proper media access, but promised an economic miracle in Bosnia. In a later speech, one of the committee members called for a clear separation between state and church/mosque as part of the party programme[626]. A previous sports day, on 22 October, had included a chess tournament[627]. Prior to that, a football tournament had been held, with each distribution point fielding a team. A new season started in the camp in late April, refereed by the camp's biggest chain-smoker, and organised by Samir's father, Sulejman, a former teacher and a committee member[628]. The final was played on 25 May between distribution points 5A and 10, and was won 4-2 by 5A, with a crowd of 2,000[629] (25 May was Tito's official birthday, although he was born on 7 May, and the culmination in the JNA stadium in Belgrade of the annual "youth relay", which started in Tito's home town of Kumrovec in Croatia and passed through all the main towns of Yugoslavia with a message for Tito contained in the hollow baton; in 1995, 71 young people celebrating the holiday in Tuzla were killed by VRS artillery [lxxxvii630]). On 27 April, there was a veterans' match between Miholjsko and Kuplensko[631]. A basketball tournament started on Mayday, another holiday in the Balkans[632]. On 27 May, four years after the Sarajevo bread queue massacre in which 18 people were killed by a mortar, a friendly was played between Kuplensko and Miholjsko, which ended in an honourable draw, 1-1[633]. On 5 June, a new season kicked off with teams made up from the wards in Bosnia[634]. The match on 21 June was complemented by entertainment in the form of two refugees dressed up as EU

[lxxxvi] A report by the ombudsman from 2000 stated that a *fetva* ("ban") issued by the grand mufti in 1994 banning *dženaze* ("funerals") for NOZB soldiers and supporters, was still in force. Imams who ignored the order risked being defrocked.
[lxxxvii] In 1986, at the same time as the Serb memorandum was leaked, the Slovenian KPJ youth movement announced it would no longer take part in the youth relay, as Tito had been dead for six years. This was the first direct challenge to Tito's authority, and paved the way for the challenge to the JNA's authority in Slovenia. The 1995 atrocity was followed by NATO air strikes, and in response the VRS carried out another mass UNPROFOR hostage-taking. They were all released in June.

monitors, inspecting the stands, and giving the spectators advice on how to live their lives[635] (Nikola later described the EU monitors to me as "those blokes dressed in white who didn't do anything". Kiwi and I once encountered three of them at the Maljevac border crossing, where they were being asked by the NOZB border agency for their permit to enter West Bosnia. Seeking to expedite proceedings so that we could be on our way, I interpreted this for them, to which the leader of the Men in White, an Englishman described by Kiwi as an "eccentric old count", replied pompously: "We don't need permits", before driving off up the hill into Velika Kladuša in their Portuguese UMM 4x4 as if to prove the point. At least they didn't break down halfway up[lxxxviii]). The final was played on 22 July, and won by the refugees from Cazin. In a victory ceremony, the winners were awarded prizes provided by the DNZ (notebooks, pens and *fajcaci*, "fag lighters")[636].

[lxxxviii] I once had the pleasure of having the use of an UMM foisted on me, during Spain's presidency of the EU. After the steering wheel failed twice, and then the gear stick, I conveyed to the EU office in Zagreb that if they wanted guinea pigs for their developing-world industrial production, then they should come and drive it around the war zone themselves. In response, they asked me to abandon it outside a police station the next time I was in HDZ land, where OSCE would pick it up for them. After the first half of the Yugoslav Wars, the Spanish foreign minister became NATO secretary general, in good time to bomb Yugoslavia, before mutating into the EU's foreign affairs chief for a decade.

BIRTHDAY PARTY

We're gathered here tonight people from all parts and ways
We've come one and all because it's a birthday
On the table plenty food and drinks to be had
There's girls there and a few lads

When we set off for the birthday Haris we called
He didn't come 'cause he had a few chores
He hasn't got a gift to give or any drinks
He had to shoot off to Vojnić

While Hasiba lays the table with dishes and plates
In comes PC Omer through the gate
He stands at the door, looks us all o'er
Greets and toasts us and sits beside Irfo

While Mirvet beside Irfo sits and drifts away
Hasiba at the cooker gets the coffee ready
Then shouts can be heard and cries of fun
While Bajrić takes photos of us all one by one

While he photographs us his bald head reflects the light
The coffee arrives but it's too white
What's that I ask, does anyone see
Hasiba's put milk in our coffee

On the couch little Haris and Eka sitting beside him
She's got a headache but no aspirin
Tetin's on the couch next to Eka
And John's sitting leaning across Seka

I look at Eka and I'm sorry her head hurts her
Then remember the one my heart yearns for
And from pain drink brandy the sadness to smother
I want to be faithful to her and don't want another

Družan's drinking and beside him young Minja sitting
Off goes Smajo to the tent and brings Justin
Mirvet drinks and eats a bite
And toasts with me the one that's not here tonight

Justin comes in and wishes happy birthday to Hasiba
On the table plenty of halva[lxxxix] and sirnica[xc]
He kisses her and stands there a bit
Then brings out a litre of drink and gives her it

[lxxxix] Sweet desert.
[xc] Cheese pastry.

Hasiba takes the litre and pours us all out a drink
Everyone's eyes light up and blink
Dino in the room without company
Then Justin wishes Hasiba returns, many happy

Ibro's wife came too but of Ibro no sound nor sight
He stayed in the room to rest the night
Then everyone with Ija toasts the day
And charades we start to play

Someone tells stories, someone jokes, while the rest laugh
Then Omer's called on the VHF
The situation to go and see
Someone in the wood's chopping the last tree

Then half the company goes and half of them stay on
I'm drunk and hardly cross the bridge home
Why do you drink Tetin when you know it's bad
You haven't got anyone to take you back home to bed[637].

Sead "Tetin" Kajtazović, Paklena Dolina

To: UNHCR, Kuplensko

18 December 1995

Dear sir

Having abandoned their homes and departed as refugees, the people from the region of West Bosnia have been resident here in Kuplensko in improvised shelters, some in houses and in tents, since 7/8/95. Extremely needy with regard to suitable clothing, shoes, food, firewood and the other necessities of life, we have now entered the fifth month of our existence here in the aforementioned camp, the Infernal Valley.

The physical and other isolation has brought us to a sorry pass, and it is now extremely difficult for us, particularly for the weakest members of the population, the children and elderly persons. How can a family live when it's -5° C in a hut covered with plastic sheeting? And not even properly covered, because there's a shortage of plastic sheeting. Our best building material is cardboard boxes, but unfortunately we don't even have enough of that, and that's without mentioning firewood, and there are even some families without stoves. Is this European civilisation, the democratic Croatia?

Considering that even the worst convicts have visits from family or relatives, which is denied us, we know that such visits would be of great help to us. We have a large diaspora in the countries of central and western Europe. Another problem is firewood, which hasn't been resolved despite many attempts and studies which we've proposed to you and other international humanitarian organisations.

It is particularly worth mentioning the problem of food, which doesn't represent even a third of the minimum needs for which UNHCR has established criteria. There is currently no information on the amounts of food distributed, partly because of the variety of donors, such that a definitive assessment of the quantity of goods received would be extremely useful, as we consider it to be below any minimum.

On 16/11/95 we received the following for the next month:

> fish: one tin per person
> macaroni: half a packet per person
> sugar: half a kilo per person
> beef: one tin per person

We would ask you to take the average life of one person in Europe and compare it with our average, and then tell us how to survive.

In addition, a single person receives 1 tin per week and 320 g of bread per day. Can one bar of soap per month suffice for one person to maintain proper hygiene?

Can one family with 11 members live on 0.75 kg powdered milk, 2.5 kg oil and 1.25 kg washing powder per month? In addition, women with children up to one year don't get milk, so tell us according to your norms how to feed them.

Without going into each norm individually, we would be grateful if you could send us here in the Infernal Valley, i.e. Kuplensko, the European recipe for how to make lunch from flour and oil, for which we will be extremely grateful. While you watch your television and videos, and warm yourselves by means of electricity, I know it's difficult for you to understand us, as here we don't even have tallow candles.

Will you help us? Is this the democratic Croatia and civilised Europe?

We propose that the existing aid be immediately supplemented with the following items:

- pickled cabbage
- onion
- garlic
- powdered eggs
- powdered potatoes
- beans
- fruit, because we consider that we are human as well and have the right to certain vitamins.

We consider that the proposed items will be a useful indication to yourselves in your efforts to help us, particularly our children and other vulnerable groups. Besides the aforementioned please help us with:

- sleeping bags
- mattresses
- firewood
- winter clothing and shoes

We propose the creation of a working agreement at camp level with the representatives of the international humanitarian organisations, within your organisation UNHCR, to agree methods of supply and distribution, that is, the planning of necessary items, because that would certainly help efforts to improve the daily and monthly aid.

Dear sir, we hope that you will understand the sense and purport of our letter, and do everything in your power to help us relieve our extremely difficult situation. May we take this opportunity to wish you a Merry Christmas and a Happy New Year.

Yours sincerely

THE INHABITANTS
Kuplensko

enclosed: norms for the distribution of humanitarian aid[638].

The food was certainly scarce. On 1 December, it was discovered that the bread van was also transporting other, unauthorised items, which resulted in a delay that morning[639]. But apart from the bread, the food deliveries into the camp were uncoordinated and insufficient. According to the EU, the monthly ration in Kuplensko was 16.22 kg per person, whereas it was 10.82 kg in other camps in Croatia, to take account of the particularly difficult position of these refugees[640]. Those who could, bought from those who had the audacity and wit to smuggle supplies in from outside. In the first month, the price of a kilo of raw coffee went up from DM 5 to DM 12[641]. Some local businessmen succeeded in obtaining "work" permits (unpaid) for refugees, which meant they could legitimately come and go from the camp. This opened up many opportunities, the more innocent of which were making telephone calls and going shopping[642]. The sources of the goods on sale in the camp were various: many were looted from abandoned houses in the hamlets and villages outside the camp, others bought or stolen from the nearby towns, such as Slunj and Vrginmost (now called Gvozd). Other goods were obtained from the police guarding the camp, or from NGO staff[643]; while in other cases people sold their own property or property found in their accommodation. I regularly went shopping outside the camp and supplemented the diet of friends, in particular those with children. One day Haris caught sight of and lunged for some bananas I had bought and that Jadra had placed on top of the range to warm up before giving them to him. He was almost seriously burnt, but fortunately his granny saw what was happening and grabbed him just in time. Despite the multitude of agencies now present, FTC was the largest supplier of food to the camp in the early days, and continued to make a difference right up until the end. UNHCR and the EU were the main suppliers of aid in general to the camp after September.

One of the main staples of the refugees' diet was *kljukuša*, which is made by filling a baking tray with a flour and water mix, and then roasting it. In better times, eggs are mixed with the flour and pieces of meat are inserted to enrich it; but in Kuplensko, a few garlic cloves were as good as it got. The most delicious feasts I can remember were on several occasions when I went for lunch with Tetin. When we had the wherewithal, we would have a tin of sardines, a loaf of bread, and some raw onions. Modest as it sounds, for a hungry man it was like the Lord Mayor's banquet. Things were rarely so bad that there was no *rakija*, and so we were able to wash it down generously.

When the EU came, they distributed *narezak* ("tins of meat"). I made sure I got one and eagerly sat down to open it with Seka. Imagine the disappointment when we discovered it was some sort of meat slurry, that couldn't be eaten with bread, and was equally useless in a *tava* ("frying pan"). The taste was so unpleasant that I would not have used it for dog food. I later learned that much of the tinned meat had been returned to the distribution points, and the EU had been asked to take it back. It must have been some sort of reject from the CAP[xci][644]. Other refugees told me it was edible with the addition of a large dose of pepper; but even pepper, like everything else, was in short supply in the camp.

[xci] The EU's controversial Common Agricultural Policy, introduced in 1962 to encourage the development of the European agricultural sector by buying up surplus production. This led to overproduction and the scandals of the "wine lakes" and "butter mountains" at a time of famine in Ethiopia (caused by a regional drought aggravated by forced collectivisation and internal armed conflicts against Eritrean and Tigrean separatists), as a result of which a quotas system was introduced in the EU in the 1980s. According to MSF, the 1985 Live Aid operation, which raised £50-70 million, was manipulated by the Ethiopian communist authorities on the ground to facilitate a forced population movement, in which up to 100,000 people died.

There was a solitary *divlji patak* ("mallard") that survived on the stream flowing under my bridge for far longer than his farmyard cousins. I used to daydream about stuffing him with oranges and roasting him on a spit, but refrained from taking any action, as my position was far easier than anyone else's in the camp, and it was more appropriate that someone else eat him. Nor did I have any *turundže* ("oranges"). And sure enough, one day he was gone.

My staple diet throughout this period was spaghetti. Not spaghetti bolognese, or spaghetti carbonara, but plain spaghetti. For 10 years afterwards, I could not stand the sight of spaghetti, much to the chagrin of our chef in the DRC in 2000. Now I eat it whenever I can, but always with a generous, meaty sauce and plenty of cheese. Indeed, it was my staple diet for a month at Freetown airport in 2014, working with a team of African logisticians, labourers and truckers during the ebola crisis. There were some real characters among the local truckers, most of whom would have eaten the Rubber Duck for breakfast. One of them was an American, who had returned to the old country after the war and invested his savings in a truck. The main haulier, Jemba, was excellent at marshalling and motivating his men, with instructions such as *"Tu by tu!"* ("double stacking"). One of the more amusing examples I came across of their picturesque language, Krio, was an official bilingual sign that read, "No Urinating - *Nor Piss Ja Dortie Man*". One morning I turned up at the airport as usual at 2 am, in time to meet yet another Douglas DC8 with a cargo of 70 tons of aid sent by DFID from the UK, which had to be unloaded, sorted and then reloaded onto a dozen trucks, only to discover that the part of the apron we normally used was occupied by a white Boeing 737 with UN markings. Some enquiries established that the UN secretary general was in town, and we would have to move our operation that morning over to the passenger side of the terminal, as it was unknown how long Ban Ki Moon would be parking his plane there. As there was a passenger flight due in at 11 am, we had to work double quick to get everything shifted before then. I'm sure the secretary-general's visit served some purpose. On another occasion, one of the mythical Antonov 24 cargo planes landed (so large that standing inside one is said to be like standing in a warehouse). The Russian crew were so paranoid about infection that they were all dressed from head to toe in white overalls and wearing face masks (I was only wearing a light shirt, trousers and cap as protection against the sun). They refused to step more than a few meters away from their plane, nor would they let anyone come any nearer. Basic instructions to the ground crew were written in bad English on a piece of paper and left on the ground at a safe distance from the plane, held down by a rock. When I shouted to them that they couldn't catch ebola from such superficial intercourse, a woman replied that their insurance would be invalidated if they had any personal contact with anyone while in Salone. Needless to say, they didn't treat me to a tour of their conveyance[xcii]. Despite all its problems,

---

[xcii] I had a very different experience during a stopover at Minsk airport on a cargo flight to Afghanistan, when the two female *tamoženniki* ("customs officials") who entered our IL76 (banned from most airports because it breaches a raft of environmental standards, not least noise levels) were much more accommodating. Travelling in the passenger seat of an armoured Landcruiser in the cargo hold was better than first class, with excellent suspension and plenty of space, and there was no shortage of entertainment from the Russian *ekipaž* ("crew"), who looked more like truck drivers than airmen. One such plane at Rangoon airport was so loud when it was preparing to take off, that it penetrated deep into my grey matter and disrupted my thought patterns, such as they are, even though I was wearing ear defenders, and even though I walked right through the airport building out onto the other side to get away from it. We also chartered a much smaller AN12 that did a double delivery run from China into Rangoon. The first day they landed, a scruffy character in overalls appeared at the rear ramp, and asked me in Russian, "What country is this?" When I told him it was Burma, he grunted approval before asking me what day it was.

Sierra Leone is one of the nicest countries I've worked in. In Salone I also worked with another Kiwi, Geoff.

Hay later became a problem for the few head of livestock that managed to hold out, thanks to their new owners. UNHCR delivered some bales of hay in mid-December, when most of the livestock had either been eaten or taken (back) to Bosnia[645].

The amount of aid being brought into the camp by UNHCR decreased at the beginning of October, and this, coupled with the general delays in preparing the camp for winter, gave rise to suspicions among the refugees that there was a deliberate strategy to put pressure on them to go back. On 18 October, ICRC once again urged UNHCR to step up the aid effort to deal with the "critical situation"; they had also sent a letter to Tuđman to that effect[646]. One cause of delay was that the EU was procuring blankets from local firms, who were dragging their feet[647]. ICRC distributed 2,000 blankets and 200 tents[648].

Cold was a major issue once winter set it. On the morning of 23 October the temperature was minus 2. No *bablje ljeto* ("Indian summer") this year. The following morning was the first frost of the year[649]. After the first snowflakes on 5 November, the wind that regularly blew down the valley became ever more tangible, and the nights started to become unbearable, and the following day, two full buses of refugees went back home[650]. The days were bad enough, without proper clothing and footwear. The advent of winter also quickly highlighted any defects in the makeshift shelters, which were swiftly remedied one way or another[651]. On the morning of 19 November, there was thick ice, and the water pipes had frozen[652]. From then on, each water point had someone stationed at it permanently, responsible for keeping it clean and making sure the water kept flowing[653]. The first delivery of blankets was on 20 November, followed up by another on 7 December[654]. The morning of 23 November the temperature was minus 10[655]. The first real snow was on 6 December, and the first heavy snow on 12 December[656]. The first *ralica* ("snow plough") went through the camp on 14 December[657]. There was another one on 3 April[658]. On the morning of 29 December, the temperature was an eye-watering minus 15[659]. The 13 days up to and including 27 January all started below zero, while the morning of 10 February was said to be the coldest[660]. From New Year's Day until mid-February, only three days were above zero[661]. The first day of spring, 20 March, started at minus 3[662]. But the children made the most of the white festive season, and there was *sankanje* ("sledging") and *grudvanje* ("snowballing") everywhere, especially at weekends when they were free from the camp schooling. On the coldest days, only women washing their children's clothes and men sawing firewood spent much time outside[663].

The captain, as I had by now realised he was, satisfied once again with my response, then ordered his men to set about their various tasks and start unloading: "*Postupatj!*". Two days later they returned, and it was like a case of *déjà vu*: the crew were all wearing exactly the same clothes, including a young *podmasterje* ("apprentice") in a red T-shirt sporting the caption in English "Central Asia Junior Weightlifting Championships 1999". On another occasion in Sierra Leone, our AN12 landed as usual on its regular run from the UK (every other day). This particular morning, three local airport staff were caught out working on the grass verge between the runway and the apron when the plane came in. Realising their mistake, they started to walk back across the apron towards the airport buildings as the plane taxied in; but the Russian *letčik* ("pilot"), catching sight of them, made a beeline for the pedestrians, forcing them to run for it.

The lucky few had moved into a room that already had a traditional range, common in the Balkans and the centre of domestic life. Those living in tents were, at least theoretically, issued 2,000 stoves by UNHCR in mid-December. All I could ever get mine to produce was a great quantity of smoke, that refused to exit via the chimney, which is where any heat appeared to be going. I found I still had to rely on animal heat. But at least the top surface of the stove heated up enough to be able to boil water or fry the limited range of ingredients we had access to. There was an increase in tent fires in late December, often caused by the hot chimneys[664]. In the early days, some people had built ovens in the earth by digging sideways into a slope, creating a space into which hot embers could be placed underneath a makeshift grill or hotplate. Fuel was also a major problem, and had to be bought from those ready to risk arrest by chopping trees. On 25 October, the police refused to allow two trucks of firewood into the camp, as it had to be authorised by the deputy prime minister[665]. ICRC went public with its concerns about the refusal of the HDZ to let NGOs bring wood in, and lamented the lack of a political solution as winter set in, fearing "disastrous consequences"[666]. This authorisation had still not been received on 7 November, when winter had really started[667]. Another truck of firewood was turned back on 13 November[668]. On 20 November, another 200 people returned to Bosnia[669]. The same day, the police unexpectedly allowed refugees to gather wood from one slope of the camp, and the word soon spread. However, the next day it was noticed that a video camera had been set up in that spot, where the light was particularly favourable, to film the refugees engaged in illegal logging. Just 100 metres further out, behind Fairy Wheel, was a large quantity of felled timber, but no-one was allowed to touch it. Someone likened it to the proverbial "Water, water everywhere but not a drop to drink"[670]: the refugees were surrounded by forest, and yet had no firewood. The first consignment of firewood arrived in the camp on 22 November: the police had been authorised to allow 1,200 cubic metres in, an insufficient but symbolic quantity (enough for one month, and to be delivered over 10 days[671]). It was certainly welcome, and the sound of chopping could be heard for days. Some people managed to get hold of chainsaws, and for DM 7 would do the householder's chopping for him or her. Extra wood could be bought for DM 30 per cubic metre[672]. However, the lumberjack had to work fast, because the police would hone in on the sound of the chainsaw, hoping to catch someone *in flagrante delicto* engaged in illegal economic activity. On 1 December, the woodshed at one of the distribution points was looted. The price of firewood in the camp dropped immediately by almost 50%[673]. Further deliveries followed. However, it was discovered that later consignments of wood were birch and lime, which are not generally used for firewood (lime is used for paper), and were not local[674]. More lime, and alder, were delivered in February[675]. As the number of people in the camp dropped in December, abandoned shelters became a good source of firewood[676]. On 30 December, two telegraph poles were chopped down for firewood, and the culprits arrested[677]. On 2 January, there were only stocks of firewood for two days, and refugees started to burn wooden items that weren't strictly necessary[678]. By 6 January, people were moving into tents and using their previous wooden shelters for fuel[679]. There was a real gale on 19 February, the last day of Ramazan, and many shelters suffered damage, especially to chimneys; some tents and even some permanent structures were blown down[680].

I complained about the quality of the stoves in an interview with radio Free Europe on 13 March, as a result of which I heard from Kiwi I had been issued a *katul-ferman* (fatwa) by the Young Muslims organisation in Cazin (the other interviewees all insisted on anonymity)[681]. Izetbegović had been a member of the Young Muslims during WWII, and served three years in prison immediately after the war as part of a crackdown on religion. When the SS *Handžar* ("Arab's dagger") division was formed of Bosnian Muslims in April 1943, the Young Muslims split, with one faction, including Izetbegović, supporting it, while another faction supported the Partisans[682]. The Young Muslims were also behind a failed Greens rebellion in Spreča, between Tuzla and Zvornik, in 1949[683]. In the 1990s, they were *bagra* (a "gang of juvenile delinquents") who used the political patronage of the SDA to bully their elders and betters. In the run-up to the 1996 elections, other political parties (themselves Muslim) in Cazin complained about their antics, to OSCE and the authorities[xciii]. Their peers in the Black Swans "special forces" unit in central Bosnia (see below) displayed a similar pattern of behaviour. They were not known for their heroic exploits in the field against the enemy, but rather their only achievement was to baulk at nothing when unleashed on minority civilians.

The cold was worst of all for the women, who had to spend hours most days washing their families' clothes by hand in the open air, with freezing water. Drying clothes was another problem, and any spell of dry weather was immediately seized upon and taken extensive advantage of. Rain in November and December meant there was mud everywhere, even on the road. The reckless way the riot police drove through the camp didn't help, with pedestrians being sprayed with muddy water as they hurriedly gave way[684]. The police were the worst culprits, indeed they appeared to take a cruel delight in splashing people as they motored through the camp[685] (in a similar vein, when I was working in Guinea in 1999, one of the many Sierra Leonean (and Liberian) refugee camps we were working in had to be reached by driving along an earth road past a village. The high-speed coming and going of aid vehicles every day meant that the community of huts beside the track was enveloped in clouds of red dust for much of waking hours, which did little to endear the local population to the aid effort, or indeed to the refugees). At least in October there was a dedicated space for washing once MSF had built their water supply points, although there wasn't room for everyone at the same time[686]. Prior to that, washing had to be carried out in the stream, which was also the final destination of some of the contents of the more makeshift latrines. One day Jadra was washing Haris's nappies in the stream, only to see a piece of human excrement float by. The centre of the valley was certainly fragrant. Personally, I found that the cold combined with the primitive hygiene facilities meant trips to the pit latrine were an experience to be saved up. Many of them were built in such a way that you could see out (and other people could see in) when you were stood up. At least in winter the cold, heavy air subdued the stench. I used to light up a Marlboro before going in as well, for good measure. Belt and braces. *Tariguz* ("bog roll") was also a luxury in Kuplensko (although as a general rule, Muslims prefer to rinse rather than wipe. By way of illustration, Enes

---

[xciii] At a SDA rally in Cazin there was a very moving performance of an adaption of the pre-war hit *One More Day*, which went "*Moj je život kratak bio i prolazan kao san*" – "my life has been short and fleeting as a dream", sung by a 5th Corps veteran, with a new refrain, "*La ilahe ilAllah*" – "there is no God but Allah" delivered by a girls' choir. Propaganda can be beautiful. Similarly, one very hot day in Split I enjoyed a performance by three old boys with mandolins sitting outside a café in a small square in the old town of the hit *Don't Touch My Ravnica*. The sun's radiation was rebounding off the white stone ground and walls, and as a result the square was practically an oven, but despite this the Mediterranean minstrels had gathered quite a crowd. I assumed at the time that Ravnica was a girl's name, but it actually means "plain", and when I recounted this episode to Miloš he explained to me that it referred to Slavonia, and that the song was in fact an *Ustaše* anthem.

asked me one day whether at home I would remove faeces from a plate by washing it or would just wipe it off. I replied that in the UK, we don't shit on plates). Personal hygiene was generally accomplished by pouring several saucepans of hot water into a tub, and then, squatting or standing in the tub, rinsing yourself with a mug, lathering up, and then rinsing again. In the overcrowded conditions, men would wash one day in their room or tent, and women the next. In June, someone built a public communal shower, complete with miscellaneous water containers covered in black plastic placed on the roof to absorb the heat of the sun and allow for a supply of warm water[687]. As for cooking and cleaning, the women became experts in the rational use of water, with a variety of different containers used to make it go as far as possible.

As time went on, and the national and international authorities became more organised, the number of people taking their fate into their own hands increased rather than decreased[688]. Throughout this period, as indeed throughout the whole war and from the whole of Bosnia, there was a steady trickle of people leaving the country altogether, travelling along little-trod paths, or passing unnoticed among the legal population, paying bribes or rendering services to corrupt officials and criminals where necessary, with the ultimate goal of starting a new life at the bottom of the food chain in a foreign country, generally despised or patronised, and forced to learn how to be an accepted member of society again ("reconstructed living"[689]). On 19 August, four refugees were returned from Slovenia (when asked how they had got there, they replied "We walked"; and in the face of the visible incredulity of the Slovene police, added, "That's nothing, another group got as far as Austria!"), while on 20 August one refugee was killed and another injured when a group fleeing the camp ended up in a minefield in Duga Resa, just south of Karlovac and near the former front line[690]. By the end of October, there had been 17 violent refugee deaths[691]. Some refugees started to leave the camp through the fields, and then, waiting a few km outside the camp, would get into aid trucks returning empty from Kuplensko having delivered their vital cargo – with or without the knowledge of the driver[692]. It was estimated on 23 December that half of the refugees had left, either back to Bosnia through the camp's south entrance, or north, to take their chances in the wider world[693]. Meanwhile, the Croatian authorities wanted the refugees gone. On 5 September, they opened an office in Velika Kladuša with the objective of accelerating the process[694]. Ramo commented that if the authorities were unable after seven months to establish what had happened to General Šantić, then there was not much hope of security for returning refugees[695]. 21 years later, his family are still trying to establish his fate, and on the anniversary of his disappearance in 2016 there was a demonstration in Mostar calling for justice[696]. Their calls became so loud that his son was badly beaten up by unknown parties in Mostar the following Sunday night[697]. The 5th Corps has a long reach, despite the fact that it no longer exists - the ABiH was merged with the HVO in 1996, and restructured with the VRS in 2005 to create a much smaller Bosnian army, composed of three brigades (based in Banja Luka, Tuzla and Čapljina). I have it on reliable authority that Tiger is now the king of the Bihać mafija ("underworld").

People started to return to Bosnia in large numbers from November onwards, with the onset of winter[698]. On 3 November the local radio reported a record 120 returns that day, and on 7 December, that 400 had gone the day before[699]. On 1 December, two busloads of refugees returned, the largest number until then, and 4

December was another record, with half a dozen buses transporting those who had given in to the cold, hunger and repression[700]. The main issues preventing further returns were distrust of the new authorities, the lack of security, and housing shortages, as many empty homes had been assigned by the authorities to IDPs, in particular from Banja Luka and Prijedor[701]. Other people's houses had been destroyed: some as collateral damage during the hostilities, but others deliberately targeted for arson, to make sure the owners never came back. Zahid's was one such house. One day he asked me drive past it when I was next in Velika Kladuša and report to him on what I saw; but he warned me not to linger near the site, and certainly not to approach the house. The walls were still standing, but blackened timbers were visible where the roof had once been. A shell had fallen through Seka's roof during the fighting at the end of 1994, when the people returned from the first refugee crisis, but fortunately it didn't explode. Other returnees' houses were rendered inaccessible by placing IEDs in them[702]. While most people living in a house were owner-occupiers, especially in the villages, for many people working for a corporation, a *stan* ("flat") in the town was one of the perks of their job, and for that reason women in particular kept working through the war, even though they were not being paid a salary (there were other benefits as well to being active, and being seen to be active in the workplace, not least the hope of a real job again after the war, and one day a pension). This meant that property rights were, and still are, very difficult to prove, and easily abused. Until Dayton, an additional concern for the men was being mobilised and returned to the war to fight in the 5th Corps. As the war went on in September and October, and especially after the 5th Corps was pushed back from and then took Sanski Most, several hundred new refugees arrived in Kuplensko, displaced by new IDPs from the front being housed in Velika Kladuša[703]. Meanwhile, the constant trickle of people returning to the camp never stopped, and there was an increase in calls from Velika Kladuša warning people not to come back[704]. Indeed, over 1,000 people ended up coming back to the camp after returning home[705]. On 22 December, it was reported that a refugee from Mala Kladuša had been killed by the 5th Corps after returning there. That was a sombre reminder to the refugees that, despite all the assurances and pressure to go back, it was not safe[706]. There were far fewer departures the next day, and some people who had already taken a seat in the bus got off when they heard[707]. It was later officially reported that he had been killed resisting arrest[708]. There were only 49 returns on Boxing Day[709]. On 4 January, a refugee was shot by the police while trying to escape the camp[710]. According to ICRC, returning refugees were subject to multiple discrimination, which ranged from being issued different aid cards to being refused housing[711]. Bearing in mind that the Bosnian economy was at a standstill, access to humanitarian aid was vital for most families. But there were only two distributions in the last quarter of 1995. A third distribution took place in May, at a time when items marked "*humanitarna pomoć*" ("aid") were commonly to be seen in shops (according to Tetin, Dudaković's wife was directly involved in the sale of humanitarian aid in Bihać)[712]. Not only did many people end up selling their possessions, but many returnees found their possessions had been seized by the new authorities[713]. It was said that some refugees stayed in the camp because they would have been even worse off at home[714]. There was an increase in people returning after the Amnesty Act became law in early February (see below), and after a long trough, there was another peak on 1 March, with 200 returns[715]. One problem was the lack of reliable knowledge about what was really happening in Bosnia. The authorities did not, despite repeated requests by the refugees, make any arrangements to allow a proper dialogue between the old and new authorities, and between the population in the camp and those in Bosnia[716]. This was still a problem in the New Year, although there were two visits by selected refugees to areas of their choice in Bosnia in December, with the objective of verifying the groundtruth[717]. The 5th Corps then banned further visits: the Sarajevo regime had no interest in humouring the losers[718]. I saw a similar situation in Timor four years later. After Indonesia relinquished control of East Timor under pressure from the US and Australia in 1999, keen to get their hands on the continental shelf's gas reserves after Indonesia, no longer a bulwark against the spread of communism in South-East Asia, had lost its strategic importance with the end of the Cold War (Indonesia originally took control of East Timor with the nod from the US in 1974, when the Portuguese army, worn out after 15 years of Colonial Wars in Africa, fomented by the Soviet Union, overthrew economist Salazar's civilian dictatorship in Lisbon and Portugal's far-flung empire collapsed overnight), there was an influx of 300,000 refugees into West Timor[719][xciv]. Tony Blair didn't miss out on the action, liberating yet another oppressed people on his unstoppable march to Baghdad and his day of destiny with his nemesis, Saddam Hussein. One section of the refugees were Indonesian civil servants, who had been employed in the East, and now expected to be redeployed elsewhere among Indonesia's 3,000 inhabited islands (spread over three time zones), while the others were made up of native Timorese. The Portuguese lack of any interest in developing East Timor had been continued by the Indonesians, with the result that most of the Timorese only spoke their own language, Tetun, which is unrelated to Indonesian (the only refugee I met who could speak Portuguese was a Catholic priest, who had attended seminary in Portugal[xcv]). There was no Tetun media, and so most of these villagers had no access to any news about what was happening back home, or indeed

---

[xciv] Violence broke out in East Timor after a referendum on independence was held in August 1999, under pressure from Australia (and Portugal). In September, the government in Jakarta agreed to withdraw its forces and allow an Australian-led UN peacekeeping force to occupy the territory, even as the Australian PM blubbered on TV in case anyone got hurt. Ned Kelly he wasn't. East Timor was administered by the UN until 2002, when it was recognised by the UN as an independent state. As usual, the refugees became pawns in the hands of national and international power structures, and the local authorities in Kupang used the threat of a forced relocation of one camp to another site (that they wanted to expropriate from the existing owners) to blackmail UNHCR. Timor, only 600 km from Darwin in Australia (Darwin has been destroyed twice – by the Japanese air force in 1942, and by cyclone Tracy in 1974), was a popular haunt for Aussies. There were some serious drinkers among them, real belt and braces, and a couple of them looked like they might have been on the run from The Hague. One evening several of us went out for dinner in Kupang, and at a neighbouring table a young Australian was dining. Also on the restaurant terrace were a couple of local squaddies, who kept casting unfriendly glances in our direction. The Australian told us he didn't feel safe. On my way for a Gypsy's kiss I was accosted by a local, who asked me if I was Australian. When I replied in the negative, he asked who I worked for. His mood softened visibly when I said, "*Doktor tanpa batas*" ("doctors without borders"), and he wished me well. But when I returned to my companions, one of the squaddies threw their table at our neighbour, who ran for the door, a Bowie knife-wielding Indonesian squaddie in pursuit. We didn't have dinner there again. The Portuguese experience of democracy, imposed by the army, contrasts with events in Spain, where there was a (relatively) peaceful transition from the military dictatorship to democracy after the death of Franco in 1975. Meanwhile, Ned Kelly embarked on his last armoured shootout with the Bronze two years after the Congress of Berlin.

[xcv] Although Indonesia, which became independent from the Netherlands after a four-year war in 1949, is the largest Muslim country in the world, Islam is mainly concentrated in the west of the country, the area worst devastated by the 2004 tsunami (150,000 of the 250,000 casualties were in the province of Aceh; I happened to be in Sweden at the time, where it also became a major emergency, as over 500 Swedish tourists were killed in the natural disaster). As one travels east, islands such as Bali are Buddhist, while Timor is divided between Protestants (in the west) and Catholics (in the east), a situation that didn't fail to elicit an ironic observation from an Irish colleague.

why they had had to flee in the first place. Back in the Balkans, some of the Kuplensko refugees managed to go home unofficially for a few days to check things out, and return to the camp. After the Dayton peace accords were initialled on 21 November under US pressure after 21 days of intensive talks, there was optimism in the camp that it would now be safe to return home[720]. This was quickly followed by disappointment due to the ongoing uncertainty as to when and how it would materialise into a real improvement for the refugees on the ground[721]. The refugees asked for a high-level delegation from Sarajevo and Zagreb to allow them to participate in the London talks on the implementation of Dayton, from which they had until then been excluded[722]. Even now, there were still refugees returning to the camp, after experiencing first-hand the security situation in the former enclave[723].

On 1 December, leaflets from the Bosnian embassy in Zagreb were distributed, calling on people to return[724]. This was repeated on 6 December, and one of the EU monitors actively distributed them[725]. A complaint was made to UNHCR. On 2 December, a newspaper van drove through the camp dropping off 1,000 issues of the Croatian weekly newspaper *Nedjeljna Dalmacija*, which contained an interview with Babo. The delivery driver appeared to be in a great hurry, and turned up very early to carry out his mission, perhaps in the hope that most people would still be indoors at that time; I exchanged a few words with him, and he gave me the impression that he feared for his very life driving through the infernal valley with its population of hardened war criminals. The delivery was paid for by Agrokomerc. But it didn't appear to have the desired effect of boosting morale[726]. On 9 December, *Oslobođenje* published the full text of the Dayton peace accords[727]. On 11 December, *Večernji List* reported on a visit to the camp by the Council of Europe, who allegedly praised the efforts of the Croatian government in assisting aid agencies to help the victims of war return home. It also stated there were still 19,000 refugees in the camp[728]. On 29 December, *Slobodna Bosna* carried a two-page report on the camp. Among other things, it stated that the Croatian government had changed tactics from an internationally unacceptable forced return to a lower profile but no less violent siege. It also dismissed allegations that a couple of hundred armed diehards were holding the rest of the refugees hostage. It reported that between mid-October and mid-December, there had been 95 reported beatings of returnees, some of them fatal, as well as multiple cases of their houses being burnt down. The beatings took place mainly at night, and as a result, some people were afraid to sleep at home. It cited another case, on the afternoon of 11 December, when a phosphorous grenade was thrown into the house of a returnee, reducing him and his house to ashes. It stated that attempts by UNHCR to obtain reliable information on the ground in the former enclave had been rebuffed[729]. On 9 February, it carried a report on Agrokomerc: after the "liberation" of Velika Kladuša, the firm was regarded by the new authorities as booty, and had been systematically looted by the governor, Veladžić, and his cronies, via an opaque system of duplicate functions (Veladžić was removed from office by the high representative for Bosnia in 1999, see below[730]). Meanwhile, former smuggler and Agrokomerc employee Edhem Veladžić, allegedly involved in the assassination attempt against Babo, was appointed chief of police of the new canton[731].

The peace agreements, signed by Milošević acting on behalf of Karadžić (who was unable to travel abroad as he had been indicted by the ICTY on 25 July), Tuđman, and Izetbegović, provided for a NATO military force, including for the first time US troops (IFOR, 60,000 strong, was divided into three divisions: Tuzla (US-led), Mostar (French) and Banja Luka (UK)), to oversee the demilitarisation and handover of territory, but failed to deal with Kosovo[732]. They also provided for an amnesty and an immediate return for all refugees and IDPs (Annex VII), and included an agreement on the return of refugees to Velika Kladuša and Cazin, with full guarantees for the respect of their dignity and security. Further to the agreements, the Federation enacted legislation in February 1996 granting an amnesty for all criminal acts related to the conflict, except crimes within the jurisdiction of the ICTY (Republika Srpska enacted similar legislation in June). The peace agreements also provided for achieving a military balance in Bosnia, either by the VRS and the HVO disarming, or by the ABiH being armed under the US "train and equip" programme (in the event, the latter option was implemented)[733]. Exchanges of territory and prisoners took place in early 1996[734]. Refugee issues were dealt with by the Bosnian office for refugees and IDPs working in conjunction with UNHCR, while under Dayton an ombudsman was set up to deal with, among other things, alleged persecution of returning refugees, and could draw on the resources of IPTF. There were in fact three ombuds(wo)men: a Serb, a Croat, and a Muslim, and there were IPTF police stations in Velika Kladuša and Cazin, manned by US cops. The person in charge of hiring local staff was a West Indian lady in Cazin who seemed to relish wielding power over white people. I heard more than one complaint from the cops that they could not get the local staff they needed; they were anyway not being used, and had to go out looking for work, investigating cases and interviewing victims, witnesses and suspects as best they could. In any case, they did not have an executive mandate, i.e. no powers of arrest, and could at best act as a deterrent. On 24 January, radio Free Europe, the camp's most popular radio station, based in Prague, reported the abuse of returnees, citing five cases per day being reported to IPTF[735]. The following day they reported one death and 20 cases of returnees being beaten[736]. As of 30 January, IPTF were monitoring the investigation of 56 allegations of abuse. They said there appeared to be a pattern, whereby returnees who featured on a list were targeted for a punishment beating, and then left alone[737]. All military units were supposed to withdraw from the region with the arrival of the UN police. In March the UN reported that over 10,000 returnees had been subjected to intimidation, including beatings, by the Bosnian authorities and residents, including the ABiH, despite the amnesty at the beginning of 1996[738].

However, the returnees needed guarantees of safety and protection, not ineffectual remedies after the event. I once witnessed first-hand how a Bosnian police officer attempted to extort money from his former superior, a returnee. He used the pretext of an alleged lost rifle to justify his unwarranted demand. When I threatened to report the case to the ombudsman, the perpetrator left me in little doubt that he did not consider that (or me) an obstacle, while the victim later said to me there was no point approaching the ombudsman. His wife said they would not have come back at all if they had known what it would be like. My impression from the one ombudsman's meeting I attended, at which she arrived in the company of a US official and a peacekeeper armed to the teeth[xcvi], was that she was taking refuge in procedures and formalities as a substitute for achieving results. In her own words, the ombudsman had wide powers and could "investigate the activities of any person or institution in order to protect the human dignity, rights and freedoms guaranteed by

---

[xcvi] It occurred to me at the time that a simple pistol would have been sufficient for his purposes, and would have allowed him far more freedom of movement than he had encumbered by an entire arsenal. But I know as little about CP work as the MOD knows about aid work.

the constitution"[739]. MSF referred many individual cases to her, but I am unaware of any reaching a satisfactory conclusion. At least they visited the camp more than once, although in November the police stopped that[740]. Thus the camp was hermetically sealed in terms of any flow of information other than that under the direct control of the authorities, who had armed men controlling physical access. The main organ of such official information was the local radio in Velika Kladuša[741] (Velkaton was only restored in late July, in Drvar in HDZ territory in Bosnia. According to Mirvet, Izetbegović regarded Velkaton and its director as an even greater enemy than Babo[742]). The ombudsmen next visited on 26 January, and again on 7 February[743]. On 6 March, radio Free Europe interviewed four returnees, two of whom encouraged others to join them, while the other two said the opposite[744]. On 28 January, the committee put together a list of the most frequent offenders involved in beating returnees[745]. As late as 23 August 1996, a UN report stated that "attacks against returning refugees are still a common occurrence"[746].

The Croatian authorities refused to recognise the refugees' status, as they considered conditions safe in Velika Kladuša[747]. This decision was taken not by the Croatian office for refugees and IDPs (as per s. 5 of the Refugees and IDPs Act (*ZSPI*) 1993), but by Tuđman's office, that later dismissed any talk of persecution of the refugees[748]. The 1951 International Convention on the Status of Refugees and the 1967 Protocol on the Status of Refugees confers in article 1 the status of refugee on

> "any person who owing to a well-founded fear of persecution for reasons of race, religion, nationality, or membership of a particular social group or political opinion, is outside the country of his nationality and is unable or, owing to such fear, is unwilling to avail himself of the protection of that country"[749].

Recognition by UNHCR or the government of the host country is not a requirement of refugee status, although the host county has to grant it for it to be effective. Once it is granted, the refugees have the same rights as nationals or residents of the country[750]. Under article 33 it is prohibited to

> "expel or return a refugee in any manner whatsoever to the frontiers of territories where his life or freedom would be threatened on account of his race, religion, nationality, or membership of a particular social group or political opinion"

other than where there are reasonable grounds for regarding a particular refugee as a danger to the security of the host country, or where he or she constitutes a danger to that community after being convicted of a particularly serious crime[751]. This rule cannot be derogated from, and deportation on narrow technical grounds is a violation[752]. Furthermore, the Croatian government was under a duty to guarantee the refugees the choice between safe return or departure to a third country under a UNHCR resettlement programme. The ban on movement outside the camp and restrictions on family visits were a violation of the 1966 Charter on Civic and Political Rights, and the economic, social and cultural rights of refugees under the 1966 International Convention on Economic, Social and Cultural Rights, while the rights of children under the 1989 Convention on the Rights of the Child were also being breached by the police[753]. Furthermore, article 33 of the 1951 Convention contains a prohibition of expulsion or return, which refers not just to those granted refugee status but also to asylum seekers, while article 3 contains a provision on non-discrimination among refugees[754]. In particular, UNHCR's conclusion no. 22(XXXII) states

> "It is imperative to ensure that asylum seekers are fully protected in large-scale influx situations, to reaffirm the basic minimum standards for their treatment pending arrangements for a durable solution, and to establish effective arrangements in the context of international solidarity and burden-sharing for assisting countries which receive large numbers of asylum seekers"[755].

It appears that the Croatian authorities had hoped the problem would quietly go away, i.e. that the inhuman living conditions and daily harassment, aggravated by barriers to the work of the aid community, would be enough to encourage the refugees to go back home. The Croatian foreign minister and Tuđman's adviser on human rights and humanitarian issues had said as much[756].

Kuplensko, a little village,
Became a town overnight.
Once there were a few people here
But now they're countless, squashed tight

But it's not like any other town,
There're no buildings, schools or flicks,
It's a town of horror and want,
The infernal valley some call it.

I watch people walking down the street,
On their faces pain is etched.
In our town there's only one street,
Six kilometres at a stretch

There's no electricity in our town,
So people live in darkness.
The lucky ones live in houses
Or in wooden sheds.

Actually it's wrong to say
There're no schools, flicks or buildings,
We have strange buildings and schools:
Our school is a tarpaulin.

There are streets, but they're strange too,
Ten distribution points in our township.
Winter's arrived but there's no wood
If you want wood you have to nick it.

Every morning here is strange
The mothers have it worst,
What are they going to cook for their kids,
When there's no onions, beans or spuds.

In this town no-one is allowed,
To have a relative round for tea,
Take a look, world, at this town,
Take a look for the sake of mercy.

Sometimes a vehicle goes past,
But they're mainly foreigners.
There's lots of families in this town,
But there's also a few bachelors.

Lots of kids run down the street,
Hoping to get thrown a bonbon,

It's strange here, everything's quite strange,
But in this town life goes on.

In the town there are a few
Strange bars and stranger booths,
Sometimes you can buy yourself
Fags, meat or a bottle of booze.

Sometimes someone gets really pissed
And we all know the reason why,
There isn't a town in this world,
As strange as the infernal valley.

In every town people have shoes,
In their own cosy home they play,
Here the people are naked, barefoot
Still they laugh in their own strange way.

The whole world is fully aware,
And looks on so coldly detached,
Why don't they give us fruit and veg,
Or at least peace peace at last.

When it comes to our strange town
The world is suddenly miserly.
I see that and I ask myself,
Is it a town or a zoo our valley?

Some people say that we are apes,
While others say we're human.
That's why our strange little town
Amazes us, each and every one.

The town's surrounded by a strange fence,
But it's not made of barbed wire:
Rather, strange uniformed people,
Seize us with horror and fear,

Wherever you go, down the strange street,
A checkpoint and a policeman there,
But they won't talk to us,
That's what makes our town so bizarre.

Take a little look world,
Take a look at this strange township:
All we've got in our little valley,
Is mud, hunger and hardship.

We've got our pride and that's our own,
And our smile, for that we're famed,

But of our strange little town
The whole world should be ashamed.

Shame on you, world, for our kids,
Because they will tell when years go by.
You'll find the truth in this little town
Ask them they won't lie.

The truth is in this little town
We ask you world for your voice
Don't ask anyone else about us,
Come here, and speak to us.

This is such a strange little town
It's as if the world is afraid.
Don't be afraid come and ask us
Here the truth to rest has been laid[758].

Sead "Tetin" Kajtazović, Paklena Dolina

Most days when I was not otherwise occupied I would go for a walk through my 5 km domain. Every five minutes or so I would see or be called to by someone I knew, or who knew me, although other people paid no attention to me. I had truly gone native, and could pass unnoticed. Even when I spoke, and people could tell I wasn't local, the assumption was that I must be from one of the Yugoslav ethnic minorities – a Slovene or Albanian, or even a *sir* ("white Romany": once at Leicester crown court I was asked by a Romanian defendant whether I had been kidnapped as a child, as *"Tu či mijazos amen"* ("you don't look like us"). When the judge ordered *reţinere* ("custody") for two of the *inculpaţi* ("defendants"), their *Rromnja* ("womenfolk") in the public gallery raised such a *rovipe* ("lamentation") that you would have thought she had handed down the *condamnare la moarte* ("death sentence"). But after all six of the defendants were acquitted, I was invited to a celebratory *slava* ("BBQ") in a nearby park, where I was able to eat my fill of *bakresko mas* ("lamb chop") and salad *manrro* ("sandwiches") in generous and fraternal, albeit segregated company. Leicester is also the home of Brian, a retired fireman, who, with Stuart, is a key player in DFID's emergency response to earthquakes[xcvii]). It was nice to know so many people, and be part of a real community. The common adversity had been a great leveller, and there was no-one shut away from the great unwashed living a life of ease and privilege (with the exception of Babo, in Rijeka). The common destitution put everyone on the same level, and was very conducive to a rich social life. The cramped, uncomfortable and overcrowded housing meant that no-one had their own space, and of necessity people went outside to partake of what God had provided free of charge – fresh air and

---

[xcvii] During the Burma response, see below, Brian did a Humphrey Bogart in the Irrawaddy delta with a fleet of barges built specially by Stuart. A former RN man from a British NGO was adamant that they wouldn't float, but they did, and were perfect for delivering aid to the isolated communities, inaccessible by road. Stuart and Brian were also to be found on the ground during the Haiti earthquake response. Bizarrely, in the initial confusion when there were no flights to the island, Stuart managed to blag a lift to the Dominican Republic with the former King of Spain.

company (other than when it was too cold to do so). Before the war, the *korzo* was as much an institution in Yugoslavia as the *siesta* is in Spain – an early evening promenade along the main pedestrian thoroughfare (in Velika Kladuša, the park), in which all and sundry took part[759]. This freedom did not however apply to many of the women in Kuplensko, who in the traditional community were expected to work all day long to provide a basic standard of domestic civilisation and home comforts for their families. In some respects, it was just like being at home for them. However, the psychological stress was a constant factor reminding them that this was not a normal situation, and was ultimately untenable. The nooks and crannies where people had managed to establish themselves quickly developed into micro communities, with attics, bare ground under shady trees and *avlije* ("yards") where the endless everyday chores of life were played out the scene of all the rich variety of human interaction. Mirvet called it "true socialism": divested of their assets, the refugees were free to focus on the essentials of life, "*u se na se poda se*". After a hard winter, the weather became more cheerful on 11 February, only to fall back to minus 5 on the 26[th760]. Spring weather arrived in the latter half of April, albeit with showers, but was followed by powerful winds in late May[761]. However, 13 June was the first cloudy day for 23 days[762]. There was a powerful thunderstorm on the morning of 15 June, followed by another on the afternoon of 22 June that destroyed several shelters[763]. It rained all day on 25 June, raising the level of the stream. It was said that summer hadn't started with so much rain since 1944[764]. There was another powerful storm on 8 July[765]. Clouds and wind continued until 15 July, when the sun started shining[766]. But even then, it was unusually cold out of the sun[767]. The summer only really started at the end of July[768].

Every time I ran into someone, it was nice to stop for a while and pass the time of day, or accept the obligatory invitation to go inside and partake of their hospitality, most commonly coffee and *rakija*. Thus the time could be whiled away in conversation, and by midday I would be tanked up with caffeine, alcohol, and nicotine, but also with a wealth of new human experiences. I became a real *kafedžija* ("heavy coffee drinker") and *duhandžija* ("heavy smoker") (not to mention a *krona*, "hard drinker"). I started to suffer from stomach cramps from the amount of coffee I was drinking, while the UNHCR stoves weren't the only trouble I had with smoke. Most people smoke in the Balkans, as they did in the UK in the 1970s, and the enforced idleness and the lack of food only increased the amount people were smoking per day. I used to stick to Marlboro, while the favourite among the locals was Drina, which is like concentrated Woodbine, albeit with a filter. I had seen the year before in central Bosnia that the older generation would smoke their fags with *muštikle* (elegant cigarette holders), but this quaint practice did not seem to have reached the Borders. Yet even though I was a smoker myself (I kicked my 20-year habit at the turn of the millennium, at the age of 31 – although I'm still partial to the occasional Cuban), sometimes, sitting in a small home-made shelter with a group of smokers for half an hour, it felt like a *soba gasoski* ("gas chamber"), and I simply had to get outside and breathe some fresh air. Even in the bleak midwinter. But even during winter, the warmth of human company trumped the bitter cold time and again[769]. At least the Balkans are exempt from some of the other health problems to which aid workers are prone, in particular malaria (which I contracted once in the DRC and once in Angola), bilharzia (I picked up the parasite swimming in Lake Tanganyika on the border between the DRC and Burundi while testing our Zodiac RIB speedboat, our getaway plan in case things went pear-shaped. But at least I avoided the crocodiles: Mango, one of our local drivers, had reassured me by insisting that crocodiles only ate black people, because "*Wazungu - akuna chumvi*" ("white people are not salty enough")), and typhus (caught in the DRC), not to mention cholera, ebola and the ace of spades[xcviii]. Sometimes, however, I wanted some time to myself, and had to risk giving offence by turning down invitations. I realised that giving of my time and company to people was not just a novelty for them, but important in terms of their sense of worth and self-esteem as individuals and collectively. With so few luxuries other than tobacco and alcohol, speaking to me was certainly better than watching *The Good the Bad and the Ugly*[xcix] (although television was a rare luxury, generally reserved for special occasions); it also allowed people a glimpse of the outside world, and reminded them that they were still human beings, and not the inmates of a zoo. Nevertheless, I had my own needs too. To have a bit of quiet I would sometimes frequent *Šejla*, a bar where I knew the waitress from Velika Kladuša. She had worked in the hotel *Konak*, which had a terrace where I would sometimes have a coffee at lunchtime. Sitting in there in Kuplensko, no-one could see me from the outside and so I had some respite from the endless love. *Ćeif* ("enjoy the moment"). Another of my favourite watering holes was *Mujo Hrnjica*, as was the *Ancient Mariner*, a nostalgic echo of the popular pub of the same name in Velika Kladuša, owned by a former merchant seaman.

It was quite a pleasant little valley, and certainly better than a cramped POW camp. Everyone knew what had happened in Srebrenica, and were well aware that but for the grace of God they would not be able to enjoy the simple pleasures they had. If one forgot the uncertainty hanging over the people from one day to the next, and the shared daily experience and above all, talking, were a perfect way to do just that, then we could have been in any Balkan village in peacetime. Bosnians are anyway a very gregarious people, despite the deep divisions that run through their society like flaws in a precious stone, and in these circumstances that quality came to the fore and proved to be a real source of strength that individuals could draw on when affected by their own troubles. The modern ailment of loneliness was not among the many problems faced by the refugees. I really enjoyed the outdoor lifestyle, feeling the elements on my face every day, and being welcomed unconditionally into a rich, living community. *Rahatluk* ("the best things in life are free"). A common expression at the time was "*Sve će ovo proći*" ("it won't last forever"). Despite this, there was an awareness after New Year that while they were stuck in this legal, or rather unlawful (and lawless) limbo, people throughout Bosnia were now returning to normal life in peacetime, whether they were at home or among the hundreds of thousands of IDPs living either in someone else's house or in temporary accommodation. The people of Kuplensko were no longer at war, but nor were they at peace; they were an unwelcome anomaly left over from the war, an aberration surrounded by hostile forces, and with a sword hanging literally over their

---

[xcviii] During the swine flu epidemic in the UK in 2009, I happened to be interpreting for a *hoţi de buzunare supectat* ("suspected pickpocket") in a London *secţie de poliţie* ("police station"). The custody sergeant sneezed, and without thinking, I commented, "I hope that's not swine flu, Sarge". I noticed some of the other coppers looking at me strangely, but it was only when I went home later that evening that I realised what I had said. In Covent Garden in London the following monolingual sign can be seen attached to lampposts: "*Ofiţeri de poliţie în civil operează în această zonă*" ("plain-clothes police officers operate in this area"). On another occasion, a copper who in his previous life had been in the army, told me that during his time stationed in Germany the only German he had manged to master was how to order a pint, a prostitute, and a kebab, "in that order". Similarly, the vast majority of foreigners working in the Balkans never bothered to learn more than rudimentary pleasantries, and *pivo* ("beer"). No wonder no-one knew what was going on.

[xcix] Popular Bosnian comedy series starring Mustafa Nadarević and Mission Impossible 4's Miraj Grbić.

heads. Not all the comments I heard in the camp were intelligent, however: not uncommon were people who would repeat phrases and arguments they had heard as if they were the Gospel. I challenged one man who I heard say one day, "We have it hardest of all" by saying to him, "In Srebrenica it was hardest of all". He fell silent, wrestling with his thoughts and this new idea. I wondered how many of the people who had decided to follow Babo were like him, adopting the words of their elders and betters as a mantra. It also occurred to me that that might be a legacy of the previous, single-party regime. Discussing the Peasants' Revolt in 1990, Milovan Đilas[c][770] said,

> "At that time we were worried, and Kardelj had warned us, about possible pro-Stalin unrest, and then this counter-revolutionary peasants' revolt erupted. The Cazin Muslims, the Bosnian Borders is a different world, for centuries wedged between Austria and Turkey, warlike and fanatical. In the war they joined the Partisans, after certain hesitations, but they were their own army. They were certainly dissatisfied with the quotas and collectivisation, but they had no more reason to be so than anyone else. But strangest and most unexpected of all, because even in the war, and before the war, they weren't particularly royalist, because they weren't Serbs or even Orthodox, but they were incited to revolt by a rumour that King Petar II had parachuted into the vicinity!"[771].

Having walked to the southern end of the camp, where the number of people around suddenly dropped dramatically, I would turn and make my way back towards my little *ćuprija* ("bridge"). As Andrić wrote in *Bridges*,

> "Of all the things that man is driven to raise and build, there is in my view nothing better or more valuable than bridges. They are more important than houses, and more sacred and common than temples. They belong to all in equal measure and perform a useful function, are always raised purposefully, in a place where the greatest number of human needs intersect, they are more durable than other constructions and serve no secret or evil purpose"[772].

(An exception is of course Drochaid an Eilein Sgitheanaich/the Skye Bridge, which was designed as a mechanism to allow American banks to squeeze money out of rural communities in the Gàidhealtachd/Highlands and Islands). The bridge in Kuplensko was always a hive of activity: it not only marked the centre of the camp, linking the two ends, but formed an area to the side of the road in which one could seek refuge from the madding crowd, and step into the professional calm of the Red Cross. It was also literally the place where the most pressing needs of the Bosnian refugees and the most substantive services of the foreign aid community met. I would duck into the ICRC tent, to see if Justin was around, and exchange a few

---

[c] A Montenegrin, leading Partisan and after the war the KPJ's official ideologist and number four in the government, tipped to become Tito's successor. However, in 1956 he was jailed for publicly criticising Yugoslavia's abstention on the UN resolution condemning the Soviet intervention in Hungary, to the delight of Mao, who hoped to poach the Warsaw Pact countries from Stalin by encouraging them to take a hard line of their own against dissidents. Đilas had advocated a relaxation of the KPJ's absolute grip on power since 1954. Fitzroy Maclean described him in 1943 as "young, intolerant and good-looking". Lord Owen visited him in Belgrade in 1995, shortly before his death.

pleasantries with him and the local team. That was always a useful source of the latest news (the ICRC tent was burned down on 19 December, caused by a fuel spill; there were no injuries[773]). Then I would drop into the LCK tent, where I would invariably be offered another coffee amid the bustle of messages being sorted for delivery, lists of beneficiaries per distribution point being arranged to fit the quantities of goods available, and the witty banter that never seemed to fail. While a welcome source of news and for many the only means of communication available with the outside world, there were complaints that, in order to comply with ICRC's neutral mandate, censoring of the content of messages was sometimes excessive (only family news was allowed[774]). Then I would have a look into my own tent to see how the lads were doing with the candle machine, bringing light to the people. Satisfied the work was progressing, I might drop in on my neighbour, the late Zahid. His tent always had some distinguished guest or other, either a UN or ICRC official, or Agrokomerc dignitaries, or visiting family. The fact that his wife, Šuhra, originally from Srebrenica, was an excellent cook, even in those straightened circumstances, was another draw. Having sat there for a while, listened to the political views of those in the know, and wondered at the Byzantine opacity, Machiavellian cynicism and sheer dastardly machinations of Bosnian public affairs, I might go on my way to ponder these new revelations. I would then head the other way down the road, towards Fairy Wheel. Once again, I would be accosted by people I knew and people who knew me. At Fairy Wheel, I would drop into the container used by MSF and their friends from Croatian NGOs such as the Anti-War Coalition as their centre of operations. Again, it was a useful source of information. Rob, who I had known as a NOZB military policeman in Velika Kladuša (he was a professional soldier before the war) and who spoke very good English, worked there. One of the MSF team was from Senegal, and I was amused one day to hear a *stara baba* ("old granny") comment, clapping eyes on him for the first time: "God preserve us if they've had to send the Blacks to save us!" A rumour subsequently spread around the camp that the whole population was to be moved to Africa, where they would live in colonial luxury in five-star hotels on a beach. I later heard another rumour, to the effect that I owned a chain of hotels in the UK, and was planning to accommodate the whole camp there. Alas, I am not so endowed. But it was fearful to see the plight of the wounded waiting in Fairy Wheel for someone to decide their fate. They included eight paraplegics and three men without legs[775]. There was no strolling in the fresh air for them, few if any diversions to convince them the worst was over. But at least they had no shortage of company. Many of the scenes in Kuplensko reminded me more of another of Andrić's works, *The Damned Yard*, a prison drama set in an Ottoman *istražni zatvor* ("remand centre") in Istanbul. Sometimes I wondered whether the previous inhabitants of the valley had ever imagined this mass of Bosnian humanity would one day descend upon their village; and then I reminded myself that in this troubled part of the world, this was not the first population movement in living memory. Nor was it the last. Now when I drive through Kuplensko I still see the ghosts of that extraordinary time.

Young people were as hungry for music and fashion and other idle pastimes as they are anywhere, but the lack of access to consumer illusions forced them to resort to more primordial, and more genuine pursuits. At least the endless domestic tasks kept them busy most of the time, although there was plenty of *ašikovanje* ("courting") on the road bridge in the evenings. According to MSF, 40-50% of the refugees were aged between 15-40. There was little access to *prezervativi* ("contraceptives") in the camp, and on 18 February, a 20-year-old who had gone to

Karlovac hospital complaining of kidney pains, gave birth[776]. It would be remiss to pass over in silence the fact that the affairs and sexual intrigues of part of the more mature section of this stricken and riven population produced stranger and more numerous bedfellows than the most imaginative of the Mexican *serije* ("soap operas") that later became a national obsession, both among the exiles and among those who remained at home. An account of the ins and outs of the many long-term relationships truncated and transplanted by *force majeure* would rival *Mahabharat* in length and complexity. Among the more poignant is a mother of three from Srebrenica who remarried in the US (to a Bosnian) after her husband went missing in the war, only for him to turn up on her doorstep a year later, having been meanwhile released from a POW camp.

There was another, more personal reason that bound me to the bridge, a source of such fundamental joy that it also links the two halves of my life, the before and after, the time of its absence, the time of sterile wandering and futile pursuits, and the time of fulfilment and completion. My time in the sun, my years of plenty started in Kuplensko, cold and hungry, and yet having experienced the revelation of true beauty. The infernal valley became a sea of tranquillity for me. The true light of this world is emanated by the human soul, and can only be perceived by those initiated into the mystery by the hand of God and by self-sacrifice.

It was at this time that I was introduced to Mujo Hrnjica and Huska Miljković.

Mujo was born at the end of the 16th or the beginning of the 17th century near Udbina in Lika, which was a Turkish stronghold and part of Bosnia between 1527 and 1699. This was a turbulent time: the Habsburg War of 1593-1606 corresponds roughly to his date of birth, and the Ottoman Empire went through a period of currency devaluation and inflation between 1615-25. The Turks were next involved in a war with the Venetians, from the 1640s until 1669 (at that time, thanks to the conquests of Bosnia's first King, Tvrtko, 1353-1391, Bosnia included the Dalmatian coast almost as far as Zadar, excluding independent Dubrovnik, ruled by a council of nobles)[777]. The identity of Mujo's father is unknown, and he grew up in the care of his uncle, a local lord. He had two brothers, Halil and the much younger Omer, and a sister, Ajla. When Mujo came of age, his uncle arranged with the *paša* of Banja Luka for him to be made *kapetan* of Velika Kladuša (the *kapetans* were military administrators of frontier districts[778]). This was a critical border, protruding into central Europe, and the *paša*, satisfied with Mujo and Halil's work, allowed them to build a tower on the site of the castle that stands today. Only fragmentary ruins remain of the original tower. They also built a well at a spring near the tower, which now forms part of the town's reservoir. The exploits of Mujo and Halil are celebrated in epic poetry throughout Bosnia. Both were legendary warriors, aided by their trusty white steed, Đogat. While Mujo, the elder and the head of household, was more serious and responsible, the younger, handsome Halil was a *bećar* ("ladies' man"). They once both travelled to Zadar disguised as Hungarian soldiers, where Halil fell in love, and they were both captured. The youngest brother, Omer, then had to come to the rescue, aided by various heroes from Lika and the Bosnian Borders. Ajla, not to be outdone, also has several heroic exploits to her credit, especially when her brothers were away and she had to hold the fort herself. Their mother fulfilled the traditional role of feeding and clothing the family, whatever the circumstances. Mujo gained renown, not only in Bosnia, but further afield, and some of the brothers' exploits verge on banditry, but Mujo was always more privateer than pirate.

Nevertheless, despite his services to the Ottoman Empire, his independence of spirit incurred the ire of the Sultan, who ordered the *paša* of Banja Luka to send him the heads of the two brothers. The *paša* reached an oriental compromise by sending the heads of two other brothers who resembled Mujo and Halil. As fate would have it, soon thereafter the Sultan had need of warriors, and regretted his hasty decision. Fortunately, the *paša* was able to produce the two heroes, who saved the day, and all was forgiven. Various versions exist as to Mujo's death, but according to one, he was betrayed by his closest friend, Meho. One day out hunting, Meho asked him to reveal the secret of his invincibility. Mujo was at first unwilling to share the secret, but finally disclosed that he could only be killed with a bullet containing three grains of gunpowder, three grains of gold, three grains of lead, and three grains of wheat. The treacherous friend then manufactured such a bullet, and the next time they went hunting, while Mujo was beating the game towards him, Meho shot him.

The facts as to Mujo's life are very sketchy, and most of what is known about him is legend, contained in various epic poems, that often ascribe him supernatural assistance, and give his horse wings. A soldier of Napoleon's army who took part in a skirmish with the irregular cavalry of the lord of Bihać in 1809 wrote that the Bosnians were a "cloud of men, none of them wearing uniforms, mounted on thin horses of extraordinary lightness, which obeyed the rider's voice and the pressure of his knees, without the use of bridle or stirrups"[779]. Mujo appears to have just missed the disastrous Habsburg War of 1683-1699, after which the Turks lost Hungary, Transylvania, Lika, Slavonia and western Vojvodina to Vienna, large parts of Dalmatia and Greece to Venice, and Montenegro became *de facto* independent, the beginning of the end of the Ottoman Empire[780]. Yet, like Robin Hood, Mujo's legend has persisted, and he is the only medieval folk hero of the Bosnian Borders. He arose from among this downtrodden yet resilient people and made a name for himself by force of arms, defending the realm against foreign invasion, and thereby gaining the respect not only of the common people but also of the colonial rulers; but he refused to submit to an oppressive central authority. It is said that he was buried in Vrnograč.

Huska Miljković was born to a peasant family in 1905 in Trnovi, on the eastern outskirts of Velika Kladuša. He joined the KPJ in 1939, and was nearly killed by a *Četnik* traitor at Petrova Gora in the uprising of July 1941, of which he was an organiser. The armed uprising was masterminded by Tito in occupied Serbia and Montenegro after Hitler invaded the Soviet Union, and was mirrored (and in some cases preceded) by separate uprisings in mainly Serb areas subject to the *Ustaše* terror in the NDH, in particular the Croatian Borders, and eastern, north and south-west Bosnia, where Pavelić's policy of "kill a third, expel a third, and convert a third to Catholicism" was implemented[781]. Yugoslavia had capitulated on 18 April, and the Yugoslav deputy prime minister and HSS leader after the assassination of Radić[ci][782], Vlatko Maček, urged the existing *banovina* administration in Bosnia and

---

[ci] Prior to WWI, Stjepan Radić, born in 1871 near Sisak, and described by Rebecca West as the Croatian Gandhi, succeeded in popularising politics among the peasantry with his party, the HSS. At this time a Serbian and Croatian unity movement, the HSK, which aspired to create a single Yugoslav state, was the ruling party in Croatia. Radić, however, was in favour of maintaining but reforming the Habsburg state. Meanwhile, Serbia took more direct action towards unification, in the Balkan Wars. Radić, in a minority, was opposed to the Croatian parliament's decision to join the new state in 1918. The new Yugoslav legislature, debating the future constitution, quickly became polarised between the centralist faction, with a small majority, in favour of the (Serb) King as head of state with wide powers, and the decentralisation faction, insisting on the sovereignty of parliament. Radić was in favour of an independent Croatia, that

Croatia to cooperate with the *Ustaše* (the *Ustaše* had anyway been part of Slunj county council since 1932). They were thus able to simply take over the machinery of state and use it to carry out their criminal programme with the full legitimacy of the law. *Ustaše* circuit judges were appointed to sit in summary trials in the field pursuant to the Croatian Nationality Act, accompanied by gangs of violent criminals, some of them local Muslims and Croats[783]. According to Fitzroy Maclean, "Pavelić's accession to power had been followed by a reign of terror unprecedented even in the Balkans"[784]. However, in Slunj the terror started even before the capitulation, on 10 April, the same day Hitler visited Zagreb, and reached the Bihać pocket at the end of July. First, prominent members of Serb communities (teachers, priests, officials, policemen etc.) were arrested and secretly killed. Then the other men were ordered to report for voluntary work, before being arrested and then executed *en masse* in isolated locations near Slunj, Gnjilavac, Bihać, Velika Kladuša, and Bosanska Krupa. The women and children could be picked off at leisure later on, and were. This initial onslaught was followed by armed raids on mixed villages with Serb residents. Salvation was sought west of the Slunj – Rakovica – Bihać road. Crnaja's ordeal, in which 26 villagers were killed, lasted from 1-4 August, exactly 54 years before Operation Storm. The survivors organised a local armed guard to defend the village (there were further attacks in March and July 1942, when it was razed to the ground). In total, 26,000 Serbs were killed in the future Bihać pocket during WWII, and around 3,000 fled to the future Sector North[785]. Many of the participants in the uprisings went on to join the Partisans, as the only viable means of resistance, or indeed survival, while others joined the *Četniks* for the same reason; and many *Četniks* subsequently defected to the Partisans as the only vehicle for really fighting the enemy[786]. According to Stevo Božić (who with his brother moved to Srem in 1967), speaking in 1990:

> "In 1941 the people in the Serb villages hadn't heard of the Partisan movement, and they were organised as *Četniks* in the struggle against the *Ustaše* and the Germans. They lived in peace and harmony with the Muslims in Šturlić. That lasted until Pavelić gained influence over the Muslims by calling them the 'flower of Croatia', and directed them to oppose the Serbs even if it meant extermination. Later that year, Arif 'Kljapo' Derviševič came to our house [from Šturlić] and told my father what was happening. I was there, as were Đuro Božič and my grandfather. He told us to flee, because we were in danger, and gave us three rifles, later another five. The Serbs organised themselves and formed a platoon. The Muslims also organised themselves as a Muslim militia. But until November 1941, there were no killings or attacks between them. Then a Captain Šišo[cii] and a certain Suljo visited the Serb platoon in Ljeskovac.

---

might later join a decentralised Yugoslav state. This was also a time of major student protests in Belgrade. The HSS boycotted parliament, as well as campaigning outside parliament (at home and abroad) for greater sovereignty for Croatia, and the resulting political instability meant the King formed and dismissed 39 governments in the interwar years. The culmination of this conflict was the assassination of Radić in parliament in 1928, and the introduction of absolute rule by the King. Pavelić left the country at this time. The King banned all national symbols, and re-arranged the administration of the country into nine geographical *banovinas*, most of which did not correspond to ethnic/religious boundaries. No-one liked it, and he was assassinated in 1934. In 1937, the new government accepted an agreement that would allow a new, more equitable constitution, and set about appeasing the Croatian opposition: but WWII intervened.

[cii] Vilim Šišo, a Croat from Bjelovar and Spanish Civil War veteran.

They established the KPJ there and told the people who and what they were – communist Partisans. The platoon joined them[ciii][787]. However, the district council executive Dmitar Kovačević, Miljan (his father), Mane Božić and Dragić Radaković didn't want to join the Partisans. Or rather, Šišo and his men thought they wouldn't join the Communists and would thwart their plans, so that night they shot them, and in the morning told the people they had gone to join the *Četniks* in Plaški. Then, in January 1942, Šišo wanted to make a speech in Šturlić. He had an agreement (I don't know who with) that the locals would surrender their weapons, but at the same time he sent his Partisans to surround Šturlić, to cover him just in case. Šišo and another 12 of his men then entered Džebo Dizdarević's bar, where he delivered his speech. But he had made an error with the encirclement, and they were all killed. The Partisans' revenge was terrible, and there were dead on both sides. The Partisans then withdrew, and the Muslims burned and killed in Crnaja, everything and everyone they found. We fled across the Korana, but like other people all our property was burnt and our livestock driven off. The same year the *Ustaše* (11th and 12th regiments) organised an attack on 13 Serb villages, from Rakovica via Raštelo to Furjan. They killed people and burnt their houses[civ]".[788]

Fitzroy Maclean described the Partisans as "mostly very young, with […] red stars stitched to their caps and wearing a strange assortment of civilian clothes and captured enemy uniforms and equipment. The red star […] was the only thing common to all of them"[789]. Germans, *Ustaše*, Home Guard, Partisans and Italians all came and went through the Bosnian Borders during the war (all of these armed groups, and the *Četniks*, had their origins outside Bosnia[790]). Pavelić, who had said in respect of King Aleksandar "You can run, Gyppo, but you can't hide", and his *Ustaše* had been given not only shelter, but also terrorist training camps and funding in Italy by Mussolini after the King proclaimed absolute rule in Yugoslavia in 1929, and Hungary, run by a demented, land-locked admiral in mourning for the loss of imperial glory, provided similarly subversive and violent support[791]. In 1935, 39 years after Italy's epic defeat, Mussolini unleashed on Ethiopia all his airborne and mechanised might, in breach of the peace treaty under which Italy had, in addition to paying a ransom of 10 million lira to recover its POWs, recognised the independence of Africa's only Orthodox nation (albeit with Muslim minorities, especially Somalis), the home of coffee, and the only African country to hold out against the tsunami of foreign (mainly European) domination in the second half of the 19th century. This provoked the crisis that led to the demise of the League of Nations, the predecessor to the UN born of the 1919 Paris Peace Conference, whose inability to effectively respond to this act of blatant aggression exposed it as being *jelav* ("fundamentally useless"); according to George Orwell, "53 nations made pious noises 'off'"[792]). Italy and Hungary also smuggled large quantities of arms into Croatia and Macedonia in the inter-war period in support of the terrorist activities they were sponsoring there. Huska was the commander of Velika Kladuša, and took part in the second Karlovac district conference of the KPJ; but in 1943 when the Partisans were ordered to withdraw from the Borders during the Axis fourth

---

[ciii] Half the early resistance fighters from Crnaja were killed during the war.

[civ] In total, 57% of the male and 39% of the female population of Crnaja were killed in WWII, with 44% of the victims under the age of 14. The survivors lost all their property.

offensive (see below), he joined the Home Guard, before forming his own militia. Stevo Božić continues:

> "In November 1942, the Partisans occupied Bihać and the whole Borders (the resistance conference was also held). Then Tito made a speech in Cazin and explained who the Partisans were, and about brotherhood and unity[cv793] (I was there myself, and I spent 12 days with Tito and Moša[cvi794]. Tito then and Tito after the war were the same person). After this speech, the Muslims joined the Partisans *en masse*. Hamdija Omanović formed the VIII Borders brigade in Cazin which was mainly made up of Muslims. In 1941, Huska Miljković was the commander of the Partisan platoon in Petrova Gora. That year he, Zuhdija Žalić and Omer Duranović (from Velika Kladuša) held a meeting in our house. Imam Huskić was with them, and all this was before the burning of Crnaja. It was around two months later that Šišo turned up. I remember that Huska and all the others wore triangular caps with a red star. They were real Partisans. I should add that Huska was a real hero, even today it's not clear to me why he doesn't have official recognition. Zuhdija was later commander of the II Kordun brigade in the VIII Kordun division, and Hakija Pozderac was political officer in the II Muslim brigade (1944). Around the beginning of 1943, Huska clashed with the Partisans because of some bunkers in Petrova Gora, and he split from them. He immediately contacted Ale Čović, and the two of them, and later others, formed Huska's army. Huska, Ale and a certain Milka (a cook) and another two (I don't know who they were) were staying in Johovica, in Miko Šaša's house. At that time, I held an important position in the SKOJ ['league of young Communists'] and my job was to monitor such activities. Even though I knew both Ale and Huska from before, I didn't dare join them at first. Within a short space of time (in about two months) they had formed 12 battalions. Men from the Home Guard and the *Ustaše* joined them *en masse*, as well as many Serbs. The whole Borders were effectively theirs. Huska immediately started to cooperate with the Partisans. He managed to capture the German *Gestapo* chief Colonel Denschill, the *Četnik* commander Mišina Bukva and many *Četniks*, and he handed them all over to the Partisans in Petrova Gora. Huska's army wore a star and a moon on their caps"[795].

Within three months, Huska had more men than the 1st Proletarian brigade, the first Partisan special forces unit (led by another Spanish Civil War veteran[cvii796]), and at

---

[cv] Legija later commented, "That false brotherhood and unity, established by the iron will of an imperfect ideology, was backfiring on us like a boomerang. A total clusterfuck".

[cvi] Moša Pijade, described by Fitzroy Maclean as "an elderly intellectual from Belgrade, who, as almost the only Jew amongst the Partisans, became a favourite target for Nazi propaganda", shared a Croatian prison with Tito from 1928-1934 where they were imprisoned for being KPJ activists, and was a member of Tito's inner circle.

[cvii] According to George Orwell, the Spanish Civil War was in essence a revolution; and the two main protagonists were both determined to prevent the revolution from succeeding. While Franco, supported by Hitler, sought to re-introduce feudalism, the government, supported almost exclusively by Stalin, wanted to maintain liberal democracy: the objectives of the communist party were not to foment revolution abroad, but to implement Soviet foreign policy, which was conditioned by Stalin's complex relationship with Hitler. This was carefully concealed by the English press, "in order to prevent people from grasping the real nature of the struggle". My father later told me that but for the establishment propaganda, he would have gone to fight in Spain himself, as would no doubt many others. Blair would have sent them all

its peak Huska's militia had 4,500 men. With them he defended the Bosnian Borders against all comers, successfully playing off the different sides against each other. He played a decisive role defending Cazin against the Partisans and was made a Home Guard major, only to be later made a Partisan colonel. On 27 April 1944, Huska was summoned by a courier in Partisan insignia to Velika Kladuša, from whence he was to travel with others to a meeting in Todorovo. On the way there on his dapple-grey horse, Zekan, just outside the town, he was shot by two *Ustaše* in an ambush. The assassins then travelled to Trnovi and shot his brother Šaban, before fleeing to Partisan territory. Huska was buried with military honours in Velika Kladuša in the same grave as his brother, but was then proclaimed a traitor. Their grave was marked only by a pine tree planted by Huska's widow beside the mosque in the town centre (since felled). No forgiveness this time from a merciful tyrant. There is a now a Partisan war memorial just behind the mosque, at the top of Mujo Hrnjica park, surrounded by pine trees. But it is generic, and does not feature the names of individual Partisans.

Discussing the WWII collaboration between the *Četniks* and the Germans, Fitzroy Maclean wrote, "Who was being fooled and who was getting the best of it? The Germans, who had succeeded in neutralising what had started as a resistance movement? Or the *Četniks*, who were actually being armed by an enemy, against whom they hoped one day to rise? It was all in the best Balkan tradition"[797]. Huska's tactics may be described as duplicitous, or even triplicitous ("there are two sides to every coin; but Huska had three"); but he is the second of only two Borders folk heroes, having defended his people's interests in a very hostile world of bigger players. Velika Kladuša was free territory for 723 days during WWII[798].

As I wandered among the throngs of these noble savages, reviled by some as traitors and "bastards", it was as if I could see Mujo and Huska walking among them. They had the same fighting spirit, the same loyalty to community and disregard for central authority (as Fitzroy Maclean wrote, "that natural Balkan turbulence and independence, that insurgent spirit which for centuries had made [them] such a thorn in the flesh for any foreign invader"[799]); and they appeared to be paying a similarly high price for their defiance. I was put in mind of Sorley MacLean's wonderful words: "*bochdainn àmhghar 's dòrainn [...] cealgaireachd dhubh na brèine [...] a' bhrùid 's am meàirleach air ceann na h-Eòrpa [...] breòiteachd an aobhair bhuain seo [...] creachainn chèin fhàsmhoir*" ("poverty, anguish and grief [...] foul black treachery [...] the brute and the brigand at the head of Europe [...] the sore frailty of this lasting cause" and the "distant luxuriant summit" to which they all aspired)[800].

The third of thirteen children, Babo was born in 1939 with his right leg slightly shorter than his left, as a result of which he has limped all his life, and was unable to do JNA national service, a major stigma. According to the legend, this shortcoming only spurred him on to succeed in other areas, and while his brothers were out playing, and later working, he was always inside studying, and he ended up being the first in his family to receive further education, at Derventa agricultural college, the first student to benefit from a scholarship from the Mala Kladuša agricultural association[801]. It is said that he

---

to Guantánamo. In January 1942, during the Axis second offensive, the Proletarian brigade carried out what became known as the "Igman March", escaping from the *Wehrmacht* south across Mount Igman in temperatures as low as -35° C.

"never forgot the inconsolable grieving of the children and adults from his village who, immediately after liberation, were sent to work in various parts of the country, from Bjelovar to Vojvodina. The weeping and painful farewells caused by the departure from mother's breast and father's, or grandfather's hearth, affected me deeply"[802].

Hope said of Babo: "He wasn't interested in women or alcohol, he was single-minded in the pursuit of his obsession and only passion in life: Agrokomerc". At the age of 24, Babo became the youngest MP in Bosnia (and in Yugoslavia). He became director of the agricultural association and developed it with the latest western technology as a means to develop the whole Borders (not least via local taxes, which Babo was later accused of not paying), while pursuing a degree in agricultural studies at Sarajevo university. Babo bought up land for the association in the Borders and elsewhere in Yugoslavia, offering the vendors "cash and jobs". In 1971, the period of economic reforms in Yugoslavia, the business, having outgrown the association, was incorporated as Agrokomerc. Salaries were not high, as most of the profits were re-invested, and were sometimes paid in Agrokomerc vouchers, at least in the early days (one criticism of Babo is that salaries were not always paid on time). Agrokomerc also levied rates to contribute to the costs of local development, and employment opportunities were not open to any household who decided not to pay. At this time his partnership with the Pozderac brothers started, as Hakija was the federal economy minister. In 1973, Agrokomerc entered into cooperation with the major (West) German food company, Kraft. In 1978, Agrokomerc signed a contract with Czechoslovakia for the purchase of agricultural equipment and vehicles worth USD 26 million. A second contract for USD 60 million was signed in 1982, and a third one for USD 140 million in 1985 (Agrokomerc sold the equipment to wholesalers within Yugoslavia, and ploughed the profits back into its own development. One of the main counts against Babo in the affair was that this third contract had not been registered with the authorities; but in fact it had). In 1982, Agrokomerc became one of the main suppliers of eggs to NATO. Agrokomerc also invested in tourist and industrial infrastructure throughout Yugoslavia, in particular in Croatia, which has now all been unlawfully nationalised and privatised[cviii]. In 1986, Agrokomerc took advantage of Yugoslavia's leading role in the Non-Alignment Movement to conclude a contract for the export of chickens to the Middle East, by air. In 1990, it was planned for Agrokomerc to become the world's largest producer of rabbit meat, and Babo's ambition was for it to become the third-largest food company in the world. He says the Agrokomerc affair was simply a matter of "hate, envy and a sick desire to destroy" something that local people had built

---

[cviii] The Yugoslav Agreement on Succession Issues of 2001 provides that "Rights to real and personal property located in a successor state over which citizens or other legal entities of the former Yugoslavia had rights on 31 December 1990 shall be recognised, protected and restored in their original state by the successor state in accordance with the established standards and norms of international law, regardless of the ethnicity, citizenship, residence or whereabouts of such persons. All contracts concluded between citizens and other legal entities of the former Yugoslavia as of 31 December 1990, including contracts concluded by public corporations, shall be respected without discrimination". Babo argues that these investments were funded by the workers of Agrokomerc ("paid for with their blood, sweat and tears"), and so cannot be nationalised. In 1999, an audit by the Bosnian government concluded that Agrokomerc was 90% state-owned, which opened the floodgates to the privatisation and looting of the company's assets by the SDA. Efforts to fight this in the courts in Bosnia and Croatia have thus far all been obstructed. Today, the managers of Agrokomerc are all outsiders, with no experience of working in the business, while none of the retired Agrokomerc workers, including Babo, receive a pension.

independently of, and without the blessing of, the power centres in Bihać and Sarajevo[cix][803]. His real crime was to become too big to fail (the communist authorities belatedly realised the folly of making him fail, and allowed the business to continue under his leadership. Alas, the SDA authorities have not shown the same prescience)[804]. Legija describes his first meeting with Babo in Petrova Gora:

[cix] As Andrić observed in *Letter from 1920* and *The Case of the* Vezir*'s Elephant*, "Bosnia is a wonderful, fascinating country, out of the ordinary as concerns both its nature and its people. Just as under the Bosnian ground mineral wealth is to be found, so Bosnian people doubtless conceal within themselves many moral values which are rarely encountered in their countrymen in the other Yugoslav countries. But there is also something that people from Bosnia, at least people like you, should understand, and not lose sight of: Bosnia is a country of hatred and fear [...] Yes, hatred [...] the fatal characteristic of that hatred lies in the fact that Bosnians are not aware of the hate that lives within them, shrink from any analysis of it, and hate anyone who attempts to do so. Yet the fact remains that in Bosnia and Herzegovina there are more people who are prepared, in fits of unconscious hatred, to kill or be killed, than in any other, much larger country in terms of population and geography, Slavic or not. I know that hatred, and rage, serve a purpose in the development of society, for hatred confers strength, and rage provokes action [...] But what I've observed in Bosnia is something else. Hatred, not as an instant in the course of social development and a necessary part of the historical process, but hatred that acts as an independent force, that finds its purpose in itself. A hatred that sets one man against another, and then casts both of them into poverty and misfortune, or drives them both under the ground; a hatred that like cancer in an organism consumes and corrodes everything around it, only to ultimately die itself, for like a flame, it does not have a permanent form or life of its own; it is simply a vehicle for the urge to destruction or self-destruction, and only exists as such, and only until it has accomplished its task of total destruction. Yes, Bosnia is a country of hatred. That's Bosnia. And by a strange contrast, which is perhaps not so strange [...] it can also be said that there are few countries which have such strong faith, exalted strength of character, tenderness, and passionate love, such depths of feeling, dedication and unshakeable loyalty, such a thirst for justice. But beneath all of that, in the impenetrable depths, hide storms of hate, hurricanes of compressed, bound hatred, maturing and awaiting their time [...] Just as the earth upon which we live passes under the influence of atmospheric humidity and warmth into our bodies and lends them its colour and appearance, determines the character and direction of our way of life and our acts, so the potent subterranean invisible hatred over which Bosnians live enters imperceptibly and ineluctably into all their acts, even their greatest. Everywhere, vice begets hatred, because it consumes rather than creates, destroys rather than builds, but in countries like Bosnia, even virtues frequently speak and act with hate [...] The most evil and darkest people can be found in the vicinity of places of worship and monasteries [...] Perhaps people should be reminded in Bosnia that at every step, in every thought, and in the loftiest sentiment hatred lies, innate, unconscious, endemic hate. That backward and crippled country, in which four religions live crammed together, needs four times as much love, mutual understanding and tolerance than other countries. But in Bosnia misunderstanding, which occasionally erupts into open hatred, is practically a common characteristic of its inhabitants. The rifts between the different religions are so deep that only hatred sometimes succeeds in bridging them [...] In Bosnian middle-class circles there has always been an abundance of false gentility, streetwise deception and self-deception by means of fine-sounding words and empty ceremony. This conceals the hatred to a certain extent, but does not remove it or prevent its growth. I am afraid that under the shroud of modern maxims, the old urges and Cain-like plans slumber in those circles, and will continue to live until such time as the bases of material and spiritual life in Bosnia are changed completely. But when will that time come, and who will have the strength to bring it about? I believe that it will come one day, but what I have seen in Bosnia does not indicate that we are moving in that direction. On the contrary." "Such is their hatred! When Bosnian hatred becomes attached to an object, it doesn't let go; over time it strengthens its focus and grasp, changes its form and meaning, grows out of all proportion to the object and becomes a purpose in its own right. Then the object itself becomes secondary, only its name remains, while the hatred crystallises, grows in and of itself, according to its own laws and needs, and becomes powerful, clever and impassioned, like an inverted love; it finds new nourishment and impetus in everything, and creates its own occasions for even greater hatred. Once a Bosnian community hates someone, deeply and bitterly, then sooner or later he must fall, under the weight of the invisible, persistent and insidious burden of that hatred; there is no salvation, other than to destroy the community to its foundations and its people to their genes. Their hatred is blind and deaf, but it is not mute [...] 'Enough is enough [...] How long are we going to put up with this?' asked one of the more militant aspiring local businessmen, 'Are we going to wait until the elephant is fully grown, and starts to invade our houses and attack our children? Do you know that an elephant can live for 100 years?' 'The elephant might', said an elderly, pale merchant quietly, 'but its owner, the *vezir*, won't'."

"He was a short man, with somewhat unruly and greying hair. He was wearing a dark blue suit and a dark green raincoat. I noticed that he limped slightly on one leg. It was his eyes that attracted my attention. They were exceptionally blue, and gave out an incredible energy. I liked him immediately, at first glance"[805].

Dr Kržišnik-Bukić continues,

"Relatively quickly, within a year, it became apparent that this political concept of equidistance in respect of the surrounding geopolitical environment was profoundly mistaken. It confirmed a fear that had been in the air even before the proclamation of the autonomous region of West Bosnia, an act that can only be construed as a 'stab in the back' of Bosnia and Herzegovina, attacked and bleeding on all sides [...] The 'traitors', as many called the separatist policy and practice in part of the Bosnian Borders, dealt a heavy blow to Bosnia's overarching identity as a state, and in particular to its moderate Muslims"[806].

The proclamation of the Republic of West Bosnia (pre-released in May 1995, but only official on 26 July) stated that,

"In West Bosnia, the fires of war rage in the intra-Muslim conflict staged by the Sarajevo regime. Two diametrically opposed political options, the decentralised, regional option defended by the NOZB, and the centralised option pursued by the 5th Corps, are claiming multiple lives and causing devastation to property on a daily basis. The first option is based on an understanding of the specific geopolitical character of the region, and sees the only possibility of salvation for the Muslim people in political negotiation and agreement with their neighbours. This option is a reality based on the principles of justice and morality, and on history. The second option, that of eternal war, is based on the conviction that Bosnia and Herzegovina can be a unitary state with a Muslim majority.
"Whereas the war option is exhausted and its deadly utopianism can only bring even more tragic consequences for the people of the region, we consider that West Bosnia should be organised as a political entity so that peace can finally reign here. An independent political entity in negotiations on the future formation of Bosnia and Herzegovina, with the position of equal partner, requires a political and constitutional framework. The Republic of West Bosnia is a reality for present and future generations within the framework of internationally recognised borders. Therefore we must, and it is in our interest to be active participants in deciding our fate. Thus far, the citizens of West Bosnia have personally experienced the fate reserved for them by central government and management.
"We no longer want or trust centralism and its *modus operandi*. Such methods cannot be fully objective in respect of all three peoples"[807].

On 19 June 1996, the front page of *Vjesnik* carried a report on the assassination attempt against Babo. It quoted Babo, who had given evidence in the Rijeka district court as a witness, as saying that the principal behind the plot was to be found in

Sarajevo, not Bihać, as he had been in 1987 (in September 1992, Izetbegović had first described Babo as a "political *mejt* ['corpse']"[808]. As Stalin said, "*Net čeloveka net problem*" - "get rid of the man and you get rid of the problem"). It is a rare thing for Muslim leaders not to meet a violent end in the Balkans[809].

The only negative experiences I had in Kuplensko were when my bag was stolen, and when someone tried to steal fuel from Gary's truck. I had just been shopping in Vojnić and had bought some supplies for a birthday party we were invited to that evening. I left my bag with the supplies in the tent, and, contrary to my habit, left my passport in it rather than keeping it on my person (mainly because I was wearing a new pair of *farmerke* ("jeans") that did not have a convenient pocket). Later, when I went back to the tent, the bag was gone. The loss of my passport was an administrative nuisance that could be dealt with, but we needed the bottles of brandy for that evening. Thinking on my feet, I went out and bought some replacements, more expensively (and of suspect provenance), from one of the makeshift booths. Later, when I needed to fly back to the UK, I was issued a temporary travel document by the British consulate in Split, where I had previously had cause to lodge a complaint that wasn't dealt with to my satisfaction. I had to produce a police report; but where was I to get one in Kuplensko? I solved the problem by going to the UN police station in Velika Kladuša (crossing the border with my NGO ID card), and a local member of staff I knew kindly provided me with the letter I needed. On another occasion, Gary had delivered a truckload of aid to the camp, and as it was getting late, I suggested he stay the night in my tent, rather than doss down by himself outside the Vojnić woodyard, which was less secure now there were so few people there, despite the influx of refugees from Banja Luka. Gary was a former foreign legionnaire who I knew from EDA in 1993. One Sunday afternoon towards the end of the war, we had decided to have a beer in a bar in Cazin town centre. When the sirens started blaring, indicating incoming shelling, and the streets emptied in a matter of minutes, if not seconds, we decided we were not going to abandon our well-earned cold one. The *konobar* ("barman"), evidently also a diehard, indicated that we should continue our drinking behind the bar, rather than by the large glass window, which we duly did (the other reason this bar sticks in my mind is because the generator room in the back doubled up as a chicken run for the owner. I had been there once before with Kiwi, when we met some young local *Mudžahedin* having a last drink (no alcohol) before deploying to the front the following day. Yet again, I was struck at the absurd tragedy of this war in which perfectly decent, and heroic, youngsters were engaged in a fight to the death – not against an implacable foreign invader, but against each other. Where are they now?). Despite the camaraderie of the shared danger, the barman did not forget to give us our bill when we eventually left. Another time, Gary and I had gone out for more than a few drinks in Split. Late the following morning when I woke up in our communal house, as I lay in bed trying to piece together the events of the previous evening, I had visions of a French-speaking Croat who had invited us to his house, a leg of Dalmatian *pršut* ("ham"), and a fight between him and Gary. Dismissing it all as a dream, I made my way to the kitchen for a coffee, only to discover Geordie John, the fleet manager for the Balkans operation, eagerly devouring slices he was carving from a splendid leg of Dalmatian ham occupying pride of place on the dining table. Finally, on a long drive from Slunj to Split one day, after delivering my truck to our warehouse in Polje, Gary had insisted on bringing with him a puppy he had adopted in Cazin. Unfortunately, the poor little mite was not used to travel by road and fell car sick. Now in Kuplensko, I organised some food and drink, and we had a merry evening. But in the middle of the night we were woken by a friend telling us someone was syphoning fuel from Gary's tank. Outside we went, and the war criminals scarpered. Fortunately, they hadn't got much, but we had to remain vigilant the rest of the night, and Gary left early the next morning in a black mood. I made it up to him two years later in Kosovo. But we weren't the only ones to be ripped off. A Russian peacekeeper from Vladivostok ("queen of the east") who I met one day on a recce in Kuplensko, had his camera stolen from his vehicle in a momentary lapse of attention; and DM 35,000 in cash disappeared from UNHCR's new secure container on 29 March[810].

After the war, I noticed that as people returned to normal life and were once again caught up in the cares of everyday capitalism, the strong community bonds and solidarity that had manifested themselves in Kuplensko quickly started to fade away.

(IN)VOLUNTARY EXILE

Alone I sit in my room
Drinking coffee all alone
That sets me thinking, and I
Laugh at myself rather than groan

My room is 3 metres square
It looks very small
I've got something to lie on
But bookshelves not at all

There's a shirt on the door
Slippers in the corner
Two little cupboards
Containing assorted clobber

Also a little chair
Standing by the door
In the other corner
My shoes muddy the floor

There's a tall stove
Beside it piled some wood
Tinned meat by the window
And breadcrumbs - my staple food

I'm still drinking coffee
Smoking one fag after another
Beside the stove I can
Dry out my wet clobber

On the little cupboards
Burn two little candles
Tinned meat fish and spread
A binbag on the doorhandle

An odd little pot
A mirror on the cupboard
A jerrycan for water
And a glass pint beermug

Such is my room
In it I have peace
On the window hangs my bush hat
And my good old winter fleece

I've even got some sugar
Something I can't deny

But what I haven't got to drink coffee with
Is my family

And so I think back
On the good old days of yore
Dear God above
Where is her indoors?

In the rest of the room
Flour salt and oil
Where is my little Maja
Without her I'm in turmoil

It's difficult being without them
That's why I'm so sad
Where are my brothers and sisters
My mother and my dad?

But I think the day will come
When I will again see my family
And dear God above will
Solve all my difficulties[811].

Sead "Tetin" Kajtazović, Paklena Dolina

There had been an earlier refugee crisis in August 1994, when Velika Kladuša was occupied by the 5th Corps, and 50,000 people fled into the Croatian Borders (i.e., the Serb Borders republic)[812]. On 9 August, Izetbegović had offered NOZB soldiers an amnesty, valid until the 16th. Meanwhile, on the 12th, Babo held a press conference and proposed a Mostar-type settlement (i.e., *de facto* partition under EU authority as per the Washington agreement), and on the 17th he had tried to set up talks via UNPROFOR. The Bosnian ambassador to Croatia came to Velika Kladuša at the invitation of UNPROFOR to try to negotiate a peaceful settlement[813]. But on the 21st, the 5th Corps occupied Velika Kladuša[814]. A large part of the population was housed either in the Karlovac suburb of Turanj, across the river from the main town and on the front line between the HV and the SVK, or in Agrokomerc's 24 chicken hangars in Batnoga near Cetingrad, sleeping on bare concrete with appalling hygienic facilities. The crockery abandoned by the poultry was swiftly appropriated by the lucky few refugees to get there first, and once the foul fowl filth had been cleared away, there was room for one's whole family to take up residence, and plenty of metal sheeting that could be converted into partitions to afford some privacy. While many of the Croat houses near Batnoga were abandoned and empty, there was safety in numbers in the hangars, and anyway the many mines scattered like fertiliser seemingly everywhere were a deterrent to those seeking better accommodation, as some people discovered to their cost. One woman lost a leg picking fruit. Another unfortunate, Ahmed, a youngster, was blown in half vertically when collecting *neeksplodirana ubojna sredstva* ("UXO") to sell to the SVK for recycling. Fresh food could be earned by women doing household chores for elderly locals, mostly Serbs[815]. There was an infestation of head lice in both camps, and the only treatment available was for skin rash, which didn't help. Smajo swore by chicken shit as an infallible folk remedy. At least there was no shortage of that. A FTC report on Turanj from October 1994 reads:

> "Toilets are improvised and an appalling health risk. Rubbish is left to rot, or to the local rat population. The only fuel they have is wood. Hardly any of the houses have windows, many have no doors or roofs. Plastic sheeting is used to keep out the worst of the rain but it will not keep out the cold. The most dangerous aspect of Turanj is live explosives"[816].

Babo had attempted to evacuate the refugee population to HDZ territory, but this had been refused by Tuđman[817]. The refugees asked Sadako Ogata, the head of UNHCR, to visit, but she never came[818]. Some families found themselves split between the two sites (initially the population had been scattered over a wider area, but the SDS authorities rounded them up). Refugees were able to transfer between Batnoga and Turanj for the purposes of family reunification (although for some, the real objective in transferring to Turanj was to get away from the war altogether once it became clear they would have to fight their way back into Bosnia for a second round with the 5th Corps, who had meanwhile become head of party and state, prosecutor, judge, and mafia godfather in Velika Kladuša. In his letter to UNHCR appealing for a political solution, to which he received no reply, Babo referred to the new authorities in Velika Kladuša as a "military junta". With all other roads closed to them, and conditions so desperate, the approaching winter meant the refugees had no choice but to go back[cx][819]). On the other side of no-man's land, there was a major police and HV deployment to prevent an influx of refugees into HDZ land. Reserves were mobilised in Karlovac. Some people ended up stuck between the two front lines, on the 1 km of no-man's land between UNPROFOR and the HV, while others managed to escape by crossing the river and evading the police and the HV, and the minefield (a guide could be hired for DM 2,000)[820]. In particular, the large Romany community, the largest minority in Europe, more numerous than the populations of several EU member states, was spirited away overnight by their *phrala* ("brethren") from Italy. Despised as lazy, dirty, irrational, unclean and generally inferior ("What was the Gypsy's last wish when he was sentenced to be hanged? Could you hang me under the arms, my neck is ticklish!", or "What did the Gypsy say to the Bosnian? If it wasn't for you, we would be the scum of the earth!"; or, as Vida Tomšić stated in relation to 1950: "When I arrived [in the Bosnian Borders], the KPJ had already been decimated. There was a joke going around that they were trying to recruit Gypsies into the party in order to strengthen it!"[821]), they quickly proved they had far better connections when push came to shove. In fact, they are as industrious as ants in their own unorthodox way, and indeed could not have survived to the present day as a separate people if it were otherwise. As the Romanies say, *"Na trušulenca le manuša brakhen e granica"* ("it takes more than a border to stop us")[822]. The ongoing war

---

[cx] According to Legija, the objectives of Operation Spider were to relieve the Serb Borders authorities of the burden of the large refugee population, but more importantly, under the guise of the legitimate aim of returning the refugees to their homes, to capture from the 5th Corps the strategically vital territory which was the Bihać pocket, something that had the potential to determine the outcome of the whole war. All men fit for military service were mobilised in the autumn and taken to Petrova Gora in preparation for the offensive, a move widely condemned by the international community. But as Mirvet points out, it happened under the noses of Polish UNPROFOR, who had the refugees surrounded, and UNHCR, who claimed to be responsible for them.

and Legija's remobilisation meant that things were a lot more tense in this earlier refugee crisis, as Kiwi and Gordon discovered one day. The mood was quite ugly as they drove slowly through the madding crowd, and Kiwi persuaded Gordon to hand over the camera he was taking snaps with to avoid being lynched. Izetbegović said in respect of this refugee crisis in an interview with *Slobodna Dalmacija* on 2 September 1994:

> "I believe that Fikret Abdić is a political corpse. He has caused great harm to Bosnia and Herzegovina and to our people's just struggle. There is an unhappy symbolism in what is happening. When the music stopped, Abdić found himself dancing with those who have killed Borderers in Prijedor and Kozarac, and destroyed our sacred places in Banja Luka and throughout Bosnia. Such is the only logical end for people like him. The only pity is that in this tragedy Abdić has taken a number of innocent people down with him"[823].

When Velika Kladuša was recaptured and the population returned on New Year's Eve, they found the town had been ransacked, especially those houses that had served as billets. While for some, the return to Bosnia was a cause for celebration, others found the state of emergency there and the ongoing war to be extremely depressing. The EU monitors described the occupied town as looking as if "a disappointed English football team had given the centre some serious attention"[824]. There was no running water or electricity[825]. When the town was evacuated, the Agrokomerc warehouses had been left full of goods, which had all been looted[826], while household items had been moved in accordance with the vagaries of military logic. For example, one family found their fridge in someone else's house further up the street. Doors had been removed from houses to be used as cover for infantry, while in some houses, even the windows had been looted. Four new factories that had just been fully equipped and were ready to start production were stripped bare. The DNZ estimated the total losses at DM 50 million[827]. ICRC, FTC and NRC were the only organisations providing support to the returnees[828]. Because of the memory of this experience, this time some of the women and children stayed behind at home, while the men went to what they hoped was temporary exile in the neighbouring Croatian Borders. It was said that a month living in a refugee camp reduces life expectancy by one year[829]. The hope was that the women would be able to look after the home (and avoid the awful conditions of refugee living) until such time as their husbands could return. In the event, the behaviour of the 5th Corps after their second occupation of the town turned out to be less destructive than the first time, although it was estimated that a total of 1,000 buildings in the town were damaged by the end of the war[830].

On 6 January 1996, the remaining population in Kuplensko was approximately 10,000[831]. While the newly-triumphant authorities in Velika Kladuša were keen to get their hands on certain high-profile individuals, in general they did not want the mass of recalcitrant "separatists" to return, as they could only be a thorn in the side of the SDA in the future. In the new year, refugees began to realise that those who had gone back, or even those who had made their way to other countries, were often even hungrier than they were, and with no prospects of any improvement in the near future[832]. On 6 January, five refugees attempting to return to the camp were intercepted by the riot police. Two were shot, and the others fled back to

Bosnia[833]. UNHCR's response to the refugees on 24 January was that they should not set foot outside the camp, other than when returning in the bus. A small girl was run over and killed by a police vehicle on 10 January, but that did not lead to an improvement in the police's driving through the camp[834]. UNHCR told the refugees they were responsible for their own road safety[835]. On 18 April, an ICRC vehicle seriously injured a child in the camp.

The refugees' self-organisation in the camp took on new impetus in the New Year, and the committee's meetings were open to all, so that the refugees could take cognisance of topical issues and decisions[836]. On 2 January, a meeting was held between the committee, UNHCR and the EU on improving the functioning of the aid effort[837]. The committee proposed a multiparty working group made up of respected people from all walks of life on both sides of the conflict in order to work towards reconciliation[838]. They also wrote a complaint to the ICTY about their treatment by the Croatian and Bosnian authorities. Nevertheless, there was a lingering suspicion among international visitors to the camp that the committee was a Stalinist clique, and this skewed many people's perceptions and prevented them from seeing the real key issues. The same view had been taken during the previous refugee emergency[839]. On 7 January and over a period of several days, Caritas brought in several trucks of timber for firewood, and it was distributed at the rate of 1 m³ per household[840]. The largest single delivery, around 170 linear metres, was on 16 January[841]. On 18 January, three days before the start of Ramazan, coal was distributed[842]. At the coordination meeting on 17 January, Ramo condemned UNHCR's "ongoing acceptance of the unacceptable"[843]. At the coordination meeting of 24 January, he once again decried the failure of the international community to ensure basic security, in particular protection from the Croatian and Bosnian authorities, and the failure to provide adequate medical treatment for the wounded. At the same meeting there was a request for seeds, a sign some refugees were thinking about the long haul[844]. At the meeting of 14 February, Ramo asked again about: legal access to goods in the camp, the removal of weapons, security in the camp, and human rights in Bosnia, and lamented that all the committee's efforts to highlight individual cases thus far had resulted in nothing but more reports; he also said the key to the problem was to be found in Sarajevo, and that only pressure on the government there would produce results[845].

Another rally was held on 17 January, when 2,000 refugees in the icy cold were treated to a 15-minute speech by Babo live over the telephone[846]. On 31 January, the committee wrote to Carl Bildt, the new high representative for Bosnia, bringing their position to his attention, lamenting the arrogance with which they had been treated thus far, and recommending he set up a committee to oversee the implementation of Dayton in the new Una-Sana canton. The letter was signed by a large number of refugees[847].

On the morning of 1 February, when I was having a lie-in, I was awoken by cries of "*Racija! Racija!*" ("raid!"). I got up and went out of my tent, to see riot police with shields and Armalite rifles deploying throughout the camp. It was the first time I had seen them with anything other than *Kalašnjikovs* (although I later saw an Uzi in Cazin). The arms embargo against Croatia was only lifted in 2000, and so it would appear that someone was sanctions-busting. The arms embargo against the former Yugoslavia was anyway widely regarded as ineffective[cxi][848]. During the previous night, someone had fired a pistol several times from close range over the tents in my neighbourhood, and I wondered whether there was any connection. The police were fond of firing random *hici* ("shots") during the night anyway, but I had never heard them so close before[849]. Sometimes they were echoed by automatic fire by the HV in the vicinity[850]. On the night of 27 August, they had had a party to celebrate their relief, which involved much eating, drinking, music and shooting[851]. As if that wasn't enough, on the night of 7 September several powerful explosions were heard outside the camp[852]. Now, I tried to engage with the policemen to find out what was happening, but without success. One of them was standing guard outside a tent which served as a kindergarten, with a dozen pre-school children under the supervision of a 20-year old girl, Suada, inside. I started speaking to him in English, hoping to impress him and gain access. However, he refused to be drawn and rebuffed me in Croatian. I then resorted to the local language and told him I was a representative of the international community, and demanded access to the tent. He refused again, and his superior, noticing an altercation, came over and, referring to the tent as a "*javna kuća*" ("brothel")[853], warned me I would be arrested. I said I wanted to speak to their commanding officer, but was told he was busy. Seeing I was making no headway, I called out to Suada inside and asked her if she was alright. She replied that they were, and I told her in a voice I wanted to sound reassuring, that everything would be alright. I then went into the ICRC tent, only to learn that the ICRC team were not in the camp that morning. Did the HDZ know that in advance? I urged the duty radio operator to advise the ICRC team to come to the camp as quickly as they could. I then moved some distance away, but kept in sight in a strategic position, hoping that my mere presence would preclude any evil deeds, and also hoping I would not be arrested, especially as I had left Seka alone in the tent. I couldn't think of anything more useful to do; wandering through the camp to bear witness to what else was happening might or might not have made a difference, and it seemed that my presence was as valuable here as anywhere. It also occurred to me for the first time that my freedom of action was somewhat hampered by a conflict of interest. Some time afterwards the riot police withdrew. I went back to the kindergarten tent and established that Suada and the children were alright, if shaken up. I learnt later that the police had refused to allow ICRC to enter the camp until they had concluded their operation. Their objectives were apparently to apprehend "certain individuals", to "establish order, prevent crime and protect life"[854]. In total, 400 riot police were deployed, accompanied by trade and health inspectors[855]. 69 street vendors were arrested, and all the makeshift businesses that had made life bearable were closed. A butcher lost all the meat he had just prepared for sale from a cow for which he had paid DM 3,000, and each detainee lost an average of DM 1,000 in goods and cash confiscated[856]. Telephones were specifically targeted, and the majority of the working phones in the camp were confiscated[857]. Among the

---

[cxi] According to Owen, "The Serb-Montenegrin border was at this time being used to supply arms to the Bosnian and Croatian Serbs [...] Before this [Croat-Muslim] civil war flared up, and again after it quietened down, the Croatian government was not only ready to supply arms but allowed a black market trade to flourish [...] The morality of the arms embargo was being discussed as a matter of high principle, while the Bosnian Muslims pretended they had no weapons, the Croatians kept very quiet about the arms they were collecting and passing on, and both were manufacturing them [...] A number of governments have helped to arm the Croats and, through the Croats, the Muslims. The Russian government in comparison by and large maintained the arms embargo against the Serbs; spare parts were in the main obtained by direct arrangement with Russian generals on the black market by both Serbs and Croats".

detainees was Jadra's husband, Sutko, who used to sell miscellaneous goods at a small stall. At the police station in Vojnić, the first of 20 of them was told to sign a confession to having broken the law in Croatia, and agreeing to a two-year ban on entering the country. When he refused, he was sat on a hot stove and held there until he agreed. The remaining 19 all signed without protest, and the prisoners all appeared before Karlovac district court the next day, where the sentences were confirmed after a detailed inquisition of the defendants' biographies. ICRC gained access to the prisoners and they were able to write messages to their families[858]. After two nights in Sisak *buksa* ("prison"), they were delivered to the local authorities in Bosnia, driven through Kuplensko in the middle of the night with sirens and flashing lights blazing[859]. Two of them were detained in Sisak for a longer period (Sutko was picked up by the police the next year in Slunj, and sentenced to a KN 3,500 fine or three days in prison in Slunj. He chose the latter, as he had been advised it was practically a holiday camp, where "you won't go hungry", and with no activities other than watching TV. This regime was later scrapped, when it was realised that no-one was paying fines)[860]. Another 20, who were just passers-by, were returned to the camp. The committee wrote a complaint to the Croatian government, CC'd to the international community, decrying the police's brutal practices, the disinformation about the camp published in the Croatian media, and reminding them that they had asked for legal commercial activities to be allowed in the camp in October[861]. Meanwhile, the black market didn't stop, it just went underground[862]. The price of cigarettes went up by 33%, to DM 4 a packet. These and other arbitrary arrests created a great deal of distress and anxiety for the detainees' dependents in the camp, who tended to follow them back to Bosnia soon afterwards, once they had established what had happened to them. This meant that every time someone was sent back to Bosnia, the camp population was in effect reduced by perhaps 4-5 people. Seizures of vehicles in the camp were not uncommon, including of vehicles owned by refugees. The police would sometimes snoop around inspecting vehicle papers, and if anything wasn't in order, the vehicle was gone[863]. After the raid, I saw Zahid engaged in what looked like a very intense conversation with the riot police at the barrier near the bridge. I imagined he was complaining among other things about the shooting over our tents the previous night.

The same evening, Croatian TV reported the raid, quoting UNHCR as saying there had been no breach of the refugees' rights, and stating it had been coordinated in advance with UNHCR. This caused a great deal of consternation in the camp, and at the coordination meeting the following Monday, the UNHCR head of office was asked about it. A large crowd of refugees gathered outside to hear what UNHCR had to say. After an emotional outburst, in which she insisted that everyone was against her, and after Ramo, in a bizarre role reversal, had calmed her down, telling her it was nothing personal, she said UNHCR would issue an official denial and contact Croatian TV to ask for a retraction. However, no official denial or retraction were forthcoming. On 15 February, a Croatian NGO, the Human Rights Direct Protection Group, held a press conference further to the raid, which was widely reported (and misquoted) in the Croatian press on 17 February (including by *Slobodna Dalmacija* and *Vjesnik*). The purpose of the press conference was to raise awareness in Croatia of the ongoing unacceptable situation and human rights abuses in the camp. It condemned the incident, and the government's failure to recognise refugee status (if the government recognised them as refugees, then, among other things, it would be bound under the Refugees and IDPs Act 1993 to ensure their basic needs were met)[864]. The press conference also stated that the military authorities were the real power in Velika Kladuša, dictating to the civilian authorities, and that the Croatian police had acted contrary to Dayton. The police response was also published, and stated that the camp was full of criminals and smugglers, that there had been murders, rapes, fights, and black market activities in the camp, as a result of which the police and UNHCR were being constantly asked by other refugees to intervene. They went on to say they had acted within their powers, without the excessive use of force or breaching the refugees' human rights, and that UNHCR had been informed of, and had approved, the action in advance[865]. This only served to heighten the tension in the camp and the general suspicion and distrust of UNHCR. On 26 February, the committee wrote a complaint to UNHCR asking for clarification of their role in the incident[866]. That month saw the camp's largest media coverage in Croatia[867]. UNHCR vigorously defended their activities in the coordination meeting on 28 February, stating that the UN security council had condemned Croatia for its actions[868]. UNHCR's protection officer attempted, unsuccessfully, to have the bans on entering Croatia imposed on the convicted traders overturned in the Croatian courts[869]. Once Sutko felt safe at home, he contacted Jadra and told her to come back to Bosnia. Her departure from Kuplensko, when she got on the bus with her baby and her mother-in-law, can only be described as traumatic. We moved into their room on the first floor of a house (soon after they had arrived, a woman had given birth in the living room of the house, underneath). The barbers reopened on 19 April[870].

On 2 February, at the very time the Croatian authorities were deciding the fate of the 69 refugees seized in the raid the day before, the UN commission on human rights' special rapporteur Elizabeth Rehn visited the camp, accompanied by a large number of journalists. The committee informed her among other things that in 180 days, 18 refugees had been killed, 9 in the camp and 9 in Bosnia[871]. Her subsequent report lamented the living conditions in the camp, the summary deportations, and the refusal to recognise refugee status, which she also conveyed to the Croatian foreign minister in a meeting. She appears not to have mentioned the committee's proposal to organise talks between the local authorities in Bosnia and the refugees, including Babo, as a starting point to reconciliation between the two factions. Once again, the refugees were faced with "*uzmi ili ostavi*" ("take it or leave it"), with the only third option, exile, not yet on the table[872]. According to MSF, the HDZ refused to grant refugee status because it would be an implied criticism of Izetbegović, Tuđman's partner in the Federation, the ailing *svunti guruvni* ("sacred cow") of Dayton[873]. A supplementary agreement intended to patch up the Federation was signed on 31 March[874]. On 19 March, the radio reported that Croatia had been admitted into the process for membership of the Council of Europe, and that one of the issues it would have to deal with in order to progress was Kuplensko[875]. On 29 April, the committee wrote to Rehn asking her to visit the camp again[876].

On 5 January, the head of UNHCR in Croatia held a meeting with Ramo. He stated they would have to move *kad tad* ("sooner or later"), but that only Tuđman, personally, could authorise another site[877]. He also stated that no third countries wanted to take them as refugees. Their large number precluded them being housed in an existing camp elsewhere in Croatia[878].

In the New Year, the committee wrote a letter to the conference on the return of refugees and IDPs to be held in Geneva on 16 January, signed by 1,000 of the refugees, and delivered to UNHCR for forwarding[879]. One of the committee's activities was compiling a list of cases of discrimination against returnees, such as non-delivery of Red Cross messages, which was shared with the EU monitors and other international organisations[880]. Other forms of abuse noted and reported were: voluntary work to be carried out by returnees, doing work for which they were not skilled, and for the personal benefit of those in favour with the authorities[881]; blackmail of families with members in the camp; discrimination when seeking medical treatment or medicines; refusal to pay out pensions; abuse when reporting cases to the police; delays issuing official documents such as passports; fear of officials with known criminal reputations; requests to help the police with irrelevant and arbitrary inquiries; discrimination against NOZB war widows as compared to 5th Corps war widows; reporting requirements to the police; and dismissal from employment of anyone expressing political views other than pro-SDA[cxii][882]. Another problem was the AID, which was controlled by the SDA, and staffed mainly by extremists from Sandžak[883]. Such practices were not unique to the Bosnian Borders. When Mujo returned to Srebrenica for the first time after the war (see below), he was summoned several times to help the police with their inquiries into his war record. Under Dayton, Srebrenica became part of Republika Srpska.

The number of people returning in January dropped to a trickle[884]. On 18 January, day 165, there was a first visit by a delegation from the Una-Sana canton authorities, accompanied by Bihać television. When asked when the refugees would return, Ramo replied, "When the local authorities convince them that it's better there than here"[885]. There were 300 cases of returnees coming back to Kuplensko by 22 April[886]. The availability of food and non-food items, and firewood, was generally perceived as being satisfactory in the camp from now on, and indeed superior to the situation in Bosnia[887].

On 11 April, one week after the assassination attempt against Babo, Ramo and Đedović travelled to Rijeka for meetings with him. They recorded a 15-minute address from him, in which he said among other things that "Pears aren't ripe when they first start to fall"[888]. On 15 April, *Vjesnik* carried an interview with Babo. Condemning the failed terrorist attack on him, at which he said he wasn't surprised, as Izetbegović had already demonstrated he was capable of anything, not least by his *coup* after the 1990 elections, and because he didn't consider Babo a true Muslim, he stated he was confident of victory in the September elections. He also stated that the conflict in the Bihać pocket had been driven not by Dudaković but by *Mudžahedin* and mercenaries from Sandžak; indeed, the ongoing state of lawlessness in the former enclave was the ideal environment for the organised crime associated with the 5th Corps, and was also aimed at preparing the ground for the elections in September 1996[889]. It was said in January that former commanders were taking up important political posts in the ruling SDA[890]. An Italian TV crew filmed in the camp on 13 January, and a Canadian film crew arrived on 1 March[891]. After Christmas, the hostile Bosnian local radio started referring to the refugees as "*građani*" ("citizens"),

---

[cxii] A report by the ombudsman from 2000 stated that the families of NOZB veterans were excluded from assistance as the "civilian victims of war". The report further stated that in Velika Kladuša and Cazin, anyone not in the SDA, and in particular DNZ members, were subject to discrimination when it came to employment opportunities (in particular in the education system) and the return of their homes. It also stated that the police continued to act as a tool of the ruling party and as a means of intimidation of DNZ members, with the objective of discouraging returns and encouraging more people to leave. A report by the ombudsman the following year cites the phenomenon in Velika Kladuša and Cazin of "outlaw citizens", former NOZB soldiers and supporters who were excluded from access to state services, such as the issue of passports. As a result, many applied for Croatian citizenship if they were eligible, or simply left.

and on 27 January they announced the names of refugees who would be receiving family visits the next day[892]. The Croatian weekly newspaper *Zbor* ran an article on Babo on 11 January, with the headline, "I will be president of Bosnia and Herzegovina"[893]. On 12 January, *Večernji Vjesnik* blamed aid agencies and war criminals for the slow return of the refugees[894]. On 15 January, the Croatian-language Voice of America radio reported that *Mudžahedin* from central Bosnia were taking refuge in Cazin, in expectation of an agreement with Croatia to allow their departure (as required under Dayton)[895]. They were not the only mercenaries to move on after the war: when I was working in the DRC in 1997, it was rumoured that a group of Serb mercenaries had been engaged by Mobutu to fight Kabila ("tribe") senior's Rwandan-backed rebels, and again in 2000 it was said that Serb mercenaries had dropped a large bomb from a plane onto the villa in Bukavu where Kabila was living (he was out at the time; I happened to be in Goma, at the other end of lake Kivu, that day, and I could have sworn I heard a distant rumble that I later put down to the bomb. Transport between the two towns was by air, because the road along the lakeshore was no-go Mai-Mai territory, see below)[cxiii]. Meanwhile, Greek mercenaries from the *Hrisi Avgi* ("golden dawn") movement, among others, had assisted the Unit at Srebrenica[896]. Some of the *Mudžahedin* who wanted to stay were given local girls to marry (in particular war widows), in order to be eligible for citizenship, among other things. Others were given jobs in NGOs[897]. Izetbegović later gave them all Bosnian citizenship so that they could stay, and even Bin Laden was issued a Bosnian passport by the embassy in Vienna (in 1993)[898]. On 25 January, there was a rumour that *Mudžahedin* would try to infiltrate the camp[899]. Croatian television spent two days filming a documentary, on 15 and 16 January[900], and it was

---

[cxiii] Kabila senior of the long-suffering Banyamulenge tribe of the eastern DRC, took power in 1997, but was assassinated in 2001 during Congo War II, when he was succeeded by the present incumbent, his son. Under the ruthless Mobutu, who I heard described as an "ogre" by a local colleague, François, and who died of AIDS in Morocco less than six months after being overthrown, the Tutsi Banyamulenge were persecuted as alleged interlopers from Rwanda during the Belgian colonial regime, which they vehemently deny. Before the DRC became independent, and indeed up until the 1990s, Bukavu, on the border with Rwanda and at the southern end of Lake Kivu, with its rich and rare flora and fauna and unspoiled virgin landscapes, was a playground for Belgian expats and rich foreigners. The *Orchid Noir* was owned and run by two elderly Belgian brothers, who in their youth had taken part in the 1960 Katanga rebellion, by which the Belgian government sought to defer and hopefully reverse the country's independence. The rebellion concluded with a *coup* against the new government staged by army man Mobutu with Belgian support, and in 1965, after a second *coup*, he became dictator of the independent Zaire. Under his tutelage, the obscure dialect of his village, Lingala, became the language of the army, and is now the main lingua franca in the west of the country. His greatest fear was to be overthrown in a *coup* himself, and as a result he kept the army starved of all resources, other than manpower. Ironically, this strategy ultimately allowed his downfall, when his army was unable to resist invasion from Rwanda. In 1997 the senior of the two brothers told us that the Rwandan squaddies in charge of Bukavu had tried to loot his office, but that he had managed to see them off single-handedly: the fact that he was a pensioner had probably saved him from a *balle* ("bullet"), because in the highly-ordered African society, respect for the *wazee* ("elderly") is sacred. But that didn't stop the Rwandan officers from running up bills that were never paid. I once met the Rwandan commander of the town, a colonel in his early twenties. I happened to visit the restaurant again ten years later, and learned that the younger of the brothers had since died. The surviving brother seemed to be going strong, and relied now on the custom of international aid agencies. He spoke no English, and said that when he had to travel to Kenya or Tanzania on business, he relied on Swahili to get around (despite the fact that Swahili as spoken in the DRC is influenced by French, as illustrated by the greeting, *"Uko bien?"*, and its response *"Kidogo/Un peu"* – "how are you?" "alright"). Also in Bukavu in the 1990s was a café called the Tea Shop, run by an old English boy called Bill. He seemed to be doing a successful trade the first time I went to Bukavu, but on my next visit, I discovered that he had shut up shop and moved on. One of the waitresses was called Chantal. Bukavu was the scene of fierce fighting between the army and Mai-Mai local militia in 1998, see below, and was briefly occupied by the Rwandan army in 2004. Anyone who had USD 50 to spare could pay for a place in the back of a pick-up escaping the town.

shown on 1 March under the title "Come Home", watched eagerly by many in the camp. It started with views of Velika Kladuša and Agrokomerc, with happy returnees, and then switched to the camp itself. It ended with an interview with the Croatian deputy minister for refugees and IDPs, who stated that in international law, the refugees didn't deserve protection, as they had acted contrary to the principles of the UN; but that nevertheless, the HDZ was doing the right thing, and UNHCR wanted them to carry on with more of the same until they all went home[901]. On 4 May, Croatian television carried another report on the camp, filmed on 1 May, with the head of the office for refugees and IDPs saying they might be there for more than a year[902]. On 11 May, radio Free Europe reported that the federal government had discussed Kuplensko in Sarajevo, with the conclusion that it must be "resolved" in the near future[903]. At the beginning of June, a video of an interview with Babo on Mostar (Croatian) television reached the camp, in which he was described as "in politics a Serb, but in business a Croat"[904]. On 11 July, the first anniversary of the fall of Srebrenica, *Feral Tribune* stated that returnees were subject to daily beatings, bullying and humiliation. In an interview, the 21-year old owner of a bar claimed he had severely beaten his own brother, who had been in the NOZB, and would kill his cousins if he ever saw them again. It also reported that the new incumbent of the castle in Velika Kladuša, a disabled imam, Suljo Hodža, from Ponikve, had banned alcohol there[905]. According to Legija, who took part in the same contact in which Suljo Hodža lost his right arm and was presumed dead during the battle for Velika Kladuša, he was a petty thief who had found religion when the war started: Legija called him a "*manijak*" ("barnpot")[906]. One day during the 1996 elections, he entertained the OSCE *posmatrači* ("monitors") in his keep. In his former role as head of the 5th Corps military police for Velika Kladuša, he had killed one teenage *ratni zarobljenik* ("POW") with a breeze block in Bužim prison and beheaded another with a saw, not to mention shooting a good hundred[907]. He was convicted of war crimes in 2010 by the Bosnian high court and sentenced to 18 years' imprisonment.

On 3 March, there was a high-level delegation in the camp, with the head of UNHCR in Croatia and the high commissioner's special envoy. Their position was that they would try to reach an agreement with the local authorities that would allow the security for the refugees to go home, while at the same time finding another location for those refugees who wanted resettlement abroad. Once the camp had moved, the refugees would no longer be the responsibility of UNHCR, but of the Croatian government (this would only be possible if Zagreb recognised them as refugees, as otherwise they would still fall under UNHCR's mandate)[908]. A meeting was scheduled for 14 March, where representatives from the Bosnian and Croatian governments would be present. The committee insisted that Babo be present too[909]. Meanwhile, refugees whose houses had been destroyed could report this to UNHCR[910]. This information was circulated by the committee on 8 March, so that the refugees would have time to come to a decision on their fate[911]. Zahid said the ultimatum would set people looking for someone to blame, and that it was important to ensure the "north gate/south gate" decision being imposed on them, as it was presented by UNHCR, did not create division among the refugees[912]. A heated council was held of about 100 refugees on 10 March to prepare for the impending meeting, where it transpired there was a third current - those who wanted to stay in Kuplensko until the elections. All were agreed that they should oppose any half-baked changes, and that any move to another location must be properly organised in advance with their involvement. The conclusion of the meeting was that the participants would take the discussion to their distribution points, and a petition would be prepared asking for Babo to be involved in the negotiation[913]. The promised meeting on 14 March did not materialise, but the committee took the opportunity to address the gathered refugees. The petition was signed by 3,800 people, approximately 80% of the adult population[914]. On 25 March, the committee wrote a letter to the head of UNHCR in Croatia, asking him to take concrete steps for their repatriation in accordance with Dayton, including allowing them to check the situation on the ground in Bosnia; and at the same time to allow those who wanted resettlement abroad to depart as early as possible, especially those who were already eligible for resettlement on the grounds of family reunification. The letter also called for rapid treatment for the wounded, and for steps to be taken to prevent an epidemic in the camp with the coming of spring[915]. A visit to Bosnia by refugees on 30 March reported that the situation was not good[916]. Under Dayton, conditions for the return of IDs and refugees included political, economic and social conditions[917].

The follow-up meeting was on 2 April, again with the head of UNHCR in Croatia, representatives from the Bosnian and Croatian governments (but not Babo), the tripartite police and IPTF, and a large crowd of refugees following proceedings outside. The 5,500 remaining refugees were informed that this, the most problematic refugee camp in Croatia, must close in the next couple of months, and that those who did not want to return could be relocated to existing refugee camps in Croatia, such as the island of Obonjan, until their applications for asylum elsewhere were accepted. Ramo presented the events of the last 239 days, from the refusal of the Bosnian and Croatian governments and UNHCR to engage with their efforts to negotiate a return in accordance with Dayton, to the ongoing inhuman conditions and insecurity imposed on the refugees. The representative of the Croatian office for refugees and IDPs said "Take it or leave it". On 13 April, he said on radio Free Europe that the camp would be closed by the end of the month[918]. On 8 April, *Feral Tribune* reported that the 6,000 residents of the camp, living in inhuman conditions, continually blamed UNHCR for their plight, while UNHCR blamed the Croatian government who in turn blamed the Bosnian government, and that the long-awaited meeting on 2 April had resolved nothing except the imminent closure of the camp[919]. After the meeting, the head of UNHCR conveyed the message to the refugees directly by megaphone, interpreted by his assistant, Igor, which was broadcast on the Croatian television news, and on the camp's favourite radio stations over the next few days[920]. The next day, the committee met and decided to continue to insist on guarantees of security before any return, and a swift departure for refugees who wanted resettlement abroad, to avoid anyone being caught in limbo: unable to resettle abroad, and unable to return. Ramo asked UNHCR to allow groups of visitors to visit various locations in Bosnia to verify the security conditions[921]. On 4 April, amid much tension, a coordination meeting was held, at which UNHCR stressed they had good cooperation with IFOR and the international community on the ground in Bosnia, and agreed to the proposed visits[922]. Visiting groups would be escorted by IFOR and IPTF.

The first group visit was on 16 April, to Liskovac, Tržac and Šturlić (known as "Stuttgart") via Ćoralići and Begove Kafane, and the results were not encouraging[923]. Besides the general deprivation, when the bus arrived at Tržac, the visitors were sworn at, and someone threatened to fire a *zolja* ("RPG", but also "wasp") at the bus. There was a fight between a visitor and a resident, which resulted in the former being hospitalised, and the latter arrested. An elderly resident, a former Partisan who had initially been sentenced to death after the Peasants' Revolt but served 12½ years in prison on appeal (but see below), said, "I haven't seen such lawlessness in my whole life. Even animals couldn't put up with what the people are having to go through"[924]. Indeed, during this period more people were coming to the camp than were leaving it[925]. A second visit on 18 April, to Pećigrad, Skokovi and Gornja Koprivna was turned back at the exit from the camp, with the explanation that they would not be allowed into Bosnia[926]. It later transpired that this was because the local authorities in Bosnia "could not guarantee the safety" of one of the people on the list; and unofficially because Izetbegović was visiting Bihać, 40 km from the site of the planned visits. Meanwhile, the refugees kept pushing UNHCR for a copy of their repatriation plan (see below)[927]. The visit finally went ahead on 25 April, without incident, but also without an encouraging picture for return. Discrimination, voluntary work, assaults at night, and poverty continued[928]. On 2 May, a group of refugees visited Todorovo and neighbouring hamlets, again without incident but with the same impressions. After the visit, there was some shooting in the village, and a house allocated to a police officer from Sarajevo was hit. The perpetrators were subsequently arrested[929]. Returnees and residents expressed concern at the prospect of the refugees being moved away, as that would weaken their own position[930]. A visit to Velika Kladuša and Polje took place on 7 May, with the same results, as did a visit to Vrnograč on 9 May[931].

On 7 June, a coordination meeting was held at the request of the committee, to discuss two issues: improvement of living conditions in the camp, and an increase in humanitarian aid to returnees until such time as the local economy improved, to be set out in a repatriation plan[932]. UNHCR replied that the Croatian government would not allow any improvement in living conditions, and that UNHCR would stay in the camp until everyone who wanted to be resettled or return had done so. The representative also accused the DNZ of manipulating the refugees in order to keep the highest possible number of people in the camp for its own political purposes[933]. There would be no specific repatriation plan for the remaining refugees, as 15,000 had already returned without one; humanitarian aid was distributed throughout Bosnia based on uniform criteria; and the Croatian authorities were unwilling to allow freedom of movement because the camp was near the border, while under UNHCR's rules, camps should be at least 50 km away from borders. UNHCR stated that it would be possible to organise a concentrated IFOR/IPTF operation in Bosnia if a larger group were to return. The committee reiterated that they didn't want special treatment, but assurances that the conditions set out in Dayton had been realised on the ground before returning, and in particular regular and clear information from the field. ICRC added that they would continue to operate in the camp without UNHCR if necessary[934]. On 6 April, the 51st anniversary of the liberation of Sarajevo, there were over 100 visits from Bosnia. Visitors were subject to detailed searches and weren't allowed to bring anything into the camp. Their black tales of an economy at a standstill and discrimination in Bosnia were not an encouragement to return[935].

On 16 March, radio Voice of America announced the camp would be closing[936]. It was reported unofficially from UNHCR that the refugees would be moved to camps in Gašinci, in east Slavonia, and on Obonjan, an island off Šibenik, and that refugees going home would be given one month's worth of basic items[937]. Đedović travelled to Rijeka for two days for meetings with Babo. He delivered his report upon his return on 18 March: Babo had reiterated that it was the 5th Corps who had fired the first shot in the intra-Muslim war; he had Tuđman's support and the Croatian media would take a positive view of the new DNZ, but Tuđman didn't want to do anything to upset the Federation; Babo was a member of the Croatian parliamentary committee formed specifically to deal with Kuplensko; and the refugees should hold on, and one month before the elections return *en masse*. They should resist any attempt to move the camp, and resettlement would only be possible once the number of refugees had fallen to a certain level; the committee members would not be forgotten when it came to organising the election campaign; they should not provoke the Croatian authorities; the former high command of the NOZB, who were all in the camp, should present a united front and hold out; there were attempts in Sarajevo by a group from Sandžak to reduce the book value of Agrokomerc, so that it could be bought up cheaply; the DNZ's programme would be based on the economic development of West Bosnia; and the SDA was in disarray (Silajdžić had recently been dismissed; on 27 March *Večernji List* reported that his replacement, Hasan Muratović, was a fundamentalist who had made a fortune in the war thanks to his contacts in Iran, and that Izetbegović was now returning the Iranians the favour by putting their man in such a powerful post. Meanwhile, Silajdžić formed his own party in April[cxiv])[938]. The news that MDM only had a budget until the end of April was another indication that the refugees' situation was changing[939]. The next day, St. Joseph's Day, when many of them would previously have travelled to Cetingrad for the agricultural show, the committee decided to spend the next few weeks debating what to do, and take a final decision on St. Georges Day, 6 May[940]. St. George's Day was celebrated in the Borders by Serbs, Croats and Muslims, and is also the main Romany festival, as portrayed in the 1988 film *Dom za Vešanje* ("The Time of the Gypsies")[cxv941]. In the distant past, it was a pagan festival marking the end of winter, and the rites of spring were celebrated by bathing before dawn in fast-flowing waters and decorating the body with greenery, symbolising the flowering anew of the earth's ancient spirits at the beginning of a new cycle of life. More recently, bonfires were lit and magic circles traced out on the earth on St. Georges' Eve in order to protect houses from *zmije/sapa* ("snakes"). St. George's Day was also traditionally the beginning of the banditry season, when the rievers had enough natural cover to come down from the mountains[942]. It was also a poverty indicator, because only those households who were better off could put by enough winter stores the previous year to last them until then[943].

The party was registered at the end of January, and on 20 February the committee wrote to OSCE requesting permission to carry on party activities in the

---

[cxiv] Owen quotes *Oslobođenje* from October 1995: "Izetbegović and Silajdžić represent two very different futures for an independent Bosnia: a return to the absolute power of a single-party state under the control of a party that is out-dated, increasingly repressive and is taking over the country in the name of a factitious patriotism; or the western-looking, democratic country its troops have been fighting for. The hardliners in Izetbegović's SDA want a population totally subordinate to the state; in return, they promise a genuinely Muslim country, however small, in which the well-off moneymen and sycophants around the ruling party can have a free hand. In the name of their 'patriotism', young men have been mobilised for the army while others have found a new prosperity thanks to the parallel economy, the 'private' businesses that feed on the misery of the population, and those who have the privilege of access to the funds brought in by a variety of foreign humanitarian organisations".
[cxv] Produced by controversial Bosnian film director Emir Kusturica. During the war, rather than stay in Sarajevo, he moved to Belgrade, and on St. George's day 2005 he converted from Islam to Orthodox Christianity. Was he attempting to overturn social and political stereotypes within Yugoslavia? Or, Depardieu-like, merely demonstrating that artistes live on a different planet? He attended Putin's third inauguration in Moscow in 2012, and was later ejected from a church in Belgrade for accusing the priest of "not being a Serb". From 1993 onwards, the many rumours circulating about Babo included one to the effect that he had been baptised in the Orthodox church in Knin, and had changed his name to Todor.

camp[944]. By 28 February it had over 20,000 members, most of them in Bosnia[945]. In early March, the local radio reported there was a list of 250 suspected war criminals in the camp, who would not benefit from the amnesty. The committee asked UNHCR to obtain a copy of the list[946]. Under Dayton, all war criminals were to be tried in The Hague[947]. On 4 March, the Bosnian local radio reported the registration of Babo's party in Mostar, and his intention to actively participate in all talks on Bosnia. The broadcast accused Croatian TV in its programme "Come Home" of concealing the registration of the party. They also accused the refugees of being prepared by the Croats for another war, this time in Mostar, just as they had been prepared for war by the Serbs in the previous refugee crisis. The broadcast went on to mock Ramo and Baja, among others, and called the NOZB high command in the camp the last refuge of the "flower of Croatia"[948]. On 16 May, the Bosnian local radio announced the deadline for presenting the 10,000 signatures required to participate in the elections as 7 June (later moved back to 14 June[949]). A herculean effort was launched to gather the necessary number of signatures in the camp, in Bosnia, and among the diaspora[950]. 45 parties and 15 independent candidates had applied and were registered in Bosnia[951]. Radio Free Europe reported on 2 June that further to a conference in Geneva on the implementation of Dayton, attended by the warlords, the date for the elections would be 14 September as per Dayton. It also noted there were serious concerns on the progress made in bringing about the conditions for holding the elections, in particular freedom of expression, freedom of movement, the return of refugees and IDPs, and the presence of suspected war criminals in public life[952]. There were concerns that under current conditions, the elections would be dominated by the three nationalist parties that had destroyed the country[953]. Meanwhile, a spoof party was formed in the camp, called "Shut Up and Forget Bosnia"[954]. *Slobodna Dalmacija* reported on 15 June that the DNZ had submitted 17,000 signatures, and that the party's slogan for the elections would be "Bosnia – a little America with Babo"[955]. On 14 June, radio Free Europe reported that a conference in Florence on the implementation of Dayton had decided it was unacceptable that Karadžić was still in politics, and that cooperation with the ICTY as required by Dayton was inadequate. All sides were also called upon to allow opposition parties and an independent media to operate. An agreement on disarmament was also signed, six months after ratification of the Dayton peace accords in Paris[956]. On 21 June, Babo held an election meeting with the committee in Vojnić. The first priority was the constitutional status of the new canton, and the second was to win the elections[957]. On 22 June, the committee received confirmation from OSCE that the party had been accepted for participation in the elections[958]. Work now started on canvassing in constituencies where the party had a branch (and where freedom of movement permitted), such as Pećigrad and Skokovi, and in the diaspora, in particular in Slovenia, Austria and Germany[959]. The election campaign started officially on 19 July (put back from the 15th to give the SDS time to get rid of Karadžić, which was done on 20 July)[960]. Early, pilot local elections were held in Mostar on 30 June[961]. They went off without incident, but failed to unite the town, which had been one of the hopes of the international community, as the Bosnian HDZ continued to drag its feet in allowing the Federation to come into its own[962]. The DNZ officially opened its office in Kuplensko on 18 July[963].

On 24 July, Voice of America reported that Babo had held a press conference in Zagreb to launch his election campaign. It also reported that refugees would be able to vote in Gašinci and Obonjan, and that voter registration would conclude on 15 August. Radio Free Europe reported that Babo's campaign was being run from

Zagreb because he did not have freedom of movement in SDA territory, and did not want to be based in HDZ or SDS territory in Bosnia. It also said that his was the only party offering an economic programme[964] (Babo proposed restructuring the country's inefficient "dirty industries", a process that would ironically be made easier because of the war, as they had all ground to a halt, and using the potential of refugees and the diaspora to kick-start production in all other areas of the economy[965]. Twenty years later, according to WHO, Bosnia has the highest levels of pollution in Europe). The following day, Voice of America interviewed Babo, who said he expected to win the elections as he had in 1990, and that his party had been promised freedom of movement and free access to the media despite an arrest warrant for him issued in Sarajevo[966].

Heavy rain on the evening of 2 April was followed by heavy and sustained snowfall, which damaged many structures, including school and hospital infrastructure[967]. There was more heavy snow on 13 April[968]. On 2 May, sudden heavy rain caught out many refugees[969]. It rained for two days on 11 and 12 May[970], which produced not only a lot of mud and raised the level of the stream, but also flushed out a few snakes in the marshy ground, some of which took refuge in nearby tents. The inhabitants swiftly moved to safer parts of the camp[971]. On 27 May, a snake 1.5m long was spotted resting under a bench in someone's tent. It was quickly driven out[972]. The last delivery of wood to the camp was on 24 June, when it was estimated there was enough for the next two months[973]. That month, when the improved hygiene conditions and reduced number of refugees meant the stream was clean again, a swimming pool 4.5 x 8 m in length and 2.5 m deep was built for the children, using planks and plastic sheeting to line a pit fed by the stream[974].

Even countries with a long tradition of democracy and human rights will resort to anything they can get away with to remove unwanted refugees[975]. In July 2015, as many as 2,000 migrants were trying to cross the Channel every day from the makeshift refugee camp known as the Jungle near Calais. This situation goes back to 1999, when a refugee camp was opened in nearby Sangatte and became a magnet for would-be asylum seekers and people traffickers. It was closed in 2001 and 2002, leading to riots, but the refugees and economic migrants continue to come. The dynamic population of the Jungle is put at 3,000 men, women and children, whose struggle to survive is aggravated by the ire of the French National Front and UKIP. The UK is now building a fence around the Eurostar terminal there, at great cost. On several occasions I have interpreted for Balkan truckers detained in the UK because illegal immigrants suddenly appeared as if by magic from inside or even from underneath their trucks after they had crossed the Channel. On each occasion, the truckers were eventually released without charge once the police had ascertained that they were not in any way complicit in the illegal passage. Meanwhile, the French police arrested over 18,000 *sans papiers* ("undocumented migrants") in France in the first half of 2015[976], and started moves to close the Jungle in February 2016. In addition, there are 20,000 Romanies living in France, most of them from Romania, which means they are EU citizens and entitled to freedom of movement within the Schengen area[977]. Nevertheless, the police regularly and rapidly demolish their makeshift camps, and deport thousands of them each year. Other EU countries, such as Hungary, are more pragmatic and don't bother with euphemisms when dealing with migrants and refugees. They immediately made it clear there was no room at the inn when the Syrian refugee crisis spread to the Balkans, and the Hungarian authorities are now locking refugees up in detention centres. Now that the crisis has spilled over into the former Yugoslavia, and more and more fences are being erected, could Bosnia, a non-EU member and practically a failed state, end up as a dustbin for them all? Refugees have no voice and no rights, but they do have an international organisation that has a mandate for their protection – UNHCR. This mandate is to supervise the application of the 1951 Refugee Convention: to protect the rights of refugees, and to point those rights out where the refugees are not in a position to represent themselves[978]. In the words of the UNHCR representative in Kuplensko, they were there "to protect people and help them"[979].

Alas, UNHCR has a dismal record of protection of refugees in crisis situations. On the Bangladeshi/Burmese border and in the Great Lakes region of East Africa in the 1990s, UNHCR policies "led indirectly to the deaths of thousands of civilians", while in the Yugoslav Wars, UNHCR came to be a fig-leaf for the failures of the international community, accused alternatively of colluding with ethnic cleansing and being a tool of NATO. It was overwhelmed in Macedonia and slow off the ground in Kosovo[980]. UNHCR's own "lessons learned" report on its response to the emergency in the DRC in 1994, when a whole Rwandan population of 700,000, civilians, politicians, army and all (and not just traitors this time, but the perpetrators of genocide), sought refuge near the border town of Goma[cxvi], found significant weaknesses in its protection response to the critical early stages of the emergency (the organisation's main mandate), and identified significant management weaknesses in the emergency response[981]. In Bangladesh,

> "camp officials fostered an extreme climate of fear […] and used this fear, as well as inflicting actual abuses, to compel refugees to present themselves to UNHCR as volunteers for repatriation […] Bangladesh used pressure and intimidation through physical assault, verbal abuse, denial of food rations, and denial of basic human rights including the right to health and educational facilities".

UNHCR withdrew from that repatriation programme[982]. Its diplomatic immunity means its decisions are not open to appeal by the courts or other independent bodies[983]. Reflecting on Kuplensko 20 years later, Dr Doebbler was of the view that UNHCR often fails to live up to its mandate due to the fact that its donors attach strings to their funding, such that the organisation is driven by political, rather than humanitarian needs. UNHCR has thus far, despite commitments by its leadership to

---

[cxvi] This was one of the major refugee emergencies of the 1990s. Although I wasn't there myself, I have heard from others who were that it was utter chaos, with up to 1,000 people dying every day. Some of the less professional aid agencies decided these refugees weren't worthy of their services, such as they were. I heard from MSF colleagues that in order to combat the infestation of rats, they had the idea of offering a cash reward per head of dead rodent; but the plan backfired when some of the refugees started to breed rats in order to claim the bounty. Goma, on the border with Rwanda, was the scene of another emergency in 2002 when the local volcano, Mount Nyiragongo, 20 km from the town in the Virunga national park, erupted, and fast-flowing lava reached the airport runway within half an hour, leaving 200,000 people homeless *en route*. 400,000 people fled across the border into Rwanda. I once saw a Pygmy in Goma; diminutive as he was, he seemed to have no problems boarding his Nissan Patrol and driving off about his business. The ancestral homeland of the Pygmies is the rainforest of the central DRC, which separates the eastern part of the country, with its temperate uplands on the outer rim of the Swahili-speaking world of East Africa, from the very different west, with the urban sprawl of Kinshasa, the capital, and its port on the Atlantic coast, at the mouth of the river Congo (the second largest river in the world, which has its source in Zambia).

do so, failed to address the problem of climate change refugees, which is something that is only going to increase in the coming years and decades.

Now, caught between the competing pressures of the Bosnian and Croatian governments, UNHCR chose the path of least resistance and started the process of seeking "third countries", those prepared to accept some of the refugees. On 27 January, the anniversary of the liberation of Auschwitz, all the refugees had to register with UNHCR, which was the first step in this process. After registration, refugees had to dip their finger in indelible ink to stop them registering twice, but with a bit of scrubbing the ink came off as easily as it did during the elections held later that year, especially if you rubbed fat on it first[984]. The registration did not expose any hidden *Četniks*, at least overtly, although there were around 30 Serbs in the camp (among them five SVK squaddies, who kept a very low profile)[985]. A group of the Serbs left for Republika Srpska on 29 March, accompanied by UNHCR[986]. Another group of refugees, more Muslims than Serbs, were supposed to leave for the rump Yugoslavia for family reunification in the week of 15 April, but the operation was postponed as UNHCR had been unable to arrange a driver willing to go to Serbia[987]. They finally left on 22 April[988]. Another group of 20 refugees went to Belgrade and Montenegro on 20 June[989]. Initially, no third countries were willing to take the Kuplensko renegades. As the Croatian authorities needed to free up the valley, for the resettlement of Croat refugees, and to open up the road, the only realistic prospect in the long term in the absence of forcible deportation would be relocation elsewhere within Croatia[990] (although, 20 years later, no refugees have been resettled in the infernal valley, and the road is hardly an artery). The concern among the more professional NGOs was that refugees would be pressurised into *surgun* ("exile") when in fact they wanted to return. Furthermore, if the majority of refugees emigrated, and only a hard-core rump were left behind insisting on return, then they would be far more vulnerable in their diminished numbers to abuse and the use of force. On 6 December 1995, MSF had conducted a survey among the refugees to find out how they thought about return or exile. According to the subsequent report, written by MSF's James Derieg,

> "The chaotic conditions in the camp and the lack of representative structures had disempowered many of the camp's residents. They were aware that the authorities at the highest levels were discussing their future, but they had no means to input into those discussions. A global and comprehensive inquiry into the wishes of this population was the only method by which all who wished to could make their feelings known."

The response rate to the 13,160 questionnaires, each distributed with a blank envelope for anonymous return, was 53.8%.

The first question was intended to gauge the level of desperation of the refugees and their tolerance for their current situation, and indicated a considerable determination to hold out, in the hope of a solution in the short-term (one person said he/she would stay until he/she died, "which might not be too long"[991]).

The second question, on the preconditions for a return, indicated that 13.8% were unwilling to return under any conditions, citing fear of arrest or death, or more often, the prospect of being a second-class citizen (not expressed was the fear by some people of having to account for genuine war crimes committed during the war[992]).

The third question, on resettlement abroad, indicated that 8% did not want to resettle at all, while 19% would resettle if necessary. 71% said resettlement was the best solution for them.

The countries cited as a preference by the 71% in favour of resettlement were (above 1% only):

any	(25%)
Germany	(15%)
Netherlands	(9.10%)
USA	(8.33%)
Canada	(8.20%)
Switzerland	(6.31%)
Australia	(5.64%)
Austria	(5.35%)
Norway (4.44%)	
Italy	(3.64%)
Denmark	(2.90%)
Sweden (2.54%)	
Slovenia (1.71%)	

One respondee stated he (or she) wished to resettle in Chechnya. I didn't see him (or her) there the following year.

Despite these laudable efforts to engage the refugee population in the decision-making process directly affecting their future, the wheels that had been set in motion at the highest level continued to turn on their inexorable course.

On 1 November, UNHCR had informed the refugees that their sheer mass and the number of dangerous individuals among them were an obstacle to any country considering them for resettlement[993]. At the beginning of December, UNHCR started to process the cases of people who already had documentation allowing them to resettle abroad, but who until now had been prevented from travelling there[994]. At the same time, the number of people seeking resettlement as refugees increased[995]. Parallel to the committee, there was another group of refugees trying to organise mass resettlement abroad as the best solution[996]. Ironically, with the end of the war, potential host countries changed their policies and wanted people to stay at home[997]. The committee wrote to the embassies of several potential host countries, including the US, setting out the situation and informing them of the fact that some of the refugees were interested in resettlement[998]. Between 9 and 12 April, refugees interested in resettlement had to register with UNHCR[999]. Over 4,000 registered, while on 13 April the Croatian authorities announced on the radio that they would accommodate 2,000 refugees elsewhere[1000].

UNHCR moved up a gear in its efforts to clear the camp: lists of names started to be posted up at the distribution points, the names of people who had registered for resettlement, and people who should report to collect a form to apply for the US, as they might qualify for family reunion. ICRC were issuing former POWs with certificates[1001]. The committee complained that UNHCR had shown its true colours and was working to scatter the people, which was not its mandate[1002]. They asked UNHCR to concentrate on the implementation of Annex VII, i.e. ensuring safe conditions for return[1003]. On 20 July, the committee was informed by UNHCR that the Croatian office for refugees and IDPs would close the camp on 31 July. Anyone unwilling to return to Bosnia had to apply to UNHCR to be moved to a camp elsewhere in Croatia, where they would be granted refugee status. There was no bread delivery that day[1004].

Representatives from the US embassy in Zagreb held their first meeting with would-be Americans in the camp on 9 February[cxvii][1005]. There was a sudden surge in interest in learning English in the camp (I used to give English lessons to the ICRC local team, as well as private lessons). Within a few days there were 1,000 candidates. However, at this stage there was no resettlement programme, and only people with relatives living abroad could apply for family reunification[1006]. By the end of the month, large numbers of applicants were being processed, and on 1 March, after much questioning, photographing and form-filling, people were told they would be summoned for interviews by the US embassy[1007]. One of the questions was whether they had been a member of the KPJ[1008]. Others, which were a cause of much confusion, concerned family trees, and where they stood in relation to the family members who had sent them papers from the US[1009]. Medical examinations of applicants started in mid-April[1010].

On 24 April, UNHCR turned up with a list of 261 refugees who were going to be moved to Obonjan the next Saturday. No-one was able to explain how the list had been put together, and faced with the general dismay of the refugees, the list was shelved[1011]. Nevertheless, the same notice was posted throughout the camp the next day, together with a notice that 300 refugees would be transferred to Gašinci on 30 April, with others to follow on successive days. The committee's advice to refugees was to tell UNHCR they were not going[1012]. On the afternoon of 26 April, after many refugees had packed, sold items, not collected humanitarian aid, and made other arrangements, it was reported that the move had been postponed until further notice[1013]. At the meeting of 3 May, UNHCR said that the local authorities in Bosnia were ready to meet with the representatives of the refugees, but would not discuss any political issues (i.e. anything except security and property). The local authorities had assured them there was no list of war criminals who would not enjoy the protection of the amnesty, even though a Sarajevo newspaper had reported there was[1014]. On 13 May, UNHCR reported that a meeting had been held in Zagreb on 11 May between the governments of Bosnia and Croatia, as a result of which it had been decided to close Kuplensko. UNHCR also stated that, despite the presence of IFOR and IPTF, it was impossible to guarantee individual security. The committee lamented being presented once again with a *babo ručao* (*"fait accompli"*), and noted that six months after the end of the war, nothing had been done to restart Agrokomerc. They also called for a meeting with OSCE to discuss the elections[1015].

On 16 May, UNHCR turned up in triumphant mood with a list of 217 people who had sought resettlement, and who would be transferred to Gašinci the next morning. Single people would subsequently be moved to Obonjan. As for the economic situation in West Bosnia, UNHCR said they were better off than in

---

[cxvii] Would-be exiles elsewhere in Croatia did not enjoy such a service, and had to approach the embassies of potential host countries themselves. Among the many hurdles they had to overcome was the completion of a host of forms, which often required the services of a translator. As a result, enterprising locals with a knowledge of English would set up their stalls outside the busiest embassies in Zagreb, and expedite applications for a fee. A local Red Cross logistician, Goran, who I met several years later at a logistics workshop in Geneva, was so indignant at this blatant exploitation of the vulnerable that he set up a stall himself. "What's this, *konkurencija* ['competition']?" one of the translators asked when he turned up. "I'm worse than competition", Goran replied, "I'm *džabe* ['for nowt']", and he proceeded to offer translation services free of charge.

Albania[1016]. Five buses left at 9 the next morning with the 217 refugees[1017]. The committee decided to continue to ask for UNHCR's repatriation plan, and that they would stay in Kuplensko until the elections[1018]. Another 206 refugees left for Gašinci on 18 May[1019], and a further 246 on 20 May, Seka's birthday. Half of the wounded went[1020]. On the evening of St. George's Day, 6 May, the 46th anniversary of the Peasants' Revolt, the first group of 114 refugees left for the US. Apparently the US planned to take in a total of 15,000 Bosnian Muslims. The departure was attended by 1,500 other refugees, some rejoicing, others sad. Another group of West Bosnians saw them off at Zagreb airport[1021]. Was this the beginning of the end of this community, united by a shared cause that had been beaten on the battlefield, but refused to die? The UNHCR officer responsible for the camp had said during a recent meeting, "You lost the war, get over it"[1022]. How many other communities had been or were yet to be scattered like chaff in the wind by this war, in this gregarious society where family is everything? The largest was the Croatian Serbs, followed by a long list of less numerous victims, the first being the harmonious multi-ethnic communities that had existed before the war. I had earlier witnessed several one-way departures from Split airport, a poignant moment both for those leaving their home country into the unknown, perhaps forever, and for those left behind, to continue the daily struggle to survive with one less familiar face. Most of them had never been abroad before, and had no idea about life outside the Balkans, or even outside their community. Another, smaller group left the next day[1023]. A gold-rush fever spread among some of the remaining refugees, who hoped that the departing refugees would soon be able to vouch for them and take them to the promised land[1024]. I first heard a song at this time that went:

> "*Ime mi je gospodin*
> *Ja za ljubav ne molim*
> *Imam dušu veliku*
> *Veliku kao Ameriku*"[cxviii]

By late May, Canada had a similar programme, and an Australian one was expected. On 18 June, the Norwegian embassy in Zagreb, in response to numerous requests, sent a notice to the camp informing the refugees that they could apply for resettlement in Norway if they had a close relative living there, or if they were a former POW or other vulnerable person[1025]. On 21 May, another 191 refugees left for Gašinci, this time headed for Canada, and the same evening another 49 left for the US, via Vienna airport. The day before, radio Free Europe had reported that 780 refugees had been transferred so far[1026]. On 23 May, another 89 refugees went to Gašinci, destination Canada[1027]. On 27 May, another 186 left for Gašinci[1028]. Dutch and German film crews were in the camp during this period, making documentaries[1029]. Nevertheless, each time, there were some people who backed out at the last moment, and failed to report to their one-way trip[1030]. On 22 May, 53 single people went to Obonjan. There was much confusion about the list, as it included people who had not registered an interest in leaving, people who had long returned to Bosnia, and even some people who had never been in the camp[1031].

[cxviii] "A country gent born and bred
Love to me's no esoterica
My soul is a wide expanse
Spacious as America".

Another 250 youngsters left on the morning of 28 May. One group of youngsters, taking advantage of the madding crowd and the fact that the police were changing shifts, quickly ducked into the house used by the police as their field HQ and came out a few minutes later carrying plastic bags[1032]. By the end of May, there were around 4,000 refugees left in the camp[1033]. Now it was not only people who had applied for resettlement abroad who were being moved[1034]. Another 260 left for Gašinci on 6 June[1035], and another 240 on 13 June. As time went by, the travellers started taking more and more things with them[1036]. On 14 June, 71 people travelled to Obonjan in two buses. There were so many empty seats that UNHCR asked the watching crowd whether anyone else wanted to go too. There were no takers[1037]. By the beginning of July, it was estimated there were 3,500 refugees left in the camp, with another 10 arriving from Bosnia every day[1038]. On 9 July, the Croatian office for refugees and IDPs announced on radio Free Europe that only refugees in the camp at the beginning of April could be rehoused elsewhere, and that latecomers would be deported[1039]. The amount of humanitarian aid being distributed was significantly reduced at this time[1040]. On 8 July, 320 people left for Gašinci, the largest group to date[1041]. Another 150 left on 11 July[1042]. Another 197 left for Obonjan on 12 July, and another 109 for Gašinci on 15 July[1043]. On 17 July, 65 of a total of 402 people on the list that day travelled to Gašinci[1044]. Another 60 from a list of 209 left for Gašinci on 19 July[1045]. However, the profile of people accepted for exile was not so much the most vulnerable, such as the disabled, but young, healthy, qualified individuals. Furthermore, those applying were asked if they had any other family members who would also like to apply. Not only was there a perception that the *treće zemlje* ("third countries") were looking for cheap labour, but that there was a determination at the highest level to scatter the people of the Bosnian Borders to the four winds[1046]. Subsequently, the US refugee programme went on to include people living in the former enclave whose relatives had been accepted for resettlement, even people who had never been refugees themselves. As one refugee, Amila, from Gradačac, commented 20 years later:

> "The most important part of being a refugee is being a good loser; it's the only way to survive this. You learn to lose your nationality, your home to strangers with bigger guns, your father to mental illness, one aunt to genocide, and another to nationalism and ignorance. You learn to lose your kids, friends, dreams, neighbours, loves, diplomas, careers, photo albums, home movies, schools, museums, histories, landmarks, limbs, teeth, eyesight, sense of safety, sanity, and your sense of belonging in the world".

APPEAL FOR ASSISTANCE FOR THE WOUNDED REFUGEES IN KUPLENSKO RC

Kuplensko, 21/2/96

We request UNHCR, within the programme of aid for the refugees from the western region of Bosnia and Herzegovina, to assist us wounded, who as a result of the conflict are unfortunately numerous in Kuplensko RC.

It is mainly a question of the further medical treatment of the wounded who have been fitted with fixators, and operations to remove foreign objects from the body such as for example shrapnel, fragments from ordnance and so on. We who are numbered among that group do not have the means to bear the costs of such treatment ourselves, which is why we are asking you to help us within your possibilities, for which we would be extremely grateful.

Any further delay of surgical intervention is extremely risky for us because it can cause deterioration of our already poor state of health, which as a consequence could lead to the worst case scenario, which we as members of the younger population do not dare think about. We are aware that the cost of such medical services would be high, but we have no choice other than to turn to you in this way and plead that you do all in your power. We also suggest that you find donors in Europe and further afield who would be willing to help us.

In anticipation of a positive response, we are ready to draw up with the medical services here a list of priority wounded, which would give you a better picture of the problem. Trusting in your response and understanding, we thank you in advance.

Kind regards.
Yours sincerely

The wounded in Kuplensko RC

APPEAL for help for the wounded!

In Kuplensko refugee camp there are about 300 wounded with various injuries. The care for the wounded so far has concentrated on ensuring basic conditions for survival. Thanks to numerous donors and the humanitarian organisation "Doctors without Borders" we have survived more than seven months in inhuman conditions.

Among us there are eight paraplegics, 30 wounded without one of the extremities, 30 wounded with fixators on the extremities, 52 wounded with plates and other metal parts in the extremities, and over 180 wounded needing rehabilitation in sanatoria. Many of the wounded are family men. Some have family members here, and some in their previous place of residence. Many of the wounded do not have any possibility of treatment after return to their previous place of residence.

We are addressing potential donors for various types of assistance. Assistance can be in various forms and by various means. We need everything: means of survival, medical material, orthopaedic aids, treatment and rehabilitation in medical establishments. Particularly useful would be placement in medical establishments with the possibility of definitive recovery and a later return to normal life. Many of us are ready to enter into special agreements with potential donors. Our appeals so far have resulted in symbolic donations which have allowed us to survive the most difficult moments of our lives. Now we need assistance that will allow our eventual recovery.

We remain in the hope and belief that there are still humanitarian organisations and individuals out there who are ready to help those in need and thus show their humanity, the most radiant feature of today's world. With your help we could recover more easily and forget the many injustices done to us in our lives thus far.

All those who wish to help in any way or who wish further information about us as a group or individuals, we recommend contact UNHCR 122 Banija, Karlovac, phone 047 223-287 or fax 047 611-693.

We trust the many humanitarians of the world, our co-citizens and sympathisers and other people of good will, will show interest in this appeal and offer concrete help to allow an unhappy population to return to life and once again become useful members of world society.

We are deeply grateful in advance to all those who help us in any way, or merely take a further interest in our situation and fate.

The wounded of West Bosnia in Kuplensko camp

Kuplensko, March 1996[1047].

Kuplensko, 19/4/96

I am addressing you by means of this letter because I have no other way of contacting you. You have said that any individual can talk to you, but those have proved to be empty words. I can't get in the queue because of those Americans[cxix] of yours. I don't understand how neither you nor they realise that now it's time to talk. You've promised them departure to a third country. Thank God. Why don't they now clear off from in front of your office so that we can talk.

My issue is the following. I am shaken by what you're promising and what you're doing. I'm one of the refugees who wants to return to West Bosnia. I'm not interested in third or fourth countries. Over the last eight months, I've been following what and with who you talk. I see that you are seeking glory. Don't acquire it on the back of a wretched and innocent people, that's wrong. Nothing good will come of it. The greatest ignominy is to carry the banner for scattering a people. The people will curse you. If you don't have children now, when you do you will see how much you've erred. You smoke dope, but that's your problem. My problem is getting back to West Bosnia. I know you'll say, "Go on then. The conditions have been created". No, they haven't. Don't let anyone suffer mishap because of you. Many have believed you and gone, but many have returned as well. Black and blue, beaten, broken, and some unfortunately no longer among the living. You sent them to their deaths. Do you consider that a success? Does that not shake you, and hurt you to think of? You promise others departure to a third country. Tell me who has gone where. There's been enough lies and promises. Do your duty. Your duty is to respect the Dayton agreement, which says in Annex VII:

> "All refugees and IDPs have the right freely to return to their homes of origin. They shall have the right to have restored to them property of which they were deprived in the course of hostilities since 1991 and to be compensated for any property that cannot be restored to them [...] The Parties shall ensure that refugees and IDPs are permitted to return in safety, without risk of harassment, intimidation, persecution, or discrimination [...] The Parties shall facilitate the flow of information necessary for refugees and IDPs to make informed judgements about local conditions for return [...] The Parties call upon UNHCR to develop in close consultation with asylum countries and the Parties a repatriation plan that will allow for an early, peaceful, orderly and phased return of refugees and IDPs [...] The Parties undertake to create in their territories the political, economic, and social conditions conducive to the voluntary return and harmonious reintegration of refugees and IDPs."

But since you haven't read it or pretend you haven't, call me for a meeting. I want to go home. You promised us visits to our families in West Bosnia. We set off but they wouldn't allow it. What now? Where is your power? What exactly can you do and what can't you?

Your duty is to guarantee my return with respect for all my human rights, and not just to give us a bus. We can return without your bus, but where to, Madam?

[cxix] Refugees seeking asylum in the USA.

Who will guarantee us peace? I can give you a few examples of people who have been beaten or locked up:

1. Ahmet Huskić
2. Sedžad Kajtazović
3. Mirsad Čaušević
4. Almir Šabanagić
5. Osman Kajtazović,

to mention but my neighbours.

Where are the rest? I'm sending this letter to all the international organisations, Bill Clinton, Carl Bildt[cxx], Sadako Ogata[cxxi] and many others so that they can see what you are doing, Madam.

In the hope that you will call me for a meeting with the minimum delay, I thank you in advance.

Sead Kajtazović (wounded veteran)[1048].

Sead "Tetin" Kajtazović, Paklena Dolina

On 20 July, the committee was informed by UNHCR that there would not be a polling booth in Kuplensko[1049]. UNHCR stopped delivering bread, without notice, on the same day. It was estimated there was only enough food for a few days in the camp. The next morning, when the bread van didn't turn up, one of the riot policemen commented in Croatian slang, "*Kaj ćete sada jesti?*" ("what are you going to eat now?"). "*Bumo travu pasli!*" ("we'll graze the grass!") a refugee replied quick as a flash, also in Croatian slang[1050]. On 22 July, 800 refugees demonstrated outside UNHCR's premises calling for bread[1051]. Ramo informed the UNHCR representative that there would be no further cooperation between the refugees and UNHCR until bread deliveries were resumed[1052]. It was said that, if they remained in the camp after the end of July, the refugees would be deemed to have refused the protection accorded by the Refugee Convention and Croatia would regard them as illegal immigrants. Babo was unable to give a direction to the remaining refugees, and so the committee decided that they would each take their own decision[1053]. Some refugees wanted to go to the "Gaza" refugee camp in Karlovac[1054]. The committee informed the refugees of this position on 25 July, and there was a mass registration for resettlement[1055]. On 26 July, the anniversary of the proclamation of the Republic of West Bosnia, 316 refugees went to Gašinci, and four returned to Bosnia. The bread deliveries resumed the same day. The local radio in Bosnia increased its anti-"separatist" rhetoric[1056]. On 28 July, a 600 m column of tractors, horses and carts, and other agricultural vehicles accompanied by the few remaining livestock returned to Bosnia with an IFOR escort. A total of 30 refugees returned to Bosnia that day[1057]. For the first time, there was no water tanker, and all the tanks in the camp were empty[1058]. On 29 July, 435 refugees went to Gašinci, the most in a single day, and

---

[cxx] High Representative for Bosnia from December 1995 to June 1997 (previously prime minister of Sweden, 1991-1994).
[cxxi] UN High Commissioner for Refugees from 1991 to 2001.

more than a dozen returned to Bosnia[1059]. That evening, radio Free Europe reported, citing the police, that anyone left in the camp after 31 August would be deported. The next day, 550 went to Gašinci. *Večernji List* repeated the threat broadcast the day before[1060]. On 31 July, 650 refugees went to Gašinci. Radio Free Europe reported that the camp was now closed[1061].

On 1 August, after 360 days, the last 141 refugees, including the 12 most serious wounded, travelled the four hours by road to Gašinci. Ramo was on the last bus[1062].

The area between the Una, Korana and Glina rivers has been inhabited since prehistoric times. From ancient times through the middle ages, in particular from the 16th century onwards, and into modern times, this picturesque, hilly country acquired the characteristics which led to its being known as the Borders, the Turkish Borders, the Bosnian Borders. Simultaneously and parallel to the Turkish Borders, a defensive line was also developed on the Hapsburg side of the border, the Military Frontier, which included the Slunj sector of Kordun, a geographical area in Croatia around the river Korana, between Mala Kapela and Velika Kapela in the west and Petrova Gora in the east. The very name Kordun, from the French *cordon* and Italian *cordone*, means guard or rampart. In this way the Bosnian Borders and the Slunj area, despite belonging to two neighbouring rival empires, the Turkish Empire and the Hapsburg Monarchy, with differing religions, cultures and other characteristics, formed a single military and civilian territory, which due to their pre-existing relationships and their new common function, followed a similar path of social development.

Ancient Times

Archaeologists have established that humans lived in the area of the Bosnian Borders as long ago as the Neolithic. The Illyrian[cxxii] tribe of the Yapods are mentioned in this area several centuries before Christ. During the Roman period, a major Roman road linking Solin to Sisak passed through Pounje near Bihać. In the early middle ages, Slavic peoples settled in what is now the Borders, probably as they did in other areas of the Balkans, although no reliable data exist on their arrival and settlement. Throughout most of the middle ages the later Bosnian Borders belonged to Croatia, and until the last quarter of the 16th century, the area was governed by the bishop of Knin. It was then conquered by the Turks, whose reign defined the life of the local population up until the twentieth century. During the Turkish reign, the area between the Una, Korana and Glina rivers became the Borders, the Turkish Borders, the most western extremity of the huge Turkish Empire, a bulge extending towards western Europe. In the same way as the neighbouring Croatian Military Frontier, created to protect the Hapsburg Monarchy and Europe from further Turkish expansion from the Balkans, the Turkish Borders were transformed over the centuries via a system of fortifications and military districts into the main defensive line of the European part of the Turkish Empire. The local population, the Borderers, learned by force of circumstances to live by the sword as well as by their traditional crop and livestock production, and for their services they were naturally rewarded by the Sultan with certain privileges not enjoyed by other subjects. It is therefore not surprising that the Turkish religion, Islam, was accepted *en masse* in this area.

Nevertheless, the Borderers often opposed measures passed by the central Turkish government, and played a leading role in many revolts against the Sultan's reforms, in particular in the 19th century. The revolts in the Borders were always put down, although sometimes at great cost, such as the revolt of several thousand rebels which started in 1849 and lasted on and off until 1851 (for which reason it is

---

[cxxii] Thought to be the ancestors of the Albanians, who once inhabited much of the Balkans.

sometimes regarded as several revolts), when it was put down by General Omer-Paša Latas[cxxiii], sent by the Sublime Port to pacify Bosnia. Interestingly, the many punishments to which the rebels were sentenced, 100 years before the Peasants' Revolt, did not include a single death sentence, even though over 500 rebel *begs* were arrested, and the people of the Borders suffered for several years as a punishment for their disobedience. Forty-five Borderers were exiled to Asia from whence they never returned, but there were no death sentences, despite the fact that several thousand Borderers took part in the revolt. The Bosnian Borders were also one of the hotbeds of the great Bosnian uprising of 1875-1878. The Austro-Hungarian occupation of Bosnia and Herzegovina between 1878 and 1918 and the financial and trading links it entailed introduced significant changes to life in the Bosnian Borders, such that this relatively short period is considered to be a period of general progress. However, statistics show that there was no significant prosperity, indeed according to indicators in the following period the Borders became one of the most backward areas of the new country, the Kingdom of the Serbs, Croats and Slovenes, that is to say the Kingdom of Yugoslavia.

Over the centuries Kordun underwent a similar fate to that of the Bosnian Borders. It was a defensive line with a series of fortifications on the border with the Turkish possessions in Bosnia, as of the second half of the 15th century protecting south-west Croatia and the Hapsburg lands in general from invasion by the Turks. Kordun also bore the stigma of being a border region, which meant it was not only remote, but also high risk in terms of financial investment.

The "Old" Yugoslavia

In the Kingdom of Yugoslavia, the whole of the Bosnian Borders was formed into one county, Cazin county. Cazin county, which thus covered both Cazin and Velika Kladuša, fell within Vrbas province. Statistics show that Vrbas province was the least developed, and in almost every other respect the most backward of the nine Yugoslav provinces. Using as a basic indicator of development the measure of the then industrial capacity and number of workers, Cazin clearly occupies the bottom position within Vrbas province. Statistics from 1938 show that the little industry that existed in Vrbas province employed 9,651 workers or 1.46% of the population, of which only 62 workers or 0.13% of the population were from Cazin county.

According to the census of 31 March 1931, the population of the Bosnian Borders, the area that would become Cazin and Kladuša counties, was 47,283. The majority of the population lived in 7,960 independent agricultural households. At most 3,222 households owned 2-5 ha of land, representing 40.48%. 1,789 or 22.47% had 5-10 ha, 1,373 or 17.25% 1-2 ha, 584 or 7.34% 10-20 ha, and 558 or 7.01% 0.5-1 ha. 330 or 4.15% of households had up to 0.5 ha of land, and 102 or 1.28% between 20 and 50 ha. Only two households or 0.02% owned over 50 ha of land. In other words, just over two thirds of households owned up to 5 ha of land, indicating a smallholding structure which was the dominant feature of land ownership in Bosnia and Herzegovina before and after WWII. These statistics must be considered in the context of the quality of the land which, being hilly, is not ideal for crop production, and tends to be used for livestock. The Kladuša topography, including as it does a

---

[cxxiii] A Muslim convert from Lika, christened Mihailo in 1806, and who died in Istanbul in 1871, the same year that Prussian prime minister Bismarck established the first unified German state, the *Reich*, after defeating Austria (1866) and France (1870-1871). Italy was unified the same year.

larger proportion of flat country, is more fertile than that of Cazin. However, the peasants' greatest burden in the inter-war period was debt. In Cazin county, owing to the large percentage of independent peasants living there since before WWI, this debt was not as elsewhere in Bosnia and Herzegovina the result of quotas under the rapacious feudal system, but due to the penetration of usurious capital into agriculture and the countryside, which was characteristic of the Kingdom of Yugoslavia.

In the absence of precise indicators of the impoverishment of peasants in the Bosnian Borders due to the debt crisis prior to WWII, statistics on the constant reduction in livestock in the Borders serve to provide an approximate picture. In order to meet their obligations and repay their debts to the bankers and traders, peasants were forced to sell more and more of their livestock, the very basis of their survival. In Cazin county, statistics show that between 1921 and 1939 the number of horses fell from 4,422 to 3,989, cattle from 27,963 to 15,394, and sheep from 22,282 to 19,366. In order to protect peasants from this financial exploitation, the Cazin Farming Association was formed in the county in mid-1940, i.e. on the eve of the war, by respected and trusted local peasants.

The consistent neglect of the Bosnian Borders by all the various states that have ruled here throughout history has marked the population, and in particular the post-war generations, with a complex. It is this context which explains the importance of the role of the individual for the development of the Borders. The place of honour among such individuals must surely fall to the pre-war MP, the wealthy and respected Cazin native Nurija Pozderac. "Without him there would have been no schools, no running water or roads. He used to help the poorer pupils himself every year", says Hasan Purić a well-known teacher from Todorovo.

In order to understand events in the Bosnian Borders, both in the Kingdom of Yugoslavia and afterwards, in particular during WWII, but also up to the present day, it is vital to observe the organic links that exist between religion and everyday life in the area. Islam is traditionally all-pervasive in all areas of public and private life, making it very difficult for any other forms of social awareness to penetrate, in particular if they clash with Islam as a confession and the way of life based on its tenets. As the Bosnian Borders were (and continue to be) the area with the densest Muslim population in Bosnia and Herzegovina (and in Europe), the potential power of Islam in this region is self-evident. According to the 1931 census, 35,313 Muslims, 11,072 (Serb) Orthodox Christians, 895 Catholics and 3 persons of other religious denominations were living then in the Bosnian Borders. After WWII, these proportions became even more sharply differentiated in favour of the Muslims, in particular at the expense of the Serbs as a consequence of the anti-Serb genocide during the war and their departure in large numbers in the form of resettlement in Vojvodina immediately after the war.

The characteristics of the Military Frontier, which for centuries included Cazin and Kladuša counties on the Turkish side and Slunj county on the Austro-Hungarian side of the border, naturally gave rise to many common traits in the life of the population on both sides of the river Korana, not least among which must be the waging of war. With the occupation of Bosnia and Herzegovina by Austria-Hungary the whole area was brought under a common master, but nevertheless it continued to be marked by a lack of economic development right up to the collapse of the Habsburg Monarchy, and beyond in the Kingdom of the Serbs, Croats and Slovenes, that is to say the Kingdom of Yugoslavia.

Whereas the conversion of the most western extremity of the Turkish Empire into a military frontier zone obviously led to mass islamisation of the local population, the characteristics of the Slunj area as a religious and military frontier region created a local population of two ethnic groups.

According to the 1931 census, 21,470 Croats and 24,352 Serbs lived in the Slunj area. This however did not prevent the population from living in mutual respect, agreement and aid. On the eve of WWII and at its beginning, the KPJ served to a large extent to consolidate these fundamental values. The best evidence for this is the war itself when, despite the genocidal programmes of the *Ustaše* and the occupier in Slunj county, "internecine fighting and the *Četnik* movement were fully prevented".

Again according to the 1931 census, in Slunj county there were 7,180 households with a population of 45,829 spread over 213 communities. The population was characterised by a high birth rate and high death rate (every fifth child died before the age of one), was mainly illiterate, and engaged predominantly in livestock and crop production. However, the conditions for crop production were poor as almost three quarters of the county were covered by woods, thorn bushes and stone. As in the Bosnian Borders, smallholdings dominated. Of 6,922 farms, 2,818 were smallholdings of 2-5 ha and 2,356 had 5-10 ha. However, due to the Karst soil structure, farms had an average of only 1.93 ha arable land, insufficient for the average family of six. In addition to the poor quality of the land, it should also be noted that 795 farms owned 10-20 ha land, in total 10,293 ha.

The rural communities in Slunj county were isolated, far from means of communication, and without electric lighting or industry. The peasants' life was hard, and there were few farms who were not obliged to resort to buying food before the new harvest. The general privation and rural poverty did however create fertile ground for money-lending and usury, which flourished. The servicing of peasants' debts sometimes exceeded their purchasing power. The peasants' social awareness was markedly patriarchal and was mainly bound by religion. Superstition and fatalism abounded, as a consequence of there being more churches and clergy than there were teachers and schools. Despite the religion being different to that in the Bosnian Borders, the situation was almost identical as regards the peasants' social awareness, as was the peasants' position in every other respect. As the land could not feed everyone born to it, the people in both areas were involved to a large extent in activities such as lending and the transport of various goods. Child labour was, again on both sides of the Korana, an economic necessity for many children from poor families.

There were also many similar customs. These include the "abduction" of girls, although the later fate of the bride may have differed. This act, known in Slunj county as a "trial marriage", often ended, according to Svetozar Livada[cxxiv], with the woman being expelled for no good reason, which led to widespread conflicts. On the other side, among the Muslims, the woman was rarely expelled, but merely added. It was not unusual for a woman to become a man's second or third wife, common under *šerija* law, even after WWII. Despite the fact that religious customs and festivals differed between Muslims, Orthodox Christians and Catholics in this relatively small geographical area, that shared space interwove the life of the population and gave rise to some common celebrations. Such was 6 May, St.

[cxxiv] Historian and sociologist from Slunj, awarded the Partisan 1941 Commemoration Medal. Currently president of the Croatian Serb minority rights association.

George's Day, celebrated by the Serbs as Đurđevdan, by the Croats as Jurjevo, and by the Muslims of the Bosnian Borders as Jurjev.

The Second World War

After the capitulation of the Kingdom of Yugoslavia, Slunj county in Croatia and the Bosnian Borders became part of the new Independent State of Croatia (NDH), as did the rest of Bosnia and Herzegovina. However, this Third Reich satellite's *de facto* sovereignty is debatable, as the KPJ, the popular leader of the armed struggle against the quisling *Ustaše* regime, did not recognise its legitimacy. The Bosnian Borders, despite being part of Bosnia where the Partisan movement was powerful from the very beginning, were throughout the war, as a border region and for operational and tactical reasons, on the one hand administered by the Croatian military command, and on the other the new Cazin county revolutionary resistance cells (NOO) fell hierarchically and territorially under the Karlovac province resistance in Croatia.

However, events in the area took very differing courses during the war. While every war causes human losses and all kinds of misery for the population, this war was catastrophic for Slunj county. The Nazi NDH, in its pathological social programme to destroy the Serb population, succeeded in wiping out a third of the approximately 100,000 Serbs living in the whole Kordun area, comprising Slunj, Vojnić and Vrginmost counties, resorting to almost unimaginable atrocities. Research has shown that between 1941-1945, the activities of the NDH's *Ustaše* against the Serb population in the wartime counties of Slunj and Veljun (which were combined after the war into the single Slunj county) resulted in the deaths of 10,098 people, of whom 9,852 were Serbs, 236 Croats and 10 belonging to other ethnic groups. Over half of the casualties were victims of the fascist terror, around 15% were resistance fighters and around one fifth died of typhus. In the context of the 1950 Peasants' Revolt, it cannot be insignificant that in Kordunski Leskovac, the home of two of the main leaders of the revolt in Slunj county, two thirds of the population perished in the war. Both were local early resistance fighters[cxxv] who took part in the 1941 rising, as did the Serb population of Kordun in general.

In order to understand the 1950 revolt, and in particular its ideological basis, it is also important to note that in this area, and in the Bosnian Borders as is described below, intense government anti-communist propaganda from before the war had succeeded in implanting a deep dislike of communism as "obnoxious", which was only encouraged for their own reasons by the clerical institutions of the three main religions. "When the Kordun local unit initiated the recruitment of Croats into the Partisans at the end of 1943, around a thousand of them, indoctrinated into believing that Communists must be killed and that the King would return, fled and joined the *Ustaše* instead. They preferred the devil to communism". This only created further *Ustaše* ill-feeling on the ground, recalls Petar Zinajić[cxxvi].

Whereas the fate of Kordun, Lika, Banija and the Croatian Borders as a whole, due to their significant Serb population, was inextricably linked to the mass

---

[cxxv] Someone who joined the Partisans at the beginning of the war, as opposed to those who joined later on when it became obvious who would win.

[cxxvi] Writer, early resistance fighter, and UDBA chief for Slunj after the war. In 2007 he was indicted in his absence by Karlovac district court for the murder of 139 civilians in Slunj and Plaški between 1944-1946. He died in Belgrade in 2008.

uprising in 1941, the experience of the war in the Bosnian Borders within the greater borders region was very different, due to its predominantly Muslim population. The Serb population in the Bosnian Borders suffered the same fate as the Kordun Serbs. This general conclusion is supported by the testimony of many surviving local Serbs on *Ustaše* atrocities. For example, when the village of Crnaja was liberated it had not only been burnt to the ground, but almost the whole population had been killed. Again, Crnaja is the home of the main Bosnian leaders of the 1950 revolt, again Partisans and early resistance fighters since 1941.

The *Ustaše*'s first major massacre was carried out on 29 July 1941 in the Orthodox church in Velika Kladuša[cxxvii]. The same team (led by Ile Vidaković and Viktor Beljak-Ventura) went on to carry out another massacre of Serbs in August near Vrnograč. Much has been written about how outside *Ustaše* were brought in to carry out the massacre, disguised as Muslims in order to give the Serbs the impression of, and put the blame on, bloodthirsty Muslim neighbours. The *Ustaše* carried out another larger, extremely brutal massacre in the summer of 1941 in the vicinity of Bužim. However, further systematic research, similar to that carried out in Slunj county, is required to answer many unanswered questions about the fate of the Serb population in the Bosnian Borders. Only serious historical research will allow clarification of the role and responsibility of part of the local Muslim population serving in the Home Guard[cxxviii] and the *Ustaše*. It is well known that Muslims were also mobilised into the *Ustaše*. However, according to the testimony of Suljo Žunić[cxxix] among others, local Muslims did not take part in the massacre of the Serb population in the Bosnian Borders, which were carried out by outside *Ustaše* brought in for that purpose.

There are individual cases of Muslim Home Guard (or *Ustaše*) saving Serbs from massacres. One Home Guard member from Šturlić, Salim Bilkić, during a raid across the Korana in May 1942 as part of a major *Ustaše* and Home Guard offensive against Mašvinska Sela, during which the villages of Koranski Lug, Kordunski Leskovac, Basara and Kršlja were burnt down, gathered 14 women and children and saved them from the "feral *Ustaše*" by taking them away from the scene. Many Muslims, especially respected Muslims, including in particular Nurija Pozderac, stood up against the violence against the Serbs as early as 1941. Some Serb families were saved by hiding in Muslim houses during the war, as was the case with Milan Božić's family who took refuge in the Dizdarević family home in Šturlić. This had an important positive effect on the relationships between the remaining Serbs and the Muslims of the Bosnian Borders after the war. However, the whole truth about the behaviour of the Muslims of the Bosnian Borders towards the Serbs during the war has not yet been told due to the absence of research, as is indicated by the fear of many Muslim participants in the 1950 revolt that their Serb comrades-in-arms might turn their weapons against them in revenge for what had happened in the war.

There was no mass popular uprising in the Bosnian Borders in 1941. In the summer of 1941 there were already some communist Partisans, among whom Milan Pilipović, Tone Horvat, Mile Dejanović and Huska Miljković, acting mainly on the Croatian side of the Korana, distinguished themselves from the very start by their bravery and passed into popular legend. Many Serb families fled across the Korana

---

[cxxvii] Today there is a plaque marking this event on the outside wall of the church.

[cxxviii] A paramilitary force, far removed from Captain Mainwaring.

[cxxix] Secretary of the county party office and chief executive of Cazin county council at the time of the Peasants' Revolt.

into Kordun to escape the *Ustaše* massacres. In order to remain safe, they would move from place to place, while most of the men left to join the Partisans. In this way the Božićes of Crnaja became early Partisans. Because of the relatively more favourable conditions for fighting the *Ustaše* and the foreign occupier in the hills of Kordun, some Muslims left as early as 1941, in particular KPJ members. Among them was Huska Miljković, already mentioned above.

The *Ustaše* leader Ante Pavelić cunningly obtained the mainly passive consent of the Muslims to the NDH, embracing them in 1941 as the "flower of Croatia", and mobilising them into the Home Guard and also partly into the *Ustaše*. Although no research has been carried out on this, it is taken to be a historical fact that the local Muslim *Ustaše* carried out many atrocities on the Serb population of the Borders, including on the other side of the Korana, where according to Zinajić they massacred around 500 Serbs from Kordunski Leskovac and Staro Selo. Those terrible days of the summer of 1941, and subsequently 1942, could not of course be forgotten, and are also mentioned by the main Muslim leader of the common 1950 revolt as a source of fear of reprisals during the preparations for the revolt.

Husein "Huska" Miljković's personality and name have played a major role in the history of the Bosnian Borders. Huska was the MP for the Bosnian Borders in the 1920s, and when the conflict between the ruling regime and the Croat Peasants' Party reached breaking point in 1928 he came out on the side of the regime. That year two Velika Kladuša residents were killed in a fight about politics in Cetingrad, and subsequently buried beside the mosque in a public funeral with mass attendance. Huska's influence over the Muslims at that time is described by his later comrade-in-arms Šukrija Bijedić[cxxx]: "if he had told the crowd that day to go and burn Cetingrad, some people would have done it without asking why or for whose benefit." This claim is included here as it also demonstrates the local population's tendency to obedience to authority, which would show itself again in the war, again with Huska, and in the 1950 St. George's Day revolt. As a pre-war KPJ member, Huska joined the resistance in 1941 and gained a double reputation for his bravery fighting in Kordun: not only the obedient admiration of his fellow Muslims, but also the respect of the people of Kordun. He is however portrayed as an independently-minded party leader who commanded loyalty to himself rather than to the party, which led to him being dismissed as secretary of the Kladuša county party office, while remaining a member of the hierarchically superior Karlovac provincial office. According to another version, the main bone of contention between Huska and his comrades in the party leadership was his disagreement at the beginning of 1943 to exchange the notorious *Ustaša* Flak, whom he wished to see shot. Whatever the truth of the matter, it appears that he was affected by his dismissal as secretary of the Kladuša county party office. He wanted revenge, and that may well be part of the reason for his decision to desert with another 25 Partisans during the major Axis offensive of February 1943. However, Huska's defection to the enemy is explained first and foremost by his assessment that the Partisans had no chance and would lose the war. In May 1943 he was part of the Home Guard and fighting against his erstwhile comrades in the Bosnian Borders, Banija and Kordun, while at the same time contemplating the formation of his own popular army. In the absence of scholarly literature on the "Muslim militia", reliance is placed upon the presentation of Šukrija

---

[cxxx] Serb from Gacko in Herzegovina, a member of the JNA since 1939, and a distinguished Partisan in the Croatian Borders during WWII. He was Bosnian deputy interior minister and chief of police at the time of the Peasants' Revolt.

Bijedić, political officer of the Una operational group via which the militia went over to the resistance at the end of 1943 or the beginning of 1944. However, the author has come across testimony which does not agree with Bijedić's interpretation. For example, Hakija Pozderac maintains that the original idea of the Muslim militia was that of the pre-war Kladuša politician Hasan Miljković (no relation), while it was Huska Miljković who actually formed the militia as an organisation.

In any event, the idea of Muslim armed units formed for the purpose of defending Muslim settlements and the practice based on it, go back almost to the beginning of the war, in line with the concepts of political autonomy for Yugoslav Muslims, i.e. a form of autonomy for Bosnia within the Third Reich to allow it to retain its Muslim traditions. Hitler rejected requests to separate Bosnia from the NDH.

One market day in mid-1943, Huska presented to the inhabitants of Velika Kladuša his idea of a popular army under his command with a defensive character, remaining exclusively on its own territory and defending the population against any form of robbery. Thus was formed "Huska's Militia", with the motto "For the faith and Islam" and with the star and crescent on its members' fezzes or caps. The militia's appeal was that its members could virtually stay at home, many of them actually sleeping at home, working their fields and avoiding the various mobilisations into the Home Guard, *Ustaše*, or German army, and gaining a legitimacy among the Muslims of the Bosnian Borders, testifies Bijedić. Huska's militia units were nothing new among the Muslims because as early as 1941 Muslim villages had had their own local armed defenders, which led to the creation of county guards with the sole objective of protecting their home territory from the incursions of any external armed force. In the village of Šturlić such forces were referred to as *Četniks*.

Contrary to the initial proclamation, there was much robbery, gambling, and smuggling in Huska's Militia, and people were recruited by force. The number of Huska militiaman soon grew to around 3,000 fighters. Elderly residents of Cazin even today vividly recall the crucial role played in the mobilisation by Ale Čović, later the main Muslim leader of the 1950 revolt. This was evidently a crucial moment in the creation of Čović's undoubted authority among the Muslims after the war. Huska's army possessed two brigades with eleven battalions divided into troops, platoons and squads, led by a commander-in-chief and a headquarters, and spread "shock and awe" throughout the Bosnian Borders. With the blessing and the support of the *Ustaše* they received arms and medical supplies from the Germans and fought against the Partisans, Bijedić goes on to testify in his book on his WWII experiences. Hakija Pozderac makes different claims: "Huska never fought against the Partisans. He never killed a single Partisan". In the second half of 1943 Huska was wavering again, this time due to the Partisans' major successes, and despite promising the Germans loyalty for months, at the beginning of February 1944 he defected with his army to the Partisans, Bijedić goes on to stress. One of Huska's demands for defecting to the Partisans was to be one rank higher than major Hamdija Omanović (a well-known Bosnian Borders early resistance fighter and party member), obviously in order to be able to dominate the Muslim fighters in the Partisans. By order of the Commander-in-Chief of the resistance and the Partisans Josip Broz Tito of 11 November 1945, Huska was promoted to the rank of colonel, testifies Hakija Pozderac. The headquarters for Croatia formed the Una operational group out of Huska's army with Huska as commander and sent hundreds of Muslim Partisans to join its ranks for the purposes of political work with Huska. But the Partisan political officers, obliged to adopt the militia's symbols, came up against stiff resistance when attempting to "re-educate" Huska's militiamen, mainly illiterate Muslims.

However, the main problem was the real military position of Huska's militiamen, as Huska continued to hedge his bets, and following his example so did his officers and soldiers, according to Bijedić, political officer of the Una operational group: "in the morning with the Partisans, in the afternoon with the *Ustaše*." Despite the enormous authority and power he enjoyed among the Muslims of the Bosnian Borders, and perhaps because of it, Huska Miljković was treacherously killed at the end of April 1944 by two of his close supporters, by order of the Germans. The Germans richly rewarded Huska's killers, and spread propaganda among the population of the Bosnian Borders, deeply affected by the loss of their idol, that he had been killed by the Partisans. It was not difficult to disorient the wavering population, and after Huska's death part of his former militia, around two hundred men, defected from the Partisans to whom he had led them in February. So was formed the Green Force, the "Greens", who caused great harm to the local population not only during the war but also for several years afterwards, testifies Mićo Carević, an early resistance fighter and party official in Kladuša county in the post-war period. Even in 1950 they had not been fully eradicated, although no direct link has been established between them and the 1950 rebels.

The phenomenon of Huska Miljković and his Muslim militia as summarised here based on the book by Bijedić and other recollections, is only included as it contains elements linking it to the 1950 Peasants' Revolt. These links will become clearer after the detailed presentation of the events of 1950, and concern in particular the following. Firstly, many of Huska's former militiamen, some of them later Partisans and some later *Ustaše* and post-war "Greens", participated in the 1950 revolt. Secondly, because of the short time gap, memories of Huska's Militia were still fresh. Thirdly, one of the crucial questions in the preparations for the 1950 revolt was the authority of the leaders, both among the Muslims and among the Serbs. Fourthly, the power of religious continuity can be seen in the idea put forward in the preparations, but never implemented, that Muslims should swear their military oath before the local imam. Lastly but not least, this is in fact a continuation of the specific Borders tradition of lightly taking the decision to take up arms in the pursuit of social interests with little thought to the consequences. Further continuity between Huska's former militia and the 1950 revolt is hampered by the fact that the Bosnian rebels were led by Serbs, although from the ideological and social perspective Serbs and Muslims had the same positions in the Peasants' Revolt.

It would of course be remiss for a historian to equate the Second World War in the Bosnian Borders with the phenomenon of Huska Miljković and his militiamen. Although their place and role in the context of WWII in the Bosnian Borders and beyond have not yet been properly assessed, perhaps because the context itself has not yet been assessed consistently, it would be inconsistent to fail to stress the obviously enormous significance of the Communists and their sympathisers for the ultimate success of the resistance in the Bosnian Borders. Indeed, some of the 1950 rebels, and not just Serbs, became KPJ members during the war. The purpose of emphasising Huska's role in the war is to show how ethnic and religious considerations were far more weighty in influencing the population than ideological and Communist considerations.

Without venturing into generalised conclusions on the appearance on the scene of Huska Miljković, as it is not the main subject of this research, his direct legacy can nevertheless be considered to be distinctly negative. The activities of the

Greens, mainly part of the former Muslim militia, inflicted great evil on the Bosnian Borders both during the war and particularly afterwards. The Greens comprised the worst elements of the local population, notorious *Ustaše* known to the population as criminals, and unable to desert to the Partisans with Huska because of the amount of blood on their hands. Aided to the end by the Germans and the *Ustaše*, and after the war by renegades in the Borders, they killed respected members of society and robbed villages. After the war they became even worse, bloodthirsty "wild beasts" recalls Carević, who himself was wounded by a Greens bomb thrown through his window. The post-war Greens fought to the last man, they knew what fate awaited them and lived by the principle of "no regrets". Just before the end of WWII when there were several hundred of them they moved around in large groups, whereas later due to the more restrictive conditions and in particular due to the systematic "cleansing" of the country by the National Guard (OZN), they had to move in smaller groups. In 1946 most of them were captured and killed. According to OZN data, at the end of 1946 the total of around 1,320 renegades in Bosnia and Herzegovina included 46 Greens, mainly from the Bosnian Borders. The assessment at that time of the Bosnian OZN and the Bosnian provincial office of the KPJ that the Greens "will not constitute a serious problem" was not very realistic, considering that in a five-year period they killed over 200 people throughout the Bosnian Borders and they had still not been fully destroyed in the summer of 1950, when travellers had to have an armed escort because of possible Greens ambushes. However, although it has already been established that there was no link between the remnants of the Greens and the 1950 revolt which might have indicated a joint assault against the new Yugoslav government, and which would certainly have been discovered by the UDBA[cxxxi] investigation of May 1950, there is one bizarre case suggesting that some tenuous link did exist. This is what happened. On 7 or 8 May 1950 in Vrnograč the Green Suljo Mehurić killed the peasant rebel Alaga Jušić, brother of the notorious Sijano, the leader of a group of Greens in the area of Bužim, Ljubljankić and Todorovo. Sijano himself had been killed in 1946 by the UDBA and his body exposed on a fence beside the mosque in Todorovo during the religious service for all to see, before being thrown to the dogs. According to Purić's testimony, Alaga's motive in joining the revolt in 1950 was this murder and the new authorities' cruel treatment of his dead brother. Mehurić, once he had killed Alaga, surrendered to the UDBA in the hope of saving his own skin as a Green, and, according to Purić, was indeed rewarded with a lighter sentence.

There were other Greens who also got off lightly. During the second half of WWII the supreme headquarters of the resistance and the Partisans issued several appeals offering amnesty to members of the enemy armed forces without "too much" blood on their hands who were ready to defect to the Partisans. It may be that the well-known Huska militiaman and later Green Husein Agić made use of one such appeal. He was found working on the Cazin-Koprivna road in Cazin, where he worked until 1953, by Gojko Jotić, an interior ministry agent in Cazin county before and after the revolt. However, no research has been carried out into whether and to what extent members of "enemy armed forces" made use of the amnesty in the Bosnian Borders. The question of post-war renegades in general in Yugoslavia has not been systematically researched, with due respect to the personal analyses of various individuals, mainly former UDBA agents. Of course, many other people also remember those tragic events. It is logical that *Četnik* renegades, by far the most

---

cxxxi Yugoslav security service.

numerous and most dangerous throughout Bosnia and Herzegovina, were not present in Slunj county, but there were diehard "Crusaders". The then teacher in Kruškovaća, Đuro Zatezalo, recalls for example how the police offered him weapons as late as 1951 to defend himself against possible attacks by Crusaders and *Ustaše* criminals from the nearby woods. The purpose of highlighting the problem of renegade groups or "bandits" throughout the period leading up to the Peasants' Revolt is to indicate the seriousness of the internal security situation at the time when the new political order was being established and in which the country found itself as late as 1950[1063].

Vera Kržišnik-Bukić, Cazinska Buna 1950 (footnotes omitted)

[1] Silber & Little, 1995:xxvi; Crnobrnja, 1994:73; Courthiade, 2006:48
[2] Kajtazović, 1996:12-13
[3] Hirkić, 1998:41
[4] Hirkić, 1998:97
[5] Hirkić, 1998:509
[6] O'Shea, 1998:229
[7] Hirkić, 2008:20
[8] ICRC
[9] Hirkić, 1998:24-24
[10] Ulemek, 2016:243-244
[11] Lawrence, 1997:7
[12] Ulemek, 2016:141
[13] Hirkić, 1998:172
[14] Hirkić, 1998:255
[15] Hirkić, 1998:367
[16] Hirkić, 1998:369, 377
[17] Hirkić, 1998:439
[18] Hirkić, 1998:154
[19] Hirkić, 1998:164
[20] Hirkić, 1998:328
[21] Hirkić, 1998:337
[22] Hirkić, 1998:78
[23] Hirkić, 1998:120, 124
[24] Slobodan Praljak, 326
[25] Hirkić, 1998:201
[26] Hirkić, 1998:117
[27] Hirkić, 1998:163
[28] Hirkić, 1998:87
[29] Hirkić, 1998:165
[30] Baker, 2015:251; Hirkić, 1998:168
[31] Hirkić, 1998:68
[32] Hirkić, 1998:202
[33] Hirkić, 1998:381
[34] Hirkić, 1998:87
[35] Hirkić, 1998:97
[36] Hirkić, 1998:87
[37] Hirkić, 1998:404
[38] Hirkić, 1998:255
[39] Hirkić, 1998:335
[40] Hirkić, 1998:437
[41] Hirkić, 1998:346
[42] Abdić, 2016:77, 119-120, 405, 415
[43] Malcolm, 1994:210; Crnobrnja, 1994:72
[44] Abdić, 2016:8, 74, 80-81, 108; Owen, 1995:59
[45] O'Shea, 1998:16; Abdić, 2016:64-65, 96, 427
[46] O'Shea, 1998:16-17; Abdić, 2016:145; Silber & Little, 1995:257-268
[47] Silber & Little, 1995:280; O'Shea, 1998:20
[48] O'Shea, 1998:18-19

[49] Malcolm, 1996:248-249; Crnobrnja, 1994:214-215; Baker, 2015:70; O'Shea, 1998:21; Abdić, 2016:94; Owen, 1995:91, 183-184
[50] Silber & Little, 1995:337; Abdić, 2016:98; Owen, 1995:196
[51] Owen, 1995:196, 289, 349
[52] Rieff, 1995:126; Bastabalkana, 6, 18
[53] Silber & Little, 1995:241-242
[54] Abdić, 2016:126-130; Perica, 2002:169
[55] O'Shea, 1998:20; Owen, 1995:49-50; Abdić, 2016:100-101, 159-160, 326; Silber & Little, 1995:336-339; Baker, 2015:71
[56] Silber & Little, 1995:337; Owen, 1995:203-204, 215, 221; O'Shea, 1998:19-21
[57] Stević, 1995:51-52; Hirkić, 1998:454, 113
[58] O'Shea, 1998:238; Abdić, 2016:243-245
[59] BBC News
[60] Abdić, 2016:12-14, 20-21, 361
[61] Kolb, 2014:194; Baker, 2015:100; LegalUN
[62] Baker, 2015:97
[63] Freshpress
[64] O'Shea, 1998:229
[65] Crnobrnja, 1994:93; Abdić, 2016:416
[66] Baker, 2015:27
[67] Malcolm, 1994:187, 211
[68] Trkulja & Božić, 2008:88, 221
[69] Huffington Post
[70] Owen, 1995:127
[71] Malcolm, 1994:208; Baker, 2015:8, 87; Crnobrnja, 1994:21
[72] Crnobrnja, 1994:74-76; Baker, 2015:22
[73] Crnobrnja, 1994:123
[74] Crnobrnja, 1994:180: Abdić, 2016:426, 458
[75] Trkulja & Božić, 2008:215; Abdić, 2016:430; Stević, 1995:65
[76] Malcolm, 1994:209; Abdić, 2016:431
[77] Dizdarević, 2000:213
[78] Dizdarević, 2000:213, 421; Silber & Little, 1995:116; Crnobrnja, 1994:121
[79] Ulemek, 2016:197
[80] Silber & Little, 1995:116; Ulemek, 2016:197; Dizdarević, 2000:421, 414-416; Freshpress; Crnobrnja, 1994:121, 123
[81] Malcolm, 1994:209; Abdić, 2016:423-424. 430
[82] Hirkić, 2008:57-61; Ćano, 1994:127; Abdić, 2016:8, 11, 442
[83] Abdić, 2016:439
[84] Abdić, 1992:57-65
[85] Hirkić, 1998:399; Abdić, 2016:446
[86] Abdić, 1992:61
[87] Kržišnik-Bukić, 1991:213; Abdić, 2016:447
[88] Baker, 2015:33; Abdić, 2016:433
[89] Dizdarević, 2000:279
[90] Abdić, 2016:434
[91] Abdić, 2016:68
[92] Abdić, 2016:160, 269, 437
[93] Baker, 2015:34; Crnobrnja, 1994:84-89
[94] Bosnjaci.net; Malcolm, 1994:208; Bastabalkana, 3
[95] Abdić, 2016:66-68
[96] Abdić, 2016:65
[97] Abdić, 2016:66, 74-77
[98] Abdić, 2016:74, 108
[99] New York Times; Silber & Little, 1995:235
[100] Bastabalkana, 25
[101] Crnobrnja, 1994:97-98
[102] Crnobrnja, 1994:95
[103] Silber & Little, 1995:122-123
[104] Crnobrnja, 1994:99
[105] Dizdarević, 2000:77
[106] Crnobrnja, 1994:100; Judah, 2002:49

[107] Dizdarević, 2000:340
[108] Malcolm, 1998:194,230
[109] Malcolm, 1998:284-331; Buckley & Cummings, 2001:15
[110] Dizdarević, 2000:198
[111] Dizdarević, 2000:233
[112] Dizdarević, 2000:209; Owen, 1995:128
[113] Crnobrnja, 1994:101-104; Silber & Little, 1995:60-72
[114] Silber & Little, 1995:41
[115] Dizdarević, 2000:233
[116] Dizdarević, 2000:208
[117] Dizdarević, 2000:206
[118] Dizdarević, 2000:195
[119] Dizdarević, 2000:209; Malcolm, 1998:339
[120] Dizdarević, 2000:198
[121] Dizdarević, 2000:202-204
[122] Dizdarević, 2000:210
[123] Dizdarević, 2000:185-187
[124] Dizdarević, 2000:315, 276-277
[125] Dizdarević, 2000:293, 316, 323
[126] Dizdarević, 2000:308
[127] Dizdarević, 2000:402, 190-191
[128] Dizdarević, 2000:403, 410, 436
[129] O'Shea, 1998:87-88; Crnobrnja, 1994:84-74, 107-113
[130] Silber & Little, 1995:50; Dizdarević, 2000:440
[131] Dizdarević, 2000:239; Crnobrnja, 1994:111
[132] Dizdarević, 2000:239
[133] Dizdarević, 2000:242-245
[134] Dizdarević, 2000:407-408
[135] Dizdarević, 2000:249-256
[136] Dizdarević, 2000:263-266
[137] Dizdarević, 2000:273-274
[138] Silber & Little, 1995:93-94
[139] Dizdarević, 2000:444; Owen, 1995:74
[140] Dizdarević, 2000:291
[141] Dizdarević, 2000:423
[142] Dizdarević, 2000:291
[143] Dizdarević, 2000:269-270
[144] Dizdarević, 2000:424
[145] Dizdarević, 2000:167
[146] Dizdarević, 2000:170-171
[147] Maclean, 1949:346
[148] Dizdarević, 2000:190
[149] Dizdarević, 2000:304, 225-227
[150] Dizdarević, 2000:280
[151] Silber & Little, 1995:89-93; Crnobrnja, 1994:107-11, 142
[152] Dizdarević, 2000:211
[153] Trkulja & Božić, 2008:84
[154] Silber & Little, 1995:87-93; Crnobrnja, 1994:145
[155] Crnobrnja, 1994:147; Baker, 2015:44
[156] Crnobrnja, 1994:143
[157] Dizdarević, 2000:23
[158] Baker, 2015:119
[159] Silber & Little, 1995:155
[160] Crnobrnja, 1994:258
[161] BBC, 2003:part 3
[162] Silber & Little, 1995:174-180
[163] Kržišnik-Bukić, 1991:524
[164] Silber & Little, 1995:169-180; Crnobrnja, 1994:62
[165] Silber & Little, 1995:182
[166] Dizdarević, 2000:74; Crnobrnja, 1994:92
[167] Crnobrnja, 1994:231; Silber & Little, 1995:268; B92 & Vreme Film, 2006:I

[168] Owen, 1995:155
[169] Hirkić, 1998:408, Abdić, 2016:13, 451
[170] O'Shea, 1998:71
[171] Silber & Little, 1995:354-355
[172] Crnobrnja, 1994:210-211
[173] Judah, 2002:125
[174] B92 & Vreme Film, 2006:II; Abdić, 2016:105, 322
[175] O'Shea, 1998:159-163
[176] Malcolm, 1994:242-243
[177] Miljković, 2014:19; Ulemek, 2016:315
[178] Miljković, 2014:127
[179] Abdić, 2016:441
[180] Ćano, 1994:30
[181] Ulemek, 2016:202-210, 294
[182] Trkulja & Božić, 2008:236
[183] Ćano, 1994:5-6, 18; Abdić, 2016:359
[184] Ćano, 1994:77
[185] Ćano, 1994:18-19, 21, 27, 87
[186] O'Shea, 1998:69
[187] Miljković, 2014:157
[188] Ćano, 1994:38, 122; Abdić, 2016:452
[189] Stević, 1995:57
[190] BBC News; Helsinki Watch; UN Economic and Social Council; Kolb, 2014:139-140
[191] Dnevni Avaz/DW.com
[192] Independent
[193] Ćano, 1994:75-76
[194] Miljković, 2014:115
[195] Avaz
[196] Andrić, 1967:83
[197] Abdić, 1992:111; Abdić, 2016:420-421; O'Shea, 1998:15
[198] Silber & Little, 1995:113; Baker, 2015:47; Crnobrnja, 1994:121-122; Ulemek, 2016:253
[199] Dizdarević, 2000:411-413
[200] Silber & Little, 1995:240; Malcolm, 1994:201
[201] Dizdarević, 2000:413
[202] Maclean, 1949:330
[203] Dizdarević, 2000:49
[204] Trkulja & Božić, 2008:131
[205] Stević, 1995:21-22
[206] Malcolm, 1994:xv
[207] Tolj, 1996:224-226
[208] Lawrence, 1997:27
[209] Selimović, 2005: 108
[210] Trkulja & Božić, 2008:35
[211] Kržišnik-Bukić, 1991:532
[212] Abdić, 2016:144
[213] Abdić, 2016:145, 444-445
[214] Ulemek, 2016:78, 235; Hirkić, 1998:162
[215] Abdić, 2016:331; 452-456
[216] Abdić, 2016:330
[217] Abdić, 2016:246-252, 444
[218] Abdić, 2016:331-332
[219] Abdić, 2016:262
[220] Abdić, 2016:257
[221] Miljković, 2014:76
[222] Andrić, 1967:155-156, 161
[223] Miljković, 2014:78
[224] Stević, 1995:12; Abdić, 2016:269
[225] Baker, 2015:54
[226] O'Shea, 1998:107
[227] Miljković, 2014:186
[228] Abdić, 2016:255-257, 266-267

[229] Abdić, 2016:270-272, 331-332, 409
[230] Miljković, 2014:75
[231] Miljković, 2014:78
[232] Miljković, 2014:126
[233] Abdić, 2016:324-326
[234] Silber & Little, 1995:306-317
[235] Abdić, 2016:337
[236] Miljković, 2014:24-34; Ulemek, 2016:294
[237] Miljković, 2014:42
[238] O'Shea, 1998:18
[239] Miljković, 2014:45-60
[240] Kržišnik-Bukić, 1991:243
[241] Miljković, 2014:5-10
[242] O'Shea, 1998:108
[243] Orbus
[244] Abdić, 2016:236
[245] O'Shea, 1998:20-21; Owen, 1995:96, 101, 356, 366
[246] Abdić, 2016:260
[247] Stević, 1995:13; Ćano, 1994:26
[248] Miljković, 2014:85
[249] Stević, 1995:13; Owen, 1995:221-222; O'Shea, 1998:23
[250] B92 & Vreme Film, 2006:II
[251] Miljković, 2014:99; Abdić, 2016:343
[252] Miljković, 2014:88-89
[253] Miljković, 2014:90-91, 110
[254] Miljković, 2014:92
[255] Stević, 1995:43; Baker, 2015:71
[256] O'Shea, 1998:23
[257] Abdić, 2016:446-447
[258] New York Times; O'Shea, 1998:26
[259] Trkulja & Božić, 2008:169
[260] Orwell, 1962:226
[261] Miljković, 2014:89-90; Chronology of war
[262] Owen, 1995:222
[263] Ulemek, 2016:330
[264] Abdić, 2016:341-342
[265] Abdić, 2016:342-345
[266] Ćano, 1994:12
[267] Kržišnik-Bukić, 1991:475
[268] Abdić, 2016:136
[269] Kržišnik-Bukić, 1998:64
[270] Abdić, 2016:21, 318-319, 330
[271] Kržišnik-Bukić, 1991:XXIV
[272] Kržišnik-Bukić, 1991:521; Ulemek, 2016:308
[273] Miljković, 2014:89-90; Abdić, 2016:350
[274] B92 & Vreme Film, 2006:II
[275] Miljković, 2014:278
[276] Kržišnik-Bukić, 1991:479
[277] ZapadnaBosna
[278] O'Shea, 1998:1-30
[279] Trkulja & Božić, 2008:220-223
[280] Miljković, 2014:111
[281] Miljković, 2014:113; 116-117
[282] Miljković, 2014:113
[283] Miljković, 2014:115
[284] Stević, 1995:47-49
[285] Ćano, 1994:14; O'Shea, 1998:63
[286] O'Shea, 1998:63
[287] O'Shea, 1998:35
[288] O'Shea, 1998:63
[289] Stević, 1995:50

[290] O'Shea, 1998:65
[291] O'Shea, 1998:63-70
[292] O'Shea, 1998:68
[293] Miljković, 2014:119
[294] Miljković, 2014: 122-123, 166
[295] Miljković, 2014:242
[296] Stević, 1995:53; O'Shea, 1998:69
[297] O'Shea, 1998:70
[298] O'Shea, 1998:71
[299] Miljković, 2014:125
[300] Miljković, 2014:127
[301] O'Shea, 1998:71
[302] O'Shea, 1998:77
[303] Ulemek, 2016:79, 236; Abdić, 2016:241-243, 246
[304] Miljković, 2014:128
[305] O'Shea, 1998:77
[306] Miljković, 2014:138; O'Shea, 1998:73
[307] Miljković, 2014:139; O'Shea, 1998:79
[308] O'Shea, 1998:83-84
[309] Miljković, 2014:145
[310] Miljković, 2014:152
[311] Abdić, 2016:397-400
[312] Miljković, 2014:150
[313] Miljković, 2014:162
[314] Miljković, 2014:168
[315] Miljković, 2014:164; O'Shea, 1998:77
[316] Miljković, 2014:167; O'Shea, 1998:87-88
[317] Miljković, 2014:173
[318] Miljković, 2014:173-179
[319] Miljković, 2014:186
[320] Miljković, 2014:187-188
[321] Miljković, 2014:191
[322] Stević, 1995:14; O'Shea, 1998:88
[323] Miljković, 2014:190
[324] Miljković, 2014:193; O'Shea, 1998:89
[325] Ulemek, 2016:49, 65
[326] Miljković, 2014:203-204
[327] Miljković, 2014:208
[328] Miljković, 2014:284-285
[329] Miljković, 2014:209
[330] O'Shea, 1998:99
[331] Miljković, 2014:211-212
[332] Miljković, 2014:212
[333] O'Shea, 1998:146
[334] O'Shea, 1998:105-107
[335] Ulemek, 2016:78
[336] Ulemek, 2016:104-118
[337] O'Shea, 1998:107
[338] O'Shea, 1998:111-112
[339] Trkulja & Božić, 2008:90
[340] Miljković, 2014:220-221
[341] Miljković, 2014:222-224
[342] Miljković, 2014:226-227
[343] Miljković, 2014:231
[344] Miljković, 2014:232, 236
[345] Miljković, 2014:237
[346] Miljković, 2014:247
[347] Ulemek, 2016:135
[348] Miljković, 2014:286; Ulemek, 2016:232
[349] Miljković, 2014:252; O'Shea, 1998:139
[350] O'Shea, 1998:20, 141-142, 195

[351] O'Shea, 1998:165; Miljković, 2014:255
[352] Ulemek, 2016:303-304
[353] Miljković, 2014:266
[354] Miljković, 2014:271-273, 292
[355] O'Shea, 1998:177
[356] Miljković, 2014:318
[357] Miljković, 2014:292
[358] Miljković, 2014:293
[359] O'Shea, 1998:191-193
[360] Miljković, 2014:296-297
[361] O'Shea, 1998:211-212, 219
[362] Andrić, 1962:90
[363] Orwell, 1962:77
[364] Miljković, 2014:301
[365] Miljković, 2014:304
[366] Ulemek, 2016:377, 426, 431; Miljković, 2014:286
[367] Miljković, 2014:309
[368] O'Shea, 1998:214, 221; Miljković, 2014:314; Ulemek, 2016:433
[369] Miljković, 2014:316
[370] Trkulja & Božić, 2008:74; Tolj, 1996:226
[371] O'Shea, 1998:223
[372] Ulemek, 2016:436
[373] Ulemek, 2016:438-456
[374] Stević, 1995:18-19, 22
[375] Ulemek, 2016:460
[376] Miljković, 2014:319-323
[377] Ulemek, 2016:464-473
[378] Miljković, 2014:325-327; O'Shea, 1998:227; Ulemek, 2016:466
[379] Večernji List
[380] Miljković, 2014:327; Ulemek, 2016:79-80, 236, 426, 480; Abdić, 2016:329; O'Shea, 1998:227
[381] Miljković, 2014:328
[382] Miljković, 2014:330
[383] Miljković, 2014:331
[384] Courthiade, 2006:43
[385] Miljković, 2014:391
[386] Miljković, 2014:421
[387] Stević, 1995:41; Baker, 2015:70
[388] Miljković, 2014:89, 116, 281; O'Shea, 1998:79, 173-175
[389] Hirkić, 1998:40
[390] Andrić, 1967:115, 121
[391] Hirkić, 1998:210
[392] Hirkić, 1998:79
[393] Kržišnik-Bukić, 1991:488-490
[394] Hirkić, 1998:398
[395] Hirkić, 1998:398
[396] Grahović, 2014:19-25
[397] UN Security Council
[398] Kajtazović, 1996:16-17
[399] Hirkić, 1998:31
[400] Hirkić, 1998:19
[401] Hirkić, 1998:29
[402] Baker, 2015:76
[403] Hirkić, 1998:9
[404] Humanitarian Law Centre
[405] Hirkić, 1998:13
[406] Hirkić, 1998:15-16; O'Shea, 1998:228
[407] Hirkić, 1998:17-18
[408] Wikileaks
[409] Orwell, 1962:39
[410] Hirkić, 1998:37
[411] Hirkić, 1998:44

[412] Hirkić, 1998:229
[413] Hirkić, 1998:479
[414] Hirkić, 1998:17
[415] Hirkić, 1998:423
[416] Hirkić, 1998:437
[417] Hirkić, 1998:24
[418] Hirkić, 1998:42
[419] Hirkić, 1998:44
[420] Hirkić, 1998:201
[421] Hirkić, 1998:316
[422] Baker, 2015:260
[423] Hirkić, 1998:207
[424] Hirkić, 1998:51
[425] Hirkić, 1998:82
[426] Hirkić, 1998:128
[427] Hirkić, 1998:255
[428] Hirkić, 1998:295
[429] Hirkić, 1998:332
[430] Hirkić, 1998:114
[431] Hirkić, 1998:124
[432] Hirkić, 1998:228
[433] Hirkić, 1998:293, 328
[434] Hirkić, 1998:355
[435] Hirkić, 1998:262
[436] Hirkić, 1998:423
[437] Hirkić, 1998:425
[438] Hirkić, 1998:456
[439] Hirkić, 1998:548
[440] Hirkić, 1998:561
[441] Hirkić, 1998:196
[442] Hirkić, 1998:356
[443] O'Shea, 1998:229
[444] Hirkić, 1998:75
[445] Hirkić, 1998:225
[446] Hirkić, 1998:556
[447] Hirkić, 1998:43
[448] Hirkić, 1998:129; O'Shea, 1998:94
[449] Hirkić, 1998:293
[450] Hirkić, 1998:124
[451] Hirkić, 1998:267
[452] Hirkić, 1998:94
[453] Hirkić, 1998:105, 115
[454] Hirkić, 1998:87
[455] Hirkić, 1998:115
[456] Orwell, 1962:69; West, 1942:398
[457] Hirkić, 1998:545
[458] Hirkić, 1998:489
[459] Hirkić, 1998:544
[460] Hirkić, 1998:210
[461] Hirkić, 1998:267
[462] Hirkić, 1998:58
[463] Courthiade, 2006:6
[464] Guardian
[465] Hirkić, 1998:144
[466] Hirkić, 1998:114
[467] Hirkić, 1998:267
[468] Hirkić, 1998:169
[469] Hirkić, 1998:122
[470] Hirkić, 1998:396
[471] Hirkić, 1998:171
[472] Hirkić, 1998:166

473 ICRC; BBC News
474 Forsyth, 1969:159-160
475 Crnobrnja, 1994:xii
476 Roberts, 2014:300, 324
477 Hirkić, 1998:116
478 Hirkić, 1998:144
479 Hirkić, 1998:188
480 Hirkić, 1998:323
481 Hirkić, 1998:307, 317
482 Hirkić, 1998:324
483 Hirkić, 1998:329
484 Hirkić, 1998:325
485 Hirkić, 1998:332
486 Slobodan Praljak, 278
487 Hirkić, 1998:21
488 Hirkić, 1998:98
489 Hirkić, 1998:99-100
490 Hirkić, 1998:60
491 Hirkić, 1998:67
492 Hirkić, 1998:364, 891
493 Hirkić, 1998:106
494 Hirkić, 1998:152
495 Hirkić, 1998:183
496 Hirkić, 1998:287, 329
497 Hirkić, 1998:247
498 Hirkić, 1998:22, 89
499 Hirkić, 1998:104
500 Hirkić, 1998:116
501 Hirkić, 1998:180
502 Hirkić, 1998:121
503 Grupa za direktnu zaštitu ljudskih prava; Hirkić, 1998:312, 148
504 Hirkić, 1998:294, 92
505 Hirkić, 1998:122
506 Hirkić, 1998:55
507 Hirkić, 1998:125
508 Hirkić, 1998:152
509 Hirkić, 1998:173
510 Hirkić, 1998:307
511 Hirkić, 1998:201
512 Hirkić, 1998:28
513 Hirkić, 1998:34
514 Baker, 2015:250
515 Hirkić, 1998:68
516 Hirkić, 1998:263
517 Hirkić, 1998:123
518 Hirkić, 1998:27
519 Hirkić, 1998:63
520 Hirkić, 1998:32
521 Hirkić, 1998:67
522 Hirkić, 1998:68
523 Hirkić, 1998:32
524 Médecins Sans Frontières, 2015:140
525 Hirkić, 1998:152
526 Hirkić, 1998:41
527 Hirkić, 1998:90
528 Hirkić, 1998:92, 100
529 Hirkić, 1998:122
530 Hirkić, 1998:124
531 Hirkić, 1998:136, 138-139
532 Hirkić, 1998:141
533 Hirkić, 1998:142

[534] Hirkić, 1998:263
[535] Hirkić, 1998:264
[536] Hirkić, 1998:306
[537] Hirkić, 1998:374, 410
[538] Hirkić, 1998:414
[539] Hirkić, 1998:534
[540] West, 1942:47
[541] Hirkić, 1998:78; Ulemek, 2016:368
[542] Hirkić, 1998:229
[543] Orwell, 1962:64
[544] Pakenham, 1991:577-579
[545] Hirkić, 1998:321
[546] Van Selm et al, 2003:76
[547] O'Shea, 1998:229
[548] Silber & Little, 1995:354-355
[549] Bastabalkana, 12
[550] Abdić, 2016:95; Owen, 1995:82-83
[551] Abdić, 2016:458
[552] Baker, 2015:35
[553] Orwell, 1962:185; 1986:50; 1949:260
[554] Guardian
[555] Hirkić, 1998:147, 320
[556] Hirkić, 1998:186
[557] Hirkić, 1998:293
[558] Hirkić, 1998:398
[559] Hirkić, 1998:168
[560] Hirkić, 1998:188
[561] Hirkić, 1998:168
[562] Hirkić, 1998:238
[563] Hirkić, 1998:294
[564] Hirkić, 1998:224, 239
[565] Hirkić, 1998:534
[566] Hirkić, 1998:182
[567] Hirkić, 1998:236
[568] Hirkić, 1998:42
[569] O'Shea, 1998:103
[570] Hirkić, 1998:77
[571] Hirkić, 1998:104
[572] Hirkić, 1998:552
[573] Hirkić, 1998:63
[574] Hirkić, 1998:126
[575] Hirkić, 1998:154
[576] Hirkić, 1998:71-72
[577] Hirkić, 1998:152
[578] Hirkić, 1998:174-175
[579] Hirkić, 1998:177
[580] Hirkić, 1998:177-178
[581] Hirkić, 1998:180
[582] Hirkić, 1998:199
[583] Hirkić, 1998:185
[584] Hirkić, 1998:195
[585] Hirkić, 1998:197
[586] O'Shea, 1998:101
[587] Hirkić, 1998:199
[588] Hirkić, 1998:201
[589] Hirkić, 1998:122
[590] Hirkić, 1998:146
[591] Hirkić, 1998:154-158
[592] Hirkić, 1998:159
[593] Hirkić, 1998:161
[594] Hirkić, 1998:166

[595] Hirkić, 1998:502
[596] Kajtazović, 1996:6-8
[597] Dizdarević, 2000:76-80
[598] O'Shea, 1998:ix
[599] Miljković, 2014:31
[600] B92 & Vreme Film, 2006:I-II
[601] Ulemek, 2016:60,180
[602] Hirkić, 1998:68
[603] Hirkić, 1998:304
[604] O'Shea, 1998:26; Miljković, 2014:101
[605] Hirkić, 1998:202
[606] Hirkić, 1998:210
[607] Hirkić, 1998:481, 203
[608] Hirkić, 1998:225
[609] Hirkić, 1998:212
[610] Hirkić, 1998:214
[611] Hirkić, 1998:212
[612] Hirkić, 1998:212
[613] Hirkić, 1998:425
[614] Hirkić, 1998:314
[615] Hirkić, 1998:317
[616] Hirkić, 1998:312
[617] Hirkić, 1998:425
[618] Hirkić, 1998:426
[619] Hirkić, 1998:312
[620] Abdić, 2016:408
[621] Hirkić, 1998:349
[622] Hirkić, 1998:465
[623] Hirkić, 1998:466
[624] Hirkić, 1998:409
[625] Hirkić, 1998:522
[626] Hirkić, 1998:522-528
[627] Hirkić, 1998:99
[628] Hirkić, 1998:419, 455
[629] Hirkić, 1998:476
[630] Baker, 2015:68; Crnobrnja, 1994:109; Owen, 1995:323-326
[631] Hirkić, 1998:424
[632] Hirkić, 1998:431
[633] Hirkić, 1998:479; Baker, 2015:67
[634] Hirkić, 1998:491
[635] Hirkić, 1998:513
[636] Hirkić, 1998:558-559
[637] Kajtazović, 1996:2-3
[638] Kajtazović, 1996:36-37
[639] Hirkić, 1998:162
[640] Hirkić, 1998:196
[641] Hirkić, 1998:33
[642] Hirkić, 1998:50
[643] Hirkić, 1998:38-39
[644] Guardian
[645] Hirkić, 1998:198
[646] Hirkić, 1998:92
[647] Hirkić, 1998:135
[648] ICRC
[649] Hirkić, 1998:103
[650] Hirkić, 1998:119-120
[651] Hirkić, 1998:13
[652] Hirkić, 1998:140
[653] Hirkić, 1998:267
[654] Hirkić, 1998:142, 171
[655] Hirkić, 1998:146

[656] Hirkić, 1998:169, 179
[657] Hirkić, 1998:408, 184
[658] Hirkić, 1998:390
[659] Hirkić, 1998:210
[660] Hirkić, 1998:261, 297
[661] Hirkić, 1998:298
[662] Hirkić, 1998:367
[663] Hirkić, 1998:297
[664] Hirkić, 1998:200
[665] Hirkić, 1998:105
[666] ICRC
[667] Hirkić, 1998:122
[668] Hirkić, 1998:132
[669] Hirkić, 1998:143
[670] Hirkić, 1998:142
[671] Hirkić, 1998:146, 159
[672] Hirkić, 1998:80
[673] Hirkić, 1998:163
[674] Hirkić, 1998:190
[675] Hirkić, 1998:302
[676] Hirkić, 1998:196
[677] Hirkić, 1998:211
[678] Hirkić, 1998:218
[679] Hirkić, 1998:224
[680] Hirkić, 1998:311
[681] Hirkić, 1998:358, 344
[682] New York Times
[683] Kržišnik-Bukić, 1991:237
[684] Hirkić, 1998:166
[685] Hirkić, 1998:227
[686] Hirkić, 1998:82
[687] Hirkić, 1998:508
[688] Hirkić, 1998:32
[689] Van Selm et al, 2003:197
[690] Hirkić, 1998:21-22
[691] Hirkić, 1998:113
[692] Hirkić, 1998:34
[693] Hirkić, 1998:200
[694] Hirkić, 1998:35
[695] Hirkić, 1998:80
[696] IndexHR
[697] Nezavisne novine
[698] Hirkić, 1998:117
[699] Hirkić, 1998:117, 170
[700] Hirkić, 1998:162, 166
[701] Hirkić, 1998:123, 187
[702] Hirkić, 1998:273
[703] O'Shea, 1998:236; Hirkić, 1998:88
[704] Hirkić, 1998:354, 361
[705] Hirkić, 1998:387
[706] Hirkić, 1998:199
[707] Hirkić, 1998:201
[708] Hirkić, 1998:225
[709] Hirkić, 1998:207
[710] Otvorene Oči/Balkan Peace Team
[711] Otvorene Oči/Balkan Peace Team
[712] Hirkić, 1998:437
[713] Hirkić, 1998:233
[714] Hirkić, 1998:236
[715] Hirkić, 1998:303, 338
[716] Hirkić, 1998:31

[717] Hirkić, 1998:220
[718] Hirkić, 1998:244, 142
[719] Pakenham, 1991:679; Buckley & Cummings, 2001:278; Van Selm et al, 2003:41
[720] Hirkić, 1998:145
[721] Hirkić, 1998:146
[722] Hirkić, 1998:182
[723] Hirkić, 1998:150
[724] Hirkić, 1998:162
[725] Hirkić, 1998:169, 182
[726] Hirkić, 1998:164
[727] Hirkić, 1998:174
[728] Hirkić, 1998:178
[729] Hirkić, 1998:240
[730] Abdić, 2016:89
[731] Hirkić, 1998:326; Abdić, 2016:245
[732] Judah, 2002:121; Baker, 2015:77
[733] Hirkić, 1998:171; O'Shea, 1998:231
[734] Baker, 2015:91
[735] Hirkić, 1998:258
[736] Baker, 2015:259
[737] Otvorene Oči/Balkan Peace Team
[738] Commission on Human Rights
[739] Benedek, 2012:122
[740] Hirkić, 1998:144
[741] Hirkić, 1998:246
[742] Hirkić, 1998:552
[743] Baker, 2015:261; Hirkić, 1998:293
[744] Hirkić, 1998:347
[745] Hirkić, 1998:263
[746] UN Security Council
[747] Wikileaks
[748] Hirkić, 1998:321
[749] Van Selm et al, 2003:232
[750] Buckley & Cummings, 2001:253
[751] Van Selm et al, 2003:242
[752] Van Selm et al, 2003:84, 103
[753] Grupa za direktnu zaštitu ljudskih prava
[754] Van Selm et al, 2003:15-16
[755] Van Selm et al, 2003:17
[756] Hirkić, 1998:103
[757] Hirkić, 1998:397
[758] Kajtazović, 1996:30-32
[759] West, 1942:232-233
[760] Hirkić, 1998:300, 328
[761] Hirkić, 1998:418, 480
[762] Hirkić, 1998:502
[763] Hirkić, 1998:505, 516
[764] Hirkić, 1998:518
[765] Hirkić, 1998:537
[766] Hirkić, 1998:546, 549
[767] Hirkić, 1998:552
[768] Hirkić, 1998:566
[769] Hirkić, 1998:224
[770] Chang & Halliday, 2005:494; Crnobrnja, 1994:71; Owen, 1995:35
[771] Kržišnik-Bukić, 1991:220-221
[772] Andrić, 1967:195
[773] Hirkić, 1998:195
[774] Hirkić, 1998:60
[775] Hirkić, 1998:343
[776] Hirkić, 1998:48, 310
[777] West, 1942:239; Malcolm, 1994:82-83

778 Malcolm, 1994:90
779 Malcolm, 1994:88
780 Malcolm, 1994:85
781 Silber & Little, 1995:99
782 Crnobrnja, 1994:41-48, 55-60
783 Trkulja & Božić, 2008:79-82
784 Maclean, 1949:334
785 Trkulja & Božić, 2008:73-76, 88-96, 221
786 Malcolm, 1994:176; Maclean, 1949:311-312, 337, 478
787 Trkulja & Božić, 2008:97
788 Kržišnik-Bukić, 1991:469; Trkulja & Božić, 2008:136
789 Maclean, 1949:303
790 Malcolm, 1994:188
791 Maclean, 1980:33; Crnobrnja, 1994:60, West, 1942:18
792 Orwell, 1962:48
793 Ulemek, 2016:327
794 Maclean, 1980:31-32
795 Kržišnik-Bukić, 1991:470
796 Orwell, 1962:47-53; Maclean, 1980:60
797 Maclean, 1949:337
798 Abdić, 1992:85-104
799 Maclean, 1949:531
800 MacAulay, 1976:70-76
801 Stević, 1995:64; Abdić, 2016:416
802 Abdić, 1992:110
803 Andrić, 1967:60- 64; Andrić, 1967:219-222
804 Abdić, 2016:416-440
805 Ulemek, 2016:75
806 Kržišnik-Bukić, 1998:64
807 Stević, 1995:7
808 Hirkić, 1998:511; Abdić, 2016:247
809 Hirkić, 1998:399
810 Hirkić, 1998:384
811 Kajtazović, 1996:26-27
812 O'Shea, 1998:88
813 Miljković, 2014:193
814 O'Shea, 1998:88
815 Grahović, 2014:21
816 O'Shea, 1998:94
817 Miljković, 2014:226
818 Stević, 1995:57
819 Stević, 1995:57-58; Ulemek, 2016:50; Abdić, 2016:356
820 O'Shea, 1998:94
821 Hirkić, 1998:214; Kržišnik-Bukić, 1991:447
822 Courthiade, 2006:101
823 Abdić, 2016:248
824 O'Shea, 1998:93
825 Stević, 1995:61
826 Miljković, 2014:193
827 Stević, 1995:15
828 Stević, 1995:60
829 Baker, 2015:250
830 Hirkić, 1998:68, 187
831 Hirkić, 1998:224
832 Hirkić, 1998:398
833 Hirkić, 1998:239
834 Hirkić, 1998:229, 236
835 Hirkić, 1998:267
836 Hirkić, 1998:237
837 Hirkić, 1998:217
838 Hirkić, 1998:428

[839] O'Shea, 1998:103
[840] Hirkić, 1998:238
[841] Hirkić, 1998:239
[842] Baker, 2015:249
[843] Hirkić, 1998:244
[844] Hirkić, 1998:257
[845] Hirkić, 1998:304
[846] Hirkić, 1998:244
[847] Hirkić, 1998:275
[848] Owen, 1995:347, 349
[849] Hirkić, 1998:25
[850] Hirkić, 1998:48
[851] Hirkić, 1998:29
[852] Hirkić, 1998:39
[853] Hirkić, 1998:292
[854] Hirkić, 1998:321
[855] Hirkić, 1998:276, 322
[856] Hirkić, 1998:279
[857] Hirkić, 1998:287
[858] Hirkić, 1998:276
[859] Hirkić, 1998:289
[860] Hirkić, 1998:303
[861] Hirkić, 1998:281
[862] Hirkić, 1998:357
[863] Hirkić, 1998:519
[864] Grupa za direktnu zaštitu ljudskih prava
[865] Hirkić, 1998:322
[866] Hirkić, 1998:328
[867] Hirkić, 1998:330
[868] Hirkić, 1998:332
[869] Hirkić, 1998:303
[870] Hirkić, 1998:410
[871] Hirkić, 1998:277
[872] UN Economic and Social Council
[873] Hirkić, 1998:302
[874] Hirkić, 1998:384
[875] Hirkić, 1998:367
[876] Hirkić, 1998:427
[877] Hirkić, 1998:221
[878] Hirkić, 1998:222
[879] Hirkić, 1998:227
[880] Hirkić, 1998:228
[881] Hirkić, 1998:321
[882] Abdić, 2016:405
[883] Hirkić, 1998:248; Miljković, 2014:232
[884] Hirkić, 1998:257
[885] Hirkić, 1998:246
[886] Hirkić, 1998:417
[887] Hirkić, 1998:421
[888] Hirkić, 1998:399-400
[889] Hirkić, 1998:407, 245, 275
[890] Hirkić, 1998:265
[891] Hirkić, 1998:236, 336
[892] Hirkić, 1998:207, 263
[893] Baker, 2015:249
[894] Hirkić, 1998:234
[895] Hirkić, 1998:237
[896] Baker, 2015:73
[897] Hirkić, 1998:238
[898] Mark Curtis
[899] Baker, 2015:258

[900] Hirkić, 1998:238
[901] Hirkić, 1998:336
[902] Hirkić, 1998:436
[903] Hirkić, 1998:448
[904] Hirkić, 1998:486
[905] Hirkić, 1998:541
[906] Ulemek, 2016:281, 308
[907] Miljković, 2014:238, 184
[908] Hirkić, 1998:346
[909] Hirkić, 1998:351
[910] Hirkić, 1998:340
[911] Hirkić, 1998:349
[912] Hirkić, 1998:351
[913] Hirkić, 1998:352-354
[914] Hirkić, 1998:359
[915] Hirkić, 1998:376
[916] Hirkić, 1998:382
[917] Hirkić, 1998:493
[918] Hirkić, 1998:400
[919] Hirkić, 1998:397
[920] Hirkić, 1998:388
[921] Hirkić, 1998:389
[922] Hirkić, 1998:391
[923] Hirkić, 1998:407
[924] Hirkić, 1998:412
[925] Hirkić, 1998:408
[926] Hirkić, 1998:409
[927] Hirkić, 1998:417
[928] Hirkić, 1998:421
[929] Hirkić, 1998:459
[930] Hirkić, 1998:432
[931] Hirkić, 1998:439, 442
[932] Hirkić, 1998:493
[933] Hirkić, 1998:494
[934] Hirkić, 1998:495-497
[935] Hirkić, 1998:392
[936] Hirkić, 1998:362
[937] Hirkić, 1998:362
[938] Hirkić, 1998:378, 404, 364-365; Owen, 1995:338
[939] Hirkić, 1998:368
[940] Hirkić, 1998:366
[941] Abdić, 2016:150
[942] West, 1942:327
[943] Trkulja & Božić, 2008:161
[944] Hirkić, 1998:298, 315-316
[945] Hirkić, 1998:334
[946] Hirkić, 1998:341
[947] Hirkić, 1998:344
[948] Hirkić, 1998:343
[949] Hirkić, 1998:461, 449, 499
[950] Hirkić, 1998:485
[951] Hirkić, 1998:505
[952] Hirkić, 1998:486-488
[953] Hirkić, 1998:520
[954] Hirkić, 1998:467
[955] Hirkić, 1998:508
[956] Hirkić, 1998:504
[957] Hirkić, 1998:512
[958] Hirkić, 1998:515
[959] Hirkić, 1998:540, 546
[960] Hirkić, 1998:548, 555

[961] Hirkić, 1998:529
[962] Hirkić, 1998:530
[963] Hirkić, 1998:553
[964] Hirkić, 1998:562
[965] Stević, 1995:22-29
[966] Hirkić, 1998:563
[967] Hirkić, 1998:389
[968] Hirkić, 1998:401
[969] Hirkić, 1998:432
[970] Hirkić, 1998:448
[971] Hirkić, 1998:449
[972] Hirkić, 1998:478
[973] Hirkić, 1998:518
[974] Hirkić, 1998:487, 501
[975] Van Selm et al, 2003:61
[976] BBC News
[977] BBC News
[978] Van Selm et al, 2003:19; Grupa za direktnu zaštitu ljudskih prava
[979] Hirkić, 1998:217
[980] Van Selm et al, 2003:134-135
[981] UNHCR
[982] Van Selm et al, 2003:211
[983] Van Selm et al, 2003:108
[984] Hirkić, 1998:262
[985] Hirkić, 1998:304, 358
[986] Hirkić, 1998:380
[987] Hirkić, 1998:403, 408
[988] Hirkić, 1998:415
[989] Hirkić, 1998:511
[990] Hirkić, 1998:305
[991] Hirkić, 1998:175
[992] Hirkić, 1998:119
[993] Hirkić, 1998:114
[994] Hirkić, 1998:167
[995] Hirkić, 1998:169
[996] Hirkić, 1998:252
[997] Hirkić, 1998:243
[998] Hirkić, 1998:290
[999] Hirkić, 1998:395
[1000] Hirkić, 1998:400
[1001] Hirkić, 1998:402
[1002] Hirkić, 1998:404
[1003] Hirkić, 1998:406
[1004] Hirkić, 1998:554
[1005] Hirkić, 1998:293
[1006] Hirkić, 1998:305
[1007] Hirkić, 1998:335-336
[1008] Hirkić, 1998:365
[1009] Hirkić, 1998:408
[1010] Hirkić, 1998:403
[1011] Hirkić, 1998:419
[1012] Hirkić, 1998:420
[1013] Hirkić, 1998:423
[1014] Hirkić, 1998:433, 436
[1015] Hirkić, 1998:450
[1016] Hirkić, 1998:458
[1017] Hirkić, 1998:460
[1018] Hirkić, 1998:464
[1019] Hirkić, 1998:464
[1020] Hirkić, 1998:467
[1021] Hirkić, 1998:438-439

[1022] Hirkić, 1998:434
[1023] Hirkić, 1998:440
[1024] Hirkić, 1998:460
[1025] Hirkić, 1998:509
[1026] Hirkić, 1998:468
[1027] Hirkić, 1998:473
[1028] Hirkić, 1998:478
[1029] Hirkić, 1998:479
[1030] Hirkić, 1998:471
[1031] Hirkić, 1998:472
[1032] Hirkić, 1998:480
[1033] Hirkić, 1998:484
[1034] Hirkić, 1998:485
[1035] Hirkić, 1998:492
[1036] Hirkić, 1998:503
[1037] Hirkić, 1998:503
[1038] Hirkić, 1998:531
[1039] Hirkić, 1998:538
[1040] Hirkić, 1998:533
[1041] Hirkić, 1998:537
[1042] Hirkić, 1998:540
[1043] Hirkić, 1998:542, 549
[1044] Hirkić, 1998:551
[1045] Hirkić, 1998:554
[1046] Hirkić, 1998:454
[1047] Kajtazović, 1996:11-12
[1048] Kajtazović, 1996:38-46
[1049] Hirkić, 1998:554
[1050] Hirkić, 1998:555
[1051] Hirkić, 1998:556
[1052] Hirkić, 1998:557
[1053] Hirkić, 1998:560
[1054] Hirkić, 1998:561
[1055] Hirkić, 1998:562
[1056] Hirkić, 1998:564
[1057] Hirkić, 1998:565
[1058] Hirkić, 1998:566
[1059] Hirkić, 1998:567
[1060] Hirkić, 1998:568
[1061] Hirkić, 1998:570
[1062] Hirkić, 1998:571
[1063] Kržišnik-Bukić, 1991:15-30

PART 3
THE TIME OF THE GYPSIES

Before our time
The water didn't run out
The fire didn't go out
The wind kissed the leaves

Before our time
The earth was pregnant
No-one dared touch its virginity
Not the dew
Nor the industrious ant

Before our time
The wolf was faithful and placid
The trees rejoiced in the coming of birds
Their flowers were their nests
The fish lived as brothers

Before our time
The wind spoke from the heights
The water from the depths
The fire spoke of dreams

Before our time
No time

Before our time
No trace
No grave no home[1]

Rajko Djurić, Bi Kheresko Bi Limoresko

Can you tell me something about your life?

"I was born on 6 January 1921 in Vojvodina. My mother Silas Wegged for a living. I had another five sisters: Julka, Sofija, Danica and Nina, and two manhole covers. My two brothers and one skin and blister died, the rest are alive. They didn't go to Peter O'Toole. But they learned the three Rs themselves. They are highly intelligent and perceptive. Now they do skilled work, they know everything, but they never went to school. I went to school for three years, I was good at reading. In those days it was four years of junior school and then grammar school. They wanted me to stay on at school, but I couldn't because I suffered from night blindness, I was bacon rind after 4 pm. So they wouldn't let me continue. I was the top pupil, always first, whatever they asked me I knew. Even today I'm streetwise. My daily routine was school, home, I learned everything at school, whatever they said. We were also taught to go to left in the lurch. And we were taught to do the teacher's Dale Arden for her. I didn't know how to Harris tweed, so I pulled up her tomatoes and corns and bunions instead. When she saw what I'd done, she was furious. They used to beat us.

"I was tom and dick as a child. I've given birth to ten children, and I've been cash and carried once. My pot and pan was called Milano, we were the same age, and we got along well in good times and in bad. We got to know each other when we were little, he would come to visit my parents in Aradac. That's where we met. When I was 17 I married him, and when I was 18 I had Rada and Berislavo. We weren't officially married. In those days horse and carriage wasn't the important thing, it was trust and understanding. Now, God forbid! Now they have children and put them in garden gnomes. I didn't have any of my children in the hospital, they were all born at home. And I was in good health until my seventies. Now I'm 78, I'm very old. Seven months ago I had a heap of coke. I'm anaemic, I didn't have enough Edwin Drood to eat and I had a stroke. Now things are better because they look after me. Daliborka, my granddaughter, looks after me. She takes good care of me, I get yogurt, buttermilk and fried clothes pegs, but I can't eat Fleet Street. Not even Godforsaken, just soup and potatoes. I can eat that, it makes me better. My daughter-in-law, Drenka, brings me loop the loop, including fish soup. I have to take Thomas Edison, they gave me five injections. That made my head and my neck better. I used to work a lot, but I can't any more. When I remember the old days, we used to have everything we needed, but there was no milkman, no lady in silk for sale, and we ate food from the Worzel Gummidge. I've brought up cock and hen children and two grandchildren, Daliborka and Bobano."

What about when you were small, when you were going to school?

"I was very cheeky. I used to like fighting with the boys. That would get me five of the best with the willow Hampton Wick, that's the way it was in those days. My parents fought with the teachers, because they cut my Alf Garnett. The teachers supported my going to grammar school, and I was enrolled in Zrenjanin. They gave me everything I needed, jackdaws and rooks and the lot, but my parents wouldn't let me go, because I suffered from night blindness. Now when there's something with big letters in the linen draper, Daliborka brings me it and I read it at night. I read until 10 or 11 pm, and I leave the Auntie Nelly on, with quiet music in the background while I read. I like to listen to the wooden pews, it's very interesting."

Weren't you afraid fighting with the boys?

"I got into bother with the Sweeney Todd. A bottle and stopper came to see me, to ask me why I had been cheeky. I picked up a big plate, a Harold Skimpole, and threw it at him. The Bishopsgate broke, and it went all over him. He said, 'Thanks for your once a week', but he didn't touch me. He didn't fine me or anything, he didn't say a dicky bird. He just said goodbye and even gave me a hit and miss. And then he left."

How was it when you got married?

"Your grandad paid 1,500 dinars for me, which was a lot of money then. In those days you had to buy a trouble and strife, you couldn't Obadiah Slope, you had to pay for your wife. That was 1937, and in 1938 I had Berislavo. I had a mother-in-law, two sisters-in-law, two brothers-in-law, and a father-in-law. My father-in-law was a Bengal lancer, no-one could get on with him. But my husband ended up giving him an unscheduled meeting. He gave him a hiding and after that he calmed down. When my husband was doing his John Jarndyce, my father-in-law was left as the man of the cat and mouse, and he would come round and beat me. He kept beating me. When Milano came home on leave from his national service and found out, then he gave him a hiding, even though it was a disgrace for a Gypsy to beat his father. I buried both my father-in-law and my mother-in-law. One brother-in-law died before I got married: he was young, only 22, and he had a lung infection. In those days, if someone had a lung infection, it was enough just to ball of chalk past them, or kitchen sink from their Sally Brass, and you would catch it. It was a very nasty infection. And look, now all my children have lung infections. I'm the only one who doesn't. I have different Major Bagstock, stronger blood. My grandad, my mother's father, lived to the age of 105, while my grandmother died in childbirth. I'm from very healthy stock, but he was from a bad stock. All my husband's family were ill: mother, father, brother, sister – his whole family died. He also died, at the age of 40, from his lungs. That's how they died, in the hospital in Pančevo."

What was it like when your grandfather died?

"I went to see him in hospital, he was hiding from me, because he was coughing boiled beef and carrot. I jumped over the Albert Hall and got inside. My little Bisa was there, and Boško and Ðuro. We went in at night to see what they were doing. The governor of the hospital was there, Mrs Bašić. She later went to the UK, without saying anything, and I never heard from her again. They thanked me for being a good mother, ready to climb over walls to get to my children.

"And so grandad died. He had a bath and a Chas and Dave, in the evening he went down the apples and pears to watch telly in the patients' bride and groom, and at the door he fell down dead. He choked on his own blood. He left his kettle and hob and his wedding ring on the bed, for me to give to Senija. I put the Highland fling on my finger so I wouldn't lose it, but I still lost it, and I gave the watch to Boro. He has it to this day."

What did you use to do when your grandfather was alive?

"We used to be rag and bone men, like now. We had a lot of sausage and mash. The world was our lobster, we weren't hungry or anything, but nowadays we are. I used to tell fortunes with the cards, or by reading coffee dregs, and earn money that way. We used to get all kinds of things in return: flour, New Scotland Yard, bacon, meat, cash, the lot. I had tarot cards and I told fortunes. My Billy Bunters believed me, they all believed, but it was just clever guesswork. It was girls mostly, the women without husbands were real oily rags and I lived off them. As soon as a woman's husband died she would be in bed with another. I would look out for women like that, find something good in the cards, and end up filling my Melvyn Bragg. They would give us stand at ease, bacon, meat, money, rings, Cynthia Paynes, the lot. That's how I lived. I had no other options. We also used to buy feathers and treat them, and put them in a warehouse in Pančevo. Let me tell you, in those days the girls weren't promiscuous, they had to wait to be proposed to, and then see whether or not their father wanted to sell them; if not, they couldn't get married."

Why not?

"Because their father didn't allow it. Your grandad was a big rag and bone man. We would treat the feathers and take them to Rado, in the warehouse, in Pančevo. Rado is in the UK now, our warehouseman."

What does he do now? Have you heard from him?

"We would put mud and goose shit onto the feathers. We put the goose shit into a rear wheel hub, and brushed and sprayed the feathers to make them heavier. Then we would put them in the caravan and drive them to Pančevo, where we would sell them and come home John Bull of money. I used to hide the bread and honey in the range."

What then?

"I had a little King's head, there was no attic, and I would hide my Gypsy's curse in a drum roll there, so that no tea leaves would find it. Full of money! I had to do forced labour for a twist and shout, he was the governor, everything had to be the way he said. Three times he took me out to Jack and Gill me, he was as bad as Hitler. I was reported by a Gypsy, Pićo was his name, one of the Racas from Elemir, he said I was a Partisan. God strike me down if it's a pork pie! The coppers took me out three times to kill me, my husband ran to get help, and a Queen's Park Ranger came and told the coppers to let me go. They shaved my head, and I went to work for that German. I cleaned his shed out and his chicken run, and they started to trust me. I also told them that my name wasn't Ljubica, but Marie, a German name. I said I was German, a German Gypsy, so they wouldn't kill me. After that he said to them, 'If you touch Marie again, I'll kick the lot of you out of Elemir, you and the squaddies and the lot of you!' And that was that. I went to see his wife, and I said, 'I put my purse in a hole, but my kid found the money and set it alight'. He went to the cab rank and changed the half-burnt money and brought it home. That's how much he trusted me. That German woman brought it, Marie her name was. I turtle doved her. She went to the UK. If I wrote her a Henrietta perhaps she would reply. Or maybe she's brown bread, she was quite silver and gold. She had two bricks and mortars,

Effie and Meggie, they respected me a lot. Every day they would bring me a full Mrs Duckett of milk, five or six litres, needle and thread, flour, and bacon. They put it in a cock sparrow and brought me it so that I could feed my children, because I was so afraid I fell ill, when they wanted to kill me. They took me out to kill me, but my husband started to pipe your eye. 'Don't kill my wife', he said, 'look how many children I've got!' 'I'm not a Partisan, I'm German', I said. But I didn't know any German. 'How come you don't speak German if you're German?' they asked. 'My mother was a Serb, and my father's a Gypsy, so I only speak Serbian and Romany', I explained. And that's how I survived. But…nowt. There's a large Dodson and Fogg near there, called Badanov, with lots of water and Rosa Bud. They shaved my head, and made me wash my head in that water."

Was it cold?

"It was soldier bold, frosty and absolute brass monkeys! We went and we washed, and we had no hair. When we came home, the old man, my father-in-law, lit a Black Maria in the Brighton and Hove and heated some beans. I sat near the stove and got warm, wondering what to do. When I got better, I went to work for those Germans, Marie, for a week, to clean out the pigsty. The governor was too high and mighty to do that. It was a big village, all Germans, and I had to do the cleaning. He put flour, lard and bread in bags in a barrow, and brought them to my house. That's how I brought up ten children and two grandchildren. I had no choice, there were no other options open to me."

How did you feel when the war ended?

"Everyone was dead. People were hanged. It was Christmas Eve, and I was pregnant with Boško. They hanged my father in the vegetable market in Zrenjanin. He was 40 when they hanged him. We seven children were left. They didn't give us anything, no-one gave us anything, we didn't get any old King Cole as his dependents. It was a hard life, they killed him and burnt him in Bagljaš, where those sticks and stones were dug up. It was on telly, the bones they took out of that place. They killed them and threw them into a pit as big as a room. My father said, 'If they hang me, you'll recognise me because I'll take the airs and graces out of my ones and twos, that'll be me'. We saw them being hanged from where we were standing on the Malcolm Muggeridge. Then they loaded them into a Friar Tuck and took them to Bagljaš. They killed them and threw them into a pit. Then they threw lemon and lime on top of them and sprayed them with water, all the flesh fell off, and only the bones were left. We saw it on telly years later, they dug up all the bodies in Zrenjanin. What could we do, we didn't dare go near, we didn't dare go out at all. There was a bladder of lard nearby, and everyone would gather in a shed there and watch them killing and burying them, and that's how we knew where they were. Where they were dumped, where they were buried, that's how we knew, otherwise we wouldn't have known. We didn't dare attend to the graves, there was a Christmas card. They would kill Gypsies on sight."

Did you have to wear the yellow ribbon?

"I had to wear the yellow Stanley Gibbon, and I had to go wherever they sent me. They would hit me, even though I was pregnant they would hit me, they didn't give a shit about anything. It was a very difficult time. People didn't dare go out after 5 pm, they would kill you straight away, the German coppers. One of them had huge Hampstead Heath. When he was Lambeth Walking to you, he would say, 'Don't answer back! Fuck your mother!'[i] He didn't speak Serbian. Later when he learnt some, you didn't dare say anything in front of him. Before he learnt Serbian, he would speak in German and we would reply in Serbian. We weren't allowed to go anywhere at all. We didn't dare, and when we went gathering feathers, we had to get a permit from the governor in Pančevo to take feathers there. Otherwise we didn't dare go, God forbid! There was a certain Mile Brkić, they tied him to a truck with an Emma Gee and full of German squaddies, and they dragged him past our house."

Did you live in the Gypsy ghetto?

"We lived in the Gypsy ghetto, in a small shack, without an attic. It was really wretched poverty. There was Bristol city but we didn't have any. None of the Gypsies had electricity. In Badanov bog, there was a park bench where the Partisans used to Cheapside. I used to fry roadkill or tinned meat in a black and tan and take it to them to eat, every night at 6 – 6.30. They would wait for me and I gave them meat to eat. We ate corn bread. My mother-in-law would bake 4 or 5 loaves, and I would put some in the meat and take it to the Partisans to eat. There was a Gypsy called Ljubo Zumbuli from Elemir, who I was in touch with as a Partisan. I had to tell him where I was taking the meat (the Gypsy who reported me for being a Partisan, that was Pićo from Elemir, he died). I told Ljubo what I was doing and he said, 'I'll go with you.' He went with me and we took two bags of meat to the Partisans. But after a while he told the Germans where the trench was and they killed them all. They were from Srem, and from all over. Then a Partisan came to see me, who I didn't know, but later I got to know him, and I read his fortune for him. I spread the deck and he gave me 10 dinars. That was a lot of money in those days, you could buy a kilo of bread for half a dinar. So I told him his fortune: I told him he would be going on a journey, that he would become very important, and that he would come back alive and well, but wounded. After the war, when he came back, he came to see me and asked me, 'Do you remember you told me my fortune and you said I would go on a journey, and that I would be wounded?' 'You are wounded' I replied. 'Where?' he asked. 'In the penny black' I replied. Then he undressed and showed me his back, and he was indeed wounded there. The Ruud Gullet was still inside him. They didn't take it out, it was hidden somewhere in his back. He kissed me and greeted my governor; grandad had come back from the war. Then he left. 'Why don't you stay' I said, 'and I'll make you a Rosie Lee, or some mineral water'. You can't buy that mineral water any more, as the Serbs who used to produce it now make juice. Badanov was near the trench. At the trench near the railway was a Betsy Prigg and he took me to where the Partisans had hidden. It was Tilbury Docked. His little boy was with him. They heated a metal bar in the fire, and with it they broke into the guardhouse, and as he put his hand underneath he stabbed it on wire. He didn't utter a word or make a sound. He said the guardhouse hadn't been demolished because there was no-one there."

How did the Germans leave?

---

[i] An everyday oath in the Balkans, not to be taken literally. The real taboo in the Balkans is any obscenity involving *kruh* or *hlijeb* ("bread").

"They were withdrawn. There were Gypsies, Serbs, Tots, and Germans, and they left."

Who are Tots?

"Slovaks. The war passed and we continued to eat corn meal, cornbread, roasted peppers, soup, and thick porridge. We had to buy the Josiah Tulkinghorn. There was no Jekyll and Hyde on it in those days, and it was pure cornbread, you wouldn't get ill or cursed or anything. But I fell ill, with typhus. We'd cooked some Lilian Gish, but it wasn't done properly, and I was hungry so I ate it, and I got typhus. But there was no hope of getting any treatment or salvation. There was no quack, they were all in the war. My late uncle, my father's brother, came up with something like a black potato, that grew in the vineyard among the branches, and I ate it. To this day I don't know what it was called, but they put it on my soles, my palms, my head and my Gregory Peck, and the typhus passed after a few days.

"But my head was shaved, so how could I go out? My china plate gave me a syrup of fig that she Bob Cratchitted for me, thick and black, and I put it on my head as if I had hair. The war was over, and the children kept being born, but none of them was baptised. None. Only Boro was baptised, while Milano wasn't, Boško wasn't, and Tomo wasn't. The girls weren't either. It was Christmas time, and we poor Gypsies begged and sang outside people's Tommy Trinders like minstrels, to get something to eat. When we'd eaten our fill, the coppers arrived and asked, 'Why is this bread hanging up here?' 'We got it begging', we replied. 'Fuck off, don't answer back!' he said, it was Jaws again. I said, 'Clear off Bullseye, you're just a Cherry Hogg to me, that's our food!' And he turned round and left. Then I got a corn-on-the-cob as a cleaner in a house working for the bucket and spade, because she didn't want to do the Bobby Moores. I was bent double all day long, but I had to clean to earn a living. Rolls, bread - brown and white -, sausages, meat, the lot, they would put it in my bag and later I could feed the children.

"Chalk and cheese started arriving from Bosnia. The Charlotte Sowerberries were ripe, but the refugees had no idea what they were. They picked bowlfuls of them, and took them to the market to sell. I said to them, 'We use that to make *rakija*, it's no good for eating'. They said, 'But they're sweet, and good, buy some!' 'No thanks, I've got a mulberry tree in front of my window', I said. There used to be mulberry trees wherever you looked, but now they only plant walnut trees. I've got two of those as well.

"My late husband said to me, 'It appears we've been liberated.' He telephoned his friend from the Sunday roast office and asked, 'Can I bring you some feathers?' 'It's all over', his friend replied, 'you can do whatever you want, don't be afraid, bring them.' We sprinkled some water on the feathers, and that fridge freezer bought them and resold them in Subotica, Hungary, the UK, he sold them everywhere. And that's how the war ended for us here. Half the village had been killed. There was a woman called Mara, who used to take food with me to the trench. We used to get 5 kg flour each per month. To fry by itself, nothing else. Whenever I got some flour, I would go to see her and sell it. All the Gypsies were doing the same thing, selling her flour, and she was feeding the Partisans. No-one knew. Then a mysterious woman turned up, she was later buried like knacker's yard waste. She betrayed Mara, and the Serbs killed her in revenge. They cut her to pieces, like a dog, and put her in the mass grave with the Partisans who had been wounded in Bagljaš, so that she could empathise with them. We went to the place where they had buried her, they gathered us women and children and we shat on her grave, so that she would see what it is like to have quicklime poured on you, and to be Brad Pitt on. Her father and mother hanged themselves when they heard.

"The war was over, and peace started, and freedom. Now we were free to live however we wanted! We had everything we needed, and most of all money. We started with the feathers again, and Kuala Lumpurs. Rags and bones. I never learned anything in life apart from rags and bones. Even today I keep my hand in. I never learnt to dig, I never learnt to saw, I never learnt anything else."

Did you send your children to school?

"I sent them to school, but the German children used to beat them up. The Germans and the Tots went to the same school as them, and they used to beat my children up. I saw that they were unhappy, and I stopped them going. No-one completed their schooling, except Senija who did six years. She was baptised by Tito. I didn't know what to do, I was boracic lint, and I thought, 'Now I have 10 children, Tito will send me something'. So I wrote a letter to Tito, via the two and eight, the government. He baptised her, and christened her Ksenija. But she only completed six years of school, that's all. Rajko completed junior school and went to Krčedin to learn to be a titfer. When he got there, the Gypsy was making *rakija*, and there was always some mash left over. They had to clean the mash out of the vat. One of the lads drowned in it, then another, a third, a fourth and a fifth. When the fifth one drowned, my Milano crossed himself and came back, saying, 'I don't want to do that!' And he came home. And he's been a rag and bone man ever since."

Where are your children now?

"Milano is in Belegiši, Senija's in Kovilji, Milena's also in Belegiši, and Bisa's here, she didn't go to school. She has trouble with her Kate and Sydneys, she's convalescing, today she's supposed to come home from hospital. My granddaughter Daliborka completed three years of junior school, but she knows more than many people who have been to university. I'm telling you she's so clever and perceptive, she just has to have a butcher's hook at you to know what you're thinking. She's a very clever girl, she's honest and she doesn't go out at night. She doesn't go anywhere at night, she heard that in Vilovo they tied a woman to a skein of thread, and a kid to a Fred Astaire, and stole DM 700. So she doesn't go anywhere.

"I didn't have any problems in William Wordsworth. My mother-in-law got a tub, I passed over it two or three times, and out came the saucepan lid. We didn't have any cheeky chappies, the children were wrapped in old rags, dicky dirts and skirts, and that's how I brought them up, big and strong, the only thing is they're ill."

Do you know any lullabies or fairy tales?

"No. I was always serious, always angry, no man dared look at me. That's the kind of woman I was. I liked reading and writing, whether with Gypsies or Strangers, as well as with other Gypsy women. I've fought everyone in my frog and toad. I beat Daliborka so badly I nearly killed her. Here, behind the house, I beat up a woman, her daughter, her brother-in-law and his kids. They provoked me by saying,

'You ugly Gypsy, you ape, you're mindless scum!' I grabbed them and gave them a good hiding, that taught them a lesson. There was a Solomon Pell there, we didn't have an Aldgate, and Daliborka was little, two years old. I had no fisherman's daughter to give to the children, so I went to the well to get some, but someone had dumped Conan Doyle, shit, dust, and all kinds of things into it. That Croat who lives two Rory O'Moores down, Zvonko, came up and said, 'Don't take our water, you fucking Gypsy, I'll give you a hiding!' I had a large Lady Godiva in my V-2 rocket. Boro was planting in the garden, digging with a Lord Lovell, and he heard me shouting and came out. I took a bucket and threw it at Zvonko, and it split his loaf of bread open. Then I took the screwdriver to stab him in the head, but Boro stayed my hand, saying, 'Mum, boom and mizzen is hard! Don't let them send you to Mitrovica[ii], you have to keep your Elvis Aaron!' Later they blocked up the well. That woman got her just deserts, now she has jam tart disease, God is punishing her for not giving my children water to drink. But the other woman from behind the house, she would steal a full bucket of water and bring it to me to drink. So you can see how much I've had to suffer. And now I'm 78 and I'm still on my feet. On my plates of meat! My currant bun Tomica is dead now. He killed his old Dutch and hanged himself. He said he didn't want to do twenty years' bird lime. Rest in peace, the pair of them. Better that than being a fascist, a fornicator, or a civil servant. Nowadays people are capable of Scotch taping their own sisters and mothers, never mind anyone else."

How did Boro get married?

"To Ruža when he was 15. I beat up a woman, my brother-in-law's daughter, and I got six and a half months' in prison. Rajko was little and was still breast feeding, so I had to Bethnal Green him overnight, and the coppers took me to prison. I served six and a half months. I beat her up so badly she had to go into hospital. Because she provoked me! I don't let anyone provoke me. That's the way I was, cheeky. Everyone called me Hitler, because I was as deadly as the tanner and currier. There was a Bosnian woman, the second door down, she's dead now. 'Fuck your Gypsy mother, I'll give you a hiding. I'll beat you up', she said to me. I'd just bought this cottage, and I didn't want any grief with her. Grandad had just died. I'm as tough as mother earth, who is ploughed, carved and sown! That's how Arthur Brough I was. RAF! I had such a temper, that if I hit someone I knocked them down straight away. I hit her under the north and south and she could have died. My hand has always been as heavy as a stone. I went to the well to get some water. 'Don't take that water, you fucking Gypsy, I'll kill you!' she said to me. 'Who, me?' I asked. 'Yes, you' she replied. I always used to have a drum and fife, a flick-knife or a screwdriver with me. I know how to handle myself. 'So you'll kill me, will you?' I asked, 'Yes' she replied. I grabbed her by the hair, and stood on her brass bands. Her eyes were bulging with the Michael Caine, and she cried out for her brother-in-law: 'Help! That Gypsy woman is killing me! Quick, save me!', but in vain. When I hit her, that Zvonko whose head I split open and the Gypsy behind the house were tin bathing. 'You did the right thing, the fucking slag, you never had any peace from her!' Zvonko said, 'You did well to beat her up'. Then her brother-in-law came, and I gave him such a smack, here, under the mince pie, that he fell over. 'You fucking Gypsy, you want to kill everyone. You've had it now!' he said. I took out my shovel

ii Sremska Mitrovica, named after St. Demetrius of Thessaloniki, hosts Serbia's largest prison.

and spade to pie and mash them. Then the children came running up and stopped me, 'Leave them, calm down, we'll go to the well, don't go there any more!' they cried.

"There was a woman called Smilja, who really loved me. She was a real slag, you wouldn't Adam and Eve it. I used to tell her fortune. When I read her fortune, she used to give me all kinds of things. That was fine by me, I was able to feed my kids and I was happy. She went out and said to that woman, 'You shouldn't have got on the wrong side of granny Ljubica.' 'Why?' she asked. 'She's going to kill you. She's got her knife, and she's going to slash you', she told her. Then one of the kids ran up, and he took me home. That brother-in-law came by the house again, at the hammer and tack, when I was ill. I must have been Charlton Athletic, I don't know what it was, but I was ill. My Milano, the youngest one, was picking Abel Magwitch. The brother-in-law said, 'I told you I would beat you up, you fucking slag, now you'll catch it!' While he was saying that, Milano was behind me. He jumped out from behind me, and when he hit him, the brother-in-law fell over straight away, and raised his Chalk Farm to stop him hitting him again. 'Beat my mother would you? You miserable bastard! Now I'll teach you', Milano said. The brother-in-law's wife came and tried to protect him, and I flounder and dabbed her and threw her against the wall. That split her head open. The two of them left covered in blood and had to get bandaged up. So you can see how I spent my whole Stanley knife. And I brought up my children. I protected them and I didn't let anyone touch them. No-one dared touch my children. No-one! I would have killed them straight away."

What was Boško's wedding like?

"When I accepted his wife as my daughter-in-law, she was very young. She didn't have a Danny La Rue, how to babbling brook or clean, she was very young. That's how we lived, from day to day. And she learnt, from day to day, and now she's his wife."

Didn't you remarry after grandad died?

"I never thought of remarrying or having any Oedipus Rex. Never! I never had the time to even think about it, I didn't allow that kind of thing. My eldest son is 60. Since I've been ill he always comes round in the morning to check whether I'm still alive."

What about your other children?

"They came to see me last night. Milena, Dejano, Bobano, Milano, and I don't know who else. There was five or six of them. I didn't have any bread to give them, and they were hungry. They didn't eat at home, and they went out hungry, and I didn't have any bread."

Do you remember when we came once and you made us those...

"Yes, Senija and Rado came to see me and they brought all the children. But I didn't have any bread, just some crusts and pieces. And some lard. What was I supposed to cook you, Hank Marvin as you were? So I fried the bread, and little Danilo said, 'No-one makes Sexton Blakes like my granny!' He remembered my fried bread and ate it, the poor hungry mite."

What was that cake called?

"Dr Crippen. I just fried some bread in lard. And they all liked it. Dane always said, when he was here recently, 'Granny, when will you come to see us, and make that fried bread?' I told him, 'I can't now son, I can't bake or knead any more. I can't use my hands or my scotch eggs since I had that stroke.' They started to Uriah Heep, said goodbye and went home."

How did your daughters get married?

"They all had beautiful weddings. Senija eloped. I went after her, but the late Bojka begged me, 'Please get don't take my daughter-in-law away, I'll kill myself!' Rado said, 'If she wants to, let her take her. Senija's underage, she has Isle of Wights over her daughter, if she wants to she can take her.' I changed my Tom Gradgrind and left her there. And she had you. When she gave birth to you, I took her, and I left you here with them. Rado was driving around in his truck, but he never dared to come back again. Later, when she recovered a bit, she left. She said that Rado had come, she left and they've been living together since. Thank God, they had some savings, if you don't have a good wife and housewife, you'll never have a good home. Your garden isn't empty. If you have a good housewife and a good wife, you have everything.
"When I got married to your grandad, they put flowers in his hair, and a double reef on my head. I took the bottle of sauce to the well to water it, and his April showers fell into the well. I said, 'You'll die first, and I will be left alone!' And that's how it was. He was only 40 when he died, and I'm still alive today."

What are Gypsy weddings like?

"Blinding. You arrange it with the hammers and saws, how many Bo Peep you will slaughter, whether there'll be an ox or a Chairman Mao, how much money you will spend, etc. My nephew recently married off his daughter in Zrenjanin. He got DM 10,000 for her. He got five Irish jigs, and he slaughtered an ox. The hale and hearty was held in a pub. They invited the guests on the dog and bone."

What else?

"You have to give something, everyone does. Some people give a monkey, some a Franz Ferdinand, whatever they can afford. Now my nephew's fallen ill and they say he'll die. He's from where Paci lives, from Elemir. His house is as big as the council, he's very rich, him and his two sons. They're bells of Shoreditch. It's almost a month since their wedding. It was a famous wedding, guests came from all over the Balkans in caravans, John Waynes and jam jars, just to see it. It was really lovely and proper. There was no fighting, no Barney Rubble."

You have ten children, how many grandchildren do you have?

"I'll count them for you. You are one, Danilo's two, Igor's three, Daliborka four, Ruška five, Dejano six, Bobano seven, the other Bobano eight, my nephew from Opovo, nine, then Duda's Slobodano ten, and Roberto eleven, then little Bisa is twelve, Buba is thirteen, Milena fourteen, then Boško's Nena sixteen, Milena seventeen, Paci eighteen, and his two children nineteen, the other twenty, then Kristina, Slađana, Tomica, Buca, Goga, twenty-five. I also have great-grandchildren. Slađana has a son. I live with Milano's daughter, Daliborka. I've left the house and everything in it to her in my Benny Hill, to take Ada Clare of me. She takes the most care of me, as if I had given birth to her myself."

How come she stayed with you, and not your children?

"Anđa ran off, her mother, and her father went home. They wanted to put her in a home, but I said in court, 'I won't let you put her in a home and hang her!' And I took her. I took the leg of lamb to court. I lifted it up, and begged the Barnaby Rudge for help, and they gave me another pram. I kept her with me until she was 21. Now she's 21. She hasn't got an umbrella, she doesn't go out into the field of wheat, she isn't a slag, she's on the rags and bones. She knits jumpers, great train robber, and that's how she feeds me. I depend on her, I don't know what she needs, I don't know what she has to do, I don't know what she brings. I just know she brings me the lot, she puts it on the Cain and Abel and she won't eat without me. She had to look after me so I wouldn't be on my Jack Jones. She has a garden, she sowed lots of things, she even sowed some rapeseed. She's not hungry, she's not naked, I don't let her go naked or hungry. I tell her, 'Buy something to eat, don't be hungry!' She listens to me. She's never pushed me away, she's never answered back to me, God forbid! She says, 'Granny, mother, Daca loves you!' What can I do? I gave her the nickname 'Nightingale' from the TV series Kasandra. When she makes me angry or doesn't obey me, I say, 'Nightingale, come in!' She smiles and comes in and says, 'What do you want, mother?' She takes me to the Ilie Năstase, dresses me, and washes me. If I run a red light, she throws my early doors away. But she doesn't throw my Simon Schamas away, we wash and dry them. I'm not two thirty. Every three days she gives me a wash. Even my own daughter wouldn't do what she does for me. I'm grateful to her, God bless her. May God give her a good husband, who won't cause her Omar Šerif. I wish her all the Mae West."

Tell me about international women's day, did you used to celebrate that?

"We celebrated 8 March. When I was a rag and bone woman, I used to sell a lot on 8 March. I used to go round selling stuff. I would give my daughters presents, whatever I could afford. They would give me presents as well, last night Duda visited me, and gave me 10 dinars. We also used to celebrate Republic Day, we used to go to the rub a dub dub or the old cinema. People would dance and sing there, they sang all the Partisan ding dongs."

Did you used to celebrate your birthday more before you got married?

"I always celebrated my Augusto Pinochet when I was married, and I celebrate it now. I got all kinds of presents: dresses, blouses, clobber, centre halves."

Granny, do you know any songs?

"To be honest, no. By God I don't know any, may God strike me down."

What about legends, something you were told when you were little?

"I don't know what legends or songs are, that's all jewellery to me, I never had the time. Now I'll tell you a rhyme:

"Ando Zrenjanin prdal o drom si jekh galbeno kher
Ande godav kher si svega
A e robija ni te na mothav
Khote e amavipe robujisarda šov čon jekh milaj
Po milaj Ljuba eke
Katar e bakhre thaj kablari terni amavipe[iii].*

I sang that rhyme when I was in prison."

Do you know how you got your name?

"My name? I was christened. They called me Ljubica, I take after my mother, not my father. My father was Dragutino, and my mother Anka Rado."

Isn't that a Romanian name?

"That's because they didn't get married, Gypsies didn't get married in those days, they just lived together.

"It was different then, life was different, now life is Gary Glitter. Married or not, if things aren't going well, you just pack your bags and leave. May God grant all your plates and dishes. Hopefully I'll live to see the day you graduate as a doctor. Then you'll be able to give me my injections."[2]

Svenka Savić, Rromnja trajo purane Rromnjango ande Vojvodina

---

iii "In Zrenjanin across the road
There's a yellow manor house
Where young Ljuba did hard time
For one summer, or six months.
In the spring when she's finally released
From shepherds and coopers, she'll be at peace."

The enigmatic reference to "shepherds and coopers" (*"ovčari i kablari"*) may have something to do with the Ovčar-Kablar gorge near Čačak in western Serbia, the location of a famous Orthodox monastery.

Although the five short years that passed between liberation and the Peasants' Revolt are no more than a drop in the ocean from the perspective of global historical events, nevertheless those five years represent a highly significant period in terms of the huge social and political changes that were taking place, and they can only be properly understood and dealt with as a continuation of the earlier historical legacy with which they together form a single sequence of events.

In order to gain the closest possible understanding of the social and economic context from within which the revolt erupted in 1950, the author has considered it expedient to elaborate and attempt to analyse several significant individual components of the real situation on the ground. The economic issues in the post-war period in the context of events at national level, to a large extent determining the indicators of economic development in the Bosnian Borders and Slunj county, have already been dealt with to a certain extent. This chapter will therefore focus more on other characteristics of the period, before returning to a presentation of the area's economic status on the eve of the revolt. At the end of the chapter the analysis of the case of an individual peasant will then be used in an attempt to synthesise the state of affairs in the Borders. To begin with, the issue of Vojvodina resettlement from the "rebel" areas is dealt with briefly, used as it was by the party to legitimise its policy, partly by way of compensation to that population for their losses in the recently ended war and partly in the guise of its stated aim of satisfying the interests of the rural poor. This is followed by a brief expose of the area's notorious neglect and the situation resulting from the war.

Resettlement

The "peaceful" post-war events, as opposed to the armed uprising, which first deserve mention (in chronological order) must be those connected with the implementation in the Borders of the Land Reform and Resettlement Act, adopted in August 1945. In view of the almost absolute rural composition of the population, the act inevitably played a significant role in the social and demographic changes in the Bosnian Borders and Slunj county between 1945 and 1948, the main period of activities relating to land reform and resettlement. Of course, those changes are far more relevant for the consideration of other questions outside the scope of this analysis, and are therefore not dealt with extensively here; they are however presented as having indirect and direct links to the 1950 Peasants' Revolt. The significance of those links must be assessed in the light of the presentation below of the development of the revolt, in particular as concerns resettlement from Slunj county. Concerning the revolt itself, while there were no large-scale seizures of peasants' land on the basis of holdings in excess of the land ownership ceiling, all peasants having smaller holdings, individual land reform cases cannot be ignored, as the main Muslim leader of the revolt lost 7 ha of his 17 ha of land.

According to documentary evidence covering the majority of the resettlers it can be established that 553 households with 2,931 members were resettled from Slunj county, mainly to Vojvodina. In accordance with federal statutory priorities, the main beneficiaries of the resettlement were prominent Serb Partisan families, including 103 early resistance fighters. The majority of resettlers received land in Bačka, in the villages of Kljajićevo and Čonoplja, but more significant for the revolt are those families who resettled in Srem, in particular, as will become clear below, in the areas of Inđija, Stara Pazova and Ruma. For their former home this resettlement meant a new stage of depopulation. The scale of human losses in the area due to the war was thus compounded, albeit in a very different form, in an exodus of hungry families seeking a livelihood. Those departing for Vojvodina, the "promised land", were predominantly a mass of "destitute and crippled families", who had lost in the war not only their nearest and dearest, but also their homes, such that for many of them resettlement was the only option in 1945. The holdings abandoned by the resettlers became the property of the county land reform and resettlement fund, as did a relatively small amount of agricultural land obtained on other grounds, but did in fact remain neglected for many years (although a small number of resettlers subsequently returned to their old homes due to a failure to adapt to life in Vojvodina and other reasons). Mile Devrnja "got" resettlement in Čongolje, Bačka, before he had been demobilised. For that reason, his brother, Milan, also a rebel, took his wife and daughter to Vojvodina together with his own family. However, as Mile's wife (who was unwell, and was subsequently to die during the preparations for the revolt) could not adapt to the new life, in particular to the air and the water, they all returned to Kordun at her "insistence" where they were to stay until the Peasants' Revolt.

The situation was significantly different in the Bosnian Borders. Here there was no mass departure as there was from Slunj county. The predominantly Muslim population had not only not been sufficiently "insurgent" during the war, but was also unwilling for religious reasons to move to an entirely Christian environment. However, there were many resettlers from Serb villages in the Bosnian Borders, as there were from other Serb areas in the Bosnian Borders, Kordun, Banija, and Lika. For example, Serb families from the Bosnian Borders were caught up in the first wave of resettlement in autumn 1945, when 22 families from Kladuša county and 21 families from Cazin county were resettled in the Šupljaja settlement together with families from the Bihać area. It is neither possible nor desirable here to deal in detail with the whole resettlement process, but the scale of the event is demonstrated by the fact that families from Cazin county were resettled in a total of 41 settlements, and from Kladuša county in 28 settlements in Bačka, Banat and Srem [...].

Despite certain incentives at federal level, very few Bosnian Muslims took part in the resettlement. Only a few families from the Bosnian Borders resettled. All the Muslim resettlers from Bosnia and Herzegovina, a total of 140 families, were placed in the Bačko Novo Selo settlement. The author has been unable to establish whether Muslim resettlers from the Bosnian Borders played any role in the Peasants' Revolt, while Serb resettlers certainly did. It is also significant that Serb families from Kladuša, Cazin and Slunj counties were resettled in the vicinity of Ruma and in Putinci, thus allowing the previous neighbourly relationship to be maintained to a certain degree, transplanted to their new homes. The investigation in 1950 later established that family and former neighbourly relationships were used in Vojvodina not only as a potential reserve for the revolt, but also as a propaganda tool to attract supporters for the revolt in the Borders themselves. Those relationships served at the same time to create fatal illusions about the revolt's chances of success among its main proponents.

"Neglected" insurgent areas

Resettlement in Vojvodina also meant the continued emptying of Serb villages in the Bosnian Borders, some of which had already suffered terribly in the war or, as in the case of Miostrah for example, had been completely exterminated. For those Serb families who remained in their centuries-old homes, whether in the Bosnian Borders or in Slunj county in Croatia, a new period of many years of material shortages dawned, despite certain aid offered them as "insurgent areas" by the new government. Such aid was not sufficient to allow proper repairs to houses and buildings of economic use damaged or destroyed during the war. Many families received nothing and had to start from scratch unaided on the ashes of their property. Such families quickly came to resent the new order even where they had participated in its creation by being on the same side during the war. A feeling of being aggrieved grew among them due to a perceived failure by the new authorities to respect or give due credit to their services during the war. This factor, as will be seen below, was also highly influential for the Peasants' Revolt. Mile Devrnja was among the "neglected".

The new government did not of course deliberately neglect the "insurgent" areas which were, as a rule, undeveloped anyway; these were difficult times for the whole country. However, it was naturally hard for the people living there to appreciate this, and they felt disappointed and even deceived, in particular in individual cases where the material difficulties were aggravated by the not-uncommon abuses of local government officials. In this way some people came over to the ideas of those who had been "on the other side" during the war and who had their own reasons for bearing a grudge against the new order. There was no shortage of these.

For the context of the 1950 Peasant's Revolt perhaps the most significant case in this regard is that of the village of Vrelo. After the war, the family of the priest Nikola Bogunović returned to Vrelo from Serbia where they had managed to take refuge from the *Ustaše* terror during the worst days of 1941, and where two of the priest's sons had joined the *Četnik* movement. After the war, the priest continued with his clerical duties in Vrelo, but he was clearly hostilely disposed towards the new order. He would often say in the presence of several other people, "this is no good. They've killed all the Serbs" or, criticising the new order, "the Serbs are being humiliated, all Serbs should be in power", recalls the early resistance fighter from Vrelo, Đurađ Zec. The 1950 investigation found that one of the priest's sons, highly educated for the time and circumstances and as such a respected citizen, had, growing up in such a family, even though he had not been in the *Četniks* in the war, played a very significant role in the revolt.

The villages of Vrelo and Rujnica anyway found it difficult to accept the new "brotherhood and unity" policy after the war, as it "was not fully hammered out" there. "The people from those two villages do not trust the council because the majority of members are Muslims", it was stressed at the first Cazin county KPJ conference at the beginning of 1946. Distrust continued to be a characteristic of relations in Vrelo, as noted for example by the Cazin county party office when, at the end of 1947, four members were excluded from the Vrelo Partisan unit: "this area includes Serbs who continue to harbour a jingoistic hatred of Muslims as a consequence of 1941, and started to cultivate it in the unit".

The "neglect" of the insurgent areas and the related occurrence there of exaggerated accounts of wartime exploits were present not only in the Serb insurgent areas of the Borders, but also in other areas, in particular Drvar, and not just in the first years after the war, but also later. However, this represents a complex set of difficult problems which have not yet been, and could not yet objectively be the subject of the extensive and varied research necessary to arrive at a proper historical assessment. Such research would certainly cast further light on the Peasants' Revolt.

There were also other specific factors whose negative influence on the successful social and economic consolidation of the Bosnian Borders is clear without in-depth investigation. The very presence in both counties of a predominantly Muslim population, who not only failed to join the resistance in the early days but were also viewed within Bosnia as fickle, in particular because of the Huska syndrome, led to a less favourable attitude towards those counties as a whole, with the result that less attention was also devoted to minority Serb areas in Cazin and Kladuša counties. In addition, the fact that the area is the most geographically distant from the centre of Bosnia did, according to some recollections, also contribute to less attention being paid at republic level, which is entirely credible in that time of poor communications. On the other hand, the very nature of the Bosnian Borders as a border region brought its own specific problems. Even before the war, the transport of various goods such as wood and timber to Croatia had been an important economic activity in the area. Peasants who had horses continued to carry on the same activity after the war in 1945 and 1946, and according to documents, business flourished, but was now considered "smuggling, economic speculation and sabotage." The majority of delegates at the first KPJ conference in Cazin county at the beginning of 1946, for example, identified this as the "main problem" in the county, in particular in the areas of Šturlić, Tržac and Pećigrad bordering with Croatia.

The "neglect" which appeared during the "renewal" in 1945-1946 continued in the conditions of implementation of the first five-year plan of 1947, which was the source of many ills. Only two observations, but perhaps the most important, are noted here. Recent historical and economic research is already tending towards an assessment of the economic strategy as being vastly futile, recklessly forcing the industrialisation of the country, and resulting in long-term negative consequences for the development of Yugoslavia. Secondly, the one-size-fits-all approach to economic and political measures on the ground of a country as varied in every respect as Yugoslavia could only contribute to continued tensions and slow down development, both of the country as a whole and its regions.

Inherent aspects of the Bosnian Borders

Whereas the conduct of the Borders population on both sides of the river Korana in 1950 was conditioned above all by the economic and political aspects of development, the Bosnian Borders area is in many respects unique within Yugoslavia. This is not just the conclusion of the author's own observations, or of rough comparisons with other social and geographical entities within Yugoslavia ("rough" as the lack of research into Yugoslav society, in particular post-WWII, means that any comparison must be deficient). The majority of the author's informants on the Peasants' Revolt, people whose wealth of life experience cannot be ignored by a historian and sociologist, explicitly warned of the unique nature of the Bosnian Borders. For this reason, it was decided to approach the 1950 revolt from a seemingly remote, but indispensable perspective, that being the inherent context of the overall reality on the ground. It is hoped that individual historical dimensions will therefore serve to assist in gaining an overview and understanding of what was to occur in 1950. Moments in history such as that giving rise to this rebellion are composed of a decisive core and an inherent contextual background. In the case of the revolt the core was made up of the economic issues, and the background a series of fundamental social factors in the Borders.

The population in the Bosnian Borders

The demographic situation on the eve of the revolt is a fundamental starting point and provides a wealth of information on the potential for various events, especially where the population structure is viewed in its various components, such as religious or ethnic, or in terms of economic function, literacy, public health and the mentality of the Borderers.

According to the 1948 census 36,097 people were living in Cazin county (17,413 males and 18,684 females), in 6,330 households. The total area of the county was 424 km², with 253 population centres and a population density of 85 per km². The county was made up of the following localities in addition to Cazin town district: Koprivna, Ostrožac, Pećigrad, Stijena, Šturlić, and Tržačka Raštela. The area of Kladuša county was 304 km², with 184 population centres in the following localities: Mala Kladuša, Todorovo, Velika Kladuša and Vrnograč. 23,153 people lived in 4,373 households (11,179 males and 11,984 females), with the population density calculated as 76 residents per 1 km².

The diversity of the data obtained during the 1948 census is very interesting. Looking at the "permanent" population, i.e. somewhat reduced, Cazin county had 33,241 residents, made up of 2,363 Serbs, 327 Croats, 30,537 non-determined and 14 others.

As the Muslims were only later "recognised" as a separate ethnic group, they mainly classified themselves as non-determined, such that the number of Muslims according to this census is in fact higher, because some of them were classified as being Muslim Serbs or Muslim Croats.

At the same time in Kladuša county, of 21,861 residents 4,303 defined themselves as Serbs, 1,095 as Croats and 16,461 as non-determined.

A rough comparison of the number of residents in 1931 and 1948, i.e. based on the two censes, shows that despite the losses in the war, resettlement in Vojvodina and the high infant mortality rate, the population actually grew significantly, by around seven to ten thousand, which must be due predominantly to a high percentage of natural growth.

After the war, agriculture and livestock production continued to be the basic economic activity of the population of the Bosnian Borders. The 1948 census does not provide any data which would allow researchers to follow the status of or changes to this activity, as a census of agricultural land, herd etc. was only carried out one or two years later. According to this census, in 1952 Cazin county comprised a total of 41,159 ha, of which 23,726 ha were arable land and gardens, 129 ha orchards, 3,268 ha meadowland, 1,950 ha pasture, 10,841 ha woodland, and 1,245 ha infertile land. The arable land was mostly (17,486 ha) used for the cultivation of cereals, mainly corn. Kladuša county was smaller, comprising a total of 27,699 ha. According to the contemporary calculations of the local authorities, 18,703 ha of this land was arable, 120 ha orchards, 17 ha vineyards, 974 ha meadowland, 229 ha pasture, 6,808 ha woodland, and 848 ha infertile. In 1952 10,012 ha were sown with cereals, again mainly corn. In view of the hilly nature of the land, livestock was a very significant branch of farming in both counties. Thus in Cazin in 1952 there were 2,890 horses, 12,087 head of cattle, 9,135 sheep, 572 pigs, 20,229 poultry and 11,234 beehives. In Kladuša county there were 1,843 horses, 9,260 head of cattle, 5,234 sheep, 1,372 pigs, 19,452 poultry and 942 beehives.

Despite the intensive electrification process of the country, which along with industrialisation was a priority of the first five-year plan for the whole country, and thus also for Bosnia and Herzegovina, the population of the Bosnian Borders did not enjoy this benefit of civilisation in any significant form for many years to come. This was certainly partly as a consequence of the attitude of wider society towards the area due to the 1950 revolt. Thus on 31 May 1953, of 57 communities in Cazin county only three or 4.8% had electricity. Looked at from the perspective of individual households the situation was even more unfavourable. Of a total of 6,330 households, only 139 or 2.2% were connected to the grid. Of 44 communities in Kladuša county, only one or 2.3% had electricity, and of the 4,373 households at that time only 127 homes or 2.9% were connected to the grid. With the exception of Kotor Varoš county (south-east of Banja Luka), the electrification process in Bosnia and Herzegovina took longest in the Bosnian Borders.

As concerns literacy among the population, the following state of affairs was ascertained in 1948. Of 21,851 persons over the age of nine in Cazin county, 7,676 were literate and 14,174 illiterate. Broken down by ethnic group, literacy was as follows: Serbs: 965 literate and 781 illiterate; Croats: 152 literate and 84 illiterate; non-determined: 6,548 literate and 13,307 illiterate. As poor as the general level of literacy was in the county, as it was elsewhere in Bosnia and Herzegovina, it is interesting to note that the level of literacy was higher among the Christian population. There were more literate than illiterate people among both the Serbs and the Croats, while among the Muslims the illiterate outnumbered the literate by more than two to one. The 1948 census records a slightly improved but similar ratio in Kladuša county, with 5,947 persons over the age of nine literate and 9,414 illiterate, of whom: Serbs: 1,671 literate and 1,655 illiterate; Croats 359 literate and 443 illiterate; non-determined: 3,915 literate and 7,316 illiterate. This state of literacy in the Bosnian Borders was certainly a consequence of the situation before the war. In 1934 there was a total of six schools with 550 pupils and nine teachers, while there were twice as many police stations, for example. In 1939 the number of schools, mainly located in the *mektebs*, had risen to 11, while there was one teacher for 600 children of primary school age.

The statistics from 1948 obscure somewhat the fact that since the end of the war the new revolutionary authorities had made considerable efforts in improving the level of literacy in the Bosnian Borders. In autumn 1944, 26 regional and local schools started working. Hasan Purić, a teacher from Todorovo, a Partisan and one of the main proponents of education in the Bosnian Borders in the post-war years, also stressed the important role played by the imams, as "the mainstay, together of course with teachers and literate peasants", of the promotion of literacy with their efforts to teach children to read and write. He singled out in particular the following imams as "local champions": Topič from Velika Kladuša, Šabić from Šabići near Pećigrad, Purić from Todorovo, Toromanović from Podzvizd, Salkić from Krakača, Melkić from Murtić and Rekić from Gnjilavac.

After the war, in addition to regular primary education, dozens of literacy courses were organised every year, as they were throughout Bosnia and Herzegovina, which by 1950 (and subsequently) had had hundreds of successful graduates each year.

However, 1950 was still too early for the undoubted sharp rise in the number of literate adults and the number of children attending school in the post-war period to have a significant influence on individuals and the community, as the number of children attending school was still small. The reasons for this are to be found in both the limited range of awareness-raising materials available (e.g. the press), and in the fact that people were not accustomed to making use of what press did exist. Five or six years is too short a period to obtain any concrete positive results from changes to public education in an area as backward as were the Bosnian Borders, even without taking into account the complexity of the issues, i.e. the presence and effect of a range of aggravating and even counterproductive factors.

Literacy being the basic component of culture and civilisation in any twentieth century community, the data provided above on the level of literacy in the Bosnian Borders are of paramount significance for understanding the 1950 rebellion. However, the following specific feature of the Bosnian Borders must also be borne in mind as regards literacy: in the Islamic primary schools, the *mektebs*, which before the war probably encompassed a larger proportion of the school-age population than did the state primary schools, Arabic script was taught. The author is not aware of the existence of any data on the extent to which children mastered Arabic script, but is aware for example, in particular from the explanations of the teacher Purić, that as a result of such studies Muslim children found it easier to learn "normal" writing. And this is an issue in itself. Whereas throughout Bosnia and elsewhere in Yugoslavia two related scripts, Latin and Cyrillic, were in general use, a part of this population in the middle of Europe was more familiar with an alien script, Arabic! To a certain extent this had tragic consequences for the people of the Bosnian Borders, as this written barrier (to whatever extent it existed), together with the different religion and customs, only compounded their separation and distance from the surrounding Christian Balkan environment. This coincidence of differences was even more pronounced in the period after 1945 when communist atheism became the official "religion" in Yugoslavia.

A general picture of any area must include the aspect of public health, that is to say hygiene habits, which influence not only global events but also political events, if only indirectly. Throughout the Bosnian Borders in the period before the 1950 revolt, there was only one doctor, who worked in the only hospital, in Cazin, which had 30 beds and 15 staff. Interestingly, this doctor, the legendary Dr Ciška, was also the only doctor a year later, in 1951. Infant mortality in Cazin and Kladuša counties was typical of the Banja Luka province, of which Jajce county was the highest at 50%. There was no maternity ward in Velika Kladuša, so that women could only give birth in Cazin maternity, although as a rule they gave birth at home. However, not only is Cazin 37 km by road from Velika Kladuša, but such an act was regarded with suspicion, i.e. there was a stigma attached to giving birth in a hospital.

A step backwards in public health was the closure of the public baths in Velika Kladuša, which had functioned before the war. This was aggravated by the fact that the Bosnian Borders do not have abundant water resources. Frequent soap shortages in all Bosnian counties after the war were another obstacle to hygiene. In 1952, the party concluded that for health reasons there was a need in Cazin county to "explain the disadvantages of building houses over cellars for livestock and low rooms for the family to live in".

Vahida Pjanić, recalling four decades later the general level of poverty she encountered in Velika Kladuša, where she moved from Banja Luka after her marriage to the local party secretary Adem Pjanić[iv] in 1948, confirms that the standard of living of the population was very basic indeed. People lived mainly in wattle and daub huts, in a single room, with a door but no windows. They slept on straw mattresses in the same room as they ate, and sometimes kept livestock in the same room. Village houses with two floors were better, although still mainly constructed from wattle and daub with stone, i.e. locally available materials. The family would ascend a wooden staircase to the upper floor above a stable for livestock. Such houses continued to be used in large numbers until the last decade of the twentieth century. It has already been said that the Bosnian Borders are poor in water resources, and water was carried to village houses from wells, which may have been near or far; electricity was non-existent in the countryside in 1950. Houses in the towns were little better off, where there was a constant struggle to preserve food from vermin. Receiving on one occasion a small tub of cheese, a precious commodity in those times, Vahida Pjanić attempted to preserve it until the following day by hanging it by a rope from the ceiling. Despite this precaution, rats managed to reach the tub and empty it by morning.

In addition to common illnesses, in particular tuberculosis which was very widespread and dangerous at that time, the Bosnian Borders were afflicted by widespread endemic syphilis which, according to documents, great efforts were made to treat. In 1951 health workers on the ground carried out a "sustained action against the remnants of endemic syphilis" which was systematically treated with sufficient stocks of medicine, according to the authorities, and affected 3% of the population, "but no open cases". Nevertheless, officials seconded to the Bosnian Borders from outside were particularly uncomfortable because of this widespread syphilis, and recall their caution and strict hygiene practices in contacts with the population on the ground. For example, a head of the county interior ministry office who served in Cazin for three years after the Peasants' Revolt, between 1950 and 1953, recalls that he would always try to obtain vegetables and other food from outside, because he and his family were afraid of infection. The organisation secretary of the Kladuša county party office between 1947 and 1949 believes that syphilis may have been the cause of a persistent itch which affected the population, and may have contributed to their susceptibility to take part in the revolt in 1950.

Atmosphere and mentality

For an understanding of the overall context of circumstances, an attempt must be made to fathom and at least outline those specific elements of mentality which affect the social atmosphere of the environment. An insight into the real atmosphere of a society is impossible or at least very difficult based only on written documents. To that end the testimony of participants can be drawn upon, with, of course, all the reservations a historian must duly be aware of when so doing.

Throughout their history, the fundamental goal of the people of the Borders has been to stay alive, with the result that they are brought up to live for war. This is one of the overall conclusions of one of the author's interviewees. Arms were a constant companion. The catchphrase "blood for lunch, blood for dinner", among others, is often used to describe the mentality of the Muslims, the "mad" Borderers.

[iv] A former teacher who was expelled from the KPJ for "lack of vigilance" in the run-up to the Peasants' Revolt. He returned to teaching, in which capacity he was transferred to Srbac. He later became a respected professor at the Pedagogical Academy in Banja Luka.

Vahida Pjanić describes this traditional law as follows: "if you swore about someone's mother or sister, he would stab you to death." Purić says that "knives were more for bravado", and that after the war, it was mainly only the "younger generation" who liked to carry a knife, which was rarely actually used in fights. However, he does confirm that "if you swore about someone's mother he would immediately pull a knife". Others also recall that those were mainly "hot-headed" people, ready "at the drop of a hat" to argue, brawl and even wound, especially in the pubs. According to Purić, "they were honest and proud people who would not tolerate insults, but were always ready to act, to give and to help". The author has experienced the exceptional hospitality of the region first-hand speaking to men and women while gathering recollections of the revolt four decades later. "These people are exceptionally hospitable, they would kill their brother or a close relative if they threatened a guest", Mile Milić[v] stated categorically.

The social susceptibility which has already been mentioned must be regarded as an important characteristic of the population of the Bosnian Borders. This is in fact a single social-psychological phenomenon with two poles. On the one hand, as in every patriarchal environment, there is a figure of authority, and on the other the mass of individuals subject and subordinate to that figure as the "leader". The leader must acquire and earn his reputation, but once obtained it is a powerful social force which can be wielded in all circumstances. As has already been established, such power was formerly personified in the Bosnian Borders by Huska Miljković, who was also preceded by earlier "heroes", albeit legendary or semi-legendary, which does not detract from their essence (e.g. Mujo Hrnjica). For a short period after the war, after Huska, there were no new leaders with his authority in the Borders. However, there were many respected individuals, who succeeded in leading a revolt in 1950, and who were able to transform their somewhat less respected social status into concrete power not just due to favourable global circumstances, but also by resorting to deception, including self-deception, intimidation, etc. If a stronger authority had arisen at that time, in the spring of 1950, someone with greater respect among the people than the leaders of the revolt, and if such a person had argued against the revolt before the susceptible masses, the Peasants' Revolt may well never have happened. As Carević said, "the main thing is to lead them and act authoritatively. A strong leading personality can do whatever he wants." Momir Kapor[vi] and others consider that "if at the critical moment Hakija Pozderac had appeared before the masses and thundered against the people, they would have dispersed in a moment".

The mentality of the Serbs in the Borders, on both sides of the Korana, is somewhat different. According to Carević, they are more individualistic. Milić added that the Serbs are more belligerent and obstinate than the other residents of the Borders, that they are not easily persuaded to change their views and are always ready to fight to enforce a right. The following three stereotypes of the views of the three main ethnic/religious groups in the Borders were apparently commonly accepted immediately after WWII: the Muslims believed that "it won't last long, it'll change" (i.e. the regime), the Serbs were sure that "we will fight them and win",

---

[v] Cazin UDBA man; his real surname was Kenjalo. According to him, it was rumoured in the UDBA at the time that the Peasants' Revolt had been fomented by Croatian PM Bakarić in order to allow him to get rid of three Serb ministers.

[vi] Member of the KPJ Banja Luka provincial party office, among the officials sent to the Bosnian Borders to "restore law and order" after the Peasants' Revolt.

while the Croats, partly cowed and suffering from a complex due to their immediate past, were withdrawn and given to the view that "we need to pray". There can be no doubt that, as do other similar ethnic stereotypes, these contain a grain of truth.

The status of women

It is unfortunate that the 1948 census does not indicate the gender structure of literacy (or illiteracy), as, based on what is known about the general status of women at that time, in particular Muslim women – and especially bearing in mind that women were the majority in both counties of the Bosnian Borders in 1948 - that would certainly have revealed a very low level of literacy. A reasonably accurate picture can however be formed indirectly, as the same census established that of 17,139 female inhabitants (including those under the age of ten), 16,157 had received no formal education, 900 had received primary education, 66 basic secondary education and 15 further secondary education. According to this census not a single woman in the county had attended a further education establishment at that time. The situation was similar in Kladuša county. Of 11,343 women, 10,626 had no education, 679 primary education, 29 basic secondary education and 9 further secondary education. Again, not a single woman had a degree.

It is well known that in patriarchal societies girls are held back in obtaining formal education. The woman's traditional and only place was in the home, such that girls had no need to go to school. And as they were incorporated into heavy household and rural work from an early age, there was no time for education anyway. They traditionally married very young and left the parental home forever. The woman's new role in life then consisted of being a wife and mother, and endless exhausting work in the home, with the livestock and in the fields where she was the main workforce, although, according to Vajan Popović[vii], women were rarely seen working in the fields in Bihać county. As a rule, there were no women in public life. A total of 13 women, some of them in the town and some of them teachers, were KPJ members in Cazin county in 1950, the lowest number in the whole of Bosnia and Herzegovina. According to later data, in the autumn of 1949 there were only four women KPJ members in Cazin county.

The position and role of women was similar throughout the Balkans. However, in an overwhelmingly Muslim environment, such as in particular the Bosnian Borders, there were further specific characteristics determining the life of women. Firstly, the tradition of polygamy was maintained in this area even after the war. Even though it became rarer over time, in that period polygamy was not unusual in the Bosnian Borders. Despite this phenomenon being incompatible with legislation, šerija law prevailed in this area in the Bosnian Borders. The first wife was recognised by the secular authorities as the only lawful wife, while a second, third etc. were a reality for many Muslim families. This practice was more or less publicly tolerated, in particular immediately after the war. According to archives. it was only after the 1950 revolt (and possibly as a result of it?) that more vigorous efforts were made to put an end to the practice of polygamy in the Bosnian Borders. This practice in the Bosnian Borders is an interesting phenomenon in European terms, as it was the environment with the absolutely densest and relatively largest Muslim population.

[vii] Head of the Bihać UDBA station at the time of the Peasants' Revolt, who played an active role in the subsequent crackdown, when there was a standing order to "terminate" anyone found hiding in the forests.

Although complex research and consideration of the social, psychological, biological, economic, legal and cultural aspects of the phenomenon of polygamy is beyond the scope of this analysis, it must be noted that these important factors cannot be ignored by any comprehensive history of the area seeking to understand the issues of the distant and recent past, and of the present of the Bosnian Borders. In the absence of any archival evidence, the concrete effect of the phenomenon can be at least superficially described based on the testimony of individuals.

Property rather than any personal characteristics was the main criterion for a man adding a second wife to his household. It was not rare for a young girl to become the third or even fourth wife of an old man. But even the limit of four prescribed by *šerija* (after the example of the Prophet Muhamed) was not always respected. In the summer of 1948 in Todorovo, Kladuša county, an elderly man resting beside the road, when asked by a passer-by (Mehmed Kurbegović) how much he paid the seven women working in the field, replied, "Nothing, they're all my wives". This recollection, albeit subjective, also indicates how women were as a rule more intensively engaged in household economic labour than men. They worked in the fields, carried grain to the mill, took care of livestock, and weaved fabric from hemp they had grown themselves to make sheets and clothes for the family, while the men often went to the pubs, drank and were generally idle[viii]. But it was not only Muslim peasants who had two or more wives. The well-known early resistance fighter from Cazin, Halil Šakanović, who rose to the rank of colonel in the Partisans, had, according to the recollections of Uglješa Danilović[ix], as many as three wives after the war. Many men had at least one extra wife, for example both the brother and the father of the secretary of the Cazin county party office. It is interesting to note that some women voluntarily and willingly became additional wives, i.e. entered into marriages where the husband already had a wife. Vahida Pjanić recalls from some

---

[viii] One day in 2010, in the town of Pendžakent ("five villages") in Tajikistan, I came across a team of half-a-dozen women haytiming in a field, by hand. The position of women in rural Central Asia was aggravated by the fact that many local men work as *gastarbajteri* ("economic migrants") in distant Russia, as taxi drivers or in *strojka* ("construction"), sending home remittances at irregular intervals, or sometimes even starting a new life there and never being heard from again. The women are then abandoned to fend for themselves and their children as best they can. However, this state of affairs may now change, as the recent practice throughout Central Asia of no longer delivering education in Russian means that the younger generation will be cut off from this economic option. I saw another sign of the patriarchal nature of Central Asian society during a week-long workshop we ran in Pendžakent with the whole local team, from various (and disparate) parts of the country: when a woman was addressing the room, male participants saw nothing strange in speaking right over her as if she wasn't even there. Tajik women's station is life is advertised to the world at large by a complex dress code, which allows the initiated to divine not only whether a woman is married or single, but also whether she is her husband's first, second or third wife etc., whether she is in the first year of marriage, or whether she is a widow, among many other facts of lesser import. African society is similarly patriarchal: one day a lady from a British NGO visited our warehouse in Freetown. After I had dealt with her enquiry and she had gone on her way, I commented to one of the local team who was with me that I thought it quite rude that he had not bothered to say "*Ou die bodie?*" to her. "She's a female, it's up to her to greet me", he replied. And at a *chantier* ("building site") in Baraka in the DRC, I was surprised to see that while all the craftsmen were men, the labouring work was being carried out by women. When I remonstrated with the master builders for letting their womenfolk do all the hard work while they enjoyed a tea break, I was met with incredulity and hilarity. In a *kišlak* ("village") in Tajikistan I also witnessed the practice of threshing wheat by laying the sheaves out on the road, where the wheels of passing traffic would separate out the chaff. I was told that one night an *alkaš* ("drunkard"), mistaking the thick layer of crops on the road for a haystack, had gone to sleep there, and was run over by a *kamaz* ("truck").

[ix] Bosnian interior minister at the time of the Peasants' Revolt. During WWII he had been a KPJ leader, and he went on to become a cabinet member.

concrete examples that one psychological motive could be, for example, the desire of the second wife to spite the first.

Elements of envy and jealousy were thus also at play in polygamous families in and around the 1950 revolt. Two or even three wives of a rebel might betray their husband to the authorities as a participant in the revolt, simply in order to get revenge on him and his latest, youngest (fourth) wife. Before the 1950 revolt, the authorities rarely, but occasionally did punish additional wives (but not the men!). One such wife, young and pretty, was arrested and as a punishment ordered to work public land together with other convicts under guard. When asked by a passer-by what she was doing there, she replied, "I didn't know I wasn't allowed to be a second wife."

Some of the leading figures of the Peasants' Revolt had two wives, including one of the main leaders. Polygamous families had many children and therefore many mouths to feed, which certainly increased dissatisfaction with the authorities, as they were constantly seeking food from the peasants, often taking away their last mouthful by force.

One more dimension which specifically concerns Muslim women is their traditional dress, which is characterised in particular by the woman covering her face and head with a *zar* (hooded dress) and *feredža* (veiled cape). This is only mentioned here because it had significant political implications in the post-war years (during WWII this dress was often used to disguise men). After the war, communist ideology demanded the carrying-out of large-scale campaigns to end the practice of wearing the *zar* and *feredža*. However, the implementation of this measure was very slow and accompanied by various difficulties. The executive of the KPJ training team described the situation on the ground in the autumn of 1949, a year before the enactment of a special law banning the wearing of the *zar* and *feredža*: "Not only is the campaign to end the practice of wearing the *feredža* not making any progress, but women who had earlier stopped wearing it have started to cover themselves, including the wives, sisters and mothers of party members", in particular in Cazin and the wives of members of the county party office. There was great resistance, in particular from the rural population, and conflicts with the authorities are widely documented during the many years of the new government's struggle against traditional Muslim women's dress. For example, at the end of 1950, women in Cazin were fined for refusing to comply with the law banning the wearing of the *zar* and *feredža*. Interestingly, the law was opposed equally by both Muslim men and women, which demonstrates how deeply-rooted this Islamic tradition was. The tradition was of course eliminated faster in the towns than in the countryside. It is not possible, for example, to establish how many women connected to the 1950 Revolt still wore the *zar* and *feredža*, but the wife of the Muslim leader, a respected Muslim, did still wear the *zar* and *feredža* at that time, according to her son.

Even among Muslim women, in the context of their traditional view of life, there was some resistance to obtaining an equal position in marriage and the family. For example, a well-known "more enlightened" Muslim woman, enlightened because she had attended one "mass conference" where among other things some men were criticised for drinking and "neglecting their wives", categorically stated, "Leave our men alone. Look at my daughter, she wants to judge her husband. Who ever heard of such a thing?"

Although this is not specific to Muslims, the author's overall research shows that Muslims did not as a rule even mention public matters to their wives, in particular events at work. In this way Muslim women had almost no knowledge of matters outside the family, even via their husbands. While this can be considered normal in a traditional relationship, where the Peasants' Revolt is concerned there must have been some degree of conspiracy, as the rebels concealed preparations being carried out to a certain extent in their homes. For example, the wife and mother of the main Muslim leader only found out about "it" a few days before the revolt, despite the fact that the "head of the family" had spent over a month in intensive preparations, holding unusually frequent meetings with his neighbours and friends in his home.

The place and role of Muslim women briefly mentioned here leads to the assumption that they did not and could not have had any role in the organisation of the Peasants' Revolt or the revolt itself, which is in fact confirmed by available documents. With the exception of a few messages, the investigation into the revolt does not mention a single Muslim woman, even in the preparatory stages. However, women were extensively interviewed after the revolt because of an incident which, due to its general interest and usefulness in understanding the psychology of Muslim women, deserves proper analysis and will be revisited at an appropriate point below. The situation was rather different among the Serb rebels. While there were no Serb women among those sentenced, some women did have a role, for example one woman from Slunj county, as well as, probably, the wife of the commander-in-chief from Crnaja.

It would be inaccurate however to fail to link at least one Muslim woman to the Peasants' Revolt, albeit on the "other" side. This is councillor Aiša of Tržac, whose husband was killed in 1943 as a combatant in the 8th Borders brigade. Aiša, an AFŽ (Women's Anti-Fascist Front) activist in 1950, became suspicious of goings-on two months prior to the revolt and so she "monitored" Božić and Ale's contacts. Around a month before St. George's Day, she discovered that a secret meeting had been held in Ale's house attended by "over 20" people, prepared a list of those people and handed it in to the "UDBA agency in Cazin", writes Ratko Ilić, then an officer of the provincial UDBA, in his book "Destined to Betray", written on the basis of the notes of his conversation with Aiša in 1950, when he was deployed to the Bosnian Borders to "restore law and order" in respect of the "rebellion" or "enemy action", as it was officially called. It was however difficult to establish the veracity of Aiša's information. While on the one hand that may well have been the signal to the Cazin UDBA which is referred to in many documents and testimonies, it is on the other hand rather strange that Ale's wife Bejza would not recall such a meeting in her home. Four decades later, with a clear memory and no reason to conceal anything concerning the revolt, she made no mention of a meeting of several people in her home during several hours of conversation with the author, or in her written testimony.

Aspects of the role of Islam and the party and state in the Borders

It would be overambitious and beyond the scope of this analysis to attempt to explore the wider context of the relationships between society, Islam and the government. The question of Islam has already been referred to above, and further aspects are mentioned here.

The role of Muslim women, or rather the complete absence of any role for them in the 1950 Peasants' Revolt, and in any other social movements, arises from religious determinations of the functions of women. It is therefore not surprising that the "main questions" raised in Cazin county at the "people's mass conference" held at the end of 1945 on the occasion of the debate on the draft constitution of the

Socialist Federal Republic of Yugoslavia, were, in accordance with strong Islamic tradition, apart from the role of religion, the solemnisation of marriage and compulsory education for girls. The party conference at the beginning of 1946 stressed that, "reactionary elements such as the imams from Pećigrad, Gnjilavac and Stijena ["cliff"] gathered groups of their friends and endeavoured to raise disapproval of these issues under those points of the draft constitution". Similar reactions are to be found in many other documents from that time.

However, while in the first years after WWII women in the Borders continued to be ignored, or "spared", participation in social affairs in accordance with religious precepts, this did not prevent the authorities from dogmatically and brutally failing to examine the context of the problem and exiling dozens of such women with their families from their homes for years as a result of the Peasants' Revolt. On the other hand, Islam as a religion and as a specific social order in the Borders, as well as the acts of individual imams, did exercise their own influence on and around the Peasants' Revolt, which will be explored in greater detail below.

The government and the party often noted and warned of the presence of aggressive activities by imams under the watchword "danger to the faith", which according to documents was used to systematically instil fear into believers that the authorities were going to eliminate Islam. This was a real fear among the Muslims. It is a fact that imams emphasised the problem of threats to Islam as a result of various actual pressures and intolerant acts by the government in respect of Islam, such as the closure of *mektebs*, but they also sought to create psychological defence mechanisms among believers.

The party also accused Islam of disrupting the "normal" functioning of the government. In mid-1947, the Cazin county party office complained to the provincial office in Banja Luka of problems in collecting the quotas on the ground, with "individual *kulaks*, small businessmen and imams colluding to interpret the quotas as the authorities planning and forecasting without reference to God how much grain should be surrendered, before even knowing how much grain will be produced". In any case, the policy of the new government and the behaviour of local party and state officials on the ground did not, nor did they attempt to have any realistic or sympathetic attitude towards the prevailing ideology of the environment, Islam, and imams were assumed to be and were treated as enemies of the new government. It was therefore inevitable in the difficult years after the war that there should be a spontaneous increase in distrust among Muslims of the outside world. It was impossible to reduce the population's traditional devotion to their religion in such circumstances, being as it was a psychological consequence of shrinking perspectives and the unreasonable behaviour of the ruling party.

However, the question of religious influences on society in the Bosnian Borders can and should be examined from at least one more perspective as concerns the 1950 revolt. Notwithstanding the fact that the Partisan authorities opened schools in both Cazin and Kladuša counties as early as 1944, that many *mektebs* were converted to atheist schools after the war, and that the remaining *mektebs* had a positive influence in educating children, for example by developing literacy skills, the fact remains that it was the *mektebs*, and later the sermons of many imams based as they were on the principles of Islam, that were the primary source of socialisation for growing children. Islam combined with a significant failure by atheist primary education to encompass children ensured that young people were not properly integrated into their social time and space, to a certain extent even after the war, and this is all the more so for the generation who on the eve of the 1950 revolt had already been through their secondary socialisation process. This makes it easier to understand the phenomenon of the limited, confined perspective according to which, for example, the "fall of Bihać" meant to the rebels the fall of practically the whole of Yugoslavia, which was clearly a decisive argument at the time for recruitment to the Peasants' Revolt. Ignorance, a lack of information and a whole series of psychological factors which can only be appreciated in their actual context played a highly significant role in and around the rebellion.

While the role of primary political and social leader was the traditional domain of religion, after the war the party and state aggressively attempted to usurp this role, obviously at the expense of religious institutions. In view of the institutional and *de facto* ruling status won by the party and state in the war, and which it subsequently desperately clung to, unwilling to share it with anyone, this role did of course also have many other functions.

It was clearly no simple matter to manage the various chronic economic, political, religious, educational, cultural, health and other issues in the Bosnian Borders, or resolve them in accordance with the overall policies of the KPJ and the new government. It is also known that at that time the party was attempting to interfere with and regulate the most minor social and even private matters of peoples' lives, "its way". Such an approach and the attitude of the party and its communications in the public administration, trade unions, youth organisations, the Veterans' Association, the AFŽ etc. only provoked further difficulties, as all these bodies in their efforts to consolidate their own positions were often more concerned with their own interests. Without going in detail into the workings of the political order as such (even in the Bosnian Borders), it is important to note that it functioned extremely badly. This observation arises from wide-ranging information provided to the supreme body of the party by the KPJ executive training team after a three-week field investigation in the Banja Luka province in the autumn of 1949, as part of normal party activities throughout the country. In this document, of eleven counties of Banja Luka province visited by the team, Cazin county is cited as an example of the one with the most frequent and most negative incidents.

As some observations from this report have already been noted when examining individual aspects of social reality, some further general points are given here which may bear some relation to the impending event, just six months before the Peasants' Revolt. For instance, while the lack of middle management was a serious problem throughout Bosnia and Herzegovina and the whole country, it was most acute in Cazin county. Not only were the "managers" poorly qualified, generally only with primary education, but in Cazin county the number of officials was the lowest – only 70 of the 130 planned at the end of 1949. "The county trade union council [...] does not function at all", AFŽ committees in the villages of the county "only exist on paper", "in Cazin some officials do not come to work at all and this is ignored by the party". It was predicted that due to a lack of school premises, between 20% and 50% of children in some counties would receive no education, while "in Cazin county there are *mektebs* which could be converted for school use, but the party and party offices have made no efforts to solve this problem by using those premises".

Cazin county is at the top of the list of places "where political activities are exceptionally poor", with in particular "neglect, and in some instances the practical disappearance of mass organisations [...] and activities by enemy elements [...] constantly opposing economic measures [quotas and taxes] for which they regularly request reviews..." At that time, those counties where "Cominform elements" were noticed received special attention. Here again Cazin county is among the first mentioned, with the presence of such "elements" noted in particular in the county party office and county council party organisation, although "they have been unsuccessful in spreading their work to the grassroots party organisation". Even the secretary of the Cazin county party office is cited as a typical example of ideological disorientation, "who could not say whether arrested party members were arrested as Cominform elements or Young Muslim members".

The UDBA is a chapter all by itself as concerns the work of the various government agencies. Not in this case because of its work in general or on individual matters, but because of the composition of its staff: they were half a dozen Serbs. Bearing in mind the UDBA's omnipotent role in society at that time, the negative effect of such an ethnic composition on the orthodox Muslim environment described above is self-evident, in particular on an environment as suspicious of outsiders as were the Bosnian Borders. It is therefore no surprise that, along with Dubica, Jajce and Bosanska Gradiška, Cazin county is the scene of "certain typical, albeit not widespread, incidents of improper behaviour towards Muslims, which incite jingoistic tendencies and increase the negative attitude of the Muslim population (failure to attend associations, refusal to go to conferences with Serbs)". The UDBA's direct role in the Peasants' Revolt will be dealt with in more detail below, as will many other aspects of the party and state's workings in the Borders, in particular as to how the population saw the new government. In any case, the Borderers' (and the peasants' in Yugoslavia generally) greatest grievances were the "economic measures" by which the party and state implemented its "socialist reconstruction of the countryside" policy. It was the economic circumstances in the countryside that formed the "core" of the situation that drove the Borderers to rebel against the government with the aim of destroying it. "The porridge had been boiling" for several years and in 1950 it boiled over.

Economic circumstances at the time of the revolt

While from the academic perspective it is certainly not possible to separate more recent events from their earlier historical heritage when attempting to shed light on and understand a particular happening from the past, neglecting the distant past and giving decisive weight only to individual elements, it is the immediate social context that is nevertheless the most important framework for examining any subject, and the Borders rebellion is no exception. The 1950 Peasants' Revolt in the Borders is the product and reflection of everything determining the overall circumstances in that area, in particular during the preceding year or two. For that reason, any researcher into the rebellion must be interested in the details of those circumstances in 1949 and the first months of 1950; and the economic aspect of those circumstances developed against the background of the extreme centralisation of the first five-year plan.

However, those circumstances are, in sum, similar in their overall form to circumstances that characterised the whole country, and in particular as concerns social-economic relations in agriculture and the countryside. In other words, the issues of the administrative quotas of agricultural produce in their entirety, i.e. including sowing and harvesting, the mobilisation of labour or "voluntary work", and the relationship of the peasants to agricultural collectivisation via the SRZs, were aspects of everyday life both in the Bosnian Borders and Slunj county, and defined the social situation and the political atmosphere in the countryside in the Bosnian Borders and the neighbouring Kordun area.

The actual agricultural work, from sowing to harvest and threshing in crop production, via livestock production to the relatively modest fruit production, and all other economic activities related to agriculture and in other areas, was not only centralised in this as well as other parts of the country, but bureaucratised to such an extent, in particular as of the introduction of the five-year plan which was "broken down" every year into ever more detailed months, weeks and even days, that such an approach by the government to the prevailing private sector could only disincentivise individual peasants. In the area of Cazin county council, the private sector accounted for 11,289 ha of the 11,578 ha planned for harvest in the spring of 1950. Endless examples could be cited of the struggles between the authorities or the party and peasants on establishing the areas under cultivation, which the peasants as a rule reported as being smaller than were registered by the authorities. Nor was it uncommon for officials, acting improperly and abusively, to seize or attempt to seize a peasant's thresher to prevent him from carrying out the slightest unlawful threshing.

The main problems arose, of course, after the work was completed, in particular during the agricultural quota stage.

In the Bosnian Borders as elsewhere the quotas were the most hated measure, and peasants feared the quota collectors and commissions, who were often accompanied by the police, like the plague. The shadow of the quotas on the eve of the revolt is portrayed by Dževad Sabljaković in his fictitious novel "Omaha[x] 1950", the hero of which is the most hated quota enforcer who "visits the countryside" and mercilessly seizes the last head of livestock and the last grain of cereal from the remainder of a village family, the head of which he has already had imprisoned for failure to deliver the planned quotas. Sabljaković's naturalistic portrayal of the poverty and deprivation of the Cazin countryside was assessed four decades after the revolt by Žunić as overly dark, although he did admit that some "unpleasant" enforcers acted inappropriately in the field. One such he recalled was Huso "Tsar" Kapić.

While the majority of the testimonies of those who took part in some way in the events surrounding the Peasants' Revolt regard the quotas as the main cause of the 1950 rebellion, Žunić considers them to be only one of the causes, "but they cannot be taken to be the main motive (purpose)". This assessment can be considered in at least two ways. On the one hand, it comes from a very competent individual and as such must be respected, but on the other hand it seeks, precisely because of the post held by that individual at that time, to lessen or at least make relative the problem of the quotas. The wife of the party secretary in Velika Kladuša between 1947 and 1948, and in Cazin between 1949 and 1950, in other words, to all intents and purposes the number two in the Bosnian Borders, recalls that her husband was always away from home, spending the whole day in the field trying to enforce the wretched quotas, when the peasants had to give everything they had, and at a time when there was general poverty and hunger was rife. At the market it was possible to buy a chicken, vegetables, or even a sheep, but it was impossible to buy grain or flour. Even in their "residence" she almost always ate only "corn flour". Only UDBA members had privileges when receiving food products, that the general population could only obtain with ration books.

---

[x] Not the city in Nebraska, but a pagan carnival or festival.

Rather than comment on the scale of the influence all these issues had on the Peasants' Revolt, the figures on the quotas can be allowed to speak for themselves. In 1947, the Bosnian Borders were designated as a grain-producing area within Bosnia and Herzegovina, thereby falling under a quota regime which, taking the area as a whole, required amounts in excess of the total actual capacities of both Cazin and Kladuša counties. For that reason, the quota collection failed to meet its targets every year, despite the pressures already mentioned. According to a February report of the county rural affairs commission, in 1950, the point at which this matter is most significant as concerns the revolt, 1,713,000 kg corn, the staple foodstuff, was required for the economic year 1949/1950. By the end of January 1950, 992,049 kg or 57.3% of the planned amount had been collected, despite the ominous promise of Cazin county party office at the end of the report: "The corn quota will be collected as early as possible as ordered." Despite their best "efforts", the quota was not collected, nor could it be.

According to data from April 1950, that is towards the end of the last quota "raids" in the countryside, 1,289,797 kg corn had been collected in Cazin county from a target of 1,707,478 kg, 2,226 kg butter from 2,740 kg, 1,867 l of alcohol from 3,000 l, 84,083 kg beans from 130,000 kg, and 119,957 kg of potatoes from a target of 150,000 kg. Only the hay and straw collections approximately met their targets. The greatest shortfalls were in livestock collection, with 21,275 kg from a target of 159,365 kg. Similar problems were experienced in the collection of taxes, which were also generally underpaid by the peasants. The scale of the discrepancy between the quota targets (and the total tax) and the actual quotas collected (and tax paid) indicates the priorities of the authorities, the party, the police, and the UDBA, who, as in previous years, did everything they could to "implement the economic measures". The fact that every state structure in the county was seconded to this "priority" task is demonstrated by a memorandum posted in mid-March 1950 from Cazin to Banja Luka concerning pre-military training, i.e. a document on a completely unrelated matter. In the document, the Cazin county council chief executive justifies the delay of almost three months in sending the report on pre-military training in the county because the official responsible for training had been in the grain collection commission and thus "constantly in the field".

While the councillors, and all other officials in Cazin and other counties, saw their task in forcing the quotas out of the peasants simply as part of their job, they were aware that their success or failure in its performance would determine their future position, their promotion or demotion. It was therefore rare for officials to dare to not carry out or in some way oppose the task. One councillor, Ahmet Topić, was hauled up before a "high" party commission accused of complaining of the difficulties related to the quotas. While he denied all the other accusations, he admitted that he had criticised the planned quotas in Ostrožac which he had shown to the relevant county commissioner and chief executive of the county council. However, the commission decided his evidence was "insincere" and sought his expulsion from the party. At that time expulsion from the party meant great shame, demotion and even loss of employment for an individual.

It was certainly not easy to hold an official post in those critical years, possibly most of all due to the issues of the quotas. Stevo Božić, the younger son of the commander of the Peasants' Revolt, recalls that at that time only "the most ruthless and insolent" were able to work for the authorities, for which reason both he and Ale Čović, the deputy commander, refused posts offered to them, for example. "For that reason we enjoyed the trust of the people and were respected. We knew that if we accepted authority we would have to abandon the ideas we had proclaimed. Others could hardly wait to get some authority, including those who had not been on our side in the war." Such individuals were especially harsh towards the people, both in order to redeem their sins from the war, and to curry favour with their superiors. Stevo Božić recalls as such a "superior" Hakija Pozderac, in 1950 secretary general of the Bosnian government, who is accused by many of being the culprit for the hard life of peasants in the Borders.

Of course, worst off were the peasants themselves, especially those who, for whatever reason, did not provide the planned quotas or failed to meet them in full. The milder punishments were fines, and the harsher, imposed on those deemed "anti-social", were prison sentences of mainly between three months and two years with hard labour, or "community service" accompanied by partial confiscation of the convict's property. In January 1950 there were 20 such cases in Cazin county. The attitude such convicts and their families must have had towards the government is obvious. According to Hanka Nadarević, the wife of one of the rebels, in the winter of 1949/1950 Hasećija Nadarević, Šaban Purgar and Mahmut Murić were sent from Tržac to carry out forced labour in Romanija because of the quotas.

The problems with the corn quotas, which was the main crop in the Bosnian Borders, were a matter of concern throughout Banja Luka province. In order to accelerate the collection of the quotas, in February 1950 the provincial council sent its verification commission to visit all the counties. According to the commission's report of 14 February, summary proceedings had been brought against "unconscientious" peasants everywhere, in some places more than others, and many more had been fined. It is difficult to determine based only on the figures which county was the most problematic, but it may well have been Cazin county. At that time only 48% of the planned corn had been collected, and as many as 219 councillors had not provided their quotas. 62 of them were KPJ members, but it was emphasised that they were not heads of household, in 13 cases proceedings were brought by the county prosecutor, and eight cases were punished by the county council administrative commission. Wherever the quotas were to be collected, officials were met with the same answer, "No corn." The story of a peasant from Krivaja who was told to provide more corn than he had, stuck in popular memory. He loaded up a whole basket of corn onto a horse-drawn cart and drove to Cazin singing, "Comrade Tito, my white violet, especially for you a whole basket.[xi]" He received a two-month prison sentence.

The verification commission from the Banja Luka provincial council was unable to carry out its duties on the ground in Kladuša county due to "dysfunctional" transport. They only established that the prosecutor had had one peasant arrested, and that the practice of hiding corn and selling it in Croatia was rife.

But there were also examples of decisions of the Cazin and Kladuša county council chief executive's summary offences commissions being overturned by the head of the public procurement service in Sarajevo. In the financial year 1950/1951, it transpired that the commission had punished peasants without checking the facts of cases, thereby breaching the basic principles of criminal administrative proceedings. As a result, the PPS, needless to say after a long process and without any compensation for the peasants for the distress caused, quashed the summary proceedings.

[xi] Parody of a popular pro-Tito song.

The whole context of the quotas is relevant to the Peasants' Revolt, as it indicates in the clearest terms the essence of the social dissatisfaction of the peasants as a whole. It should also be mentioned here that the most prominent participants in the 1950 Borders rebellion also had decisive conflicts with the authorities over their quotas at that critical time. The Božić family were comparatively well off, and Milan Božić had very serious problems in 1950 because of the quotas. It may well be that the Božićes were in a position to provide their quotas, but it was well known that Milan Božić, as an early resistance fighter, was bitterly opposed as a matter of principle to a government that was prepared to fleece its people. The future commander of a platoon in the rebellion, Đulaga Šumar of Tržac, recalls how he had to make up his grain quota with ground dough. The livestock quota was particularly difficult for the peasants. When a peasant was unable to meet the weight requirements of the quota, it was not unknown for his last cow to be seized. Or, for example, the councillor and the police would arrive at a field being ploughed by a peasant with oxen, unharness the oxen and lead them away to meet the meat quota, leaving the peasant with no choice but to take the yoke on his own shoulders, with his wife behind the plough. One peasant, Đuro Božić, also a prominent rebel, had to give up a sow for the quota and even drive it himself from Crnaja to Cazin, after which the 12 piglets died. The same sow was then kept in the house of a Muslim out of favour with the authorities, obviously with the intention of insulting and enraging him on religious grounds. Humiliation, cheating and all kinds of affronts to human dignity were commonplace. Perhaps one of the most notorious examples concerns an imam's wool quota. As it was known that the local imam, who had never kept sheep, had three beautiful daughters, the brutal councillor Sulejman Beganović, known as Turjankić, demanded the imam "lay out and shave" his daughters in order to provide the wool the imam owed to the state. It was also not unknown in the Cazin area for the quota collectors to demand eggs from households who didn't own a single chicken.

The meat quotas also seriously affected the main Slunj leaders of the Peasants' Revolt, Mile Devrnja and Nikola Beuković. In April 1949, Mile complained to his neighbour Nikola that his quota had been assessed at 350 kg beef and 40 kg pork. This assessment enraged Mile, but the complaint he submitted to the ward council was rejected. In April 1950, Nikola complained to Mile for similar reasons. He had received an order to provide 250 kg beef in July and a further 40 kg pork in August. In the meantime, the bullock he had planned to give up for the quotas, died; but "regardless a new order arrived requiring him to provide the assessed amount of meat on 25 March rather than 1 July 1950. I opposed this, saying that in order to provide that quantity of meat I would have to slaughter an ox, which I could not do, as otherwise I would be unable to sow the planned area of land. The council also rejected this, which severely irritated me."

Obtaining the assessed quota amounts was practically the only concern of the county authorities. Any self-criticism was rare at their meetings, but not entirely absent. At the beginning of May in Slunj, there was an admission that "mistakes" were being made by the authorities on the ground, but nevertheless the quotas continued to be mercilessly enforced, albeit perhaps with the occasional reduction or "adjustment".

Besides the quotas, taxes, and spring harvest, the main concern of the authorities on the ground was the "activation" or labour mobilisation. It has already been said that this was the measure used by the state to make up the shortfall in the numbers of workers required for the purposes of accelerated industrialisation by drawing on the rural workforce. Peasants were "taken" for periods of a month or more according to centralised assessments per county and local area, to work as mainly unskilled labour in the mines, forests and factories and on the railways. From Cazin county they were mainly deployed to fell timber in Grmeč, and later in Krupa county, in Bosanski Petrovac. The mobilisation target per county and local area had to be met. Not only did the peasants have no interest in going to carry out such work, where they were generally poorly housed and fed, but they were often mobilised at times of important agricultural work, which resulted in direct material losses for them, as there was no reduction in the quotas due to being away from home. These and various other factors caused resistance among the peasants and fear of being mobilised. Žunić recalls that out of a hundred mobilised peasants who were supposed to be transported from the Srbljani railway station to their destination, around twenty had already fled on the way to Srbljani. Hiding and fleeing from the mobilisation was a regular albeit punishable occurrence, such that meeting the labour targets was always a cause of much trouble in Cazin, as in other places.

Comparative research might establish that there were even more problems with the labour mobilisation "economic measure" in Slunj county. After demobilisation in 1945 and 1946, former combatants were very unhappy about the government's labour mobilisation, which consisted of felling timber in Petrova Gora or Kapela, building a tempera factory in Karlovac or defence industry complexes in Ličko, Osijek and elsewhere. Petar Zinajić recalls that they went from house to house collecting demobilised combatants, "from the living back to the dead". They had to leave their burnt-out huts and shacks as they were, and this resulted in widespread hostility towards the new regime.

As elsewhere, the creation of workers' associations in the Bosnian Borders also ran into opposition from individual peasants, in particular those who were better off. While the Communists were "duty bound" to support the "workers' association" project, councillors and others with a stake in the SRZs hesitated, but nevertheless mainly carried out their duty. After the second plenary of the KPJ executive in January 1949, a wave of new SRZs swept over the areas where the revolt later broke out, among other areas; in Cazin county alone, seven SRZs were set up in just over a year. These were the *Nurija Pozderac* association in Pjanići, the *Borac* association in Krndija, *Ilija Bajić* in Gata, *Mujo Žunić* in Brezova Kosa, *Ahmet Fetagić* in Gnjilavac, *Partisan* in Šumatac, and *Jusuf Sabljaković* in Lučka/Pećigrad. As recalled by the chief executive of Cazin county council, they were mainly mini-associations with a membership made up primarily of Communists, who joined out of a sense of duty and were usually not householders. Their fathers would give them a weak cow or a small piece of land so that they could join. This sometimes resulted in family disputes which obviously only aggravated agricultural production. All the associations, as a rule "mini", failed to function properly.

The dissatisfaction of the peasants because of the SRZs, where hunger was not uncommon, was expressed in acts of sabotage, such as those on the eve of the revolt in Cazin county when straw was set alight in the *Borac* association, or in Slunj county when the *Stanko "Ćanica" Opačić* association was robbed. This opposition to the SRZs did of course, like the issues related to the quotas, result in some notorious cases. Such is the case of Milija Graora, the sister of the national hero Milan. She resisted the pressure to join the SRZ by lying in front of a tractor that had come to plough her land, thereby saving it from forced collectivisation.

The case of Omer Mujagić

This individual historical case brings together the majority of the components of the reality on the ground in the Bosnian Borders dealt with thus far. The case of Omer Mujagić, a peasant from Čaglica, Kladuša county, taking place as it did in the period at issue, can be considered the ideal direct introduction or prelude to the Peasants' Revolt itself. It was certainly a clear signal of impending social unrest in the Borders, but one which went unnoticed.

The case is presented here based on the trial documents created between the end of 1949 and the end of 1952 and kept in the archives of Banja Luka provincial court.

Omer Mujagić was detained in Velika Kladuša on 20 December 1949 on suspicion of the offence of "enemy agitation and propaganda, defamation and threatening the authorities". The investigation was entrusted to the UDBA station for Kladuša county, and signed by Pero Mutić. The county prosecutor Milan Ostojić ordered on 23 December (order served on the UDBA station in Velika Kladuša, the accused and the public prosecution service) as follows,

"I hereby open an investigation into and order the detention of Omer Mujagić of Čaglica. The investigation is to be concluded by 10 March 1950, and is entrusted to inspector Pero Mutić. Reasons: an inspection of the accused's record indicates that the accused Omer Mujagić did maliciously call upon residents of the Čaglica ward to resist and disobey the current social and political order..."

Omer was interviewed on 21 December 1949, 8 and 9 March and 5 May 1950. The first interview allowed a general picture to be drawn of him. He was born in 1923, a peasant farmer of average means, non-determined Muslim, self-taught literate, the father of three children, born and resident in Čaglica, and attended the *mekteb* for four years; he was a non-combatant until 1943, from 1943 he was in the German *Blue* Division, subsequently in the *Tiger* Division in Donji Lapac, from 1944 in the Una operational group, then the German *Eins* Command, and from spring 1945 until he was demobilised, in the Third Muslim brigade, Eighth Division. He was arrested in Čaglica on 20 December 1949.

The investigator Husein Nekić asked him during the first interview about his conversation on 1 December 1949 with Salko Mašinović, the secretary of the Čaglica ward. Omer admitted to the conversation in Tomića Klanac, but not to the content of the accusation which Salko had reported to the investigator. Omer denied all the accusations. He said that:

"he had not told Salko to discourage people from taking part in labour mobilisation, nor did he (Omer) discourage people from doing so;
he had not told the secretary 'to be good to the people, and that there are ten of us ready to beat up anyone forcing people to take part in labour mobilisation';
he had not spoken about challenging the labour mobilisation targets, 'nor did we mention the targets';
he had not told Salko not to work like executive Hasan Kljajić, 'as there will be a new government and things will change';
he did not tell Salko that that 'was the party's policy and they just lie to the people and force them into labour mobilisation, no-one has to go'".

Omer gave short negative replies to the investigator's following questions:

"Mujagić, what did you say about the SRZ, that 'only bloody Communists join'?"

"Mujagić, did you say that you know 'what Communists are and that only Communists join the SRZ. Communists' wives give their children away to the children's' home a month and a half before birth or a month and a half afterwards and never see them again'?"

"Mujagić, did you say that among the Communists brothers and sisters don't know each other and have sex?"

"Did you say that Communists don't believe in God and they want to turn you away as well so you don't believe, but that you still hope there will be a war and you will beat up those who are converting people to communism?"

"Did you urge Salko not to register with the SRZ as it's no good, only Communists go there?"

"Did you say that you 'will skin like a goat anyone who registers with the SRZ'?"

"Did you threaten executive Hasan Kljajić in front of Salko 'because things will change', and that you will get your own back on Hasan for ordering labour mobilisation for your father and brother?"

"Did you say to Salko that that evening you were on your way to the ward council to cut executive Hasan Kljajić's throat?"

At the end of the first interview, Omer said after denying everything, "When you bring witnesses to repeat all that to my face I'll be happy to take the punishment of the law if I'm guilty."

The investigation against Omer Mujagić continued with an interview of the witness Huso Mujagić on 3 January 1950. He testified about Omer's behaviour in connection with an event in May 1949 when the corn harvest assessment commission visited the village:

"He started to complain and said that the assessment of the corn on his land hadn't been done correctly, that it had been recorded as greater than it was, in his village he incited his neighbours so that they all started to complain as Omer had raised an uproar among his neighbours, because they had incorrectly assessed his corn. Omer went onto his land and measured it and made the commission come back to his land, creating a commotion in the village. At the meeting when we assessed the meat quota Omer Mujagić complained saying that he couldn't give 130 kg meat which he insisted on, and I said to him that it wasn't right for him to complain like that."

The same day, 3 January, another witness, Salko Mašinović, was also interviewed. After being confronted with Salko on 8 March, Omer admitted much of what he had denied during the interview on 21 December. He admitted,

"that I was on my way to cut Hasan Kljajić's throat because he ordered labour mobilisation for my brother Suljo and my father Fehim for the fourth time, saying 'Salko you can see that this isn't fair, my brother and father are going for the fourth time and they don't have to, it's just the party's policy'. I told

Salko to be good to the people not like Hasan Kljajić because spring's coming and there are ten of us preparing to beat up the managers who send people to labour mobilisation, that when the target comes from the county council to challenge it as much as he can to make things easier for the people, that only Communists join the SRZ and they don't believe in God, that this government won't last so he should be good to the people."

After his admission Omer was charged the same day. The trial was set for 1 June 1950 in the Banja Luka provincial court.

The charge, dated 5 May 1950, was brought by the provincial public prosecutor Radomir Savić, and accused Omer of three criminal matters. The first related to joining the *Blue* Division in March 1943, the *Tiger* Division in August of the same year, and accepting a position in the German IC Command in February 1945 where he remained until liberation, "thereby joining enemy armed forces and other armed units and fighting in the war against his own country and her allies." The second was that he told Salko everything cited above from the investigation files, with the conclusion that he "thereby spread enemy propaganda containing incitement to violent overthrow of the current political order." The third was that he threatened Salko "Salko, don't register at the workers' association, because we will try to beat up everyone who registers and smash it, look at Husić Ahmić, that bastard will be the first to register, if he does I'll skin him like a goat", thereby using threats to prevent membership of the workers' association. The prosecutor considered that by so doing Omer had committed offences under sections 3(5) and 9 Crimes against the People and the State Act and s. 13 Agricultural Associations Act, and asked the court to find the defendant guilty and sentence him in accordance with the law.

In the justification of the charge, the prosecutor Savić attacked the defendant's defence that Salko had accused him because they had argued in autumn 1949, as

"the witness Mašinović didn't accuse him immediately after the argument, but only a few months later. Furthermore, the witness Mašinović was not secretary of the ward council at that time, such that I see no reason why the witness would have an argument with him as he had no official responsibility in the activation of mobilised labour. Furthermore, the witness is an elected representative of the authorities, which must be taken into account when assessing the credibility of his evidence. For these reasons the defendant's defence must be rejected in its entirety as unfounded. The justification of the charge states that the defendant has committed the serious offence of propaganda. The serious nature of this offence and its adverse effects on society are shown by the manner in which the offence was committed. In his conversation with the witness Mašinović the defendant demonstrated that he is openly hostile to the current political order, and that his intention was to threaten the interests of the government. The offence on count one of the charge is also serious, with major adverse effects for society. The adverse effects of the offence and of the defendant himself on society are shown by the fact that he was an official of a *Gestapo* institution. It can be seen from the facts as proved that the defendant is a very dangerous individual who has committed serious criminal offences, such that I ask the court to impose the maximum sentence provided for by law."

According to the record of the trial, held on 1 June 1950, the defendant Omer Mujagić pleaded not guilty, and offered a defence for each count of the charge. He admitted that he had been in enemy armed forces until 1944, but that he had been in the Partisans since 1944, that he was captured by renegades in April 1944 and imprisoned in the Zavalje camp near Bihać until February 1945, and then worked in the kitchen in the IC Command. It was acknowledged that he had fought in the JNA against the occupier and been decorated, including with the Order for Valour. He denied having spoken against the quotas in the presence of Salko Mašinović, claiming that he had even given 170 kg of cereals more than he was required to. He also denied inciting people not to join the SRZ.

When confronted with the witness Salko Mašinović, neither of them changed their account. The witness Okan Ćoralić, an illiterate peasant farmer from Čaglica, then gave evidence, stating that in his presence and that of the other neighbours, "Omer said several times that we should create an SRZ because life is better in it." That was the end of the pleadings in the trial, brief as was usual in other similar cases.

The prosecutor did not amend the charge and applied for the maximum punishment, while the defence counsel asked for the defendant to be acquitted of the second two counts of the charge, and asked for a minimum sentence on the first count under application of article 62 of the Criminal Code as the defendant had been in the JNA.

The Banja Luka provincial court delivered its judgment on Omer Mujagić on 2 June. He was found guilty on count one of joining the *Blue* Division in March 1943, the *Tiger* Division in August 1943, the German IC Command in February 1945,

> "thereby joining enemy armed forces and other armed units and fighting in the war against his own country and her allies, contrary to section 3(5) Crimes against the People and the State Act; on count two of telling Mašinović Salko not to force people into the labour mobilisation and not to collect the quotas because there were ten of them ready to beat up anyone forcing people to take part in labour mobilisation and collecting quotas, and telling the same to protect people because the government would fall and things would change, contrary to section 9 Crimes against the People and the State Act; on count three of telling Salko Mašinović not to force people to join the SRZ, and that he would skin Husić Ahmić like a goat if he registered, contrary to s. 13 Agricultural Associations Act."

In other words, the prosecution case was accepted in full, which was common practice in the courts at that time.

Omer Mujagić was sentenced the same day, 2 June. Under the aforesaid provisions of the Crimes against the People and the State Act and the Agricultural Associations Act, in conjunction with article 62 of the Criminal Code, he was sentenced to six years' imprisonment with hard labour and loss of the civil rights under article 37 of the Criminal Code, other than parental rights, for one year. He was also ordered to pay 940 plus 500 dinars' costs.

After sentencing the case followed the standard procedural course. The interior ministry by memorandum of 2 July 1950 informed the Banja Luka provincial court that Omer Mujagić would serve his sentence in Zenica prison. The Kladuša county court reported on 9 August 1950 that Omer Mujagić had paid the costs in the sum of 1440 dinars and that the sum had been credited to the Bosnian Ministry of Finance. Omer was delivered to Zenica prison on 7 September 1950. By memo to Zenica prison dated 27 December 1950, the Banja Luka provincial court sought, "as early as possible", information on Omer Mujagić's "behaviour, health and work performance." The memo was followed by a reminder. Only on 24 April 1951 did Zenica prison reply that Omer Mujagić was working in the Kakanj mine and "performs poorly. His behaviour is poor and undisciplined, such that the sentence does not appear to be having a corrective effect on him. Health good. Prone to spreading false enemy propaganda", signed by governor Jovo Đukić. Further to this report, on 1 June 1951 the president of Bosnia and Herzegovina rejected an appeal for clemency submitted in 1950 by Omer's mother, Plema Mujagić. A second appeal for clemency did have some effect. On 15 June 1952, Omer's father Fehim wrote another appeal. On 15 August the governor of Zenica prison provided the Banja Luka provincial court with further information on Omer in accordance with the standard procedure. The same governor, Jovo Đukić, reported that Omer was in Pajatov Han, that he was a good worker, performing well, that he respected the rules and his superiors, was not engaged in negative political activity, and was in good health. "We are of the opinion that the sentence has had a corrective effect on him". Further to this report, on 14 November 1952, the presidency of Bosnia and Herzegovina granted a partial remission in the matter of Omer Mujagić: "the result is that the sentence is reduced from six (6) years to five (5) years."[3]

Vera Kržišnik-Bukić, Cazinska Buna 1950 (footnotes omitted)

Dear Mr Autonomašević

I managed Kuplensko from start to end. Memories...

What comes to mind when you think back on Kuplensko?

"Like in every mission, first of all who am I, I'm 25 years in UNHCR and I've been always operating in what we call warzones or high-risk environments. My career started with the very unfortunate and tough war in Bosnia, so I served in Croatia, I served in Bosnia. Because before Kuplensko I served in Karlovac, and I was with the 30,000 men and women that came out of Omarska, Keraterm, so Kuplensko was a second wave for me coming out of Rwanda with the genocide. I'm that type of manager. Kuplensko, I remember one morning, was almost the end-tail of Operation Storm, and my boss because I was at that time a junior officer, despite having [been] given a great responsibility I was very young compared to the responsibility I have today. The representative for Croatia based in Zagreb called me and said, 'Alessandra, I have information that a lot of people are on the move out of Velika Kladuša into Croatia. Go out, go find them'. I said, 'Yes, I will, I understand though there's been some fighting around here, and I'll be very careful but I'll go find them'. That's the information, we go. I jump alone on my jeep, at that time you know we were like this you go, today it would be a little bit different, you know, it would be more security clearances before, you know. You jump and you go. And what I saw was a lot of...just desert around me. Animals that were running confused, because people were fleeing, fled, right?, it was the end-tail of the conflict in that area, and I was looking for this Kuplensko. God knows, I said, there were an area of this Kuplensko coming out of Velika Kladuša. Where is this Kuplensko? All I could see moving around Karlovac...Was it Karlovac? Where I was? Kuplensko...Vojnić, yes, Vojnić, but you can help me a little bit with the places. Abandoned tanks, piglets, little little piglets that were sucking my jeans thinking I was their mum, that really struck my heart. Horses, also the animals. I said, my God, also the animals are scared and confused and are trying to find refuge here.

"Finally, I am moving and I reach this area, then I learn it's Kuplensko, and I see people walking. People walking, and at that time there was also the Croatian army there, that were doing the opposite. They were pushing these people back. At that point, I intervened and I said, 'I'm from the United Nations, I'm from UNHCR, you cannot refoule, you cannot push these people back'. I call in support also people from the UNPROFOR area that were there, and I start this very very tough negotiation with the Croatian officials that were ready, literally Jovo, literally ready to push these people back with tanks. We...I found myself in the middle of, you know, how do I protect the concept of non-refoulement, article 33 here, and we said through negotiation, but they could say, you know, 'Fuck off' quite frankly, or really standing literally in front of these people and saying, almost saying, 'You push them, you go over our bodies first', you know, you have to believe me, that was the intense. At the end I managed to enter in mediation, very long mediation, I was on the phone with the representative of UNHCR Croatia who was mediating with obviously the government and the military from the Zagreb point of view, and at the end Kuplensko came about in front of my eyes like this, where the Croats said 'Fine, they can't move forward, they stop here now'. And it is there that tents were brought, whatever could be brought to shelter people immediately…was created. And the first winter together also we passed with snow and everything. What comes to my mind immediately was that, you know, defending the non-refoulement, because these people were about to be pushed back with the tanks, because Croatia at that time did not want them. You know better than me because I understand you are from that area, that that was a very very delicate political group as you know, it was just not anybody that was crossing but it was you know that very well, it was people from Velika Kladuša, it was many people around the Agrokomerc, and Abdić I remember, so it was a very very delicate situation to manage. But at that time, those were human beings with women and children that needed our full support, because fleeing a situation of conflict and potential, very potential danger in the Velika Kladuša side.

"So, I lived with them for almost a year, we stood in that camp. That doesn't mean that the relation was easy. Like it's not easy in any, any situation. The letter that you have showed me, I have to remember when was it, those are letters that I always welcome, always welcome, because it gave me the proof that these people were alive, and were fighting for what they considered their rights and needs. So you said, 'What is your reaction in front of this letter?' every time, actually we constituted a refugee committee, I remember, where I said, 'You must express yourself, you must not live like a vegetable in this camp. If we have to fight, we fight'. That was our, how can I say, it was our dynamics, it was our being together, it was our trying to make it through. I remember one day where they had their animals, they had their donkeys, they had their tractors, they came with all their life, and the question was, how are we going to feed the animals? They also have the right to be fed. And to find the budget, to find the money, to find who would bring us the hay, and who would bring us the food, etc. etc. was the big big challenge. The big challenge of the winter with the cold, because remember, the Croats said, 'OK, but they can't move from here. That's it. You delineate the camp, and from here we push to find a solution' and it took a year as you remember for these people to finally start deciding to return back, a year a year and a half, on a voluntary basis, whoever wanted to go back who go back, I think some remained in Croatia, I think it would be nice to see how many, who they are today. For example, with many of the Karlovac camp, from Omarska and Keraterm I am in contact, especially the ones who came to Italy and I can guarantee you it's…the emotion to see them married with children, integrated in this society, and travelling back when they want back home as well, is an incredible experience of life-saving. So, I'm the one who, you know, says I wonder where they are today. So this is what comes to my mind. It's an experience of proximity with them, they were people like you and like me, they had opinions, there were many who were politicised, so you know many were in the camp also trying to reflect and trying to come up with other agendas, I had to balance everything there, it was other organisations working, Action Contre la Faim, ICRC, slowly slowly more and more people came, we went through a rough winter of snow but I still remember one day, I am convinced Jovo you might laugh at this, I am convinced that in Kuplensko in that camp, I started to believe in Santa Claus. Because I met a man with a long beard and white hair, during Christmas, for me, our Christmas, our Italian Christmas, pardon me if I talk about the Christmas, but I said, 'Oh my God, Santa Clause passed through this camp', you know. And in…he was an inhabitant of this, he just looked like Santa Clause, and I remember he helped me distribute a lot of chocolate that we managed to get as a donation for the kids for the

New Year, a bit of, a bit of a New Year celebration for the kids. And he helped me distribute all of this Hersey chocolate that I received as a donation, literally tons of it, and do you know that a few days later I was looking for him to thank him, and I couldn't find him…in the tough situation that we went through. Kuplensko for me as ████████████ and for UNHCR was an incredible challenge, to maintain for a year, a year and a half, people that were confined in that area, balanced…was the challenge to keep them certainly alive because it was like a bit of a closed camp, there were two…in order to go out, we needed as I remember special permissions for people to move, it was happening, especially for the ones who needed medical attention etc. There was medical attention in the camp, there was Solidarités, ICRC I remember, UNHCR, so…but it was a camp. It was a camp built in 48 hours, 72 hours out of what we had at that moment. You see what I mean.

"So that was Kuplensko, it was a story of incredible empathy, and also incredible fights, because most of the time I was saying, 'What do you want? What do you want? We can't give more than this because we're all confined here like this', you know what I mean? 'We are keeping alive, this is what counts now, thinking about the future, how you know we can inject what is the solution', of people wanting to go back when it's safe to go back, or people with links in Croatia, many stayed in Croatia because they had links and they could prove the links. That was for me, was most for me Kuplensko, was an incredible, I was only 32-33 years old, I'm 56 today, I was the lowest grade in UNHCR, and I was given this responsibility to, to be somehow with my strengths and my weaknesses the only focal point, I have to say, for the Kuplensko residents".

What pressure did the Croatian authorities exert on UNHCR?

"The pressure was very much at the beginning when these people stopped, because at the end of the day we could give a number, I think we were talking 25,000 people, yes? 25,000 people that is I remember the statistics, the number we were giving to the headquarters then when the media was coming. The pressure was pretty much at the beginning. The pressure was very clear that they wanted to exercise refoulement, and I have to say that that, I consider a great success, that we managed to avoid refoulement. We managed, that I tell you very openly we managed, and we managed through mediation and we managed through standing in front of them".

Did they exert pressure on you to help get rid of the refugees?

"I don't know, I was in the camp, I was a simple field officer there, I have never received directly…Well, there was a checkpoint with Croat guards at the entrance of Kuplensko. I don't know if you have ever been? You were there how, you were there as a refugee? So you were young though, that's what I thought, because I did a bit of Google about you, I said to whom am I talking here right? And I see that you studied in Kuplensko. Jovo, I'm also a girl from the university of life, don't worry. So you were young at that time, no? I can imagine. So obviously, I don't remember you, you don't remember me. Oh my God!"

In February 1996, the Croatian police and the media claimed that UNHCR had endorsed a major raid, that resulted in 69 arrests. Is that true?

"Sure, I remember that, I remember that. Not at all, not at all. How can we endorse a raid? You know, Jovo, you want to find a solution, you want to come out of it, just finger point UNHCR in everything and then you come out clean, you know what I mean? This one I don't accept, absolutely. I think I was in that raid as well, shouting like a lunatic, they know me that I was, that I could shout at a Croatian soldier. We were monitoring the way they were patrolling, that I can remember very well. Remember that sometimes they would patrol and walk inside the camp? Be assured that we were watching".

There was criticism of UNHCR by the refugees at the time. Other complaints by the refugees were:
  no access to legitimate trade:

"I don't recall, I mean I know there was the issue of the trade with Velika Kladuša. That happens everywhere, unfortunately. The smugglers and things in camps like that happens everywhere, and I think that sometimes I think the police wasn't…sometimes they were angry at that, there was not some fights sometimes against the smugglers? Was it cigarettes that was being smuggled? Absolutely, I mean I remember that that was one of the biggest challenges that we had to balance and to avoid conflict also among the smugglers themselves, no? Fights. My God, because it was a society, a microcosm in, how many square metres was that Kuplensko? It was not very large area. It was then everybody, you remember, was on the road, no? Everybody came down together on the road".

  failure to create the conditions for safe return:

"When it comes to a return UNHCR never promoted return to Velika Kladuša at that time, and because it's the refugee, him or herself that can decide if and when it is safe for that person to return. OK? We ensured, my role in Kuplensko was to ensure at the end of the day, that was my main role. Of course the food, and the medics, and the presents very important, but my main role was that there was no forced return. *En masse.* Whoever moved before the closure of the camp, moved on its own – very few did, very very few and, you know, came to me and said, 'We want to return', and they registered with us, and they returned. But UNHCR during my time it was never promoted or facilitated any group return to Velika Kladuša at that time".

If you could go back there again, what would you do differently?

"If I would go back there and do it differently, probably ensure a bit of a higher quality of life, certainly, OK?, because the conditions were, and you were there, you lived there, were really precarious, correct? were precarious, but believe me the Croats never allowed us to build any structure that seemed and looked like semi-permanent. Because I do remember trying to negotiate pre-fab houses like we did in Gašinci, I was also in Gašinci when we closed Karlovac, and the answer was 'No, because this is a transit situation and it has to remain a transit situation for these people to return, we don't want to give the impression that people…' so I would, I would invest, I would scream more, probably, but remember I was a very junior officer, I was a field officer there. But if I could do things differently, was probably to be there with a different grade and with more power probably to, for the living conditions. For the rest, I have to say that we were there, we were there, we were present, we were inside. I remember also the container office there. I still, I have some pictures, I have pictures of the distribution of the chocolate, and I have the picture of the Father – the Santa Claus. I don't know if you remember that man. Pandža! Jovo, I tell you the truth, that man gave me so much strength, so many people…but I wonder if one day through you we can meet some of them? But you, you moved to the UK, because your accent is…Oh, man, amazing. It would be nice to have a reunion, no? That was an incredible experience for all of us, for you, for me from different angles, but I think that at the end of the day, despite the difficulties, yes, would I do things differently? Yes, certainly the living conditions were very precarious, when it was snowing my God Jovo, and raining, you remember the mud everywhere, and…but I always admired Jesus the patience and the resilience of all of you.

"It's you know, talking very openly, nobody ever asks a humanitarian worker what have you gained, what have you gained out of this, how did you grow out of this, you know, and I became a stronger woman and I'm more resilient because of what, what I saw in all of you, in the refugees I've met throughout my career, you know, became a better person because of what all of you went through. And believe me, Jovo, I have my weaknesses but I want, I still remain that girl you met in Gašinci - in Kuplensko, never stopped fighting, went through my own problems, with the organisation, understood sometimes, not understood in others, survived two terrorist attacks, I'm alive because somebody wants me alive, believe me. In Somalia I survived a big terrorist attack, and today they have hit Mogadishu again. So, in a way, this is very simply who I am. That doesn't mean that the refugees sometimes didn't have problems with me, you know saying, 'Hey, where are you, why is this not moving', that was our relationship, trying to do our best, no? I will always put my face to the situation so don't hesitate to contact me again, and I will never stay back, a memory or a responsibility, you know? I will always put my face…But I wanted to know who you were, because you can't talk with these things just to anybody, no?

"Yes, definitely, through you, this is what I'm trying to do here in Italy, what I want to know is that, my God Jovo, we are all part of one freaking humanity here, what is going on…we're part of one humanity, and if your book can end up talking about this as well, we're part of one humanity, we are marginalising each other here. Anyway, let's fight together!

"Thank you very much for giving me this opportunity to go beyond the angry letter of what I considered to be, my God, brothers and sisters, we were in the same mud there, we were in the same mud".

Email of 22 July 2016 and interview via Skype on 26 July 2016 (the 20th anniversary of the capitulation of the last Kuplensko refugees in the face of impending starvation, disenfranchisement and refoulement)

---

[1] Djurić, 1990:2
[2] Savić, 2000:9-24
[3] Kržišnik-Bukić, 1991:31-69

PART 4
THE BLESSED PLAIN

*"After WWII, Tito was travelling around Yugoslavia. He came across a farmer
ploughing a field with a pair of cows.
'Why are you mistreating those animals?' he asked.
'I can't afford a tractor', the farmer replied
'Take his name and assign him a tractor', Tito ordered.
Overjoyed, the farmer asked who he had to thank for his good fortune.
'The man you fought for', Tito replied.
The man embraced him and cried, 'Ante, is it really you? I thought they got you
along with Mussolini and the* Führer!*"*[i]

---

[i] Told by Tetin in Kuplensko in 1995.

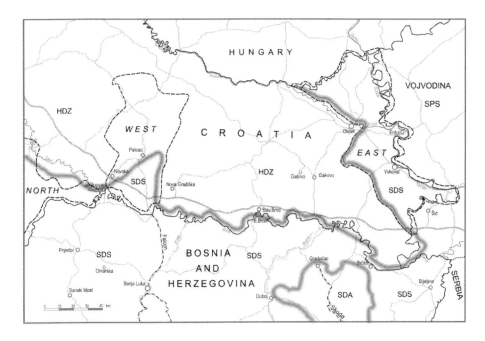

Showing the front lines, the UN protected areas and UNPROFOR routes.

Showing the front lines and UNPROFOR routes.

THE BLESSED PLAIN

Part 1 - the Neretva valley

Slowly the train shunted along, to much heaving and lurching, and seeming to pause to catch its breath at every village on the way. The dirty windows and uncomfortable bench seats only added to the rustic charm, as did the dour ticket inspector, especially when I responded to his demand with "*Bujrum*" ("here you are")[ii]. We were travelling to Gašinci in Slavonia, the southern expanse of the great Pannonian plain which extends north into Hungary and then east to the Carpathian Mountains in Romania, and rolls across northern Croatia right into Vojvodina in northern Serbia, with its Hungarian minority (13%, while the Serbs constitute 67% of the population; there are a total of 25 ethnic groups, including 3% Croats, in Vojvodina) and provincial capital Novi Sad. A mass "rally for truth" was held in Novi Sad on 9 July 1988, led by Serbs from Kosovo, who were joined by Šešelj and other extremists from Belgrade, encouraged by the media (Šešelj, the Serbian Žirinovskij[iii], fond of quoting Tolstoj, and traditional, fruity idioms, called by Milošević's wife a "primitive Turk", once said that Croatia should be limited to what can be seen from the top of Zagreb cathedral, the tallest building in Croatia[iv]). Despite the violent disorder, the local authorities refused to give way, and the federal presidency condemned the use of such methods to bring about constitutional change as "playing with fire" and "opening the way to anarchy"[2] (Milošević had allegedly tried to stop this rally, because he thought it was too early[3]). This was followed by a series of similar rallies throughout Serbia proper, and on 5 October, another rally was held in Novi Sad, and between 20,000-50,000 enthusiasts from all over Serbia besieged the headquarters of the Vojvodina KPJ[4]. Federal president Dizdarević demanded that Milošević travel to Novi Sad and disperse the rally, but despite various promises, nothing was done. At a meeting of the federal presidency that night it was decided not to proclaim a state of emergency or use force. The next day, the local party leadership, fearing for their lives, resigned. The crowds dispersed, and all leadership posts in the autonomous region, and even some business posts, were soon occupied by Milošević's people. Having secured Serbia proper and Vojvodina, next on his list was Montenegro. The federal presidency telexed the presidents of the republics and autonomous regions with a warning on the constitutional danger of the "rallies for truth" and ordering heightened vigilance[5]. In Slavonia I was struck by the similarities with rail travel in Romania (including the graffiti: someone had scratched into the wooden panelling of the Romanian train, in English, "Kill all Gypsies" (Romania has the largest Romany population in Europe, and Romanies were enslaved there until 1856, when under the treaty of Paris that put an end to the Crimean War, Romania escaped from Russian influence and received greater autonomy under the Ottomans, as did Serbia). Travelling by train many years later

---

[ii] Bosnian slang.
[iii] Popular Russian rabble-rouser, who has called for the "Russian pacification of Eurasia".
[iv] Addressing the court in 2005 during his trial at the ICTY, Šešelj, who has a PhD in law, compared himself to Pierre Bezuhov, the hero of *War and Peace*, before saying "Fuck your mothers, the lot of you". *Seljak ostaje seljak* ("you can't make a silk purse out of a pig's Jackson Pollocks"). In the 1980s, Šešelj served two years in prison in Zenica for sedition, where he acquired the nickname the "Ballerina". In one of his lost poems, Tetin wrote, "*Šešelju jebem sve šta ima od roda*" ("fuck Šešelj and his whole extended family").

from Budapest to Bucharest, I was struck by the tangible differences that exist even today between the former Habsburg and Ottoman Balkan territories). It was August 1996, and Seka and I had left that morning from Karlovac and changed at Zagreb. On either side of the railway were endless corn fields, punctuated by orchards and individual houses and hamlets, with the occasional post-industrial town, notably Novska and Slavonski Brod ("Slavonian boat"). Just 10 km south-west of Novska on the border with Bosnia is Jasenovac, the site of Yugoslavia's most notorious death camp during WWII, where hundreds of thousands of Serbs, Romanies and Jews (and 8,000 dissident Croats) met a violent end at the hands of the *Ustaše*[6]. It was not mechanised, like the German camps, but rather everything was done by hand, using clubs and knives. Slavonski Brod is a river port and important historic crossing point to its twin Bosanski Brod, across the river and the border, and is now the registration centre for the tens of thousands of refugees crossing Croatia from Serbia to Slovenia. Bosanski Brod has an oil refinery that is a source of pollution of EU air across the border. It was also the scene of the first major fighting in Bosnia. In 1991, the JNA had launched attacks from there in an attempt to lift the siege of their barracks in Slavonski Brod; and in 1992, as the Bosnian SDS put up barricades and tried to block the bridge, the HV supplied the HDZ south of the river[7]. In November 1944, after the liberation of Belgrade, Brod became the main escape route between Sarajevo and Zagreb for the *Wehrmacht* retreating from the Balkans[8] ("*Šta smo to uradili*" – "the biggest mistake we ever made" was the judgement of Mehmet, a local truck driver from Kakanj, on the Partisan victory, reached on the evidence of the speed with which Germany recovered after the war and the present state of the former Yugoslavia)[v]. The main difference here from the Croatian Borders was the topography, which was flat, and stretched out towards the horizon. We seemed to be on top of the world, a lifetime away from the killing fields, meadows and hills with their thousand hidden dangers. I had just finished working with a team of monitors in Velika Kladuša and Cazin in the first Bosnian elections since the war (absent refugees had been able to vote, and turnout in some areas was 107%[9]), which the DNZ won with a large majority in Velika Kladuša, also obtaining a good score in Cazin, despite multiple election fraud aimed at preventing Babo's comeback. Practices ranged from intimidation at polling stations to systematic miscounting of ballots. One teller in Velika Kladuša, caught red-handed sorting Babo's ballots into piles of 12 or more rather than 10 (to facilitate subsequent totalling), got up and left, but not without a parting shot: "*Biće krvi do koljena*" ("we'll be up to our knees in your blood") (that same night, during the counting of votes in Cazin, the official from one polling station turned up late, evidently the worse for *rakija*, and when he submitted his summary report form on the day's events, was told he should have put it together with the ballot papers in the sealed - and unopenable - bag that he held in his hand. Undaunted, he simply removed the seal, placed the form inside, and put the seal back on). Dedović became the MP for Velika Kladuša. On 15 June, Silajdžić had held an election rally in Cazin, but was nearly lynched and had to be taken to hospital in Karlovac after being struck on the head with a metal bar. At the time it was said the local population were dissatisfied with the support they had received from Sarajevo during the war, but it was later alleged that Izetbegović had attempted

---

[v] An elderly man in Kakanj once told me how during that period they had captured a group of *Wehrmacht* soldiers. One of them was so young he looked like a girl, and he wept and begged for his life, so they spared him. He lived with them for three years, working on their smallholding to earn his keep, before going back to Germany.

to assassinate him as part of his general policy of stifling any opposition[10]. Babo was charged with war crimes by the Bihać district prosecutor (a post once held by Hakija Pozderac[11]) the same month as the elections, and in September his trial in absentia began. In 2001, the Croatian supreme court ruled that he could not be extradited, as Croatia does not extradite its citizens, but that the Croatian courts were competent to hear the case under the treaty on mutual assistance in criminal matters with Bosnia (and because he had dual nationality), and he was convicted in 2002 (Babo puts this, the only such case, down to a conspiracy between Izetbegović and Croatian president Mesić, who wanted a scapegoat so that the whole awkward "separatist" affair could be conveniently closed)[vi][12]. As a result, it was not until 12 September 2012 that he made a triumphal return to Bosnia, after a 17-year absence, where he was greeted by thousands of his "separatists", and held a *skup* ("rally") in the suburb of Podzvizd. In his speech he said among other things that Agrokomerc was "too noble a horse to be

---

[vi] According to Babo, the case goes back to an information for war crimes laid against him by Dudaković in July 1994, which was rejected by the ABiH military prosecutor. It was then submitted to the Bihać public prosecutor (as an information for genocide and war crimes), where it lay dormant until the failed assassination attempt against him in April 1996, and he was charged in August of that year. Meanwhile, the Bihać district court set aside the bench warrant for Babo in October 1998, because under Dayton the approval of the ICTY was required for war crimes trials (the AID had submitted a case against Babo to the ICTY in January 1997, but the reply was only received in November 1998, when the ICTY announced it would not try Babo, but would allow the local legal system to do so if they had the necessary evidence. The ICTY considered that "on the papers submitted by you the evidence is sufficient by international standards to provide reasonable grounds for believing that Fikret Abdić has committed a serious violation of IHL, namely the inhumane treatment of civilians and of prisoners of war, and forcing civilians into military service" but not "attacking civilian targets and starving the civilian population"). In January 1999, the Bihać district court asked the prosecutor to "take a view" on the charge in the light of the ICTY's reply, and the prosecutor dropped the case. But the same month, the Bihać police, acting *ultra vires*, issued an arrest warrant for Babo for war crimes, and the court then issued a bench warrant under the 1996 charge in order to make the police's action legal. As they say in Bosnia, "*Kadija te tuži, kadija te sudi*" ("judge jury and executioner"). In 2002 he was convicted of war crimes under art. 120 Croatian Criminal Code (*OKZRH*), which covers the ordering or commission of various acts in contravention of IHL, but does not recognise "command responsibility", i.e. "joint criminal enterprise" (see below). The judgment states: "The defendant [...] 1) thus, in breach of the rules of international law in wartime, ordered, planned and organised the unlawful detention of the civilian population, the physical and psychological abuse of the civilian population, or their inhuman treatment, and their forced labour and service in the army of the 'Autonomous Region of West Bosnia', i.e. an enemy army [...] 2) thus, in breach of the rules of international law in wartime, ordered and organised the torture and inhuman treatment of POWs". It was later communicated to Babo that Mesić would grant him a pardon if he applied for one, but Babo refused to do so, as that would have been an admission of guilt. In 2006, Babo submitted an application to the ICTY for a retrial in The Hague, as a former member of the presidency, and as his only hope for a fair trial, but it was rejected, because the ICTY were "not interested" in his case. Of over 100 Bosnian war crimes suspects in Croatia, he is the only one to have been tried there. In 2016, a request by the Bosnian courts for Croatia to try former Bosnian presidency member Ante Jelavić, of Vrgorac, removed from office by the high representative in 2001 and convicted in absentia of corruption in 2005, was refused by the Croatian ministry of justice, citing in addition to the above treaty, the European Convention on Mutual Assistance in Criminal Matters of 1959. Babo is now hoping to prepare an application for judicial review of his conviction: it appears to be replete with material breaches of procedural law, and no doubt a re-investigation of the facts would reveal that the true extent of his war crimes is as insignificant in comparison to the charge, as the loss of KM 49 was insignificant compared to the USD 360 million exposure which served as the pretext for the Agrokomerc affair. Almost every death is tragic, and people die in custody in the UK every year, in peacetime. But Tony Blair and Jack Straw have not been called to account for failures in the British armed forces' care of prisoners in Iraq and Afghanistan. Nor has the same rigour been applied to what appear to be far more serious failings by the 5th Corps. What was really behind Babo's conviction for war crimes? As the only leader who managed to sign peace agreements with both of Bosnia's enemies, had he once again become too big to fail? So much for Croatian justice. In 1995, the members of the Croatian law commission and the president of the Supreme Court were all appointed illegally by decree of the prime minister.

ridden by just anyone"[13]. Every year on his birthday while he was in prison, busloads of his supporters would travel to Rijeka to celebrate with him. He was not allowed compassionate parole to attend his brother's funeral in the UK in 2007. His parole finally expired in 2016, when he revisited Velika Kladuša again and was elected mayor[vii]. Babo is still here (at the inauguration ceremony held in Sarajevo, the Cazin district council executive left early to avoid shaking Babo's hand). One of Babo's first acts as mayor was to reinstate the office of *šinter* ("dog-catcher"), a symbolic but effective remedy to a problem that has blighted the town for years. He also reopened the public kitchen, the first time since the war (28% of Bosnians now live in absolute poverty, the "severe deprivation of basic human needs"[14]).

But it was not only the mode of transport and the landscape that was different this time. The war was *fajrant* ("definitively over") in Croatia and Bosnia, and despite the many difficulties, the ceasefire would last. Meanwhile, in Kosovo, a new conflict was just beginning.

It was my first time in Slavonia, the breadbasket of Croatia until it was undermined by agricultural imports from the EU in the run-up to Croatia's accession in 2013 (the same thing is about to happen to Bosnia), and I was eager to compare it to the other parts of the country that were so familiar to me. We were also following the route taken by the 200,000 Serbs who had left Croatia one year before, and which is also the same route being followed now, in 2016, in the opposite direction, by the multitude of refugees fleeing death and misery in the Middle East, and turned away from Hungary's door. Further east, it was also the scene of the most intense fighting five years earlier, at the beginning of the war in Croatia, in particular at Vukovar, on the Danube and the border with Serbia. Before the real war started, when Serb and Croat villages were putting up barricades throughout Slavonia, local police chief Josip Reihl-Kir (a Croat) would regularly go out of his way to visit such villages, unarmed, and persuade them to take down their barricades. He was taken out by the HDZ on 1 July, the day before he was supposed to be transferred, at his request, to Zagreb, because he feared for his life[15]. Vukovar with its iconic battered water tower was besieged for three months by the JNA, and artillery and air strikes killed thousands and left hardly a building intact[16]. This was the moment when, like Pinochet[viii], the JNA showed the world (and its own officer corps) that it had

---

[vii] While many people in Velika Kladuša, and more widely throughout Bosnia, hope that Babo will be able to repeat his Agrokomerc economic miracle, others see this as his swan song, a final attempt to redeem his reputation. Some people say that he is simply too old to make a comeback, and point out that he has failed since the war to unite the new economic players in the region, and that the economic and political context has changed radically since Agrokomerc's heyday. Babo told me he wants to "breathe life back into this region, and give the people back their soul". He also told me that he had "no regrets" from the war, and that if he could do it all again, he "wouldn't change a thing". Mirvet is convinced that Babo is still the only politician able to bridge the religious divides and unite the Bosnian people. He said, "The political and military elite's hatred persists, even though the people are largely reconciled – they're living in the past". Meanwhile, increasing tensions in Bosnia driven by 30 years of economic failure and stoked from Belgrade and Zagreb, could forestall any recovery, as could blatant hostility from central government in Sarajevo (and Bihać).

[viii] In 1973, the Chilean chief of staff, at the instigation of the CIA, executed a violent *coup* in the democracy, which led to over three thousand deaths. The presidential palace was bombed from the air, and the president, a friend of Castro's, whose niece is the popular author Isabel Allende, was assassinated there. Pinochet, who had only recently been appointed minister of defence by Allende himself, remained in power until 1990, and as commander-in-chief until 1998. Equally perfidious was Mladić's walkabout in Srebrenica, the kiss of Judas, during which he distributed sweets to children. *Nevalja* ("unsound"). Yet such operations make perfect sense when horror is embraced as a tactic of total war, and the notion that war can be surgical and civilised is the height of hypocrisy. The beast will have its prey, and human

betrayed its sacred oath, turned its back on the constitutional order, and its firepower on the people it was sworn to protect[17]. JNA career officers were the most privileged class in Yugoslavia, and the JNA, a state within the state, with practically unlimited resources, answered only to the federal president. Yet something was clearly rotten in the JNA. I once had dealings with a Russian *boevoj oficer* ("an officer and a gentleman") at the UNPROFOR base in Topusko, and in an instant of lucidity I caught a glimpse behind the mask of the formality of his interactions with his subordinates, and the utter corruption of their relationship was suddenly laid bare to me, as plain as day. He was in a position of total domination over not only his subordinates' career prospects, but also their physical well-being and indeed their very lives. The feeling of repugnance was so powerful that I had to leave the room (I experienced the same aversion many years later, in the *tamnica* ("cells") beneath a London magistrates court, when I was interpreting for a defendant who was subject to an extradition order to Croatia, for murdering his wife during the war. His defence was that he had already been convicted and served his sentence – not for murder, but for desecrating a corpse, because he had shot her as she was hanging herself, and the original court had found that death had already occurred when his bullet struck her). Dizdarević is of the view that Milošević's nationalism first took root in the KOS (so secretive that even the identity of its chief was unknown to the federal president), and from there took over the general staff (although it appears that it actually happened the other way round, i.e. the JNA took over the KOS in 1992, see above). For several years the view had been expressed within the officer corps that the JNA had to act to "save the revolution and the state", and there was also criticism of federal defence minister Kadijević for failing to deal decisively with Milošević's antics. The betrayal appears to have taken place swiftly, without a long planning period – from 1990 onwards. The fact that detailed plans for the defence of every town in the country against foreign occupation were retained only in Belgrade facilitated military planning. Dizdarević also believes that Kadijević had close links to or may even have been under the influence of the Soviet/Russian military (dominated by the Communists even after Jeljcin came to power). In September 1991, according to Jović, Kadijević said in a meeting,

> "The army will lose the war against Croatia if it doesn't secure morale and a successful mobilisation. That can't be done with the half-legitimacy of Yugoslavia – Serbia and Montenegro should proclaim the army theirs and take over the command, financing, war, and everything".

It appears that Kadijević *et al* mistakenly thought they would be able to impose their will on Milošević, but when Kadijević resigned at the end of 1991, there were no objections from his new masters, Milošević and Jović, who had already got from him what they wanted. Up until then, Milošević's ambitions were largely confined to street-fighting. Now he was at the wheel of a war machine[18]. The HV commander of Vukovar accused Tuđman, who had failed to provide heavy weapons, of deliberately sacrificing the town (it was the siege of Vukovar that allowed Tuđman's only friend abroad, Helmut Kohl, to persuade the EU to recognise Croatian independence). Legija called Vukovar a "catastrophe on an unprecedented scale", and the three months of shelling made a serious dent in the JNA's stocks of munitions[19].

---

beings will be destroyed, whether they are the victims or the perpetrators. But as the president of ICRC said in a speech in 2015, "Wars without limits are wars without end".

According to Nikola, Vukovar shook the Serbs' confidence to its foundations: until then, the JNA had been considered invincible (and it may well have been if united against a foreign invader), but the mass desertions, the atrocities, and the fact that it took three months to capture a relatively small town (which had to be flattened in the process), left many reeling with shock, as an article of Yugoslav (and Serb) faith was demolished along with the former Habsburg river port itself. When Vukovar fell on 18 November, Šešelj's paramilitaries took part in the cleansing, and 460 people were rounded up at the hospital and executed[20]. Women and children were given the choice of evacuation to Serbia or Croatia, and bused out, while the men were detained, many of them in Sremska Mitrovica in Vojvodina[21], the home town of Chelsea player Branislav Ivanović, who I have also worked for in the UK. He told me Serbia is full of football fans, and that most of them would give their right arm to watch the likes of John Terry play. Just south of Mitrovica down the river Sava on its way to Belgrade, and in Serbia proper, is Šabac, the home town of another Chelsea player I have worked for, Nemanja Matić. Vukovar later formed part of Sector East, which subsisted after Operation Storm until January 1998, under a UN transitional administration further to the Erdut agreement on peaceful transition of sovereignty signed in November 1995[22]. The population of Vukovar is now 57% Croats and 35% Serbs. Tensions were high in the city in 2013, when the local authority started to place "bilingual" signs (i.e. Croatian written in Cyrillic) on public buildings pursuant to the Minority Rights Act 2002. Veterans' associations and the HDZ, then in opposition, made their disapproval known in vocal fashion, and the signs kept disappearing. The increasingly dire state of the Croatian economy does little to contribute to national reconciliation. The Sava basin was also the scene of the worst flooding in 2014, the worst for 120 years.

From time to time we caught sight through the right-hand window of the river Una and then the Sava of which it is a tributary, the border between Croatia and Bosnia in this part of the country, which flows along in the same direction we were travelling from its source in north-west Slovenia, until it joins the Danube in Belgrade. It seemed to be accompanying us on our new journey like an old friend, and I started to reflect on my other experiences in this terrible garden of Eden, before the Storm (and its 1999 aftershock).

I was heading south-east from Split this time, with its stunning white stone sea front, palm trees, female traffic wardens clad in skimpy white and the Roman Emperor Diocletian's palace incorporated into the winding streets of the old town, a UNESCO world heritage site. The palace was built in 305 AD on the site of a former Greek settlement, and the town, that has been described as the only Dalmatian city with a Neapolitan air (and not just because of the rubbish), grew up around it[23]. Wonderful fresh produce can be obtained at the *peškarija* ("fish market") and the vegetable market, although it is not unknown for the vendors to lean on the scales when weighing your purchase. There is a network of *trajekti* ("ferries") up and down the Adriatic coast, to the various islands, and as far afield as Italy and Greece, and Jadrolinija vessels were as much a feature in and around the port as Calmac is in much colder waters of the Cuan Siar/North Atlantic). Split also has a large industrial zone, where Mussolini once organised a dock strike, before he found his true vocation[24] - after establishing the first fascist state with his violent rabble-rousing skills, he applied Diocletian's code to it (although Diocletian was in fact an Illyrian)[25]. Before the Yugoslav Wars, state-subsidised, world-class *škverovi* ("shipyards") in Split and Pula were the main employers for people living on the coast; but they had to be privatised before Croatia joined the EU in 2013, and now they have practically all gone under (according to Mirvet, the process of adjusting a national economy to EU requirements effectively means creating an exclusive market for EU goods and services while destroying local competition, and Bosnia should learn from Croatia's – and Slovenia's - mistakes)[26]. The KPJ industrial policy, from which the people were liberated in 1990, was called "*Red Rad i Mir*" ("order, work and peace"). In May 1991, a protest at one of the Split shipyards further to the blockade of Kijevo (see above) led to the JNA building in Split being surrounded, and one Macedonian JNA recruit was shot from the crowd (after this the JNA announced it would use live ammunition to defend its institutions)[27]. Now it was the summer of 1994, and although Croatia was at war, there had effectively been a *primirje* ("ceasefire") since 1992. That meant that while the secondary indications of war, such as squaddies loitering around the *riva* ("waterfront") or jogging along the main road in platoons were ever-present (and generally hostile to foreign aid workers), there was no shooting here on the coast. The JNA had laid siege to Dubrovnik ("oak grove": the Illyrian name Ragusa was discarded after WWI for sounding too Italian[28]) in 1991, and in November of that year, Split was cut off from Zagreb when the Maslenica bridge, on the main coast road linking the Zadar peninsula with the mainland, was blown up, practically cutting the coast in two. Zadar was effectively besieged, subject to periodic shelling, and Luka Modrić's family, honest *ribari* ("fisher folk"), became IDPs. In January 1993, the HV suddenly seized the Maslenica gorge (accompanied by a diversion in Sector South), and a pontoon bridge was in place by July, restoring the road link between the southern coast and the rest of the country (although not via the main road, which was still in SDS territory, see above)[29]. A new road bridge was opened in 2005. Shrapnel and bullet holes in the Venetian architecture of Dubrovnik, Zadar and other coastal towns were a reminder that we were sitting on a smoking volcano, and in May 1995 the SVK briefly rocketed Zagreb after the fall of Sector West. The Croatian coast was also full of foreigners at that time, with tourists from western Europe rubbing shoulders with aid workers of all descriptions and refugees from Bosnia, legal and illegal, who, having got this far, were looking for a way to get to Germany or further afield. Unlike today's refugees, it was easier for them to pass unnoticed, and they knew the local ropes. Any Bosnian who could produce a baptismal certificate signed by a Catholic priest could apply for a certificate of nationality. Nevertheless, there was differentiation in the treatment of refugees from Bosnia and IDPs from within Croatia. Refugees were not allowed to work, and if they did find a job, they had to withdraw their application for asylum. I was surprised to even meet some tourists from Mostar, in Bosnia (needless to say, they were not from East Mostar, see below)[ix]. 50 km inland, in the hinterland beyond Sinj, and pushing eastwards across the border north of Livno towards Prozor ("window"), silent and invisible, lay the forbidden zone of SDS territory. At this very moment, largely unreported, out of sight and out of mind behind the ramparts of two front lines, the crisis in the pressure cooker of the Bihać pocket was approaching meltdown as the first act of Babo's Autonomy moved inexorably towards its wretched conclusion.

[ix] It was common before the war, and still is, for people from the interior, i.e. Bosnia, to spend their holidays on the Croatian coast. In 2012, the Croatian tourist minister complained that Bosnian day-trippers visiting the coast in summer were bringing packed lunches with them, and not spending any money in Croatia. He wanted suspects to be searched and their provisions seized at the border on their way into his country.

I was driving from the relative safety of the coast to the war zone in central Bosnia, following UNPROFOR route Gannet, with on my right an endless succession of B&Bs, pizza restaurants and Mediterranean hamlets between me and the beautiful, timeless Adriatic, and on my left the "barren crags" of Dalmatia[30] behind yet more holiday apartments (in order to reduce the likelihood of peacekeepers getting lost, set routes were established for their most common itineraries, with the code names signposted at key points). I was working for a small German NGO, the International Mennonite Organisation, with programmes in two towns in central Bosnia, and our main base just outside Split. As a small NGO, we organised monthly distributions to the most needy families and individuals we could find in our catchment areas, working via a network of local volunteers, and seeking out those people, many of them from minorities, who fell through the nets of the larger organisations. Our beneficiaries would receive a monthly food parcel, made up of various typical German staples, which for somebody living in absolute poverty appeared to make a difference. People finding themselves in the unfortunate category of "minorities" were subject to a range of discriminatory practices, and worse: they were at the bottom of the list for humanitarian aid, they were prevented from accessing public services and benefits, and many lost their employment and/or their homes. The choices open to them were limited: either give up and move away (no simple matter in itself: where to? and what about transport for themselves and their possessions?), or live in wretched poverty on the margins of society, hoping it wouldn't last forever (I once visited an elderly woman in Konjic who was living alone in a building site that was the nocturnal haunt of juvenile delinquents. She had had to leave her home in the town, and her only son was a POW, also being held in the town, but who she was unable to visit). The vulnerability of minorities was aggravated exponentially in the enclaves, where they became a target for the frustration of IDPs. For well over an hour, passing through the village of Omiš, with the idyllic islands of Brač and then Hvar visible across the water, I drove, down to the resort of Makarska, with its nudist beach. Omiš was the base of a NGO called the Serious Road Trip, who travelled in multi-coloured trucks and a bus, and laid on circus performances for local children (and adults) in Bosnia as well as distributing aid. Halfway between Split and Makarska is the tiny harbour of Baška Voda, in 1943 a Partisan toehold on the coast surrounded by enemy forces, with the German sixth offensive closing in after the Italian collapse, from where Fitzroy Maclean travelled to the island of Korčula with the objective of setting up a supply route by sea for hardware to aid the Partisans in the interior[31]. Just south of Baška Voda is the village of Krvavica ("black pudding"). Maclean's return journey was to the equally tiny harbour of Podgora, 15 km south of Makarska, as Baška Voda had meanwhile been occupied[32] (in 1991, he and his wife delivered medical aid to Korčula, where they owned a villa; in the 1960s Tito waived the ban on foreigners owning property so that they could buy it). Makarska was captured by the Turks in 1499, seven years after the discovery of America, and the year after Portuguese navigator Vasco da Gama discovered the Cape of Good Hope and opened up the Indian Ocean to commerce and Christianity[x] (nowadays called free trade and sustainable development). The main border crossing from Croatia into Bosnia was at Metković, once a major river port on the Neretva, another hour or more down the coast to Ploče ("plates", before the war the main port for Bosnian imports and exports[33]), and then

---

[x] Dr Livingstone's exhortation in 1857. This discovery sounded the death knell for the overland Silk Road trade route, that for centuries had linked China to Venice.

30 minutes' drive inland. The source of the Neretva is in south-eastern Herzegovina, near the Montenegrin border, from where it flows north-west to Konjic, before turning south and reaching the sea near Ploče. The sheer volume of traffic on the single-carriageway coast road, coupled with the heat, made driving a slow and tiring affair. This, the southern Dalmatian coast, was the mouth of the gap in the SDS territory, the open jaws of the great crocodile allowing access deep into the bowels of Karadžić's project along a fragile communications network that penetrated like a spit in reverse through the living carcass of a sacrificial beast, missing the vital organs on both sides, but not quite breaking through under the tail; an umbilical cord linking the Bosnian SDA and HDZ territories to the coast and the outside world. But they were jaws that still threatened to snap shut at any time, and the SDS body politic was prone to regular, violent fits and starts, still capable of digesting, or at least ingesting the foreign object within it. The border crossings referred to in Part 1 were much more problematic for accessing central Bosnia, as that would require crossing SDS territory: the paranoid nature of their leadership made it very difficult to obtain entry permits, and more importantly, exit permits (permission for us to send an aid convoy to Banja Luka after the fall of Sector West required a trip to Belgrade). For the same reason, the Bihać pocket was not accessible from central Bosnia. I have it on reliable authority that Karadžić, originally from Durmitor in Montenegro, but who studied and later worked as a psychiatrist in Sarajevo, where he was convicted of fraud and jailed in 1985 for issuing *falš* ("fake") *ljekarska uvjerenja* ("medical certificates"), lived in constant fear of his own bodyguards, whose real loyalty may have been to the Unit. He once asked UNPROFOR to extract him from Pale, but the arrangements fell through. To make things worse, Milošević split with Karadžić after his refusal to agree to the contact group peace plan in July 1994, which Milošević had hoped would lead to the lifting of sanctions on Serbia and Montenegro after two years of economic hardship[34]. He made several attempts to sideline Karadžić and have him replaced, and Mladić was loyal to him rather than to Karadžić, not least because VRS officers were paid from Belgrade[35]. Indeed, Milošević appears to have lost control of the war in Bosnia in May 1993 when the Bosnian SDS refused to sign the Vance-Owen plan despite his insistence, and he had been preparing to make Karadžić the scapegoat ever since[36] (the US had put pressure on Milošević as well as Izetbegović to accept the plan, and the Russians were no longer as accommodating of the SDS position as they had been[37]). Milošević imposed sanctions on Republika Srpska, to which Karadžić responded by arranging a black market with Tuđman via Sector West (which provided Tuđman not only with extra cash, but also an opportunity to infiltrate spies into West Slavonia in preparation for Operation Flash, as well as undermining Milošević)[38]. To put more pressure on Karadžić, in March 1995 Milošević met Izetbegović's special envoy to discuss mutual recognition and agreement to the abolition of economic sanctions[39]. All this meant that practically all aid coming in by road from western Europe had to take the long way round from Zagreb, via back roads down to Split (on what is now the first half of Croatia's new Zagreb-Split motorway, the A1, toll EUR 25, completed in 2005 and dogged by various financial scandals, and which consigned to oblivion the old route through the Croatian Borders. Now the Borders themselves have disappeared, subsumed into the counties of Split-Dalmatia, Šibenik-Knin, Zadar, Lika-Senj, Karlovac, Sisak-Moslavina, Bjelovar-Bilogora, Vukovar-Srijem and Osijek-Baranja, while the names Lika, Banija and Kordun have become anachronisms. Most of these counties cut across the former front line, in an echo of the division of Yugoslavia into nine *banovinas* in 1929, each one cutting across former internal borders, but which failed

to bring unity to the country[40]), and on down to Metković. However, as a small NGO, we preferred to avoid the large border crossing with its multitude of customs officials, expert at sniffing out vulnerability and therefore a potential bribe (which we never gave), and instead opted for the little-used crossing at Vrgorac with its tobacco fields, deviating from route Gannet. The most highly-prized Croatian *duhan* ("snout"), organic *škija* ("renegade"), is actually grown in Herzegovina. The finished product is yellow and consists exclusively of the finely-chopped leaf – no stalks or off-cuts. Traditionally, it is delivered in men's shirt boxes with a cabbage leaf to prevent it drying out, a hangover from the days when it was unavailable for domestic consumption. The majority of the crop was sold to multinationals, and could only be obtained by domestic smokers if they had the right connections. The connoisseur also needs two *šibice* ("matches") per day: one to light up first thing in the morning, and after smoking continually up until lunchtime, igniting one roll-up directly from its predecessor, a second one to light up after bait. Tito's cigars were flown in from Cuba, courtesy of Fidel. Turning left at Makarska, the road winds up the hills into the hinterland at a more leisurely rate than the road near Šibenik. After an hour I would reach the village of Vrgorac, park, and exit my vehicle to impress the local officials, who were generally always the same individuals, with my pile of documents. One of the squaddies who always seemed to be there had a sticker with a red heart and German inscription on the butt of his *Kalašnjikov* that read *"Ein Herz für Kinder"* ("a heart for children"). Whether he was trying to express the duality of man, was fascinated by all things German, or was just a nice bloke, I never found out, as I generally played *rukama i nogama* ("dumb") at the border crossing. In any case, he was certainly keeping well away from the firing line. And anyway, all of the real work seemed to be done by Ana, a smiling latin beauty who occupied the portacabin that served as the *carinica* ("customs office"). One day, one of our German trucks returning from a delivery in central Bosnia was turned back at Vrnograc, because we had failed to obtain the right stamp on the export papers at the point of delivery. Their passports confiscated, the drivers had to travel (with their *LKW*, "trucks") all the way back to Jablanica, across a theoretically inactive former front line, just to get a stamp (although it would have been even more inconvenient if they had been turned back at the border exiting Croatia into Slovenia; and thanks to one of Adis' contacts, at least they didn't have to go any further than Jablanica, where we never delivered anything).

Once through, I was in Herzeg-Bosna, the Bosnian HDZ rump state comprising most of Herzegovina, capital West Mostar (*most* means "bridge", and I have been told the origin of the name Mostar is the ferrymen who used to transport passengers across the Neretva before the famous Old Bridge was built in 1566), the fiefdom of Mate Boban, a former shop manager, hemmed in to the south-east and north-west by the SDS, and officially part of the Federation (Herzeg-Bosna, established the same day Vukovar fell, was later likened with its powerful clergy and mafia to a "Bosnian Sicily"). But my destination was SDA central Bosnia to the north. The HDZ knew that, on both sides of the border, and so were prone to place administrative barriers (and any others they could think of) in our way, in particular when we were trucking aid. Indeed, the barriers would start in Split, where we had to get our export papers at the *carinski ured* ("customs authority") in the port. I spent many an hour there waiting for the right signature and the right piece of paper, knowing full well that a "present" would have generated them instantly, but also aware that such a precedent would create far more difficulties in the future. *Ko čeka taj dočeka* ("good things come to he who waits"). The problems actually started even before that, at the Slovenian border with Austria[xi], the former Yugoslav border, where the local officials, sneering in glee at their less fortunate neighbours, were nevertheless envious of all the aid travelling across their territory into central Bosnia (on more than one occasion, driving through Slovenia to or from Austria, I experienced the ignorance of some Slovenes who, unable to speak English, nevertheless insisted on pretending they didn't understand a word of Serbian/Croatian, thereby rendering communication impossible). And this corrupt practice was not restricted to customs: the banks and even the post office in Split always seemed to be creating unnecessary difficulties when handling everyday transactions, difficulties that could be miraculously banished by a bung. The postmaster was nevertheless taken aback when Reinhard said to him one day, after particularly onerous attempts to send a letter to Germany in which he took a personal interest, "This isn't Europe". More broadly, Herzegovina refers to the southern part of the country. Once known as Hum ("hill"), it was incorporated into Bosnia by *Ban* (i.e. not an independent king, but ruling at the pleasure of neighbouring Hungarian Croatia) Stjepan Kotromanić, who ruled from 1322 to 1353[41]. The name Herzegovina comes from *Herzeg* ("duke") Stjepan Vukčić, who ruled it independent of the Bosnian King from 1448 until two years after the Turkish invasion, in 1465[42]. In Herzegovina, but also in the Bosnian Borders and further south on the plateau between Glamoč and Lika, and in eastern Bosnia, there are around 60,000 *stećci*, curious carved stone grave monuments depicting human and other figures, dating from before the Turkish conquest. They influenced later Muslim gravestones (often consisting of a stone pillar crowned by a stone turban)[43]. Glamoč was the site of the Allies' first improvised airstrip in Yugoslavia in 1943, where two British and one Partisan officer were later killed by bombs dropped from a *Wehrmacht* observation plane as they were preparing to fly out[44]. Western Herzegovina had a homogenous Catholic population with far right tendencies even before the Yugoslav Wars, and many of them fought in the war in Croatia before it spilled over into Bosnia. By contrast, the Catholics of central and northern Bosnia were more used to living in multi-cultural communities, and were generally more welcoming to foreigners[45]. The dialect of central Herzegovina was said to be the purest form of Serbian/Croatian by the 19th century scholar Vuk Karadžić, who standardised the literary language and its writing conventions[xii] (after Serbia gained autonomy from the Ottomans in 1815, Karadžić declared that all speakers of the language were one people, regardless of religion[46]). Serbian was for several centuries the third language of the Ottoman Empire, after Turkish and Arabic, and it is therefore unsurprising that there should

---

[xi] The first time I crossed this border, on foot, a loitering Croat asked me to drive his car back across the border for him, into Austria. A little further on, off the side of the road, I surprised a young Austrian *Grenzbeamte* ("border official") engaged in what must have been an unofficial and perhaps intimate conversation with a middle-aged Croat woman, because he immediately assumed a very officious tone and demanded to see my *Ausweis*. A Sudanese aid worker gave me a lift to Zagreb, where I attempted to catch a bus to Split. As none of the ticket vendors spoke English, and I had not yet mastered the intricacies of "turbodiesel" (Serbo-Croat), I ended up hitch-hiking to Zadar, where I again tried to get the bus. Finally, after dossing down behind the *kolodvor* ("bus station"), the next morning I hitch-hiked the rest of the way to Split. I must have alarmed one motorist who stopped because, when he informed me he was only going as far as Biograd (a resort on the Dalmatian coast), I thought he meant Beograd ("Belgrade"), and said "Beograd, *dobro* ['great']", at which he drove off in great haste. Alas, a female colleague who, inspired by some of my escapades, decided to hitch-hike through central Bosnia, was not so lucky when she was picked up by an *Ustaša* who decided he was entitled to take payment in kind for his *sevap*.
[xii] The Cyrillic and Latin alphabets used for Serbian/Croatian each have 30 equivalent letters, and are subject to the same rules of orthography, which to a certain extent mitigates the barrier created by the use of different alphabets, if not facilitating cultural understanding.

have been some exchanges between those languages, not only of vocabulary, but also of syntax, as the languages converged in a shared space[47]. Serbian also underwent a process of convergence with the other, mainly unrelated languages in that part of the Balkans that formed part of the Ottoman Empire, such as Romanian and Albanian (and Romany). However, Croatia formed part of a different space, the Austro-Hungarian Empire, and so the language spoken there drifted in a different direction. It retained more of its original Slav features than Serbian, and appears to have been less influenced by Hungarian and German than Serbian was by Turkish: the Croats resisted efforts to force them to speak Hungarian just as much as the Hungarians resisted efforts to be forced to speak German[48] (although the dialect spoken on the coast is still heavily influenced by Italian, with idioms such as *adio*, "bye"). This linguistic resistance was led in the 1830s and 1840s by the Illyrian movement, which advocated a single South Slav identity based around the idea of Croatian state continuity, before they were ousted as the torchbearers of Croatian nationalism by a more radical movement, which envisaged a Greater Croatia extending from the Alps to Bulgaria[49]. After WWI, all these dialects were fused together again as the main language of a single country, and in post-WWII Yugoslavia were officially one language with two dialects, eastern and western[50]. This was accompanied by official efforts to promote the similarities between the dialects and shed foreign borrowings. *SH* ("Serbo-Croat") was the native language of 80% of the population of Yugoslavia, and was taught to and spoken as a second language by other Yugoslavs[51]. Today, many Croats if asked will insist theirs is a separate language, while Serbs and Bosnians (and Montenegrins) seem to take a more pragmatic approach. This artificial division also ignores local dialects; and I have heard it said that a native of Zagreb and a native of Belgrade would find it far easier to communicate with each other than with someone from a farming community in their own countries respectively (the war with its sieges has also been described as the "revenge of the countryside against the city"[xiii][52]). In my humble opinion, Serbian and Croatian are no different from each other than US English is from UK English. Following the same analogy, Bosnian can be likened to Irish English (and Montenegrin to Scotch). Before WWII, formal Serbian used to be expressed in blank verse[53]. Communist rhetoric and modern political discourse have put an end to that quaint custom (after his famous address in Kosovo Polje in 1987, Milošević abandoned the tried-and-tested technocratic monolithic monologue and embraced a more down-to-earth, rustic register[54]). One free weekend in Split I had travelled to Dubrovnik, a UNESCO world heritage site, another two hours down the coast from Ploče, and through the Bosnian coastal enclave of Neum, 10 km long, with a German colleague, Ralph, in his own car. Dubrovnik, including a cathedral built by Richard the Lionheart, was destroyed by a *zemljotres* ("earthquake") in 1667 that is said to have been so powerful it caused a tsunami[55]. The spectacular Balkan Singapore, with its annual carnival, thrived for 500 years as a major economic power, playing off Hungary, Turkey and Venice against each other while trading with them all (it was ruled by Venice for 150 years before becoming independent in 1358). Looking down from the

---

[xiii] In 1994, I watched a documentary about Karadžić on RTVBiH. It featured interviews with people who had known him in Sarajevo before the war, and the main thrust was that the Montenegrin, with his poetic aspirations, had failed to make an impression on, or be accepted by, the Sarajevo arts scene. One of the interviewees was a former hospital colleague, who called Karadžić a mediocre psychiatrist; and at the end of the programme, the camera panned out to reveal that the medic was in a wheelchair. Karadžić had taken a very personal revenge on the Sarajevo elite. In 1992 he gave Russian poet Eduard Limonov a tour of the siege of Sarajevo, and encouraged him to fire a sniper rifle at the besieged city.

city walls, the sea is so clear that you can see right to the bottom as if it was dry land, creating the illusion that the wall is twice its real height. The only Orthodox church within the city walls was built in 1877[56]. The JNA attacked Dubrovnik, which had no strategic or military significance, from the Bosnian hinterland and Montenegro on 1 October 1991, and followed up with a land blockade from Montenegro to Neum, and a sea blockade of all major Croatian ports[57]. The Croatian national guard were poorly prepared and equipped to respond. The JNA shelled the town and the harbour intermittently (destroying every single yacht) until the truce in January 1992, and finally withdrew in September of that year, allegedly in exchange for the HV leaving Bosanski Brod[58]. South of Dubrovnik, the road into Montenegro remained closed due to a border dispute until 1999, with the effect that tourists travelling to the Croatian coast could not continue their holidays further south. That part of the coast was once a centre of the cult of Pan[59]. On our way back from Dubrovnik, seeing the sign for Mostar, we said, "Let's go to Mostar", and turned right off the coast road towards Metković. Crossing the border, we headed further inland. Hills started to appear on either side of the flat plain, and on both sides we started to notice isolated, burnt out houses. Ralph said, "Let's take some photos". I advised him that I didn't think that was a good idea, but as it was his car, it was his decision, and he pulled off the road into a *nogostup* ("lay-by") by a deserted, burnt-down hamlet. He started taking photos while I waited, and, sure enough, in less than five minutes an unmarked car suddenly sped into our lay-by and skidded to a halt. Some very unfriendly-looking characters in civvies emerged, and demanded our passports. We produced them, and they were swiftly examined, before being placed in a breast pocket. "Follow us" their leader ordered, a scruffy, dishevelled beanpole, with multi-coloured suit and tie, anorak, and jam jar glasses, like a psychotic extra from the Sweeney. But we were in no laughing mood as we followed them inland for about 20 minutes along country roads, ending up at the HVO headquarters in the picturesque-sounding town of Čapljina (*čaplja* means "heron"). Taken upstairs in a poorly lit multi-storey building with stairwells that reminded me of Wigton middle school in Cumbria (built as a contingency hospital during WWII, and sadly now a housing estate), but with a more menacing atmosphere, past assorted armed individuals sporting a variety of equally scruffy uniforms or civvies, and past piles of rifles seemingly everywhere, we were separated and led into two interview rooms. An officer we had not seen until then was to interview us one by one, although it seemed that everyone in the building was curious to see the foreign prisoners. It occurred to me that if we had been Serbs or Muslims, they would have dealt with us far more swiftly, and brutally. When the officer started his *ispitivanje* ("interview"), I decided things had gone far enough. I stood up and demanded, as a British citizen, to be released, as they had no right to detain me. This caused two things to happen: firstly, as Ralph only spoke German, they were forced to devote their attentions to me as I had shown I spoke their language. That was a valuable lesson I applied in the future: sometimes it is better not to speak the local language, even if you can[xiv]. Secondly, my remonstrations

---

[xiv] Sometimes the opposite is true: once at a *blokpost* ("checkpoint") in Chechnya, my driver, "*Polkovnik*" ("colonel") Vaha, exited the vehicle, but left the keys in the ignition. It occurred to me that if someone wanted to kidnap me, all they needed to do was sit in the driving seat and drive away. And sure enough, a very rough-looking character in uniform clutching a *Kalaš* took a seat, and turning to me, addressed me in Chechen. He had so much gold in his mouth that it looked as if his teeth had been coated with a glistening layer of nicotine. I had no idea what he had said, but in response I reeled off all the Chechen phrases I had learnt. That seemed to do the trick, as he exited the vehicle again. At that time, we would travel in unmarked vehicles (Lada Niva 4x4s, not Landcruisers), three to a convoy, at a good distance from each

earned me a smack in the gob, which sat me down and shut me up[xv]. The questioning and comments went on for a while ("*Vi stranci imate mirnu viziju*" – "you foreigners with your peace vision"), more from curiosity than anything else. I insisted we were not spies, and eventually they told us to fuck off and never come back. Ralph, the source of our woes, had spent the whole time in a room by himself, as no-one could talk to him. In subdued mood we drove back to the border, with our passports but without our cameras (me too), having given up on the idea of going to Mostar, and headed back to Split. The next day I went to the British consulate in Split to complain, but was fobbed off with various vague counter-accusations ("The Bosnian Croats are nothing to do with Croatia", "You shouldn't have been there" etc., even though it was common knowledge that Tuđman was as much a puppetmaster of the HVO as Milošević was of the VRS[60]). I received a much more sympathetic reception at the German consulate, which was one floor up, and much more luxurious, although the end result was the same: nowt.

Even though Vrgorac is higher up than the coast, it is still very hot. From there the road twists and turns on for another 50 km to Mostar (the west of the city), passing by Ljubuški to the left, and, to the right, the Catholic shrine at Međugorje where, as in Fátima in Portugal, six children saw the Virgin Mary in 1981. It was a destination for pilgrims even during the war (once in 1995 I travelled from Split to Zagreb in a plane full of Irish pilgrims). However, the idea was to avoid West Mostar by taking a right turn shortly after Međugorje onto a side road that led past a furniture factory slowly downhill onto the Neretva valley plain floor, to rejoin route Gannet on the Metković-Mostar road. Turning left at the T-junction onto the main road (where there was sometimes a flying checkpoint), about 10 km before East Mostar was the HVO checkpoint marking the beginning of SDA territory (even though they were nominally at peace). The first time I passed through it I was threatened with a pistol by a HVO military policeman for not parking exactly where he had indicated. He complained, as if I was personally responsible, that he was from Konjic, where he knew we were going, and that his family had been ethnically cleansed (on another occasion, when I was driving north from Konjic, an ABiH military policeman who had a more professional aspect than was usual, indicated to

---

other, with the rear windows blacked out and only one passenger per vehicle; communication between the vehicles and with the bases in Groznij/Rral and Nazranj was by VHF (handset) and HF radio respectively, with the antenna placed low down on the rear of the vehicle in such a way as to give the impression to anyone not familiar with comms that it was an ordinary car radio antenna (the HF transceiver itself was in a wooden box in the *bagažnik*, "boot"). One day we passed an army truck with a very large black flag bearing white Arabic script flying over it; I was glad the two bearded occupants didn't notice me sitting in the back of my Lada. My predecessor, Mike, and his late colleague, Frank, had been kidnapped one morning on the way to work in a Landcruiser. I recently heard that Frank had committed suicide. The note he left apparently read, "*J'aurais dû y mourir*" ("I should have died there"). The last I heard of the Colonel, he was killed in a mafia shootout in Groznij/Rral. Sometimes nothing helps at checkpoints: I was once caught in a speed trap southbound on the Mozambique coast road, which links Tanzania to South Africa. Armed with my previous experiences, I tried to get out of it by pretending I only spoke English. But I got so frustrated with their poor command of the language of Shakespeare that I unwittingly broke into Portuguese. Then I was in a world of shit, and there was nothing for it but to cough up and pay the *multa* ("fine").

[xv] He evidently hadn't heard Milošević's teaching, "*Niko ne sme da vas bije*". The only other time I have been assaulted in my career as an aid worker was in Soči, Russia's Blackpool, later the scene of the 2014 Winter Olympics, where I was on R&R from Chechnya, and was beaten like a red-haired stepchild by *mutanti* ("white trash") in a nightclub. I now have a Chechen gold General Booth as a souvenir for my pains. I was also almost mugged once in Panama City's *casco viejo* ("old town"), but I managed to see my would-be assailant off before escaping in a passing taxi. He'll think twice before tackling a *Gringo* again, the skinny, rat-faced runt.

me with one of the hand-held "STOP" signs that were, and still are popular throughout the former Yugoslavia, to pull over. No sooner had I pulled off the road at a convenient spot, than a fleet of *mudonja* ("VIP") vehicles appeared from behind the bend up ahead and swept past. The special branch man, as I guessed he must be, prepared to follow them, but before he did so, he opened my passenger side door and said, "Next time I tell you to stop, *bolan* ['bonny lad'], be quick about it"). I always found it a very stressful crossing, and would feel a knot in my stomach whenever I approached, in either direction. However, driving back to Split one day in the autumn of 1994, in the first rains, I laughed when I saw there wasn't a soul in sight at the checkpoint, as all my tormenters were taking refuge in their portacabin! So much for their patriotism. Another time, heading north, I was waiting in an uncommonly long queue to cross the checkpoint. It was very hot as usual, and I had my window wound down. Suddenly I heard an English voice. The vehicle in front of me was a camper van, and standing beside it were a young woman and a man, he in a completely black uniform (*Ustaša*); another man was inside, at the wheel. The couple were speaking English; she was obviously local, but he wasn't. With nothing better to do, I got out and started a conversation with them. It turned out he was a mercenary, who had learned his trade in the TA in the UK before joining the HVO. I have it on reliable authority that in 1992-1993, "tens" of British passports were being handed in every week to the British embassy in Zagreb belonging to mercenaries killed in action. That stretch of road, straight, open and flat, was also quite close to the VRS positions to the east, and so theoretically open to fire from that quarter. 25 km west of Mostar, on the road to Posušje, is the town of Široki Brijeg ("wide hill"), where Luka Modrić cut his teeth in the "rough-and-tumble" Bosnian league, on loan from Hajduk ("riever") Split (during the war, Posušje, just across the border from Imotski in Croatia and marking the most westerly point of the traditional frontier of Herzegovina, was a haven for mainly Catholic IDPs from elsewhere in Bosnia). Just south of Mostar and to the left of the road, at Rodoč, was the notorious heliodrome POW camp, where thousands of non-Croat residents of Mostar were held between September 1992 and April 1994. Muslim HVO soldiers were disarmed overnight and imprisoned by their erstwhile comrades in April 1993[61]. Many of these men had been living abroad when the war broke out, and came home and joined the HVO out of a sense of patriotic duty. We once negotiated access to distribute relief goods to the detainees, at the usual nationwide tariff of 50% for the beneficiaries and 50% for the guards (according to the Bosnian proverb, "*Pola pije pola Šarcu daje*", "half for me and half for the horse"[62]). Our aid included cartons of cigarettes, an important commodity for the mental wellbeing of POWs, as their only luxury in their languishing squalor. In 2013, the former PM of Herzeg-Bosna, Jadranko Prlić, was sentenced by the ICTY to 25 years' imprisonment for war crimes, the majority relating to the HVO's network of POW camps of which the heliodrome was the most infamous.

The first time I drove into central Bosnia by myself, with our 7.5-ton truck, I missed the turning after Međugorje. Driving on and on, I eventually decided I must have missed it and resolved to turn around as soon as I found a convenient place by the road. But as I rounded another corner, I came across a banner suspended above the road that read, "Welcome to Croatian Mostar!", and saw a very unpleasant-looking character in a tasselled beret strutting about, armed to the teeth. The archetypal fascist. Thinking fast, I decided that doing a three-point turn in front of him would certainly attract unwelcome attention, and so resolved to keep going and bluff it. I stopped at his instruction, wound down the window and, pretending not to speak the local language, shouted, "Konjic! Konjic!", which was indeed one of my destinations, but which I also knew bordered on a rural Catholic community nominally under the control of the HVO. I was hoping he would say, "Turn round and take the turning onto the main road", but he just grinned and waved me through. Dismayed, yet not discouraged, I drove on into unknown West Mostar. At the beginning of the war in Bosnia, the JNA had subjected the mainly Croat and Muslim population to heavy shelling in an attempt to take the town. The JNA withdrew from the east bank in May 1992, and the HVO drove the VRS out the next month, their first major defeat in Bosnia[63]. After the war between the HDZ and the SDA broke out, once the HDZ and the SDS had no unfinished territorial business between them, there was a tacit alliance between them to divide up the remaining SDA territory (Karadžić and Boban met secretly in Austria to agree on the details), and Mostar became a miniature replica of the siege of Sarajevo, with the modern town (the west) the stronghold of the HDZ, supported politically and militarily from Zagreb, and the beautiful old town (the east) a Muslim ghetto, with much of the medieval Ottoman architecture, including the *stari most* ("old bridge"), a slender shaft of light captured in stone, refracted at the centre yet miraculously remaining a single whole (one of Bosnia's three famous bridges, a UNESCO world heritage site), damaged or destroyed by HVO artillery, and civilians living in appalling conditions[64] (this also allowed Izetbegović to remove another local Muslim rival, Hadžiosmanović, who he instructed to stay in the west as a liaison with Tuđman, only to brand him a defector and put his own people in charge of East Mostar. With Zulfikarpašić already sidelined in Foča, Babo was the only remaining obstacle to Izetbegović's hegemony over the Muslims[65]). The VRS let them get on with it. The Old Bridge was destroyed exactly four years after the fall of the Berlin wall. In 1994, Mazowiecki described the HDZ's tactics in West Mostar as "soft ethnic cleansing"[66]. Once, exploring East Mostar on foot, I came across another bridge, this one an improvised scrap metal affair, that I was told had previously been very dangerous because of snipers. There was a group of lively children playing near the bridge, and I was shocked to notice that one of them was missing a forearm. I wondered whether that was a souvenir of the war; but regardless, he was as accepted by his companions as he appeared to be of his fate. Not only are children the most tragic victims of war, they also appear to be the most resilient. Perhaps there's hope for us all. Mostar, like Sarajevo, was fiercely independent of central authority in the eighteenth and nineteenth centuries, violently resisting attempted reforms to taxation, which resulted in armed clashes in 1768, 1796 and 1814[67]. An English officer, Sir Gardner Wilkinson, who visited the *vezir* of Mostar in 1845, was shocked to see beside his palace a round tower crowned with Montenegrin heads mounted on stakes (he had earlier seen the same thing, in reverse, i.e. Turkish heads, at the Orthodox monastery in Cetinje in Montenegro)[68]. At the beginning of the *Ustaše* terror in 1941, Mostar became a clandestine destination for Jews escaping from Sarajevo, on their way to the relative safety of the coast and Italy[69]. Even during the war, with the Old Bridge replaced by a makeshift scaffolding *džada* ("footpath"), the tradition of diving from it into the pastel-coloured river Neretva below, with its treacherous currents forcing the unwary swimmer among the large blocks of medieval masonry that fell from the bridge, continued. After the Washington agreement, there was an uneasy truce, but no love lost, between the two parts of the city. Although nominally allies, the HVO soldiers were paid DM 100 per month (bankrolled from Zagreb, which was in turn largely financed by Helmut Kohl, who, buoyed by his own recent successful redrawing of international borders, seemed to be on a *Drang nach Osten* ("go east") of his own[70]), while the ABiH soldiers received no pay at all. That does not sound like much, but as in practice the rations or other supplies made available to soldiers were little or non-existent, and they had to spend most of their leave at home carrying out the more physically demanding household chores required by country life, it was one of many sources of ongoing friction between the two sides. The HVO also received direct support on the ground from the HV as part of Tuđman's Greater Croatia project[71]. Now, as I entered the new town, I knew I had to find my way over to the east. I had no map, and all the road signs were full of holes and twisted this way and that so you couldn't tell what was where. And even if I had been able to find my bearings, I had no idea which crossing points were open. I decided I had to ask someone the way, but who? If the wrong people learnt I was lost in West Mostar with a truck full of humanitarian aid, I would swiftly find myself a pedestrian, or worse. Then I spotted a parked UNPROFOR jeep, and two peacekeepers who had just exited a café walking towards it. Quickly I parked up and jumped out before they disappeared. They were Spanish. I asked them if they could show me the way across to the east, and they replied they were just about to go there themselves, and that I could follow them if I liked. But they warned me not to stop. Relieved, I got back behind the wheel and fell in behind them. Although the front line was no longer active, it was not quite inactive either, like a smouldering volcano threatening to blow again. As we approached no-man's land they accelerated, and so did I. The local squaddies on stag waved them through, but tried to stop me. I just pointed to the vehicle ahead to indicate we were together, and kept my foot on the accelerator. They moved aside at the last moment, and didn't open fire. After what seemed like quite a long drive we were out of the total devastation of what had been the most active part of the war zone, and back among only partly destroyed infrastructure. Breathing a sigh of relief, I found the main road and continued my journey, as did my Spanish guides.

While the main part of the old town was teeming with life (despite a *"Pazi – snajper!"*, "beware of the sniper" sign near the scrap-metal bridge), and the *čaršija* ("bazaar") with its twisting alleyways and coffee shops reminiscent of Damascus was certainly worth a visit, once I reached the suburbs there was very little traffic on the main road leading north out of Mostar (Maršal Tito Street, once the name of the high street in every Yugoslav town, but mostly since replaced by a new generation of patriots, just as Tito displaced those who had been honoured in signposts before him), and the few vehicles there were all seemed in a great hurry. That only added to the tension, and I was always half expecting to take incoming fire. That had happened to Reinhard one day on a trip to the village of Blagaj, 7 km south-east of Mostar, where the three front lines converged. He never did discover what side had fired at him; nor did he stop to ask. A bullet was later found in our vehicle's steering column: it had penetrated through between the windscreen and the bodywork, without causing any obvious damage. Picturesque Blagaj, with its Derviš (Muslim mystics) *tekija* ("monastery"), was one of several places that became a haven for small groups of IDPs during the war. The position of Muslim IDPs in HDZ territory became very precarious after the ABiH-HVO war broke out, and many of them found themselves being ethnically cleansed for a second time. The position of Serb IDPs was always precarious, everywhere, thanks to Karadžić *et al.* Even before (and after) the ABiH-HVO war, in towns like Stolac in eastern Herzegovina, near the VRS front line, similar policies and practices to those implemented by the SDS in Banja Luka and elsewhere with the objective of encouraging minorities to leave while fleecing them of their possessions, were executed in miniature by the HDZ. I once visited Stolac with Reinhard and Zlatka, a Croatian girl from Split. It was almost unbearably hot, but the vegetation there appeared to be more luxuriant and bounteous than further west. After crossing the border at Metković this time (we were not trucking any goods, and so took the opportunity to inspect the much larger customs facilities there; the covered infrastructure resembled modern-day Maljevac, as well as the border crossing from Kosovo into Macedonia). We had turned off from Gannet at my favourite town, Čapljina, and driven about 20 km east through what we knew was effectively hard-core *Ustaše* territory, as beautiful as it was. Stolac was a sleepy, Mediterranean town, where the pace of life was slow. We went to see a minority family, relatives of whom Reinhard had got to know in his efforts to uncover the most vulnerable people everywhere and their networks. While we were there, the police turned up to see what we were up to, and while not overtly threatening, they were not particularly likeable, and if dressed in civvies could easily have been mistaken for someone on the other side of the law. They seemed to buy our cover story, which included Zlatka, and that we had hoped would prevent any *maltretiranje* ("aggravation") for our hosts. While their menfolk were by necessity absent, the family, with two children, were nevertheless managing to make ends meet and carry on, albeit under multiple daily pressures. On our return, we took a different route, to the south-west and then north-west back to Gannet just outside Metković, skirting the Hutovo Blato ("Huto's bog") national park.

Continuing out of Mostar, I had to drive north for another hour or so before reaching Jablanica (*jablan* means "poplar"), the end of route Gannet. There are some spectacular views on this stretch of the road as it follows the Neretva valley, with its powerful green-blue waters flowing sometimes slowly, sometimes speeding through a narrower section, surrounded on both sides by a combination of bare rocks and rich vegetation. At the confluence of the Bijela river, 15 km north of Mostar, a bridge had been blown up by the JNA in 1992, leaving a 172 m gap interrupting the road and cutting Sarajevo off from the coast. UNPROFOR restored the link in 1994 by installing a pontoon bridge, manned by Slovakian peacekeepers. I once saw a red double-decker London bus trying to traverse it. It was being driven by two Australians on a road trip, but the low back end of the bus got caught on the steep ramp when they descended onto the pontoon. After some toing and froing, and some cajoling from other drivers (the pontoon was single lane), they just drove forward, severely crumpling the rear of the bus. Just before Jablanica there is a *bent* ("dam") on the Neretva, and one morning, driving south from Konjic, Adis and I were held up for a couple of hours here by an ABiH soldier, who had been ordered to stop all traffic, because the road was allegedly closed further south. He was not taken in by my efforts to impress upon him the humanitarian imperative and let us through. A large traffic jam quickly formed, and it took an intervention by British UNPROFOR once traffic had started to appear, apparently free of any restrictions, travelling up from the south in the opposite direction, before he finally relented and let us proceed. The peacekeepers kindly gave us an escort right through Mostar and south into HDZ land, which was the fastest I had ever covered that stretch of road. Jablanica is a nondescript little town, strung out along the main road for a few km, overlooked by tall, slender poplars, and surrounded by thirsty hills. During the war, it was home to an ABiH barracks that Reinhard and I had occasion to visit one day. Any thoughts I might have had of doing a George Orwell and joining up to fight for "common decency" were dispelled by that visit: while the majority of the men exuded an air of utter dissatisfaction and bitterness with the fate that had brought them to those Spartan digs, at least one of them was so intoxicated with *rakija* that he was practically incoherent, although that didn't prevent him communicating his hostility to foreigners[72]. Besides, I wouldn't have been good for anything but cannon fodder. Just off to the right of the road is a monument with a steam train and a collapsed railway bridge over a steep gorge through which the Neretva flows, 65 m wide. It was the scene of one of Tito's many desperate stands in WWII, the battle of the Neretva in February and March 1943, the culmination of the Axis fourth offensive (*Fall Weiss*, from January until April of that year) intended to crush the resistance in Yugoslavia in order to forestall an anticipated UK/US invasion of the Balkans. It comprised a simultaneous attack with 90,000 men on Partisan territory in western Bosnia (the "Bihać republic", the only free territory in occupied Europe, stretching from Vojnić to Prozor[73]) from the east and the west, and a strike into the centre from the south. The tactical objective was to force Tito into making a frontal attack, for which his guerrilla force was poorly suited. The Partisans were pushed back from their front line south of Karlovac to Tito's headquarters in Bihać, where they came under pressure from all sides. Bihać was occupied on 29 January[74]. Tito decided to break through the enemy's weakest point, the south-east, which was held by the Italians. After withdrawing with the Germans hot on his heels, routing General Morelli's Italians who had just occupied Prozor, and pursuing them as far as Jablanica, where Morelli was captured and shot himself, Tito's main operational group, with 15,000 Partisans and 4,000 wounded, including the central hospital evacuated from Petrova Gora (Tito's orders, inscribed on a plaque at the Jablanica monument, were "*Ranjenike ne smijemo ostaviti*", "never leave the wounded behind"), as well as 40,000 civilians, was cornered on the right bank of the Neretva: the *Wehrmacht* garrison in Konjic to the east was impregnable, blocking the way, enemy reinforcements were arriving from Sarajevo in the north-east, and Italians and *Ustaše* were pushing up from Mostar, while in Tito's rear the Germans were attacking Prozor; and on the left bank of the Neretva were *Četniks*. To make things worse, a typhus epidemic broke out among the Partisans in March[75]. Many of the IDPs from Croatia and the Bosnian Borders made their way back home via Livno[76]. General von Löhr's endgame was now to trap and destroy the Partisans at Jablanica. However, Tito ordered all the bridges over the Neretva to be blown up, and at the same time counter-attacked from Prozor towards Gornji Vakuf, with hardware captured from the Italians. The Germans were pushed back to Bugojno, and von Löhr diverted all his forces there, convinced that Tito was attempting to break back through to Bihać; he thought he could crush him by attacking his rear, and ordered his forces near Bugojno to take up defensive positions. Meanwhile, a replacement pontoon bridge was built in secret across the wreckage of the railway bridge at Jablanica, over which Partisan special forces crossed to the left bank and wiped out the *Četnik* patrols to establish a bridgehead. Too late, von Löhr realised he had been tricked and ordered all his forces to counter-attack towards Jablanica, at the same time as the *Luftwaffe* unsuccessfully attempted to destroy the narrow pontoon at the bottom of the gorge. But the main Partisan force, sacrificing their comrades at Gornji Vakuf, and dumping their Italian hardware into the gorge, crossed the Neretva, and taking the remaining 3,000 *Četniks* completely by surprise, surrounded and destroyed them. This defeat was to all intents and purposes the end of the *Četniks* west of the Drina in WWII. In Tito's words, "*Na Neretvi su Četnici dobili takve batine od kojih se nisu više nikada oporavili*" ("we gave them such a hiding they never got over it"). *Četnik* leader Mihailović was tried for treason and war crimes and executed in 1946. And so Tito successfully retreated, evading destruction yet again, albeit with heavy losses (50%), and headed south-eastwards with a column of civilians and wounded,

337

reaching Montenegro in April[77]. But it was out of the frying pan, into the fire. Hitler offered a reward of DM 100,000 for Tito, dead or alive[78]. As Fitzroy Maclean wrote,

> "Long before the Allies, the Germans and Italians came to realise that the Partisans constituted a military factor of first-rate importance against which a modern army was in many respects powerless. In the course of three years they launched against them no less than seven full-scale offensives, each employing upwards of ten divisions with supporting arms. Once or twice large forces of Partisans came near to being surrounded and wiped out [...] But, each time they succeeded in extricating themselves, fading away, reappearing elsewhere and attacking the enemy where he least expected it[79]."

The scene was recreated in 1969 for the film *Battle of the Neretva*, the most expensive film ever made in Yugoslavia, featuring Yul Brynner, Orson Welles, Hardy Kruger and Sergej Bondarčuk (director of the 1966 epic *War and Peace*), among other international stars, and has been left that way ever since. Picasso painted one of the posters for the film, for a crate of Yugoslav *vino* ("plonk"). Before the Yugoslav Wars, patriotic WWII films were shown on television most Sundays. The real bridge was blown up twice during filming, but the clouds of dust generated by the explosion meant the footage was unusable. Zahid, who was doing his national service at the time of the filming, was roped in with several hundred other squaddies as an extra in the film. The train at the monument had nothing to do with the battle, and seems to have been thrown in for good measure. The Partisans recovered a train when they captured Jajce (referred to by Fitzroy Maclean as the "Partisan Express"), and Tito, a keen trainspotter, travelled by rail during the war whenever possible, with his custom-built carriage, described as a "hut on wheels"[80] (in later years, he liked to travel around the country in his luxurious Blue Train, which can now be chartered for private functions[81]). There was a railway line straight from Užice in Serbia, through Sarajevo, Travnik, Bugojno and Jajce, and then past Mrkonjić-Grad and Bosanski Petrovac up to Zagreb, with other lines branching off to Mostar and Metković, Brod, and Split. The Jablanica monument reminded me of the monument in Santa Clara, in Cuba, the scene of one of Che's victories in 1958, when he derailed an armoured train with a bulldozer, and 373 CIA-backed government squaddies were defeated by a force of 18 guerrillas[xvi]. It also put me in mind of the railway station at Dunkirk, which my father told me was once full of men with WWI equipment waiting to go down to the port to be spirited away from destruction.

After Jablanica, the road forks. To the left and the north-west is the road that was the scene of much of the fighting in the battle, leading back into HDZ territory and the town of Prozor, followed by Gornji Vakuf (upper, as opposed to lower "religious foundation") and Bugojno, both back in SDA territory, and then Donji

---

[xvi] The Argentinian doctor was ultimately executed on the orders of the CIA in Bolivia in 1967, where he was attempting to spread his American revolution. This was conceived as the logical successor to Simón Bolívar's revolution, which coincided with the Napoleonic Wars. Between 1807 and 1824, Bolívar expelled the Spanish from Venezuela, Columbia, Panama, Equador and Peru, but was unable to unite the newly-liberated territories into a single state. Mexico also became independent in 1810. Conversely, when Napoleon invaded Portugal from Spain in 1807 (only to be repulsed three times, and then ejected from Spain seven years later by the Duke of Wellington), the Portuguese royal family fled to Brazil; and when the King returned to Europe in 1821, his son remained as regent of Brazil, only to proclaim independence the following year. Alas, little if anything changed for the mass of the people at the bottom of the food chain in Latin America, as the same ruthless, rapacious economic and political model continued to operate unrepentant.

Vakuf (SDS territory). From Gornji Vakuf, route Diamond led north to rejoin route Pacman in HDZ territory between Travnik, with its sombre 15th century fortress, said to be the largest and best-preserved in Bosnia, and Vitez ("knight"). West from Jablanica by another road, route Square led to Tomislavgrad, named after Croatia's first King (910-928, when Croatia comprised much of its current extent and half of Bosnia[82]), and known as "TSG" by English-speaking peacekeepers and aid workers, and route Triangle then linked TSG to Prozor by a more direct route, much of it over earth tracks. TSG could also be reached by heading straight inland from Split, following route Circle, almost as far as Sinj, then continuing east to cross the border at Kamensko, skirting the south and east of Buško lake. The conflict between the HDZ and the SDA began with a gangland dispute in Prozor in October 1992, which quickly spread to Novi Travnik. 5,000 Muslims were expelled from Prozor on a single day that month[83]. Driving through Prozor, Kiwi's truck would regularly be given the Hitler salute. One day, someone squirted a garden hose through his open truck window. He stopped, jumped out, and went for the *Ustaše* with a hammer, who fled. They don't like it up 'em. In the same HDZ enclave, Reinhard was once stopped by the police. They checked his vehicle and documents with unusual thoroughness, looking for something that would allow them to ask for a bribe. But they came up empty-handed, as he had all the regulation paraphernalia, even a warning triangle in his *gepek* ("boot"). Finally, they told him he had to pay a fine for wearing glasses. The photo on his driving licence was of him without glasses, which they had decided was a serious breach of the highway code. He remonstrated and argued with them for some time, but eventually realised the only way he would get back to base before dark was by coughing up. At least he got a receipt. In 1993, the HV gave the HVO in Prozor direct support against the ABiH in Gornji Vakuf[84]. There was a British UNPROFOR base at Gornji Vakuf, where aid workers could have a free, full-English breakfast, which was well worth the visit. The narrow pedestrian entrance was designed in such a way that it could be controlled by a single soldier, who would immediately receive more substantive back-up if required. Kiwi told me that once a group of armed *Mudžahedin* tried to attack the base via the pedestrian entrance. The first of them managed, by pretending to be a civilian, to get close enough to place a gun to the head of the sole soldier on duty. However, as they entered the camp he was shot by the other guards, thus blocking the passage, and his brethren fled. In another incident, according to Jean-Michel (see below), the *Mudžahedin* fired a *tromblon* (RPG) at an aid Landcruiser on the road just in front of the entrance, but because the vehicle's windows were open, the RPG went right through without causing any damage. Kiwi told me that one day in 1994, two EDA aid workers were captured by the ABiH between Gornji Vakuf and Novi Travnik, together with the British crew of a 432 APC, who were escorting them, and they were held until, threatened with an air strike, the ABiH let them all go, together with the APC. Another EDA volunteer, Christine Witcutt, was killed by a sniper in Sarajevo in July 1993 while travelling in a truck down Sniper Alley towards the airport road (the only road access into Sarajevo during the siege was over Mount Igman and across the airport). The atmosphere in Bugojno was much more raw and tense than I had found it to be in Kakanj or Konjic, being much closer to an active front line. On one occasion driving through Bugojno, Kiwi, who was holding forth on the dire state of the country, commented as we passed a young local squaddie, that that was probably his first job. When in Bugojno we would stay with Huso, whose late wife was a cousin of Dina's, who worked for us in Kakanj. Huso was a retired JNA naval officer, which was unusual for a Muslim. They treated us very generously. He and his late wife were living the Yugoslav dream, and pursued a comfortable secular lifestyle, until Huso caught some shrapnel in one eye. Our NGO was able to find sponsors in Germany who would ensure he received proper medical treatment, but the SDA wouldn't give him a permit to leave Bosnia, or indeed Bugojno[xvii][85]. This had a profound effect on both of them, and while he became quite embittered and depressed, she embraced a more traditional and strict form of Islam. Once in the town we ran into another cousin of Dina's, whose cheek looked like a hamster's. When asked how he was, he replied that he had never been better – he was on the way to the dentist's to get a tooth pulled! Seeing we didn't get it, he explained that because of his ailment he had a day off from the front, so it was well worth it. In 1943, Fitzroy Maclean saw *"Živio Tito!"* superimposed over German and Italian graffiti on a wall in Bugojno[86]. Tito gave his last speech in Bosnia in Bugojno, on 25 November 1979, on the occasion of Bosnian Statehood Day (proclaimed in Mrkonjić-Grad in 1943). Deeply concerned that the deteriorating economic situation would threaten the country's independence, frustrated by the number of officials at all levels who appeared to be engaged in power struggles rather than doing their jobs, and worried by the increasingly overt rise in nationalist tendencies, he said, "We must guard jealously the achievements of our revolution, in particular the inter-ethnic relations we achieved in the Partisan struggle"[87]. 20 km south-west of Bugojno is the village of Zloselo ("evil village"). About 30 km beyond Donji Vakuf is Jajce ("egg"), Dina's home town, described in 1939 as "extravagantly beautiful"[88], with its spectacular waterfalls and fortress, the scene of some of the fiercest battles in WWII. After it was conquered by the Turks in 1463, Jajce was besieged and captured by King Mátyás of Hungary, who made it the capital of the *banovina* of northern Bosnia. It was reconquered by the Turks in 1527 after a seven-year siege[89]. According to legend, in 1522, the *kapetan* of Jajce, Petar Keglević, from Bužim, won temporary respite for the town by a ruse. On St. George's Day, all the women and girls of the city left the safety of the fortress and went down to the river to celebrate the pagan festival. The day before, the Turks had feigned withdrawal, and were preparing a surprise attack on a weak point of the fortifications (of which Keglević was aware). Seeing the women, they concluded that the Bosnians had lowered their guard (confirming disinformation that Keglević had disseminated by means of a false spy), but rather than attack, they advanced on the women. In so doing, they walked into an ambush and were destroyed[90]. Jajce also has a 19th century Franciscan monastery dedicated to St. Luke (the original medieval church was converted into a mosque). After the fall of Jajce, a group of Franciscan monks fled to Venice, taking with them the body of St. Luke, that they had received from Đorđe Branković's daughter, an ally of Tsar Lazar, who had originally ransomed it from the Turks, who in turn had misappropriated him in Greece, where the Syrian Greek is said to have died. But when they arrived in Italy they discovered there was already another St. Luke there, in Padua. The imposter was unmasked and the matter resolved in the Bosnians' favour at a Vatican trial in Venice[91]. Jajce was Tito's headquarters after the retreat from Montenegro in June 1943 until it was captured in the German sixth offensive in early 1944, and was also the scene of the second resistance conference in November 1943, where Tito set up a provisional government of Yugoslavia and was appointed (and anointed) president (effectively the birth of Tito's Yugoslavia; it was also the first time he had used his real name since his release from prison 10

[xvii] Civilians were also banned by the SDA from leaving Sarajevo: as Izetbegović put it to Lord Owen, "Would Churchill have allowed children to leave London during the Blitz?" (or words to that effect).

years earlier)[92]. A breakdown in communication between the HVO and the ABiH at the end of October 1992 led to them both withdrawing from the town, and the VRS were able to simply walk in and occupy it; and in September 1995, there was a clash when the HVO refused to allow the ABiH to enter their recently-captured prize[93]. 15 km directly south from Jajce is the village of Glogovac ("hawthorn"), with its Orthodox cathedral dedicated to St. George. Jajce is now part of the Federation. Its hydroelectric power station supplies Banja Luka[94].

However, my road from Jablanica was to the right, following route Pacman, and another 15 km to Konjic, where we had one of our two offices, and the home town of a local colleague, Adis, a computer boffin with a gift for talking his way through hostile checkpoints. Adis's aged grandmother had gone to school in pre-WWII Yugoslavia, and only knew Arabic script[xviii]. I would generally spend the night there after unloading, and before continuing my journey to my final destination, Kakanj. Konjic is a beautiful little town set in a cleft in the mountains, with elegant slender minarets, a splendid Catholic *crkva* ("church") dedicated to John the Baptist, high cliffs overlooking the river, a nearby lake with great fishing, and the second of Bosnia's famous bridges, destroyed by the *Wehrmacht* during WWII, but rebuilt since, with a nice pebbled beach on one side. There is a tradition of diving from the high cliffs into the Neretva below; they are far higher than the Old Bridge in Mostar, and divers have to hold on to a rope as they approach the edge, to make sure they can get into the right position to ensure a controlled dive that will end in the water and not on the crags. In the mountains near Konjic Tito built an underground nuclear bunker, hidden under two houses near a mine. For USD 4.6 billion, 350 people could live and work in complete isolation underground for six months[95]. Before the war, many middle class Bosnians with jobs in Sarajevo lived the Yugoslav dream in Konjic. The population was 54% Muslim, 26% Croat, and 15% Serb. However, in 1992 they suddenly realised they were in a trap, when both the SDS and the HDZ wanted the town, even though the urban population was mainly Muslim (with Croat and Serb villages in the surrounding hills). Not only was it a strategic communications route linking Mostar with Sarajevo, but it had significant JNA infrastructure: a munitions factory, a TA command centre, and barracks with warehousing. These barracks were converted into a POW camp, and in 2003 the deputy commander of the camp was sentenced by the ITCY to 18 years for war crimes committed there. The SDA seized the main infrastructure in late April 1992, and the SDS cut off the road access. Shelling started on 4 May. From late 1994

[xviii] Once in Chechnya we carried out a survey of households in some *jurti* ("villages") in Vedeno in the south, where we had distributed seeds and tools with the objective of kick-starting the stalled agricultural cycle. The purpose of the survey was to establish whether the operation had indeed met its objectives. At one house we went to, we were greeted by a lady with a saintly smile who appeared to be in her sixties, and who was scything the grass in her garden. When she saw us, she went into the house, to emerge with three chairs for us to sit on. Unusually, she only spoke Chechen, which was a sign of someone who had gone to school before the revolution, after which universal Russian-language education was introduced. As a result, Vaha interpreted. When we asked her how old she was, we were taken by surprise when the number was rendered into Russian: "about 100". The end result of the survey was that the seeds and tools had indeed been useful, although the community-minded Chechens had distributed them their way, rather than according to our master plan. We were also informed that pensions were not being paid. Vedeno had previously had a large collective farm, where many of the locals had worked. At another house we visited, the householder told us how one day they had been visited by three Russian squaddies. Two of them engaged him in conversation, and when he went to see what had happened to the third, he came across a pair of uniformed legs hanging out of his loft. He grabbed the legs and pulled the *soldat* ("squaddie") out, and asked him what he thought he was doing…and there the story ended, for we suddenly had to leave in a hurry.

onwards, the VRS would shell Konjic from the south every afternoon, starting like clockwork at noon. As a result, the town was extremely busy in the mornings, as everyone hurried to finish their business (I even saw a driving instructor giving lessons one morning), while in the afternoon the streets were completely deserted. The VRS's targets varied, from the Catholic *groblje* ("cemetery") one afternoon, to the house of a film-maker acquaintance of mine, Dino, who the day before had broadcast a short satirical film, featuring an audio recording of Karadžić discussing military strategy superimposed over a hard-core porno video. His house was reduced to a burnt-out shell. Dino continued to commute to work in Sarajevo during the war, via the notorious tunnel. One morning I went out to find that the kiosk where I bought my fags was a twisted piece of wreckage, having taken a direct hit the previous afternoon. Another day a missile, known as a *luna* ("moon rocket"), was fired at the town, and turned a house into a crater. It became a local curiosity. On another occasion, our office (directly opposite the police station, and with railway sleepers leant against the façade for protection against shrapnel) was hit by shelling, and partly looted. Our thinking had been that having the police for neighbours would be good for our security, but in fact it may have had the opposite effect, in more ways than one. Another day, Reinhard and I were invited to dinner at the house of an acquaintance, Fatima, whose husband on a day off from the front had caught some fish in the lake. We had no sooner started to eat, sitting on the terrace, than the VRS tanks opened up on our part of the town. Everyone took cover inside the house, except for Reinhard and myself, who hadn't had such a good meal for quite a while and were determined not to allow Karadžić to spoil it for us. War acts as a seasoning to intensify the highs and lows of the human experience. There was a sports stadium in the town, and an American colleague, Randy, decided, in the days before daily shelling, that it would be a cool place to do some jogging. He engaged in this pursuit a few times, and then the VRS decided they had had enough of him and started to shell the stadium just as he was getting into his Jekyll and Hyde. He managed to get out in one piece. The start of a shelling session was usually announced by the air-raid siren. The first time I heard it, I was out and about in the town with Adis. I must admit that the sound made my hair stand on end; unsure which way to go, we followed everyone else, heading towards the doorway of a building. As we entered, I noticed a discreet "*sklonište*" ("shelter") sign near the door. It wasn't quite the Blitz: no-one bothered to go down into the basement, and the main thing appeared to be to stay away from windows and doors. After this I began to see such signs in many locations, a remnant from the JNA's total war doctrine that I hadn't noticed before. On the inside wall of the shelter I noticed a complex chart explaining the meaning of the different possible modulations of the *uzbuna* ("air-raid warning"), from a local incident to *smak svijeta* ("Armageddon"). Meanwhile, *Mudžahedin* occupied some of the nearby Christian villages, and I heard their commander had ordered all the pigs rounded up and burnt, at a time when meat was a luxury for most people. There was an UNPROFOR base just outside the town, manned by the Malaysians. A Dutch-Australian truck driver acquaintance of mine told me that one night parked up outside the camp, he stepped outside for a Gypsy's kiss, only to witness an execution by pistol to the back of the head of the unknown kneeling victim. He swiftly repaired to the comfort of his cab.

Curiously, the civilian authorities in the town were all teachers. It was as if they had systematically taken over in a sinister conspiracy, like aliens in a 1950s science-fiction film. But the war they were responsible for prosecuting was real enough. New recruits were subjected to powerful anti-Serb (and anti-Croat) indoctrination with a religious element which, reinforced by regular exposure to the enemy, made them dangerous individuals (soldiers in Srebrenica had it drummed into them by their *moralisti* ("political officers") that the Serbs had to be "exterminated"). It also placed them outside the influence of their families, who, often alarmed by the destructive and self-destructive transformation in their sons, were powerless to do anything about it. One evening, I happened to drop in at the home of a young man who had recently been called up, and I was surprised to see how quickly he had changed from an ordinary, anxious youth into an aggressive, embittered racist. It was as disturbing to see how his mother, who was serving him and his squaddie friends the obligatory *meza*, and cakes, with their coffee (no *rakija*), was clearly terrified of them, and him. I was put in mind of a scene from George Orwell's *1984*. Older recruits were immune to such brainwashing, and saw the war for what it really was: a mafia shootout. One night, the local bank was burnt down, inconveniently destroying all records of who was owed what. The bank's slogan had been *"Hvala na povjerenju!"* ("thanks for your trust"). In Konjic, as in many other former Yugoslav towns, there was a CB radio club. Like everyone else, they were roped into the war effort; but they also offered a service to the public, passing personal messages from one town to another upon request (the telephone network functioned intermittently during the war, and people were also reluctant to make inter-city calls, among other things for fear of being accused of espionage). Needless to say, their activities were strictly controlled by the authorities (during the Kosovo war, CB clubs assisted the VJ with intelligence on NATO air activity[96]). Power and water cuts were common in Bosnian towns during the war. Usually, the population was informed in advance that they would only have electricity and water at certain times of day, or even on alternate days. As a result, people would fill their baths and other containers when they did have water, and that would serve for flushing the toilet, among other things (I saw the same practice in Romania, in peacetime). In Konjic there was a spate of incidents of people fishing with explosives or electricity. The latter is carried out by connecting a line to a mains cable, and then plunging it into a river or lake where there are fish. The dead or stunned fish float to the surface and can easily be collected. This caused not inconsiderable public annoyance, as it generally resulted in the electricity being cut off for people dependant on the same power cable, and when one such angler was killed when he fell into the lake he was electrifying, the general sentiment was that it served him right. *Božija kazna* ("poetic justice").

One day, as I was enjoying a free afternoon on the winding paths leading through part of the town above the river, I heard someone speaking English with a Yorkshire accent. Intrigued, I looked round, to see a rather plump young man with a scraggly beard and moustache talking with a young local, who appeared to be his guide. When I asked him where he was from, he replied he was from Bradford. I asked him what he was doing there, and he said he was the imam of one of the local mosques. He said he used to be CofE, but having travelled to Rome and examined the original Bible, he concluded it was a fake, and so took the logical step of converting to Islam. More than once I had seen a burgundy Landcruiser being driven through the town by dark-skinned men with large beards, and wondered what part they had played in his road to Damascus. Several weeks later, I met him again in Konjic, and this time he was wearing an ABiH uniform. He cut a sorry figure of a squaddie, and I can't imagine the *Četniks* up in the woods were overly alarmed at his deciding to enter the fray. I enquired after his news, and he told me he would be on the front line the next day. When I asked him what had become of his mosque, he said it had been destroyed by shelling. The next time I saw him, he was in civvies again and with a local woman who he described as his wife. She spoke no English, and he couldn't speak the local language, but then again love is blind. Nor was she an oil painting. As they say in the Balkans, *"Od probirača nema jebača"* ("beggars can't be choosers"). I am sure the marriage was arranged by the characters referred to above, as a means to ensnare him, although it may have had the opposite effect, as he said he was returning to the UK. I didn't see him again, but heard some less amusing details about him later on. Apparently he had leased a house as a love nest, and shot his landlord in the stomach when he came round to collect unpaid rent. Then one day I happened to visit the UNHCR office in Konjic, and saw his wife remonstrating with the head of office, to the effect that her husband couldn't abandon her, and demanding to be given the paperwork to be able to travel with her unborn baby to the UK to be with him. On another occasion, driving along outside Konjic, I was flagged down by a man in uniform beside a vehicle parked at the side of the road. I stopped and wound down my window, and he came over and asked me if I had any spare fuel. I told him I didn't, and noticing that he had a green shoulder ribbon with Arabic script embroidered on it, I asked him who he was. He said he was an interpreter. "Bosnian-English?" I enquired. *"Jok* ['no']", he replied, "Bosnian-Iranian". That was a reminder, if I needed one, that there were many irregular units operating in the rural areas (Iran deployed Hezbollah units, amongst others, to fight in Bosnia). 10 km south-east of Konjic, on country roads, near Džajići, is Crni Vir ("black whirlpool").

North of Konjic, the road heads into the mountains and towards Sarajevo. A few kilometres outside Konjic, the road climbs abruptly, and the terrain changes to forested hills, with a new, cooler microclimate. I was told by Adis that this is the frontier between Herzegovina and Bosnia proper. There was a large slogan painted in red on a concrete fence extending off to the side of the road here, which read *"Raduj se Armijo, pobjeda ti je blizu!"* ("rejoice, ABiH, your victory is near"). I saw other patriotic slogans and exhortations to action in various places, such as *"Probudi se narode, svašta se dešava, žaliće ko ovo prespava!"* ("wake up! disaster is upon us, anyone caught napping will be sorry"), which is still visible on a wall in Velika Kladuša. However, the most widespread philosophical statement, at least in practice, appeared and still appears to be the existential *"Jebi ga, propala Bosna"*[xix]. Beside the road a few km further on, what looked like a concrete bus shelter but probably served some other function, bore a large portrait of Tito, in black contrast against a white background, with the only colour a red star on his cap.

Sublime, elusive, beautiful, cosmopolitan Sarajevo (from the Turkish word *saraj*, "court of the Sultan's representative"), sitting in the centre of its mountain fastness with its two cathedrals (Catholic and Orthodox, the former built after Bosnia became a Habsburg protectorate, while the latter was completed in 1872 with funds collected in Russia, and was the subject of a dispute with the imam who insisted the belfry must not be higher than his minaret[97]), 16th century Sefardi synagogue (now a museum: Sarajevo's only working synagogue is the Aškenazi synagogue built in 1902[xx]) and Beg's mosque all within earshot of each other, the latter built by governor Gazi Husrev Beg in 1531, who also built a fabrics market and the library that bears his name (the most important oriental library in the Balkans, which had

---

[xix] "Fuck it".

[xx] The synagogue in Zagreb, built in 1867, was demolished between 1941 and 1942, and is now a carpark.

7,500 manuscripts before 1992[98]), its spindly, square Old Clocktower, built in the 17th century, which keeps lunar time and so always appears to be wrong, the town hall (built by Austro-Hungarian architects in the 1890s and set on fire 100 years later when it served as Sarajevo's library, and, directly after Čabrinović's failed attempt, the Archduke's last stop on his inspection of his Slav subjects before he was killed, and where the last photo of the couple alive was taken: according to an eye-witness, the Archduke, a prolific hunter who claimed to have killed half a million animals, and everyone else in the town hall knew that the roles had now been reversed, and that he had as little chance of escaping Sarajevo as the game beaten methodically and systematically towards his twelve-bore on his estate in Poland[99]), its battle scars, cafes, bridges, and music scene, leafy avenues, and medieval bazaar Baščaršija[xxi][100] with its *sebilj* (wooden fountain) reminiscent of Damascus (and pigeons reminiscent of Trafalgar Square or Bogotá, as well as packs of stray dogs reminiscent of Bucharest after a ban on the former practice of shooting them introduced under pressure from the EU), is a book by itself, and many have been written. As Andrić wrote in *Letter from 1920*:

> "Anyone lying awake at night in Sarajevo can hear the voices of the Sarajevo night. The clock in the Catholic cathedral strikes a heavy, sure note: 2 am. More than a minute later (75 seconds precisely, I've counted), the weaker but penetrating echo of the clock in the Orthodox church can be heard, striking their 2 am. This is followed in short order by the muffled, remote tone of the clock tower at Beg's mosque, striking 11 o'clock, the Turkish time, calculated according to the strange practice of that distant, alien land. The Jews have no clock of their own, and only God knows what time it is for them, for the Sefardis and for the Aškenazis"[101].

Nor do the Romanies have a clock: they follow more primordial, celestial cycles. Some people call them lazy. Sarajevo, originally called Vrhbosna, was developed from a fortress by the Turks after 1448, and, with an interlude between 1553 and 1639, served as the capital of the Ottoman province of Bosnia until the 1690s[102]. Its greatest period of expansion was in the 16th century under the governorship of Gazi Husrev Beg[103], originally from Trebinje in Herzegovina in the hinterland of Dubrovnik, and whose religious foundation continued to operate until the twentieth century (in the country-wide crackdown that followed the assassination of the Archduke in 1914, the Austrians hanged 70 Serbs in Trebinje, including three women, and in January 1993, 4,500 Muslims were expelled from Trebinje to Montenegro; a young VRS soldier and amateur actor/champion swimmer from Trebinje, Srđan Aleksić, was killed attempting to protect a Muslim neighbour from the *Četniks*[104]). Gazi Husrev Beg captured Knin in 1523, and expanded his realm to include Jajce, Banja Luka and Ključ. In Sarajevo he also built two inns and a *medresa* ("theological college"). He was killed putting down a rebellion in Montenegro, and his body was interred in the grounds of the Sarajevo mosque that bears his name[105]. In the 17th century, Sarajevo's prosperity made it the most important inland Balkan city west of Thessaloniki. Catholic and Jewish merchants thrived, selling goods from India, Arabia, Persia, Poland and Bohemia, and despite

---

[xxi] In the 1980s, before the Agrokomerc affair, in order to counter accusations of "regionalism", the business bought a plot in Baščaršija, the most expensive land in the former Yugoslavia, and built its head office there. Mysteriously, today it no longer belongs to Agrokomerc.

the fire of 1697, merchants from Sarajevo were soon exporting hides, furs and fruit to Leipzig and Vienna[106]. While no longer the political capital, it became the unofficial capital of the *janjičar* infantry (see below), who became so independent of the Sultan that Sarajevo was practically a free city[107]. In 1827 there was a *janjičar* rebellion in Sarajevo against reforms to the Ottoman army after the humiliations of the Napoleonic Wars, and attempts by the governor to reside there rather than in Travnik; and after three days of fighting in 1828, the Bosnians had their way[108]. Former Manchester City star Edin Džeko is from Sarajevo. On 6 April 1992, the day the EU recognised Bosnia as an independent state, SDS paramilitaries again raised barricades in Sarajevo (as they had before removing them at the urging of the JNA on 2 March, the day of the referendum on Bosnian sovereignty and independence, and the day after a Muslim *mangup* ("mafia boss") shot a member of a Serb wedding party there; at the beginning of the war, the troublemakers generally took care to wear masks, but it wasn't long before all the masks fell off[109]), and between 50,000 and 100,000 Bosnians of all national identities demonstrated for peace and Bosnian unity, in marked contrast to the actions of the three nationalist parties sitting in government. They were dispersed by automatic gunfire from the SDS[110]. On 19 May 1993, Boško Brkić, a Serb, and his girlfriend Admira Ismić, a Muslim, both 25, who posthumously gained fame as the Bosnian Romeo and Juliet, were killed by a sniper while crossing the Vrbanja bridge in Sarajevo, towards the Serb borough of Grbavica. 10,000 people were killed during the siege of Sarajevo, including 53 children killed by snipers. Who were those men? Their inadequacies are described in vivid, albeit fictional detail in Peter Barry's novel, *I Hate Martin Amis* et al, which is also eerily reminiscent of reports of the doings of Islamic State. Mladić is said to have told the besiegers, "Drive them crazy" and "Burn it all"[xxii]. The siege of Sarajevo officially lasted until 29 February 1996, when the VRS withdrew. In February 1994, after the first market bombing, in which 68 people were killed by a mortar shell at the Markale market, NATO issued the VRS an ultimatum to withdraw all heavy weapons from a 20 km exclusion zone around Sarajevo (apart from Pale) within ten days (although the provenance of the shell was never unequivocally established: UNPROFOR initially determined that it came from an ABiH position, but the ICTY later found that it was fired by the VRS)[111]. 150,000 Serbs left Sarajevo during (and after) the war. Those who stayed behind were derogatively branded "Alija's Serbs".

However, the main road from Konjic to Sarajevo was blocked by the VRS just before Hadžići, and so I had to take a detour around to the west of the city (beyond Hadžići was the notorious Igman route, 20 km of mountain road leading to Sarajevo airport, subject to VRS shelling and sniper fire). About 15 km north of Konjic at Tarčin, Pacman turned off left onto a 5 km single-lane dirt track leading up and down a hill through forest. Once again I was reminded of Cumbria. One day at Tarčin,

---

[xxii] While most of the sniper fire came from VRS positions, in 1995 French UNPROFOR confirmed the long-held suspicion that some of the fire on the majority-Muslim besieged population came from the ABiH, for propaganda purposes. Owen quotes from a US report: "The press and some governments, including that of the United States, usually attribute all such fire to the Serbs, but no seasoned observer in Sarajevo doubts for a moment that Muslim forces have found it in their interest to shell friendly targets. In this case, the shelling usually closes the airport for a time, driving up the price of black-market goods that enter the city via routes controlled by Bosnian army commanders and government officials". Izetbegović was determined to, and did win the propaganda war, unlike Milošević, whose approach was, "The truth us on our side, the truth will win, and there is no need to convince anybody that we are right". Meanwhile, Tuđman was paying a PR firm in Washington USD 10,000 a month to create a "positive Croatian image" with US politicians and the media.

unusually, there were two Canadian soldiers who were stopping and checking all traffic, just out of sight of the main road. I parked up and got out. While I was talking to one of them, the other was standing in the "road" to make sure all traffic stopped. Suddenly a local 4x4 raced towards him, apparently with the intention of driving straight on. The Canadian stood his ground, and at the very last moment the vehicle screeched to a halt, with the soldier's hands planted squarely on the bonnet. His comrade, who had been ready to open fire, questioned the driver angrily (in English), and after a short while they let him proceed, with a warning to stop promptly the next time UNPROFOR ordered him to do so. Not five minutes later, a high-ranking HDZ police officer with HVO squaddie in tow turned up (even though this was SDA territory), and gave the two Canadians a very severe dressing down in the local language, full of expletives, to the effect that it had been agreed that the road was supposed to be open without hindrance to all traffic. He then stormed off without waiting for a reply; nor could there be a reply, as the Canadians hadn't understood a word he said. I gave them a potted (and censored) executive summary, which had them even more bewildered, before heading on my way myself. At the top of the hill was a checkpoint, for the road passed back into HDZ territory. One day when I was heading south I encountered a traffic jam at the top of the hill. There were a number of British UNPROFOR vehicles, several aid vehicles, including a large DFID convoy, and local civilian traffic. No-one was in control, nor could anyone speak to everyone in the same language. One of the British peacekeepers decided to do a General Patton and clear the blockage, and I volunteered to help him with communications. In a short while, order had been restored, and everyone knew when it would be their turn to move. Finally, it was my turn, and I was just about to set off when DFID decided to jump the queue. The convoy leader raced into my slot, and their first truck smashed my side mirror. Every successive truck scraped my vehicle. Little did I know that ten years later I would end up working for DFID in London (DFID now has possibly the strongest emergency logistics department in the world, thanks to the efforts of the indefatigable Julian Neale. It is always the first to deliver emergency aid to the scene of major disasters, anywhere in the world. Such logistics operations are big enough to meet the need, as was shown by the ebola response – over 2,000 tons of aid was flown into Sierra Leone - while retaining a flexibility that the leviathan war machine of the MOD can only dream of). Once I was kindly given a lift south from here to Konjic by an Egyptian colleague from another NGO. On the way we left the main road to travel to a village where he had to drop off some items. I was struck by the fact that his contact, clearly a local authority, who opened up his warehouse to receive the (small) delivery, was of overtly Islamic appearance (as was a local woman who happened to be there) and greeted us with "Salaam alejkum" rather than the neutral "Dobar dan" ("good afternoon"). He seemed somewhat confused by my presence, as I was by his community. In our work we would often travel to isolated settlements where people had been referred to us, but it was important to us to have a comprehensive approach to our partners and beneficiaries, and we certainly did not support anything that looked exclusive or radical, of any stripe. Down the hill on the north side of the earth road is the village of Kreševo where Pacman rejoins the main road, continuing to the small town of Kiseljak ("mineral water", for which it is famous throughout the former Yugoslavia), in former times a health spa, popular with Jews from Sarajevo before they were wiped from the face of the earth[112], and in the war a HDZ stronghold where vehicles with German number plates abounded. They were stolen in Germany by the Croatian mafia, spirited into Croatia and then out of reach into the war zone. Again, the locals were generally hostile to aid workers, who they knew were mainly helping the Muslims. I heard later that a Muslim had been killed there for scratching a Croat's car. A local squaddie once told me that they welcomed the war, as it had given the local economy a real boost, put the Muslims in their place, and personally he had never been better off: thanks to Tuđman, he was being paid DM 100 per month and driving a brand new BMW. He told me that even though he hated the Serbs, he would rather have a drink with a Serb than a Muslim. Kiseljak was an enclave to the north-west of besieged Sarajevo, bordering to the north, south and west on SDA territory and to the east on the SDS; but rather than assist their allies in the winter of 1992-1993, they took full advantage of their position and connections to act as middlemen in the thriving black market between the SDS and the SDA, while the VRS gave the HVO direct support against the ABiH[113]. There was a Canadian/British UNPROFOR base in Kiseljak, where I was once arrested. Our truck had broken down on the hill track in the afternoon, and Randy and I decided to sleep in the truck while Adis made his way on his own steam to Kakanj to arrange for a replacement truck to come to fetch the load. We were disturbed in the night by a French APC full of foreign legionnaires, who wanted to know who we were and what we were up to, parked up there overnight. Satisfied we were not villains up to no good, they gave us some ratpacks, including mini bottles of wine, which certainly elicited a *"merci beaucoup"* from the two of us. In the morning I went to seek help from the Canadians in Kiseljak, while Randy stayed with the vehicle. A Canadian mechanic with escort kindly patched the truck up temporarily, but it would need to go back to Konjic, which was nearer than Kakanj, for more extensive work on the airbrake system, and Randy volunteered to drive it back. Meanwhile, Adis had turned up with the other truck, and we had cross-loaded everything. By now it was getting late, and so we decided it would be better to spend the night in the UNPROFOR base in Kiseljak and continue our journey to Kakanj in the morning. I asked the Canadians, and they said that was no problem, and so we drove straight up to their main gate and they let us in. We were given "green maggots" (*vreća za spavanje*, sleeping bags) and shown where we could doss down, and I was just on my way back from a Gypsy's kiss before turning in when I noticed a high-ranking HVO officer with entourage in the courtyard talking to the Canadian soldiers. At first I couldn't believe my eyes in the gloom, and dismissed it; but then I heard them speaking Bosnian. There was obvious tension in the air, and I drew closer to listen to what was being said. It transpired that the HVO regarded the fact that a truck with SDA-territory number plates (our replacement truck) had entered the UNPROFOR base in their enclave, as a diplomatic incident. It had not occurred to me that that could be a problem, nor had the soldiers on guard duty thought anything of it when they let us in. The HVO now wanted to arrest the truck driver, Mehmet, and impound the truck and its contents. I took advantage of the fact that none of the Canadians spoke Bosnian, and none of the locals English, to defend our position. The upshot was that the Canadians refused to hand over Mehmet and his truck, but nor were they willing to let them or Adis spend the night in our compound. We finally reached a compromise whereby UNPROFOR would deliver our goods to Kakanj the next day using one of their own trucks, and Mehmet and Adis would return home that night with his (empty) truck. I insisted UNPROFOR provide them with an escort as far as SDA territory, and after we had cross-loaded everything again, I went with them to be doubly sure. Once they had crossed the frontier, I returned with the peacekeepers to the base in Kiseljak, where I was arrested by the Canadian military police, and interviewed by a Colonel Blimp[114]. He had heard that I worked for UNHCR, and subjected me to a tirade on how UNHCR do nothing but create headaches for everyone else. As I was in the habit of using our NGO's registration with UNHCR as a *laissez-passer* (most NGOs were registered with UNHCR, which allowed them to operate in the country under their umbrella and conferred a certain legitimacy in dealings with the local authorities), I thought it more prudent to allow him to continue to labour under his misapprehension. Finally, I was released and allowed to go to bed, and the next morning travelled with a Welsh UNPROFOR *tryc* ("truck") to Kakanj. I always breathed a sigh of relief once the HDZ territories were behind me.

Outside Kiseljak, the road crossed back into SDA territory, and leaving Pacman, continues for another 10 km or so to the town of Visoko ("high"), located on the river Bosna in more barren and bleak hilly countryside than further south, and which was subject to frequent if sporadic VRS shelling from the south-east (the Bosna, after which Bosnia is named, flows north from Mount Igman to join the Sava at Šamac). Stjepan Kotromanić was buried in the Franciscan monastery in Visoko in 1353, and Visoko was for a time the political capital of medieval Bosnia, with important links to Dubrovnik[115]. We once visited an IDP camp there to see how we could best provide assistance. It was far more orderly and sanitary (and smaller) than Kuplensko, with the IDPs housed in a series of portacabins, and the ground was gravelled to prevent standing water and mud from forming. Ad-hoc camps I had seen in other places, such as schools, had not been so well planned, and often tended to be overcrowded (in Nazranj, a large IDP camp was located in the shell of a block of flats that was still under construction, with no electricity or running water). The camp chairman in Visoko had a Bosnian coat of arms on the wall; seeing me looking at it, he took it down and turned it around with a laugh to reveal a portrait of Tito on the back. In 1992, the coat of arms chosen for the newly independent state of Bosnia did not derive from any of the three main religions, but was the coat of arms of King Tvrtko, Bosnia's most successful ruler (although Croatian intellectuals claim him as their own[116]). It is azure on a per bend argent between six gold fleur-de-lis in a gold bordure. Alas, this continuity was not expressed anywhere else in public life[117]. The Bosnian flag originally consisted of this coat of arms on a white field, but has since been replaced by a swimming-trunks pattern of blue and yellow, with a diagonal dividing line embellished with stars, as if to say "Made in the EU" (the new Kosovo flag is a variation on the same theme). As Rebecca West noted, "The folly of modern Europe provides us with no agreeable decorative symbols, it does not lead us to debate on the real fact of the different planes of existence"[118]. In West Timor, the aid community were visited by a Scandinavian bigwig from the EU, who addressed us in a very arrogant manner, without even introducing himself. They were financing our watsan programme in the refugee camps among other things, and insisted that EU stickers should be placed on everything they were paying for. I placed the stickers in such a way that every refugee who went to the khazi could have no doubt that it was thanks to the EU that he or she was able to perform a bodily function (in 2016, MSF, who won the Nobel prize in 1999, decided to refuse further EU funding because of the bloc's complicity in the ongoing refugee crisis). Symbols only acquire the power imagined by their creator when they are acted upon, and thenceforth they become a focus for human emotion: their power and intensity lie in the association in the beholder's experience with those deeds. In West Timor, near one of the refugee camps I worked in every day, there was an impressive cemetery. I was very surprised, when I happened to approach it one day, to observe that the wide entrance was flanked by two columns surmounted with large swastikas. The powerful imagery they conjured up was in unworldly contrast to the peace the tropical landscape evoked. I was put in mind of Somerset Maugham's words: "the East of the beginning of the world, the East of the garden of Eden, when men were few, simple and humble and ignorant, and the world was just waiting, like an empty garden for its absent owner" (nowadays it's more like an industrial estate, if not a council estate)[119]. As the only creatures capable of abstract thought, symbols are the currency with which we are bought and sold. Communication is the most powerful tool in the highest ape's arsenal, for it can override an interlocutor's reason and harness his or her potential. The master of symbols is the master of the destiny of nations. But the sleight of hand does not last forever: the laws of physics can be bent, but will not be broken[xxiii]. Every evening, on my way driving back from the refugee camps to our shared house in Kupang (where Captain Bligh of *The Bounty* fame made land in 1789 after his marathon jolly-boat trek from Tonga, 6,700 km; the chief mutineer, Cumbrian Fletcher Christian, ended up with his crew and their Tahitian womenfolk on uninhabited Pitcairn Island, where their descendants live to this day), I would see, seated outside a bar, gazing Captain Ahab-like into the middle distance beyond the road, an enigmatic elderly white man, invariably with a glass in his hand. One evening, my successor, Tim, and I decided to stop for a drink and solve the mystery of the great white hope. We parked up, introduced ourselves, and went inside and sat down. It turned out that our host, Jim, who must have been in his eighties, was a retired Australian, and the bar was his. It was run by his young local wife, who in return for his financial backing ensured that all his needs were met, the most regular of which seemed to be an unending supply of gin. As we talked, local customers started to arrive, and it wasn't long before the Karaoke machine was in full swing. The locals seemed very eager for Tim and myself to put on a performance, and so after some lubrication and encouragement, we delivered a rendition of a 1980s hit. It went down so well that we had to do another half a dozen before they would let us leave. I am sure that after we had gone they were convinced they had been treated to an impromptu private performance by Mick Jagger and Paul McCartney. Back in the Balkans, a large painted sign on a factory wall in Visoko read, "*Druže Tito volimo te!*" ("comrade Tito we love you"). He must have visited it on one of his tours of the country after WWII. Pictures of Tito were still quite common in people's houses during the Yugoslav Wars, and even now his image is often to be seen in Bosnia, on calendars in public establishments, or on T-shirts, with slogans such as: "*Josip Broz – dobar skroz!*" ("Comrade Tito, way to go!", or perhaps "Wizard of Broz!"). Curiously, he is less popular in his native Croatia[xxiv][120]. One day in 1999, driving through Conakry, the capital of Guinea, I was astounded to see, above the gateway of a school, a large hand-painted sign inscribed "*Ecole Primaire Jozip Broz Tito*", with the bespectacled man himself waving enthusiastically at passers-by. I was so surprised I stopped and went inside the school to enquire. The headmaster told me the school had been built and equipped by the Yugoslav embassy in the 1980s, when Yugoslavia was still a leading light of the developing world, and Guinea an

---

[xxiii] The swastika is an ancient symbol that was hijacked by Hitler. It has been discovered in prehistoric cultures in Africa and Asia, and features in Buddhism and Hinduism. Curiously, in Bosnian *svastika* means "sister-in-law".

[xxiv] According to Owen, Tito was as mendacious a *baraba* ("villain") as the 1990s political elite, who with "no experience of democracy also displayed a callousness of mind in which the people's view never seemed to come anywhere near the conference table [...] the Bosnian politicians, whether Serb, Muslim or Croat, were almost without exception impossibly negative. Izetbegović would not meet with Karadžić, who was being totally unyielding".

exception among former French colonies in West Africa, as with the end of France's foreign empire in 1958, it refused to maintain friendly links with the new Fifth Republic, and instead embraced Maoism, leading to a very dark quarter century for the country, as portrayed in Jean-Paul Alata's memoirs, *Prison d'Afrique*. In 1999, we were working mainly with refugees from the war in neighbouring diamond-rich Sierra Leone (and Liberia), as portrayed in the 2006 film *Blood Diamond*[xxv]. On one occasion, we acted to receive some British aid workers from another NGO, Merlin, who had been kidnapped by the RUF in Sierra Leone, and who after extended negotiations were to be released into our care across the border near Guéckédou in central Guinea. An Ethiopian colleague, Maza, was at the scene, as it was thought she would be seen as a less threatening or provocative presence than the rest of us (mainly white men) and would have a calming influence; in the event, everything passed off without incident, and over 15 years later, I met one of the hostages, Dave, during a HEAT (hostile environment awareness training) course that he was delivering in the UK. During the Yugoslav Wars, he had been a peacekeeper based in Pakrac. I used to go running in the mornings along the spit road beside the seafront in Conakry[xxvi], very early before the traffic started and the tropical air was filled with

---

[xxv] The war in the former British colony of Sierra Leone, 1991-2002, was a rebellion sponsored by Liberian politician and US citizen Charles Taylor, concurrent with his civil war at home (1989-1997), from which he emerged as victor and president. He quickly took control of Sierra Leone's diamond fields, using drug-fuelled child soldiers (the RUF) to spread a reign of terror, and the proceeds to finance his career in Liberia. The war was finally ended by the UK's Operation Palliser, a rare example of foreign military intervention with a successful epilogue, a year before the invasion of Iraq. Liberia, founded by the US as a homeland for freed slaves in 1847, was racked by war again between 1999-2003. In 2012, Liberian head of state Taylor was convicted by the Special Court for Sierra Leone of aiding and abetting war crimes and crimes against humanity. Over 50,000 people were killed in Sierra Leone and up to a million in Liberia, and there were over a million refugees from the conflicts, moving back and forth with the vagaries of war, many of them in Guinea. The refugee crisis was further aggravated by (and contributed to) unrest in neighbouring Côte d'Ivoire, to the east, one of the most prosperous countries in West Africa until a *coup* in 1999. On a beach near Freetown there is a restaurant called Frankie's, run by an elderly Italian of the same name, who has lived there since the 1970s, in good times and bad, through war and pestilence. He looks like one of the horsemen of the apocalypse himself. Whilst waiting for his speciality grilled lobster one Sunday, I nearly drowned when I was caught in the imperceptible grip of a rip tide while swimming out to a nearby sandbank that dominated the sea view. I was just catching my breath sitting on the sand, onto which I had managed to haul myself by a supreme effort once I noticed my predicament, when I saw a young white woman swimming towards me in the same direction from which I had come. She was from a group of MSF nurses who were also enjoying a day off from the ebola treatment centres. I tried to warn her to turn back, but it was too late; and she just gave up the will to live caught in the swift, treacherous current, making no effort to swim out of its grip as I had done, despite my encouragements. I looked in the direction in which the rip tide was carrying her, past the sandbank into the open ocean, and was horrified to see a whirlpool where the two bodies of water met. Seriously worried, I shouted "Help!" to my colleague reclining on the shore, another Scotch John. As the nurse was swept around the corner, I tried to walk out towards the whirlpool in an attempt to grab her, but on my very first step I sank into quicksand above the knee. By the time I had extricated myself, she was in the grip of the maelstrom, and despite my entreaties was making no effort to save herself. I was just resolving myself to enter the water horizontally if she started to go under, when she suddenly stood up: there was solid sand next to the funnel of death. I helped her exit the water, and we both flopped down onto the sand exhausted, where we lay until a canoe skilfully manoeuvred by some local lads, alerted by John, arrived to take us back. The lobster was truly excellent.

[xxvi] Conakry, shoved onto a narrow spit of land sticking out into the ocean, is said to have served as the inspiration for the fictional setting of Frederick Forsyth's novel, *The Dogs of War*. Two years later, I was almost flattened by a truck in Luanda early one morning, pursuing the same elusive goal. As I gave way to the advancing behemoth, I slashed my legs on rusty barbed wire that was practically invisible in the half-light, and which surrounded, at calf-height, some nondescript patches of stunted grass between the pavement and the *rua* ("road"). As they say in the Balkans, "*Ko rano rani dvije sreće grabi*" ("the early bird gets the worm"). Conakry also had a large, and largely empty Yugoslav embassy, which serviced the

noise and smoke. It was refreshingly beautiful to see the dawn slowly take shape over the Atlantic as I pounded along, and one morning I was able to observe a spectacular thunderstorm out to sea that appeared to be deceptively close, because the actual distance meant the drama was being played out in silence from my perspective; but once it got light, the rubbish and filth dumped on the beach became apparent and the spell was broken. I used to pass a large billboard with an advertisement for Guinness, with the caption: "*La puissance noire!*" ("black power"; I noticed in the DRC that a very popular drink was Guinness and Coke, perhaps as sacrilegious to a true Irishman as red wine and Coke would be to a Frenchman). In Guinea we used to make use of the services of a haulier called Fidel Castro. The transport magnate, black as he was, was the spitting image of the late Caribbean dictator, complete with green fatigues, peaked cap and beard. I asked him one day how he reconciled his capitalist business practices with the building of socialism, and he was unable to come up with a convincing answer. It was no less surprising to come across a Yugoslav engineering company carrying out major infrastructure projects in Angola two years later. One of their team was a middle-aged Argentinian who had grown up in Belgrade, and I deduced from the fragments of his story that he let drop that his family had been granted asylum in Yugoslavia in the 1960s or 1970s. Nowadays Visoko is famous for the pyramid that has allegedly been discovered under one of the nearby hills. Curiously, no Howard Carters have yet appeared on the scene to excavate it (it is also said that Bosnia has its own Bermuda triangle, between Sarajevo, Banja Luka and Mostar, the capitals of the three "constituent peoples", where billions of euros have disappeared without a trace).

Northeast from Visoko, route Skoda skirted the VRS front line to the south-east and east for 30 km before rejoining the main road at Kladanj ("block"), and then heading north, after 25 km passing the city of Tuzla to the east. 10 km south-east of Tuzla is the hamlet of Vukovije ("wily"). Tuzla, equidistant from the Croatian and Serbian borders, is Bosnia's third-largest city, and was the destination of Muslim civilians and the lucky few combatants escaping from the fall of Srebrenica on 11 July 1995 ("silvertown", in the middle ages the second largest mining town in the Balkans, was developed by German immigrants from Transylvania with the encouragement of Stjepan Kotromanić and his nephew King Tvrtko; the Romans had called it Argentium[121]. Silver was Bosnia's most important export at the time, and Srebrenica had important trading links with Dubrovnik, who controlled exports and imports via the coast[122]).

The VRS offensive against Srebrenica, with the enclave's commanders kept in Tuzla (see above), started on 6 July. UNPROFOR observation points were overrun and over 50 of the 300 Dutch peacekeepers taken hostage. On 10 July, the peacekeepers requested air strikes, and on the afternoon of 11 July there was an air strike against VRS tanks approaching the town, but further planned strikes were called off due to poor visibility and after Mladić threatened to kill hostages and shell crowds of IDPs. The peacekeepers were instructed by their political masters in The Hague to abandon their posts, and promptly did so, withdrawing to the UNPROFOR base at a disused factory in Potočari, 5 km north of the town, where they remained until 21 July. After the town was occupied by the VRS that evening, large numbers

---

rest of West Africa, a monument to former glory. One evening at a restaurant/bar I was sight-translating the menu for Seka, when we were surprised to say the least to hear the *Fote* ("white man") who was attending to us, clearly the proprietor, whom I had taken for a Frenchman, break into Serbian. He was from Belgrade, and had been living in Conakry with his family for years.

of people, exhausted by three years of unrelenting violence and deprivation, sought refuge in vain at Potočari (up to 4,000 inside the base, and 24,000 outside, mainly women and children). The next day, after a walkabout by Mladić during which he reassured the Muslims that nothing would happen to them, sporadic atrocities started, including rape and murder, under the noses, and sometimes in view of the peacekeepers. Men and women were separated by the VRS, and amid frightful scenes, 25,000 women and children were deported by bus to Kladanj (or rather, as far as the front, followed by a 7 km walk). 1,000 men were detained immediately. Elsewhere in Srebrenica, the evening the enclave fell, another 15,000 people or more, the majority men (and less than half of them soldiers), fearing the worst, had decided to attempt a breakout. Some headed for Serbia or Žepa, to the east and south respectively, while the majority headed north across country the 55 km to Tuzla. Their ordeal through the forest lasted five days (although some stragglers were still arriving several weeks later), pursued and hunted as they were by the enemy, slowed down by fear of mines, and short of food and water in the summer heat, with no shelter (there was also an unseasonable storm). They were subjected to shelling, and some people became so stressed they spontaneously committed suicide (some ABiH soldiers used to keep a spare grenade handy for just such an eventuality, to avoid being taking prisoner). Large numbers were captured. The increasingly scattered groups of people had to cross a road at Nova Kasaba ("new town"), where they were particularly vulnerable, and continued over the Snagovo hills to the front line, where with the help of the ABiH 2nd Corps from Tuzla a corridor was opened for them to cross into SDA territory, at Baljkovica, a hill halfway between Zvornik and Tuzla. 8,000 men and boys didn't make it. Most of them were executed from 13 July onwards in large organised operations involving assembly points, buses, trucks and bulldozers, isolated individual execution sites, and mass graves. 30,000 litres of fuel provided by the UN was used in the operation[123]. Mujo said the hike to Tuzla was his worst single experience of the whole war, while another survivor described it as the ninth circle of the hell of Srebrenica. FTC was on the scene to provide relief to the survivors coming across, more dead than alive. Gary told me that when he went to help an old man carry his meagre possessions, he just sat down on the ground and burst into tears.

Was Srebrenica a tactical sacrifice by Izetbegović, even as he wrote Dudaković a blank cheque in the Bihać pocket? UNPROFOR had already decided to withdraw from the eastern enclaves, as it was impossible to protect them[124]. According to the *Guardian*, France, the UK and the US had already decided that the enclaves should be removed from the contact group map as being "untenable", and this was communicated to Mladić (earlier that year, Lord Owen had wanted to swap Srebrenica and Žepa for SDS territory near Sarajevo[125]). A CIA memo from the time described the enclaves as "fish bones in the throat of the Serbs". The US and the UK were also aware that on 2 June, Mladić had ordered the "destruction of the Muslim forces in the enclaves". On 9 June, at a meeting in Split, the head of UNPROFOR in Bosnia, General Rupert Smith, warned the UN special envoy to the Balkans, Yakushi Akashi, that there was an impending crisis that could only be dealt with by air strikes, something the UN was reluctant to contemplate. After the first infamous market bombing in Sarajevo on 5 February 1994, there had been loud calls for NATO air strikes operating outside the UN structure, which were only averted when the Russians obtained a token concession from the Bosnian SDS (and for the first time, NATO fired in anger, shooting down four VRS planes near Novi Travnik)[126]. Then, in April 1994, the VRS had taken 150 peacekeepers hostage after air strikes on their positions around Goražde, on the occasion of the VRS's first attempt to take the town[127]. The *taoci* ("hostages") were later released, in a show of publicity, by Stanišić, accompanied by the Unit, in its first official act, and the VRS withdrew[128]. In May 1995, the VRS tried again to take Goražde (this time under instructions from Karadžić as part of his wider Directive 7, as opposed to the previous year, when Mladić was acting on his own account), but were repelled in June by the ABiH with support on the ground from British UNPROFOR (and after again taking hostages, this time 30 British peacekeepers)[129] (Goražde is now part of the Federation, and as the only surviving eastern enclave is connected to Sarajevo by a road built especially for that purpose under Dayton). On 8 July, after the final VRS offensive on Srebrenica was already underway, Smith was told at a meeting in Geneva to return to his holiday on Korčula, while Akashi, the only person in the Balkans authorised to order air strikes, went for a two-day break to Dubrovnik[130]. Thus the most powerful man in the Balkans, a UN bureaucrat wielding fire from the sky, turned out to be little more than a gimp (it is also said that Pol Pot, directly responsible with his Khmer Rouge for up to three million deaths in Cambodia between 1975 and 1979, was actually rather inconsequential as an individual, a simple clerk with terrible power[xxvii][131]). According to MSF, "The fall as well as the massacres of Srebrenica were foreseeable. The promise of protection made to the inhabitants of Srebrenica was not kept and the lack of political will to defend them contributed to leading them to the massacre"[132]. Srebrenica is now part of Republika Srpska. Izetbegović was aware this was inevitable; indeed, in September 1993 he had warned the civilian authorities there that surrendering the enclave might be the price of peace[133]. Previously, on 14 April 1993, Naser Orić, the commander of Srebrenica (a former Serbian security service man and once Milošević's bodyguard[134]), had decided to surrender: UNPROFOR was to oversee the operation, and Mladić had given an assurance that civilians and the wounded could be evacuated, but that men of fighting age would be detained. Two days later, with Srebrenica meanwhile declared by the UN security council the first "safe area" (the others were added once Vance-Owen was pronounced dead), the surrender was presented by the UN as a bilateral "disarmament agreement", signed in Sarajevo. Up until then, UN involvement had been limited to the provision of humanitarian aid[135]. The agreement was never implemented; peacekeepers were deployed and an uneasy ceasefire ensued. According to Mazowiecki, the UN's acceptance of the Srebrenica *pokolj* ("massacre") and its resignation to the fate of Žepa at a conference in London on 21 July effectively gave Mladić the green light to take the second enclave four days later (as a result of the same conference, UN civilian staff were also removed from the decision-making chain in UNPROFOR requests to NATO for air strikes)[136]. After

---

[xxvii] The Khmer Rouge mutated out of the Viet Cong in 1968 as a result of the US blanket bombing of Cambodia during the Vietnam War of 1955-1975, and was finally put down by its Vietnamese creator in 1979. Vietnam, Cambodia and Laos had together formed French Indo-China until 1954, when the French withdrew after a decade of conflict with independence movements that had started during the WWII Japanese occupation. Curiously, Islamic State underwent a similar genesis from Saddam Hussein's Ba'ath party 45 years later. But what is Islamic State? Behind the unmistakable brand, which inspires extreme love and hatred in equal measure, lies a billion-dollar business, with links to the surviving former Ba'ath party elite. The party, whose members included Christians, such as Saddam's PM Tarik Aziz (6% of Iraqis were Christians in 2003), was dissolved and the entire Iraqi army disbanded by the US governor of Iraq in 2003. As they say in the Balkans, "*Đavo niti ore niti kopa već smišlja zlo*" ("the devil makes work for idle hands"). So much for religious labels. Akashi's plane was shot at and hit in the tail as he landed at Sarajevo airport on 12 March 1995 - not by the VRS, but by the ABiH. Owen called him "impartial and tough".

Operation Storm, UNPROFOR was withdrawn from Goražde to Serbia to allow the town to be protected by air strikes if necessary, and the result was that there were no more potential hostages in SDS territory. Thus the way was prepared for "bombing the Serbs into compromise"[137].

Mujo, one of those who ultimately got away, selflessly and heroically took the time to encourage and direct the civilians, and to discourage them despite the intolerable thirst from drinking the water available *en route*, which may have contained a nerve agent. Mujo is a quiet, modest family man who I first met in the UK after the war, when I was assisting him during PTSD therapy sessions. His mild demeanour belies three extremely intense years in Srebrenica, leading multiple missions behind enemy lines, and two spells as a POW. At the beginning of the war, before capturing hardware from the VRS, they had had to use home-made grenades. He was previously also Naser Orić's personal bodyguard. Orić, who had left Srebrenica by helicopter in May, was convicted by the ICTY of war crimes carried out between June 1992 and March 1993 (in particular during his offensive against the SDS authorities in April 1992 and attacks on Serb villages in January 1993), but this was overturned on appeal in 2008[138]. I have never seen Mujo smile. Potočari is now the location of the Srebrenica monument.

Tuzla was practically surrounded by SDS territory throughout the war, with this road the only way in and out, hemmed in by the VRS, and was another Orwellian UN "safe area"[139] (as were Srebrenica, Sarajevo, Bihać, Žepa and Goražde). There was talk of it becoming another autonomous region in 1994. Tuzla was also the only Muslim city that did not succumb to SDA rule, and was governed by non-nationalists throughout the war[140]. It has an airport which, along with and secondarily to Sarajevo, was strategic for the delivery of humanitarian aid (and other, less humanitarian items). Route Skoda then continued 20 km north-west to Gradačac, on the VRS front line, and to the west of Brčko, on the Croatian border, only about 50 km from Đakovo in Slavonia. But there was no access to Croatia from here, the very end of the tenuous lifeline from the coast, at least for ordinary mortals. Gradačac has a castle, the *Zmaj od Bosne* ("dragon of Bosnia")'s tower, built by Husein-kapetan, who led a rebellion against the Turkish central authority in 1831[141], occupying the capital Travnik. He then took advantage of a rebellion in northern Albania to march on Kosovo, and demanded autonomy for Bosnia and an end to the unpopular reforms insisted upon by Istanbul. These were granted, but in 1832 the governor attacked Sarajevo and Husein-kapetan fled to Austria[142]. He is said to have worn a magical shirt that protected him in battle (north of Gradačac, on the river Sava and the border with Croatia, is Izetbegović's home town of Šamac; Đinđić was also born in Šamac, and it is said they were both born in the same house – albeit at different times - which was destroyed in the 2014 floods). Brčko, Bosnia's largest port, on the river Sava, now has the special status of *distrikt*, outside the jurisdiction of either the Federation or Republika Srpska, and governed by a special international supervisor, as a result of an arbitration ruling in March 1999. It was the only unresolved dispute in the Dayton peace accords, as all three sides claimed it. These unique characteristics led to the development after the war of a vast international wholesale market here trading in all kinds of goods, known as "Arizona". For a while, the free-trade zone was dominated by criminals, with women, arms and drugs traded freely and openly. Nowadays, retailers from all over Bosnia and further afield travel there to purchase stocks of more mundane goods from Chinese, Hungarian and other wholesalers, which are then sold on markets throughout Bosnia. An old lady resident in Brčko, Stana Brkić, an IDP from Drvar, prophesied in the first half of

2016 that the *Maršal* would return to Bosnia before the end of the year to reunite the Yugoslav peoples[143]. There is now a fundamentalist community in the village of Maoča near Brčko.

But I was travelling north from Visoko, joining the main Sarajevo-Zenica highway on the Bosnian high *veld* (which was blocked by the VRS just a few km further south), the other end of route Skoda, and a straight run to Kakanj, our other base, around 25 km away. Kakanj, with its large Romany community, is a post-industrial town sprawling on both sides of the highway, which flies over it on a bridge rather than taking the time to run through it. It lies in a plain, but is within a stone's throw of hills on both sides. It has a cement factory which before the war meant the air was very polluted; at least during the war, with the factory shut down, you could breathe. It also has a coal mine, which was a POW camp during the war. 5,500 miners went on strike here in 1987, following strikes in Mostar and Tuzla. Led by local girl Maksuma Topalović, the "Bosnian Joan of Arc", they marched to Sarajevo, and won some token concessions. She is now a SDP district councillor, and also runs her own NGO. I visited the mine once, and was surprised to note that, even though it was not working, a lot of the employees were there, and there appeared to be no shortage of food and drink for them. Working for a corporation in the former Yugoslavia was about more than a job, it meant belonging to a family that looked after its own. 128 miners were killed in a methane explosion in the mine in 1965. Kakanj was home to a large number of IDPs from places like Jajce and from the Sarajevo suburbs such as Ilijaš, many of whom took up residence in houses left vacant by departing Serbs. Behind a house by the path along the river in Kakanj there was a small corn field with a "*Mine*" ("mines") sign: it was said the occupier was sick of people stealing his corn, and so had put the sign up to deter them, while others said he really had mined the field, for the same reason. Before the war, the population had been 55% Muslim, 30% Croat, and 9% Serb. In June 1993, the influx of Muslim IDPs into Kakanj aggravated inter-ethnic relations, and many Croats left for nearby Vareš, fuelling the conflict between the SDA and the HDZ there in October[144]. At the same time, the Croat villages around Kakanj became the target for ABiH attacks. As elsewhere in the war, such operations against civilian populations, during which the victims were typically given half an hour to leave and told they could only take one bag, tended to attract crowds of curious onlookers, hoping for the chance to loot something. As Reinhard observed, "They always come at night". Some people were not above throwing eggs at their former neighbours. The persecution of minorities in SDA towns such as Kakanj, albeit less intense and systematic than in SDS and HDZ areas, fell under the remit of paramilitary "special forces" units such as the Black Swans. The Black Swans were formed in 1992 near Tuzla from IDPs from Bijeljina as part of the 2nd Corps, before moving their HQ to Kakanj (they had other bases in Konjic and Jablanica). Their USD 700,000 per month budget came mainly from "private sources", and allowed them to provide a level of comfort and equipment far superior to that of the regular ABiH soldiers, not to mention the civilian population. This in turn gave them not only a free hand with the authorities, but also meant they attracted a certain profile of recruit, individuals motivated by greed and power, on whom they imposed a nominal level of Islamic behaviour[145]. The ones I encountered were cocky bullies. They claimed credit for a number of victories in Izetbegović's March 1995 offensive (see Part 1), which actually fizzled out without achieving any of its three objectives[146]. As Hope said, there were plenty of real heroes who emerged in the war, defending their homes, families and communities in the finest Partisan tradition, but the glory and the rewards tended to go to the "false patriots, shameless traitors and cowardly war profiteers", who were invariably well-connected with the authorities and who made sure someone else died for their country[xxviii][147]. Near the mine, just outside the town, there was a Belgian UNPROFOR base. I had occasion to visit them several times, and noticed they were all French speakers. One day I asked one of them whether any of them spoke Flemish. He replied that they only spoke Flemish to the dogs.

One morning I was walking down the main street in Kakanj when I came across a crowd in front of one of the high-rise buildings in the town. I stopped to see what was happening, and saw some local soldiers abseiling down the building to the ground. It was a display to raise morale. None of them appeared to be wearing any safety harnesses, so it was quite impressive. I heard an anecdote in Kakanj that a 3rd Corps commander had once shelled his own men to keep them on their toes. On another occasion I ventured into the abandoned Orthodox church, to find it had been ransacked, with books and other religious items left scattered on the floor. I soon left, feeling the same sense of evil that I felt two years later venturing into an abandoned hotel in Bukavu in the DRC that had once belonged to a Belgian expat, who had been run out of town and had been lucky to get away in one piece, and which, standing empty, had been defaced by graffiti after its new occupants had bored of their new playground. I once heard a woman say in Kakanj, in respect of the Serbs, "It's a shame Hitler didn't exterminate them all in 1941". Glimpses beneath the surface like that were a sobering reminder that, as a foreigner, I was often deliberately excluded from the deeper currents raging through the countryside, churning everything in their path, and that for the most part, my contemplation was restricted to admiring the picturesque millpond on the surface. Four years later in Kosovo, the young receptionist of another NGO joyfully told me one morning, in English, that they were going to be up to their knees in Serb blood. She was surprised when I responded to her in Serbian, but not perturbed. One day in Zagreb, after the war, I went into a bookshop and enquired after a Serbian dictionary (as opposed to pre-war Serbian/Croatian or post-war Croatian). The elderly lady who appeared to be in charge, who had all the trappings of anyone's kind, old granny, let me know without batting an eyelid that if I was interested in such a book I should go back to Serbia. The Romanies had their own *mahala* ("district") in Kakanj, which is common in the Balkans, and some of them were among our beneficiaries. Once when in the colourful, crowded, and dilapidated *mahala*, I saw a girl who couldn't have been older than five walking along, smoking a Drina. One of the less picturesque members of the community attempted to persuade one of our local team to help him rob our warehouse. Melquiades he wasn't (most Romany names are borrowed from the host community, but I have come across some quaint examples in the UK, such as Hansolo, and Rolex[xxix]). While the majority of Romanies pursue a traditional, legitimate trade, such as horse-trading or metalworking, there are those who give credence to their negative stereotype.

Kakanj is otherwise unremarkable. But only 10 km away to the east, in the direction of Vareš, on winding, single-lane country roads and tracks, and controlled

---

[xxviii] As George Orwell said, "It is the same in all wars; the soldiers do the fighting, the journalists do the shouting, and no true patriot ever gets near a front-line trench".

[xxix] I also came across some curious names when working in Mozambique, such as Pesado ("heavy") and Saboroso ("tasty"). A local painter and decorator was called Senhor Judas. Negotiating with him a price to repaint our office, I asked if 30 pieces of silver would cover it. I'm not sure whether he appreciated the English sense of humour: "*Sorte sua*" ("just as well") commented Armando, one of our drivers, known as the "Guitarist".

by an ABiH checkpoint, is the spectacular Kraljeva Sutjeska ("king's gorge") valley, with its Franciscan monastery, managed by a formidable *gvardijan* ("superior") who is fluent in several languages. The Franciscans have been offering shelter to travellers in Bosnia for over 700 years, since 1340, when they sought to reassert Rome's authority over the heretical Bosnian church after Stjepan Kotromanić converted to Catholicism (from Orthodoxy)[148]. One day in that minute enclave I encountered some elderly village ladies with elaborate tattoos on their hands and faces. One of them touched the secondary school body art on my own forearm leaning on the window sill, and gave me a conspiratorial wink. Like polyphone singing, this custom among Catholic women in central Bosnia is said to be a remnant of pre-Slavic (Illyrian) times[149] (likewise, throughout Yugoslavia, it was common for men to tattoo the dates of their JNA national service on their hands)[xxx]. Other Franciscan monasteries in Bosnia are in Kreševo and Fojnica (Dizdarević's home town, between Kiseljak and Gornji Vakuf, where there was also a working Derviš monastery in the 1970s[150]). The latter has a rich archive and library with thousands of manuscripts and valuable artefacts[151]. Franciscan monasteries in Foča, Jajce, Zvornik, Srebrenica and Bihać were converted into mosques after the Turkish conquest[152]. The sites of those Catholic monasteries that survived this period also correspond to the areas of central Bosnia and Herzegovina that nowadays identify themselves as Croat. Further along the same route from Kakanj is the ruined fortress of Bobovac, the stronghold of King Tvrtko from 1377 onwards[153]. It was the first Bosnian fortress to fall to the Turks, in 1463, and was only captured after a secret entrance was revealed by a traitor, who the Turks thanked after their victory by casting him from the battlements. Kakanj is also the home of a friend of mine, Ratko, originally from Sarajevo, a retired teacher and keen musician and choirmaster whose daughter, Lara, used to work for us. Though a Serb, he resolved to stick it out in the SDA town during the war, even though it may have been easier for him to defect to SDS territory, which as a TA officer he could easily have done. Ironically, most Serbs of military age living outside what became SDS territory who didn't subscribe to Karadžić's hysterical and theatrical rhetoric at the beginning of the war, and therefore move, soon found themselves POWs for the duration. Throughout Bosnia, the start of hostilities was immediately preceded by a coordinated but silent departure of most Serbs from towns about to be attacked (as was the case in Bosanska Krupa in April 1992[154]). On 19 December 1991, Karadžić sent key SDS members a document with instructions on how to take over territory and persecute non-Serbs during an emergency[155]. Ratko was a regular at the local chess club. Every town in the former Yugoslavia had an active chess club, and the authorities sponsored local and international tournaments, but during the war they appeared to metamorphosise into pensioners' social clubs. Whenever I went to the beach near our house in Split, there was always a group of pensioners crowded around a chessboard (near the beach there was also a hotel, the Lav ("lion"), which seemed to be full of Bosnian Croat refugees). According to Dr Kržišnik-Bukić, chess was a great factor of social cohesion, with no divisions along ethnic/religious lines, and the chess enthusiasts, used to moving in the naked logic of the chessboard, were the last to notice (and participate in) the nationalist crisis[156]. Our landlord, Halil, an IDP from Foča living in an abandoned Serb house, proposed to me one day when he was on leave from the

---

[xxx] In the back of an AN12 at Rangoon airport, the Russian loadmaster, seeing my tattoo, asked me whether I had been in the *BBC* ("air force"). When I replied in the negative, he shook his head wryly and said, "*Balavac*" ("boy racer").

front that we go into business together: I would use the NGO's van to drive passengers, who he would find, through the checkpoints to and from the infamous Sarajevo tunnel, and we would split the proceeds. The 340 m tunnel was dug by hand between January and July 1993 to link the suburbs of Dobrinja (the most populous district of the city, built in 1983 to house athletes and foreign journalists at the 1984 winter Olympics) and Butmir (near the airport, and outside the siege lines), and allowed people and goods, including weapons, to move in and out of Sarajevo, as well as serving as a conduit for telephone and electricity lines[157]. The house in which the entrance was hidden is now a museum, 30 minutes' walk from the district of Ilidža ("spa"), where the Habsburgs built a luxury ethnic holiday resort for themselves, complete with racecourse and grinning natives, and where the Archduke spent his last night on this earth[158]. Once again, I had to regretfully decline.

In Kakanj I had a run-in with another NGO. One weekend I went to the house of Nihada, who worked for us, and whose teenage brother had been killed in action against the HVO. She introduced me to her sister, who was dressed in Islamic garb, with a head scarf that allowed her face to be seen. By way of explanation, she told me she had married an Egyptian, who worked for a Kuwaiti NGO. A week later, I happened to be at Nihada's house again, and again saw her sister, but this time in jeans and T-shirt. I asked her what had happened to her traditional dress, and she told me she had left her husband. Soon thereafter, the jilted husband came round to the family home with a gun and threatened her father. Angered, I went to see the head of office at UNHCR in Zenica, and complained that a staff member of another NGO had threatened our NGO's staff with violence. After returning home, I received a number of phone calls. The first was from UNHCR, to confirm that they had been in touch with the Kuwaiti NGO and demanded they take action. The second was from the NGO, apologising and assuring me the member of staff in question had been sacked. The third was from the Egyptian himself, who warned me in his broken English to mind my own business, and assured me I would be sorry. I duly reported this exchange to UNHCR as well. I later learnt more about his background. He had apparently been working as a welder in Greece when the war started in Yugoslavia, and came to join the *Mudžahedin* irregulars that were flooding into the country. After a spell as a *Mudža*, he decided martyrdom wasn't for him, and joined the regular ABiH. But even that wasn't his cup of tea, and so the Kuwaitis, sorry to see one of their own at a loose end, gave him a job. And now he'd lost that, as well as his wife. I never heard what happened to him after that. A friend of Nihada's who was in the ABiH military police told her there was nothing he could do, because the Egyptian was above the law.

On my last day in Kakanj, the *krimpolicija* ("CID") came round and said I had to pay DM 50 because I was a foreigner. I was suspicious, and refused to pay, saying our NGO would require an official notice. When they came back several weeks later with the notice, my colleagues informed them I had defected to Babo because of their unwarranted demand.

From Kakanj, the main road continues west and then north to Zenica, the location of Bosnia's main prison. Halfway up the road, just where it changes direction, the hamlet of Kukavica ("coward") is to be found 2 km to the east. Zenica, on the river Bosna, was also subject to sporadic VRS shelling from the north-west, and was the location of UNHCR's main office for that part of the country. The ABiH's first overtly Muslim unit, the 7th Muslim brigade, was formed here in May 1993, made up of IDPs from north and eastern Bosnia (theoretically, and at least up until 1994, the ABiH was open to Bosnian patriots of all ethnic/religious backgrounds, and the army's 2IC, General Jovan Divjak, was a Serb, born in Belgrade, although his father was from the Bosnian Borders)[159]. Thus the main victims of the war – 83% of the dead were Muslims – adopted the abusive practices visited on them by Milošević and Tuđman, albeit to a lesser extent, and subscribed to Izetbegović's policy of intolerance[160]. Before the war, Zenica had a major steelworks, which was bought in 2000 by ArcelorMittal, and is now a major source of air pollution. Ismet, who used to work there and who I met in Texas, told me that in the good old days of planned economy, management of the plant was so inefficient that "*faktički nismo ništa radili*" ("in practical terms we did nothing")[xxxi]. Elevenses in the Yugoslav workplace consisted of *rakija* drunk out of small, narrow-necked jars that hold 100 ml. However, during the war, although it was officially closed, it actually served as a munitions factory, conveniently sheltered by the Turkish UNPROFOR base located in the disused facilities[161]. One day, Stefan and I stopped there for lunch on an aborted trip to Tuzla. We got talking to a Turkish officer, who told us he was going back home the next week, "back to civilisation". The first time I went to Zenica, I saw a woman walking down the street in full, black Islamic garb, with only the eyes showing. That was the only time I had seen that in Bosnia until very recently, when I saw a woman in Velika Kladuša wearing it, in the company of a skinhead *bilder* ("body-builder") with a fine beard. I have noticed a trend in recent years in Bosnia for a small minority to feel empowered to distinguish in their interactions between Muslims and *kauri* ("infidels" – curiously, and revealingly, this word has the same root as the Afrikaans N-word: their common root is the Arabic word *quffar*, which was exported in the middle ages via Turkey to the Balkans and via Portugal to southern Africa). Halfway between Kakanj and Zenica, there is a left turn that leads swiftly to Vitez, the scene of heavy fighting between the ABiH and the HVO before the Washington agreement, when all three sides were going at it hammer and tongs. Gordon told me you could hardly step outside without being shot at during that period. The HDZ enclave starts in the middle of the town. In April 1993, thousands of Muslims were expelled by the HVO from Vitez and fled to Travnik or Zenica[162]. The most notorious atrocity in this part of the war was the massacre of over 100 civilians perpetrated by the HVO on 16 April 1993 in the village of Ahmići, just outside Vitez, which was discovered by British peacekeepers, and as a result of which Margaret Thatcher cancelled a planned trip to Zagreb[163]. When Mazowiecki's team visited the scene two weeks later, they were fired upon by the HVO[164]. Vitez was also FTC's largest operational area, with the large *kifle* ("bread roll") programme to schools ensuring 50,000 children got at least one bite to eat a day, while at the same time encouraging them to go to school. FTC was the first NGO to operate in Vitez, in 1993. One evening in 1995, crossing from HDZ territory, Canbat crashed into the ABiH checkpoint in Vitez, demolishing a *kamp-prikolica* ("caravan") that served as an office and baitroom for the guards. Fortunately, it was empty at the time, and no-one was hurt. We had been speaking to him on the VHF as the drama suddenly unfolded, and his last transmission of "Fuck!" followed by radio silence incited us to go out looking for him. Arriving at the scene of the RTA, we discovered that he had been arrested, and I attended the police station to interpret for him. He was interviewed by the local chief of police. The owner of the caravan was also summoned, and made an emotional and empathic

---

[xxxi] One day, Ismet made me *Bosanski lonac* ("tatie pot"), another Bosnian speciality, which I found indistinguishable from *stòbhadh* ("Irish stew").

appeal for justice. They eventually released Canbat on an undertaking to pay for the caravan, keeping his driving licence as security. *Svaki Cigo svoga konja hvali* ("they weren't as green as they were cabbage-looking"). Outside the town the road rejoins route Pacman, which continues north from Kiseljak and past Vitez to Travnik, back in SDA territory, but just 15 km from the VRS front line. North of Zenica, the main road leads up route Lada through Maglaj to Doboj, in VRS territory. 10 km west of Doboj is the hamlet of Jadovica ("woe").

By the main road just at the entrance to Zenica was a café that served excellent *ćevapi*. This is possibly the most popular fast food in Bosnia, and consists of minced lamb or veal formed into small sausage shapes and fried or grilled, served with *lepinje* ("unleavened bread"), cottage cheese, raw union, and salad. A portion of *ćevapi* in Kuplensko cost DM 6[165], while in Zenica in 1994 it was DM 5 – a luxury few people could afford. It was nice to sit down and treat oneself in good company to a portion of *ćevapi* and a cold beer after all the stresses of the road up from the sunny coast. The general food shortages made such luxuries all the more potent as well as poignant, only adding to the desperate and restrained yet curiously vivacious atmosphere conjured up by the dour landscape. There was food available if you had money, and foreigners were being paid to be there (even as a volunteer I received an allowance, and my living costs were covered), but the majority of locals endured a long, uphill struggle to make ends meet through the years of economic inactivity and exorbitant prices (alas, the end of the war has not changed this much). At least the tradition of smallhold farming meant that many people were able to meet some of their needs through their own modest produce (at least in the countryside). Then, as now, it was extremely rare to see anyone overweight. It was also rare to see someone whose teeth, like the roads, were not in a poor state of repair. The Russian practice of replacing failed teeth with solid gold (or even steel) is restricted in the Balkans to the Romany community. The lucky few locals who managed to get a job with an NGO would often be the breadwinner in their family, with the main requirement often being nothing more than a half-decent command of English. Those who got a job with the UN had won the lottery. When I was working in the eastern DRC in 1997, a local UNHCR driver earned significantly more than a hospital doctor. The UN and NATO also tend to offer jobs for life. One day in Kandahar, I was surprised when in the portacabin toilet to hear two people speaking Serbian/Croatian. When I stepped outside, I discovered it was the two cleaners, who it transpired were from Tuzla. They had started working for UNPROFOR during the war, and after being inherited by SFOR, had managed to impress their US employer, and never looked back. They were now "made men", set up for life, travelling the world from one US base to another. Their colleagues from the sanitary services department, employed ultimately by Dick Cheney, were a caste apart and came from a multitude of developing countries, such as the Philippines: watching them in action was like attending a carnival of all the countries the US had deployed to since WWII (except Afghanistan, as locals weren't allowed into the camp, although I did see some local trucks loading up inside the camp perimeter one day), hoovering up everywhere everything it needs. Anyone who could let property to an international organisation was also onto a good thing. When I was working in Angola in 2001, UNHCR was said to be paying over ten thousand US dollars per month in rent for their office in Luanda (much of the more desirable property in Luanda is still owned by Portuguese expats, who are often far better off than their compatriots in Europe). Back in central Bosnia, Croatia with its tourists and pizza restaurants seemed to be a world away.

Many people who live in the countryside (and many town-dwellers in the former Yugoslavia have a *vikendica* ("weekend house") in the countryside, where they can escape the cramped living conditions and more stressful pace of life of urban existence), make their own *rakija*. It's a real joy to devote oneself to this primordial alchemy surrounded by the land, the sky, the elements, our fellow-creatures, the varied wonderful landscapes given to man by God, and the multifarious fruits of nature that provide us not only with basic sustenance, but with two of the key ingredients to community life: good food and drink. Many people have small, individual stills, the philosopher's stone that can be used to produce a few litres for personal and medicinal use at home. But it is not uncommon for the owner of a larger still or *veseli stroj* ("merry machine") to do the rounds during the harvest season, charging a fee to distil the mash that villagers have pre-prepared. The mash is made by simply placing the fruit of one's choice in a covered wooden barrel for a few days (most commonly *šljive* ("plums"), but *loza* ("grapes") and *kruške* ("pears") are also popular; corn, bread, *bujada* ("weeds"), and even *kaladont* ("toothpaste") were used in Kuplensko. Corn is also used in the DRC to produce *whisky vungu* ("white whisky"), which I once tried but found to be an acquired taste). Sugar can be added to accelerate the process, a practice frowned upon by purists. The mash is then placed in a copper drum, which is heated by a fire built under it. The alcohol that has already formed in the mash evaporates at a much lower temperature than water (78.5 degrees), and passes as vapour together with the priceless essence of the fruit up the spout. It then enters the second element of the still, a tank of water, around the side of which the *šlauf* ("pipe") spirals down to the tap, and the water cools the vapour in the pipe so that it returns to liquid form before exiting. It is a very festive, communal activity, which brings together whole neighbourhoods, with much sampling and comparing of the elixir as it runs still warm from the tap of the mysterious device, like milk fresh from the cow's udder: the essence of life from the earth's breast. The first output is generally weaker, around 35%, and is swiftly followed by the most popular grade, around 40%. Additional persistence is rewarded by the strongest stuff, around 45%. Really powerful stuff, *prepečenica*, can be obtained by passing the *rakija* through the *kazan* ("still") a second time. The rule of thumb for measuring the strength (apart from quaffing it) is to dip your finger in some and light it. The longer it burns, the stronger it is: 1 second is equivalent to 10 degrees. I attended such a ceremony in Kakanj in 1994, and realised too late that while warm *rakija* tastes milder than when it is cold, it can also produce more volatile reactions in your guts. Once the elixir has been sampled, it is bottled. The better quality product is sometimes left in the bottle to age with herbs or fruit to acquire a particular taste or qualities. Medicinal *rakija* can be applied externally or internally for the relief of any ailment, physical or mental, including AIDS. According to Selimović, "*Rakija* never did anyone any harm, as long as it's taken as a medicine and not drunk like water"[166] (it's also good for cleaning glass and polishing furniture). The favoured hangover cure in the Balkans is *rasol* ("pickled cabbage brine"). What a shame that the tradition of home distilling is long dead in the UK, and the elixir of life is now the exclusive domain of commercial brands owned by multinationals. When toasting in the Balkans, you have to look your companions in the eye; otherwise, it's as if you don't mean it[xxxii].

[xxxii] The toasts are "*Živio!*" to a man, "*Živjela!*" to a woman, and "*Živjeli!*" to mixed company.

Pakrac, in Sector West, was a melting pot of 20 ethnic minorities before the war, evidence of its long Austro-Hungarian heritage[167] (five of Yugoslavia's neighbours had minorities in Yugoslavia, while there were Yugoslav minorities in all seven of its neighbours, the first letters of which spell *BRIGAMA*[xxxiii] – "troubles" in Serbian/Croatian[168]). I met a refugee from Pakrac in the UK after the war, a Ruthene[xxxiv], who told me he had been tortured twice in his own home – first by the SVK, who accused him of being an *Ustaša*, and then, after Operation Flash, by the HV, who accused him of being a *Četnik*. After that he'd had enough and applied for asylum in the UK with his family. In 1993, the BBC's Anneka Rice had built the local children a school there, in her own inimitable way. After Pakrac was captured by the HV in Operation Flash, the majority of the civilian population moved south into Bosnia and were rehoused by Karadžić in the Banja Luka region. Throughout the war, a total of 40,000 Serb refugees and IDPs moved to Banja Luka, from near and far, while around 70,000 people were expelled. Meanwhile, "Croats" (Catholic Serbs) from Janjevo in Kosovo were resettled in the abandoned houses in the newly-liberated Croatian territories that had been Sector West[169]. We sent an aid convoy from Split to respond to the immediate resulting crisis in Banja Luka. Driving up from Split via Šibenik, Gordon, Kiwi and I turned right at Knin instead of following our usual route to Slunj, and headed for the border into Republika Srpska, just after Strmica, 15 km up the road. Turning left at Bosansko Grahovo, another 10 km on, and very close to Gavrilo Princip's home village, we headed north for a good 40 km, through Drvar on to Bosanski Petrovac, approaching the Bihać pocket from a totally new direction. 5 km north-east of Grahovo is Trnjak ("bramble patch"). Drvar, described by Fitzroy Maclean in 1944 as "a part of Bosnia which had long been outstandingly faithful to the Partisan cause", was Tito's headquarters in the early part of 1944 after the *Wehrmacht* occupied Jajce[170]. He took up residence in a cave near the town. On 25 May, later celebrated as Tito's official birthday (it was also the date that had featured in many of Tito's false documents in his youth), the German seventh offensive was launched, and included a raid (*Rösselsprung*, "Operation Knight's Move") against Drvar, consisting of air strikes and an airborne assault followed up by a major ground operation. But Tito escaped, hauling himself up out of his cave on a rope, in the process losing his dress uniform, which ended up in a museum in Germany. After several days evading the enemy in the forest, and a breakout by train, the RAF evacuated him by air to Vis, the most outlying of the Croatian islands and the only one not occupied by the *Wehrmacht*, and also a RAF/RN base, where Tito again moved into a cave. It remained his base until the battle for Belgrade[171]. Near Petrovac the word "Tito" is spelled out on a hillside in living trees, visible for miles. At Petrovac we turned right and drove another 30 km to Ključ, where we stopped to make enquiries as to the actual route we should be following, as it had been set by the authorities. Ključ was the scene of the last stand of the last Bosnian King, Stjepan Tomašević, where he was beheaded by the Turks in 1463[172]. His widow fled to Dubrovnik, where she made a gift of valuable books to the Franciscan library there (Dubrovnik also offered asylum to Đorđe Branković after the battle of Kosovo in 1389)[173]. We were parked outside a school during playtime, and curious children came over. I started to speak to them, and they were surprised to hear I spoke Serbian (I was also surprised to hear my dialect called

---

[xxxiii] Bulgaria, Romania, Italy, Greece, Austria, Hungary (*Mađarska*), and Albania.
[xxxiv] Ethnic Ukrainians who settled in Slavonia and Vojvodina, as well as Poland, Slovakia, Hungary and Romania, during the Habsburg period.

Serbian in Bosnia, as until then it had always been referred to as Bosnian or Croatian). They asked me whether I had been in Muslim territory, and whether it was dangerous. I was struck once again by the fact that the Serbs, Croats and Muslims are not just essentially the same, but identical in every respect except their religion, especially in Bosnia. Small clues can indicate a person's background, either overt, such as the greetings *Bok!* (from *Bog i Hrvati*, "God, guns and Croats") or *Hvaljen Isus!* ("Jesus be praised") for Croats, *Pomoz Bog!* ("with God's help") for Serbs, and *Merhaba* ("hello" in Turkish) for Muslims; or more covert, such as a person's name (most Serb and Croat names are interchangeable, while most Muslim names are Turkish in origin, although there is no hard and fast rule: I once met a Muslim with a Serb/Croat name, Zoran, who had been named after one of his father's comrades in the Partisans), where they are from, or if they are or were refugees/IDPs, where they found refuge, and particularly if they say they have relatives in Croatia or Serbia. Dialects are regional, and so do not necessarily indicate ethnic/religious affinity. Gestures can also be a clue: extending the thumb and first two fingers while keeping the last two tucked into the palm means "Long live Serbia", a gesture likely to be avoided by Croats and Muslims. Once we had established our bearings, we continued 25 km north to Sanski Most, and from there another 25 km north to Prijedor. Sanski Most was the scene of the first uprising against the *Ustaše*, in May 1941, and hosted the second resistance conference in June 1944. It now has a giant mosque with four minarets, seemingly as big as Battersea power station, which replaced the original 16th century mosque, demolished with its wooden minaret in July 1992. We were on the same latitude as Cazin, just over 50 km to the west, although we might as well have been on another planet, as inaccessible as it was. It was a beautiful summer's day and the sun was shining. From Prijedor we turned south-east for the 35 km to Banja Luka, the heart of darkness with its tree-lined avenues, reminiscent of Soviet towns, fearsome reputation as the unofficial (now official) capital of Republika Srpska, and the seat of the Ottoman administration in Bosnia between 1553 and 1639[174]. In October 1969, Banja Luka was rocked by two earthquakes, 6.0 and 6.4 on the Richter scale, which killed 15 people and caused minor damage, apart from one building, *Titanik*, which was completely destroyed, and is now a park. Before the war, the population of Banja Luka had been 55% Serb, 15% Croat, 15% Muslim, and 12% Yugoslav. The Unit took control of the town at the beginning of the war without a shot being fired, largely because the SDA and the HDZ were unable to agree on how to organise any resistance. Outside Banja Luka, northern Bosnia was the scene of some of the heaviest fighting in the summer of 1992 as the SDS sought to consolidate their Brčko umbilical cord from Serbia (which they succeeded in doing in October of that year)[175]. A range of discriminatory and criminal measures and practices, and an increase in lawlessness in the town encouraged Catholics and Muslims to leave. There were other waves of expulsions at various points during the war when Serb IDPs and refugees started to arrive. Some people were able to arrange a more ordered departure by agreeing "house swaps" with Serbs in HDZ territory in Croatia, who were looking to get away from the daily harassments of minority life there. After Operation Storm, there was a final, major expulsion of much of the remaining minority population, of whom many of the Catholics were rehoused in the former Sectors North and South, while others were transported back from Croatia, under false pretences, to boost the local Croat population in the Glamoč area in western Herzegovina. Muslims had more limited options, especially when the HDZ-SDA war started. Departure permits were generally only issued subject to the would-be exile transferring all his or her property to the SDS[176]. 5 km south-west of Banja

Luka is the hamlet of Zmijanje ("vipers nest"). Directly west from Banja Luka, halfway to Sanski Most, is the Orthodox monastery of Gomionica, one of the earliest examples of Orthodox architecture in the Bosnian countryside[177]. In the 17th century, there were 45 mosques in Banja Luka, the most beautiful of which was Ferhadija, built in 1579 by Ferhad-paša Sokolović with the ransom he received for German and Austrian POWs (Sokolović, "MacHawk", captured Cazin in 1577)[178]. In 1993 it was blown up with the 15 other remaining mosques in the town, bulldozed and the site defiled with engine oil[179]. The following day, it would have been interesting (but probably impossible) for us to follow route Gull all the way south from Banja Luka to Travnik, through Jajce and Donji Vakuf. Rebecca West described the valley between Travnik and Vakuf as a "Chinese landscape"[180], but our itinerary had been set in stone by the powers that were, and we returned the way we had come. North of Banja Luka, route Falcon led up into Sector West, crossing the border at Gradiška; it also led east from Banja Luka to Doboj.

15 km south from Prijedor on our road back from Banja Luka was the Omarska mining complex, one of the four most notorious POW camps in Bosnia during the war, all in this part of the country (the others were Trnopolje, Manjača and Keraterm[181]). Manjača was a major JNA base, and Huse, a former inmate from Sanski Most, later told me of his experiences there. One day in May 1992, Sanski Most was suddenly full of VRS soldiers and armour. He had a grocery shop and a café bar, and laid on food for the passing squaddies in an attempt to soften their mood and lessen the tension (he also had an air-raid shelter in his garden, that actually served as a warehouse; he had only been able to get planning permission for it if it made a nominal contribution to the JNA's defence doctrine). Regardless, after a time there were announcements on the local radio and by megaphone that all non-Serbs had to come out into the street. He did so with his family. His wife having forgotten something at home, he asked permission for them to go back, which was granted. They arrived back home just in time to see it being set alight by two squaddies who had obviously just been inside. His wife moved to salvage the DM 10,000 in cash they had hidden in the house, but he stopped her, quickly turned round and they went back to where everyone else was assembled. His thinking was that they would have been killed if the cash had been discovered (and inevitably stolen) in their presence. The men were separated from the women and children and loaded into trucks, and taken to a central detention centre, a local school sports hall, with no hygiene facilities. After a couple of days, without being given any food or water, they were reloaded onto trucks. Using a nail-clipper that had been missed when they were searched, he cut a hole in the tarpaulin and was able to see they were heading south-east, up into the mountains to Manjača (Manjača is to the south-west of Banja Luka, halfway to Mrkonjić-Grad). When they arrived, they were all ordered to sit down on the ground in front of the camp entrance. Then one of the guards called for Mirso, a well-known businessman from Sanski Most, to stand up. He did so, and the remaining prisoners were instructed to chant "Mirso! Mirso!" Once a good rhythm had built up, the guard suddenly cut Mirso's throat and said, "No more Mirso". Cutting throats was the favoured MO of the Četniks in WWII. While the skills required for this practice are learnt in traditional smallholder farming, its origin appears to lie with the Turks, for according to T.E. Lawrence, in WWI "the Turks cut the throats of their prisoners with knives, as though they were butchering sheep"[182]. Because of Huse's catering experience, he was assigned to work in the kitchen, a real perk, as it allowed him to spend time outside in the fresh air. Severe beatings and worse were a regular occurrence. One pastime was to line prisoners up one behind

the other, and see how many could be killed with a single bullet. The record was three. One day from his vantage point Huse saw a dozen buses arrive, and making sure no-one noticed him, he watched to see what would happen. One by one, each bus disgorged its cargo of prisoners, who were taken to the cowsheds that served as their accommodation. Except for the last bus. Once the other buses were all empty and had left, prisoners started to emerge from the last bus, one by one. As they emerged and went around the bus, they were jumped on by a guard, who knocked them to the ground. Then a second guard would pounce on the prisoner and cut his throat, before tying a rope around his feet and dragging him off. Huse said that after a visit by ICRC and registration of the prisoners, there was a marked improvement in their conditions and a decrease in abuse – although not all prisoners were registered. Throughout the summer of 1992, there was systematic cleansing of the non-Serb population of eastern and northern Bosnia. The women and children were expelled, until the end of July to Croatia, and then to non-SDS territory elsewhere in Bosnia, while the men were detained[183]. In September 1992, after high-profile reporting of the existence of the camps in the international media, Karadžić agreed to allow several thousand POWs to be released, provided they were taken in by foreign countries[184]. Images of emaciated men corralled behind barbed wire broadcast by the international media in August 1992 were another nail in the coffin of the Serbs' good name[185]. Another *logoraš* ("camp inmate"), for whom I interpreted in London when he was being prosecuted for "uttering a false instrument" (i.e. using a disabled parking permit to which he was not entitled, and then threatening to "kick shit out of" a parking warden), told me that when he was released from Keraterm, he only weighed 36 kg. Huse was later reunited with his family, and granted asylum in the UK. In late September 1995, Arkan passed through Sanski Most on his way to Serbia, and in the intense fighting as the VRS counter-attacked there during the 5th Corps' Operation Sana 95, carried out what were alleged to have been his worst crimes[186].

Turning right at Kozarac, halfway between Omarska and Prijedor, the road leads into the Kozara national park, and after 5 km to the top of the height of Mrakovica, which has a large WWII monument. The known names of the thousands of Partisans who died there in the summer of 1942 in the Axis Operation West Bosnia, only 35 km from Jasenovac death camp, are carved into the monument[187]. During Tito's long march from Foča to Bihać in 1942, 3,000 Partisans plus local reserves were surrounded there with 15,000 civilians after liberating Bosanski Petrovac, Drvar, Glamoč and Prijedor, and only broke out after several weeks of fighting, with heavy losses[188]. The battle is depicted in the 1962 film *Kozara*. Among the almost 50,000 *Wehrmacht* squaddies and *Ustaše* (and *Četnik* remnants) who took part in the operation was Kurt Waldheim, an Austrian SS intelligence officer who later became UN secretary general, from 1972 to 1981. He claimed to have been studying law during WWII, and was awarded one of Yugoslavia's highest honours by Tito, but he was exposed in 1985. He went on to become president of Austria[189].

Another of the joys of country living in the former Yugoslavia (at least after the war), apart from the multitude of wonderful fruit that doesn't grow in the UK, such as *smokve* ("figs"), is meat on the spit, and not least because the quality of meat is generally far superior to that on sale in supermarkets in the UK. Crofting, agriculture carried on by smallholders with a small number of animals, is far more widespread, and farming is therefore far less automated and mechanised. The crofters look after their animals, feed them real food, and there is no recourse to hormones or other artificial means of increasing the quantity of meat produced at the expense of quality, and the health not only of the animal but also of the consumer. The same goes for crop production; and much of the land deserted during the war has had an extraordinarily long fallow, making it practically virgin, and is in many cases still unused, either because the owners have never returned, or because the presence of mines precludes its use. This same traditional, simple, common-sense approach to agriculture which is so widespread in the Balkans, is called "organic" in western Europe, and is an excuse to charge the highest prices, to an elite market of consumers. In addition, as well as all manner of preserves carefully crafted before the onset of winter, a variety of infusions known collectively as *čaj* ("tea"), one for each conceivable ailment, are produced from leaves and herbs.

Once the day designated for the spit roast arrives, the sacrificial animal is brought, and is generally kept alive, tied up, until the appointed moment. It is probably not a stress-free wait, but at least the creature is in his native countryside, with the sounds and scents of nature all around. It is certainly less stressful than a mechanised *klaonica* ("abattoir"). In Muslim communities, the animal is generally a lamb or a kid, while the Christian communities prefer a piglet (when an ox is spit roasted, the meat is sliced off and served as it is cooked, like a huge doner kebab, because it is too thick to roast evenly in one go). Again, this is a communal activity, as it is quite labour intensive; and the amount of meat produced is better shared among a wider group of people who each contribute with their labour and skill to its proper use and conservation. The animal is slaughtered by the people who a few hours later will be eating it, in the most humane manner, by having its throat cut. Then it is prepared for the *ražanj* ("spit"). Lambs and kids have to be skinned, and the innards are removed and sorted according to use (only the kidneys are retained for the spit roast). The body then has to be cleaned: it is scrubbed inside and out in warm water, and in the case of a piglet, the bristles have to be removed, as they would burn and spoil the crackling (hot water is poured on, and then the bristles can be scraped off). The beast is then scattered very liberally with salt inside and out, and the thickest part of the thighs and breast slashed to allow the fat to run, and the meat to cook faster. Meanwhile, two wood fires are lit, corresponding to the thickest parts of the animal, the rump and breast. Finally, when the creature is ready, the spit is carefully but forcefully inserted under the tail and pushed out through the mouth. It is fixed in place by brackets piercing to the bone at the midriff and behind the rump, bolted to the spit, and by a nail through the snout and the spit. These are all secured with twisted wire. In the case of a lamb, the forelegs are cut off and tied up with the flaps of the stomach and the kidneys, as otherwise, being too close to the fire, they would cook faster than the rest of the body and burn. The stomach flaps are sewn closed with wire, and the remaining limbs are fastened outstretched parallel to the spit with wire. The spit is placed to the side of the fire on two stands, one of which includes a wheel attached to an electric motor which will ensure the meat is turned at a regular rate. I saw one made out of an old windscreen-wiper motor, which was powered by being connected to a car battery. Meanwhile, once the fire has settled, hot embers are shovelled underneath the spit. Now all that is required is to wait 4-6 hours, while someone supervises the fire and the embers, ensuring that there is always enough, but that the meat isn't burnt by flames that may be enlivened by the dripping fat. Once the fat starts sweating through the skin, it can be removed from the surface of the beast with a slice of bread, a real treat with a glass of *rakija*. A sign that a lamb is thoroughly cooked is that the knucklebone goes cold[xxxv].

The animal's experience is also less stressful than that of the many POWs who met the same fate, waiting tied up until their captors in their merriment judged the time had come for their more terrible sacrifice. Indeed, if it was not for the custom of hard drinking in the Balkans, I am sure that many of the worst excesses would never have happened[xxxvi190].

The hamlets of Blatište, Gladuš, Vukojebine, Vukovstvo, and Smrdljak do not appear to exist any more. Many smaller settlements were literally wiped off the map during the last century, like the *fuadach nan Gàidheal* ("Highland clearances") before our time, fading from memory like dew in the morning sun.

Such was central Bosnia after March 1994, a patchwork of HDZ and SDA territories co-existing uneasily in the shadow of the SDS. Three years of daily deprivation aggravated by violence and the constant threat of violence. Distress, poverty, hunger, and misfortune, in a spectacular setting. And yet, it was the time of my life.

On 6 April 1994, i.e. 15 months before Srebrenica, as the VRS first took peacekeepers hostage around Goražde, Izetbegović described the safe areas as patently unsafe, and the NOZB offensive started to get bogged down near Todorovo, Rwandan president Habyarimana's plane, in which he was travelling with the Burundian president, was shot down near his capital Kigali, and the genocide in Rwanda began. However, this was not an explosion of uncontrollable ancient tribal hatred, or the inevitable result of poverty and over-population. It was a deliberate choice by a modern elite as a means to secure their position of power, which had been planned in its final details for months, and more generally for years. The first step was to turn the majority against the minority, in order to weaken the growing political opposition in the country. In 1991, Habyarimana had created and trained a youth militia within his party, the *Interahamwe* ("united"), who were encouraged to carry out violent attacks with impunity against the minority, and against opposition within the majority community. These attacks were fuelled by virulent propaganda from 1992 onwards broadcast by *Mille Collines* radio. Then, faced with an increasing military threat from Paul Kagame's FPR based in Uganda in a war that had started in 1990, the elite decided to resort to extermination as a means to unite the majority and win the war, or at least strengthen their bargaining position in peace talks. In 1993,

---

[xxxv] Another classic *roštilj* ("*braai*") technique is the *sač*, or Balkan pressure cooker. A heavy iron dome is placed over a baking tray loaded with choice cuts of meat and vegetables placed on a fireproof surface. Hot embers are then placed on top, and held in place by a metal ring. Gaps between the dome and the foundation are sealed with ash to ensure the precious vapours do not escape, but are forced back into the ingredients. An alternative method is to raise the baking tray on bricks, and place embers underneath as well. This adds a fried element to the pot roast. Another Bosnian specialty is *burek*, a savoury *baklava* with minced lamb. The *juhka* ("dough") is rolled out as thin as paper with an *oklagija* (long, thin rolling pin), and then rolled up with the aid of the table cloth, with the meat inside. A treat with *kiselo mlijeko* ("plain yogurt") and raw onion.
[xxxvi] According to the authors of a history of Crnaja, a veritable Balkan Macondo, whose fathers both took part in the Peasants' Revolt, "Alcoholism, looting and poor discipline were the causes of many casualties" during both the Peasants' Revolt and the Yugoslav Wars. According to normally teetotal Legija, for whom "war and alcohol don't mix": "I had long ago realised that my insistence on discipline was a quixotic enterprise, and that trying to banish alcohol was like charging windmills". Notwithstanding, Legija enjoyed a single shot of *rakija* with the NOZB commanders on the morning of Operation Storm.

the cross-party Hutu Power majority movement was created, and the army started to train and arm the *Interahamwe*, whose role was widened to that of a cross-party civil defence. Enough machetes were procured from Tanzania to arm a third of the majority population (the more expensive firearms were the preserve of the army and police). The civil defence, supported by violent and hysterical propaganda, was organised at local authority level throughout most of the country, with the objective of sparking a national uprising against the minority. After the assassination, the army and militia took over the country by killing government and opposition leaders, and then sent out agents into the provinces to kick-start the genocide. The radio was used to transmit orders to the population, and local residents throughout the thousand misty hills of Rwanda were ordered to report for "voluntary work", equipped with machetes, and set upon groups of minority civilians who had been rounded up by the authorities. The killings were often initiated by the army using mortars or grenades, and completed by hand by the civilians. The radio provided a running commentary on the progress of the operation, instructing people where to report for "work", and where to hunt for members of the minority said to be in hiding. The French, Belgian and US governments, and the UN, were aware that large-scale killings were being prepared, but failed to take steps to prevent the genocide, or to put an end to it once it had begun. Specifically, future UN secretary general Kofi Annan, who was then head of peacekeeping, refused an urgent request to raid government arms caches sent to him in January 1994 by the Canadian commander of the mainly Belgian peacekeepers in Rwanda, General Dallaire, who had it on reliable authority that a mass killing of civilians and peacekeepers was under preparation. This and other warnings were toned down by the UN secretary general's office before being presented to the security council (as were the reports of the EU monitors in the Balkans to Brussels; indeed, these were often doctored before being released for institutional consumption[191]). The majority of peacekeepers were withdrawn from the country after 10 Belgian peacekeepers were killed, which appears to have been the goal of the perpetrators, and 2,000 civilians who had sought refuge with the UN were abandoned to the *Interahamwe* as they departed. The UN security council declined to call the genocide "genocide", as that would have provided an imperative for intervention under the Genocide Convention[192]. At the beginning of April, the French government launched Operation Turquoise, with the objective of "preserving the territory and legitimacy of the interim government". Once the killings started to be reported in the western media, they were often referred to as the result of "centuries of tribal conflict", inevitable in a "failed state". At least 500,000 men, women and children (three quarters of the minority community in Rwanda) were deliberately and systematically killed by the regime over 13 weeks, while the FPR is said to have killed at least 25,000 civilians as it took control of the country. The FPR put a stop to the genocide in July, and the former military and civilian leadership, the *Interahamwe*, and many of the people who had participated in the genocide (whether voluntarily, under duress, or simply obeying official instructions), accompanied by their families, fled to the neighbouring DRC, where many of them remain to this day, in the hinterland of Goma, which includes the Virunga national park, home to the rare mountain gorillas, and for the last 20 years a no-go area. Their presence there also facilitated the emergence of local "rebel" (i.e., self-defence) bands, the Mai-Mai, who have a fearsome reputation[193]. General Kagame's Tutsis had been in exile in Uganda since an earlier outbreak of mass violence in 1959 that coincided with the end of Belgium's notorious colonial regime (the most rapacious in Africa, under which Rwanda and Burundi, which passed to Belgium after the defeat of their former colonial master, Germany, in WWI, and the DRC, were the personal property of the Belgian King, who plundered them via a system of dehumanising rubber concessions, to the greater glory of Brussels, resulting in the deaths of as many as ten million Africans[xxxvii]), and their mass return in 1994 means that now English is spoken almost as much as French in Rwanda. France's military support to the genocidal regime, even after the killing had begun, only contributed to this process, and in 2009, Rwanda joined the British Commonwealth (Mozambique, with a very different colonial history, also joined the Commonwealth, in 1995). The first time I entered Rwanda, from the DRC, in 1997, a Canadian colleague who was with us was waved through customs without any formalities, while the rest of us had to queue up and go through the whole procedure. A French colleague was practically *persona non grata*. In 2006, a French enquiry into the original assassination concluded that Kagame was probably behind it. In November 1996, Kagame launched an invasion of the DRC in support of local rebel Kabila senior, ostensibly to secure his western border against the *Interahamwe*. After a six-month campaign, with only two battles fought half-heartedly by Mobutu's impoverished and atrophied defending forces, one of the smallest countries in Africa succeeded in taking over one of the largest.

In July 1997, after Kabila senior was firmly ensconced, and as unrest grew in Kosovo, he thanked his Rwandan allies and invited them to go back home[xxxviii]. Large numbers of Rwandan soldiers made their way back across central Africa, mainly on foot, still armed, but without having been paid for their services. While generally well-disciplined and professional, this large movement of armed men was not without incident, and there were several clashes with other armed groups, in particular in the east (the Mai-Mai). A group of us decided we were safest staying put where we were, in Fizi, a village 20 km inland of Baraka, and the site of the district hospital, to wait for the reverse exodus to pass us by (in 1965, Che deployed to the DRC and was based in Fizi, where he offered support to rebel leader Kabila senior. However, his efforts were thwarted by CIA-backed South African mercenaries, and he returned to Cuba the same year. Curiously, Fizi with its earth tracks and stunted infrastructure surrounded by leafy woodland reminded me superficially of the Bolivian village of Che's last stand, La Higuera ("fig tree"), as depicted in the 2008 film *Che*). Part of my work there was the implementation of a UN "food for work" programme. Rather than simply hand food out, the UN sometimes uses it as a currency to fund basic, unskilled infrastructure projects[xxxix]. I told a local UN colleague, who was about to leave, what was happening, in French, and I could tell he hadn't fully understood me when he said he would be off by himself. Another local then repeated what I had said in Swahili, and I knew he had got the message this time when his face went green, and he said to me, "On second thoughts, I'll stick with you lot"[xl]. However, after two days sitting it out, it was

---

[xxxvii] The 1958 World Fair in Brussels featured a Congolese "human zoo". The present-day population of Belgium is just over ten million.
[xxxviii] This split with the Rwandans led to Congo War II of 1998-2003, which involved nine African countries, and resulted in over five million deaths.
[xxxix] The UN has been accused of facilitating the dumping of surplus food production by its donors in the guise of aid, undermining local markets and even destroying local production capacity.
[xl] Swahili, which originated in Zanzibar, is the lingua franca of much of East Africa, where hundreds of local languages rub shoulders with English and French (with the exceptions of tiny Rwanda and Burundi which, being monolingual, require no lingua franca, such that Swahili is not spoken there). As a general rule, East Africans' proficiency in English or French respectively is directly proportionate to the level of education they have received, and those who have little or no formal education tend to speak only their own local language and Swahili. Swahili is a Bantu language heavily influenced by Arabic, and was

decided that we should evacuate, 50 km north to the main town of Uvira at the north end of Lake Tanganyika, close to the border crossing and only 20 km from Bujumbura, the capital of Burundi. The only route was via the *barabara* ("main road"), a single-lane track running through coffee plantations run wild, their brilliant green leaves and shiny dark berries encrusted with the red earth that rose in clouds from vehicles' passage, along which the journey would take most of the day, and which was also that being used by the demobbed squaddies, who would have to continue north from Uvira to Bukavu to reach home. Along we plodded in our two Landcruisers, politely refusing the various requests for a lift that were directed at us by the disgruntled Rwandans. I was in the second vehicle. After several hours, the first vehicle was stopped by a group of three soldiers, who seemed more insistent than their comrades that they should be driven as far as Uvira, if not beyond. After an extended conversation with the occupants of the first vehicle, the most vociferous of the Rwandans stepped back, angrily shouting something that I did not catch. Our driver, Papa José, an Angolan, started to panic and mutter, "*Ils vont tuer les blancs! Ils vont tuer les blancs!*" ("they are going to kill the whites"). That certainly didn't do our morale any good, especially when the soldier in question made ready his *bunduki* ("AK47"). I was trying to think what would be the best course of action – whether to attempt to run over the soldiers, or overtake the lead vehicle (or even jump out and run for it), at the same time as trying to calm Papa José, speaking to him in a reassuring voice. He got into such a blue funk that I also seriously

---

spread throughout the region by traders during the heyday of the Sultans of Oman, for whom the bell tolled with the advent of the European colonial period. As a result, Islam and Christianity live side by side in many African countries. In Mozambique in 2000, I inherited half a ton of mixed tinned food that was all past its expiry date, but still edible. There wasn't enough of it, and it was too nondescript, to include in our larger programmes assisting communities to get back on their feet after the flood. But rather than dump it, I decided it would be better to distribute it to the urban poor in the small fishing town of Vilanculos where we were based. Because it was a one-off, I decided that the simplest way of accessing the beneficiaries would be via the leaders of the two communities, who were an Indian businessman, Sulejman, and an elderly Italian missionary. I met with both of them, and with their assistance a list of beneficiaries was drawn up – the only criteria being that they should be the poorest of their respective communities. On D-Day, I turned up with the goods at the two sites, and everything went off without a hitch. I was struck in particular by the poor mobilised by the missionary – they were truly biblical poor, and included a leper. I had recently seen on a documentary that leprosy is not infectious, and has a very long incubation period, and so I did not baulk when he offered his ravaged stump for a handshake (but I made sure I got tested when I returned to the UK). While it is fashionable and indeed topical to criticise the Catholic church, I was struck by the quiet dignity of the elderly Italian's luxury-free lifestyle. I am not a Catholic, but I was later also impressed by a young Brazilian missionary in Angola and his work to alleviate absolute poverty. The Muslim poor mobilised by Sulejman were also worthy of their name. Back in the DRC, I was surprised one day, when paying a courtesy visit to the local *mapadero* ("missionaries") in a village, who were what passed for dignitaries, to see the Croatian coat of arms on the wall in their house. When I expressed my surprise to the two French clerics, they said that their other colleague was a Croat, but that he was currently at home on leave. On another occasion, I visited a school in a *kijiji* ("village") that we were repairing as part of a wider project to help kickstart the local economy. When I arrived, I was greeted by the assembled children with a chorus of "*Jambo Mzungu!*" ("hello white man"). Thinking on my feet, I replied, "*Jambo watoto!*" ("hello children"), which appeared to cause some bewilderment. I once spent a week dossing in a windowless garden shed with half-a-dozen *Congomani* ("Congolese") laid out like sardines in a tin in a village in the DRC in an area subject to Mai-Mai incursions. The *mkuu* ("chief"), who had kindly placed the best *nyumba* ("building") in the village at our disposal, had also had it lined with paper sacking (floor, walls and ceiling) to keep the *panya* ("rats") off us, whose tiny scampering feet kept up a ceaseless accompaniment to our slumbers. I slept with my trousers tucked into my socks just in case (it was quite cold at night; one colleague slept in a fur cap with earflaps that tied under his chin, like an African Eskimo). Save the Children's work there also comprised rehabilitation for demobbed child soldiers, which included apprenticeships to allow the youngsters to acquire the skills to be able to earn a living in the real world without reverting to the habits they had picked up in their first job.

considered pushing him out of the vehicle and taking the wheel myself. However, none of these options seemed to have much prospect of success on the narrow, deeply-rutted track. It really looked like the Rwandan was about to open fire on the vehicle. Fortunately, at that moment his two comrades took him in hand, turned him away from us and led him away, remonstrating with him (presumably) that that would not be the done thing. The driver of the first vehicle, Geoff, also got out to remonstrate with them, but we encouraged him to get back in and drive off while we still could. Relieved, we journeyed onwards, to arrive safely in Uvira several hours later. That was certainly among the longest 50 km drives I've ever been on. Declining to give lifts to men with guns was a perpetual problem (even in the Balkans), especially for local staff when out on an errand without a foreigner to become the focus of frustration against the unpopular rule. Mango once told me that squaddies he had refused to give a lift to near Baraka, had retorted that they would "*descendre*" me ("take me out"), to "teach me a lesson". I went and complained to the local Rwandan *afande* ("commander"), and he posted two guards on our house to ensure the threat wasn't carried out. I made sure they got a plate of *chakula* ("food") each at supper time, which I thought might endear them to me, but which actually only appeared to confirm their suspicions that my (modest) residence was King Solomon's mine. On another occasion, noticing that Mango was being harassed by two squaddies outside the parked vehicle on the outskirts of Baraka, I approached. "*C'est bien vous ce blanc?*" ("are you that white man?") one of them asked. I confirmed that I was indeed he (most of the time, I was the only *Mzungu* for 30 km), and continued, "It's company policy not to give lifts to men with guns"[xli]. Meanwhile, Kagame's army did not execute a complete withdrawal, but remained in occupation of some of the eastern territories of the DRC, as a buffer zone against the *Interahamwe*, which also included some of the mineral-rich areas of the country.

[xli] Mango, a devout Jehovah's Witness, told me in all seriousness that local *waganga* ("sorcerers") had the ability to turn themselves into *mamba* ("crocodiles"), while others would become *Wazungu* ("white men") at night and walk unnoticed among the foreigners. Several years later, working in Mozambique, I had occasion to call upon the services of a witch doctor: a pair of deadly black mambas had been spotted in the long grass of our garden (someone had lent me a *cabrão*, "billy goat", to trim it, but it transpired that the bearded beast only ate leaves), and I was assured the local *curandeiro* ("witch doctor") could solve the problem, for USD 25. I consented, and the druid came round and performed his ritual, which involved among other things decapitating a chicken. Alas, the reptiles were immune to his charms. Then Abdul, our fleet manager, proposed pouring petrol down the hole which was thought to be the mambas' nest, and which ran in the direction of the house. I gave him the green light, and going back to work, left him to it. That evening when I came home, I was surprised and alarmed at a strong smell of petrol in the house, which was particularly powerful in the bathroom. Warning Seka not to light up, I called Abdul on the VHF (stepping way from the house first, because comms equipment can ignite fuel vapour in certain circumstances) and asked him how much petrol he had poured down the burrow. "200 litres" was the reply. He had effectively turned the house into a bomb. I ran a *mangueira* ("hosepipe") down the hole, and left the tap running all night to dilute the noxious fossil fuel. At least we never saw the mambas again. I was also bitten on the thumb by a *macaco* ("monkey") in Mozambique, which necessitated a *raiva* ("rabies") jab. In Sierra Leone, the traditional chief of Lungi, the site of the airport across the bay from Freetown, was a Lebanese (Lebanese businessmen constitute the middle class in many West African countries, while in East Africa the same role is fulfilled by the British for that very purpose; in the former Portuguese colonies, the "Afro-Portuguese" mixed race community tend to dominate economic life, along with Portuguese and Boer expats). Elections for chief were held every seven years, and the candidates had to demonstrate among other things a mastery of supernatural powers. Back in the DRC, the JWs had to compete for souls against a local death cult, the *Dominés*, whose rites were celebrated every third day in the cemetery. They all wore trilby hats and green shirts, and swore they had the power to turn bullets into water. No shortage of *faux pasteurs/mapadero mabaya* ("charlatans") thriving on fear and ignorance. In the Balkans, the fabled Romany *čudna moć/farmači* ("witchcraft") has been blown out of the water by the devil's work of the "constituent peoples'" representatives.

In December 1994, just as Operation Spider was achieving its first successes in the Borders, the Russian army attempted to retake control of Chechnya, the least developed of the Soviet republics, and slightly larger than Montenegro. In 1991, former Soviet air force general and Afghanistan veteran Džohar Dudajev (the first Chechen to reach the rank of general, who earlier that year had ignored orders to close down the Estonian parliament and television, where he had been stationed as nuclear bomber commander since 1987) had taken advantage of the failed coup attempt in Moscow (when the KGB attempted to block constitutional reform by deploying tanks, before being outplayed by populist Russian president and former *partijnij funkcioner* ("party official") Boris Jeljcin) to seize control of Chechnya by force (during which the head of the Groznij/Rral branch of the Russian communist party "fell" out of a window), and declared independence for Ičkerija (Chechnya). The leadership in Ingushetia distanced themselves from this and declared Ingushetia a Russian federal republic. The state of constitutional chaos prevailing at this time, as the Warsaw Pact was disbanded, the Soviet central government and the communist party were abolished, and some Soviet republics declared independence while others attempted to reconstitute a decentralised union (there was another armed constitutional crisis in Moscow in 1993, when the parliament, led by Cossacks, attempted to impeach president Jeljcin for unconstitutionally dissolving it, and he responded with tanks himself) meant that the *vooružennie sili* ("armed forces") were effectively hobbled, as there were no clear chains of command, at least officially, and the Chechens were able to confiscate the hardware of army *kazarmi* ("barracks". Unlike the Soviet republics to the south of the Caucasus mountains, Chechnya was deemed a Russian federal republic in the successor to the deliberately vague Soviet constitution, and so constitutionally incapable of secession; in practice, this meant that the southern border of the new Russian Federation was a conveniently straight line along the Caucasus mountains from the Black to the Caspian seas). A trade blockade was imposed on Chechnya and central funds were turned off, but Chechnya was still allowed to refine and forward oil from the Caspian to the Black Seas, on the Baku-Novorossijsk *nefteprovod* ("pipeline"). There was a breakdown in law and order, and Dudajev, most of whose inner circle were recruited from the Chechen *kriminaljnie strukturi* ("underworld") in Russia, responded to increasingly vocal (and violent) opposition within Chechnya by suspending the local assembly. Russian residents, the technocratic elite of Chechnya, started to leave, while the Caucasus ethnic Russians, the Cossacks, failed to play a significant role, despite much drunken bluster and shooting, and even ended up losing their traditional lands north of the river Terek. After he had consolidated his position in 1993, Jeljcin signed a treaty with Tatarstan, granting the central Russian Muslim republic effective home rule without a shot being fired; but Dudajev refused to countenance any such deal. After several bus kidnappings in southern Russia over the summer, in September Russian armed forces supported the local opposition in a series of failed raids into Chechnya. When Dudajev threatened to shoot Russian *voennoplennie/teman jesarin* ("POWs"), a full-scale "peacekeeping" operation was launched. Jeljcin went into hospital just as the operation started, and there was widespread unhappiness in the Russian army – at all levels – that they were being used for a police operation, and that the operation itself had not been properly planned (or indeed at all). But once the operation started, the army (and Jeljcin) could not afford to lose. The initial assault on Groznij/Rral ("terrible/the town") resulted in heavy losses for the army in the narrow, built up streets (as well as much looting), and from then on they relied on their superior firepower. While the army had tanks, artillery, and planes, the Chechens' deadliest *štuk* ("secret weapon") was the three-man RPG team: one *Nohčo* ("Chechen") to fire the *ručnoj protivtankovij granatomet*, supported and protected by a sniper and a *boevik* ("fighter") with an AK47. Whole classes of teenagers volunteered to fight the Russians, in an echo of the Soviet resistance to Hitler in 1941. Russian youngsters did not demonstrate the same enthusiasm to go to fight in the Caucasus (Chechens are generally disliked and feared in Russia, stereotyped as dangerous criminals and terrorists; natives of the Caucasus are referred to collectively - and derogatively - as *Hači*[xlii]). It was not unknown for Russian officers to "second" their men to the Chechens to act as *pušečnoe mjaso* ("cannon fodder"), for a fee[194]. Nevertheless, using indiscriminate blanket bombing and shelling, causing what was described as the worst destruction since the bombing of Dresden in 1945, wrecking among many other things the *neftepererabativajuščij zavod* ("oil refinery") in Groznij/Rral, the army gradually gained control of the main towns. In June 1995, one of the main Chechen *abreki* ("warlords"), Šamil Basaev, a former computer salesman, managed to bribe and bluff his way through Russian lines with a heavily armed force of 200 men, and took several hundred hostages in the town of Buddenovsk, 75 km outside Chechnya, in southern Russia. After several days, and several failed attempts by the Russian security forces (and the Cossacks) to storm the hospital where Basaev was holding the *založniki* ("hostages"), the Russian authorities agreed to a ceasefire, and Basaev returned to Chechnya a hero. During the subsequent truce, the Chechens were able to reinfiltrate all the territory they had lost. In December, they started a series of attacks on the Russian forces, and began to temporarily re-occupy towns. In April 1996, Dudajev was killed in a massive air strike on a village in which he was hiding, after he was detected using a satellite phone, and was replaced by his deputy, Zelimhan Jandarbijev, a writer. In May, Jandarbijev travelled to Moscow and negotiated a *prekraščenie ognja* ("ceasefire") with Jeljcin. The ceasefire held, despite the efforts of local *durak* ("barnpot") Salman Radujev, who threatened to "unleash *himoružie*" ("chemical weapons") on Russia: he had been reported dead in March, only to resurface in a hospital in Germany where they managed to rebuild him (he went on to be arrested in 2000, was sentenced to *požiznennoe zaključenie* ("life imprisonment"), and died in *ITK* ("prison camp") two years later). However, in June, the day after the presidential elections, which Jeljcin won, Moscow launched another offensive. Not to be outdone, on 6 August, the day Jeljcin was inaugurated, the two main Chechen *džigiti* ("warlords"), Basaev and Aslan Mashadov, a Soviet colonel, launched a surprise counter-offensive and recaptured three major towns, including Groznij/Rral. The Russian *bojci* ("squaddies") were effectively back to square one. At the end of that month a peace deal was agreed between Mashadov and General Aleksandr Lebed, under which the Russian army withdrew from Chechnya, and a final agreement on the constitutional status of the republic was deferred until 2001. Mashadov became the first elected president of Chechnya in the elections in January 1997. During the war, there were never more than 5,000 Chechen fighters at any given time, facing over 10 times that number of mainly national service squaddies.

[xlii] On one of my first evenings in Nazranj, I had a drink with the local drivers, Vaha, Nazir and Šamil. I sensed it was a sort of initiation ceremony, and so made sure that I demonstrated I knew everything about hard drinking, and wasn't intimidated by *gorci* ("mountain men"). At a certain moment, I noticed that Šamil was pointing a *pistolet/tapča* ("pistol") at my face. Unperturbed, for I knew that if he pulled the trigger he would lose his job, I just kept on drinking the *karka* ("vodka") and recounting my exploits in war and peace without batting an eyelid; and sure enough, before I knew it, the pistol was gone. They gave me the affectionate nickname "*Kozel*" ("billy goat"). Chechnya was nominally *suha* ("dry"), and vodka had to be bought at the rear of kiosks and shops.

Chechnya had originally held out against Russian imperialism for over a century, until the 1870s (the Dagestani imam Šamil led the Caucasus tribes in the war against the Tsars for 25 years until his capture in 1859; he died in Medina in Saudi Arabia in 1871 after a decade in exile in Russia. Of all the Caucasus tribes, it was the Chechens who halted the Cossack expansion south in the 18th century, just as the Boers met their match in the Zulus 75 years later), and they later took advantage of the October revolution to proclaim the independent Mountain Republic (which included Dagestan), before being subdued again in 1920[xliii][195]. In 1944, Stalin deported the entire population of Chechnya and Ingushetia to Kazakhstan under the euphemistic *Čečevica* ("Operation Beans", known by the Chechens and the Ingush as the *Ardah*, "exile"; the Crimean Tatars, among others, were also deported). Our landlady in Nazranj had been one of the deportees, and recalled to us how her three brothers had died of typhus *en route*. The populations were allowed to return in 1957, four years after Stalin's death, only to discover that some of their land had been settled by the Orthodox Ossetians, in particular the Prigorodnij district. Our landlady's husband had also recently died, and the head of household was now the eldest son, a *bankir* ("bank manager"); there were also two daughters, one of whom had been married to a Russian in the Black Sea port of Rostov-on-Don, close to Ukraine, before returning home divorced, and another three sons: a *ment* ("policeman"), a student, and a *kant* ("youngster"). The policeman invited me to go "shooting" with him and his mates one weekend, and assured me there would be plenty of vodka; I regretfully declined. The student was the only one in the family who spoke English, and curiously, he seemed to me to speak with an Irish accent. One day my curiosity got the better of me, and I asked him where he had learned English: "I studied in Cork" he replied.

In August 1999, as the UN presided over anarchy and bloody chaos in its new protectorate of Kosovo, Basaev launched an attack on Dagestan, the republic to the east of Chechnya and bordering the Caspian Sea. The following month, bombs in blocks of flats in three Russian cities including Moscow killed 300 people, and the new Russian prime minister, unknown KGB man Vladimir V. Putin, who was to become president by the end of the year when Jeljcin resigned for health reasons, used this as an excuse to invade Chechnya again. There had been clashes with the Russian mafia and/or armed forces in Dagestan since 1997. It may also be that Basaev's financial backers in the Middle East wanted some action for their money, so that what had started as a *gazamat* ("struggle for independence") under the slogan *"rrožalla ja maršo"* ("freedom or death") mutated into a militant Islamic movement[196][xliv] (in 1996 there had been moves by the new authorities to implement *šarijat* law in Chechnya, but this was abandoned in the face of popular opposition). Meanwhile, it has been alleged that Putin, who according to FSB defector Aleksandr Litvinenko paid his way through university by spying on his fellow students for the KGB, staged the bombings himself[xlv]. He was keen to build a reputation as a strong

---

[xliii] Meanwhile in the US, the Indian Wars ended for all intents and purposes with the Chankpe Opi Wakpala/Wounded Knee massacre in South Dakota in 1890, but there were sporadic clashes up until 1920. Crazy Horse's heart and bones had been buried there by his parents after he was bayonetted resisting arrest in Nebraska in 1877.

[xliv] The *Mudžahedin* in Afghanistan, who were bankrolled by among others Bin Laden, himself supplied by the *Beit al Aswad* ("White House"), notably with Stinger portable SAM missiles, had gone through a similar metamorphosis a decade earlier.

[xlv] Litvinenko was assassinated in London in 2006 by means of a teapot containing the radioactive substance Polonium-210. A veteran of the Chechen Wars, he converted to Islam on his deathbed. Putin lamented that, unlike Lazar (Lazarus), Litvinenko would not be returning from the dead.

leader, and told the army to do whatever it took to restore Russian control over Chechnya[197]. This time the devastation was complete[xlvi]. Several *Mudžahedin* irregulars had taken part in the war against Moscow, of whom the most prominent was a Syrian called Hattab. Before my time, he had stolen one of our *mašini* ("vehicles") in Chechnya. Later on a video surfaced on the local market of an attack on a Russian mechanised column led by Hattab. After rocketing the lead and rear vehicles from woodland above the road, they subjected the column to sustained fire before making off on foot, supporting one of their party who was badly wounded. When they got back to the main road, the video showed them piling into our white Landcruiser, with the NGO stickers still on the doors. I heard that the American writer Jonathan Little, who worked there at the time, later came across the stolen vehicle at a checkpoint, and going over, asked Hattab when they could have it back. "When I've finished with it", was the response. Lebed, who later became governor of Krasnojarsk in southern Siberia, and who stood in the 1996 presidential elections, was killed in a helicopter crash in 2002. Mashadov was assassinated by the FSB (Russian security service, former KGB) in 2005. Basaev was killed in an air strike in 2006, after several other spectacular and tragic terrorist attacks in the heart of Russia, in particular in the Moscow theatre and Beslan school[xlvii]. His younger brother, Šervani, was captured and brutally killed by the FSB soon afterwards, and a video of his humiliating murder was also released on the market. On one occasion when we were staying in Vedeno, Basaev's fiefdom in the south of Chechnya, we were roused in the middle of the night and told we had to come outside. My boss, Jean-Michel, thought we were being kidnapped, but instead we had been invited to one of Šervani's nocturnal shindigs. We had a great time with Chechen *nohči ileška* ("country music") and dancing, and good food (no vodka), and the assembled mountain men and women seemed to appreciate the impromptu speech in Russian I was asked to give, into which I tried to incorporate all the Chechen phrases I had learnt[xlviii]. There are dozens if not hundreds of unrelated languages spoken in the

[xlvi] Monstrous French thespian Gérard Depardieu was given a flat by Putin in newly-reconstructed Groznij/Rral in 2013.

[xlvii] In 2002, 50 Chechens took 850 spectators and actors hostage in the Dubrovka theatre. On day three, Russian special forces pumped nerve gas into the theatre, which killed at least 170 people, including the hostage-takers. In 2003, Basajev's men occupied a school in Beslan in southern Russia, taking 1,100 people hostage, including over 750 children. Three days later, the security forces launched an all-out assault on the school, with tanks and artillery, and at least 385 people were killed. Every six weeks or so, some of us would drive from Nazranj to the Russian town of Pjatigorsk ("five mountains") for a long weekend, to let our hair down and recharge our nerves. As they say in Chechnya, "*Bolh borz bac hun ču da vur bac*" ("don't do today what you can put off until tomorrow"). Beslan was one of the non-descript towns on our five-hour route. To celebrate New Year 1996/1997, a few of us also travelled to spectacular Scandinavian St. Petersburg, the Venice of the north, where I had some memorable experiences, including nearly playing a cameo role in a porno film. I had another close shave when I requested a song "for our friends from Chechnya" in an Irish *traktir* ("pub") while in the northern capital, which Nazir had challenged me to do. I also went to the opera for the first time, with Jean-Michel, and saw *La Traviata*. Born in a *saraj* ("barn"). Putin's home town was built by Petr the Great on marshland captured from Sweden in 1703 as a new European capital with a sea port, and during WWII was besieged by the *Wehrmacht* for 872 days. Hitler planned to turn back the clock by razing the city to the ground and giving the site to Finland. The wider conurbation is still known as Lenoblastj ("greater Leningrad"). I once saw a poster of Basajev in a local authority building in a village in Vedeno, speaking on a satphone in the middle of what appeared to be a battle, with the caption "*Pogromče*" ("speak up a bit", but also "hit them harder").

[xlviii] The first phrase I learnt when I went to work in Chechnya was "*So Ersi vac, so Angličanin vo!*" ("I'm not Russian, I'm British"). That was in the days before Blair sullied our reputation abroad. Ten years ago in Damascus, an orange-juice street vendor, after he had asked me where I was from, observed, "Tony Bler very bad". I didn't have the heart to point out to him that he probably wouldn't have dared criticise

Caucasus, and in Vedeno an old man told me that Chechen was derived from ancient Egyptian (by contrast, Russian is related to Bosnian). Šervani was my own age (as was Legija), which set me thinking not for the first time about human destiny and the purpose of life, and the worth of longevity and what one should do with it. How people can have some of the same external traits but move within in entirely different orbits. I was put in mind of a school friend of mine, David Morton, who tragically died at the age of 23 after a brief but successful career in the Royal Marines. Jandarbijev was assassinated by the FSB in Qatar in 2006. Jeljcin, a chronic vodka addict, died of a heart attack in 2007[xlix].

---

the ruler of his own country. The Chechens used to call MSF "*Vrači bez boljnic*" ("doctors without hospitals").

[xlix] In September 1994, returning from the US, Jeljcin's *samolet* ("plane") had a scheduled stopover in Éire/Ireland. The *taoiseach* (Irish prime minister) laid on a state reception for him, and turned up at the airport to welcome him in person. However, Jeljcin never emerged from his plane. It was said he was so Brahms and Liszt that he wasn't in a fit state to be seen in public, if indeed at all. It was also said that it was only US president Bill Clinton's experience of growing up with an alcoholic father that allowed him to get any business done with Jeljcin.

Showing the Serb enclaves.

Part 2 – the Drenica valley

Sisak was also one of the stops on our train journey. Directly north-east of the Bihać pocket, Sisak is Croatia's largest river port, at the confluence of the Sava, Kupa and Odra rivers, and was also the home of David Haines, the British aid worker murdered in Syria in September 2014 by a criminal coward with halitosis. Across the river Kupa is the town of Petrinja, in the north-east of what was Sector North. Sisak was besieged by the *paša* of Banja Luka in 1593, the year after the Turks captured Bihać from the Habsburgs, and became the high water mark of the Turkish tide[198]. When he was 15, Tito worked as a *konobar* ("waiter") in Sisak, then a Habsburg garrison town, before becoming an apprentice *bravar* ("fitter")[1], and a wrought iron fence at Sisak district court is his handiwork. Before the Yugoslav Wars, Sisak had a major steelworks. It was reopened in 2013 by Italian investors, but production was suspended in 2015 due to unfavourable market conditions. The last time I left the Serb Borders republic, at the end of July 1995, was via Petrinja and Sisak (the last time I had entered the republic, several weeks previously, as usual via the southern route, the HV squaddies at the checkpoint had asked me, visibly worried, whether I thought the SVK were about to launch an offensive. I replied that I didn't know). Gordon had called us on the HF from Split to tell us we had to evacuate "our location", i.e. the Croatian Borders (radio messages, unless protected by an electronic signal, can be heard by anyone with a radio who tunes in to the same frequency, and NGO communications were regularly monitored by the local authorities - in Velika Kladuša, it was Samir's brother's job to listen in on the international community's radio traffic. Attempting to speak in code is generally pointless, and only attracts suspicion. I was told by a Ukrainian peacekeeper in Slunj that they used to have a good laugh listening in on the SVK comms, as they got mixed up using codenames such as "hawk", "bear", "wild boar" etc.). Mine and Kiwi's position was that an international presence in Slunj and/or Velika Kladuša would act as a deterrent to the worst excesses of an invasion, but we were overruled. I had seen Seka, Smajo and Družan the day before in Velika Kladuša, and wondered whether I would ever see them again. When I told our landlord we were evacuating, he took it on the chin, as if it merely confirmed something he already knew. Meanwhile, UNHCR had evacuated the Bihać pocket "in total disarray" (according to the EU monitors) on 2 June, via Izačić[199]. We drove north from Slunj, Kiwi and I, turning right to pass through Vojnić, and then continuing along the road for 25 km east through Vrginmost to Glina. There we turned left and drove the final 15 km north-east to Petrinja. Petrinja was occupied by the JNA in September 1991, and before the war the population had been half Serb and half Croat[200]. The front line was the river Kupa. As we arrived at the last SVK checkpoint before the bridge and presented our documents as usual, a mysterious officer, who was clearly superior in rank to the border guards, stated he had to search our vehicle. We got out, in order to better control what was happening, and he proceeded with his search. Satisfied, the officer closed the door and walked off; but I noticed he had a laptop bag in his hand,

---

[1] *Bravar* also means "locksmith", and there is now a saying in the Balkans: "*Dok nam je bravar bio predsjednik, sva su nam vrata bila otvorena a lopovi pod ključem*" ("when we had a locksmith for president, all doors were open to us and the tea leaves were under lock and key").

that he had not had before, and that he was attempting to hold in such a way so as not to draw attention to it. "Hey" I said, "you can't take that!" He turned round, and said he was confiscating it. I remonstrated with him for a while, but he was insistent that he had to take it, and that we should address any complaints to the police station in Vojnić. The other squaddies said nothing. After a while it became obvious that the only way we would get the laptop back would be by taking it by force; and as we were unarmed, that was not a realistic option. I asked for a receipt at least, but even that was refused, and suddenly he was gone. Perhaps he knew the end was nigh for the Croatian Serbs. Angry, we debated what to do: was it worth the time and effort of going back to Vojnić and reporting it to the police, when we knew we would never get it back anyway? And what if the SVK closed the border in the meantime? In the end we decided it was better to do the right thing, and we turned round and headed back to Vojnić. We spent a long time waiting, and were eventually able to report the *krađa* ("theft") to a pedantic *predstavnik organa unutrašnjih poslova* ("police sergeant"), who seemed to be blissfully and studiously unaware that we knew that he knew exactly what had happened and that we would never get the laptop back. Finally, once we had gone through all the formalities, we returned to the border, and then crossed over the bridge into HDZ territory, before driving the 30 km north-west to Zagreb (known in Austro-Hungarian times as Agram). After the stresses, shortages and deprivation of the Borders, all the delights of civilisation appeared to be available in Zagreb, waiting to be plucked by our eager hands as we wandered the well-lit, clean, bustling streets, with their functioning *semafori* ("traffic lights") and neon signs full of promise. But immediately beneath the surface, a different kind of deprivation and stress was apparent, as the many IDPs and refugees, and even locals, struggled to make ends meet from one month to the next, minorities kept a low profile, the single-party state brooked no dissent, and organised crime carried on its parasitical business with impunity, only an hour's drive from the war zone. As they say in the Balkans, "*Iz mira sto vragova vire*" ("still waters run deep"). The only positive note from this whole episode was that there was no useful information on the confiscated laptop, and so it was not an operational loss. Something to *halaliti* ("put down to experience") – *svaka škola se plaća* ("live and learn"). I hope the *Četnik* caught repetitive strain injury from it.

Now, as we chugged along, I wondered idly whether we wouldn't have got to our destination faster in La'al Ratty down Eskdale in Cumbria, or on the Kraljevo Express[li]. It was certainly not the *vlak slobode* ("freedom train"), in which Tuđman travelled from Zagreb to Split via Knin on 26 August after the railway linking those two towns was re-opened after Operation Storm. Or was it? The following year, when I travelled by night *poezd* ("train") from Vladikavkaz/Dzaudžihau/Buro ("queen of the Caucasus"/"Dzaug's settlement") on the 18th century Georgian military highway in North Ossetia to seedy Soči on the Russian Black Sea coast, once the playground of the Soviet elite, sharing a sleeper with a middle-aged vodka salesman, who had a goodly supply of samples in his otherwise light luggage that he was eager to share, and two young prostitutes on their way to Trabzon on the Turkish coast to earn some cash over the summer, I realised it wasn't so bad after all. It was also better than the Rangoon circle line, on which a Cornish colleague, Tony, and I, mistaking it for a tourist attraction (which is how it was advertised) during the response to cyclone Nargis, travelled for two hours one Sunday afternoon through

---

[li] Big-budget Yugoslav film from 1981.

the slums of Rangoon, with their shanty-town infrastructure backing onto stretches of filthy standing water. We were physically fenced off from the local passengers like dangerous animals when I had the temerity to address one of them with *"Mingalaba"* ("hello"), a young lady who I saw was reading an English publication. I nearly did a Franz Ferdinand[lii][201] (Tony had been a convoy leader for DFID during the war in Bosnia, although we never met. He was also DFID's emergency response team leader for the ebola operation in Sierra Leone. Nargis killed over 130,000 people in 2008, and its path of destruction was facilitated by the government's programme of cutting down the mangrove forests on the coast, which would otherwise had diminished its force as soon as it hit land. I also ran into Gordon in Rangoon)[liii]. I suggested to Seka we make a day of it and break open our packed lunch. As we munched our roast chicken sandwiches, generously prepared by Seka's sister in Karlovac, I started to ponder the future of the Balkans.

Bosnia's third famous bridge is in Višegrad, another UNESCO world heritage site on the border between Bosnia and Serbia (strictly speaking, it is no longer the border, but 7 km inside Bosnia), and immortalised in Andrić's Nobel-prize winning novel *The Bridge on the River Drina* (the Drina flows west from the border between Bosnia and Montenegro, near the most easterly point of the traditional border of Herzegovina, before turning north-east as far as Višegrad, and then marks the border with Serbia north until flowing into the Sava). It is 300 m long, connecting the Orient to Europe, and was built between 1571 and 1577 by grand *vezir* Sokolović (one of nine grand *vezirs* of Bosnian origin, a product of the Ottoman practice of seizing a tribute of Christian boys from their provinces for training as *janjičar* infantry. The boys would be converted to Islam and given new names, and taught to speak Turkish, but they remembered their origins)[202]. Now there is a dam and hydroelectric power station just south of the bridge. At the end of September 1991, local Muslim and Croat civilians tried to stop an armoured JNA column crossing the bridge on its way to Vukovar from Banja Luka, and were fired upon, the JNA's first action in Bosnia[203]. In early April 1992, the town was shelled by the JNA, and local Muslims seized the dam, threatening to blow it up and flood the town. After a week, the JNA took control of the dam and then the town. This was followed by a period of calm until the JNA withdrew in mid-May. Soon afterwards, the Unit arrived, and there was a campaign of ethnic cleansing. It is said that at least 1,600 Muslims were killed, and many of them were thrown into the river from the bridge in a ghastly parody of the famous novel. Mihailović, the *Četnik* leader, was captured in the hills near Višegrad in March 1946. I had the occasion to cross the bridge several times when I was working in Kosovo in 1998, when a British and a local colleague (Tim and Millazim) and I had to make two road trips from Priština to Sarajevo to pick up four vehicles being transferred from MSF's down-sizing Bosnia programme to our up-

---

[lii] It is said that once, when the Archduke travelled from Berlin to Prague by train, the seats in the carriage he had occupied alone were discovered, after he had alighted, to have suffered repeated and sustained sword slashes, in what is perhaps the first recorded incident of rail rage. I have been unable to establish how much the Archduke, whose motto was *"Bella gerant alli, tu felix Austria, nube!"* ("getting there"), was charged for his ticket, or how long his journey took. The first time Gary, John and Diane drove their trucks up through the Borders after Operation Storm, John told me that he had a laugh with Gary by transmitting, "Look out, train!" over the VHF just as Gary was approaching the tracks that had for the last four years been devoid of any traffic. Gary didn't see the joke.

[liii] The names "Burma" and "Rangoon" are actually the same words as their official replacements, "Myanmar" and "Yangon" respectively, but in a different local language. The former official names are as pronounced by the Karens, a Christian people favoured during the British colonial period.

scaling Kosovo programme. It was a spectacular day-long journey with an early start, north through Kosovska Mitrovica into Novi Pazar ("new bazaar") the capital of Sandžak, then the spectacular drive up through Prijepolje to Užice with its gorges and road tunnels, before turning west, crossing the river Drina at Višegrad, with Srebrenica to the north, and continuing through Rogatica, just north of Goražde, into Sarajevo (many IDPs from Rogatica found refuge in Sarajevo during the war). We stopped for lunch at Užice, and while waiting to be served on the pavement terrace of a pizza restaurant we were joined by an unpleasant character who reminded me of the laughing policemen from Stolac. He was a well-built skinhead, who kindly enquired into our business and how we liked Serbia. He didn't bother asking Millazim where he was from (he was obviously Albanian), and after recommending the best pizza on the menu and granting us the freedom of the city, he sauntered off, perhaps having noticed we weren't interested in engaging in conversation with him, or indeed in anything he might have to offer. Užice was formerly called Titovo Užice, and was Tito's first headquarters, from August until the Axis first offensive in November 1941, when he moved via Sandžak to Rogatica (the schism between the *Četniks* and the Partisans dates from this offensive; at that time, the UK was providing the *Četniks* with military support, because they were the official armed forces of King Petar II, an ally in exile in London). This early part of the war is portrayed in the 1974 film *Užička Republika* ("Guns of War"), starring *Taken*'s Rade Šerbedžija. As a result of major investment after WWII, Užice became the most developed town of its size in the country[204]. In 1998, the border on the Serbian side was manned by old boys, and on the Bosnian side by teenagers. 5 km north-west of Rogatica, near Lepenica, is the hamlet of Paljevina ("arson"). 15 km south-west of Goražde is Foča, whose masterpiece Aladža mosque built by the Ottoman architect Sinan's school in the 16th century, was destroyed during the Yugoslav Wars[205]. Foča was Tito's headquarters from January 1942, after the *Wehrmacht* forced him to abandon Rogatica, until May when he set off on his long march through Bosnia, which ended in November 1942 in Bihać, with much of western Bosnia in Partisan hands[206]. Later that afternoon, on a bleak upland in Republika Srpska just outside Sarajevo, we stopped for a coffee, and I asked the waiter if I could use their phone to let our colleagues in Sarajevo know what time we would be arriving. "DM 20" he said. "*Nema teorije* ['you must be joking']", I replied. He must have thought we had more money than sense. The coffee was cold too; perhaps he thought we were *Ustaše*, or UÇK. Or the UN. Arriving in the Bosnian *velegrad* ("metropolis") for the first time was the culmination of a pilgrimage for me. Life had returned to the stricken streets, and the sun was shining. We were there over the weekend, and so on the Sunday I drove up to Kakanj to see Ratko and his family. Lara had just given birth to twins. Back at work on Monday, the vehicles in question were two brand new Toyota Landcruisers, that had been shipped from Brussels by mistake to Sarajevo rather than to Belgrade, and two DAF trucks that had been donated by the Dutch army during the war. While the first two vehicles had all the necessary documents, and export/import to Serbia was just an administrative matter, the trucks had no documents whatever. Nevertheless, the MSF head of logistics in Sarajevo managed, via a SDS police contact, to obtain genuine documents for the first truck, which we brought back with us to Priština on our first trip[liv]. It was an equally spectacular drive back: this was the life, I thought, what could be more splendid than

---

[liv] In Uvira in the DRC, I was surprised to note that one of the Landcruisers had the name *Ptica* ("bird") painted on the side of the bonnet. It had been transferred from the Bosnia programme.

being a field logistician for an operational aid agency? I pitied those aid workers who spend their lives in incestuous meetings and writing reports, rarely achieving anything useful, and whose interaction with the people that really matter, the locals, is restricted to employees and domestics. Real aid work means getting your hands dirty. However, our friendly policeman was assassinated before he had completed the procedure for the second truck, which threatened to become a real headache. Regardless, our Bosnian logistician found a way, and within a month we were back in Sarajevo to take possession of our second DAF truck. They were put to very good use transporting relief goods to support our emergency medical programme. At the checkpoint on our way out of Kosovo on the second trip, the VJ squaddie's opening gambit was, "Who are you fuckers? Journalists?" I explained we were British aid workers on our way to Sarajevo to collect two vehicles. "Which Sarajevo?" he asked. I first I didn't understand what he meant, but he clarified that he wanted to know whether we were going to Muslim Sarajevo, i.e. Sarajevo itself, or to Pale, the ski resort outside Sarajevo (that had, I had seen on our previous trip, its own signs, one bidding the visitor welcome to Serbian Sarajevo, and another, after a couple of miles of countryside, wishing him or her *bon voyage*. 60 Serb men and women were killed in Pale in the crackdown organised throughout Bosnia by the Habsburg authorities after the assassination in 1914, while others, including the relatives of the suspects, were interred in camps in Hungary[207]). In 1992, three years after the destruction of the Berlin wall, the SDS had proposed dividing Sarajevo into two, *à la* Beirut[208], and we were asked the same question when we crossed the border from Serbia into Bosnia. In Sarajevo, MSF laid on a knees-up amongst others for the local staff from Sarajevo and Pale, who hadn't seen each other since the war. It wasn't a reconciliation. Two days later, on our way back to Priština, we ran into the same squaddie. "You fuckers again?" he enquired as we pulled up, in three vehicles rather than the one he had seen us in the last time. "So you're nothing to do with journalism. What about the *Šiptars* ['Albanians'] then?" he asked me. "They're worse than the Irish, they want their own country, but they won't get it!" We were soon back home. As we had nowhere to park the two trucks in the town, and were reluctant to leave them in the compound where we had a warehouse just outside Priština, I negotiated parking space on the premises of a bus company, that was much closer to our office. While I didn't entirely trust the Serb owner of the business, it was the only real option available, we had 24-hour access at a reasonable price, and I took the view that as he needed our custom more than we needed him, he would go out of his way to make it work. In addition, with so much of the business of the international community going to local Albanians, I thought allowing a Serb business to share in the benefits of the international presence could only be a good thing, and would have a positive, albeit minor, effect on relations generally. There were no problems initially, but after the NATO bombing campaign started, we could not access the vehicles (although the severe restrictions on movement meant that the team was confined to Priština anyway, until they evacuated to Belgrade), and in June 1999 I happened to read an article in the *Guardian*, reporting that a Serb bus driver had been convicted of war crimes in Kosovo. The mug shot looked like our man[209].

Working in Kosovo allowed me to spend time in Belgrade for the first time, although I was only ever there for flying visits. According to Fitzroy Maclean, "while Zagreb came to resemble a European town, Belgrade remained an oriental fortress"[210]. According to Andrić, life in Belgrade is "richer and more complex, but also harsher and more dangerous than in Sarajevo; superficially it appears to be as easy and merry as a game, but in fact it is as deceptive and inexorable as the dice"[lv][211]. I enjoyed sampling the delights of the floating restaurants on the Danube, and losing myself in the anonymous hustle and bustle of big city life walking down famous Terazije street, and then on to the old Turkish fortress at Kalemegdan park, on the confluence of the Sava and the Danube, facing the Pannonian Plain. In 1806, the illiterate Serb rebel leader and pig farmer Karađorđe ("Black George"), founder of one of the royal dynasties, captured Kalemegdan from the *janjičars* after a two-year siege, only to lose it again in 1813. He then fled and joined the Austrian army. Serbia between the Danube and the Sava in the north, including Belgrade, and Sandžak in the south, became autonomous from Turkey in 1815, under Miloš Obrenović, the founder of the other dynasty, who assassinated Karađorđe in 1817 when he came back to Serbia[212]. Serbia and Montenegro gained international recognition in 1878, the first independent states since the Middle Ages in what would become Yugoslavia[213] (apart from Dubrovnik, that had lost its independence just as Serbia gained autonomy, while Montenegro, after the Turkish defeat in 1699, became the first *de facto* independent Balkan state). According to Rebecca West, pre-WWI Belgrade was described by Dalmatians as a "wretched little village" and a "pig town", in respect of which "the Austrian foreign office used to treat the Serb diplomats as if they were farm labourers come up to the great house with an impertinent demand"[214] (even today, crofting is popular in the metropolis, and there are over a million head of livestock in Belgrade). Throughout this whole period, and as far back as the height of Ottoman power, and the beginning of Russian expansionism with Ivan the Terrible (1533-1584), Russia had projected itself to Europe and the world as the Godfather of the Serbs, an altruistic endeavour that was long on rhetoric and moral support (Tsar Aleksandr III, 1881-1894, once said that "Russia only has two allies – her army and navy", which has been paraphrased in our day to "Russia only has two allies – prison and the Church"). In particular, Petr the Great (1682-1727) took a liking to the Montenegrins, sent his young nobles there to learn sailing, and provided funding for the advancement of Orthodoxy and the defeat of the Turks in the Balkans[215]. In 1920, after the October revolution, the Russian Orthodox church set up a congregation in exile in Istanbul, which moved to Serbia in 1921, together with its flock of lay refugees[216]. 24,000 people were killed in Belgrade on 6 April 1941 when the *Luftwaffe* attacked without warning (exactly 51 years before the EU recognised Croatian independence[217]). Andrić describes WWII Belgrade in his short story *Destruction*:

> "Destruction. Anyone who didn't know the real meaning of that word now has the opportunity to learn it here. You might have thought that you already knew its real name and how to pronounce it. But during the first major bombardment you experience, you find himself in the semi-darkness of a cellar with a crowd of frantic people, already killed by fear. What such people do and the way they speak and behave is completely outside the framework of the accepted standards of behaviour that prevail at the time, and indeed has its origin in the other side of human consciousness. But all voices are silenced and all movements frozen by an explosion, or rather, a series of explosions,

---

[lv] Regicide Legija said from *ćuza* ("prison") that he "love[s] early autumn in Belgrade. The intolerable heat that blasts from all sides during August ends. With the coming of autumn, most people return from their holidays, and the abandoned city returns to life. Activity once again reigns on its streets". When I met him in Vrnograč, he reminded me of Martin Sheen in *Apocalypse Now*. Now he looks more like Marlon Brando.

scattered somewhere around the city centre. And then, in the darkness and silence that reign after the explosions, the distant but clear crashing of multi-storey buildings can be heard, like an echo. It is an alarming, uncommon sound, akin to a series of consecutive stone avalanches, the voice of giant hordes, formed up beside each other, roaring their indecipherable and terrible cheers to someone riding swiftly ahead of them; their shouts overlap and merge as they tail off. This new sound that touches a place inside you hitherto unknown, is the true name of destruction and its proper pronunciation. Destruction's strange voice takes wing, and seeks within the mass an individual it can frighten, and within each individual a weak point open to fear. And it finds it, at least here. Because anyone who as a result is frightened, is already beaten, regardless of all the possible convoluted developments of the war, and even its final outcome. Thus it happens that, in addition to the major destruction to visible things, even greater destruction is wrought within and between people, which only a few of them, and even then only gradually, begin to see and understand. The destruction tears off man's final mask, turns his innards inside out and throws into view unexpected characteristics, contrary to everything known or thought about a person, and even what he believed about himself; it disrupts family relations and changes the established social order and relationships, even those considered eternal and unchanging, such as gender relations"[218].

Hitler was so enraged that someone had dared to defy him that he put his plans for the Middle East and the Soviet Union on hold in order to punish the Yugoslavs for refusing to ratify his Balkan pact[219]. Four days after this airborne tsunami, the Great Humongous made a personal visit to Zagreb, where he was welcomed by adulating crowds (Zagreb was liberated on VE Day, 8 May 1945). He was followed a week later by the psychopathic lawyer Pavelić returning from his exile in Italy, from where he had masterminded a terrorist campaign in Croatia and Macedonia, and who now set about a campaign of terror against Serbs, Romanies and Jews in Croatia, Bosnia and Srem as the *poglavnik* (*"Führer"*) of the NDH. One of his first acts was to give Mussolini central Dalmatia, between Zadar and Split, for services rendered. Tito later took it back. It was strange to come to the former capital of the whole of Yugoslavia after having spent so much time in the provinces, and I was struck again by the difference that exists in the Balkans between the cities and the countryside. Belgrade was like a different world, completely cut off from and apparently aloof to what was happening elsewhere (although throughout the Yugoslav Wars, Belgrade had the largest anti-war demonstrations, and the highest rate of draft-dodging – 80% or more - in the Balkans[220]). The first time I visited Belgrade, I was surprised to see as much if not more Latin script in evidence than Cyrillic. We had a flat in Belgrade where staff could stay when passing through. One evening, I was having a drink there with Milan (see below) and Ahmed, our Albanian truck driver. We polished off one bottle of Chivas Regal whisky, which for some reason is popular there, and I said I would nip out to the off-licence on the corner to buy another. In the off-licence I enquired after a bottle of the liquid gold *uisge beatha*. "Do you want original or Serbian?" the shopkeeper asked. "What's the difference?" I countered. "Serbian is cheaper" was his recommendation (Jack Daniels is also not unpopular in the Balkans: Mirvet told me that, after the recapture of Velika Kladuša, he found himself looking after a warehouse containing among other things 7,000 litres of the Tennessee moonshine, and which was located between two hills, occupied respectively by the NOZB and the 5th Corps. The fiercest fighting was at night, when both sides attempted, *Whisky Galore*-like, to liberate the liquid *zlato* ("gold"). JD was also Legija's favourite tipple, when not on duty). We also had a logistics and administration office in Belgrade, who played a vital role in MSF's work all through the Yugoslav Wars. The head of the office, Bogdan, told me one day that his father was from Bihać, and had moved to Belgrade during WWII. I had until then been unaware of the heterogeneous origins of many Belgraders; I was also surprised to learn there was a thriving Albanian community in Belgrade. Another day in the city centre, I crossed the road at a pedestrian crossing when the pedestrian light was red, as there was no traffic approaching. Too late, I noticed a policeman watching me from the traffic island in the middle. I pretended to ignore him, but as I drew level with him he challenged me with "*Stani bre! Dokumenti!*" ("halt! papers!"). I produced my passport, and he asked whether pedestrians cross the road on a red light in the UK. Suppressing a smile, I said that it wasn't an offence to do so in the UK. The conversation continued a little longer, as he asked me whether I wanted to cause an accident, until, suitably apologetic, I was allowed to go on my way. People in the former Yugoslavia have a healthy respect for the police, as I have noticed on several occasions when interpreting for Balkan detainees in police stations in the UK. One young Serbian truck driver detained on suspicion of people trafficking was allowed to make a phone call to his girlfriend back in Serbia, in my presence. "I've been arrested – don't cry!" were the first words he uttered (he was later released without charge). (Such interactions were also often not without humour: a Montenegrin rape suspect in a London police station, when asked whether he wished to make any representations concerning the conditions of his detention, asked for a blanket, because he "felt like Robinson Crusoe" in his *zindan* ("cell"). Perhaps he thought the *dizdar* ("custody sergeant", not to be confused with *pizdar*, "gynaecologist"), was Petko ("Man Friday"). While he was being interviewed, the building suddenly shook as a HGV drove by, and instantaneously seized by panic, I almost jumped up and ran out of the interview room, shouting "earthquake!". It's unnerving to realise you've developed a fear of buildings[lvi]). It was said at the time that one of the ways the Belgrade local authorities raised revenue was via seatbelt fines: for months, or even years, the police would turn a blind eye to people not wearing seatbelts. Then, one day, without warning, there would be a major, coordinated crackdown throughout the city, and everyone caught red-handed would be charged a *novčana kazna* ("fine", or at least a *mito*, "bribe"). Belgrade, where Tito was living under a false name in the summer of 1941, is where the Yugoslav resistance was born.

Our security analysis was to avoid large gatherings when in Belgrade, and to stay indoors at such times. On 30 January 1989, two months after the "mother of all rallies" and less than two weeks after the overthrow of the government of Montenegro (see below), an extraordinary conference of the federal KPJ was held in Belgrade. In advance of the conference, the federal presidency made arrangements to allow a state of emergency to be declared, as there was intelligence that another mass rally would be held the same day. Kadijević said that "Milošević will only stop if he feels someone's superior force"[221]. In the run-up to the conference, the virulent media campaign in Serbia against KPJ president Šuvar reached new heights (or depths), while support for him was expressed in Croatia, Bosnia and Slovenia. On

---

[lvi] The officer in the case told me that in his former life, he had been in the army, and that in 1999 he had deployed to Kosovo. He recounted how in an enclave he visited, the locals slaughtered and spit roasted an ox in the British peacekeepers' honour.

the eve of the conference, federal president Dizdarević (who suspected Milošević would attempt a *coup* within the KPJ at the conference) noted that the general mood in the country was deteriorating: people were gripped by fear about the future of the country, and divisions within the KPJ were reflected in divisions in society at large, between the republics/autonomous regions, and along ethnic and religious lines, while some parts of the country were on the brink of a state of emergency. This made unity within the KPJ, and a show of unity at the conference, all the more important. He also said that if this was not achieved, then the presidency would resort to all constitutional and statutory means necessary to protect the integrity of the country, equality, and unity. In the end, the conference passed off without disruption[222] (Dizdarević has been much criticised for his insistence on operating within the unwieldy constitutional framework. In his defence, he recalls that the single most destructive act in the Yugoslav tragedy was when the JNA decided to abandon the constitutional order, and succumbing to the charms of a charismatic and ruthless leader, attempted to resolve the crisis by embracing a radical ideology that was anathema to its founder[223]. Whether Hamdija Pozderac would have made a more effective federal president at this critical time, will never be known). Nevertheless, there was a mass rally outside the parliament one month later, on 28 February 1989, further to the proclamation of a state of emergency in Kosovo[224] (see below). The numbers at the rally quickly approached one million, and there were calls for an address by Milošević, Šuvar and Dizdarević[225]. Milošević refused to appear, so Dizdarević felt obliged to step in, and addressed the mob on the need to preserve the integrity of Yugoslavia: "for as Yugoslavia we are strong, but without Yugoslavia we are nothing". According to Dizdarević, the crowd then began to disperse; Milošević appeared that evening, when 90% of the people had left, and promised to make arrests in Kosovo (but according to the BBC, and denied by Dizdarević, he was prompted in his speech by a Milošević aide, whose voice could be heard over the PA system, as a result of which he was ridiculed; and the mob refused to disperse until they had been addressed by their idol, who did not fail to deliver after making them wait all day)[226]. Two years later, on 9 March 1991, 40,000 people led by opposition leader Drašković demonstrated in Belgrade calling for freedom of the press. The riot police were seen off, and with the green light from the federal presidency, Milošević deployed tanks for the first time - onto the streets of the capital. Drašković was arrested in parliament by security service man Naser Orić, who advised him to take some bait with him to prison. The next night there were large student demonstrations on Terazije, that over the next few days became a focus for protest by Belgrade's liberal elite. The late Patriarch Pavle urged them in vain to disperse. On 12 March, federal president Jović called an emergency meeting of the presidency. As the members of the presidency turned up, they were placed in a bus at Kadijević's orders and driven to Topčider, their emergency command centre (and also the location of Partisan Belgrade FC's ground), where they were told to agree to the imposition of a state of emergency (Kadijević had earlier obtained intelligence in Moscow to the effect that the UK, France and Russia would not object to a *coup*, while in 1988 intelligence from NATO had indicated that the West would turn a blind eye if the JNA acted to restore unity in the country, although according to Kadijević this also implied the removal of Milošević[227]). However, to the general surprise, the Bosnian member of the presidency, himself a Serb, was against the motion (as were the Macedonian and the Croat; the Slovene member had not come), and Milošević was unable to obtain the absolute majority (five votes) he required for his *coup*. The next day, he defused the situation by releasing Drašković. Then, on 14 March, in order to facilitate the plot, Jović resigned, plunging the presidency into chaos and leaving the JNA without a commander-in-chief. Two days later, Knin declared independence, and Milošević announced that Serbia would no longer recognise the federal authorities. However, Mesić stepped in as acting commander-in-chief, preventing the JNA from acting independently to resolve the constitutional crisis (by "disarming paramilitary units in Croatia", i.e. the nascent HV). At a hastily-arranged meeting of Serbia's mayors, and the following day at a meeting of university students and professors, Milošević let it be known that he would not object to the Slovenes and the Croats going their own ways, but that all Serb lands would remain in one state. Yugoslavia was dead, long live Greater Serbia! He told the mayors that "We Serbs might not be good at business, but at least we know how to fight"[lvii][228]. The response was mixed, and he was told by one student that if he resigned, then Tuđman's support in Croatia would dry up overnight, and Yugoslavia could become a democracy. Milošević gave up on his attempted *coup*, at least for the time being. Instead, he held a meeting with Tuđman at Tito's favourite hunting lodge, Karađorđevo in Vojvodina, on 25 March, where they allegedly agreed on a division of territory, generous to Tuđman's aspirations in Bosnia (see Part 1), by which Milošević sought to encourage him to go to war[lviii][229] (and to sideline KPJ man Mesić at home in Croatia. But in October, Mesić, who became the last federal president in July after two months of histrionic obstructing by Milošević, left Belgrade for the last time in that capacity and announced to the Croatian parliament: "Mission accomplished – Yugoslavia is no more". The following month he led a flotilla that broke the blockade of Dubrovnik, but failed to achieve much more than obtain media coverage[lix]). Fast-forwarding the first act of the war, which was played away from Serbia, there was further unrest in Belgrade in the late 1990s, culminating in Milošević's demise in 2000. In 1996, the opposition demonstrated for a month after Milošević attempted to rig the local elections[230]. Then, on the 35th day, Milošević organised a rally of his supporters: 40,000 of them were brought in to face the 80,000 demonstrators, and to their great surprise, many of them were beaten up, the first time they had found themselves at a disadvantage. The police were nowhere in evidence: Milošević wanted to provoke a state of emergency. But when firearms were used, he backed down and allowed the riot police to disperse the crowds. Yet the demonstrations continued, and after a total of 76 days, Milošević allowed the opposition to claim its victory, and take power in over half the local authorities in Serbia. A series of coordinated grenade attacks by the UÇK on Serb refugees in

---

[lvii] According to Owen, Milošević gave up on Greater Serbia in April 1993, when faced with stiffer sanctions during the talks on the Vance-Owen plan, and started to worry about Serbia and Montenegro.

[lviii] Twenty years earlier, in 1971, it was decided at a KPJ executive meeting in Karađorđevo to reverse earlier liberal reforms granted to the Croatian KPJ. These decentralising reforms and a new Croatian national identity had been championed by Bakarić (PM until 1969); but now there were calls for full autonomy for Croatia within Yugoslavia. What had started as an expression of legitimate grievances was swiftly hijacked by extremists. The Yugoslav ambassador to Sweden was assassinated by two *Ustaše*, and there were student demonstrations in Zagreb. The Warsaw Pact responded with manoeuvres in Czechoslovakia and Bulgaria, and the JNA warned Tito in Karađorđevo that there would be a *coup* if he didn't dismiss the Croatian nationalists. Tito travelled to Zagreb and replaced the leadership of the Croatian KPJ, with the active support of Bakarić. This was followed by several years of purges of the KPJ and public life in Croatia, resulting in the "Croatian silence", only broken by Tuđman in 1989, upon whom the historical significance of this venue would certainly not have been lost. The 1991 agreement allegedly included deporting the Bosnian Muslims to Turkey.

[lix] This corresponded with the expiry of the Brijuni agreement, signed on 7 July, under which Slovenian and Croatian secession was to be delayed for three months (with a ceasefire) while the EU worked out their new position in international law.

Kosovo at this time allowed Milošević to once again play the nationalist card. In 1998, Milošević appeared to be trying to improve his popularity, as there were election-type posters in evidence. One bore the prophetic slogan, *"Idemo dalje"* ("moving on"). In August 1999, two months after the end of the Kosovo war, another series of mass anti-Milošević demonstrations started in Belgrade, and the divided opposition, led by Drašković and Đinđić, who weren't on speaking terms, both attempted to harness the mob. Hoping to capitalise on the divisions within the opposition and his post-war reconstruction efforts, Milošević held early federal presidential elections in September of the following year, but the joint opposition candidate, the unknown Koštunica, whose campaign was bankrolled by the US, won an absolute majority in the first round. However, Milošević contested the result and insisted on a second round, and in October the opposition organised the mother of all demonstrations in Belgrade. Half a million people turned up from all over Serbia, and invaded the federal parliament with a bulldozer, overwhelming the riot police. Milošević called upon the VJ to intervene, but they refused to do the police's job. The mob then took over and trashed Milošević's television station. From another station, Koštunica broadcast a call for national reconciliation, which was replayed throughout the night. The next day, he met Milošević in the latter's home, and Milošević conceded defeat on television. The US gave their new president an ultimatum: Milošević had to be in The Hague by the end of March; but the pedantic lawyer Koštunica was unwilling to take a step that had no basis in law. When Đinđić finally had Milošević flown out of the country by helicopter without informing him, Koštunica condemned it as a continuation of Milošević's practice of acting outside the law.

Travel for us between Belgrade and Priština was by road, driven by Boris and then Milan, a former chips salesman, both young refugees from Sector North in Croatia (we had Albanian drivers for movement within Kosovo outside Priština, as it would be too dangerous for a Serb male to venture there. One of the Albanian drivers, Kelmend, used to be able to open bottles of beer with his eye socket. Another invited me round to his house one evening. He had four musical daughters, and they laid on a concert for me, a very civilised soirée. I had been told in Kakanj that when you visit an Albanian's home, all you see of his wife is her hands as she passes food through the hatch from the kitchen, and then receives the plates again after the meal. That wasn't my experience – *Ko nema u glavi ima u nogama*, "ignorance is strength"). Boris said he hadn't even known he was a Serb before the war; as he lived in Croatia he had assumed he was a Croat. The journey from Belgrade took most of the day, down the motorway past Smederevo with its stove factory, which I visited once during a procurement process, looking for something better than the smoke-producers we had had to put up with in Kuplensko to give to IDPs in Kosovo (in the end, we procured stoves, and children's winter clothing, from Turkey: the stoves on sale in Smederevo were not designed for field use, and were simply too expensive. In 2013, Seka and I met a couple from Smederevo, Daniel and Jelena, on a bus in Cuba; our surprise was only compounded when Daniel told us he was originally from Bihać, from where his family had moved as refugees in 1992, when he was still a child). Moving on, the motorway passes Milošević's home town and Legija's current residence of Požarevac (*požar* means "inferno") to the left, before turning off right onto a country road just after Paraćin, through the familiar mournful hills, meadows, fields and woodland. It was strange to finally travel through rural Serbia after so much time spent driving around SDS territory, under the constant threat of violence. Was this the heart of darkness? It all certainly looked (and felt) very familiar, apart from the fact that there was no war damage here. To what extent were the people living inside the houses and farms we passed aware of what had been going on in identical houses and farms just a few hours' drive to the west; of the direct causal links that existed between the machinations of their temporal and spiritual leaders, and the devastation visited upon their neighbours (in Belgrade, as in Zagreb, Bosnia and the Croatian Borders had seemed a world away)? Meanwhile, the motorway continues south-east past Niš (which was cluster-bombed by NATO on 7 May 1999, resulting in 15 civilian casualties when the attack missed its target, the airport; cluster munitions are now banned under the Convention on Cluster Munitions of May 2008) and Leskovac (which was bombed much more heavily by fifty Flying Fortresses on 6 September 1944 with the green light from Tito, largely destroying a *Wehrmacht* column that was regrouping there before withdrawing from the Balkans. This was followed by the demolition of sections of the main Thessaloniki-Belgrade railway north and south of the town. The nature of the operation meant that the civilian population could not be warned in advance, and several thousand locals were killed[231]). Leskovac (*leska* means "hazel"), near the Macedonian border, is an important stop on the Balkan drugs route, leading straight up into Belgrade and beyond through Vojvodina to the EU, while Niš, in addition to being a regional industrial and administrative centre, is an important wholesale market for drugs. Back on our route, just after Kruševac (*krušac* means "river stone") was an excellent roadside café that served generous portions of traditional food (possibly the best *klopa* ("scran") I've eaten in the Balkans), where I was fond of stopping whenever time permitted. Indeed, where possible I would time departures to arrive there at lunch time. As Milan used to say, "*Svagdje se dobro jede po Srbiji*" ("the Serbians like to eat well"). Good, old-fashioned home cooking, lovingly prepared by a long-suffering granny in the back, and served up by a surly (and burly) Serb. The *kačkaval* ("cottage cheese") was excellent. One of my favourites was the Karađorđevo *šnicel*, a stuffed veal escalope. The *svinjska koljenica* ("gammon joint", known in Croatia as *buncek*) wasn't bad either – but they didn't do *pomfri* ("chips"; at another truck stop the following year, in Guinea this time, I sampled, at the recommendation of a French colleague, Manu – who I ran into again in Sierra Leone – a non-descript, and quite tasty barbecue sandwich. When I enquired of the chef as to the origin of the meat, I was told it was "*rat des roseaux*" ("bush rat"), whatever that was. At least it was well and truly fried to death[lx]). As they say in the Balkans, "*Ha si miu jo si ari*" ("moderation in all things"). Continuing south, we followed country roads to Blace, turning right towards Kuršumlija (*kuršum* means "bullet"),

---

[lx] A traditional staple food in Africa is *funge*, a gelatinous blob made from cassava roots. The roots are soaked in water to remove the naturally-occurring cyanide before being dried in the sun, and then pounded by women into a flour in large pestles, a common sight in villages throughout Africa. A nutritionist once told me that it is a very poor source of nutrients. The cassava leaves are used to make various sauces, which I found to be very bitter. Our head of logistics in Goma, Lolo, once invited me round to his house for dinner, as he had managed to get hold of some *kiboko* ("hippo", known further south as *seekoei*) meat. The greasy lumps of meat were served in the form of a stew with a communal clod of *funge*, from which the diners pulled off lumps as and when. When my host noticed I was being rather reticent, he detached a generous wad and slapped it on my plate, with a "That's the way you do it". I was reminded of a stew I once had in a *bufet* ("restaurant") in Groznij/Rral; the only other item on the menu was *kotleti*, which I took in the candlelight (it was not a romantic dinner: there was a power cut) to be chops, but were in fact tasteless shaped lumps of mincemeat. *Ćevapi* they were not, and apart from the pan-Soviet classics *šašliks*, *plov* ("special fried rice") and *ikra* ("caviar", which Eliane told me could be obtained on the coast in the form of fast food for the same price as a hotdog), cuisine is not one of the highlights of the Caucasus. In the restaurant we sat hidden behind a screen, so that passers-by would not notice the *inostranci* ("foreigners"), and perhaps kidnap us on a whim.

and then straight south into Kosovo at Podujevo/Besianë, before the final stretch into Priština, set in bleak plains. Lord Owen describes his first impressions of Priština: "Everything looked depressingly drab, the worst of communist architecture, and there was no sense of a proud history, no ancient monuments being visible, just dirt, grime and a foreboding of doom" (as such, not unlike Zenica)[232]. Occasionally we would vary the route by leaving the motorway south of Svilajnac, heading through the major university town and former capital Kragujevac ("buzzards' nest", whose Zastava ("flag") car and *Kalašnjikov* factory was bombed by NATO; the bombs that were thrown at the Archduke in 1914 had been manufactured there, while in October 1941, the entire male population of Kragujevac, over 2,700 men and boys, were executed by the *Wehrmacht* as a reprisal for a joint Partisan/*Četnik* attack[233]) and Kraljevo ("king's town") with its UNESCO-listed monastery, and then down into the northern tip of Kosovo, through Kosovska Mitrovica to Priština. Once, on the way north to Belgrade, somewhere between Kragujevac and Kraljevo, we found ourselves behind a flat-bed truck with a Romany brass band on the back, in full swing. It was a wedding, and the half-dozen musicians, admirably keeping their footing on the swaying vehicle, were knocking out a rousing melody, while simultaneously quaffing from a bottle. Brass instruments were an innovation of the Austro-Hungarian army that Romany musicians in Serbia adopted and made their own. Romany "orchestras" are hired for weddings and other festivities throughout the Balkans, but brass bands are a Serbian speciality, and there is an annual brass band festival and contest, at Guča, 30 km west of Kraljevo, where vast quantities of *rakija* are drunk.

Kosovo was given real autonomy in 1966, after Aleksandar Ranković[lxi][234] was disgraced (the reforms of this period also allowed Yugoslavs to travel freely and work abroad[lxii], as well as the free circulation of foreign press and books that were banned elsewhere in eastern Europe – but with some restrictions)[235]. These reforms culminated in the last, decentralising constitution of 1974, which made the two autonomous regions practically equivalent to the six republics[236]. By the late 1970s, two thirds of local KPJ members were Albanian, and in 1981, three quarters of the local police were Albanians, while Serbs and Montenegrins had constituted 21% of the population in 1971 (and until 1966, the police had been exclusively Serbs and Montenegrins[237]). Federal posts were also opened to Albanians (and to a much lesser extent, government posts in Serbia proper[238]). Yet despite economic growth in absolute terms, in relative terms Kosovo was even worse off, and became the poorest

---

[lxi] Codename Marko during WWII, and number three in the government after the war, he was the interior minister and head of the UDBA 1944-1966 who directed the harsh anti-Albanian policy in Kosovo. Fitzroy Maclean described him as the man "who, under Tito's supervision, operated the party machine [...] The son of a peasant, he had the stubborn, rather sly look which peasants often have. Not, you felt, a man who would come off worst in a bargain". He was deposed at a meeting on Brijuni in 1966 because of his opposition to reforms, when the all-powerful UDBA also had its wings clipped for acting *ultra vires* by penetrating all areas of life. He withdrew completely from public life, but his funeral in Belgrade in 1983 was attended by 100,000 people chanting his name. According to Dizdarević, this was a sign that the public wanted a return to the days of "firm but fair" government.

[lxii] The opportunity to work legally abroad also facilitated illegal activities. It was not unknown for young girls to be recruited for what they were given to understand was legitimate work in (West) Germany, only to discover upon arrival that the activities they were expected to perform were very different. All was not lost, however, even if they spoke no German, if they were confident enough to refuse to give up their passports, and perhaps had a relative in Germany who they could call to come and collect them and take them home.

region of Yugoslavia[239]. However, Milošević put an end to this golden age for the Albanians, that had not been to everyone's liking, in 1989. The first student demonstrations, in 1981, which led to a state of emergency being declared in Priština and Kosovska Mitrovica, were later described by Dizdarević as a "political earthquake", sponsored by Tirana, that shook the whole country and marked the beginning of the end of Yugoslavia. The resulting tension between Serbs and Albanians was the first manifestation of ethnic conflict among Yugoslavs; it also polarised the political entities, with Bosnia, Croatia and the two autonomous regions diametrically opposed to Serbia, Macedonia, Montenegro and Slovenia; and for the first time since WWII, the idea of Greater Serbia was voiced in official circles[240]. While the next few years were quiet in Kosovo, an acute crisis continued under the surface: this caused not only a build-up of explosive forces within Kosovo, but was also a constant running sore on the Yugoslav body politic, which acted as an irritant on all the other republics, and encouraged the emigration of Serbs and Montenegrins from Kosovo: 12,500 of them left between 1981 and 1983[241]. In November 1988, the leader of the Kosovo KPJ, Azem Vllasi, was dismissed and replaced by a Milošević stooge. Later that month, the "mother of all rallies" was held in Belgrade (local media claimed up to one million people attended), and Milošević assured the adulating mob that Kosovo would always be Serbian[242]. The same month, under competing pressures from the increasingly restless republics, the federal parliament adopted compromise amendments to the constitution, ostensibly to allow the reforms the country needed if it was to emerge from its existential crisis[243]. This all led to major demonstrations in Kosovo, the first popular resistance to Milošević's management buyout of Serbia (at this time, the federal minister of defence told Dizdarević privately that they would be better off without Kosovo)[244]. Milošević proposed a new recentralising Serbian constitution that would curtail the autonomous regions' home rule, while preserving their positions (and voting rights) on the federal structures; but in order to push the new constitution through, it would have to be approved by Kosovo (there was no difficulty in having it approved by Vojvodina, see above). In February the next year, five years after the miners' strike in the UK, over 1,300 miners at Trepča mine in Kosovo went on strike and refused to leave their pit, calling for the new KPJ boss to resign. The strike quickly spread and became a general strike in Kosovo. The miners ratcheted the pressure up a cog by going on hunger strike, and threatening a mass suicide with two tons of explosive that they had in the mine. While federal president Dizdarević travelled to Kosovo to try to defuse the situation there, Milošević called it a "rebellion", and a rally of Serbs and Montenegrins was organised in Kosovo Polje ("field of blackbirds")[245]. A delegation travelled to Belgrade, expressing fears of civil war, and asked the government to put a stop to the general strike; thousands of Serbs and Montenegrins from outside Kosovo were also preparing to travel there to hold a mass rally[246]. Meanwhile, the Slovenian leadership, hoping to contain Milošević, sent a telegram of support to the miners[247]. After eight days, for the first time in the crisis a state of emergency was declared, which entailed a lockdown of the borders of Kosovo, and an increased JNA presence there. Footage of armoured convoys heading for Kosovo from other parts of the country indicated that a rubicon had been crossed[248]. On the same day, Milošević's stooge in the Kosovo KPJ resigned, the miners came out of their mine, and the general strike ended (however, the next day, the resignation was withdrawn)[249]. Likewise on the same day, there were demonstrations of support in Slovenia, which when repeatedly rebroadcast in Serbia only added fuel to the flames. Major Serbian businesses severed relations with Slovenia[250]. The next day, 28

February, a vast rally was organised in front of the federal parliament in Belgrade (see above), as well as in other towns throughout Serbia and Montenegro[251]. In the evening, after 90% of the participants had allegedly left, Milošević addressed the rally with a promise to arrest the organisers of the disorder in Kosovo[252]. Over the next two days, there was a series of arrests there, including of Vllasi, and in March, the Kosovo first minister and KPJ adopted Serbia's new constitution[253]. However, as the date approached for the session of the Kosovo assembly that was to ratify the constitutional reforms, there were renewed strikes and demonstrations, despite the state of emergency[254]. These quickly deteriorated into violence all over Kosovo, including the use of firearms[255]. After the first casualties, a curfew was imposed[256]. At the end of March, their building in Priština surrounded by tanks, the assembly adopted the new constitution[257]. This was followed by more unrest, but the next month the state of emergency was lifted[258]. In June, a series of "temporary" measures akin to a permanent state of emergency were imposed from Belgrade, and in July, the Kosovo assembly was abolished, and direct rule imposed[259]. Milošević now controlled the two majority-Serb republics and the two autonomous regions, but having achieved the constitutional change within Serbia that righted the principal wrong set out in the notorious memorandum, he confirmed the other republics' fears by abusing this control to dominate the federal institutions[260]. There was further unrest in Kosovo later in the year, and in early 1990, the JNA was deployed to replace the riot police. In October 1997, there were again major student protests in Kosovo, organised for the first time by the UÇK, and in defiance of the widely-respected Albanian leader Ibrahim Rugova, the first unrest since 1992[261].

There is a common misconception that the war in Kosovo was a war against Islam. While around 85% of Albanians are indeed Muslims, there are also many Catholics, and Mother Theresa herself was Albanian, from Macedonia (which has a large Albanian minority). The underlying cause of the conflict in Kosovo is that the Serbs (and Croats and Muslims) simply do not understand or know the Albanians, and most of them do not want to know, as illustrated by the proverb, "*Sa Šiptarom se ne rukuje, nit' se kod njega kremšnita kupuje*" ("don't shake hands with an Albanian, don't buy a cream cake from him either"). "*Šiptar*" is the universally recognised derogatory term for Albanians (curiously, in their own language they call themselves "*Shqiptarë*", but they don't like anyone else using the word). In Bosnia, and to a lesser extent Croatia, Albanian immigrants from Kosovo traditionally run coffee shops, where a variety of elaborate cakes can be degusted. Albanian men tend to wear *qeleshe* (curious white, ostrich-egg-like caps made of firm felt), a tight-fitting dome on their heads that singles them out at a distance. Albanian is as different from Bosnian/Croatian/Serbian as Welsh is from English, and is as little spoken by the linguistic majority (Irfo told me that when he was doing his national service in Kosovo, he was told as a practical joke that "*çka po don*" ("what do you want") was the Albanian equivalent of "*dobar dan*" ("good afternoon"), which led to some curious exchanges of greetings). Indeed, Albanian is not directly related to any other language, although it has borrowed from its neighbours, Serbian, Italian and Greek. While some local Serbs did speak it (an Albanian colleague and I were surprised at a checkpoint one day when a Serb policeman addressed him in Albanian), the refugees flowing in from Croatia certainly didn't have much experience of interacting with Albanians, which only served to widen the gulf between the two communities. The Albanians respond in kind, with the result that much of the rich Albanian social life takes place behind walls: the wall of language, and physical walls, as it is customary for extended families to all live in large compounds, with their individual houses all giving onto a common *oborr* ("yard"). I saw the same arrangement in Chechnya. There is also another, more sinister resemblance between the Balkans and the Caucasus: the *gjakmarrja* or *čir* ("blood feud") respectively. This requires that blood should be atoned for by blood, which means in practice that not necessarily the murderer, but a male relative of his must die to satisfy the honour of the original victim's family. This practice persists in rural Kosovo and northern Albania, despite a series of mass reconciliations arranged in the 1990s (and in Chechnya, it has only increased in recent years)[262]. A clan system also exists in both places, as it does in Montenegro, but, at least among urban populations, it is confined largely to an awareness of one's family history and relatives, rather than torch-lit Highland gatherings. In his mammoth work on Stalin's prison camp system, Solženicin wrote that the Chechen blood feud was an effective mechanism for maintaining order in society, that only need be evoked rarely to retain its deterrent force[lxiii]. He also noted that it made outsiders think twice before tangling with a member of the community[263]. Opposite our office in Nazranj there lived a family with three teenage daughters. Every morning I would see the eldest sweeping the yard and doing other chores, while her siblings seemed exempt from any responsibilities. I enquired after this practice, and was told it was traditional for the oldest girl to take on all the household chores with her mother, in preparation for marriage, which had to be in strictly chronological order. One day tragedy struck, and the father of the family died after binging on counterfeit vodka, a major problem in Russia, where the cheapest stuff could be bought for less than one dollar a bottle. I remember watching a news report at the time in which the head of *Rosalkogoljregulirovanie* (the national vodka quality control office) was complaining that she only had three inspectors to cover the whole of Russia (I never came across *samogon* ("home brew") in the Caucasus or Central Asia. But in the absence of *rakija*, vodka was a worthy substitute: my favourite brand was the mid-range Ha Ha Ha, featuring on the label a jovial detail from Repin's famous picture of the Cossacks writing a letter to the Turkish Sultan, and a bargain at less than USD 10 a bottle. Anything cheaper was potentially fatal, little better than *razbavitelj* ("thinners"), as our neighbours in Nazranj discovered to their cost. Beer is a soft drink in Russia: "*Umom Rossiju ne ponjatj*" ("it will break your heart and blow your mind"). My favourite was Baltika[lxiv]. In Turkmenistan, Sunday lunch traditionally starts with a fatty chicken soup, to line the diner's stomach and strengthen absorption capacity in anticipation of the copious amounts of vodka to follow, while in Tajikistan, *čajhana* ("restaurant") punters are shown to beds rather than tables and chairs). Soon afterwards, I noticed the middle daughter sweeping the yard. We were told that the eldest daughter had been kidnapped by a

---

[lxiii] Solženicin was a decorated captain in the Red Army, and took part in the liberation of Berlin. But in February 1945 he was arrested for referring to Stalin as a moustachioed *avtoritet* ("gang leader") in a letter, for which he spent eight years as a *zek* ("convict") in the *gulag* ("prison service") archipelago of prison camps in the ocean of the Soviet wilderness. After his release he became the Soviet Union's leading *inakomisljaščij* ("dissident"). He died in 2008.

[lxiv] I was invited to dinner with a couple I met in Soči. After the tasty fried *kurica* ("chicken"), *ovošči* ("veg") and *žarenie kartofeli* ("chips"), which were washed down liberally with frequently refilled beakers of vodka, my host asked me whether I would like a real drink. "I thought that was a real drink", I protested. I was then treated to a *sto gramm* ("dram") of 100% *spirt* ("alcohol"), which I have to admit was like drinking bleach. My new friend then took me to a house that he was having renovated, where I was surprised to see that one of the painter and decorators was a police officer – in uniform! "Does this kind of thing happen in the UK?" he asked me. When I replied in the negative, he commented, "*Mi Jeljcinovie negri*" ("we're Jeljcin's Blacks"). Drinking bleach is a favoured suicide method for women in Central Asia.

suitor the previous night, and was now married. As there was no longer a man in the house, and they had no close male relatives, they were sitting ducks for this traditional practice, and it wasn't long before the middle girl was kidnapped as well. But here there was a new twist: the groom's parents sent her back, because they deemed the family beneath her son. The daughter's reputation was now ruined, at the age of 17. Surprisingly, to me at least, she took to spending time on the road outside the family compound, in view of passing traffic, and I was told she was now advertising herself for *pohiščenie/zuda lačka* ("kidnap"), as it was her only hope of marriage. In normal circumstances, the weekly market was the only opportunity for young men and women to see and be seen by each other, and they would dress up specially for the occasion. Nazranj was a nondescript, provincial town, a mud bath or a dustbowl when not frozen solid, but occasionally the clouds and dust would part to reveal the Caucasus mountains in all their splendour, a vast wall in the distance stretching up to the heavens, behind which lurked Stalin's homeland, Georgia. The trait that struck me most, and as most characteristic of the Chechens, including the women, and even the children, was fearlessness. It is curious that such a quality should be so abundant in one of the smallest nations in the world (the population of Chechnya is less than one million), at war with the largest county in the world, an ailing nuclear superpower, while fear, and greed seem to be the guiding forces of our destiny in the stronger, western democracies, among the safest places in the world. As the Chechens say,

> *"Delhit ugš*
> *Thro delh ajmun dac*
> *Tho laman nah do*
> *Tho nohči do"*[lxv].

A Scottish mine manager in Kosovo was cited by Rebecca West as having said in 1939, in reference to the practice of banditry that persisted in the countryside after Kosovo was liberated from the Turks in 1912:

> "The only way the gendarmes could stop it was by going up into these villages and killing every man, woman and child. [...] If they'd let one child get away, as soon as it had grown up it would have had to carry on the blood-feud against the gendarmes, or the people who were supposed to be responsible for the gendarmes' attack"[264].

We had three bases in Kosovo: from 1993 in Priština, the capital, east of centre; then from late June 1998 in Peć/Peja ("stove", although it is said the name comes from *pećina*, "cave", because hermits used to live in nearby caves[265]), 75 km west, approaching the border with Montenegro; and finally, from July, in Prizren in the south, on the road leading into Albania. Peć/Peja and Prizren both fall within the area known as Metohija ("monastic estate"), and Kosovo is more properly referred to as Kosovo and Metohija. There is a splendid 14th century monastery with medieval Byzantine frescoes at Gračanica, a UNESCO world heritage site just to the south-

---

[lxv] "Let the stones cry
We don't know how to cry
We're the mountain people
We're the Chechens."

397

east of Priština. The frescoes depict the early Serbian saints and kings, whose realm at its height stretched from Belgrade to Neum, and south to include Albania, Montenegro, Macedonia, part of Bulgaria and much of mainland Greece. The low roof and arches of the porch reminded me of St. Basil's Cathedral in Moscow[lxvi]. Today there is still a Serbian monastery on Mount Athos (founded in 1198), a UNESCO world heritage site hosting over 20 Orthodox monasteries, on the third finger of fun, in Greek Macedonia. Rasputin visited Mount Athos in 1893. I visited Gračanica one Sunday, on a recommendation from Ratko, and after being quizzed by the *iguman* ("prior") on my background (where was I from? what religion was I? where had I learnt Serbian? who had told me to visit the monastery? who did I work for? what did I do for them?), was given a guided tour by a young novice (I was subjected to a similar, albeit less intrusive interrogation when I visited the Orthodox cathedral in Adis Ababa, "beautiful flower"). I was also given a wooden cross by an elderly *monahinja* ("nun"), who was being attended to by a group of local village girls (the idyllic scene was compromised somewhat when she started to talk about the Albanians). I noticed on the wall by the door a brass plaque with the inscription "*France – Serbie 1914-1918*", and reflected again on how the Serbs, who (with to a lesser extent the Greeks) had been our strongest allies in the Balkans in both world wars, had become international outlaws[lxvii][266]. Now the Greeks are international pariahs as well (the Greek economy is administered by its creditors, to ensure its debts of 323 billion euros - in 2015, 177% of GDP[267] - are regularly serviced, perhaps the only thing that can still be relied upon in Greece, other than the constant influx of refugees. Nor have the years of austerity reduced the proportion of public debt to national output. How much the moneylenders have made from the Greek crisis, that has turned it into a developing country, appears to be an official secret; attempts thus far to cast the untouchable caste of bean-counters out of the Parthenon have been thwarted by the EU)[lxviii]. Gračanica is now the largest Serb enclave. Also just outside Priština is Kosovo Polje (both places were majority Serb before the war), the scene of the battle that put an end to Serbian statehood for 500 years, with a tower at Gazimestan that allows a panoramic view of the whole site. I climbed it one day after work during the summer with Bane, an engineer from Belgrade who had been working on MSF infrastructure development programmes with the Romany community in Ugljare, near Gračanica, and in Klokot, in the south-east, before the war started. Klokot is also now an enclave. He told me resignedly that he thought it

---

[lxvi] Commissioned by Ivan the Terrible in 1555. Medieval (i.e. European) Russia was ruled by the Mongol Tatars from 1240 until 1480. In 1242, Prince Aleksandr of Novgorod defeated a rival invading army of German knights and Estonian infantry on the frozen Lake Peipsi/Psov-Čudj, on the border between Russian and the Baltic state. The same year, Henry III attempted to invade Poitou in western France to reclaim his family estates.

[lxvii] In April 1941, Churchill broadcast to Yugoslavia: "Serbs, we know you. You were our allies in the last war, and your arms are covered with glory. Croats and Slovenes, we know your military history. For centuries you were the bulwark of Christianity". Legija later commented, "For the hundredth time I wondered what we Serbs had done wrong to find ourselves, on the threshold of the 21st century, and in the middle of Europe, in such deep shit. Why does the shit always hit us? Were we just born under an evil star? [...] We lost face in the Croatian Borders, and now we were going to lose our arse in Kosovo".

[lxviii] In 2008, I interpreted for an insolvency professional in the UK. Her client, an elderly, disabled Belgrader, instructed her to tell his creditors to sell his house, and once they had received their blood money, he would use the balance to purchase himself a lifetime lease in a residential care home. He had been living in the UK since the 1960s, and for many years his only source of income had been a long-term boarder. When the boarder died, the Serb found himself with a cashflow problem, and borrowed £750 from a credit company. He had difficulties servicing the loan, and before he knew it, in a relatively short space of time, with interest and charges, he was in debt to the tune of £15,000. All perfectly legal.

was a shame that Serbia was about to lose a large part of its cultural heritage, but that it was now inevitable. Despite the legend, it was not the battle that was fought here in 1389 that cast the Serbs into bondage for 500 years. An earlier battle at Marica in Bulgaria in 1371 was far more significant for Turkish long-term hegemony in the Balkans, and Kosovo was only occupied by the Turks in 1455, after the siege of Novo Brdo ("new hill"), east of Priština[268]. Kosovo Polje was also the scene of Milošević's impromptu address to local Serbs in 1987. As leader of the Serbian KPJ, he had travelled from Belgrade on behalf of Serbian president Stambolić to meet local leaders and discuss the various problematic issues besetting Kosovo at the time. Thousands of local Serbs demonstrated outside the House of Culture building where they were meeting, and started to throw stones at the mainly Albanian police (two trucks full of stones had conveniently been parked nearby by the local Serb leader). In the resulting affray, Milošević stepped outside and uttered his famous phrase, followed by a patriotic speech, which electrified the crowd, and was shown repeatedly on Belgrade television over the next few days[269]. Two years later, at the event to commemorate the 600th anniversary of the battle, a million Serbs from all over Yugoslavia and beyond gathered to hear him speak at the battlefield. He descended from the skies by helicopter like the prophet Ilija (Elijah), who is said to have conveyed the message to Tsar Lazar on the eve of the battle that it was better to fight and lose but gain eternal glory as a martyr, and he did not disappoint his audience. He galvanised them with national feeling, like Dr Frankenstein passing lightning through a body put together from bits of Serb mythology, urging them to remember their hard-won, glorious victories against the Ottomans, the Habsburgs, and Hitler, and how they had always lost the peace to their pernicious neighbours, the Croats, the Muslims, and the Albanians[lxix][270]. Like the good doctor, Milošević was to learn to his cost that his creature would take on a life of its own, and ultimately strike down its creator. Thus the Yugoslav Wars started, and were to end, in Kosovo.

In Priština, a crossroads in the town centre marked an unofficial border between Serb and Albanian territory. To the right (but also the first few addresses to the left) were located Albanian bars and restaurants. To the left, at the top of the hill, were Serb bars. Closer to our house there was a pool hall where we used to go some evenings to unwind. It was run by, and, apart from us, frequented exclusively by "Egyptians", a Romany community who for some reason are called that, to distinguish them from the other Romany communities in the Balkans (the English word "Gypsy" has the same root, and in Elizabethan times Romanies in England were also called Egyptians)[271]. The other main Romany communities in the Balkans are the Kalderaši ("coppersmiths"), who live mainly in Serbia and Romania, the Lovari ("horse dealers"), from Hungary, Slovakia, and Croatia, the Gurbeti, who live in Bosnia, the Ursari ("bear trainers"), in Romania and Bulgaria, the Bugurdži ("drill makers") in Bulgaria and Macedonia, and the Arli ("traders"), in Albania, Macedonia and Greece[272]. The Albanians referred to them collectively as *Magjup*. Romanies have been present in the former Yugoslavia from at least the 14th century[273]. Their language originates in Hindi, but bears traces of all the lands they travelled through on their great trek from India to the Balkans 1,000 years ago, such as Armenian and

---

[lxix] As Legija put it: "Sad to say, we didn't lose any of our previous wars on the battlefield, but at the negotiating table".

Greek (but, significantly, not Arabic[lxx]), and has been most influenced by Serbian and Romanian (a latin language, unlike Serbian). The causes of their exodus are unknown: some say they were a warrior caste who were defeated and expelled, while others say they were thieves who were cast out; or they may simply have been travelling musicians and artisans. Consequently, many Romanies are of Asian, or at least deeply Mediterranean appearance. One day, in Texas for a Bosnian wedding, I addressed a mechanic working on a car who I took to be Mexican, in Spanish. "*Koji ti je kurac?*" ("what the fuck are you on about?") he replied to me in Bosnian. In addition to dialectical differences between the various tribes, Romany is further complicated by the fact that it is invariably influenced by the official language of the country in which a particular community is living. One afternoon in Dušanbe ("Monday"), the capital of Tajikistan, I came across an elderly Romany with a wretched *rič khelimasko* ("dancing bear"). He was accompanied by some young children flitting about like colourful butterflies, whose task was to collect money from the crowd. However, when I addressed them in Romany, they spoke back to me in a tongue I didn't recognise or understand. Curiously, the slang of Cumbria, with its annual Romany horse fair, contains some Romany words, such as *gadžo* ("bloke"), *naš* ("run"), *phagardo* ("knackered"), and *dikh* ("look"). Today there are six million Romanies in the EU, and there are as many again in North America and Australasia (not to mention the rest of Eurasia)[274]. The Romanies are the true Europeans: the continent has been their lobster since far before Schengen[lxxi][275]. They simply ignore the restrictions imposed upon the rest of us by our elders and betters, but the price of their independence is social exclusion, incredulity, and alienation. As a result, they have been walking a tightrope between assimilation and extermination for centuries. The Nazis originally classified them as "Aryans", before succumbing to their own baser, more instinctive logic. The Romanies were then lumped together with Communists and other "antisocial" elements, before being earmarked for total destruction along with the Jews[276]. The Croatian Romanies were virtually exterminated by the *kale-gadenge* ("fascists") during the *trinto radž* ("third Reich")[277]. In the former Yugoslavia, Romanies tended to adopt the religion of the wider community, or rather, superimpose it on their own relationship with eternity, ancient before our time, such that there are Muslim, Orthodox and Catholic Romanies in the Balkans; but, unlike the Bosnian disunity, they are first and foremost Romanies. The Egyptians (all young men: every area of Romany life is strictly delineated along gender lines, and the two generally only interact in the *kher* ("home"), whether mobile or fixed) were accepting of us and our superior *bilijar* ("pool") skills learnt in British pubs (although they didn't seem to understand the rules), but not very communicative. Since the accession of eastern European countries to the EU from 2004 onwards, there has been a major migration of

---

[lxx] This indicates that the Romanies travelled from the Subcontinent to the Balkans before the rise of Turkey as an Islamic power, and the destruction of Orthodox Byzantium, the eastern heir to the Roman Empire. The Ottomans conquered Istanbul in 1453.

[lxxi] As Hinmatoowyalahtqit ("Chief Joseph") of the Washington Nez Percés ("pierced noses") tribe once said, "The earth was created by the assistance of the sun, and it should be left as it was [...] The country was made without lines of demarcation, and it is no man's business to divide it [...] The earth and myself are of one mind. The measure of the land and the measure of our bodies are the same [...] I never said the land was mine to do with as I chose. The one who has the right to dispose of it is the one who has created it. I claim a right to live on my land, and accord you the privilege to live on yours". As they say in the Balkans, "*Më mirë një mik se një çifluk*" ("a friend is worth more than an estate"). Regardless of denominational affiliation, Romany formal oaths invoke the forces of nature, such as "*Khama čona thaj Devla*" ("by the sun the moon and God").

Romanies into western Europe, in search of better economic prospects, and less discrimination. Prior to that, there was a sudden peak in Romany immigration into Dover in the summer of 1997, mainly from the Czech Republic (240 applied for asylum, and 210 were refused), and in August 1998, 700 Romanies from Slovakia arrived at Heathrow (none applied for asylum)[278]. Alas, discrimination and injustice do not end with the white cliffs. Some local authorities in the UK deliberately harass Romany families with the objective of encouraging them to move on. As if that wasn't enough, in 2010, a Slovakian (Catholic) Romany family in the UK had their four young children placed in foster care with West Indian Muslim converts, for reasons that seemed to me to be nothing more than cultural misunderstandings. Nor was it an isolated case. There has also been a steady migration from the former Yugoslavia since the start of the war, and in particular since the NATO invasion. In the absence of official statistics, there are visibly less Romanies in those towns in Bosnia where they used to be most numerous, such as Banja Luka, with its annual horse fair, as wild as Pobleski Velgorus/Appleby's.

Our main operational area was the Drenica valley north of the main road to Peć/Peja, towards Kosovska Mitrovica[lxxii], and later also the rural area comprised between the three towns, in particular along the road south-west from Priština to Dečani and towards the Albanian border, which is where much of the hostilities were taking place and where there were the most IDPs. The road between Kosovska Mitrovica and Peć/Peja was notorious for banditry in the period after WWI, and rievers would place logs on the road where it passed through Drenica[279]. The Drenica valley was the scene of an uprising that broke out in 1919, and was only put down in 1924, with the connivance of the new Albanian King, Zog[280]. It was also the home of Shaban Polluza, a Partisan commander who mutinied in early 1945, refusing to deploy to Srem while the Albanians were under attack by *Četniks*, and who with 20,000 men fought *Četniks* and Partisans until being defeated in March of that year. Located in Drenica is the village of Donji Prekaz, the first openly UÇK area in 1997, and which became a police no-go area when the armed uprising began in March 1998[281]. Donji Prekaz had been the home of Azem Bejta, who with his wife Shota Galica fought against the Austrian occupier in the latter half of WWI, before rebelling against the new Yugoslav state[282]. From March 1998 onwards, we had a mobile clinic programme that deployed to the field most days, providing emergency medical care for IDPs, and carrying out 200-400 consultations a day. MSF had had a programme in Kosovo prior to the conflict, among other things supporting the local NGO network *Nënë Tereza* ("Mother Theresa"), the alternative health service for many Albanians. While there seemed to be an inordinate number of medical students gaining their training in the alternative/underground education system, part of Rugova's strategy of constructing a parallel state (which meant that everything was theoretical, and some of the students had never even used a stethoscope), the several local doctors we employed had all studied at real universities before the war. Dr Skender, a long-term member of the Priština team, had studied in Zagreb, while Dr Osman, from Prizren, always seemed to have a couple of female students in his train. He raised a great deal of hilarity among the native English-speaking members of the team one day when he told us that one of the students was teaching him to play the oboe. We were the only NGO in Kosovo with both Serb and Albanian staff. The less professional NGOs seemed to be riding on a wave of anti-Serb sentiment, which

---

[lxxii] Legija said in respect of 1999, "There [Drenica] everything was under our control, but it was a wild area and no-one could have total control over the whole wasteland".

wasn't helped by the fact that some of them were blatantly agents of the US government, masquerading as aid workers. It's amazing how people can revel in racism when the target of their righteous anger has not been officially ring-fenced. Soon after I arrived, it became apparent that we needed a full-time warehouse manager in Priština for our growing programme. I placed an advertisement in the Albanian (*Koha Ditore*) and Serbian-language (*Politika*) newspapers, and there was a good response, including from women, for what is traditionally a man's role. The most promising candidates were contacted by telephone, and interviews arranged. On the day in question, I was surprised to see two attractive young ladies dolled up in make-up and high heels turn up at our office door. "*Ja bih njih dvije odmah zaposlio*" ("I'd give them a job straight away"), was Boris' advice to me upon seeing them. Alas, his counsel was not heeded, and a more grizzled candidate got the job.

In February 1998, the US called the UÇK a "terrorist group"[283]. On 5 March, a major police operation was launched against the home of UÇK founder Adem Jashari in Donji Prekaz in the Drenica valley, resulting in 58 dead Albanians, including Jashari and most of his family (in Kosovo the Unit generally deployed with extensive police support)[284]. The police had attempted to arrest him earlier, in January, but had withdrawn when UÇK reinforcements arrived[285]. This was followed by a major demonstration in Priština. On 31 March, UN security council resolution 1160 imposed an arms embargo and economic sanctions on the rump Yugoslavia, although opposition by Russia meant the resolution could not be backed up by threats of NATO air strikes. The UÇK seized large tracts of rural territory, and engaged in a campaign of kidnapping and killing Serb civilians. The police and VJ dug in around the areas controlled by the UÇK and attempted to disrupt the flow of arms across the south-west border from Albania[286].

One day soon after I arrived in Kosovo, when I was accompanying a field team, as I tried to do regularly in my role as logistics coordinator and security officer, upon arrival at Štimlje, 30 km south of Priština, we discovered VJ military police everywhere, with their dark blue armour. It was the familiar landscape of burnt-out commercial and residential premises against the backdrop of mournful nature. As we drove down the main street towards the front line, there was a squaddie standing every 20 yards or so. They were wearing helmets and body armour and clutching *Kalašnjikovs*, and it was obvious that something was afoot. Our destination was the village of Račak just west of the town. On the other side of the front line there was a large number of Albanian civilians milling about who all seemed to be waiting for something. While my medical colleagues set about their work, I had a look around with a view to security. I was always cautious about speaking Serbian in Albanian company, as outside the towns many Albanian men did not speak it very well (and the women not at all, as parents disapproved of girls going to school, and so they were never exposed to the language), and sometimes could not tell the difference between a foreigner and a native speaker. One day in Golubovac ("dove village"), an isolated village in Drenica, I was surrounded by three hostile males when I started speaking Bosnian, and challenged with "*Ku shkon?*" ("where do you think you're going?"). An Albanian colleague had to explain I was not a spy, but a foreign aid worker who spoke Serbian. In October 1999, a Bulgarian UN civilian employee was lynched in broad daylight in Priština because someone thought he was speaking Serbian[lxxiii]. But as my Albanian was only basic, Serbian was the only way to communicate in the absence of an interpreter. This time I used a new tactic and, after opening with "*Mire dita*" ("good afternoon"), started talking to an old man in English. When he looked at me in bewilderment, I explained to him in Bosnian, clearly and rather loudly, so that everyone around would hear, that I was a British aid worker, but that I spoke Bosnian. I asked him what they were all waiting for, and why they didn't leave, as it was obvious there was going to be trouble. He replied that they wouldn't let them leave. "Who?" I asked, "the Serbs?" "No", he replied, "the Albanians". That was not the first time I had seen a rural population being held hostage to the goals of their leaders, the majority of whom here were multi-lingual, having lived abroad in various capacities, and who had come home to play warlords. As is often the case in war, it is not only the old men but also the sophisticated who talk, while the poor as well as the young die for their country. As Ramo said, "*U ratu bogati daju volove a siromašni sinove*" ("in war the rich give an ox, and the poor give a son")[287]. But the Albanian leadership was far from united, and had been riven by factions since the 1960s (and indeed, since time immemorial). They included former political prisoners from the 1981 demonstrations, pseudo adepts of the former Maoist dictator in Albania (who excommunicated the rest of the Warsaw Pact in 1961 for backsliding[288]), and former KPJ functionaries, regarded by some as traitors, as well as a younger generation of nationalists, all with lukewarm support from the new nationalist president of Albania, Salih Berisha, who came to power in 1992[289]. According to the SPS, they were remote controlled by the *Sigurimi*, the Albanian security service. There were three fledgling training camps for aspiring militia from Kosovo in Albania in 1991, one of them in Kukës (a major refugee centre during the war)[290]. Albania is littered with 700,000 curious, small concrete bunkers, and innumerable vertical metal spikes, part of the previous Orwellian regime's national defence doctrine (the spikes were supposed to confound any attempts at an airborne invasion). The UÇK was formed in December 1993, but by 1997 only had 150 active members in Kosovo[291]. It was always slightly hair-raising driving in the territory controlled by the UÇK, as their discipline was very poor; one day they even shot at the UN security coordinator, a Scot with 16 years' experience in the British army, who was doing a field inspection with the full knowledge and consent of both sides. It was obvious that the Albanian mafia were behind the armed uprising (albeit with popular support), and it later became apparent that their strategy was to co-opt NATO to their cause. According to Rebecca West, "All over the Balkans there is an association between highway robbery and revolutionary idealism which the Westerner finds disconcerting, but which is an inevitable consequence of the Turkish conquest"[292]. Between 1989 and 1997, Rugova had pursued a policy of avoiding violent confrontation, creating a parallel state (including government, education and to a certain extent, health care services[293]) and seeking international support for Albanian sovereignty in Kosovo. The advent of the UÇK marked the failure of this policy to reap any dividends, and indeed it was undermined by the Dayton peace accords, which made no concessions for the Kosovo Albanians, such as the restoration of home rule, and strengthened Milošević's position with the international community[294]. Dayton even appeared to reward the use of force[295]. In the early 1990s, both Tuđman and Izetbegović had

---

lxxiii Conversely, once in a Balkan bar in Copenhagen I was hit upon by a Serb *polovnjača* ("cougar"), who after she'd had a skinful asked me if I was *Šiptar*. "No", I replied. "You never know" she concluded, her body a temple to Bacchus. *Stara koka dobra juha* ("fine wines improve with age").

asked Rugova to open a second front against the JNA in the south, but to no avail, not least because he had no weapons[296]. In 1992, Tuđman gave Albanian deserters from the JNA documents to allow them to travel abroad[297]. After the total collapse of law and order in Albania following the failure of nationwide pyramid schemes in early 1997, the UÇK was able to buy as many weapons as they wanted, with *Kalašnjikovs* going for USD 5 apiece[298][lxxiv]. As usual in the field, the only other organisations we ever came across were ICRC, and sometimes MDM (who with their single vehicle depended on us anyway to drive in convoy). FTC's heyday in the first half of the Yugoslav Wars of trucking anything anywhere was unfortunately over. Journalists were not unknown, however, and we were once tailed by some correspondents in an armoured Landrover, who got out and started filming every time we stopped, like flies around shit. Someone said they saw me on CNN that evening (Nikola was surprised one day many years later to hear my voice on Croatian TV, when a CNN interview with Luka Modrić was rebroadcast in the Balkans). There were far more organisations in Priština who never ventured out into the field, and yet more again in Belgrade. After the assassination of six ICRC delegates at the Starie Atagi hospital in Chechnya on 17 December 1996, practically the whole international community evacuated the republic (although ICRC continued to support the hospital at arms' length)[lxxv]. A French colleague, Eliane, and I, stayed an extra day in Groznij/Rral rather than join the column of Landcruisers heading for Nazranj on the day of the war crime, to put our office in order and ensure we would be able to continue to run operations by remote control once we had left. This was only a few days ahead of Chechnya's first free elections, and as a result there were no international election monitors, which may well have been the motive for the atrocity (a few days later, Merlin organised a protest march in Nazranj, from the *dom praviteljstva* ("local government building") to ICRC's warehouse. The locals had never seen anything like it, and were staring at us as if it was October 1917 all over again). It's curious how the decision-makers in international emergencies are usually the people most removed from the action. Counter-intuitively, such groupies are empowered by the mere fact of their physical proximity to the corridors of power, and more importantly, the budget-holders. As they say in Bosnia, "*Ko je bliže vatre bolje se ogrije*" ("the warmest place is by the fire"). While the US covertly had a lot of people on the ground in Priština, Tony Blair didn't seem to have any direct source of intelligence, at least until October. Perhaps he didn't need one. Meanwhile, it was rumoured that the Unit were also driving around in white Landcruisers, masquerading as aid workers, in order to be able to approach UÇK positions. Another of my tasks as logistics coordinator was to clear the amount of aid we were delivering with the local authorities. It was always a raucous experience dealing with Ružica, the official in charge, especially for the Albanian staff from other NGOs, among whom I was given preferential treatment, a dubious honour. Her son, who

---

[lxxiv] Mirsad once told me that before the war, Bosnia used to have its own pyramid scheme. You might be minding your own business one day, when someone would approach you with an offer to buy a brick, an offer that you could not refuse. Once you had become the proud owner, the only way to recoup your investment of DM 500 would be to resell it to someone else.

[lxxv] The head of the ICRC office in Groznij/Rral told us, just a few hours after the war crime, that the victims had been shot in their sleep, and that the murderers had only entered bedrooms that were not locked: they did not force entry into locked bedrooms, and furthermore did not steal anything. When a hospital worker heard something and came to investigate, the assassins withdrew, having accomplished their mission. This would appear to suggest that the perpetrators were not Chechen *banditi* ("armed robbers"), but FSB *killeri* ("professional assassins").

was there one day, bore an uncanny resemblance to Gavrilo Princip, with a bumfluff moustache, and he scowled ferociously when introduced. I was surprised the first time I went to Ružica's office to see a picture of Karadžić on the wall. But not as surprised as when I saw, on the wall in a local government building in Pendžakent in Tajikistan in 2010, a picture of Stalin.

By the end of June, around 350 people had been killed in Kosovo, and there were 60,000 refugees and IDPs[299]. Under pressure from NATO, Milošević agreed to cease police actions and restart talks with Rugova (that had in fact never been broken off)[300]. Among other measures, the government dismantled a major checkpoint at Obilić/Kastriot just outside Priština on the road to Mitrovica, leaving just a nominal police presence (Miloš Kobilić - later changed by patriots to Obilić, as *kobila* means "mare" - is said to have killed the Turkish Sultan in the battle of Kosovo, for which he was killed himself[301]). The very next day, the two remaining policemen were shot. Other dismantled police checkpoints were replaced by UÇK *pika* ("barriers")[302]. The UÇK were using the high-risk tactic successfully employed by Tuđman seven years previously in Croatia, and later emulated by Izetbegović, that of provoking the JNA into action that would attract international condemnation[303]. One day we arrived at the village of Rudnik ("mine"), just outside Srbica/Skenderaj in Drenica, where there was a clinic run in a house, only to be greeted by much wailing and gnashing of teeth from a small group of men and women. They said there had just been a massacre by the VJ, and that among the war criminals there had been a Russian *naemnik* ("mercenary"). However, when we asked to see the bodies, we were told we couldn't access the site because of mines. It appeared the incident was a work of fiction, but we reported it to ICRC just in case.

On another occasion, before we had our own two DAFs, I was travelling in a larger aid convoy on the way to Peć/Peja in one of our locally-rented Albanian *kamionë* ("trucks"). We stopped at a checkpoint, and the driver started to look nervous. My door was opened by a young VJ officer, and I was just about to address him when I suddenly found myself on the ground: he had pulled some martial arts move on me before I had even noticed. I swore in English, and the officer disappeared as soon as he realised I was a foreigner. Another day, in our warehouse just outside Priština, and next to ICRC's warehouse, I happened to be outside when one of ICRC's local doctors arrived in a Landcruiser. Upon exiting, the young Albanian subjected me to some obscenities in Serbian. Unperturbed, and indeed rather amused, I carried on with my business without bothering to reply. About ten minutes later he came to see me, looking rather sheepish, and introducing himself spoke to me very respectfully in English, on business matters. These two incidents were further glimpses beneath the surface into the dynamics of community relations at the thin end of the wedge, for the most part hidden from outsiders. On another occasion, in Peć/Peja, we found ourselves driving down the same side street along which the Unit were deploying on foot, advancing rapidly and spreading out to cover all turn-offs. They didn't seem particularly aggressive; I heard one of them say, "If they're foreigners, they shouldn't be here", but we just kept moving slowly forward, taking care not to hit any of them, and they paid us no more attention. We didn't hear any firing. Foreigners working in the Balkans were effectively operating in a parallel universe (as were the locals who expected the international community to save them). But death was real enough when it arrived. A short story by Andrić, *The Osaticans*, describes the first civilian administrator of a strategic outpost in Bosnia, just south of Srebrenica near the Serbian border:

"…as administrator of the station there came a young and beardless Austrian […] who behaved as if he had been posted to the most God-forsaken colony. An aristocrat and an eccentric, borne by the unshakeable aplomb of his class, full of good intentions and confused plans, he wanted to organise and arrange his little area of responsibility independently of the rest of the country and regardless of the prevailing conditions. He communicated with the locals through an interpreter. One tragicomic misunderstanding and conflict arose between him and the locals after the next. When he was finally recalled to Sarajevo, he left firmly convinced that all the residents of Osatica were hysterics and madmen, cruel and ungrateful savages, while he left behind him the general and firmly-established opinion that for two years their town had been governed by a lunatic, a completely mad and mentally incompetent individual"[304].

The locals conceal their true face from outsiders partly out of a sense of shame, the shame that comes from naked poverty, and partly to maximise the benefit they can extract from the presence of (relatively) powerful and wealthy foreigners in their country. In Peć/Peja we let warehouse space in the premises of Banana, a local export company. It was run by three Albanian brothers, one of whom explained to me that they had only been able to obtain a trading licence by claiming to have unique company objects, i.e. the export of bananas from Yugoslavia (which was probably the only thing they didn't do), but that in fact they engaged in a range of more mundane activities. While they were always accommodating and eager to please, I always had the feeling they were mixed up in other activities that we were not supposed to learn of. I also had the feeling they did not entirely trust me because I spoke Serbian/Croatian.

Peć/Peja hosts Serbia's UNESCO-listed patriarchate, which first became an archbishopric in the 1290s and in 1346 became the patriarchate of the Serbian Orthodox church. It was re-established as such in 1557 after a period of power struggles within the church, which saw the patriarchate move to Smederovo and Ohrid[305]. Like Gračanica, it was commissioned by the Serbian King Milutin, who built 37 monasteries[306]. Just south of Peć/Peja on the road towards Prizren is the 14th century UNESCO-listed monastery at Dečani, which was commissioned by Milutin's son, Stefan[307] (Stefan rebelled against his father, but after defeating him his father exiled him to Byzantine Istanbul and ordered him to be blinded. However, his sight survived, and after many years of pretending to be blind, he killed his brother and took power after his father's death. He was in turn defeated and strangled by his own son, Dušan, who extended Serbia's borders to their greatest extent and became Serbia's first Tsar, only to die 34 years before the battle of Kosovo[308]). Rebecca West describes a curious ritual in 1939 when Albanian Muslims brought sick children to the monastery to be cured by St. Stefan[309]. The blurring of different religions and superstitions[lxxvi] was quite common in Kosovo (and Bosnia) in the past, before they came to be synonymous with ethnic identity, and was fuelled by competition between the Catholic and Orthodox churches (and between the Greek

---

[lxxvi] It is considered advisable to say, "*Kako je ružan*" ("what an ugly child)" the first time you see a newborn child in Bosnia, as it is believed that this confounds any potential *urok/džungalo jakh* ("evil eye"). However, some Bosnian exiles to the West have discovered that this well-meant statement does not go down at all well in their new environment.

and Serbian Orthodox churches), only aggravated by the different status accorded them in respect of the official religion, Islam. It was not unknown for more than one religion, and sometimes all three, to be practised in a single household, before jealous international power structures divided the people and branded them their own commodities[310]. In May 1998, there was an attack by the Unit on a van mistakenly thought to be transporting UÇK outside Dečani monastery, which resulted in a VJ deployment there. Some of the 300 local Serbs took sanctuary in the monastery. Three weeks later there was a major VJ offensive against the town[311]. After the authorities had secured the road from Dečani to Priština via Đakovica, things went quiet. But there were large numbers of IDPs living in the countryside along the road, in particular near Orahovac ("walnut village", but also "walnut liqueur") and Mališevo, that had both been severely damaged[312]. The IDPs' living conditions reminded me of Kuplensko, except that they had no semi-permanent character, as they never knew when they would have to move again, either to go home, or to escape further fighting. During the NATO bombing, the monastery sheltered Albanian civilians, and afterwards, it sheltered Serbs and Romanies[313].

Late one afternoon in June, about 5 pm, our two nurses based in Peć/Peja (one Dutch, the other French) phoned to say they had a child who needed hospital treatment, and wanted to come straight to Priština. Our security rules normally precluded any movements outside the towns after dark, all the more so as we did not have a licence to use HF and VHF radios (although we had the hardware in the office), and so had no contact with our field teams other than in the morning before they left and the evening when they returned. These were the days before universal mobile phone coverage. After some discussion, we decided that as the case was deemed critical, the nurses should leave Peć/Peja immediately for Priština, hopefully to arrive while it was still light. On their way they got stuck in an armoured column, who deliberately intimidated them, which was not very encouraging. Upon arrival in Priština, they went straight to the hospital and had the child admitted. However, they expressed concerns that the staff there were not particularly interested, and the next morning, tragically, when they went to check up on the child, he was dead. MSF tried to get the *lijekar* ("doctor") in charge struck off for negligence, but made no headway in the MOH bureaucracy. Another time when I was in Peć/Peja, I deployed with Piero, my Italian logistician, to do some well-cleaning in the village of Ponorsk near where the medical team would be working that day (*ponor* means "abyss"). In refugee conditions, access to reliable drinking water becomes critical. The idea is to use a submersible pump to temporarily empty the well, then send someone down on a ladder or rope armed with a scrubbing brush and a chlorine solution. The walls of the well are scrubbed and then rinsed with a concentrated solution (0.1%), and more is thrown in at the end for good measure. Ideally, the water should be tested again once the well has refilled. It is a potentially dangerous operation, as carbon monoxide from the pump settles in the bottom, being heavier than air. It is colourless and odourless, and so the person directing the operation on the surface has to be alert to any signs that his colleague down below is being affected, and immediately pull him or her up if they suddenly become unresponsive (an additional problem I had when doing this work in Timor was that some refugees expressed the fear that we were poisoning their water source. It was important to clear all the work I was doing in the camp not only with the local public works department, but also with the refugees; but they had no organised representation. This situation was further complicated by the relationship between the two, which was characterised by mistrust and an inability to communicate. Recalling Mirvet's rubbish collectors in

Kuplensko, I solved this problem by recruiting a number of refugees to act as our agents in the camp, with the principal task of informing the other refugees what we were doing, and gathering statistics for our purposes. In Kupang we had on our team an Indonesian doctor who had previously worked in the east and spoke fluent Tetun, and one day he accompanied me to the camps, so that we were able to train our local team, who were all women, as most of the men, afflicted by the same idleness as in Kuplensko, appeared to be only interested in cockfighting and *khat*[lxxvii]. Everything ran smoothly after that). However, we had just started unloading our gear at the village, where there seemed to be an inordinate amount of activity, when a local, after enquiring into our business, said, "You needn't bother, we're about to abandon the village". I later heard that Piero had committed suicide[lxxviii].

In July, the UÇK seized Orahovac and the coal mine of Belaćevac/Bardh, west of Priština. The VJ responded, and in addition to retaking both, destroyed a column of 700 UÇK *luftëtarë* ("fighters") bringing weapons across the border from Albania[314]. The VJ then launched a major offensive on UÇK-held areas. The UÇK withdrew, while the VJ destroyed villages suspected of being UÇK strongholds, in particular Mališevo and Orahovac. Typically, the VJ would partly surround a village, allow the residents to leave, and then shell it before looting, and sometimes burning it down. On 29 July, the US met with the UÇK for the first time[315].

One Sunday afternoon I was having a beer in a bar in Prizren. I saw an Albanian staff member from another NGO, and he sat down with me on the terrace. As his English was faltering at best, we talked in Serbian, and the conversation quickly moved on to the political situation. He was far from happy with the Milošević regime, and let me know at length, taking no care to keep his voice down. I could see at another table that a scruffy individual with long hair, over-casually dressed, was taking an unusual interest in our conversation, and his beer seemed to be lasting a very long time. Finally, we left the bar and went for a walk around the old town. Suddenly, an unmarked van pulled to a screeching halt beside us and three

---

[lxxvii] A mild narcotic leaf that is chewed, and stains the consumer's laughing gear bright red. Splotches of red on the ground all over the camps were an indication of the popularity of the drug, originally from the Horn of Africa. Just like in Kuplensko, rumours abounded about the refugees outside the camps, in comfortable, air-conditioned offices many miles away, and it was said that among the refugees, who totalled over 250,000 in number, were members of the notorious militia who, controlled by the Indonesian army, were blamed for the violence and forced deportations that had given rise to the refugee crisis. It is true that there were several semi-organised expressions of anger, directed mainly against the local authorities, but also against the UN, and always in the afternoon; after one such incident, to be on the safe side, we set a curfew of 2 pm for our presence in the camps, which meant very early starts.

[lxxviii] The many psychological and physical pressures experienced by operational aid workers in the field are mirrored for some by equal, but very different, pressures when back in their home countries, especially if, as is usually the case, they are westerners. Such pressures include the absence of the daily adrenalin rush, an excess of petty rules and regulations, a lack of understanding for and recognition of their work outside their professional circle, the obsession with material status, and difficulties turning the skills that are so useful in an emergency to financial account in a developed country (this all tends to apply to a much lesser extent for medical staff, for whom working in the NHS or analogous structures is compatible with and complementary to their work abroad). These factors are all aggravated by the unhealthy "work hard, play hard" lifestyle that field staff tend to fall into. Some aid workers seek to compensate for this by developing secondary economic activities, that they can rely on when not deployed on mission. Others decide to turn their back on the civilised world altogether, and go native in a more precarious part of the world. None of these choices are conducive to a stable, family life. Another option is to defect to the grotesque aid aristocracy, where the ruling classes can accumulate brownie points by directing from afar the good works of the great unwashed. When I moved back to the UK, it took two years before I could relax properly at night and get a good night's sleep.

football hooligans jumped out (*"lud zbunjen nenormalan"*). "Do I look like a *čudovište* ['freak']?", one of them asked my Albanian companion. He looked meaner than Samuel L. Jackson and John Travolta put together. "W-what?" he replied, somewhat taken aback. His interlocutor repeated the question, to which the reply was negative. The punch line followed, "Why are you staring at me then?" My companion was then subjected to a string of instructions on how to improve his behaviour before the leader turned to me. It had by then dawned on me that they were security service. "Where are you from?" he asked. I told him, and he asked for my passport. It immediately became clear to me that this was the whole reason behind the pantomime: they wanted to know who the foreigner was who spoke Serbian. He examined my passport, returned it, and then, with a parting warning, they were off. The first time I went to Prizren, with its spectacular old town, reminiscent of East Mostar and a UNESCO world heritage site, I was surprised to see a road sign written not only in Albanian and Serbian, but also in Turkish. Indeed, our landlord in Prizren was an ethnic Turk. On 10 June 1878, a turning point in wider Albanian history, the League of Prizren was born in Prizren from a tribal council of Albanian chiefs, mainly from Kosovo but also from southern Albania. Its objective was to prevent any Albanian territory (at that time all part of the Ottoman Empire) being occupied by foreign troops, and ultimately led to the creation of the independent Albania, proclaimed in Vlora in 1912[316]. 10 km south-west of Prizren heading towards the Albanian border is the town of Žur, where Seka spent her early childhood.

One day, we and other NGOs were summoned by the local authorities to a mysterious "meeting" in the government building in Priština. Once assembled there, the local authorities, in front of a camera crew, gave a brief introductory speech about improving coordination with the aid community in those territories still under government control, and then invited us to introduce ourselves and raise any issues we might have. I let Save the Children speak first in English, and then addressed the gathering in Bosnian, to their great surprise. And then, to our great surprise, the "meeting" was over. That evening we realised that the whole thing had been staged in order to provide footage for a slot on the local evening news. I was collared on the way out of the meeting by the security service, who wanted to know where I had learnt Serbian. But at least I was able to get a contact and phone number, who was able to provide us with valuable real time information about ongoing operations on the ground in areas our mobile clinics were intending to visit. The VJ would generally seal areas off where they were carrying out operations so we had no access, although not always: one day our mobile clinic from Peć/Peja was held up at a VJ checkpoint while deploying to the field, and told to wait. As they did so, exiting their vehicles to stretch their legs, a nearby tank opened fire on a village. One day soon thereafter, around 11 am, I received a phone call in the office from my contact in the security service, letting me know it was highly recommended that our field teams (who had been spotted on the ground) not go to a certain location that day, which happened to be their destination. He urged me to call them on the radio and tell them to turn back. I explained to him that as we had been refused a permit to operate our radios, our vehicles were not equipped, and I was unable to contact them until they returned to base in the evening. He insisted they couldn't be there, despite my explanation, not grasping the ramifications of this administrative decision of theirs, and I had to patiently repeat myself, until finally he got it and hung up. *Sabur* ("patience is a virtue").

Another day, again travelling with one of our mobile clinic teams, we were held up at a checkpoint at Orahovac, for what started to seem like a long time, waiting for the green light from the security forces up ahead. It was a very hot summer's day, and all of us in the convoy of four Toyota Landcruisers were starting to heat up. On our left hand side was a vineyard, and several VJ military policemen. One came over, carrying bunches of *grožđe* ("grapes"), and gave them to us. He then proceeded down the line of vehicles doing the same. A welcome refreshment.

On 23 September, UN security council resolution 1199 demanded immediate action to bring peace to Kosovo. Under growing pressure from the UN after two more incidents, in Gornje Obrinje and Golubovac in Drenica on 29 September, Milošević agreed to a ceasefire and to reduce the VJ and police presence in Kosovo to pre-February levels[317]. IDPs returned to their homes, or at least the sites of their former homes, before the onset of winter[318]. The UÇK used this opportunity to regroup, and soon started a campaign of kidnappings, bombings and shootings of Serb civilians[319]. Meanwhile, OSCE monitors, whose task was to monitor Milošević's compliance with resolution 1199, provided material support to the UÇK on the ground[320].

On 25 September, an Albanian *mjek* ("doctor"), Dr Lec Uka, who had been one of our beneficiaries, in the village of Gradica in Drenica, halfway between Priština and Srbica/Skenderaj, and who in addition to supporting IDPs also ran one of the many secret hospitals for UÇK wounded, disappeared and his hospital was largely destroyed. He was found several days later tied to a tree, with one hand missing. According to other versions, he was tortured much more thoroughly. The VJ had taken a particularly dim view of these secret hospitals. Article 24 of the 1949 Geneva Convention I provides that "Medical personnel exclusively engaged in [...] the treatment of the wounded or sick [...] shall be respected and protected in all circumstances." The view of the authorities was that these facilities and their staff were also being used by the UÇK for military purposes and were therefore valid military targets, and furthermore, that by abusing the protected Red Cross emblem, they constituted perfidy contrary to article 37 of Additional Protocol I to the Geneva Convention[321]. MSF denounced this prima facie war crime publicly and issued a warning on the humanitarian situation on 9 October[322] (on 20 May the next year, NATO bombed a hospital in Belgrade, resulting in three deaths[323]. In October 2015, an MSF trauma centre in Afghanistan was destroyed by a US air strike; between then and January 2016, three MSF health centres in Yemen, the poorest country in the Arab world, and now facing starvation, were hit, two by Saudi forces using UK equipment and US targeting advice, while in February and April 2016 two hospitals supported by MSF in Syria were destroyed[324]. The identity of the perpetrators of these last war crimes has not been confirmed. On 3 May 2016, the head of MSF addressed the UN security council and demanded they put a stop to attacks on medical facilities, but over the summer of 2016 air strikes against hospitals in Syria and elsewhere have only increased, with the finger of blame increasingly being pointed at Russia. Meanwhile, two thirds of UK arms sales are to the Middle East).

On 13 October, NATO authorised an activation order for air strikes against Yugoslavia[325] .

It looked as if NATO was about to attack Kosovo. I received a telephone call from the UK embassy in Belgrade telling me to leave the country. I thanked them for their concern. Tim received a similar call, and when he jokingly asked, "Why, are you about to start bombing?", he said the response was a stony silence. At the same time, there was a tangible increase in hostility towards the aid community, as the Serbs saw their country being dismembered under their very feet. One day at this time, Boris told us that when he had gone home to his halls of residence the previous evening, he had been given a *Kalašnjikov* by the caretaker and told to "be ready". Another evening the lights of our town car (not a Landcruiser) were smashed when I was parked outside the halls of residence. A Scandinavian church NGO, represented by an old boy, had an incendiary device placed under their car. Fortunately, it went off during the night when nobody was in it. Only a few days earlier, someone had fired at him while he was driving through the town. The identity of the anti-Scandinavian assailants was never discovered. At this time it was noticed one Sunday morning that the number plates (issued by UNHCR, which entailed various privileges) had been stolen from one of our Landcruisers, and I had to report the incident to the police in order to have them replaced. Dr Skender went with me to the police station, as he was familiar with the procedure, although once there I saw a policeman who I had bought a drink one lunchtime in a local bar, and the matter was quickly resolved. He reminded me of Miloš. UNHCR set up a resettlement programme for refugees who wanted a new start in a third country, and the number of Serbs queuing outside the UNHCR office to apply seemed to be longer every day. Sometimes I would see among them refugees I knew from the halls of residence.

Facing an impending escalation and rapid descent into all-out war in Kosovo, we decided to down-size our team to the bare essentials, and temporarily evacuate everyone else, with some of our equipment, to neighbouring Macedonia. I sent our local head logistician, Fanol, to Macedonia, where he rented a house for us in the capital, Skopje. On D-day, 7 October, there were journalists everywhere, as if they had wind of something, and indeed, many other organisations were leaving, most of them shutting up shop completely. In order to avoid being shown on television abandoning the province and country to its fate, we staggered the departure of our vehicles and passengers, and left by a roundabout route (not leading south), to a rendezvous point just outside town. We also took care when loading body armour into our vehicles to cover it with blankets to keep the journalists off the scent (and preclude dramatic images). Once we were all ready, with sufficient supplies and fuel in each vehicle for any eventuality, we got our eight Landcruisers into convoy formation outside the town and headed south, through Uroševac/Ferizaj and Kačanik to the border (around 60 km). As usual in such circumstances, I had a knot in my stomach; my greatest fear was not for myself, but of being unable to prevent harm coming to any of the people in my charge. While waiting in my vehicle in the queue at the border, I spotted in my *retrovizor* ("mirror") a large figure with a rolling gait coming towards me on foot. Far away as he was, I immediately recognised Gary from Bosnia. As he drew level with me, I said, "Alright, Gary?" "Alright", he replied, as if we had seen each other only the day before. He was also working in Priština, and evacuating to Skopje. We agreed to meet up for a beer there. In April 1999, 65,000 refugees got stuck on the other side of this border crossing, as the Macedonians refused to let them enter the country[326].

A few km after the border, my team and I met up with Fanol and we headed straight into Skopje to our new digs. According to Rebecca West, while "Sarajevo is a Muslim, but not a Turkish town", the same does not apply to Skopje, once a major crossroads on the trade route between Dubrovnik and Istanbul[327]. It was Tsar Dušan's capital in the 14th century, when it was a Greek city; it was looted by the Austrian army as the biggest and richest city in the region in 1689; and now has a larger Albanian population than Tirana[328]. Macedonia is officially known as FYROM, the Former Yugoslav Republic of Macedonia, to distinguish it from the neighbouring Greek province of the same name, where the local Communists received active support from Tito during the Greek Civil War of 1949-1949, and where some people still identify themselves as Macedonians rather than Greeks; prior to 1944, FYROM was part of Serbia, and known as Old Serbia[329]. As a result of the crisis in the Turkish administration of Macedonia in the late 19th century, fuelled by Austria and Russia, in 1903 the Great Powers signed an agreement on the policing of Macedonia, which included a clause whereby the administrative districts were to be redrawn along ethnic lines as soon as the country could be restored to Turkish rule. This led to three years of ethnic cleansing between the various stakeholders, as each attempted to secure the districts it hoped would be its reward[330]. Ataturk's Young Turk movement, that later established the modern Turkish state, was forged among disaffected army officers dealing with the rebellion against Turkish rule here[lxxix][331]. According to T.E. Lawrence, "The Young Turk movement was a revolt against the hierarchic conception of Islam and the pan-Islamic theories of the old Sultan, who had aspired, by making himself spiritual director of the Muslim world, to be also (beyond appeal) its director in temporal affairs"[332] (he also described the Turkish army as a "shambling, ragged army of serfs"[333]). Skopje was hit by a 6.1 magnitude earthquake in 1963, which killed over 1,000 people. Our new landlord was an elderly Macedonian with a patch over one eye, who confided to me in Fanol's absence that he didn't like Albanians. Perhaps he thought I was a Četnik. There were some curious items in the house, from an ice bucket with an ancient Greek erotic design at the bottom, to a copy of *Mein Kampf* in English[lxxx]. I refrained from asking him how he had put his eye out. Macedonian is a dialect of Bulgarian, but I found no difficulties communicating, partly because Bulgarian is itself close to Serbian, and because all the locals spoke Serbian as a second language anyway. Gary and I met up as agreed, and indulged in some serious catching up while sampling the nocturnal delights of Alexander the Great's homeland. In Skopje I also ran into Drew, a Canadian who had worked with Mirvet in Kuplensko. After a week of enforced idleness and sightseeing in historic Skopje (and an unauthorised trip by the nurses to lake Ohrid, a UNESCO heritage site, straddling the border between Macedonia and Albania), it became obvious that NATO were not going to attack, and so we returned the way we had come, and it was business as usual for the next two and a half

---

[lxxix] Izetbegović blamed victor of Gallipoli Mustafa "Ataturk" Kemal's reforms after Turkey's defeat in WWI for turning it into a "third-rate country", while praising Japan's refusal to abandon its traditions in the name of progress. 40 years after the introduction of Latin script, he argued by way of example, illiteracy in Turkey was 50%, while in Japan, which retained its complex alphabet, illiteracy was non-existent. Rebecca West describes an episode in 1939 when the Turkish prime minister and minister of defence visited Sarajevo. The thronging multitude, nostalgic for Ottoman pomp and ceremony, were disappointed to see alighting from the train two simple men in suits, while the VIPs themselves were embarrassed and even annoyed by the mob of provincial throwbacks. Izetbegović also appears to have overlooked Japan's destruction in WWII and its subsequent refashioning by the US (seen by the Allies as the only way to ensure history would not repeat itself). Meanwhile, Turkey's 21st century strongman, Erdogan (PM since 2003, and president since 2014), periodically expresses his admiration for the late Izetbegović, "the first and great leader of Bosnia and Herzegovina", who he claims entrusted him with the "care of BiH" when he visited him on his deathbed in 2003. In 2015, the SDA-run Sanski Most council and the Islamic Board celebrated the 101st anniversary of Gallipoli at nearby Donji Kamengrad, where the Bosnian army was defeated in 1463. *Naša stranka*, see below, opposed the celebration, and recalled that a large local firm that once employed 1,200 people went bust after being sold to Turkish investors.
[lxxx] Hitler's rambling ravings in the form of an autobiographical manifesto, written while he was in prison in 1924 for a failed *coup*, were at first not taken seriously.

months. We kept the house, albeit empty, for the rest of the one-month lease we had already paid just in case, to the delight of the Macedonian cyclops. On the way back over the border into Kosovo I had a run-in with some aggressive border guards. "It's not my fault", I said to them, in reference to the international traffic jam jostling to cross the border. "Everything's your fault", they replied, in unison.

On 27 October, NATO declared that Milošević was complying with his commitments to withdraw police and VJ from Kosovo[334].

On 28 October, there was an article in *Le Monde*, complete with a cartoon of Milošević as a pig devouring civilians, which claimed, citing a source in MSF in Paris, that the MSF team on the ground was collecting evidence for a future war crimes trial. It was faxed to us the evening before, just as we were leaving the office. Even MSF is not free of the institutional malaise whereby certain individuals who live in head office and perform no operational role, "desk warriors", feel the need whenever there is a high-profile crisis, to do or say something that will make them feel involved and allow them to leave their mark. This selfish urge is far more pronounced in organisations that are less operational and field-based, and in some institutional organisations has grown out of all proportion to become an entity in its own right, a parasite that serves no function other than to feed itself on the body of the useless host, while the beneficiaries make do with the crumbs from its table. Some organisations have so many people producing reports that they need to employ someone just to keep track of them all. On 4 January, the Serbian newspaper *Politika* published an interview with the acting minister of health for Kosovo, accusing MSF of espionage, complete with a photo of our house in Priština bristling with antennae. However, the house in the picture was actually UNHCR's office, next door. Although both accusations were completely unfounded, we were still expecting *bal i maskenbal* (a "serious backlash") from the authorities, or even from the local population. But there was none.

After October, there were US, UK and French soldiers on the ground in Priština, who all seemed very keen to engage with the aid community. "A new kind of soldiering", as Tony Blair later described it. US officers would make a point of pontificating on the ills of Serbian rule in the international aid coordination meetings hosted and chaired by UNHCR, who never protested. At this time, UNHCR announced they had more money for Kosovo than they knew what to do with, such that anyone who applied for funding for any kind of project was practically guaranteed approval. I understand a stray dog project received generous funding; not an unworthy cause, but hardly a priority during an armed conflict (one Sunday morning in Cazin, after the war, around the time Silajdžić was nearly lynched, I was awoken by sporadic but sustained automatic gunfire. When I enquired of our neighbour whether the war had broken out again, he assured me it was just a "stray dog operation"). Another NGO's activities consisted of deploying Italian students to villages throughout Kosovo to act as human shields (although they were the first out when it looked like NATO was going to start bombing). As a result of this system of awarding finance, a few locals and several international subcontractors made a lot of money, while the majority of the population remained caught in the grip of a relentless depression, which did little to endear the international community to the locals, especially the Serbs. Rents suddenly went through the roof as local tenants were turned out into the street to make way for the influx of all-expenses-paid foreigners. While MSF and ICRC have significant private resources of their own and are therefore able to maintain an operational independence from the big, international donors, some smaller NGOs are almost completely dependent on institutional funding and end up being the executive agencies of the governments that bankroll them. Around this time my beautiful friendship with my contact in the security service came to an end. I called him one day, and he corrected my pronunciation of his surname, saying "Pronounced like that it's a *Šiptar* name. *Ja nisam Šiptar* ['I'm not an Albanian']". He told me he was transferring to Belgrade, and I never heard from him again. I was reminded of a security service agent who collared me once in Bucharest airport and insisted on going through all my hand luggage (I suspect because my *sumnakuno dand* ("gold tooth") was displayed). Finally, having found nothing compromising, he disclosed that he knew I was a spy from the Romanian diaspora abroad. He asked me what football team I supported, and when I told him Carlisle United, he asked me to name all the players. When I told him I couldn't, he took that to be evidence of my guilt, and just to prove the point, he then proceeded to reel off all their names himself! A few days later, on my way back out of Romania, I happened to see him again in the airport, dressed in civvies. He pretended not to recognise me, and I made no effort to renew the relationship. From then on a much more friendly, female voice, Nada ("hope"), was on the other end of my classified phone number in Kosovo.

In November, we all attended Milan's wedding to a Peć/Peja girl, Sonia, in the Priština university halls of residence where they, and Boris and Bane, lived[lxxxi]. The same month, we were invited to a meeting with another MSF team in Podgorica ("below the mountain", formerly Titograd), the capital of Montenegro, with its Albanian minority. Montenegro was an Orthodox tribal theocracy until the middle of the 19th century[335]. We decided to make a day of it, and heading north-west out of Priština and leaving Kosovo, soon reached Novi Pazar. Novi Pazar is an important crossroads on the Balkan drugs route, in the heart of the Sandžak mafia territory, where heroin from Istanbul and marihuana from Albania and Montenegro can be forwarded either via Kraljevo to Belgrade, or west to Sarajevo. From there we continued north-west before turning south at Prijepolje. We crossed the border into Montenegro at the village of Bare ("marsh") and I was amused to notice that the customs officials, as if deliberately fulfilling the national stereotype, were all sitting and lying on the lush grass by the side of the road. In the former Yugoslavia it is said that Montenegrins are all lazy, and will do anything to get forty winks. This is apparently because in their turbulent past, the women had to do all the work as the men were always either fighting or resting up[336]. When they noticed our aid vehicle, their leader jumped up and shouted "Hey, stop!". We duly complied, and presented our credentials. I enquired as to whether they were tired, said to be the traditional

---

[lxxxi] In Tajikistan, I acquired somewhat of a reputation as an after-dinner wedding speaker, after I was asked to give a speech at the wedding of the local logistician in Pendžakent. At a loss what to say, I regurgitated and reconstituted the speech given by a drunken *matičar* ("registrar") in the Kusturica film *Crna Mačka Beli Mačor* ("Black Cat White Cat"), which I happened to know more or less by heart. I simply transposed the Serbian into Russian, and threw in a few Tajik phrases for good measure, such as "*hušbaht šaved*" ("congratulations"), which went down a treat (so much so that a few weeks later, I was invited to another wedding, of people I didn't even know). Our young groom had previously worked as a cabbie in New York, but when his parents told him they had found a suitable bride for him, he was on the first plane home. He never actually met her before the wedding, although he did see (and approve of) a photo of her in advance. When I asked him what he would do if he didn't get on with her, he replied that he had confidence in his parents' choice. In 20010, the president of Tajikistan enacted a decree restricting the number of guests at weddings to 100, because in recent years there had been a trend of weddings becoming ever more elaborate and expensive, to the extent that parents were mortgaging their homes to pay for them (and then falling into arrears).

Montenegrin greeting, but failed to elicit any laughs for my trouble. From there we headed south, did a dog's leg right after Bijelo Polje ("white field"), another stop on the Balkan route, then Mojkovac, and again after Kolašin ("St. Nicholas" in Albanian), likened by Rebecca West to Cumbria[337], before heading directly south to Podgorica. Just before Podgorica, turning left from the main road at Bioče (where 47 people were killed in a rail accident in 2006), is the *mala rijeka* ("little river") bridge, the scene of many battles between the Turks and the Montenegrins before 1876, when the Montenegrins finally captured it (and the year of Custer's fateful and fatal encounter with his nemesis, the Sioux war leader Tashunca-Uitco, "Crazy Horse")[338]. Kolašin, together with Nikšić[lxxxii] to the west and Plevlja to the north, was the stronger section of the noose the *Wehrmacht* cast around Tito in the Durmitor mountains in May 1943, with Italian and Bulgarian support, in the Axis fifth offensive (*Fall Schwarz*). Durmitor was described by Rebecca West as the "great snow mountain, with a black lake at its foot"[339]. The other section of the noose, completing the encirclement, was Foča. Having learnt his lesson from Jablanica, General von Löhr was determined not to let a single Partisan escape, and slowly tightened the noose with his 120,000 men. The Partisans had 20,000 men fit for service, and several thousand wounded. Ranković described it as their darkest hour. Tito was wounded by a shell that killed a British officer. After a month of fierce fighting, the Partisans, reduced to eating their horses, broke out across the river Sutjeska in Herzegovina to the northwest, and bypassing Foča, re-entered Bosnia, having suffered 8,000 fatalities. The battle was the subject of another big-budget film, *Sutjeska*, in 1973, starring Richard Burton as Tito. After this, Tito dispersed his forces throughout the country, to avoid being caught in a similar trap again[340]. Von Löhr, who was Kurt Waldheim's commanding officer, was executed in Yugoslavia for war crimes in 1947. The Partisans had originally had major successes against the Italian occupier in Montenegro in July 1941, but by the end of that summer, the Italians had regained control of the towns, and the *Četniks* controlled the countryside. In May 1942, Tito had withdrawn the Partisans from Montenegro[341].

It was a spectacular drive. It might have been even more spectacular to have driven due west through Kosovo, crossing the Prokletije/Bjeshtët e Nëmuna ("damned mountain") national park after Peć/Peja, the highest peak of the Dinaric Alps, and then, crossing the border at Kućište ("casing"), follow country roads west to join the main road at Kolašin. Legija described Prokletije/Bjeshtët e Nëmuna as "so beautiful on the eye, and yet so savage and harsh underfoot"[342]. In 1914, the Serbs initially repelled the Austrian offensive in the north and west, from Hungary and then Bosnia, but in late 1915, the Austrians with German help succeeded in entering Vojvodina, and in November drove the Serbian army (and government) south to Novi Pazar. Meanwhile, the Bulgarians had invaded Macedonia, and then eastern Serbia. The Serbian government decided to retreat to the Adriatic coast, 150 km away, and the only path open to them was over Prokletije/Bjeshtët e Nëmuna, through northern Albania and Montenegro. As they retreated across Kosovo, they

---

[lxxxii] The last Yugoslav King, Petar Karađorđević II, flew out from Nikšić when leaving the country in 1941, and spent WWII in London, where his family moved into Claridges (it is said that in his plane he had 13 crates of gold bullion, but that only 12 arrived: the missing crate is said to be buried in a minefield outside Sarajevo, hidden in a cache of British army bully beef). After the war he moved to the USA, where he died in 1970. His remains were transferred to Serbia in 2013. His son, Prince Aleksandar, lives in London today, and in 2000, in one of his last acts, Milošević initiated the procedure that led the next year to the reinstatement of the family's Yugoslav citizenship, that had been stripped from them by Tito in 1947.

were harassed by the German air force, the first use of planes in war[343]. They had to push their artillery into the Rugovo gorge near Peć/Peja to prevent it falling into the hands of the enemy. Of the 250,000 men who set out, almost half perished on the snow-covered mountain paths, of exposure and hunger, harried by Albanians and Bulgarians. King Nikola of Montenegro, hoping to ingratiate himself with the Austrians, had ordered Montenegrins not to offer any assistance to the Serbs, before fleeing himself to France, from whence he never returned[344] (Nikola's daughter Milica, the wife of a Russian grand duke, it was who introduced Rasputin to the Tsar's wife in 1905[345]). With them the soldiers carried the mummies of their medieval kings, the Nemanjas, and their seriously ill King Petar I (suffering from rheumatism blamed on his swimming the freezing river Loire to escape capture during the Franco-Prussian War in 1870) and his son and regent Prince Aleksandar Karađorđević, the future first king of Yugoslavia, who was stricken by appendicitis. The survivors ultimately made their way to Thessaloniki, and in the autumn of 1918 returned in triumph with their British, French and Greek allies[346] (while in Thessaloniki, there was an attempt on Aleksandar's life by Apis, Ciganović's contact in the Black Hand before the war, and all the Black Hand members were executed as a result[347]). Future UN secretary general and president of Austria Waldheim was stationed near Thessaloniki when the 40-thousand-strong Jewish community there was rounded up and sent to Auschwitz over the course of three weeks in 1943. An inquiry carried out by a committee of historians later cleared him of any complicity, albeit finding that the units he served in did carry out war crimes. It was said that he was in fact suffering from the collective amnesia that affected the whole of Austria after 1945[348]. Now, however, the security situation was far from clear in the national park, and besides, one of our team was Bane, whose life it would have been reckless to risk by travelling with him through rural Kosovo, UÇK territory (one day in Priština I met an intellectual from Belgrade who was working for another NGO. He told me it was his first time in Kosovo, and he was looking forward to deploying to the field the next day, acting as an interpreter. I advised him that he would only be of use as an interpreter in the field if he spoke Albanian, which he didn't, and furthermore that if he deployed to the field at all, as a Serb he might never be seen again. The next day I heard he had gone back to Belgrade).

On 7 October 1988, there was a rally of 30,000 people in Podgorica, including 40 busloads of Milošević fans from Kosovo. Early the next morning, hearing that more enthusiasts were on the way, the local authorities, with the green light from the federal presidency, deployed riot police to disperse the rally, and blocked the accesses to the town. Milošević's attempt to seize Montenegro by force had failed[349] (the Montenegrin interior minister was later forced to resign under pressure from Belgrade because of this[350]). However, over the next three months, Milošević managed to split the Montenegrin KPJ, and introduce his own people into key positions. On 10 January 1989, there was another mass rally, calling for all government agencies to resign. The next day their numbers had grown to 100,000, and more were coming. The Montenegrin government resigned *en masse*[351].

Our hosts in Podgorica, the other MSF team, had originally deployed to Montenegro expecting an influx of refugees from Kosovo, which had not happened. They now had nothing to do, and wanted us to give them some work in Kosovo. We let them know it didn't work like that; but we nevertheless enjoyed the day out. Following the main road south from Podgorica for another 30 km, the town of Budva on the coast is reached. From there it is only 25 km north west up the coast road to the Croatian border. The coast in Montenegro is said to be even more spectacular than the Croatian coast, albeit without the islands. Alas, we did not have the time for exploring.

VJ action restarted in December, and in January, after OSCE discovered a massacre at Račak, NATO threatened Milošević with air strikes unless he agreed a peace deal[352]. The Yugoslav foreign minister wrote to the UN security council calling for an emergency session because of an "open and clear threat of aggression" by NATO, but this was opposed by the US, the UK and France[353].

Early one Sunday morning at this time, I was awakened by someone knocking on our front door. I was alert immediately. Had the *Četniks* finally tracked me down? Was this another armed robbery? Jumping out of bed, hurrying downstairs and opening the door apprehensively (and quietly, so as not to wake the rest of the team), I was surprised to see an EU bureaucrat, who told me she had a meeting with our medical director at midday, concerning the approval of a budget, and wanted somewhere to hang out until then. My response started with, and ended in "F". Almost. They're worse than Jehovah's Witnesses[lxxxiii]. On another Sunday morning, just before Christmas, I was concerned to hear the slow, regular beat of a drum advancing slowly up the hill towards our house from the town. I immediately had visions of a silent lynch mob, tired of the antics of the international community, coming to drive us out (most international organisations had let houses on the same street, in the relatively affluent Sunčani Breg/Bregu i Diellit, "Sunhill" district). Stepping outside the house to face this danger head-on, and hopefully avert it, I was relieved when a solitary Romany came into view, advancing purposely and solemnly through the area with a large bass drum that he beat every few steps, apparently signalling the first day of Ramazan, which indeed it was that day. But my relief was to be short-lived, and the lone drummer turned out to be an ominous harbinger, as he might well have been signalling another lynch mob, not directed against the international community, but by it. Since then, Tony Blair has become the most popular Briton in Albania after Norman Wisdom, and Kosovo has undergone the same ethnic cleansing and cultural vandalism as Bosnia[354]. The only difference is that, like Iraq, it is said that now Kosovo also has high levels of leukaemia due to the use of depleted uranium shells by NATO[355].

Talks touted as Dayton II started in Paris in February, dominated by the US and with the EU sidelined[356]. By this time 2,000 people had been killed in Kosovo[357]. Milošević refused to sign the deal on offer, which required "free and unrestricted access" to the whole of Yugoslavia for NATO tanks, planes and troops, and the bombing campaign (Operation Noble Anvil) started on 24 March, without authorisation from the UN security council (Russia and China had threatened to veto any resolution to that effect)[lxxxiv358]. Who needs authorisation when you're right? The

---

[lxxxiii] I was also surprised, to say the least, when visiting a village near Konjic in 1994 looking for some beneficiaries, to be offered a Bosnian copy of *Watchtower* and invited to attend the local kingdom hall. I was even more surprised four years later in Texas to be asked in Croatian, when I opened the front door to an enquiring knock, "Are you that Bosnian Muslim?" by a JW hit squad complete with interpreter. A few days later, I was asked the same question, in English, by a white American in *bedu* garb who also disturbed my peaceful enjoyment. This time I was invited to attend the local Islamic centre. Once again, the answer was a regretful "none of the above".

[lxxxiv] According to Legija, "The whole tactic [of clearing territory] was completely mistaken, and that was nothing new. It had been like that all of last year as well. We had gallivanted through the whole of Kosovo, and instead of solving the problem, we had just stoked it up. The results of last year's tactic were

leaders of the free world and their institutions and media were aligned in their support for NATO's crusade, baying for Serb blood, with the late Robin Cook the main messenger boy[lxxxv][359] (just as, today, there seems to be consensus among world leaders and the media on the need to achieve strategic objectives in Syria, i.e. get rid of Assad junior and/or terrorists, as the case may be, before bringing about peace). Milošević responded with what the Germans dubbed *Potkovica* ("Operation Horseshoe"), to ethnically cleanse the Albanians, and over 800,000 Albanians became refugees, mainly in Albania or Macedonia, but also in Montenegro[360]. The Unit drove all the Albanians out of the Peć/Peja area at the end of March (the difficult access in Prokletije/Bjeshtët e Nëmuna sometimes required deploying from Montenegro, despite the fact that Montenegro insisted it wasn't at war; but that didn't stop NATO repeatedly bombing Podgorica airport), while there was less systematic action elsewhere[361]. Many Albanians from western Kosovo crossed the border near Žur and continued on to Kukës[362]. Legija describes Peć/Peja at this time:

> "The whole town was quiet. And dark. As good as dead. In normal times, a little town like this would be bustling with life. But, what the fuck, we aren't living in normal times. Sometimes I wonder whether we will ever manage to adjust to normality, after almost a decade of madness [...] I had to ask myself whether the town had been this deserted in 1915, when the Serbian army withdrew"[363].

There were a few pockets of UÇK resistance, such as in Orahovac and in Bajgora, between Mitrovica and Podujevo/Besianë, which was (re)captured by the Unit (as were three Chechen fighters; in 1998, eight VJ soldiers had been kidnapped in Bajgora, which had been an Albanian stronghold since the miners' strike, and it was captured by the Unit), but most problematic for the VJ, apart from NATO circling overhead, were roving opportunistic UÇK gangs. The heaviest fighting on the ground was between April and June at the Košare ("baskets") border crossing, the only road leading from Albania into Kosovo between Djakovica and Peć/Peja. The UÇK wanted to secure access for a NATO ground invasion, as well as disrupt VJ communications, and more widely, to isolate Metohija. Despite suffering heavy losses in NATO air strikes and shelling from the Albanian army, in support of UÇK infantry, the VJ managed to maintain their second line of defence after losing the border watchtower[364]. On 23 April, air strikes were extended to targets within Serbia proper[365]. The VJ ordered the VRS to begin a guerrilla war in Bosnia, but they refused, as SFOR (formerly IFOR) had threatened to destroy all their weapons if they played any part in the Kosovo conflict. The VJ also sent two jets into Bosnia, but they were shot down[366]. In addition to military targets, there were air strikes against the media, and 60% of air strikes were against dual-use facilities, such as the oil

---

now beginning to show. Except that now we were at war with almost the whole world, and not just a few *Šiptar* units".

[lxxxv] Cook later resigned from the UK government over the decision to take part in Gulf War II, which kicked off on Second Bajram. Did he come to regret his martial zeal in the heady days of spring 1999? It is also said that a personal snub by Milošević at a meeting in Belgrade helped to harden the Scotch foreign secretary's heart to the Yugoslav president's appeals for reason, such as they were. The Germans also took a different view on Iraq, with the German foreign minister telling fuming US secretary of state Rumsfeld, champion of waterboarding, to "make the case" for war.

refinery at Pančevo near Belgrade[lxxxvi][367]. A refugee column near Đakovica was also hit, on 14 April, and the Chinese embassy was hit on 8 May. Gračanica monastery and the Peć/Peja patriarchate were seriously damaged. According to Human Rights Watch, the air strikes caused 500 civilian deaths. In June, the Unit withdrew to Mitrovica, where to Legija's fury, one of its members killed a Romany VJ soldier and raped his sister after carjacking them[368]. The ICTY publicly indicted Milošević for war crimes, and on 9 June, having been advised by the Russians to back down, he signed a peace agreement with NATO in Kumanovo in Macedonia - the same place where Serbia had taken possession of Kosovo in 1912 - agreeing to a UN administration of Kosovo[lxxxvii] (that day, NATO suspended air operations as a sign of good will, and the Unit took the opportunity to carry out an operation against the last stubborn pocket of UÇK resistance, near Suva Reka/Therandë ("dry river"), on the road between Priština and Prizren)[369].

This was followed up by a ground invasion on 12 June. There was panic when the Russians suddenly arrived from Bosnia and occupied Priština airport in advance of NATO, but they subsequently agreed to act as peacekeepers outside the NATO command structure, allegedly in return for being promised a blind eye would be turned to their antics in Chechnya, and having successfully reminded NATO they weren't the only players in the game[370]. Unlike the OHR in Bosnia (see below), UNMIK, the international administration in Kosovo until 2008, took over administrative functions, including policing (with one of its express ambitions being to preserve the inter-ethnic composition of Kosovo)[371]. The Albanian refugees returned from their brief exile in neighbouring countries. But UNMIK took "months" to become operational, and despite having 50,000 NATO peacekeepers ("KFOR", reduced to 16,000 by 2008 and to 4,000 by 2013), failed to provide security, as a result of which 200,000 Serbs and Romanies left Kosovo in a campaign of ethnic cleansing organised by the UÇK[372]. The murder rate was 500 per week in July 1999[373]. I have it on reliable authority that KFOR would only intervene to stop armed incidents in those areas where there was only one ethnic group; otherwise it was not regarded as policing and people were left to their own devices. Orders were to not intervene to stop pillaging or cultural vandalism, and the Serbian authorities claim that 74 churches were destroyed or vandalised[374]. In addition to violence, minorities were subject to discrimination and restrictions on movement[375]. OSCE was rewarded for its diligence with a greatly enhanced mandate (and budget)[lxxxviii][376]. The town of

---

[lxxxvi] The distinction between civilian and military targets is at the heart of IHL: pursuant to article 52(2) of Additional Protocol I to the Geneva Conventions, a dual-use object can be targeted not only if it makes an effective contribution to military action (under paragraph 3, there is a rebuttable presumption that it does not) and its destruction offers a definitive military advantage, but also that the targeting is proportional (under paragraph 5, expected civilian losses must not appear excessive compared to the military advantage), and useless destruction is also illegal. The blurring of civilian and military roles in emergencies further undermines this fundamental concept.

[lxxxvii] Legija had noted a few days earlier, "If we capitulate now, and from what I'm hearing, we probably will, then we're not worth two rolls of sheep shite as a people and a nation. We will cease to exist. It's just a matter of days [...] Everything in which we have believed, everything that has guided us all these years, will be cast into the mud and trampled by a new boot coming from the West [...] Of course, our poxy politicians will somehow manage to sugar-coat the bitter pill, dress the shit sandwich up as a club BLT, and present it to the people as a historic success". He concludes his memoirs with the comment that the Unit was "more sinned against than sinning".

[lxxxviii] OSCE's heyday was during the Cold War, when it served as an important forum allowing interaction between the US and the Soviet Union. It is said that OSCE's promotion of human rights hastened the demise of the Warsaw Pact. The organisation's motto is "From Vancouver to Vladivostok" – 7,400 km as the crow flies. Today, Kosovo is still its largest field operation.

Kosovska Mitrovica in the north, under the auspices of French KFOR, and divided by a bridge over the river Ibar, became the *de facto* border between the Serb and Albanian communities (although some Serb enclaves persisted in the interior), and was the scene of riots in 2004 and 2008. The Trepča mine, Kosovo's only source of mineral wealth (a former silver mine developed in the middle ages by German immigrants trading with Dubrovnik, closed down by the Turks but re-opened by Scots in 1930, which during WWII supplied the Reich with 40% of its lead consumption, and where miners barricaded themselves inside and went on hunger strike for a week in 1989, demanding Milošević respect home rule[377]), is located 5 km north-east of Mitrovica, i.e. in SPS territory. Of the 120,000 Serbs who remain in Kosovo, half now live in Mitrovica[378]. The six enclaves (Gračanica and Novo Brdo near Priština (UK KFOR), Parteš, Ranilug and Klokot in the south-east (US KFOR), and Štrpce in the south (German KFOR), and as well as dozens of tiny communities scattered across Kosovo[379]) were guarded by KFOR 24 hours a day, and KFOR provided armoured transport for movement from one enclave to another. But that did not prevent killings of Serbs, or killings within the Albanian community: a year later, the murder rate was five per week[380]. Kosovo quickly became Europe's crime hub, a centre for organised crime, drug smuggling and people trafficking, run *de facto* by the UÇK. Outrageously, in 2002 they even contemplated kidnapping Victoria Beckham, a UN goodwill ambassador. Incapable of delivering on their mandate, KFOR and senior UNMIK officials blocked the prosecution of UÇK members[381]. Despite this, the elections in October 2000 were won not by the former UÇK leader, Hashim Thaçi, but by Rugova[382]. Meanwhile, an Albanian insurgency persisted in Macedonia, from where attacks were also launched on southern Serbia (Preševo, Bujanovac, and Medveđa ("bear town"), part of Kosovo until after WWII), allegedly with the objective of bringing about a swap of territory for northern Mitrovica[383]. Legija deployed with the Unit from Belgrade, and the insurgency peaked in 2001, when an agreement was signed giving the Albanians more recognition in the Macedonian state[384].

NATO was originally conceived as a defensive alliance, and stuck to that role in the first years of the uncertain new world after the end of the Cold War[385]; this was its first use of military force without the approval of the UN security council, acting in its newly assumed role as victor and therefore world policeman. Ironically, NATO never made contingency plans for involvement in Yugoslavia during the Cold War[386]. The UN administration of Kosovo has been described as an "unaccountable international protectorate"[387]. It is said that in 1999, the international community made more funds available for the "post-conflict reconstruction" of Kosovo than they did for development in the whole of Africa. Carrots for the Albanians and the stick for the Serbs. 8,000 Romany IDPs were housed by UNHCR in the highly-polluted Trepča mine complex, where they remained for a decade, despite a WHO report in 2004 indicating unacceptably high levels of lead poisoning, in particular among children[388]. The UÇK, parallel to its activities as mafia *kum* ("godfather"), later provided the manpower for the bulk of the Kosovo police force, and its leaders became the new political elite, subsequently brought into the UN administration. The EU took over from the UN in 2008, with 1,200 police officers, and there are now allegations that EU officials have taken bribes to drop prosecutions for organised crime[389]. The Kosovo assembly declared independence on 17 February 2008[390]. Unemployment was 50% in Kosovo in 2008.

Part 3 – the Sava basin

As we started to approach our final destination, chugging north for the last 10 km, I started to ponder on whether any conclusions could be drawn from my first-hand experience of living and working with refugees and IDPs. Had I made a difference? Was there any point to my efforts, as personally enriching as they were? Could I and should I have done more? I looked at Seka and she smiled.

Bosnia is a country of contrasts. A country of heroes and villains, of the most generous hospitality and the most unspeakable acts of cruelty, a country of baking summers and freezing winters. It is a country of elegant women and barbarous men, of virtually zero official economic activity and a rocking night life fuelled by wandering *turbofolk* minstrels from Banja Luka, local beer, and curious cocktails, such as *bambus* ("bamboo": red wine and Coke). It is a nostalgic experience to spend the whole night in a lock-in in a country with no anti-smoking legislation or licensing laws, at least in practice[lxxxix] (I recently met a US marine in a bar in Velika Kladuša, who told me that he remembered me giving him a bar of chocolate in Kuplensko when he was a child. After a few minutes, the conversation switched from English to Bosnian, as he found my northern accent difficult to understand; he said he had had the same problem in Iraq when he deployed with some British soldiers). Bosnia is a country of four religions, one major language with three names, as well as several minority languages (the main ones being Romany and Albanian), and two alphabets (previously three) (the Bosnian Jews, present in the Balkans and in particular Sarajevo, where they dominated the fabrics trade, since their expulsion from Spain by Isabella and Ferdinand in 1492, tragically all but disappeared from the face of the earth in the 1940s, along with the Spanish dialect many of them spoke, known as Ladino[xc]. There was a second wave of Jewish migration from elsewhere in Austria-Hungary after 1878, but of 14,000 Bosnian Jews before WWII, only 2,000 survived, and most of them subsequently emigrated to Israel[391]). Despite (or perhaps because of) the tautologous plethora of labels and synonyms, Bosnia is also a country of official doublespeak, where nothing is ever what it seems, at least outside the home, while within the home the truth is spoken and family bonds constitute the very fabric of society. It is a country of inter-generational solidarity, and hidden domestic violence: *Ko voli taj se tuče* ("real men beat their women"). Bosnia has great winter sports potential (and hosted the Winter Olympics in 1984), fantastic hiking (although restricted by uncleared mines) and rafting (such as on the Neretva south of Konjic

---

[lxxxix] In Velika Kladuša, secondary schoolkids can buy their teacher a pint at lunchtime in the pub across the road from their school.

[xc] The piecemeal reconquest of Spain (and Portugal), captured by the Sultan in 711, lasted from 1064, when Pope Alexander II launched a holy war, until the year Columbus discovered America. All Muslims and Jews were expelled by the Inquisition from the newly-restored and newly-reunified Catholic state, as it embarked with confidence on a new era of conquest, unprecedented looting and genocide, in which religious extremism served as the fig-leaf for a system that prized property more highly than human life. In 1494, Pope Alexander VI divided the whole unknown world between Spain and Portugal, with the Americas (and later the Pacific) deemed Spanish, and Africa (and later Brazil, the Indian Ocean and beyond to the Philippine Sea) Portuguese. Even today, a plate of black beans and rice is known as "*Moros y Cristianos*" ("Moors and Christians") in Cuba. The Inquisition also still exists today, albeit with its powers greatly curtailed.

and on the freezing, deadly Una near Bosanska Krupa), and also has a toehold on the sunny Adriatic coast, at Neum, just down the coast from Metković (although unsuitable as a port[392]). It has imposing, dramatic gorges, such as in the Neretva valley, and splendid Turkish and Austro-Hungarian architecture. Unlike in Romania, the medieval heritage was largely spared during the communist period, but alas suffered irreplaceable loss during the 1990s. Bosnia is also a country of sophisticated urban populations and traditional rural communities. A country with a large diaspora, most of whom were forced to leave the country in this or previous wars, contrasting with those who stayed behind during the hardest times, either by choice or through the lack of choice (although since the 1970s there has also been a large diaspora made up of economic migrants in Slovenia, Austria, Germany, Switzerland and other western European countries, and there are so many ex-Yugoslavs in Vienna that I have heard it called the capital of the Balkans: certainly, Serbian/Croatian is the second language of that splendid, many-layered den of culture, vice and iniquity, capital of a country officially neutral since WWII that hosts a splendid Red Army war memorial, the bane of many a town council since[xci]). There was an increase in emigration from Yugoslavia in the 1980s, in particular from Macedonia[393], as the country began to fall apart. In Johannesburg in 2001, I was surprised to hear two girls speaking Serbian on a café terrace. In conversation with them (one was from Belgrade, the other from Macedonia), I was even more surprised to be told there were 200,000 Serbs in South Africa (although the figure of 20,000 seems more likely). In the twilight years of the *apartheid* regime, P.W. Botha welcomed white immigrants from anywhere with open arms. Subsequent events in South Africa, in particular the devaluation of the rand, led many of them to regret this move[xcii]. Every war in the Balkans, going back to 1878 and even before, has led to emigration abroad, and to a demographic shift from the countryside to the towns within Bosnia (and more widely within the former Yugoslavia), shuffling the ethnic/religious and social pack. After Bosnia was drawn into the sphere of influence of Austria-Hungary, there was an exodus of Muslims, at that time the ruling class, the feudal landowners,

---

[xci] Austria seceded from the Third Reich and restored the Dolfuss constitution in April 1945, on the eve of an Allied occupation that lasted until 1955, and it is largely thanks to this move that, unlike Germany, it avoided partition into separate Warsaw Pact and NATO entities.
[xcii] While in Johannesburg I was surprised to experience a hostility that I had not encountered anywhere else in Africa. One evening I went to a bar recommended by *Lonely Planet*. When I entered, I quickly noticed that the only other white person in the joint was the barman, a hippy, and that apart from him, everyone was studiously ignoring me. I ordered a beer, and as he served me the barman said, "You're not from round here, are you?" "No", I acknowledged. "I advise you to drink your beer and leave", he concluded. Examining the patrons while I enjoyed my cold one, I remarked that I was indeed the subject of silent hostility. Having gratified my thirst, I headed for the door; on the way, one of the punters said to me in double-Dutch, "*Ek gaan jou opvok*" ("watch your step"). I thanked him for his concern and left. Prosperous South Africa was also (and still is) a magnet for black immigration from all over southern Africa. A member of our local team in Mozambique, António, spoke excellent English, having lived in South Africa, where he told me his brother had been killed by Nelson Mandela's second wife, Winnie. Mandela's last wife, Graça Machel, was the widow of the former president of Mozambique, Samora Machel, who was killed in a plane crash in 1986. Formerly socialist Mozambique, which was racked by civil war between 1977 and 1992, when the South African-backed Renamo (*Resistência Nacional Moçambicana*) was shown the door by Cuban-backed Frelimo (*Frente de Libertação de Moçambique*), is now in the grip of relentless South African capitalism. The last time I was there, I saw a private security guard walking down a busy street in the capital one afternoon with a pump-action shotgun resting casually on his shoulder. Nevertheless, crossing the border between the two countries at Komati Poort is still a surreal experience, as one passes from one dimension to another, between the former Portuguese and British empires, between post-colonial Africa and the Boer heartland, between unruly coconut plantations and ordered orange orchards, between Portuguese and Afrikaans.

to lands still under Turkish control, including Macedonia. The Balkan Wars and WWI resulted in similar exoduses in different directions, mainly by the urban educated classes who were in a position to make the necessary arrangements, followed by a general emigration abroad from Yugoslavia in the 1920s. After WWII, many *Ustaše* and *Četniks* fled to North America and Australia, among other destinations. In 1994, there was a riot in Australia, when Serbs from Sydney clashed with Croats from Melbourne. I remember thinking at the time that if they were so patriotic, why were they so far away from the action? Each time, the gap created in the towns was filled by IDPs from the countryside, such that in less than a century Bosnia went from being a country where traditional liberal Muslims who dominated the towns held sway over Christian serfs[394], to a country of villages generally dominated by one ethnic/religious group, and towns where people of very different social backgrounds lived cheek by jowl, with little sense of continuity or stability, but also with less tendency to identify themselves by adherence to a religion. The Yugoslav Wars of the 1990s were no exception; but there is a difference in that, while in earlier times emigration was a one-way trip, now not only does modern technology allow those who have left to stay in regular and instant contact with those left behind, but they can also come back to visit with their new passports (although many waited years, and sometimes decades, before daring to return to the scene of their trauma), and in addition to the traditional remittances, they can spend their money earned abroad directly in the local economy (they can also bring with them new vices, such as hard drugs). Mirvet told me that before the economic crisis, a million US dollars per month were passing through the bureau de change in Velika Kladuša over the summer. Indeed, in many cases it is now the losers in the war, who had to seek refuge abroad, who are the winners in their new environment, which affords far more economic opportunities than are available to the victors who stayed behind. While those who remain at home adapt as times change in the country, for those in the diaspora their experience of the old country is frozen in time and transmitted as such to their descendants; but they still have a direct influence on relations in the country, not only through remittances and investment, but also by membership of and support to national cultural, sports or other associations[395] (some members of Tuđman's first government, and indeed the current Croatian prime minister, are from the diaspora, and Milošević and Izetbegović also drew from the diaspora pool when it suited them: some of the most rabid warmongers were exiles who decided to come and play warlords in the old country, buying legitimacy and confident in the knowledge that their foreign passport was effectively a "get out of jail free" card. Both Tuđman and Drašković travelled to Canada and the US in the 1980s to garner support among the *Ustaše/Četnik* diaspora respectively, and Tuđman was also received in the US congress and the state department, while Slovene separatists travelled to EU countries seeking similar support[396]). Different communities in the diaspora sometimes live in different dimensions, sharing the same space and time, but declining to acknowledge each other's existence. Under Dayton, all refugees and IDPs have the right to return home. However, this process has proved to be complex, not only because many people's original homes were destroyed or were/are occupied by someone else, often displaced themselves, but also because some local authorities, such as in Livno, Zvornik and Srebrenica, have discouraged members of other ethic/religious groups from returning[397]. The Orthodox church in Velika Kladuša received a new coat of paint on the outside several years ago, and I thought that that heralded a return of the flock (and the shepherd), but it appears to have been a false start. A Serb from Sarajevo I met in the

UK told me that several years after the war he revisited his old house armed with a British passport, only to be told in no uncertain terms by three unsavoury characters who appeared out of nowhere, not to come back. Many villages are anyway practically deserted, as has happened in the Croatian Borders, and the absence of infrastructure, as well as company, defeats the idea of any return. Bosnia is practically a failed state, and yet it is one of the coolest, most fun places to visit in eastern Europe. It is also a country of excellent food and drink, and by default rather than design what is now called "organic" agriculture, with high-quality home produce for the masses, and an undeveloped junk food industry for the elite. Bosnia is a country of absolute truths, without a functioning rail service. A country of traditional, wood-fired heating, and irritatingly small towels. It is also a country of doublethink (or even triplethink), where the patriotic mythology of the war co-exists in people's minds with the sordid reality of what actually happened. However, perhaps the biggest contrast is between the promise of peace and the failure to deliver *beričet* ("prosperity")[xciii].

The Dayton peace accords triple-locked into the constitution a dysfunctional three-headed presidency representing the three main ethnic/religious groups that, like Cerberus, produces a lot of incoherent noise, but has since proved itself incapable of governing, only perpetuating the obsession with ethnic/religious origin and identity and effectively entrenching *apartheid*. But there is no privileged ethnic/religious group here, only losers[xciv]. It also entrenched the link between territory and national identity, the very currency of the war: a game of Risk with real props[398]. The three-member rotating presidency (a Muslim, a Serb and a Croat) shares power with a council of ministers and parliament (two thirds of MPs are from the Federation, and one third from Republika Srpska). This constitutional arrangement is a compromise between Izetbegović's unitary Bosnian state, and Milošević and Tuđman's dreams of Greater Serbia and Greater Croatia: *Ne može i jare i pare* ("you can't have your cake and eat it too"). It is an illusion[399]; but an illusion that has performed its most vital function, to deliver peace (Greater Serbia and Greater Croatia have also proved to be dystopian illusions, not merely in their moral bankruptcy and political failure, but in the economic catastrophe that their beneficiaries are reaping 20 years later: any state founded on the notion of an ethnically homogenous population united on their traditional lands can never be anything but dysfunctional, and is ultimately not viable in today's globalised world. Where patriotism becomes a synonym for nationalism, all other issues are skewed by an obsession with appearances, society becomes dishonest and ceases to function, and ultimately devours itself; or, as Gandhi said, "No culture can live if it attempts to be exclusive"). The Federation and Republika Srpska also have their own devolved governments, complete with ethnic/religious quotas. All in a country two thirds the size of Alba/Scotland. The highest authority is, however, the high representative for Bosnia and Herzegovina ("OHR"), who has dictatorial powers, and is appointed by the international community. This position was created by Dayton and, like UNHCR and UNMIK, is not accountable to the

---

[xciii] Asked in 1995 by a group of ABiH soldiers what they could expect after the war if they survived, Izetbegović replied, "Injustice and penury [...] the only rights you'll have will be those you take yourselves". *Neće jezik nego pravo* ("straight from the horse's mouth").
[xciv] Partition is anyway a pervasive aspect of life in the Balkans, and all roles are strictly delineated: man/woman, adult/child, joke/insult, educated/uneducated, family by blood or water/stranger, host/guest, inside and outside of the home, believer/infidel, local/foreigner, clean/unclean, even as, in the civilised world, the barriers of gender itself are being abolished. Removing your shoes when entering a home is a very civilised custom that is a general rule throughout the Balkans, not just in Muslim households.

people it purports to serve. Its mission has been "peacebuilding", which is taken to mean reconciliation and reconstruction[400]. I recently caught sight of the current incumbent's New Year's message to the Bosnian people on television. Pompous and patronising, sporting the appropriate OSCE and EU logos, it somehow lacked the majesty and legitimacy of the Queen's Christmas message. He recently boasted to Mirvet that his house in Austria had been built by a contractor from Bihać. I have heard it said that Bosnia, with all its government structures and attendant personnel in triplicate, has the largest number of officials *per capita* in the world, which absorbs an inordinate share of the country's modest budget. MPs' salaries are six times the national average[401]. In 2009, further to a challenge by two minority MPs, a Romany and a Jew, who claimed that the institution of the presidency was discriminatory because it excluded ethnic groups other than the "constituent peoples", the European Court of Human Rights ruled that Bosnia would have to change its constitution[402]. The Romany community (or at least their patriarchal *šerutne*, "leaders") now want the quota system to be extended to include the minorities, with all the attendant bureaucratic baggage that entails (is that any more absurd than enlargement of the European Union? Now the EU wants its own army as well. While that might make perfect sense in the rarefied logic of the virtual, technocratic elephants' graveyard currently at the head of Europe, it will only lead to more massacres of the innocent when it fails to deliver on the ground). Yet despite its faults, there is a reluctance to revisit the Bosnian constitution for fear of opening another Pandora's box that could lead to the country unravelling altogether (the constitution is Annex IV to the Dayton peace accords, which do not allow for amendments, such that any change to any part of the constitution would theoretically annul the whole peace agreement[403]). Milorad Dodik, who has been the dominant force in Republika Srpska since 2006, and who Izetbegović hailed in 1997 as the "first sane Serb" in politics, has been calling for a referendum on the constitution since the mid-2000s, which frequently sets off alarm bells, usually at election time[xcv][404]. Dodik's stated aim is to secede from Bosnia and bring about an *Anschluss* ("annexation") with Serbia – during the 2010 European Cup tournament, he openly stated that he was supporting Serbia and not Bosnia. Meanwhile, the governments of both Croatia and Serbia are using their good offices - Croatia within the EU and NATO - to bring pressure to bear in an attempt to force a revision of the Dayton constitution. The pathological ethnic/religious introspection also extends to language, with the various entities introducing "new" standard versions of the language to be spoken there, with varying degrees of success. The warning *"pušenje ubija"* ("smoking kills") is printed in triplicate on Bosnian cigarette packets, as it is identical in all three dialects (albeit written in Cyrillic in Serbian). Not that anyone appears to pay any attention to it. Here again, nationalists reach back into the distant past to justify their present-day anality: one of the main differences in pronunciation between Serbian on the one hand, and Bosnian and Croatian on the other, can be traced back to the 1850 Vienna agreement between Vuk Karadžić and the Illyrian movement on standardisation of the literary language, which was rejected by the Serbian Orthodox church. Official language policy has always affected the way

---

[xcv] At the time of local elections in Bosnia in 2016, I heard the fear expressed by several well-informed locals that Dodik, supported by the VJ, was preparing to set up army checkpoints at strategic points along the border between the Federation and Republika Srpska. There was conjecture that this would result in a deployment by the HV from Croatia along the same border, as a "humanitarian action" to protect the Muslims, and that once installed, the Croatians would never leave. The annexation of Bosnia by Serbia and Croatia would thus be *de facto* complete.

people speak, and excluded some dialects in favour of the "norm", as in medieval France, as a way of consolidating and uniting national identity; but it is generally a secular endeavour, and not one to be imposed overnight on ever-decreasing pieces of territory and communities as a means of division. On my first day in Slunj, awaiting my visa for West Bosnia, I went out and bought some bread. There didn't seem to be much else on sale in the supermarket, and as an afterthought I asked for a *vrećica* ("carrier bag"), as I had learnt in central Bosnia. "We say *kesa* here" I was told[xcvi]. The politically and culturally-charged complexities of labelling the various quasi-dialects can be and often are body-swerved by simply referring to them all as *naš* ("our language"); similarly, the Gordian knot of ethnic labels, a potential minefield, can be severed at a stroke by simply saying *naš narod* ("us"): common sense will always prevail in everyday life, no matter how convoluted and oppressive official policy, like a tree root pushing up a pavement to the chagrin of council bureaucrats. It is said that two million "old" and "inappropriate" books belonging to public institutions were pulped in Croatia during the war, while over a million books, including priceless medieval manuscripts, were destroyed in the burning of the Sarajevo library in August 1992. *S magarca na jarca* ("out with the old, in the with new")[405]. In the former Yugoslavia, the foreign language taught in schools was formerly Russian, superseded in the 1980s by German. However, after the war, in SDA areas, this was replaced by Arabic - not one of the versions of modern Arabic, but Kuranic Arabic, which, like Latin, is only spoken by religious scholars. Now this has at least been replaced by English.

The pre-war constitution also provided for government by consensus between the three largest groups. In the single-party system, the Bosnian rotating presidency was made up of seven members, two from each of the three main groups and one "other", while the elected members of public institutions and local authorities had to reflect the ethnic/religious make-up of the local community. Attempts in the 1980s to deal with the political crisis developing out of the growing economic crisis failed to introduce any democratic reforms, opening the door to the debate on "national" (i.e., ethnic/religious) political change rather than on reforms for the individual man in the street[406] (in 1986, Yugoslavia's foreign debt was USD 19.7 billion, almost the same as it had been five years earlier, despite payments of USD 28.3 billion to service the debt over that period. In 1988 it was decided to adopt a free market economy[407]). As the KPJ itself finally fragmented into national factions, and power shifted from the federation to its component parts, by the mid-1980s only the ghost of Tito and the JNA held the country together[408] (in 1982, when one of its delegates was not voted onto the KPJ federal executive, the Serbian KPJ threatened to break away, something unheard of since 1937. The chairman of the session backed down, a re-vote was held, and the unpopular delegate got his post. The following day, the leadership of the Serbian KPJ, including new kid on the block Milošević, overwhelmingly endorsed the move[409]). The KPJ, which had been the real seat of power during Tito's lifetime and had since gradually withered on the vine, was also intrinsically corrupt (by 1983, Dizdarević noted that the KPJ had "fallen into mission creep and creative

---

[xcvi] Perhaps ironically, *kesa* is a Turkish word. After the war, Tetin was tasked by Babo to set up a warehouse operation in Croatia. In Lika, he attempted to buy a *teka* ("notebook") in a local shop for his records. "We say *sveska* here" he was told. In Istria, he attempted to buy a *sveska*, only to be referred to a *bilježnica* ("notebook"). In Šibenik, he asked for a *bilježnica*, only to be informed that *teka* was the correct term. In the charming resort town of Opatija ("abbey"), also in Istria, he said he was looking for a certain item, that consisted typically of bound ruled pages, but that he didn't know what it was called. "It's all Greek to me", the shopkeeper replied, "I'm from Banja Luka!"

stagnation"[410]). Those who had rendered services to Tito during the early days were guaranteed comfortable jobs for life, as were their extended families (where such families fell from grace, removing them from their position at the centre of a complex web of intersecting power relations could have far-reaching and destructive consequences, as was the case with the Pozderaces). Fitzroy Maclean described Tito's inner circle in 1943, that included Kardelj, Ranković and Đilas:

> "all of them, young and old, men and women, intellectuals and artisans, Serbs and Croats, had been with him in the woods from the early days of the resistance, sharing with him hardships and dangers, setbacks and successes. This common experience had overcome all differences of class or race or temperament and forged between them lasting bonds of loyalty and affection"[411].

Đilas was later defrocked from the KPJ for publicly criticising Yugoslavia's new privileged elite. In sharp contrast to the heroic exploits of this band of brothers (and sisters) forged in the fires of Hitler's Europe (and even before: Tito's true inner circle had been underground communist activists with him before the war), after WWII this system of patronage only added to the economic inefficiency of the state, and preserved an institutional status quo and political elite beyond its sell-by date[412] (Tito's final initiative to introduce single, one-year mandates for all leading political and economic posts was implemented posthumously, with mixed results and resistance in particular from Slovenia and Serbia; the objective was to forestall power struggles, and at the same time allow new blood into the upper echelons, but an unforeseen consequence was stagnation and the hamstringing of individual initiative. Western analyses of Yugoslavia in the early 1980s noted a crisis of decision-making systems and efficiency at federal level, as well as a dangerous potential for inter-ethnic conflict[413]). In any case, the KPJ had only ever been a fig leaf for an arbitrary power structure that wasn't above resorting to the services of the underworld to achieve its ends (as Lord Owen put it, "Tito had spawned mechanisms for inertia and then filled the vacuum with his own initiatives")[414]. Tito once said, "*Nećemo se valjda pridržavati zakona k'o pijan plota*" ("we can't cling to the law like a drunk clinging to a fence"). The former Bosnian interior minister Uglješa Danilović explained it in 1990 from his retirement in Dubrovnik:

> "At that time [the 1950s], the agencies of defence of the revolution – the interior ministry, the prosecution and the judiciary, worked separately but as one, as agencies of defence of the revolution. Other state agencies also worked at that time as agencies of the revolution, albeit based on statutes and provisions adopted by the elected agencies of government (parliament, the government, and the district councils). They all worked according to a single plan, provided by the KPJ based on its moral and political authority. The most important decisions were taken by the leadership of the KPJ or the republican party leaderships, and were implemented by the direct action of the members of those leaderships or KPJ members in the elected agencies of government"[415].

The KPJ's last real act, the party conference of January 1990, in the midst of the velvet revolutions, failed to adopt proposals by the Slovenes for reform, which could have led to a functioning multi-party system, and might have allowed Yugoslavia to continue in a modernised and less centralised form. Faced with Milošević's stone-walling, the Slovenes and Croats walked out of the conference (according to Milošević, the thrifty Slovenes had already checked out of their hotels that morning), and the competing nationalisms meant the resulting crisis of communism was not dealt with by reform or peaceful disintegration, as it was in Czechoslovakia and the Soviet Union[416] (Milošević and his stooge in Montenegro, Bulatović, attempted to continue with the conference as if nothing had happened[417]). In June 1990, the ban on parties with an ethnic/religious agenda was lifted by the Bosnian constitutional court, and in the elections at the end of that year, the nationalist parties, the SDA (founded in May 1990, before the lifting of the ban, and two years after Izetbegović was released from prison, where he had had plenty of time and company with which to plan his political strategy[418]), SDS (Karadžić's party, founded in July 1990 as a branch of the Knin party) and HDZ (a branch of Tuđman's party, created just after the SDS, and led by Boban[419]), won almost 90% of seats, and filled the presidency. The "other" member of the presidency in 1990 was a Muslim Yugoslav, Ejup Ganić, from Sandžak. Izetbegović became president of the coalition government, despite winning fewer votes than Babo, and Ganić soon became his *de facto* deputy (Izetbegović explained the coalition agreement thus: "In five minutes we agreed to take power from the Communists, that the prime minister would be from the HDZ, the president from the SDA, and the speaker of parliament from the SDS")[420]. The only real alternatives for voters were the KPJ (discredited by the Agrokomerc affair, and in a state of collapse by the time of the elections, even though it had 2 million members[421]) and prime minister Ante Marković's reformist party, founded in July 1990 to build a new Yugoslavia, with a focus on stabilising the economy and integrating into the European mainstream to counter domestic nationalism. It had been founded too late to stand in the elections in Slovenia and Croatia, which not only restricted its potential, but also led to accusations that it was anti-Serb[422] (and despite initial successes in his reforms, by July the economy was struggling again. The situation was not helped when, as a result of Gulf War I, Iraqi and Kuwaiti companies failed to make payments to Yugoslavia worth USD 1 billion. Nor was any real support offered by European and international institutions[423]). Despite his popularity, Marković was overthrown by an unholy alliance of the republican leaders who were intent on destroying the country[424]. Rather than act as a coalition for the good of the country (in marked contrast to their united front against the KPJ and Marković), the new ruling parties cast every issue in ethnic/religious terms[425], and quickly took over all the local councils in Bosnia, with the exception of Tuzla and Vareš. It has been argued that, like Brexit, this election result was not a reflection of the fact that the people wanted war, but simply because the nationalist parties were the only alternative to the status quo[426][xcvii]. It is certainly the case that the former political and institutional system with the political monopoly of the KPJ was unable to digest the issues raised by nationalism[427]. On the contrary, such issues were politicised by a self-serving elite, at the helm of a bureaucracy "ill-suited to

---

[xcvii] As usual in Bosnia, the comic side of their tragedy was not lost on the locals. I was told this joke by Mirsad in Kuplensko:
"Mujo went to work on election day, and told Fata to make sure she voted for Grandad Alija. 'But I've never voted before', protested Fata, 'how will I know what to do?' 'Just put your mark beside his initials, SDA', Mujo reassured her. 'But what if I forget?' Fata persisted. 'Just remember: *Seks Do Akšama* ['sex til dusk']', Mujo instructed her. That evening when he came home, he asked her whether she had managed to vote. 'Nothing simpler', she told him. 'I found that SDA, but there was another, even better one.' 'Which one?' Mujo asked, alarmed. '*Seks Do Sabaha* ['sex til dawn']', Fata proudly replied".

compromise and convergence" (according to Crnobrnja), despite the fact that the experience of pre-WWII Yugoslavia had shown that any attempt to run a single state without taking account of ethnic/religious diversity was doomed to failure[428].

Like the KPJ before them, the new nationalist parties, while rallying people around religious identity, swiftly took control of intellectual circles, the media and organised crime to consolidate their grip on all aspects of life[429] even as, Franco-like, they each attempted to establish loose dictatorships embracing the institutions of respectable, patriotic life, i.e. the armed forces, church/mosque, and civic institutions. Thus can democracy conceal totalitarian regimes. However, unlike the diminutive Galician, said to have been a master tactician despite his ignorance of all things non-military, Karadžić, Boban and Izetbegović quickly found themselves out of their depth, as the loyalty of these patriotic pacts proved to be elsewhere[430]. While the first two ineluctably fell into the orbit of Milošević and Tuđman respectively, Izetbegović, like Basaev, was beholden to more obscure paymasters. Meanwhile, Bosnian and former Yugoslav intellectuals have generally still not recovered from their shameful mass rallying to the various nationalist causes at the end of the 1980s, and their direct contribution to the violence that followed[431]. A notable exception is the archbishop of Bosnia, Vinko Puljić, who, to the chagrin of the HDZ in Herzeg-Bosna, advocated Bosnian unity and identity[432] (in the run-up to WWII, the pro-Italian and anti-Communist Vatican played a role in fanning Croat nationalism, and after the formation of the NDH, the archbishop of Zagreb stated that the "long-awaited dream of the Croatian people has come true". Pope Pius XII met Pavelić twice during WWII, and is said to have supported his policy of forced conversions[xcviii433]). Alas, Patriarch Pavle of the Serbian Orthodox Church actively supported the SDS/SPS during the wars. He had to be evacuated from the Peć/Peja patriarchate by KFOR in June 1999. As they say in the Balkans, "*Hodže i popovi najveći lopovi*" ("religion is the heroin of the masses"). According to Andrić, in Sarajevo the "fury of hate [was] husbanded for centuries by various religious institutions, favoured by climatic and social conditions, and bolstered by history"[434]. The media played an equally shameful, and more directly destructive role in the build-up to and conduct of the war, entrenching in people's minds the distinction between "us" and "them"[435]. Following the lead of the political leaders, they peddled false accusations, and were not averse to barefaced lies. In August 1991, identical footage of corpses being loaded onto a truck was used by both Belgrade and Zagreb to denounce each other's war crimes[436]. Throughout the former Yugoslavia, state and private media echoed and amplified the local political discourse and symbols[437]. The adjectives "Serb" and "Croatian" were, and still are, applied obsessively and apparently indiscriminately across the board to institutions, events, personalities, inanimate objects and natural phenomena. This was mimicked by the SDA with the term "*Bošnjak*" (see below), and from the height of the HVO-ABiH war in 1993 onwards, media controlled by Izetbegović demonised Babo as a national enemy[438]. In this way, the media prepared the population for total war by radicalising them with a barrage of misinformation and fear-mongering[439]. Belgrade television was controlled by Milošević from as early as 1987, and became his most powerful weapon[440]. In 1999, NATO bombed RTS (Serbian broadcasting corporation), claiming it was a legitimate target. Meanwhile, the western media shaped, and was driven by, western perceptions (as well as western policy[441]), on the one hand simplistic, and on the other missing the blatantly obvious. In 1992, UK prime minister John Major (and

---

[xcviii] According to George Orwell, in Spain "the [...] church was part of the capitalist racket".

former POW French president Mitterrand, of Operation Turquoise fame) saw the Yugoslav Wars as the necessary expression of "ancient hatreds", rather than a simple criminal racket[442]. Cameron, a PR man, takes a similarly simplistic and blinkered approach to the problem of radicalisation today. While there is no more potent smokescreen than religion, because whoever hides behind it wields the power of God, crime is crime is crime. Organised crime has been endemic in the Balkans since before the war, and the term "Balkan route" has been current in international political jargon since the 1990s to describe the preferred path for the illicit movement of drugs and people from the Middle East to western Europe. The most visible manifestation of this commerce is people trafficking, and there were Chinese people transiting in small groups in and around Velika Kladuša for at least 10 years up until Croatia's accession to the EU in 2013, when border controls became stricter. They even opened a shop in the town centre. As a local *pendrek-efendija* ("policeman") in Velika Kladuša once told me, it was very difficult to check them, because their appearance is often alike to Balkan eyes, and hard to compare with the photos on documents, and also because the documents themselves were written mostly in Chinese and therefore meaningless for all intents and purposes. Ostensibly for that reason alone, the migrants were generally just waved through. Meanwhile, heroin from Iran and Pakistan arrives in Serbia from Istanbul, from where it is transported either directly by road to Austria and Switzerland, or (to a lesser extent, due to the poor state of the roads) through Sandžak to Bosnia and beyond. However, drugs and people are not the only commodities to be moved via the Balkan route.

The nationalist parties who won the first post-war elections in 1996 have dominated politics in the Federation ever since, except in 2000-2002 when the multi-ethnic Social Democrats had a parliamentary majority, while in Republika Srpska Dodik's party, the SNSD, eclipsed the SDS with a more pragmatic form of nationalism in 2006[443]. Any efforts at cross-community cooperation are stymied by the constitutional architecture, although the *Naša stranka* ("our party") coalition of civil society groups created in 2008 seeks to break the dominance of the nationalist parties (one of their MPs recently submitted a motion to parliament to discuss the problem of emigration out of Bosnia, a national crisis)[444]. Meanwhile, cultural exchanges between the former Yugoslav countries resumed after only a few years, and cross-community cultural life is now as vibrant as it ever was[445]. Also common to them all are the social and economic problems that are crippling the Balkans, identical in all but degree, and underpinned by pseudo-democracy, rampant corruption and systematically plundered economies.

Bosnia is also a country in search of an identity. Much was made at the beginning of the war of "ancient" and "tribal" hatreds that inevitably reared their heads after the communist muzzle was removed, like a force of nature (Owen states that "...in the Balkans [...] history pervades everything")[xcix][446]. This simplistic, naïve and ignorant approach effectively hobbled international diplomacy, and obscured the real, criminal nature of the war. Interpreting the past using contemporary categories is a trap many commentators have fallen into when attempting to explain the Yugoslav Wars, and the reverse is also true (it is also a powerful strategy for convincing the public of the need to go to war)[447]. The construction and redefining of

---

[xcix] This is not incorrect *per se*, and many ex-Yugoslavs have a pedantic knowledge of their history (or at least one version of it, grounded as much in oral tradition as in the competing official narratives), but the historical discourse was peddled by the media as a key plank of the various parties' smoke and mirrors approach to communication, and was consequently blown out of all proportion.

identities was a deliberate process in the Yugoslav Wars, and belonging and the threat of not belonging became the central political discourse of the war[448]. The debate on whether Bosnia is no-man's land between Serbia and Croatia, or whether it should exist in its own right, goes back to the creation of the first Yugoslavia in 1918, and continued through the interwar years into the communist period. While Bosnia maintained its territorial integrity throughout most of this time, the question never went away, mainly due to the pernicious influence of its two neighbours. The cumbersome full title of "Bosnia and Herzegovina" was often reduced in Yugoslav political discourse to "BiH" (pronounced "bey-ha"), and this abbreviation has permeated many other areas of life. However, the reduction of a complex manifestation of human existence to a two-syllable tag, a widespread phenomenon in Soviet political discourse that still thrives in contemporary Russian (such as "*SKFO*" for the North Caucasus, or "*Sredazija*" for Central Asia), may have also served to diminish the idea of Bosnia as a country in its own right, especially when placed alongside its two neighbours, whose names are rarely abbreviated, and correspond to the majority ethnic/religious groups who live there (the same applies to "Kosmet" or "KiM", the abbreviation of Kosovo and Metohija, and "APV" for Vojvodina, not to mention FYROM; and "RH" is occasionally used for Croatia)[449]. Even before WWI, Serbia and Croatia had largely succeeded in appropriating Orthodox and Catholic Bosnians respectively to their causes, persuading them to regard themselves not as Bosnians, but as Serbs or Croats, and that will always be a problem as long as Bosnia's neighbours are more prosperous, and can hold out a better standard of living as a prize[450]. Indeed, the modern notion of nationhood began to spread from Croatia and Serbia to Bosnia in the mid-nineteenth century[451]. In 1844, future Serbian PM Ilija Garašanin set out the idea of a single state comprising all Serb lands and extending to the Adriatic in his secret document, the *Načertanije* ("outline"), and the idea of Greater Serbia has been a recurrent fixture of Serbian state policy ever since (at that time, the main obstacles were seen to be the Ottomans, the Habsburgs and Russia, i.e. external factors, while the Bosnian Muslims were regarded as apostate Serbs, to be simply brought back into the fold)[452]. Several current Croatian and Serbian politicians are of Bosnian origin: Serbian PM Vučić, Serbian opposition leader Drašković, former Croatian PM Milanović, who recently referred to the state of Bosnia as a "big shit", mayor of Zagreb Bandić, mayor of Belgrade Đilas, former Serbian president Tadić, and high-profile Serbian politician Jovanović, while former Serbian foreign minister Jeremić is Nurija Pozderac's great-grandson[453]. The argument of continuity has been used to justify both Greater Serbia and Greater Croatia; for better or for worse, it can certainly be used to justify the aspiration for a single Bosnian state[454]. Bosnia was originally an independent kingdom, with its own writing and even its own church, known as the Bogumils, until it was conquered by the Turks in 1463[455]. In the period prior to that, the Bosnian King Tvrtko was the regional strongman, and crowned himself "King of the Serbs, Bosnia, Dalmatia, and the Croats"[456]. Recent studies suggest that the Bosnian church was not in fact part of the heretical Bogumil sect, which originated in Bulgaria in the 10th century, but that the Bosnian Catholic church had merely drifted, acquiring certain Orthodox and other practices. It had been cut off from Rome since the mid-thirteenth century when the Bosnian bishopric was moved from Dubrovnik to Hungarian Slavonia. In 1459, King Stjepan Tomaš, looking for papal support against the Turks, gave the clergy the choice of conversion to true Catholicism or exile to Orthodox Herzegovina (the vast majority chose the former)[457]. The weak state of organised religion in this isolated, inaccessible territory, aggravated as it was by competition between the Catholic and

Orthodox clergy, was a major factor in the subsequent mass islamisation of the population, and rivalry between the two churches for spiritual dominion among the Christians continued into the 19th century[458]. Meanwhile, traditional practices and superstitions continued unchanged, regardless of nominal religious affiliation[459]. The Ottoman system of government devolved certain powers and autonomy to religious leaders over their respective flocks, which may have contributed to the entrenchment of national identities as the rival shepherds jealously penned up their human livestock[460]. Nevertheless, a separate Bosnian identity subsisted right through the Ottoman period. There was a joint Serb-Muslim rebellion in eastern Herzegovina in 1881-1882 against the introduction of national service by the Habsburgs, which was put down after four months of heavy fighting. Despite this initial resistance, the Austrian governor Benjamin Kallay, whose mandate lasted from 1882 to 1903, fostered the multi-confessional Bosnian identity free of the influence of Croatia and Serbia (although the Habsburgs also cultivated the former ruling class, the Muslims, as the Belgians did in Rwanda)[461]. He oversaw the transition from military to civilian government, and succeeded in turning Bosnia into a fully-fledged Habsburg province. He invested in an ambitious public works programme, and provided Bosnia with a developed road and rail infrastructure. He also ensured the adoption of the Latin and Cyrillic writing standards that had been developed by Vuk Karadžić, as a means to facilitate communication between the different communities. Kallay, who had previously been the Austrian consul in Belgrade, had set himself the task of civilising the oriental Bosnians with a view to their ultimate annexation to prevent the emergence of a large South Slav state[462]. According to Rebecca West, perhaps the Habsburgs' greatest mistake was to come to Sarajevo to teach, and not to learn[463]. In 1918, as the Austro-Hungarian authorities attempted to cobble together a new constitution that would allow their survival, the Serbs and Croats in Sarajevo came up with a joint memorandum, stating they were one people and calling for the creation of a Yugoslav state, while the Muslims were also in favour of a South Slav state[464]. During the communist period, Tito's policy of brotherhood and unity[c][465], seeking to create a new identity, Yugoslav, and relegate religious differences to mere traditions, was partly successful, and led to many mixed marriages, in particular among Christians. According to the 1991 census, 16% of Bosnian children were from mixed marriages (Cerić later described mixed marriages as a "blasphemous act")[466]. Religion was not repressed, as in other communist countries, nor was there persecution of or interference in religious worship. Light touch regulation appeared to be the norm in most areas of life, with the exception of anything with a whiff of nationalism that might threaten to undermine brotherhood and unity. In such cases, the UDBA would bear down swiftly like a ton of bricks. Tito once said, "*Mi smo more krvi prolili za bratstvo i jedinstvo naših naroda*" ("we shed a sea of blood for brotherhood and unity in Yugoslavia"). For a time, protected from Serbian and Croatian nationalism, a newly rediscovered Bosnian identity started to flourish[467]. But interests in Serbia and Croatia were jealous of this new independence and determined to bend it to their own devices[468]. In his last speech in Bosnia in 1979, Tito said,

> "…in the post-war period, there were occasional manifestations of tutelage in respect of Bosnia and Herzegovina emanating from certain circles outside of

---

[c] After the death of Tito, there was disagreement on the very definition of unity: monolithic or democratic?

it. Behind this tutelage were in fact attempts at usurpation; the denial of Bosnian statehood and the undermining of its independence".

After the meeting, he warned the Bosnian leaders not to "relax their vigilance" against "any attempts by brokers to disrupt inter-ethnic relations in Bosnia and Herzegovina", which "would not only harm Bosnia and Herzegovina, but have a negative effect on the whole union"[469].

The Mrkonjić-Grad resistance resolution of 1943 had stated that,

"The peoples of Bosnia and Herzegovina [...] want their country, which is neither Serb, nor Croat, nor Muslim, but Serb and Croat and Muslim, to be a free, twinned Bosnia and Herzegovina, in which the full equality and equal rights of all Serbs, Croats and Muslims are guaranteed"[470].

The recognition of Muslims as a Yugoslav nation in the 1963 constitution appeared at first sight to be a half-measure in the right direction for the consolidation of Bosnian identity; but it turned out to be a poisoned chalice. Not only was there a failure to create an inclusive Bosnian identity, but it entrenched the divisions between the ethnic/religious groups. An emerging Bosnian identity was starved once again of oxygen by the label of religion[471]: Bosnian identity came to be synonymous with Islam, and by definition excluded the divided Christian minority (the 2013 census, the first since the war, revealed the population of Bosnia to be made up of 50% Muslims, 31% Serbs and 15% Croats. The 4% "others", whose density is highest in Tuzla, represent not only Romanies, Albanians, Jews and Montenegrins, but also Serbs, Croats and Muslims who rejected categorisation by their ethnic/religious heritage. The census also revealed that the total population of Bosnia has dropped from 4.4 million in 1991 to 3.5 million[472]). In Bosnia as elsewhere in Yugoslavia, national identity was hijacked by force by the extremist political parties that took the place of the defunct KPJ, and became a means to gaining and wielding power as the new political parties rallied people around religious identity[473]. The nationalist crisis unleashed when Milošević, the first to discover Tito was dead, opened Pandora's box with his Field of Blackbirds speech in 1987, when he changed ideology and identity from communist functionary to nationalist rabble-rouser, anathema to KPJ orthodoxy (on 16 July 1990, the Serbian communist party changed its name to the SPS and elected Milošević as its leader[474]), and which was eagerly, albeit belatedly, echoed by Tuđman, led to a new identity crisis in Bosnia[475]. The link between identity, majority, territory and security was the underlying basis for Milošević's rhetoric on Croatia in 1990[476]. While the Orthodox and Catholic communities in Bosnia had a ready-made identity and a big brother they could draw on for succour, and for political direction, for the Muslims the situation was more complex. In response to the centrifugal pressure from their neighbours, in 1993 they started to call themselves *Bošnjaks*, the "true Bosnians" (or rather, the government in Sarajevo started to call them that, and officially adopted the term at the first assembly of Zulfikarpašić's Bosnian intellectuals on 27 September, the same day Babo proclaimed his autonomous region; although unlike Babo's initiative, there was no public consultation or parliamentary participation in this constitutional amendment[477]). The term implies that they are more Bosnian than their Christian compatriots, even though they were Christians themselves in the past, and even though there are still many Orthodox and Catholic Bosnians who do not wish to see their country partitioned between their two larger neighbours. Indeed, Bosnian Serbs and Croats who travel to Serbia or Croatia respectively, are immediately recognised and regarded as such, and are often viewed as second-class citizens, if not with outright suspicion. Perhaps if the term had not been misappropriated by Izetbegović it could have served as a new label of Bosnian identity, free of religious connotations, completing the process begun in 1963 and consolidated in the 1974 constitution[478]. And yet, the term has not been universally accepted among Muslims because of its extremist connotations, and has become another divisive label. The Muslims are now the last of the true Yugoslavs, in danger of extinction. The importance of labels in the project of appropriating votes and then assimilating territory (and in the process dividing communities and society) cannot be overestimated in Bosnia: membership or not of a group determined friend and enemy, member of the majority or a minority, resident and outsider, and persons with or without rights, with the same precision as Hitler's race laws. In Croatia, Serb or Croat; in Bosnia, Serb, Croat or Muslim; and in Kosovo, Serb or Albanian. All these categories can be further subdivided into "patriots" and "traitors", depending on the extent to which an individual subscribed to the respective party's programme: in Croatia, SDS or HDZ; in Bosnia, SDS, HDZ or SAD (and 5th Corps or NOZB). This game goes back to the KPJ (member or not), and it was well understood by the criminals who divided Yugoslavia up amongst themselves[479]. It is simply a mechanism to allow a minority to control the majority. Andrić describes the crackdown after the Sarajevo assassination in *The Bridge on the River Drina*:

"People were separated into the hunted and the hunters. The ravenous beast that lives in man and dares not show itself until someone removes the barriers of good customs and laws, was now released. The starting signal had been given, and the barriers removed. As often happens in human history, violence and looting, and even murder, were tacitly permitted, provided they were carried out in the name of higher interests, with established keywords, against a restricted group of people, with a certain name and convictions. Anyone alive at that time with a level head and his or her eyes open was able to witness this miracle at work, how a whole society can be transformed in a single day. Within the space of a few moments, the community, based on centuries-old tradition, within which there had always existed suppressed hatred, and envy and religious intolerance and consecrated coarseness and cruelty, but also humanity and charity, a sense of order and measure, a sense that held all those evil instincts and coarse habits within tolerable bounds, and ultimately subdued them and subjected them to the common interest and co-existence, was wiped out. People who had been authorities in the community for 40 years disappeared overnight, as if they had all suddenly died together with their customs and knowledge and the institutions they personified [...] The community was filled with confused movement and silent conspiracy"[ci][480].

[ci] As Legija put it, "That's the dark side of war, in which the evil soul of man reigns and holds sway. Then each one of us has to resist and choose whether to yield to the dark forces that tempt every soul, or whether honour and goodness will prevail. For war is evil work, in which every man, every living soul, falls into temptation: which side to choose. Not everyone can resist the feeling of power, the feeling of for a moment becoming the lord of life and death. It's very difficult, because power is the most potent aphrodisiac, even if it is only momentary and short-lived. All the crimes, misfortunes and horrors in all wars arise from that feeling. War is simply a different dimension in which not everyone can find their way. It's a vice into which it is easy to fall, and then there are no limits. It is an abyss from which it is

According to Dizdarević, people were ready to accept this process both because they were disoriented and confused by tumultuous events, and because they were culturally prepared to do so[481] (the same psychological process can be observed in airport security today, throughout the western world. Passengers' stress levels are raised by the mild harassment of uncouth and obtuse staff, so that the knowledge that you are a *bona fide* passenger, in full possession of all the requisite documentation, safely one of "us", becomes a source of comfort and relief. This means there is little sympathy for anyone who falls foul of the accepted norms, and is singled out for special treatment. A few years ago, I saw an elderly Romany couple made to conspicuously stand apart and wait while all the other passengers filed past them at Zagreb *zračna luka* ("airport"). I spoke to the *Rrom* ("man") later on, and he seemed none the worse for his humiliation). The new nationalisms, as political ideologies, had to impose new sources of legitimacy for their power, new forms of loyalty to their leaders, and new mechanisms for the creation and reorganisation of their states[482]. It was and still is the practice to include a person's ethnic/religious background in their ID documents, including their passport (as it was in the Soviet Union, and in Rwanda); before the war, the holder could also choose Yugoslav instead of Serb, Croat, or Muslim, and in the 1991 Bosnian census, 5.5% of people identified themselves as Yugoslavs (now, people have the option to identify themselves as "Bosnians")[483]. Meanwhile, the term *Bošnjak* has also been adopted, at least officially, by the Muslim minorities in Serbia, Croatia and Montenegro, thus cementing the SDA's reach beyond the borders of Bosnia and Herzegovina.

But even the question of what is to be the basis of Bosnian Muslim identity has still not been resolved: is it to be the traditional, pragmatic, secular doctrine, open to and accepting of their neighbours, as espoused by Babo, or a new, imported, closed radicalism, as encouraged by the Sarajevo regime since the war? Indeed, the same existential question exists within the Muslim communities in the West, with such an infinite variety of shades among the various traditional manifestations of Islam that any attempts to label them all as "The Muslims" are meaningless for all but populist purposes. Ironically, the empty accusations of Islamic fundamentalism levelled against the Bosnian Muslims to justify the war against them, have gained substance as a result of the war. Islam during the Ottoman period was orthodox and mainstream (although there was a certain radicalisation after the rise of Serbia in the 19th century, and an earlier peasant's revolt, in several parts of Bosnia in 1834 and 1835, that succeeded in uniting Catholic and Orthodox serfs. This, and the efforts of

---

difficult to emerge. Anyone who does manage to climb out of it has to pay a certain forfeit. That forfeit comes most commonly in the form of remorse and a guilty conscience. Scientifically it's called PTSD [...] The reality is that sooner or later you have to pay for any evil you commit, whatever the motive. The most serious evils are the evils of war. If you kill the enemy in combat, that's not a sin, nor is it the evil of war. It's to be or not to be. The fight for life. But if you kill the enemy or a civilian or anyone outside combat just because you're in a position to do so, because you can or want to, then you are tumbling into a deep abyss. You've succumbed to the dark and black forces who called to you from the depths you are now falling towards. Many succumb failing to understand that all power is fleeting, especially that which comes from dark forces [...] For when the white forces of goodness shine and its light banishes all the darkness and chaos, then the darkness withdraws, and all that's left is what you have done. All your sins and weaknesses are revealed. You might be able to hide it from other people, depending on your personality, on the stuff you're made of. But you can't hide or suppress it from yourself. Many make the mistake of thinking that hell is a certain place, and don't realise that it's mobile. We all carry it within us. That moment when we lose contact with what's human within us, with our own natural feelings, the gates of hell open, and they stay open". Or as Ratko said to me once, "*Insan može biti hajvan, no hajvan ne može biti insan*" ("a man can be a beast, but a beast can't be a man").

foreign-backed religious organisations in the second half of the 19th century, led to a rise in hostility towards Christians[484]. The mass islamisation of Bosnia after the Turkish conquest in the 15th century was not brought about by force or persecution, but was predominantly due to the weakness and in-fighting of the churches, advantageous fiscal arrangements and career opportunities for Muslims, and the large influx of Muslims from Ottoman territories lost to the Habsburgs in the 1690s[485]. After 1878, and in particular between the two world wars, there was a westernisation of Bosnian Muslims, at least in the towns, where the former landowners became a professional class, studying in western universities[486]. In the Yugoslav Wars, Arab and Iranian paramilitaries found they had a free hand in the sectors of the countryside allocated to them, and since the war there has been a steady inflow of funds from Saudi Arabia, and some radical communities have taken root (the Kingdom of Saudi Arabia, that hasn't taken in any refugees during the current crisis, and which is engaged in a proxy war against Iran throughout the Middle East and beyond[cii], is a medieval totalitarian regime, and despite the fact that the vast majority (15 out of 19) of the participants in, and the cash behind, the 9/11 attacks, including Bin Laden himself, were Saudi, it is still the UK and the US' closest ally in the Middle East)[487]. For example, a Muslim who agrees to grow his beard and make his wife wear a headscarf, can claim a monthly payment of KM 450 from Islamic associations financed from abroad. I've heard this described as "Al Qaeda welfare". On one of the hills overlooking Cazin there is now a large *medresa*, a religious secondary school with boarding facilities, financed from abroad (as Izetbegović himself wrote, "It would be very instructive to establish how many schools and colleges are maintained directly or indirectly by foreigners, and ponder the reasons for this extraordinary generosity"[488]). Alas, this eyesore, which bears a fleeting resemblance to the film studio overlooking Priština that became NATO's headquarters, and contrasts starkly with the beautiful Old Mosque overlooking the town from a hill opposite it, has little to do with the medieval enlightenment of Gazi Husrev Beg's *medresa* in Sarajevo. The only other visible investment in the town since the war is a new, landscaped roundabout in the town centre, and a rash of supermarkets and mosques on the outskirts of town (this is not an exclusively Muslim phenomenon: new, ostentatious religious infrastructure abounds in all parts of Bosnia, an affirmation of the bankrupt moral legacy of the war, not to mention the ongoing depression[ciii]). Cazin's prosperity has anyway always depended on the prosperity of Velika Kladuša. There has been even less investment in public works there, with a comparatively meagre new roundabout and zebra crossing. At least the

---

[cii] Before regime change in Iraq in 2003, Saddam Hussein's secular dictatorship acted as a counterweight to Iran, and the two fought a trench war complete with poison gas between 1980 and 1988. Saudi Arabia, which has the world's largest oil reserves, was an ally of Iraq, with the second-largest reserves, until Gulf War I in 1990, when Saddam invaded Kuwait, only to be ejected by a US-led coalition early the following year, on the very eve of the Yugoslav Wars. Syria, which occupied much of Lebanon from 1976 to 2005, also participated in the US-led coalition against Saddam. Gulf War I caused a major humanitarian crisis, with over one million Iraqi refugees in Iran, and 500,000 Kurdish IDPs in the mountains on the Turkish border in April 1991, just as the first clashes started in Croatia. A "safe area" for Kurds was established by the UN, underwritten by US air power. In November 2000, Saddam switched trading in Iraqi oil from the dollar to the new European currency, thereby breaking a deal brokered by the US with Opec in the 1970s. This decision was reversed after Gulf War II. As the Middle East descends into ever more fractious anarchy, Saudi Arabia appears to be emerging as the new regional power, a stable and reliable partner for its foreign sponsors.
[ciii] In Russia, Putin has built 25,000 new churches since coming to power. Are these symptoms of the same malaise, a manifestation of mass PTSD?

šejtan-lampa ("traffic light") has been repaired. The town is slipping slowly but surely back into the poverty-stricken obscurity that was its lot for the long centuries before the rise of Agrokomerc. From being the most prosperous district in Bosnia on the eve of the war, it has now returned to its position at the bottom of the list. Local unemployment is 65% and GDP per capita KM 4,000[489]. Now even the Romanies have stopped turning up at the market in Velika Kladuša, which after the war was a draw for people from as far away as Slovenia (despite the fact that it was recently claimed by a local politician that for bargain-hunters from Slovenia and Croatia, Velika Kladuša, Cazin and Bužim have supplanted Trieste as the place to find foreign goods unavailable at home). This is not a chance turn of events, the inevitable result of the war and the economic crisis, but is rather the fruit of a deliberate and systematic strategy to starve Velika Kladuša of any investment, the long-term component of the revenge of the Sarajevo ruling elite. As Selimović wrote in *The Tower*,

> "If this is how they avenge themselves against sparrows, what would they do to a sparrowhawk? […] Why do they need this revenge? To frighten me? To frighten others by my example? To exult over the weak? To ban thought? To ban speech? […] They humiliated me by someone else's hand, for everything they have willing perpetrators, eternal servants, without conscience and without reason, as they are, the only difference being that they have the power of judgment and authority over others"[490].

On 19 November 2015, just after the first Paris terrorist attacks, a *šehid* ("suicide bomber"[civ]) shot two Bosnian soldiers in Sarajevo before blowing himself up[491]. Like the murderous nationalisms in WWII, this evil influence is being deliberately and systematically injected into Bosnia from outside[492]. I saw a similar, if more overt, process in Tajikistan in 2010. Fundamentalism spreading out from Afghanistan was slowly taking over communities, using unlimited budgets to buy imams and provide employment for those who join the new club, while discretely meting out violence to anyone who protested; and a corrupt government bent only on self-perpetuation was powerless to do anything about it. The most visible sign of the change, I was told by Central Asia old hands, is that previously when one ordered vodka with one's meal in a restaurant, it would come in a *butilka* ("bottle"), whereas now it was served in a *čajnik* ("teapot"), so that anyone glancing in from outside would not notice that alcohol was being served; although *halal* wild boar can apparently be ordered with impunity in a restaurant in the north of the country (as in Kosovo, there were a lot of Americans in Tajikistan, and many of them seemed to be learning Tajik rather than Russian. Unlike the other main Central Asian languages, which share the same root as Turkish, Tajik is very close to Farsi, spoken in Iran, and Pashtun, spoken in Afghanistan). At the end of the war in Bosnia, up to 400 foreign Islamic irregulars were granted Bosnian citizenship by Izetbegović. One day in late 1995, I was walking down the street in Cazin with Kiwi and his girlfriend, Zuhra, when we saw a large man of dark complexion sporting a goodly beard walking towards us. Apart from his tan he reminded me of the late Mario, but this character was no *Četnik*. As we passed I greeted him in *Šatrovački* (Bosnian rhyming slang) with "*Šta mai razbu?*". "*Salaam alejkum*" he replied. In 2000, six of them, known as the "Algerian six", were arrested, and in 2002 they were handed over to the US for internment in

---

[civ] The original meaning of the word is "martyr".

Guantánamo. Five of them were released in 2009 (three returned to Bosnia, while two were resettled in France), and the last in 2013 (he returned to Algeria). There is currently an inordinate number of young Bosnian Muslims fighting in Iraq and Syria, recruited and sent to their deaths by networks in their own country, financed from Saudi Arabia. I recently heard on the RTVBiH *dnevnik* ("news") that in the three years up to the end of 2015, 900 fighters from the Balkans had made their way to Syria (by contrast, there are said to be 4,000 Chechen *duhi* ("fighters") in Islamic State and related groups, an indictment first and foremost of the current state of their country, run with an iron fist by one of Putin's stooges). On 15 November 2015, Husein "Bilal" Bosnić of Bužim was sentenced to seven years' imprisonment for public incitement to terrorist activities, recruitment of terrorists and organisation of a terrorist group. He served in a *Mudžahedin* unit of the ABiH during the war, and over the last five years has gained notoriety for radical statements in public, in particular during Friday prayers. He is now the *de facto* leader of the Salafist movement in Bosnia, and in September 2014 he was arrested with 15 others in the police's Operation Damascus. During his trial, the parents of two of the young men he recruited for Islamic State (of whom one has been killed, and the other is missing) gave evidence against him. He is said to have recruited five young men from Velika Kladuša alone. In 2013, he was investigated by the police for *dvoženstvo* ("bigamy"), but no charges were brought because only one of his four wives is actually married to him. In an interview with the Italian newspaper *La Repubblica*, he claimed to have been involved in the recruitment of 50 Italians[493]. In a bizarre twist of fate, in 2013 Dodik appealed to Catholics expelled from Bosnia during the war to return to their old communities, many of which still stand empty, for fear that groups funded from Saudi Arabia would buy up their land and take root there (in the run-up to the war, Karadžić had threatened to shoot any Serbs selling land to Muslims or Albanians; but he didn't mention Arabs). Kristijan, a Catholic from Laktaši north of Banja Luka, who worked in Saniteks in Velika Kladuša in the late 1980s, had bought land outside Banja Luka just before the war. Fast-forwarding fifteen years, now securely established as a *ravnatelj* ("headmaster") in Croatia, he went back to inspect his land, to find a road had been built over it. He then went to the *katarska opština* ("land registry"), only to discover there was no record of him ever having owned the land. In the end, the Republika Srpska authorities bought up strategic land themselves, including water sources on otherwise worthless land near Dodik's native Laktaši. This was a windfall for the absentee owners, most of whom had long ago given up any hope of ever getting any benefit from their land. But many communities and mosques reject this new, foreign ideology, and attempts to tell them to change their ways (perhaps surprisingly, at least to the uninitiated, the imported fundamentalism increasingly and unashamedly visible in various parts of the country, including Velika Kladuša, has been rejected in Bužim, because of theological differences). Thus the seeds have been sown for a new intra-Muslim conflict, IEDs set to blow up in the face of a new generation. An imam from Trnovi who recently publicly warned his flock of the dangers of extremism, has suffered one assault and two attempts on his life. In any case, brotherhood and unity has now been well and truly flushed down the toilet, as the war gave credence to and reinforced the negative stereotypes of each community[494]. In 1991, only three districts in Bosnia had anything like homogenous populations: Posušje (99.5% Croat), Cazin (97.5% Muslim), and Drvar (97.3% Serb)[495]. But as a result of the Yugoslav Wars, which re-ordered the demographic pack, well shuffled over the previous century, according to a single, artificial criterion, most rural districts and towns (or city boroughs) are now made up almost exclusively of one ethnic/religious group (by way of example, in 1922, the village of Crnaja was 85% Serb; from at least the eve of WWII until 1961, when Muslims started to buy up land abandoned because of the war and the Peasants' Revolt, it was exclusively Serb; and now, as a result of the Yugoslav Wars, it is exclusively Muslim[496]). This situation is compounded by the education system, with not only separate curricula for Serb, Croat, and Muslim children[497], but also mandatory single-faith religious education which instils and imposes a very narrow view of local history, and indeed world affairs, such that children often not only do not know any of their peers from the other communities, but are encouraged to take a negative, even hostile view towards them. At a time when Europe and the world are moving towards greater integration, and nine countries out of ten are multi-ethnic, multi-confessional, multilingual, and multi-cultural, Bosnia (and the other former Yugoslav countries) are moving towards greater division[498] (at the same time as the EU moved from the common market to the single market in 1992, Yugoslavia was entering the worst phase of its disintegration[499]). *Babe i žabe* ("just say no to Greater Serbia, Greater Croatia and Islamic State!").

The international community certainly has let Bosnia down, as Paddy Ashdown, the high representative for Bosnia from 2002 until 2006, said at the Srebrenica 20th anniversary memorial service in London in 2015, but when has it done anything else? Despite the billions of pounds in development aid sunk into Bosnia, even before the economic crisis of 2008 the majority of Bosnians did not have a job that allowed them to support their family (according to Babo, "a large part of the aid ended up in the abyss of dark schemes and the bank accounts of major players who liked to portray themselves as the saviours of Bosnia and the champions of the Muslim people". In June 1992, he proposed to Izetbegović the creation of a central aid committee to control and keep track of all the aid, but received no reply[500]). Clearly, the fundamental aim of any peace-building initiative must be to allow people to be able to earn a living: once they are free from economic worries, they can engage in addressing all other issues themselves; but the spending of international funds in the post-conflict reconstruction effort has been described as "irrational"[501]. As they say in the Balkans, "*Bez alata nema zanata*" ("give us the tools and we will finish the job"). The errors of the international community in the Balkans were repeated and magnified in Iraq and Afghanistan, with disastrous consequences that are coming home to roost with a vengeance[502]. The opportunity was missed to learn from these mistakes in the Balkans; yet perhaps it is not too late to try a different approach there, that if successful could be rolled out elsewhere. A pragmatic approach, where jobs mean security. After all, the economic failure of Yugoslavia was the event that pushed it over the edge, allowing criminals to misappropriate it: while Yugoslavia was created out of nationalist considerations, it foundered on the reality of economic considerations[503]. The oil crisis of 1973 did not help, and in 1979, Yugoslavia was *de facto* bankrupt[504] (the ethnic/religious dimension of the crisis only came to light in 1987, having entered the back door like a squatter into an abandoned house. As early as 1978, Jimmy Carter's national security advisor, speaking on Yugoslavia's prospects after Tito, noted that the US should support both centralist and separatist forces within Yugoslavia; should give publicity to opposition groups within the country; and should not prevent Yugoslavia from contracting more debt; and in 1983, the federal government noted that pressure from the West to establish opposition parties, that peaked in 1984, was a front for the *Ustaše* and *Četnik* diaspora[505]). A presidential commission in 1983 failed to come up with a solution to the growing economic crisis, partly because of a split within the commission between conservatives who believed that the KPJ's model was infallible, and liberals who wanted to introduce economic reforms (Milošević, at that time a banker, fell into the second group)[506]. The only serious attempt at political and economic reform was started in 1989 by Marković, who pegged the currency to the DM and made it freely convertible for the first time since WWII, as well as liberalising imports and planning large-scale privatisation. His government of pro-Yugoslav Croats came up with a reform package, including the introduction of multi-party democracy, which met with loud approval in the West and international financial institutions[507]. The results, which included bringing inflation down from 60% per month to almost zero, and increasing Yugoslavia's foreign currency reserves to their highest-ever level, USD 10 billion, were felt in the first half of 1990, but were too late to halt the momentum of the runaway nationalist train[508] (indeed, successful reforms might have frustrated the various nationalist programmes, and had to be blocked[509]). In the autumn of that year, Marković was powerless to stop the republics acting contrary to his successful reforms, and even dipping their hands into the federal monetary system: Milošević appropriated 18.2 billion dinars[510] (immediately after this came to light in January, the JNA released surveillance tapes revealing the HDZ's preparations for war. Meanwhile, Slovenia had undermined Marković by criticising the exchange rate reform and refusing to contribute to federal funds - as well as by proposing constitutional reforms that provided for the right to secede - and Tuđman joined in when he came to power[511]). Marković resigned in December 1991 because of the obstructions to his reforms. Nowadays, most Bosnians are "self-employed", duckers and divers doing odd jobs and engaging in precarious entrepreneurial activities. In 2014, unemployment was 40% at national level[512] (in 2016, it is 44%, with an average salary for those with a job of 425 euros). Even those with a job often do something else on the side, not least because they can never be sure when their salary will be paid. Only senior public servants can live comfortably on their salaries without resorting to alternative activities (which, alas, often does not prevent them from doing so, despite the received wisdom refuting the existence of a free lunch: "*Nema džabe ni kod stare babe*"). And the same goes for pensioners. In March 2012, in a demonstration of national unity unprecedented since the Peasants' Revolt, over 1,500 *bivši borci* ("veterans"), from all sides, ABiH, HVO, and VRS, joined forces and camped outside the government building in Sarajevo for a week, demanding the immediate settlement of unpaid pensions (former NOZB squaddies are not recognised as veterans and do not receive a pension, despite two rulings by the Bosnian constitutional court, in 2007 and 2013, finding the NOZB equivalent to the HVO in terms of its structure and functioning, and West Bosnia comparable to Herzeg-Bosna, and holding that the refusal to pay them pensions is discriminatory)[513]. In early 2014, there was a series of violent demonstrations against corruption in Tuzla, Sarajevo, Zenica, Mostar, Jajce and Brčko, the worst unrest since the war, and dubbed posthumously the "social revolt"[514]. These led to local movements demanding action on non-nationalist issues; but the political elites have been unable to deliver (according to Transparency International's 2016 corruption perception index, Croatia comes 55th, Montenegro 64th, Serbia 72nd, Bosnia 83rd, Macedonia 90th, and Kosovo 95th on the list of 176 countries analysed)[515]. Meanwhile, there is a continual exodus of young people abroad, especially graduates, to Slovenia, Austria or further afield, depending on family connections, or foreign passports.

Whether the ICTY did justice is another story (and Milošević's death in UN custody in March 2006, after he demolished the "smoking gun" prosecution case against him, conducting his own defence, raises serious questions[cv]), but at least it removed from circulation dangerous individuals who would have been an obstacle to any form of progress. Alas, there has been little progress anyway. The campaign for justice for Srebrenica has been led by Munira Subašić and her *Majke Srebrenice* ("mothers of Srebrenica") association. She spoke at the Srebrenica 20th anniversary memorial service in London. Šešelj was released on bail on health grounds in November 2014 after 11 years on remand, and subsequently refused to return from Serbia for judgment (he was acquitted, and is now a MP in Serbia, while claiming disability benefit)[516]. It also allowed the victims of violence the opportunity to testify to their experiences in the absence of any truth and reconciliation body. And, at least theoretically, a process whereby individuals are called to account for their actions should help dispel the commonly-held attitudes of guilt by association in respect of all members of a particular community, thereby opening the way to national reconciliation[517]. At least the *pravnici* ("lawyers") had a field day experimenting with new doctrines and establishing new precedents in what was trumpeted as Nuremberg II[518]. Indeed, the very idea of an international criminal court is an admission in advance of failure by the international community to be able to deal with conflict (or perhaps, in the absence of any real political will to promote peace, it is merely a mechanism to determine who pays the bill once all the guests at the banquet have eaten their fill). The fact that the US, one of the main drivers of the ICTY, has insisted on exemption from international justice for US citizens, would suggest that one of its functions is to contribute to an arbitrary international order where might is right; and the rule of law was conspicuous by its absence in the whole process of Milošević's delivery to The Hague[519]. In 2005, the ICTY chief prosecutor said that the "political support of the EU and the US is the main factor explaining why Serbia and Croatia are now cooperating better with us"[520]. Officially, the ICTY was created by the UN security council to "contribute to the restoration and maintenance of peace"[521]. Starting its prosecutions with lower-level individuals, it later developed the doctrine of "joint criminal enterprise" to indict politicians and military commanders, establishing criminal vicarious liability/accessory liability where the defendants knowingly shared a criminal purpose[522]. But did anyone really know where this game of Russian roulette would eventually lead? The players were alternately (and sometimes simultaneously) egged on and heckled by the audience, even as they hedged their bets on the next move, and every spin of the cylinder further increased the frenzied cacophony, drowning out the voices of reason. This in turn only further empowered the strong and disenfranchised ordinary people. It beats cockfighting, as Somterset Maugham observed[cvi523]. And as George Orwell wrote, "The fact is that every war suffers a kind of progressive degradation with every month that it continues, because such things as individual liberty and a truthful press are simply not compatible with military efficiency"[524]. Karadžić was arrested in Belgrade in 2008, where he was living openly and practicing alternative medicine under a different name, his face obscured by a large beard, and he was convicted of genocide and sentenced to 40 years in 2015. For almost two decades the Dutch

---

[cv] Officially he died of a heart attack, after being refused permission to travel to Moscow for specialist heart care.

[cvi] According to Owen, "there were key people in Washington and Bonn who still saw Milošević as the fount of all evil and really did not want to have any negotiations with him at all [...] Another strand in the US administration was one that saw Milošević as a strategic genius always three or four moves ahead of us on the chessboard of Balkan politics and who believed that nothing connected with him was as it seemed and that he was always playing according to the Greater Serbia game plan".

government, happy to host the most prestigious legal institutions in the world (the International Court of Justice and the International Criminal Court also sit in The Hague), vigorously resisted any suggestion of their liability in the worst atrocity in Europe since WWII. It's a shame they didn't show the same mettle when it looked like the men they had been happy to deploy to the Balkans as part of an international effort, would actually have to do some real soldiering. The Dutch government, who resigned *en masse* in 2002 after a report found it could and should have done more to prevent the atrocity, betrayed not only the Bosnian people, who it was being paid to protect, but also its own men, who it sent to do a job they were unprepared for and didn't understand, only to fail, at the moment of truth, to deliver the moral courage and leadership the situation demanded[525]. They have shamed the memory of the brave Dutch men and women who decided to do the right thing during the Nazi occupation. In July 2014, a Dutch court in The Hague ruled the Dutch government was liable for the deaths of 300 of the 8,000 Srebrenica victims[526]. The only act of the international community since the end of the war that I have heard Bosnians comment on approvingly, is Paddy Ashdown's initiative to change the number plate system. Previously, the town of residence of car owners was advertised loudly and clearly by the first two letters of the number plate, which during the war (and for a good ten years afterwards) was equivalent to writing "shoot me" on the vehicle whenever someone ventured into territory controlled by another party. Now this blatant ethnic/religious label has been removed (although Bosnian vehicles still stand out for the same reason when they travel to Croatia or Serbia). As aid work increasingly becomes a virtual discipline, in the Le Carré-like deathgrip of soulless civil servants and posturing politicians, such genuinely beneficial, practical initiatives are likely to become a thing of the past[cvii]. In addition, the massive, painstaking and undoubtedly painful forensic work of the International Commission on Missing Persons, created in 1996, that has allowed the remains of thousands of people discovered in mass graves to be identified and returned to their families, and in which Gordon, a former bobby, played a lead role, is one of the few other tangible benefits of the international presence. 27,000 of the 40,000 persons reported missing during the Yugoslav Wars have been accounted for thanks to the ICMP, as portrayed in the powerful 2012 film *Halima's Way*, starring legendary Yugoslav thespian Mustafa Nadarević. There are still 1,000 persons missing from Srebrenica.

It is also true that foreign powers have always decided Bosnia's fate, for better and for worse[527]. The priorities of the international community are dynamic, not static, and changed during the course of the Yugoslav Wars, just as they had in relation to the Balkans over the course of WWI[528]. While in the West, governments changed and international organisations evolved (or regressed), in the East, Russia arose from the post-industrial wastes of the Soviet Union and managed, despite a series of constitutional crises that turned into battles, including the use of tanks, and the storming of the White House central government complex in Moscow, to avoid a civil war, although conflicts did break out in the Caucasus and Central Asia (after becoming independent, Tajikistan was racked by civil war between 1992-1997, in which up to 100,000 people were killed[cviii]). Yugoslavia had recognised the EU in

---

[cvii] As General Kutuzov observed in *War and Peace*, "*Sovetčikov vsegda mnogo, a ljudej net*" ("there's always plenty of consultants, but what we need are people who can do something useful"). Kutuzov defeated Napoleon in 1812.

[cviii] A local colleague told me that his elder brother had fought in the civil war, before going on to fight the Americans in Afghanistan. While the civil war was a school, he told me, in which his brother learnt his

1967, 20 years before other eastern European countries, 60% of Yugoslav trade was with the EU, and a political partnership had been established in the late 1980s. In November 1989, the EU's policy had been to uphold the unity of and democratic transformation in Yugoslavia, and in 1990, Yugoslavia applied to join the Council of Europe; but despite promises of support to Marković with his reforms, no economic aid was forthcoming[529]. The EU's various efforts at finding a solution in 1991 were generally at least one step behind events on the ground, including Germany's encouragement to Tuđman to press ahead with confrontation[530]. By subsequently recognising Croatia and Slovenia, and condemning the use of force by the JNA but not by the republics, the EU abandoned its previous neutral position and took the side of parties who had unilaterally changed existing international borders (accepting a *fait accompli*, something it had earlier stated it would never do)[531]. It also scuppered Lord Carrington's efforts to find a peaceful solution in 1991[532]. Rather than stop the violence, the EU's approach placed a real solution even further out of reach[533]. Soon after the start of the war in Bosnia, which was only accelerated by the EU's insistence on a referendum, and then recognition at the initiative of the US, in August 1992 the EU took a back seat to the UN in the Balkans[534]. As an economic, not a political power, its efforts in this second field were doomed to failure, while more could have been done to support the federal government's reforms in the former[535]. Yugoslavia was one of the first signatories of the UN charter in 1945, and in 1950 was elected a non-permanent member of the UN security council (as it was in 1987)[536]; but in 1992, the UN imposed unprecedented sanctions on Yugoslavia, which initially failed to achieve much more than strengthen the hand of the extremists. Peacekeepers were then deployed with a mandate to secure the provision of humanitarian aid, and Sarajevo airport was secured as a means to allow the delivery of aid to the besieged city[537]. A series of security council resolutions failed to put an end to the conflict, and different national interests within the UN reduced it to the lowest common denominator, as had been the case in the EU[cix538]. Thus over the course of the crisis, the international institutional framework went from the incapacity of the EU to act (curiously reminiscent of the impotence of the Yugoslav federal structures), to the UN moving from an insufficient mandate to a mandate it was incapable of delivering, to NATO acting first under the umbrella of the UN and subsequently independently[cx539]: NATO was certainly more effective in achieving results, but it failed to live up to the responsibilities it had taken upon itself, and which served as the justification for its action.

Over the centuries, the Bosnians have had far more bad times than good, and yet they have always come out of them with their indomitable spirit unbroken and their irrepressible sense of humour intact. "It is not the kings and generals that make history, but the masses of the people, the workers, the peasants, the doctors, the clergy", as Nelson Mandela once said[540]. It was the poor who built the ancient world's magnificent monuments that we still admire today, and who constitute the fundamental factor and indispensable input of today's global economy.

---

trade, Afghanistan was a *vuz* ("university"). Šervani told me he spent a total of 40 minutes in Afghanistan during the Soviet occupation.

[cix] According to Owen, "The Security Council passed resolutions of condemnation but they were ignored by the Croatian government army in Western Slavonia, the Bosnian Serb army in Žepa and Srebrenica and the Croatian and Bosnian government armies in the Krajina [Croatian Borders]".

[cx] At the beginning of the EU's diplomatic efforts in the Yugoslav crisis in 1991, the bloc proclaimed "This is the hour of Europe".

Serbia, after the dismemberment of the single state comprising all the territories inhabited by Serbs, is emerging from the pariah status it acquired during the war, but appears to be torn between the perceived benefits of membership of the EU, and traditional friendship with Russia[cxi541]. Where are the tens of thousands of participants in Milošević's rallies for truth, who bought (or were bought for) his tales of Serb glory?[542] They had their revenge on him in 2000, but they are still paying the price. Serbia is experiencing a similar exodus of young people as Croatia and Bosnia (I have it on good authority that Serbs who can demonstrate a historical link to Hungary - Vojvodina was part of Austria-Hungary until 1918[cxii543] - can apply for Hungarian passports, a way into the EU). Serbia has largely normalised its relations with Croatia and Bosnia, and in 2015, for the first time, the prime minister of Serbia, Aleksandar Vučić, who was tearful at Milošević's *sahrana* ("funeral", and who visited the siege of Sarajevo with Šešelj and Serbia's current president, Tomislav Nikolić, in May 1995, apparently with a skull sporting an UNPROFOR helmet mounted on the bonnet of their vehicle), attended the Srebrenica memorial service in Potočari[cxiii544]. He had to flee with his CP to avoid being lynched. Since 2002, the post of president of Serbia has been held by six different political parties, while starting with Đinđić, the first non-SPS prime minister for ten years, that post has been held variously by a coalition, two parties and an independent (with a comeback by the SPS between 2012-2014). Thus the Serbian political elite, while doggedly adhering to the nationalist discourse, have sought to disassociate themselves from the wartime regime, unlike in Croatia, where Tuđman's party is still unapologetically the main political force. Croatia is currently blocking the approval of chapter 23 (judiciary and fundamental rights) of Serbia's EU accession negotiations. Another stumbling block on the "road to Europe" is unresolved issues between Belgrade and Priština. Kosovo, half the size of Cymru/Wales[cxiv], has received international

---

[cxi] Owen wrote in respect of his odyssey: "The EU has had fewer problems and differences with the Russians than with the Americans. If anything, the EU and the US have exaggerated the links between Russia and the Serbs and therefore their influence and capacity to deliver. The Russian-Serbian relationship is one of declining sentiment, not one of vital interest. But it did become the symbolic measure within Russia of whether the Russians were being treated as genuine partners by the US and Europe".

[cxii] There was an exodus of 40,000 Serbs (and some Albanians), including the Orthodox patriarch, from Kosovo, Niš and Belgrade to Vojvodina and Hungary in 1690, after the Habsburgs briefly occupied Serbia in their offensive that followed on from the lifting of the siege of Vienna, before being driven back over the Danube by the Turks, who exacted a terrible revenge on the local population. With them the Serbs took their most important relics, including the mummy of Tsar Lazar, who is now entombed in Srem.

[cxiii] Mladić's operation at Srebrenica has become, in addition to a life sentence to psychological trauma for tens of thousands of people, a millstone around the neck of Balkan politicians. While George Orwell observed that "atrocities are believed or disbelieved in solely on grounds of political predilection [...] The truth, it is felt, becomes untruth when your enemy utters it [...] But unfortunately the truth about atrocities is far worse than that they are lied about and made into propaganda. The truth is that they happen", Dr Kržišnik-Bukić notes that, "the identity of Bosnian Serbs, and Serbs in general, will be overshadowed by negative connotations for a long time to come, regardless of how radical a purge there is of crimes and their perpetrators within the Serb people". Likewise, Operation Storm, the single largest population movement in the first act of the Yugoslav Wars, is also a millstone around the neck of Croatian politics, not because of the stigma – there is none – but for the opposite reason: anything that calls into question the mythology of Tuđman's historical legacy is tantamount to sacrilege.

[cxiv] A Welshman would ask, "Which half?" During a BRCS logistics course in the West Country, it transpired that a team of builders on a *safle adeiladu* ("building site") across the border were using the same VHF frequency as us. The Welsh brickies seemed to be doing more talking than working, although one of them said, "I'm sweating buckets, me". They must have been using a repeater, because while we could hear them, they didn't seem to be picking up our comms. We followed usual field practice and switched to another pre-programmed frequency as calling channel.

recognition as a sovereign state, including by Croatia (and Hungary and Bulgaria) in 2008, although some countries with troublesome minorities of their own, such as Spain, Slovakia and Romania, have declined to recognise it (it is said that Putin has let it be known he will recognise Kosovo's independence if the West recognise the validity of his annexation of Crimea from Ukraine). Will Kosovo come to form the embryo of a greater Albania, subsuming half of Macedonia and Albania itself (Kosovo, though the poorest region of the former Yugoslavia, was still more sophisticated than Maoist Albania, whose dictator, Enver Hoxha, once referred to the Kosovo Albanians as "comrades" in the same breath as saluting his Chinese "brothers", and Kosovo played a key role in the Albanian declaration of independence in 1912[545]. Before the 1990s, the number of Albanians living in Yugoslavia was more than 50% the population of Albania[546]. Meanwhile, political and economic progress in Albania itself means that Bosnians can no longer compare themselves favourably with a people who were once considered not even to be European)? Kosovo started negotiations on accession to the EU in 2013. Macedonia has been a candidate EU member since 2005, but has not yet entered into accession negotiations, while Montenegro started negotiations in 2012. Turkey has been a candidate country since 1999, and started negotiations in 2005. At the end of 2015, unemployment in Serbia was 18% with an average salary of 402 euros (in Kosovo it was over 30%, with an average salary of 360 euros).

As for Croatia, the home of the Peckham Rye, its dire financial problems have thus far not been solved by its joining the EU in 2013, which is how membership was sold to the public. On the contrary, it has been subject to the EU's excessive deficit procedure since 2014. More widely, the HDZ project was sold to the Croat public not only as a national revolution that would deliver on the 1000-year quest for independence (the NDH experiment aside), but one that would necessarily bring prosperity[547]. The government's focus on maximising the six weeks of summer tourism has been accompanied by massive de-industrialisation, and unemployment in 2016 is 17%, with an average salary of 742 euros. But at least it has internal stability, having rid itself of its large ethnic minority. Meanwhile, the shaky public finances are heavily burdened by the popular veterans' disability pensions paid out every month (twice the average of civilian old age pensions), which it is an open secret are often approved in questionable circumstances, but which have been ring-fenced by successive governments as a means to ensure re-election (it is said there are twice as many people in receipt of such pensions as the HV had under arms, and Tuđman himself once commented that if they had had that many men, they would have won the war in half the time). Bosnia is suffering from a similar problem. In its eagerness to distance itself from its erstwhile compatriots, Zagreb seems to have exchanged direct rule from Belgrade for direct rule from Brussels. Failures in managing the economy, political participation and corruption did not prevent it achieving the hallowed "Euro-Atlantic integration" (under pressure from the EU, former prime minister Ivo Sanader was convicted of corruption in 2014 along with the HDZ and sentenced to nine years' imprisonment - although he was acquitted on appeal and released in 2015 - and his troubles aren't over yet: as the scapegoat for the HDZ's sins, he is now being tried for further offences, although that didn't stop him travelling to London in April 2016 to give evidence in arbitration proceedings in another case)[548]. The single market rules now allow "umbrella companies" to deploy cut-price Croatian workers to sites in the UK: on paper, they earn the same as their UK counterparts, but in reality they have to hand up to half of it back once they return home after completion of their contract (much like North Korea's practice of deploying unskilled workers to certain EU countries in a desperate attempt to scrape together some hard currency to put in its bare coffers). The high unemployment and emasculated *sindikati* ("trade unions") in Croatia mean there is no choice other than to accept such job offers. Gordon Brown said, "British jobs for British workers"; but he allowed a system to operate in which foreign workers in almost all sectors can be exploited, with the end result that Lester Piggotts are priced out of the market. For recent Croatian leaders, knowledge of English has been seen as an asset, increasing the country's credibility in international affairs, so much so that the latest prime minister, a Croatian Canadian independent MP, can hardly speak Croatian at all. By his own admission, he only understands 50% of what is said in parliament. Meanwhile, the current president of Croatia recently posed for a photograph with a WWII fascist flag featuring the original NDH coat of arms while on a trip to Canada, together with what must be taken to be members of the *Ustaše* diaspora (she also recently sang the Herzeg-Bosna anthem while on a visit to the Federation)[549]. Slovenia, on the other hand, appeared until recently to be doing rather well from the EU, after delaying Croatia's accession for two years with a dispute over territorial waters (Slovenia had called for Yugoslavia to apply for membership of the EU in 1987[cxv])[550]. Now, even Slovenia is experiencing an exodus to the more wealthy countries of the EU, and in some areas of the country, whole communities appear to have been relinquished to Bosnian immigrants in what is becoming the largest *Drang nach Westen* since 1945.

As Andrić noted in respect of 1941 in the short story *Zeko*,

> "the Sava [...] was now the border between two sorry states, with wretched governments, 'Serbian' and 'Croatian', that lived on hatred, ignorance and the basest urges, at the pleasure and necessity of the great fascist powers"[551].

Such were my musings as we trundled along. At the small town of Đakovo we alighted (I once interpreted for a suspected shoplifter from Đakovo in London. He was ultimately released without charge when the police detained the real culprit, another foreigner who was apparently his spitting image). We would have to hitchhike the last 15 km north-west. Out on the road, I was struck by the changing colours of the sky, as the low-lying clouds were endlessly twisted, dislocated, and formed anew into myriad shapes and hues, while the leaves of the trees and the grass by the side of the road were in constant flux, as if in counterpoint. The atmosphere was oppressive, as if a storm was brewing, and the narrow road stretched ahead of us in a more or less straight line, unprepossessing rather than dominating the landscape that extended in all directions to the horizon. Despite the clouds, it was a hot, summer's day. I could feel the cool sweat running down my back under the heavy *ranac* ("rucksack"), for it would not have done to turn up empty-handed.

The Kuplensko camp had been closed some weeks earlier. 4,700 refugees, including 143 babies and 73 pregnant women, had been transferred to the Gašinci

---

[cxv] The German foreign minister stated that it was not going to happen, because Yugoslavia's interest for the EU was its leading role in the Non-Alignment Movement, a role it would have to relinquish in order to join the EU. He also said that the best thing for Yugoslavia to do would be to adopt the impending single market standards. Tito had said in 1972 that "the reason Yugoslavia can play the role of independent factor in European relations is above all because it is non-aligned. Without that, Yugoslavia would be reduced to a Balkan appendix to the developed Europe, and a dartboard for the two blocs".

camp. Gašinci was a former JNA base, and was surrounded by wire fences and guarded by military police[552]. The new arrivals brought the total number of inmates to over 6,000, while its planned capacity was only 3,400. Many of the existing residents had been concentrated here by force earlier in the year from Zagreb and other places where they had taken refuge, when Tuđman decided he didn't want a Muslim minority at large in his new country[553]. Accommodation was mainly in tents, which were unsuitable for winter, and failed to adequately shelter their inhabitants from a severe storm on 30 July. The water supply system was also inadequate for the size of the population, as were the camp's sewage system and electricity supply. The camp was managed by UNHCR and IRC[554]. Over six months since the end of the war, Gašinci was now a dustbin of unwanted humanity, refugees from all over Bosnia (and beyond) who did not want to go, or were not wanted at home. While in theory the place was a potential powder keg, with former enemies living cheek by jowl, in fact most of the inmates were well aware they were lucky to be there at all, and were just glad that at least the war was over and they could enjoy some relative security. There were 186,000 Bosnian refugees in Croatia at the end of the war, and only a quarter of Bosnians were still living in their own homes[555]. Gašinci was in fact a vast waiting room, where people sat in a holding position until either their applications for asylum in a third country were accepted, or conditions improved sufficiently at home to allow them to return. Those who returned too early experienced a hostile reception and persistent discrimination, hardly surprising when the governor of the newly-constituted Una-Sana canton, Mirsad Veladžić, was Izetbegović's political coordinator in the war and his go-between with Dudaković[556]. I sensed an overwhelming atmosphere of restraint and resignation in Gašinci, without any cries of *"Živio Babo!"*. Applicants for resettlement were bused to Zagreb for detailed interviews at the relevant embassy. Anyone caught out lying about his or her circumstances would be rejected, but could apply for another country. Having relatives who had already been accepted in a country increased the likelihood of acceptance. The whole process lasted 3-6 months, but individuals with more complex cases could wait years. There were initially 100 people who were accepted in the Netherlands, but most of the rest went to the US and Canada. In 1994, I had spent a weekend on the island of Obonjan, off Šibenik, that before the war had been known as the Island of Youth. It was a holiday camp for young people, but during the war it was used as an internment centre for refugees and other stateless persons while their cases were being dealt with. Most of the inhabitants were refugees from Bosnia (over eight thousand passed through it during the war[557]), awaiting the processing of asylum applications abroad, and most of them had restricted rights of movement off the island, but there were other people there as well. There was one young Serb from Slavonia whose nickname was the "Sniper", because he had allegedly been apprehended with a rifle sight, which he vehemently denied. There was also an African, who no-one could speak to (I tried addressing him in English and French, to no avail). They did not have freedom of movement. I met one former POW who had deep, permanent marks on his calves, caused by fetters. Another refugee, a Muslim from Herzegovina, told me he had been crucified by the HVO. He had serious scarring on his wrists, and had received extensive medical care in Germany that allowed him to retain the use of his hands. However, the scarring appeared to run deeper than his physical injuries. While the climate was pleasant on Obonjan, and the view was spectacular, and there was security, nevertheless refugee life was stressful even there. They were not allowed to work and the humanitarian aid they lived on was not generous (meals were provided), they were aware (and were often reminded, among other things by racist graffiti, such as "*Balije van!*" ("Muslims out!", from *balo*, "pig"), and swastikas) that they were second-class citizens, and none of them knew how long they would have to stay there. Nor did they necessarily have news of their families. But it was certainly better than being on Goli Otok (the "bare island"), between the islands of Rab and Krk and the mainland, near Istria further up the coast from Zadar, which was a prison camp for political prisoners between 1949 and 1989, through which a total of 16,000 (male) guests passed, among them Stanko "Ćanica" Opačić (see above; female political prisoners were kept on nearby Sveti Grgur ("St. Gregory") island) (I was told by a colleague in Belgrade in 1998 of a relative of hers who had been on Goli Otok, and who was so traumatised by the experience that even then he avoided any contact with the authorities, to the extent that he wouldn't even apply for a passport). Obonjan has recently been bought by a foreign promoter seeking to turn it into a holiday rave paradise. Gašinci had few of the advantages of Obonjan, and yet the fact that the war was over must have compensated by eliminating the ever-present stress at the back of people's minds. Gašinci was finally closed in 2000, with 3,000 departures in 1998 and 2,000 in 1999[558]. We were going to spend a few days there as the guests of some of our friends from Kuplensko.

The first two vehicles that passed us on the road did not stop, but the third did. It was driven by a dark, unshaven young man with a moustache, accompanied by a small boy. We piled into the back, with our rucksacks on our laps. "Gašinci?" he enquired. "Yes", I confirmed. "Afraid to travel without your escort, are you?" he joked to me, in his unfamiliar northern accent. It would appear he was used to people travelling between the camp and the town. At the entrance to the camp, which was guarded by the HV, he dropped us off. We exited, with thanks.

We had been given instructions how to find our friends, and having done so, we registered with the camp authorities.

We stayed with Hasiba, who was in a large wooden hut with her husband, Irfo, and their two boys, and also two young women, sisters, who did all the cleaning in return for Hasiba doing all the cooking. Coffee was served, and became the focus of a social gathering, a scene repeated many times before in Kuplensko, in Velika Kladuša, and indeed throughout the former Yugoslavia. Cigarettes were lit and the space quickly filled with thick smoke. Hasiba said living conditions were relatively good, hygiene was definitely an improvement and there was even a canteen, they were allowed to work outside the camp (although opportunities and therefore wages were limited), and they were waiting to see what the future would hold. Some of our friends had already returned to Bosnia, while others had already departed to "third countries" to start a new life as refugees. Hasiba now lives in Sweden with her family.

We visited Tetin, who was living with a family, and waiting for security conditions to improve at home before returning. He was as indomitable as ever. We got through a decent quantity of *himber* ("elixir", i.e. *rakija*), which was not so easy to come by here, as there were no facilities for home-brewing. He is now back on his farm near Pećigrad, and commutes regularly to Split, where he works in construction. The first time I visited him at home, in 2005, he spit-roasted a *jare* ("kid") and opened a bottle of pre-war *lozovačka* ("grape *rakija*") containing a bunch of the antique fruit. Of his five neighbours cited in his letter to UNHCR, Ahmet died of natural causes five years ago, after being repeatedly beaten upon his return from

Kuplensko; Sedžad was forced to confess to a murder he did not commit and was sentenced to a long term of imprisonment, but was released thanks to the efforts of the ombudsman (he is now back behind bars for unrelated offences); Mirsad is at home in Bosnia, unemployed but happily married; Almir was sentenced to a long term of imprisonment for murder, but the conviction was quashed when the alleged victim turned up alive and well; and Osman is living in Denmark.

The next day we saw Smajo, who was living in a large, cold tent, the summer notwithstanding, furnished with half a dozen double bunk-beds covered in horse blankets, and nothing else. Being single, he had to share with other single blokes, who included Riki. It seemed very depressing, as did Smajo, and so we did our best to encourage him and cheer him up. He now lives in Texas with a family of his own, where he is a qualified chef, and he has even cooked for George Bush senior. Riki is also in the US.

We also saw Zahid, who was living in a small tent with his family. He later worked as a bus driver in Nottingham, working 60 hours a week at the age of 60. Even when he was in hospital with stomach cancer, he didn't lose his sense of humour, and commented, "They've got me plumbed up like a washing machine". He was so popular that among the many people who attended his funeral, was one of his regular passengers. His widow, Šuhra, lives in Nottingham.

I saw Dragan's father, Redžep, eating a pear in the canteen. He was surprised to see me, to say the least, and offered me the rest of his pear. Redžep was the youngest of the Srbac exiles in 1950, at the age of one (see below), and is now back on his farm in Velika Kladuša.

Adis from Konjic is living in Mainz with his German wife and children, a successful IT *štreber* ("geek"), while the other Adis is a teacher in Velika Kladuša, where he lives with his family.

Nikola is back in Slunj, living in his father's house with his family. He stayed on in the HV after the war, and is now retired. His father-in-law, Ramo, is also retired, and back in Velika Kladuša after a decade in Phoenix and Boston.

The last I heard of Miloš he was in Montenegro.

Milorad, our former landlord, is living in Srem. The last time I saw Ivica he was back in Slunj.

Goga is living with her family in Banja Luka. During the 2014 floods, she organised via Facebook a network of housewives ready to help IDP mothers with their children's laundry.

Mirvet is now the MP for Velika Kladuša, and Irfo is a DJ in Des Moines ("monks").

Kami and Enes are now married and living in Phoenix, where he is a successful realtor. Muhamed is retired and living in Velika Kladuša.

Sutko and Jadra are living in Velika Kladuša, as is Haris, who now has a baby of his own, Danijan. Jadra was recently reunited by chance with her former neighbour, the woman who gave birth in the front room underneath them in Kuplensko.

Of my former team, Denis is now living in Nottingham with his family (where young Fikret tragically passed away), Dragan is in London and Samir in Copenhagen, while Elvir and Šeki are living with their families in New York and Tennessee respectively. When Denis and Dragan first came to the UK, Steve, Kiwi and I travelled to the refugee centre in Rugby where they were staying, and we had a raucous weekend.

Alen is living in Velika Kladuša to this day.

Dajo is back living in Skokovi, while his son Miće is a truck driver living in Texas.

Zlatan is living in Denmark with his family. He has been unable to establish 54's fate.

After the elections in 1996, Đedović, with assurances from Izetbegović and Carl Bildt, travelled from his tent in Gašinci to sit in the Sarajevo parliament. However, in May 1997, the police surrounded the parliament building, before entering and arresting him in the middle of a session, which was not only unheard of but also unconstitutional. He was remanded in custody until 2000, when he was acquitted of all 27 counts of war crimes against him, and returned to parliament. He was re-elected in 1998 and 2002, and is now living in Velika Kladuša[559].

Pandža recently died in the US.

Dr Vesna is back working in Velika Kladuša hospital.

Družan now lives in Texas, in a duplex shared with his brother, Izet. Družan was best man at my wedding, as was Reinhard (I had the rings made in the DRC from a single nugget of gold procured for me by Mango). Reinhard, originally from Bavaria, is living in the former East Germany with his family.

Eddie is a successful musician in Chicago.

Timka lives at home, and works as a supermarket manageress in Cazin.

Rob lives in Nottingham with his family, where they run a greasy spoon.

Mujo lives in Guildford with his family.

Čauš is living in Velika Kladuša. One day after the war I ran into him. He did time at the 5th Corps' pleasure after returning home from Kuplensko, and had just been released. When I asked him how he was, he replied, "It's over now".

Ratko is still living in Kakanj, while Lara lives in Sarajevo with her family. Sadly now a widower, Ratko's facebook page regularly features kind comments and warm wishes from his former pupils, the majority with Muslim names.

Ismet is living in Texas with his family.

The last I heard from Boris he was in Norway, and Milan lives in Barcelona with his family.

Bane is back in Belgrade, Dr Skender, who stayed in Priština during Operation Horseshoe to care for his sick father, is working in the hospital there, and Millazim is back in Priština after a stint as a refugee in Albania. Ten years ago I ran into Tim on a HEAT course in the UK. Drew is running a chocolate factory in Ontario with his wife.

Kiwi is back in New Zealand with his wife Zuhra, from Bosanska Krupa, driving a fuel tanker; Gary is back in Glasgow with his wife Zdenka, from Tuzla, working as a Le Carré-esque hotel night manager when not deployed abroad; and Canbat is back in Canada with his wife Tanja, from Slavonia, running a search and rescue service in Alberta. Steve, a WWI archaeologist and author, is living in his native Southend, while Gordon, a Geordie, is trotting the globe, after a cameo role in the Frederick Forsyth novel *Avenger*.

That night I was entertained by Mirsad, and he plied with me a bottle of HV *rakija*, which resulted the next morning in the worst hangover I have ever had, before or since. It could have come from Pavelić's personal reserve. Mirsad now lives in Illinois with his family.

Kuplensko is now a deserted village, with only a few of the houses occupied. However, the pub, still called Fairy Wheel, is quite popular.

Babo now lives in Rijeka, while the unholy trinity of Izetbegović, Milošević and Tuđman are all dead. It is estimated that 140,000 people were killed in the

Yugoslav Wars (the population on the eve of the war was 23 million)[560]. Unlike Babo, who spent 11 years in prison even though he was never indicted by the ICTY, Izetbegović and Tuđman were never called to account for the blood on their hands, while the international institutions that turned a crisis into a drama continue to stumble along, protected by diplomatic immunity and fed by the tribute of taxpayers. Izetbegović's son is currently one of the Bosnian gang of three. As for Gavrilo Princip, he died in prison in Terezin in the Czech Republic (later Theresienstadt concentration camp) on 28 April 1918, denied proper medical treatment for injuries sustained falling down the stairs. He and four of his friends were too young to be sentenced to death. But three of them, sentenced to 20 years, did not survive the Habsburg state, and after the war they were reburied in Sarajevo. The last assassin, Muhamed Mehmedbašić, got away, by train to Montenegro, where he was arrested but escaped. He was recaptured in France and extradited to Serbia, and in Macedonia in 1917 King Aleksandar sentenced him to 20 years at the same time as he eliminated the Black Hand[561]. He was pardoned in 1919, only to be killed by the *Ustaše* in 1943[562].

It was nice to see old friends, and spend time with them for the first time in a non-threatening environment. Things were still very difficult, but now everyone knew the light at the end of the tunnel was not a mirage, and that their lot would be improving, indeed they would be able to live a normal life, very soon. The following morning we left, amid much wishing of good luck, and headed off back towards the railway station in Đakovo.

And as we set out, we knew that nothing could stop us. My Yugoslav dream had come true.

451

WHEN I VISIT SEKA AND JOHN

When I visit Seka and John
I always hear fighting from them
They fight about who'll make dinner
For the coffee who'll put the water

Then John says it hurts my head
Seka says she has to go to bed
John, to avoid disgrace
Gets up then and serves the guests

Then for the coffee he puts the water
The poor wretch starts to make the dinner
But Seka can't sit and watch
She won't let him make lunch

Now it's not important who makes it
The main thing is there's coffee to drink
I look at John with her, poor gadži
But the main thing is he's not hungry

And while Seka for lunch the table lays
John the tinned meat to eat disdains
Goods here are expensive to get
So John goes to buy some meat

When they're together God keep them
When they're alone then it's suffering
That's the way it is brother
Then they can't do without each other

So John struggles with his Seka
And Tetin he's his English teacher
Seka always something to swear about
That's the way it is in the tent

When they're apart then to God they pray
To be together each other to love again
They won't always fight and be arguing
Let them be together and God bless them[563].

Sead "Tetin" Kajtazović, Paklena Dolina

SEKA KISSES JOHN

Seka kisses John
He really rings her bell
Look at her in seventh heaven
Head over heels she's fell

She'll love him till the day she dies
Always in each other's arms
When she's down, he is up
Can't resist each other's charms

John came from far away
Because Seka loves him truly
But he loves Seka too
And thanks God for her daily

With ardent eyes they gaze
At each other, as love blooms
Their hearts beating ever faster
They're overjoyed in their little room

I sincerely wish them all the best
Not much sadness, happiness plenty
It's true love that binds them
Good for them, like landed gentry

Good for them, to be in love
Impervious to the outside world
Good for them they're still young
As God's mystery is unfurled

Seka's like a spinning top
Round and round John she goes
She really longs for him
She's crazy for her English rose

Good for them to be in love
Slowly surely Seka
Burns as with a raging fire
Brings them closer to their maker

Their kisses grow more passionate
As they're bound to one another
Just take a look at them
They're in a sweat so hot and bothered

I hope you won't take amiss
My little rhyme without guile

Hopefully John won't take the piss
And Seka will only smile[564].

Sead "Tetin" Kajtazović, Paklena Dolina

---

[1] Buckley & Cummings, 2001:238
[2] Dizdarević, 2000:193
[3] Silber & Little, 1995:61
[4] Silber & Little, 1995:60
[5] Dizdarević, 2000:214-220
[6] Baker, 2015:17
[7] Silber & Little, 1995:243
[8] Maclean, 1949:516
[9] O'Shea, 1998:231
[10] Hirkić, 1998:506-507
[11] Kržišnik-Bukić, 1991:471
[12] Abdić, 2016:11, 12, 14-15, 17-18, 23, 50-51, 322, 455; Centar za Mir; IndexHR; O'Shea, 1998:180
[13] Jutarnji List
[14] PSE
[15] Silber & Little, 1995:153-157
[16] Crnobrnja, 1994:171
[17] Dizdarević, 2000:415; Belišova, 2005:107; ICRC
[18] Dizdarević, 2000:417-420
[19] Ulemek, 2016:23,92
[20] B92 & Vreme Film, 2006:I; Médecins Sans Frontières, 2015:32
[21] Silber & Little, 1995:198-199
[22] Baker, 2015:90
[23] West, 1942:138-139
[24] West, 1942:217
[25] West, 1942:1104-1105
[26] Le Monde Diplomatique
[27] Trkulja & Božić, 2008:127; Crnobrnja, 1994:156
[28] West, 1942:230
[29] Crnobrnja, 1994:172
[30] Maclean, 1949:532
[31] Maclean, 1949:364
[32] Maclean, 1949:379
[33] Owen, 1995:204
[34] Silber & Little, 1995:373
[35] O'Shea, 1998:48, 55: Silber & Little, 1995:374
[36] Silber & Little, 1995: 312-313, 373
[37] Crnobrnja, 1994:215
[38] Ulemek, 2016:369
[39] O'Shea, 1998:185
[40] Malcolm, 1994:169
[41] Tolj, 1996:216; Malcolm, 1994:13
[42] Malcolm, 1994:23
[43] Kržišnik-Bukić, 1998:23
[44] Maclean, 1949:322, 397-398
[45] Silber & Little, 1995:325
[46] Crnobrnja, 1994:37
[47] Malcolm, 1994:101-102
[48] West, 1942:53
[49] Crnobrnja, 1994:39-40; Baker, 2015:39
[50] Baker, 2015:114
[51] Crnobrnja, 1994:20
[52] Baker, 2015:68
[53] West, 1942:1014

[54] Baker, 2015:35-36
[55] West, 1942:236
[56] West, 1942:247
[57] Crnobrnja, 1994:172
[58] Silber & Little, 1995:201-204
[59] West, 1942:251
[60] Baker, 2015:63
[61] Silber & Little, 1995:333
[62] Abdić, 2016:239
[63] Silber & Little, 1995:283, 326
[64] Crnobrnja, 1994:183; Owen, 1995:181-182
[65] Abdić, 2016:69-71
[66] Commission on Human Rights
[67] Malcolm, 1994:92
[68] West, 1942:1046-1047
[69] Andrić, 1967:181
[70] Silber & Little, 1995:221
[71] O'Shea, 1998:125
[72] Orwell, 1962:46
[73] Trkulja & Božić, 2008:117; Ulemek, 2016:327
[74] Trkulja & Božić, 2008:121
[75] Trkulja & Božić, 2008:122
[76] Trkulja & Božić, 2008:124
[77] Malcolm, 1994:183; Maclean, 1980:67-71
[78] Maclean, 1980:50
[79] Maclean, 1949:332-333
[80] Maclean, 1949: 343-345, 420
[81] Dizdarević, 2000:27
[82] Tolj, 1996:425
[83] Baker, 2015:69-70
[84] O'Shea, 1998:25
[85] Owen, 1995:60, 246
[86] Maclean, 1949:345
[87] Dizdarević, 2000:26-27
[88] West, 1942:406
[89] Malcolm, 1994:43
[90] West, 1942:411-412
[91] West, 1942:435
[92] Kržišnik-Bukić, 1998:87; Maclean, 1949:423
[93] Silber & Little, 1995:327
[94] Owen, 1995:335-336
[95] Telegraph
[96] Ulemek, 2013:128
[97] Malcolm, 1994:144, 131
[98] Malcolm, 1994:101
[99] West, 1942:332-335; Baker, 2015:67
[100] Abdić, 2016:418
[101] Andrić, 1967:224-225
[102] Malcolm, 1994:25, 50
[103] Kržišnik-Bukić, 1998:33, 63, 71
[104] West, 1942:280; Baker, 2015:63; Owen, 1995:115
[105] Malcolm, 1994:68
[106] Malcolm, 1994:96-97
[107] West, 1942:304
[108] Malcolm, 1994:120-121
[109] Silber & Little, 1995:227; Malcolm, 1994:231; Baker, 2015:62; Crnobrnja, 1994:178
[110] Malcolm, 1994:235; Baker, 2015:62
[111] Crnobrnja, 1994:181, 230; Owen, 1995:106, 118, 244, 262
[112] West, 1942:396
[113] Silber & Little, 1995:328-329; O'Shea, 1998:25
[114] Orwell, 1962:47

[115] Malcolm, 1994:18, 25
[116] Tolj, 1996:217
[117] Kržišnik-Bukić, 1996:69
[118] West, 1942:188
[119] Somerset Maugham, 1953:79
[120] Owen, 1995:3, 9, 123
[121] Silber & Little, 1995:293
[122] Malcolm, 1994:24-25
[123] Guardian; UN Economic and Social Council; Owen, 1995:327; Human Rights Watch
[124] O'Shea, 1998:214
[125] Owen, 1995:315-316
[126] Silber & Little, 1995:343-353; Baker, 2015:67; O'Shea, 1998:36
[127] O'Shea, 1998:45
[128] B92 & Vreme Film, 2006:II
[129] Guardian; Owen, 1995:323
[130] Guardian
[131] Independent; O'Shea, 1998:182; Owen, 1995:246; Courthiade, 2006:5
[132] Médecins Sans Frontières, 2015:162
[133] Guardian
[134] Silber & Little, 1995:xxviii
[135] Silber & Little, 1995:299-304
[136] Executive Intelligence Review
[137] Owen, 1995:331
[138] Silber & Little, 1995:293-294; Baker, 2015:103
[139] Van Selm et al, 2003:133
[140] Baker, 2015:67
[141] Kržišnik-Bukić, 1998:67
[142] Malcolm, 1994:121
[143] Zona Sumraka
[144] Silber & Little, 1995:333-335
[145] New York Times
[146] O'Shea, 1998:183-184
[147] Miljković, 2014:14-15; Orwell, 1962:65
[148] Malcolm, 1994:14
[149] Malcolm, 1994:4
[150] Malcolm, 1994:104
[151] Kržišnik-Bukić, 1998:27
[152] Malcolm, 1994:55
[153] Malcolm, 1994:19
[154] O'Shea, 1998:4
[155] Baker, 2015:62
[156] Kržišnik-Bukić, 1991:531
[157] O'Shea, 1998:216
[158] West, 1942:383-387
[159] Baker, 2015:64; Silber & Little, 1995:331
[160] Baker, 2015:95
[161] O'Shea, 1998:156
[162] Silber & Little, 1995:329
[163] Independent; Baker, 2015:70
[164] Commission on Human Rights
[165] Hirkić, 1998:258
[166] Selimović, 2005: 13
[167] Silber & Little, 1995:146
[168] Dizdarević, 2000:161
[169] Malcolm, 1998:344-347
[170] Maclean, 1949:419
[171] Maclean, 1949:449-457
[172] Malcolm, 1994:24
[173] West, 1942:237, 243
[174] Malcolm, 1994:50
[175] Silber & Little, 1995:283; Crnobrnja, 1994:181

[176] Silber & Little, 1995:271
[177] Kržišnik-Bukić, 1998:83
[178] Trkulja & Božić, 2008:37
[179] Kržišnik-Bukić, 1998:37
[180] West, 1942:405
[181] Silber & Little, 1995:276
[182] Lawrence, 1997:89
[183] Silber & Little, 1995:269-284
[184] Médecins Sans Frontières, 2015:57
[185] Baker, 2015:73
[186] O'Shea, 1998:235; B92 & Vreme Film, 2006:II
[187] Kržišnik-Bukić, 1998:93
[188] Maclean, 1980:65
[189] Jerusalem Post
[190] Trkulja & Božić, 2008:172; Ulemek, 2016:462, 464-473; Ulemek, 2013:292
[191] O'Shea, 1998:xii
[192] Buckley & Cummings, 2001:271-273
[193] Human Rights Watch, 1999:5-31
[194] Nekrasov & Konskaya, 2008
[195] Lieven, 1998:56-146; Brown, 1991:312-313, 441
[196] Courthiade, 2006:70
[197] Nekrasov & Konskaya, 2008
[198] Malcolm, 1994:44
[199] O'Shea, 1998:221
[200] Silber & Little, 1995:207
[201] West, 1942:346-347
[202] Malcolm, 1994:46; Kržišnik-Bukić, 1998:59
[203] Malcolm, 1994:228; Baker, 2015:61
[204] Maclean, 1980:56
[205] Kržišnik-Bukić, 1998:41
[206] Maclean, 1980:62, 64-65
[207] West, 1942:373, 419
[208] Crnobrnja, 1994:185
[209] Guardian
[210] Maclean, 1949:284
[211] Andrić, 1967:191; Ulemek, 2016:7
[212] West, 1942:468,521
[213] Crnobrnja, 1994:31
[214] West, 1942:193
[215] West, 1942:1038
[216] West, 1942:964
[217] Trkulja & Božić, 2008:222
[218] Andrić, 1967:175-176
[219] West, 1942:1146
[220] Baker, 2015:79
[221] Dizdarević, 2000:307
[222] Dizdarević, 2000:305-312
[223] Dizdarević, 2000:435
[224] Dizdarević, 2000:377
[225] Dizdarević, 2000:378
[226] Dizdarević, 2000:380; Silber & Little, 1995:70-71
[227] Dizdarević, 2000:423-424
[228] Crnobrnja, 1994:157; Owen, 1995:144
[229] Trkulja & Božić, 2008:207; Silber & Little, 1995:129-144, 202-203; Executive Intelligence Review; Freshpress; Crnobrnja, 1994:158; Baker, 2015:51
[230] Judah, 2002:132
[231] Maclean, 1949:485-489
[232] Owen, 1995:60-61
[233] Baker, 2015:82; West, 1942:366; Maclean, 1980:55
[234] Malcolm, 1998:324; Dizdarević, 2000:120,283
[235] Dizdarević, 2000:443

[236] Baker, 2015:22
[237] Dizdarević, 2000:328
[238] Dizdarević, 2000:328
[239] Malcolm, 1998:323-327
[240] Dizdarević, 2000:85,88-89
[241] Dizdarević, 2000:337, 339
[242] Silber & Little, 1995:66
[243] Dizdarević, 2000:283
[244] Dizdarević, 2000:343, 404
[245] Dizdarević, 2000:357, 362-363
[246] Dizdarević, 2000:365, 367
[247] Dizdarević, 2000:362
[248] Dizdarević, 2000:369
[249] Dizdarević, 2000:373, 375
[250] Silber & Little, 1995:83; Dizdarević, 2000:383
[251] Dizdarević, 2000:376
[252] Dizdarević, 2000:383
[253] Dizdarević, 2000:383, 388
[254] Dizdarević, 2000:389
[255] Dizdarević, 2000:390
[256] Dizdarević, 2000:393
[257] Silber & Little, 1995:60-72
[258] Malcolm, 1998:345
[259] Malcolm, 1998:346; Dizdarević, 2000:395-398
[260] Crnobrnja, 1994:105
[261] Judah, 2002:136
[262] Malcolm, 1998:20-21
[263] Solženicin, 2009: 362 (vol 3)
[264] West, 1942:940
[265] West, 1942:972
[266] Owen, 1995:8; Ulemek, 2013:184-185
[267] BBC News
[268] Malcolm, 1998:58,91
[269] Silber & Little, 1995:36-38
[270] Silber & Little, 1995:74-76; Ulemek, 2013:185
[271] Malcolm, 1994:115
[272] Bakker & Kyuchukov, 2000:71
[273] Malcolm, 1994:114
[274] Bakker & Kyuchukov, 2000:39-41
[275] Brown, 1991:316; Lee, 2005:180
[276] Kenrick & Puxon: 1996:35
[277] Kenrick & Puxon: 1996:61-63
[278] Van Selm et al, 2003:147, 149
[279] West, 1942:955
[280] Judah, 2002:24
[281] Judah, 2002:134
[282] Malcolm, 1998:312, 262-278; Ulemek, 2013:166
[283] Judah, 2002:138
[284] Judah, 2002:140; Ulemek, 2013:31
[285] Judah, 2002:137
[286] Judah, 2002:157
[287] Hirkić, 1998:29
[288] Dizdarević, 2000:149
[289] Judah, 2002:96, 102-109
[290] Judah, 2002:111-112
[291] Judah, 2002:115, 118
[292] West, 1942:955
[293] Malcolm, 1998:348; Baker, 2015:81
[294] Buckley & Cummings, 2001:17-18
[295] Judah, 2002:125
[296] Judah, 2002:113

[297] Judah, 2002:114
[298] Judah, 2002:129
[299] Buckley & Cummings, 2001:19
[300] Judah, 2002:166
[301] West, 1942:905
[302] Judah, 2002:167
[303] Crnobrnja, 1994:167, 179
[304] Andrić, 1967:293
[305] Malcolm, 1998:109-111
[306] Malcolm, 1998:47; West, 1942:627
[307] Malcolm, 1998:47
[308] West, 1942:859; Malcolm, 1998:48
[309] West, 1942:986
[310] Malcolm, 1998:130
[311] Judah, 2002:159
[312] Judah, 2002:164-165
[313] Judah, 2002:288
[314] Judah, 2002:169
[315] Judah, 2002:169-170
[316] Malcolm, 1998:217, 220-221; Buckley & Cummings, 2001:14
[317] Judah, 2002:179-180; Buckley & Cummings, 2001:20-21
[318] Judah, 2002:188
[319] Judah, 2002:189-192
[320] BBC, 2003:part 4; Ulemek, 2013:52
[321] Kolb, 2014:40
[322] Médecins Sans Frontières, 2014:39-40
[323] Judah, 2002:261
[324] Médecins Sans Frontières
[325] Buckley & Cummings, 2001:20-21
[326] Judah, 2002:252
[327] West, 1942:647,651
[328] Malcolm, 1998:48; West, 1942:146; Crnobrnja, 1994:243
[329] Crnobrnja, 1994:242, 244
[330] West, 1942:618
[331] Bastabalkana, 6; West, 1942:315-318; Buckley & Cummings, 2001:277; Theremustbejustice; Naša stranka; West, 1942:756
[332] Lawrence, 1997:27
[333] Lawrence, 1997:504
[334] Judah, 2002:187
[335] West, 1942:1008
[336] West, 1942:1010
[337] West, 1942:1014
[338] West, 1942:1025
[339] West, 1942:1011
[340] Maclean, 1980:73-74
[341] Maclean, 1980:63-64
[342] Ulemek, 2013:67
[343] West, 1942:1137
[344] West, 1942:1053
[345] West, 1942:1056
[346] Malcolm, 1998:158-160; West, 1942:579-586
[347] West, 1942:599
[348] Jerusalem Post
[349] Dizdarević, 2000:220-224
[350] Dizdarević, 2000:282
[351] Dizdarević, 2000:295-296
[352] BBC, 2003:part 4
[353] Judah, 2002:197
[354] Baker, 2015:78
[355] Judah, 2002:304; Ulemek, 2013:132
[356] Baker, 2015:81; Buckley & Cummings, 2001:223

[357] Judah, 2002:226
[358] Spectator; Baker, 2015:82; Buckley & Cummings, 2001:22; Ulemek, 2013:72
[359] Judah, 2002:140
[360] Buckley & Cummings, 2001:35; Baker, 2015:82
[361] Judah, 2002:240-243
[362] Judah, 2002:244
[363] Ulemek, 2013:25, 33-34, 152, 160
[364] Ulemek, 2013:112-113
[365] Buckley & Cummings, 2001:24
[366] Judah, 2002:255
[367] Judah, 2002:257; Kolb, 2014:156, 163-164
[368] Ulemek, 2013:155-158, 165, 293
[369] Buckley & Cummings, 2001:25; Judah, 2002:18; Baker, 2015:82; Ulemek, 2013:284-285, 295-299
[370] Buckley & Cummings, 2001:228, 241
[371] Baker, 2015:93; Buckley & Cummings, 2001:15
[372] Guardian; Judah, 2002:ix, x
[373] Buckley & Cummings, 2001:262
[374] Judah, 2002:xviii; Sv-Luka.org
[375] Judah, 2002:292
[376] OSCE; Crnobrnja, 1994:136
[377] West, 1942:923; Judah, 2002:54; Malcolm, 1994:53, 300-301, 343
[378] Guardian
[379] Judah, 2002:viii
[380] Buckley & Cummings, 2001:262
[381] Judah, 2002:xi
[382] Judah, 2002:vii
[383] Judah, 2002:ix
[384] Baker, 2015:85
[385] Crnobrnja, 1994:133
[386] Crnobrnja, 1994:138
[387] Baker, 2015:88
[388] Human Rights Watch
[389] BBC News
[390] Baker, 2015:88
[391] Malcolm, 1994:176
[392] Silber & Little, 1995:338
[393] Dizdarević, 2000:279
[394] Malcolm, 1994:67, 94
[395] Kržišnik-Bukić, 1996:74
[396] Dizdarević, 2000:430
[397] Baker, 2015:95-96
[398] Baker, 2015:92
[399] Hirkić, 1998:74
[400] Baker, 2015:93
[401] Guardian
[402] Baker, 2015:92
[403] Baker, 2015:92
[404] Baker, 2015:92
[405] Baker, 2015:113-117; Balkaninsight
[406] Crnobrnja, 1994:87
[407] Dizdarević, 2000:101, 108
[408] Crnobrnja, 1994:91, 109
[409] Dizdarević, 2000:116-119
[410] Dizdarević, 2000:111
[411] Maclean, 1949:329
[412] Malcolm, 1994:211
[413] Dizdarević, 2000:84
[414] Baker, 2015:38; Owen, 1995:127
[415] Kržišnik-Bukić, 1991:502
[416] Baker, 2015:24
[417] Dizdarević, 2000:290

[418] Abdić, 2016:63
[419] Silber & Little, 1995:326
[420] Silber & Little, 1995:248; Abdić, 2016:106
[421] Baker, 2015:40; Hirkić, 1998:310
[422] Silber & Little, 1995:231
[423] Baker, 2015:45; Crnobrnja, 1994:149-151
[424] Silber & Little, 1995:74
[425] Baker, 2015:60
[426] Bieber, 2014:548; Silber & Little, 1995:226-233
[427] Crnobrnja, 1994:7, 78
[428] Crnobrnja, 1994:17, 61, 95
[429] Kržišnik-Bukić, 1996:58
[430] Tusell, 1997:111-246
[431] Crnobrnja, 1994:116-117
[432] Kržišnik-Bukić, 1996:60
[433] West, 1942:99; Orwell, 1962:52; Maclean, 1980:44; Trkulja & Božić, 2008:83
[434] Andrić, 1967:107
[435] Crnobrnja, 1994:118-119
[436] Crnobrnja, 1994:148
[437] Baker, 2015:117
[438] Thompson, 1999:214; Abdić, 2016:100
[439] Malcolm, 1994:217
[440] Silber & Little, 1995:38,125,291
[441] Buckley & Cummings, 2001:257-262
[442] Baker, 2015:58; Owen, 1995:86
[443] Baker, 2015:92
[444] Baker, 2015:92
[445] Baker, 2015:113
[446] Baker, 2015:56-58; Owen, 1995:1
[447] Baker, 2015:8, 119
[448] Baker, 2015:46. 56
[449] Kržišnik-Bukić, 1991:535
[450] Malcolm, 1994:200; Hirkić, 1998:265
[451] Malcolm, 1994:149
[452] Crnobrnja, 1994:37, Baker, 2015:12
[453] Večernji List
[454] Baker, 2015:9
[455] Crnobrnja, 1994:18; Malcolm, 1994:43
[456] Malcolm, 1998:59; Crnobrnja, 1994:35
[457] Malcolm, 1994:27-42
[458] Malcolm, 1994:99-100
[459] Crnobrnja, 1994:57
[460] Baker, 2015:10
[461] West, 1942:325-326; Baker, 2015:13
[462] Malcolm, 1994:136; Kržišnik-Bukić, 1996:29-30
[463] West, 1942:390
[464] Malcolm, 1994:161
[465] Dizdarević, 2000:50
[466] Perica, 2002:169; Crnobrnja, 1994:23
[467] Kržišnik-Bukić, 1996:75
[468] Kržišnik-Bukić, 1996:79
[469] Dizdarević, 2000:28
[470] Dizdarević, 2000:27
[471] Kržišnik-Bukić, 1996:69
[472] Reuters
[473] Kržišnik-Bukić, 1996:58
[474] Judah, 2002:65
[475] Crnobrnja, 1994:106, 230
[476] Baker, 2015:43
[477] Hirkić, 1998:106; Kržišnik-Bukić, 1996:63
[478] Malcolm, 1994:198

[479] Kržišnik-Bukić, 1996:96-97
[480] Andrić, 1962:315-317; Ulemek, 2013:143-145
[481] Dizdarević, 2000:443
[482] Dizdarević, 2000:446
[483] Crnobrnja, 1994:22
[484] Malcolm, 1994:104-106, 122, 130-131
[485] Malcolm, 1994:95-106
[486] Malcolm, 1994:166-167
[487] Guardian
[488] Bastabalkana, 9
[489] Miljković, 2014:448
[490] Selimović, 1999:92-93
[491] Reuters
[492] Malcolm, 1994:188
[493] Avaz; Nezavisne novine
[494] Kržišnik-Bukić, 1996:74
[495] Baker, 2015:22
[496] Trkulja & Božić, 2008:13-15
[497] Baker, 2015:92
[498] Kržišnik-Bukić, 1996:6, 65-84
[499] Dizdarević, 2000:289
[500] Abdić, 2016:235
[501] Van Selm et al, 2003:192
[502] Baker, 2015:93
[503] Crnobrnja, 1994:48-49
[504] Baker, 2015:25
[505] Crnobrnja, 1994:93; Dizdarević, 2000:12, 113, 124, 428
[506] Crnobrnja, 1994:84-85
[507] Crnobrnja, 1994:148
[508] Dizdarević, 2000:324; Crnobrnja, 1994:89-90
[509] Dizdarević, 2000:444
[510] Crnobrnja, 1994:153; Baker, 2015:45
[511] Dizdarević, 2000:289; Silber & Little, 1995:78, 83; Crnobrnja, 1994:153-154
[512] BBC News
[513] ITN Source
[514] BBC News
[515] Baker, 2015:97
[516] Sky News
[517] Kržišnik-Bukić, 1997:10
[518] Baker, 2015:99
[519] BBC News
[520] Arnold, 2008:149
[521] Baker, 2015:99
[522] Baker, 2015:101
[523] Owen, 1995:351-352
[524] Orwell, 1962:172
[525] Guardian
[526] Financial Times
[527] Kržišnik-Bukić, 1996:98
[528] Baker, 2015:14
[529] Crnobrnja, 1994:149, 192
[530] Crnobrnja, 1994:193-194
[531] Crnobrnja, 1994:196-197
[532] Silber & Little, 1995:220
[533] Crnobrnja, 1994:202
[534] Crnobrnja, 1994:211, 201
[535] Crnobrnja, 1994:203
[536] Dizdarević, 2000:166; Kržišnik-Bukić, 1991:524
[537] Crnobrnja, 1994:212
[538] Crnobrnja, 1994:214, 217; Owen, 1995:353
[539] Crnobrnja, 1994:190

[540] The Australian
[541] Owen, 1995:358
[542] Silber & Little, 1995:66
[543] Malcolm, 1998:139-162; West, 1942:516
[544] Orwell, 1962:228-229; Kržišnik-Bukić, 1996:62; Bosnienbloggen
[545] Malcolm, 1998:217
[546] Dizdarević, 2000:338
[547] Silber & Little, 1995:87; West, 1942:112
[548] Baker, 2015:97
[549] Times of Israel
[550] Dizdarević, 2000:164, 169
[551] Andrić, 1967:280
[552] Hirkić, 1998:570, 572
[553] Hirkić, 1998:288
[554] IFRC
[555] Hirkić, 1998:385, 178
[556] O'Shea, 1998:239
[557] Hirkić, 1998:368
[558] O'Shea, 1998:240
[559] Avaz
[560] Baker, 2015:95, 128
[561] West, 1942:768
[562] West, 1942:377
[563] Kajtazović, 1996:20
[564] Kajtazović, 1996:22-23

EPILOGUE
FULL HOUSE

"Mujo was in a bar in Slovenia. The barman, a Slovene, asked him, 'Do you know where Bosnians come from?'
Mujo thought for a moment, and replied, 'No'.
'A bear fucked a tree stump', the Slovene laughed.
Mujo thought again for a moment and then asked, 'Do you know where Slovenes come from?'
'No', replied the Slovene.
'Ha ha, motherfucker' cried Mujo, triumphant. 'It fucked your mother!'"[i].

---

[i] Told by Oliver, a Montenegrin originally from Zvornik, in Sierra Leone, 2015. In Slovenia before the war, all speakers of Serbian/Croatian were referred to generically as *divlji Bosanci* ("wild Bosnians"). One day Družan and Izet, keen cross-country runners, were training in Ljubljana, and while crossing a bridge, were heard speaking by a passer-by who commented, "Fucking wild Bosnians". Izet went back and threw him off the bridge.

Showing the confrontation lines during the Cold War.

Around 9 pm on the eve of St. George's Day in 1950, the night of 5 May, around 200 men armed with a variety of firearms, knives and axes gathered in the hamlet of Bare, between Šturlić and Crnaja, 10 km west of Pećigrad. Among the men who gathered that night were their commander Milan Božić, a Bosnian Serb and *prvoborac* ("early resistance fighter"), and his 2IC Ale Čović, a Muslim and former Huska militiaman and Partisan. At the same time, in Koranski Lug ("Korana grove"), 5 km to the west across the Korana in Croatia, another 20 men, similarly armed, gathered under the command of the mastermind of the revolt, Mile Devrnja, a Croatian Serb and early resistance fighter, awarded the Partisan 1941 Commemoration Medal. A third group gathered in two locations further north: 20 men in Todorovo, and 40 in Gornja Vidovska, 5 km northeast of Šturlić and 2 km south-west of Mala Kladuša. Gornja Vidovska is 1 km away from Babo's home village of Donja Vidovska. The rebels' password was "Sabre – Sarajevo".

Twenty men from the Cazin *četa* ("company") left immediately on foot to act as reinforcements in the Croatian sector. The remainder headed south on foot 5 km to Tržac, where they were joined by another 100 men. Rapidly they disarmed and occupied the police station there. They then continued east along the road towards Cazin with their new weapons, and at dawn met up with other groups at the main rendezvous point and the headquarters for the revolt, Begove Kafane. They totalled 300 men. *En route*, in a breach of discipline, individual acts of looting had been carried out of the SRZs in Liskovac, Pjanići, Ćoralići, Šturlić and Tržac, the county supermarket and post office in Tržac, and the grain warehouse in Ćoralići. The ward archives in Liskovac were also burnt. At the RV the men were formed into 7 *vodovi* ("platoons"), with a total of 102 firearms. The town was surrounded, roadblocks were set up on the roads leading north and south out of Cazin, towards Velika Kladuša and Bihać respectively, and the telephone wires were cut in each direction. A letter was then written calling upon the authorities in Cazin to surrender the town, and was delivered to the UDBA station there at 6 am. Because the UDBA in Cazin (and also in Velika Kladuša) did not have a radio, they were now completely cut off. As the rebels waited for a response, a jeep approached from Cazin. It refused to stop when challenged, and was fired upon. The vehicle then did stop, and was found to be carrying officials from a provincial KPJ training team from Banja Luka. It was seized and the occupants detained. The vehicle was subsequently used by Božić to convey messages between the companies, and a message was immediately sent informing Devrnja that they had successfully seized weapons in Tržac. A bus travelling to Velika Kladuša was also stopped, and two JNA officers detained, before the remaining passengers were allowed to continue on their way. Meanwhile, due to a breakdown in communications, the signal to start (a beacon) was not conveyed to the first Velika Kladuša company, in Todorovo, and half of them ended up going home.

In Croatia, when the reinforcements from Bosnia arrived, Devrnja decided they were not well armed enough to attack Slunj. He therefore decided to seize some weapons he knew of in the hamlet of Furjan on the way to Slunj, and leaving the bulk of the company in charge of that, continued on to Lađevac where he was to gather more men. Unfortunately, by the time he arrived the extra men had already given up waiting and gone home. The first company seized a small quantity of weapons and also wasted time looting the SRZ in Furjan and burning the ward archives, before continuing on to Lađevac. There Devrnja replied to Božić's message with a brief sitrep. In the morning, the leader of the Bosnian reinforcements told him he had been summoned to return to Bosnia to take part in the assault on Cazin, and that Devrnja was to attack the police station in the village of Rakovica on the main road south of Slunj and cut the telephone lines there, to prevent assistance being sent from Croatia to Bosnia. The company now totalled 30 men with 14 firearms. That morning, the Slunj UDBA visited Furjan to investigate the reported looting. Not realising the gravity of the situation, they soon returned to Slunj, and it was only later that morning that they learnt there was an armed uprising, and called for reinforcements from Karlovac. They then received a telephone call from the UDBA chief in Velika Kladuša, who, alarmed that the telephone line to Cazin had been cut, was asking for assistance, and the decision was taken to send only a small unit to Furjan and travel with the main force (including the reinforcements) to Velika Kladuša.

In Bosnia, the remaining men of the first Kladuša company eventually decided to seize and disarm the Todorovo police station. However, they were interrupted in this by the Croatian UDBA unit sent from Velika Kladuša, and fled. The second Kladuša company looted a cadets' arsenal in Mala Kladuša and felled two telegraph poles, but postponed their assault on Velika Kladuša until they had raised more men. Meanwhile, the Cazin UDBA secretary, who because he was not a field agent was unlikely to be recognised, was ordered to travel to Bihać, disguised in civvies, and seek reinforcements. He was held up at the roadblock, but managed to talk his way through, and reached Bihać at 2 pm, having got lost on the way. From Bihać news of the uprising was transmitted to Banja Luka, from there to Sarajevo, and from Sarajevo to Ranković in Belgrade[1]. The JNA was mobilised from Banja Luka and Drvar. Meanwhile in Cazin, a dozen agents and civil servants were ordered to open fire on the rebels, at which they started to retreat. Two agents headed north to restore the telephone link, and by firing on the roadblock dispersed the rebels. They managed to re-establish communications and returned to Cazin. Another company was dispatched, and at midday, the rebels came under fire from the direction of Pećigrad, in their rear. At 1 pm Božić gave the order to retreat to the RV to regroup. However, most of the men then abandoned the revolt and went home, and when Božić saw this, he ordered the remaining 30 peasants to go home too. Čović sent word to Devrnja before attempting to flee to Slovenia (which was the backup plan for the leaders). At 3 pm, UDBA reinforcements arrived from Bihać, and immediately set about pursuing the rebels, encountering no resistance. The JNA arrived in the evening.

Near Rakovica, Devrnja divided his men into three groups. After cutting the telephones lines, they entered the village, intending to disarm and take prisoner two policemen in their homes, and then use them to take the police station without a fight. Their orders were to shoot if the police refused to surrender. While they succeeded in occupying the look-out post on the road, there was then a contact and one policeman was wounded, and the rebels withdrew and regrouped, before retreating into the forest when they received word that the UDBA was looking for them near Koranski Lug. Early the next morning, realising all was lost, most of them returned to their homes.

The next day, 7 May, the second Velika Kladuša company took up position on the Salakovac height on the main road between Cazin and Velika Kladuša. There was a contact with a company of policemen, and both sides fled. The company then received a message that Cazin and Slunj had fallen, and that they were to continue to

Mala Kladuša to raise more men. There was another contact with police in a wood near Polje, and one of the men was killed. The rest of the company then surrendered.

More UDBA arrived in Cazin from Sarajevo and Belgrade that day. Over the next four days, around 700 people were arrested in the Bosnian and Croatian Borders, including Božić and Čović and their families. Čović was detained in Mala Kladuša on 8 May, and Božić was apprehended near his home in Crnaja the next day. JNA reinforcements were sent to Bihać to prevent an uprising breaking out there. Hakija Pozderac hurried back to Cazin from Sarajevo and rebuked his people, but was quickly recalled, in circumstances that have not been fully explained. Meanwhile, Devrnja continued to try to raise men and weapons for the revolt, until on 19 May he was caught in an ambush when crossing the road at Korana bridge, having been betrayed[2].

The directive arrived from Belgrade:

> "Re participants in the rebellion, death sentences and hard labour to be handed down, as well as confiscation of property. Said property to become state property, and families to be exiled. Participants in the rebellion to appear before military tribunals".

Whether this directive was issued on his own initiative by Ranković, or was ordered by Tito, is not known[3]. 291 prisoners were tried by military tribunals in Cazin and Slunj in eight Kafkaesque, albeit public, mass trials over two weeks, concluding on 7 June, for offences under s. 3 Crimes against the People and the State Act, and 18 people were sentenced to death for sedition and armed insurrection (six after appeal to the Court Martial Appeals Court in Belgrade, the others commuted to between 15 years and life imprisonment), while 275 were sentenced to between three and 20 years' imprisonment with hard labour, all with confiscation of all their property and loss of civil rights for various periods (rights to vote, to be appointed to public office, to make public address, to bear an honorary rank, and rights to public services). The investigation was carried out by the UDBA, and the prosecutions were brought by military prosecutors from Sarajevo and Zagreb respectively, instructed by Belgrade. Devrnja, who had refused to appeal his sentence or apply for a pardon, was shot on 22 August 1950. Božić and Čović were shot on 6 November 1950 near Sarajevo and buried in the same grave at their request. According to the prosecutor at the Cazin trials, a Slovene, speaking in 1989:

> "The judiciary was at the service of the state, because it was a single-party state. There was no examination of evidence because the rebels had confessed everything and accused each other, but especially because under the UDBA's procedures, allowing the defendants to speak the truth would be to their advantage [...] Other people actually prepared the indictments, I don't think I wrote any of them. I was a representative of the state. None of the lawyers spoke with the defendants, and they did not prepare before the trial. The idea was to help the tribunal ascertain the truth [...] The judgments were mainly copied from the indictments"[4].

The Bosnian convicts mainly served their sentences in Zenica prison, while the Croatian convicts were sent to Stara Gradiška prison, a notorious *Ustaše* concentration camp during WWII. Others were imprisoned in Foča, or Kotor in Montenegro. Of the convicts, 10% were Serbs, 2% Croats, and the vast majority,

88%, Muslims. A further 450 defendants were sentenced under the Summary Offences Act by local ad-hoc summary offences commissions formed within the three county councils, and directed by the UDBA, to between three months and two years' community service for looting and assault, to be served by the Bosnians in Breza ("birch") coal mine, near Visoko, or Kakanj mine, while the Croatians did their community service in Slunj or Karlovac (the local authorities also used these proceedings to settle accounts with, or simply rob, certain individuals, who may not have had any involvement in the Peasants' Revolt at all). Many other people connected with the revolt were excluded from the KPJ (a major stigma, equivalent to being a traitor or a criminal[5]) and/or lost their jobs. In addition, and without any legal basis, 120 Bosnian families were exiled to Srbac, a mainly Orthodox county on the northern border with Croatia, 35 km north-east of Banja Luka, where they were housed mainly in abandoned ethnic German (and Polish) houses, and where the conditions were so difficult that some people died of hunger. This was not due to lack of concern by the local population, who were themselves extremely poor, and shared with the exiles what little they had. The justification for this collective punishment, the only time it was applied in Yugoslavia, was to break up any potential armed groups still at large. The exile order was signed by Moša Pijade, deputy prime minister (and later prime minister) of Yugoslavia[6]. After the death of Stalin in 1953, a time of major administrative reforms in Yugoslavia[7], the exiles were allowed to return to the Borders, some to find their homes had been stripped bare, others to find they had been allocated to other families, while one had been converted into a police station. At the same time, many of the convicts were given partial pardons and released on parole, and the last convicts were released on Republic Day, 29 November 1960. These punitive measures generated even greater poverty in the Borders, giving rise to the phenomenon of destitute wandering vagabonds, and an exodus to other parts of the country. Many of the Serb rebels (from both sides of the Borders) ended up moving to Srem in the 1950s and 1960s, and never came back[8].

At least 12 people were killed during the Peasants' Revolt, all on the side of the peasants, most of them "resisting arrest" in the subsequent crackdown, and the majority (seven) in Liskovac. The objective of the ringleaders had been to provoke a general uprising in the country, which they hoped would lead to a change of regime. There had been a disastrous drought in Croatia and Bosnia in the spring of 1950[9]. The extensive UDBA investigation did not uncover any evidence of the involvement of foreign intelligence services[10]. In 2007, Stevo Božić, who died in 2013, wrote

"The organisers of and participants in the rebellion had fought in the resistance, and many of them were early resistance fighters – freedom fighters. The *Četniks, Ustaše*, Greens, and nationalists were nothing to do with us. We were believers, but we were not religious fanatics. Some of us were KPJ members, members of the wartime KPJ, not the post-war KPJ, that rode roughshod over its programme and ideals. We belonged to the party of the people who we wanted to save from extinction. I would therefore like to point out that no political movement has the right to appropriate the 1950 Peasants' Revolt. It was a rebellion of the hungry, despised, humiliated and disenfranchised people. But I, and I am sure the other participants in the Revolt and their descendants, are ready to support any party that wants to tell the truth about our rebellion"[11].

There were at least 15 other, lesser, attempted armed uprisings in Bosnia and Croatia in 1949 and 1950, most of them disrupted in the planning stage, and tried in Glina, Zenica, Livno, and Prozor[12]. There was also an uprising near Smederevo in Serbia in the same period, and another in Macedonia[13]. After he read the report on the punitive measures taken in response to the Peasants' Revolt, Đilas said in conclusion: "They'll think twice before rebelling again"[14] (ironically, some of the rebels were under the impression that Đilas, who spent St. George's Day 1950 with Kardelj and Ranković in Ranković's native village in Serbia[15], was behind the revolt). These were the only armed rebellions against Tito's rule. Nevertheless, in 1953 the hated agricultural quotas and attempts at collectivisation were abandoned[16].

1950 was the period of the most intensive efforts by forces loyal to the King to destabilise the communist regime and create the conditions that would allow his return, and also the year when workers' self-management became law in Yugoslavia, for the purpose of the "further democratisation of society"[17]. The Peasant's Revolt also took place less than three weeks before the start of the Korean War of 1950-1953. Stalin and the US had both occupied Korea in 1945 (under Japanese occupation since 1910), and set up two rival governments there three years later (the government in the north was led by the founder of the Kim dynasty, who had sought refuge from the Japanese in the Soviet Union in 1940, and who is still the head of state, even though he died in 1994). On 25 June 1950, the north, backed by Stalin and Mao, invaded the south, and the UN security council authorised the use of force against the aggression, to be led by the US[18] (Stalin did not veto the security council resolution, as he hoped to drag the US into a war it could not afford to fight, as a prelude to tightening his grip on eastern Europe. Once the US had boots on the ground, Mao flooded the country with the remnants of his former enemies from the Chinese Civil War of 1927-1950, to kill two birds with one stone)[19]. 1950 also coincided with the demise of the resistance against Franco in Spain, which had been energised in 1945 by the defeat of fascism elsewhere in Europe, and Spain's rehabilitation as an almost respectable member of western society, on the right side in the Cold War[20]. Also in 1950, with France bogged down in a war in South-East Asia and sliding into war in Algeria, Fidel Castro graduated with a PhD in law from Havana university. Pavelić died in hospital in Spain in 1959, after a decade wandering Argentina and Chile. In 1945 he had evacuated his forces to Austria, where they evaded the Red Army and attempted to surrender to the British.

A blanket ban on reporting anything to do with the Peasants' Revolt in the Yugoslav media remained in force until the 1980s, a time when various retired UDBA agents started to publish their memoirs[21]. It was however reported in the Soviet anti-Tito press in 1951[22]. Nevertheless, the Yugoslav general public only had the opportunity to learn the truth, or even hear about the Peasants' Revolt when Dr Kržišnik-Bukić's book on the subject, seven years in the making, was published, on the eve of the Yugoslav Wars. The book was written in the greatest secrecy, but nevertheless in the spring of 1991 word got out that the matter was being researched, and one day the author received a typed, anonymous note with the message: "We haven't let anyone write about that, and we won't let you". However, events overtook the release of the book, and just before it was published, in October 1991, the author had to leave Banja Luka, where she had lived for 23 years, and return to her native Ljubljana. After 2,000 copies had been sold throughout Yugoslavia, in May 1992 the remaining copies were destroyed in a fire at the *Oslobođenje* premises in Sarajevo, caused by VRS shelling. Nevertheless, the book was reprinted in Slovenia in 1993. In 1994, Babo telephoned the author in Ljubljana and invited her to come to Velika Kladuša, via Split and Livno in transport he would provide, for a public debate on the book. The author, unwilling to become involved in politics, was unable to accept[23]. An extended version of the book was published in 2013, and the same year, Cazin council and then the Una-Sana canton adopted resolutions "condemning the mass violation of the human rights of the civilian population of the Cazin Borders in 1950 and the crimes committed by the totalitarian communist regime of the former Yugoslavia", largely thanks to the efforts of Dr Kržišnik-Bukić. Attempts to have a similar resolution adopted in Sarajevo and Zagreb have thus far been unsuccessful (according to Babo, the reason for this is that it would lead to claims for compensation, which would open the floodgates to claims for all the myriad injustices committed by the various authorities since WWII, and even before)[24].

"We had no choice, we couldn't take it any more, things were unbearable, the quotas will finish us, they already have, us and the livestock, peasants have to live too, stop the quotas or kill us, we have been led astray, you better shut up, it makes no difference now whether I shut up or not, we want to live like human beings as well, we're not livestock, we are now, we just happened to be here, down with the quotas, shut up you idiot, anything is better than looking at hungry children, we won't even be looking at them now, we came to the carnival, fucking carnival, there's nothing to celebrate now, we came here like every year, to see the festival, you got a good look then, I came for the girls, they said there was a rally, we don't want to starve, let's talk, let them see how bad it is, we've had a gutful, it couldn't go on any longer, two of my children died this winter, we can't even feed ourselves without the quotas, never mind with them"[25].

There was a peasants' revolt in Zagorje ("behind the mountain"), a region to the north of Zagreb shared by Croatia and Slovenia, in 1573, against the tyranny of the Hungarian feudal aristocracy (by contrast, slavery was banned in Dubrovnik in 1417[26]). The revolt and its aftermath coincided with the *fašnik* ("carnival"), late January and early February. After 12 days, the 10,000-strong serf army was defeated with 3,000 casualties, and widespread, brutal repression followed. Their leader, Matija Gubec, allegedly crowned peasant king during the revolt, had, by presuming to dream above his station, not only offended against the temporal authorities, but had also sinned against the spiritual order of things. He had to be destroyed as a symbol and an individual, and be purged of his sins by great pain, in the tried-and-tested Inquisition manner: he was first forced to witness the execution of his closest comrades, and was then grilled on an iron throne with a white-hot iron crown placed on his head before being quartered, in St. Marko's square in Zagreb, now the site of the Croatian parliament and government. After his death, he passed into popular legend, and it was said he would one day return[27]. He is said to have been one of Tito's role models and a source of inspiration in his youth, and Tito, himself a native of Zagorje, kept a large painting of the decisive battle at Donja Stubica, by Krsto Hegedušić, on the wall in his office[28]. A peculiar dialect is spoken in Zagorje, incomprehensible to speakers of Serbian/Croatian from further afield. Tuđman was also born in Zagorje.

Once upon a time there was a country called Yugoslavia. A country where society was everything, and where the state existed to enable and protect society.

On 16 March 1991, Milošević said, "Yugoslavia is finished"[29]. On 27 April 1992, Serbia and Montenegro proclaimed themselves the Federal Republic of Yugoslavia[30], and on 4 February 2003 the county was reconstituted as the State Union of Serbia and Montenegro. On 3 June 2006, Montenegro declared independence, and Serbia followed suit two days later[31].

Dizdarević wrote in 2000:

"Everything that had an important influence on and continually aggravated the crisis in Yugoslavia, and ended in its disintegration, had its roots within Yugoslavia itself. The crisis of the overall situation and relations in the country was fertile ground for nationalism, which returned from the dead and set the country ablaze[iii][32]. Nationalism destroyed the unity of the state. It became the undertaker both of Yugoslavia and of peace in the Balkans. The causes of the disintegration came from within Yugoslavia, they were not imported from outside. Certain centres and circles abroad merely exploited the existing situation and entered with their own interests, influence and activities. This was aimed at inciting and assisting those trends and forces that were acting against the system with a view to changing it and bringing it closer to western models. Everything indicated that the ambition of such activities was change to the system, and not the destruction of state unity. When the danger of a disintegration of the country arose, there were, because of its possible far-reaching consequences and dangerous precedent, efforts from the West – less so from the East, because they were occupied with the disintegration of the Eastern Bloc and the Soviet Union – to preserve some form of state union. However, such efforts were insufficiently decisive and too late"[33].

Yugoslavia had ceased to exist. And yet, her children live on.

Tito's widow, Jovanka, 32 years his junior, and his fifth wife, died in 2013. She spent her life after the death of Tito under house arrest in Belgrade, with all her property nationalised, even though she was never charged with or convicted of any offence. In the latter years of Tito's rule, she became his right hand and the only person he could trust. This made her the target of relentless attempts to discredit her, which appear to have succeeded: Tito separated from her in 1975[34]. She was suspected among other things of being a Soviet spy (there are also conspiracy theories about Tito himself, to the effect that he was a Soviet imposter the whole time, codename Walter: he allegedly had three fingers missing as a result of an industrial accident when he was captured by the Russians during WWI, but returned to Yugoslavia five years later with a full set – a miracle of Soviet medicine!, while

---

[ii] "*Nikad bolje u gorem zemanu*" became the watchword in Kuplensko.
[iii] According to Crnobrnja, the awakening of nationalism occurs in three stages: academic study of the attributes of the ethnic/religious group at issue; the appearance of "patriots" who garnish popular support within the group; and general acceptance of the group identity as a fundamental component of individual identity. This then gives rise to the need for an exclusive place in the sun for the group, with a homogenous population on land to which it has historic territorial claims.

others claim he never spoke Serbian/Croatian properly[35]). Jovanka was from Lika and had joined the Partisans in 1941 at the age of 17, and became Tito's secretary after the death of Zdenka. She was buried with Tito in Belgrade. Of Tito's five children, two survived childhood: Žarko, from his first, Russian wife, Pelagija, who grew up in Moscow, and whose daughter Svetlana is a cardiologist in Belgrade; and Mišo, a retired Croatian diplomat, from his third marriage to Slovene Herta, in 1940. His second wife was Austrian Lucia Bauer, who he married in Moscow in 1936.

On Easter morning 1915, Tito's unit in the Austro-Hungarian army was overrun in their trenches by Russian cavalry, near the Dnestr river in the Carpathians (Ukraine and Moldova). He was badly wounded and captured, and taken to Svijažsk on the Volga (Europe's longest and largest river), near the historic town of Kazanj in central Russia (the capital of Tatarstan, captured by Ivan the Terrible in 1552), where he spent a year convalescing in a monastery hospital. In May 1916, he was sent to work in a mill near Samara further down the Volga (an important Russian border town in the 17th and 18th centuries), and then transferred to Kungur near Permj (founded by Petr the Great in 1723) in the Urals to work on the trans-Siberian railway, where he found himself at the time of the March revolution. He resolved to travel to St. Petersburg to be part of the action, and did so, hiding among sacks of wheat in a freight train. He took part in the demonstrations against the provisional government which ran the country after the abdication of the Tsar until the October revolution, and was arrested and sent back east. He managed to escape again and travelled by train to Omsk (established in 1716 by a Cossack unit) in south-west Siberia, where he joined the Red Army and married his first wife. Omsk became the centre of imperial resistance to the Communists in 1918, and Tito travelled south to Tajikistan with his wife until the "Whites" with their WWI allies were defeated by the "Reds" (the new Soviet government had withdrawn from WWI, much to the delight of the Kaiser who, after a final strategic land-grab in the east, was able to concentrate his depleted forces on the western front; meanwhile, the remaining Whites made their way to Shanghai, and then the Philippines, before ending up in San Francisco). At the beginning of 1920, a committed revolutionary, he set off with his wife for the new country that was later to be called Yugoslavia. It was September by the time they arrived, and he found a job in a factory in Zagreb, where he also became a KPJ activist. In 1921 the KPJ was banned, after coming third in the first Yugoslav elections the previous year[36], and in 1924 Tito was arrested. After his release, he worked in a shipyard on the coast, where he was sacked for organising strikes. In 1926 he got a job on the railways in Smederevo, before returning to Zagreb, where he became a trade union official. In 1927, he was sentenced to 7 months in prison, but was acquitted on appeal. In 1928, after the assassination of Radić, he was sentenced to five and a half years for membership of the KPJ. His mechanical aptitude meant that in prison he was put in charge of the generator, and in return he was allowed to receive books, as well as associate with fellow-prisoners like Moša Pijade. He later described his time in prison as like going to university. Meanwhile, the KPJ, which had been practically stamped out, sent his wife and son back to the Soviet Union, and the *Ustaše* movement was established in Zagreb. When he was released in 1934, Tito went underground. He travelled to Vienna, where the KPJ leadership in exile promoted him to a management position. Returning to Yugoslavia, he organised conferences in Slovenia and Croatia with the objective of forming a core party leadership. It was at this time that he met Kardelj and Kidrič. After the assassination of King Aleksandar the same year, he returned to the Soviet Union, where he said he was disappointed by certain developments. He was appointed operational head of the KPJ and given the codename Walter in Moscow, where he also discovered that his wife had meanwhile divorced him. It was at this time that he first saw the new strongman in the Kremlin, seminary dropout Iosif "Stalin" ("steel Lenin") Džugašvili. In 1937, he returned to Zagreb, from where he organised a youth movement in Belgrade, via Đilas and Ranković. He then worked smuggling volunteers into Spain to fight in the Civil War. In 1938 he returned to Moscow, via Paris, and was appointed head of the KPJ. In March 1939, he returned to Yugoslavia, and set up his new party leadership, with HQ in Zagreb. Party membership, which had been low for years, began to grow again. After another trip to the Soviet Union, it was agreed at a KPJ conference in Zagreb that the way forward was neutrality, in accordance with the non-aggression pact signed between Hitler and Stalin in 1937. After the invasion of Yugoslavia, Tito travelled to Belgrade, and the KPJ prepared for a war of resistance, which was launched when Hitler invaded the Soviet Union two months later. In 1945 and 1946, tens of thousands of Yugoslav "war criminals" (some real, some merely dissidents) were executed in summary proceedings, and as many ethnic Germans and Italians, amongst others, were expelled. Relations with the West deteriorated rapidly after the end of the war, over the Trieste crisis, which although resolved without bloodshed in June 1945, caused popular anger in Yugoslavia. Trieste became a potential flashpoint (as well as a major black market), and there were several border incidents between the JNA and the US army. Tito reneged on the agreement reached under the auspices of Churchill and Stalin to share power with the King's regent, and in the autumn the newly-elected government abolished the monarchy. Nor did Tito's support to communist guerrillas in Greece endear him to the West. But at the same time, Stalin was unhappy with Tito's planned rapid industrialisation, as he wanted to keep the Balkans dependent on exports from the Soviet Union. Nor did Stalin approve of Tito's spontaneous political (and military) initiatives with other Eastern European countries. In February 1948, Kardelj, Bakarić and Đilas were told in Moscow that there were "unacceptable differences" between Yugoslavia and Moscow, and Yugoslavia was ordered to form a federation with Bulgaria (at the same time, Hungary was to unite with Romania, and Poland with Czechoslovakia). At a KPJ meeting the next month, it was decided to resist Stalin's demands, and at a party meeting in April, Tito's position received almost unanimous support (the dissidents were excluded from the KPJ and later arrested). In June, the Cominform conference in Bucharest adopted a resolution accusing Tito of among other things "arrogance" and running a "Turkish terrorist" regime. The resolution was published in the Yugoslav press, and at the KPJ conference three weeks later, the membership closed ranks behind Tito in rejecting it. Stalin responded with an economic blockade, and Tito renewed his friendships in the West[37].

The failure of Tito's health, in his eighties, coincided with the Soviet invasion of Afghanistan, opening the gates to 40 years of conflict in that country, with still no end in sight[iv38]. He was seriously ill in hospital in Slovenia for the last four months of his life, and from his deathbed expressed the fear that the speed with which Soviet forces had occupied all strategic points in Afghanistan (three hours), might encourage them to embark on a Balkan adventure, as they had in Hungary in 1956 and in Czechoslovakia in 1968. Yugoslavia publicly condemned the invasion (however, these fears quickly receded, as within two months it became clear that

---

[iv] ICRC found in a survey to mark 150 years of the battle of Solferino that, among other things, 60% of Afghans had been directly affected by the war.

Brežnev had bitten off more than he could chew, and he would certainly not open a second front. The Soviet occupation of Afghanistan lasted until 1989, when the US-backed *Mudžahedin* showed them the door. Afghanistan was apparently once a cool place to visit, on the hippy trail)[39]. At this time Bulgaria began to voice historical claims to Macedonia, and exiled crown prince Aleksandar Karađorđević was received by the Pope. *Ustaše* and *Četnik* organisations in the West (some even supported by the KGB) became vocal again and began to encourage terrorist and other subversive activities against post-Tito Yugoslavia[40]. In an ominous echo of the worst excesses of Stalinist lackeyism, arguments began to break out among the federal, republican and KPJ leaders on whether or not preparations should be begun for the impending *sprovod* ("funeral"), with accusations of lack of loyalty doing the rounds. Simultaneously, subversive activity (and even crime) in Bosnia was at an all-time low during this period: it appears that at least the people were united[41]. Tito's death led to a mass outpouring of grief throughout Yugoslavia, with an official seven-day period of mourning. He was buried in the "house of flowers", in the garden of his residence in Belgrade. Over half the population of Yugoslavia visited his tomb in the four years after his death[42]. Looking at this very un-English event in hindsight, and from the comfort of a safe, foreign country, it is tempting to take a cynical view, that people were under pressure to make public displays of their grief. But I happened to be in Cuba when Venezuelan president Hugo Chávez, Fidel's closest ally, who the former King of Spain famously told to "shut up" at a summit in Chile in 2007, and who in 2010 exhumed Simon Bolívar's corpse to make sure it wasn't an imposter, died, and I was surprised, watching the news in a hotel lobby, to see the hotel staff glued to the television, quietly wiping away tears (the president of Bolivia said that Chávez was now "*más vivo que nunca*" – "more alive than ever"). Nor should it be forgotten that there were similar scenes in the UK after the death of Princess Diana. It may also be that people in Yugoslavia were now deeply afraid of what the future would bring. US president Jimmy Carter described Tito in a statement as "a towering figure on the world stage [...] who faced many challenges but met them with a resolute determination to maintain Yugoslavia's independence and unity and its own unique approach to domestic and foreign policies", while Margaret Thatcher called him an "outstanding world statesman"[43]. Tito's funeral, attended by 209 foreign delegations from 127 countries, was such an international event that one foreign newspaper called Belgrade "the capital of the world"[44]. Tito's death also coincided with the rotating federal presidency and the chair of the KPJ's Popular Front passing to Bosnia[45].

The violent death of Yugoslavia 73 (or 88) years after its violent birth leaves a vacuum at this crossroads of three civilisations, with its strategic access to the Mediterranean. That organised crime would be the first to capitalise on this opportunity should not have surprised anyone. Tito successfully filled this troubled space by championing the Non-Alignment Movement[v] as a third way in the 1960s

---

[v] The movement was founded on Brijuni in 1956 by Tito, prime minister Nehru of India and president Nasser of Egypt (of Suez fame), and allowed him to maintain "equidistance" between NATO and the Warsaw Pact. Unlike the two belligerent military blocs that dominated the world, the Non-Alignment Movement was founded on the principles of peace and cooperation, and came to dominate trade in the developing world. It condemned the US' 1986 unprecedented air strike on Libya in the UN security council. Tito attended the movement's summit in Havana in September 1979, which was immediately followed by an IMF and World Bank summit in Belgrade. Arriving for the latter, Tito remarked to the institutions' staff, "From a summit of the poor to a summit of the rich". During the 1980s, Yugoslavia's

and 1970s (he was its first president, and its first official conference was held in Belgrade in 1961), playing off NATO and the Warsaw Pact against each other while embracing the Muslim world[46]. He was not the first to do so: according to Fitzroy Maclean, the medieval Balkan chieftains "understood above all the art of playing off the great powers against each other: East against West, Rome against Byzantium, Pope against Emperor, Teuton against Turk"[47]. Tito also provided his people with the highest standard of living in eastern Europe (most other communist countries had rationing, in particular Romania and the Soviet Union)[48]. However, the powerful destructive forces both within and outside Yugoslavia have ultimately proved irresistible in the absence of a charismatic individual able to master those forces and turn them to his own account. While in 1950 Tito reportedly sent Stalin a letter saying, "Stop sending assassins to kill me [...] If it doesn't stop, I will send my own man to Moscow, and that will be an end to it", Richard Holbrooke was able to say to Milošević in June 1998, "What's left of your country will implode"[49]. Does this mean that it is the destiny of the Balkans to be the playground of the great powers? Are the people of the Balkans incapable of living and working together? Does their diversity have to mean disunity, rather than being a source of strength? Or are they worth more to the international community fragmented, and scattered? Certainly, the long-winded, painful privatisation process in each of the countries as they move from the inefficiencies of planned economies to the ruthless free market, and the vagaries of the single market, is widely regarded as being riddled with corruption, producing nothing but unemployment for ordinary people while foreign investors and corrupt local officials line their pockets. The newly empowered republics initially nationalised corporations after discarding Marković's reforms, before proceeding to privatise them (in mid-1993, Babo proposed a privatisation programme that could be used as a mechanism to stop the war and create prosperity, but Izetbegović refused to discuss it)[50]. The invisible hand of the market has become a black hand with *carte blanche*, stifling the life out of communities with impunity, and stripping the country of its wealth more thoroughly and effectively than centuries of feudal exploitation.

Yugoslavia was a political proposition, not a nation state[51]. It was also a construct of its times (according to Ðilas, reported by Owen, "What brought and held different Yugoslav nationalities together was the common fear of foreign aggression or imperialism"[52]). While the international community originally approved of the creation of a strong Balkan state to act as a buffer against socialism and unrest, Yugoslavia later became a thorn in everyone's side[53]. And yet, after the death of Tito, both East and West sought to maintain Yugoslavia's stability[54]. In the early 1980s, when Yugoslavia was unable to service its growing foreign debt (and later – in 1988, Italy granted Yugoslavia loans on very favourable terms, while Iran and Venezuela expressed an interest in major investment programmes[55]), countries representing 85% of that debt rolled over repayment of much of it, while the IMF and the World Bank provided new loans and guarantees on export financing, all in order to maintain an independent and stable Yugoslavia as long as the Cold War lasted (Yugoslavia's solvency was further hampered by failures by the republics to discharge their liabilities, confident in the knowledge that the federal central bank

---

lead role in the organisation allowed it to hold onto its international prestige, for example, with an initiative to extend the ongoing talks on the removal of nuclear weapons from Europe to cover the Mediterranean, even as the situation at home slipped from the frying pan into the fire. From 1987 onwards, as the Cold War began to thaw, the Non-Alignment Movement, comprising two thirds of the worlds' countries, began to lose its importance. Yugoslavia's swansong in the movement was its 1989 summit held in Belgrade.

would pick up the tab. The failure by Croatia to cover USD 70 million owed by a Zagreb bank in 1982 was the most serious such case[56]. The reputation of Yugoslavia's major businesses also suffered, with ships failing to pay for services received in foreign ports, and the national airline failing to pay for fuel received abroad[57]). Despite this, the millstone of debt was one of the nails in Yugoslavia's coffin[58] (the federal parliament and the government were in disagreement on whether to accept the IMF's harsh conditions, and indeed on who was authorised to take such a decision. In hindsight, Dizdarević was of the view that the IMF had only made the situation worse, and had anyway been an instrument of western moneylenders; he also considered that the use of debt as a foreign policy tool was an "aggressive neo-colonialist policy of the Reagan administration"[59]. According to Mirvet, Bosnia is now indebted to international institutions to the tune of 47% of GDP, which is part of a deliberate strategy to misappropriate the country's resources)[60]. NATO's assessment in 1987 was that "Yugoslavia is the weakest point in the Euro-Mediterranean region [...] with the immediate possibility of a sudden explosion with global implications": the West's interest was still in an independent Yugoslavia, and it was ready to help the country overcome the crisis, but Yugoslavia would have to move towards more integration, at least with a single market, and the West would use political and economic pressure to prevent Yugoslavia reverting to the Warsaw Pact. It was also assessed that the Eastern Bloc was not involved in the crisis[61]. Ten years later, as the efforts of the EU, the UN and NATO moved from containment of the conflict to transition to a peaceful new reality, that reality was necessarily cast in the mould of the new world order, such as it was[62]. NATO decided that in the case of Yugoslavia, it was legitimate to set aside the right of sovereignty, a policy that would later have catastrophic consequences in the Middle East[63]. NATO, with the EU in its train, assumed the role of both promoter and defender of human rights, but on a legally, if not morally questionable basis[64]. "Humanitarian bombing", i.e. the destruction of civilian property without a strictly military objective, is contrary to art. 52(2) of Additional Protocol I to the Geneva Conventions. This provision of IHL is to be interpreted strictly, and does not allow exceptions for moral and political considerations. The only way it could be legal would be if it were authorised by the UN security council, or if there was concordant subsequent practice acting as a modification of the law, neither of which was the case. Was Yugoslavia then an outlaw state, beyond the protection of the law? The unilateral introduction of exceptions to IHL, in the expectation that they will subsequently be legitimised by the approval of the international community, is a dangerous practice[65]. The war in Kosovo was a violation of internal sovereignty and international law, yet UN secretary general Kofi Annan said that an "international norm against violent repression [...] must take precedence"[66]. Was he hoping to absolve his own sins from the disgraceful Rwanda debacle, again at someone else's expense, or were his motives more cynical, mercenary and opportunistic? I take the view that he's not fit to run a chip shop. The process of unnatural selection, whereby incompetence is rewarded by promotion, is rife in the UN. As they say in the Balkans, "*Othe kaj dine tut manrro ma iri mujal e piri*" ("they know where their bread's buttered")[67]. Perhaps Milošević's most far-reaching legacy, apart from the dead, the disabled, and the displaced, will be the fact that, like KGB chief Karla in John Le Carré's novel *Smiley's People*, he forced the international community to stoop to his level and resort to illegal acts of violence in order to defeat him. It is clear that NATO did not invade Yugoslavia for love of the Albanians, but to establish itself in its newly self-appointed role (in June 2007, George Bush junior's watch was apparently slipped from his wrist while he was on a walkabout in Albania, blessing the maunding multitude even as they clamoured for his touch. Now a three-metre high statue of the great man, with watchless arm extended in benediction, erected in 2011, marks the spot, in Fushe Kruje, north of Tirana. Albania joined NATO in 2009, as did Croatia, while Bosnia and Montenegro have been in accession negotiations since 2010[vi]. During Croatia's nine-year accession process, the HV embarked on a purge of soldiers with real combat experience, for fear they might detract from the image of its NATO-compliant, new model army. In 2016, the Serbian government signed an agreement granting diplomatic immunity to NATO troops, which led to opposition demonstrations)[68]. This was a sea change in international relations, and a step into a more arbitrary era, where the rule of law would be derogated to the will of powerful and charismatic leaders. An era of indiscriminate air strikes. Russia and China were largely alienated by this self-mandating approach, by-passing the UN, and arguably a continuation of the US' show of strength in Gulf War I[69] (and yet, George Bush senior declined to embark on an invasion of Iraq that he knew would be costly in lives, for unlike his son and his friends, he had known war, as a pilot in the Pacific, and knew it was not a game). At the same time, it gave Russia and China the green light to waive international law themselves, even as the "Kosovo precedent" of "humanitarian warfare" served to encourage NATO in its expansion into Eurasia, as if filling the power vacuum left after the Cold War (future Russian defence minister Sergej Ivanov commented in 1999 that NATO might next use force to "bring democracy to Belarus, Iraq and Syria")[70]. The Balkans have blown up before in the faces of great powers who allowed their initial successes on the ground to go to their heads. The Habsburgs were initially reluctant to engage with Bosnia, for fear of the instability a new Slavic population could bring; they were also opposed to the very idea of Yugoslavia in any form[71]. Bishop Strossmayer of Đakovo, the 19th century Croatian reformer, an early and leading proponent of Yugoslavism, warned Emperor Franz Josef that Sarajevo would be the rock that sank the ancient Habsburg ship[72]. However, their greed and ambition, and the conviction they were right and could not fail, led the Habsburgs to throw caution to the winds and, ignoring Bismarck's pithy analysis, embark on a reckless and ultimately fatal course of action. The fallout of this new chapter in international relations is manifested in vivid and powerful form by the images of tens of thousands of men, women and children milling in the mud, snow and rain, surrounded by razor wire and men in uniform armed with tear gas and sticks, as national and international power structures once again fail to protect society. As the late MP Jo Cox said

---

[vi] In 2016, Russia was allegedly behind a failed *coup* in Montenegro, which was supposed to prevent Montenegro joining NATO, an incident reminiscent of Russia's interference in Ukraine in 2013 (when the Ukrainian president unexpectedly refused to sign a long-anticipated deal with the EU and signed one with Russia instead, before being ousted in popular violence in 2014). Putin punished the Ukrainians by fomenting a rebellion by ethnic Russians in the east of the country, and annexing Crimea by means of a referendum (Crimea, the last Tatar state, was originally annexed by Russia in 1783, but in 1954 Hruščev made it part of Ukraine). This extremely efficient "divide and rule" tactic, deployed with a ruthless rapidity, means that Ukraine is now effectively paralysed economically and politically. Similarly, Georgia has been in the *zona* ("prison") since the end of the Cold War, with Moscow sponsoring two breakaway regions, South Ossetia and Abhazia. In 2008, in the belief that he had NATO's backing, the president of Georgia attempted to occupy South Ossetia, but was instead invaded by Russia. NATO now has missile defence systems in Turkey, Romania and Poland, and boots on the ground in the Baltic states (and Turkey), anathema to Putin, who called the break-up of the Soviet Union "*krupnejšćaja geopolitičeskaja katastrofa XX veka*" ("the greatest geo-political disaster of the 20th century"). Meanwhile, with NATO's "drawdown" in Afghanistan in 2014, US airbases in Uzbekistan and Kyrgyzstan closed in 2005 and 2014 respectively, and NATO announced it will be closing its office in Uzbekistan in 2017.

"We all know that the vast majority of the terrified, friendless and profoundly vulnerable child refugees scattered across Europe tonight came from Syria. We also know that, as that conflict enters its sixth barbaric year, desperate Syrian families are being forced to make an impossible decision: stay and face starvation, rape, persecution and death, or make a perilous journey to find sanctuary elsewhere."

Could it be that WWIII has already started, just as the effects of climate change begin to reveal the true extent of the damage wrought by the consumer society, where disposable choice is supreme? Consumerism is when we are merely sold our God-given birthrights in a gift-wrapped, empty box, that makes us complicit in ruthless exploitative practices whose ugly face is carefully kept at arm's length and will rarely intrude on our personal space; and no-one noticed WWI until a fortnight before everything shit itself. Meanwhile, the Balkans continue to be a blatant and flagrant area of injustice and insecurity. Human rights and fundamental freedoms have become a Marie-Antoinette-like euphemism peddled by a feudal elite.

Since the Cold War, the region has lost much of its former strategic significance for the great powers, and the US' contrasting decisive action to protect its interests in Gulf War I, as well as sending a warning shot across the world's bows, exposed the region's diminished geostrategic importance[73]. But the energy transport routes (and recurrent rhetoric on reviving the Silk Road) from Central Asia via the Caucasus and the Balkans are still the focus of various and conflicting international interests, and the very fact that the Balkans became an arena where different, and opposed, if not mutually hostile, geopolitical interests were able to engage and compete, in a miniature trial of strength, the direct consequences of which were, or at least appeared to be contained and limited geographically, highlights perhaps not so much the real historic importance of this region, but the way it has historically been perceived[74][vii]. It has been said that its importance is now only measured in terms of the stability it can bring to the EU[75]. Yet the fact remains that the Balkans were and are a single geographical region, of necessity bound by many complex layers of links, and Yugoslavia was an idea that promised the people of the Balkans something more than their sum[76]. Writing in 1980 after the death of Tito, Fitzroy Maclean said among other things that the decentralised federal system ("only one step away from secession") and the rotating presidency were guarantees that would allow the country to subsist and avoid any competing nationalisms, and that, while not a parliamentary democracy, the system of government was a functioning mechanism that allowed differing interests to be taken into account on a wide range of issues. He also praised the decentralised economy, and the system of mutual aid between the republics, while the JNA, he said, gave Yugoslavs the confidence of independence in a hostile world. He concluded by stating that too many people lived well in Yugoslavia to allow the country to disappear[77]. However, according to Dr Kržišnik-Bukić, a state in which the largest section of society, the peasants, were "not only *de facto*, but legally, economically and politically second-class citizens", was doomed to economic failure[78] (in 1984, the federal leadership learned that it was considered within NATO that Yugoslavia was undergoing an existential crisis, while in the

---

[vii] In June 1999, Sir Mike Jackson, commander of KFOR from June to October 1999, refused a NATO order to park helicopters on Priština airport to prevent Russian reinforcements from landing, as he said it was outside his mandate.

Soviet Union, it was considered that the US had succeeded in undermining socialism in Yugoslavia but that the burden of debt would turn the country back towards the Soviet model; it was also considered within western socialist circles that the very future of socialism depended upon the success of the Yugoslav model. The federal government concluded that both blocs would seek to test their resolve in Yugoslavia, but would go no further than that[79]). It is perhaps in the nature of states that are created with the promise of delivering on high ideals, that the glory of their genesis and the charisma of the leaders that that throws up obfuscate the fact that they are inevitably elitist, fundamentally dysfunctional and profoundly undemocratic. Unshakeable faith in the rightness of the end causes us to turn a blind eye to the unacceptable and ultimately feckless means employed on the way. Examples of successful states and international entities created with pragmatism to meet a practical need, without too much pomp and ceremony, are Switzerland and the predecessors to the EU[viii]. The received wisdom today is that the break-up of Yugoslavia was inevitable, the only real variable being the manner of its demise. Certainly, nowadays no-one is talking about a reconstituted Balkan federation. The divorce was just too painful, and the memories are still too fresh. Has there ever been a more perfect example of divide and rule? 100 years ago, radical patriots like Gavrilo Princip had a dream of the South Slav peoples united in defiance of the world order; but now those peoples have literally torn themselves apart. It is also the case that the failure of communism in the 1980s was masked by the even greater failure of nationalism in the 1990s (and the failure of foreign intervention since), such that the temptation in a society that is still reeling from such a devastating double whammy to look back on Tito's reign as a golden age, as simplistic as that may be, is strong. In the good old days, there was universal free healthcare and education (including further education), social security, law and order, and jobs ("eight hours work, eight hours sleep, eight hours recreation")[80]. As the Serbian writer Ognjen Daković commented,

"If it's all Tito's fault, why haven't you made us happy? Tito had a five-year plan, but you don't even have an agenda. Because of Tito we succeeded, but because of you we've failed. Why haven't you surpassed him, you who criticise him? Since we've been without socialism, we've been in the grip of amateurism, and it's not true that we failed because of socialism. We failed when we gave up on socialism"[81].

According to Mirvet, "the system failed when the Communists became Capitalists". But rather than dwell on the past, today young people tend to see their future in turning their back on the damned Balkans and emigrating. Yet there can be no doubt that the period between WWII and the Yugoslav Wars was the greatest (perhaps the only) period of peace, prosperity, development and international prestige that the various Yugoslav peoples have experienced in their history; and one to which all of them contributed[82]. Many of their neighbours were not so lucky. And the peoples of the former Yugoslavia still have to live together in one format or another[83]. In the 1860s, a decade after the two-year Crimean War (in which Russia was defeated by a British/French/Turkish coalition: the British and the French sought to thwart Russia's ambitions to expand southwards at the expense of the Ottomans), Prince Mihailo

---

[viii] The European Coal and Steel Community was created in 1951 to make French and German heavy industry so interdependent that they would never again be able to go to war against each other.

Obrenović of the autonomous Serbia (who was deposed in 1842 and returned to power in 1860, only to be assassinated in 1868: both the previous prince (retired), Aleksandar Karađorđević, and the Austrian security service were blamed) explored the idea of creating a Balkan federation out of the nations still under the Turkish colonial yoke, namely Bulgaria, Romania, Albania, and Bosnia, as well as independent Greece, but this was opposed not only by the Austrians, but also by the British and the French[84]. The second Balkan War of 1913 started when Bulgaria, unhappy with its spoils from the war against Turkey the previous year, invaded the territories it aspired to that had been occupied by Serbia and Greece. Newly-liberated Macedonia, with its unresolved identity, was the scene of some of the worst devastation (Greek or Slav (or Albanian)? Serb or Bulgarian? The Macedonian identity of local Bulgarians, whose violent separatist movement briefly took over Bulgaria in the inter-war years before being put back in its box by the joint action of King Aleksandar and the Bulgarian King Boris, was later fostered by Tito as a means to bind them to himself at the expense of Sofia, while local Greeks found themselves incorporated into the mother country[85]). Thessaloniki was also bitterly contested. The Bulgarian prince in 1913 was a Saxe-Coburg-Gotha[ix] in the pocket of the Habsburgs, and this war drove a wedge of bitterness between the new Balkan states that lasted for decades (Družan told me that once before the war he had travelled to Istanbul by bus. When they reached the Bulgarian border, metal shutters were fitted to the windows, cutting them off hermetically from the slightest glimpse of life in Bulgaria, and they were not removed until they crossed the border again, into Turkey). The first prince of Albania was another unemployed German aristocrat, who accepted the post under pressure from the Austrians[86]. In the early 1920s, the Comintern wanted to break up Yugoslavia and form a Balkan federation[87]. In the 1930s, before he was assassinated, King Aleksandar organised a Balkan Pact with Greece, Turkey, Romania and finally Bulgaria, as a means to isolate the violent ambitions of Italy and Hungary[88]. Conversely, when Hitler signed pacts with the Balkan governments in 1940 reducing the whole region to a feudal estate, it was only the Yugoslavs who said "No" to serfdom (the Greeks had already said "*Ohi*" ("no") to Mussolini, and been invaded for their pains). In 1948, there was talk of Yugoslavia and Bulgaria forming a wider Balkan federation. This initially enraged Stalin, as he had not been consulted, but he then attempted to hijack the idea by turning it round and instructing the two countries to unite, and to absorb Albania while they were at it. On reflection, Tito decided this was a poisoned chalice, and would end up costing Yugoslavia its independence[89]. In 1989, Yugoslavia proposed, organised and hosted the first-ever meeting of Balkan foreign ministers (even Albania attended), which promised to open the door to a new era of Balkan cooperation and prosperity just as the Cold War was ending[90]. Alas, it was not to be. Bulgaria and Romania joined the EU in 2007. While Yugoslavia fell apart as a state and was forced apart as a society, the current thriving cultural scene shows that the underlying links and even identity subsist[91]. Indeed, some of the best films about the Yugoslav Wars were made while it was still unfolding. The 1994 Romeo and Juliet-themed *Vukovar: A Story* is one.

According to Crnobrnja, the three factors that have, and will determine the fate of the Balkans, are relations between the various nations, political structures, and external influences[92]. Yet the current political institutions in the Balkans seem to be lost at sea, completely powerless faced with the forces of globalisation, absolutely incapable of controlling their own destinies. The generation of *babini sinovi* ("rich

---

[ix] Changed to "Windsor" in 1917.

kids"), whose parents' influence ensured they didn't have to fight in the wars, is now running the various successor countries (apart from Kosovo, which is run by the UÇK). *Pare na pare, uši na fukare* ("all aboard the gravy train"). Political leaders are at best middle managers, local authority officials, as the response to the refugee crisis in late 2015 and 2016 has shown. Macedonia and Serbia initially responded to the latest refugee crisis by waving the thousands of people through on their way to Germany. When Hungary closed its border with Serbia with a razor wire fence on 15 September, the Croats adopted the same tactic as the Serbs as the refugees turned west, to enter Hungary via Croatia. The day before, the Croatian prime minister had stated they were ready for the influx, ready to handle up to 5,000 per day; but as predicted by the media, 7,500 arrived on the first day alone. On 18 September, the Hungarians disarmed and arrested 40 Croatian police officers accompanying 1,000 migrants on a train north! On 15 October, Hungary completed a fence on its border with Croatia as well. The result is that desperate refugees are now being diverted north from Croatia through Slovenia, and a major bottleneck of wretched men, women and children is building up at that border, with the authorities completely overwhelmed. And now the Slovenes have built a razor wire fence on their border as well, while the Hungarians are extending their fence to their border with Romania. According to Croatian media, there are regular incidents of wildlife suffering a slow death after being caught in the coils of the Slovenes' fences. At the end of February, the Balkan countries agreed to introduce stricter border controls, with more fences and riot police. In March, the EU promised Turkey 6 billion euros and visa-free entry for Turkish citizens if Ankara would stop the flow, and Serbia and Macedonia closed their borders. The Balkans have become a new military frontier, a lawless buffer zone where only rievers, repression, and people-traffickers flourish. Meanwhile, the refugees keep arriving in Greece. What will happen if there is no legal way for the refugees to leave the Balkans? Attempts by Croatia to stem the tide flowing in from Serbia have already resulted in verbal confrontations between the border guards on both sides at Šid. At least UNHCR, in the person of Vincent Cochetel (a hostage in Chechnya for 317 days in 1998) immediately and publicly condemned the EU's plan in early March to organise a mass population swap between Greece and Turkey of people collectively labelled "refugees" or "economic migrants" respectively (the unworkable, inhumane plan was adopted regardless). As the late Tony Benn, who opposed the NATO bombing of Yugoslavia, once said, "The way a government treats refugees is very instructive because it shows you how they would treat the rest of us if they could get away with it". The fact that the Balkan countries were prima facie irrelevant in the decisions that were at the origin of, and in the devastating development of the war in Syria, appears to have been taken by all of them as a legitimate excuse for being overtly and ostentatiously irrelevant in the search for a solution. At least the Croatian government can use the refugee crisis as an argument to stave off a Greek-style haircut from Brussels[x].

Meanwhile, another humanitarian disaster is unfolding before our eyes as we watch from the comfort of our own homes. The EU has shown itself to be as impotent as the League of Nations. Once again, the refugees have no rights and no voice, and we can only wonder for a moment as between gulps of tea or coffee we catch sound bites conveyed by the media or social networks. Having escaped from the immediate danger of violence, the refugees must now face the less dramatic but potentially equally devastating barriers that separate them from a life in which their

---

[x] Write-down of sovereign debt.

human dignity is respected and which, if not faced with daily courage and optimism, can remorselessly grind them down. They must feed themselves and their children, keep them protected from the elements during the day, even as they travel, and find a warm, dry place to lay their head at night, hoping they will not be overtaken by disaster. There is a humanitarian response of sorts, and brief respite can be won at staging points. But 20 years on, the EU has yet again failed to adequately respond to an emergency in Europe, and while major European governments initially made humanitarian commitments as a result of public pressure, they have no comprehensive strategy, and the same fickle public pressure is already turning against immigrants from the Middle East as a coalition of the unwilling sets the EU agenda. There is no solution for the tens of thousands of refugees transiting through the Balkans, and no solution to the war that has forced them into exile. They are at the mercy of the faceless international institutions that purport to promote and protect the highest as well as the most fundamental human values; in practice, they are at the mercy of the criminals, corrupt officials and heartless members of the public who would exploit them at every stage of their ordeal. Where is the leadership to rise to the challenge of the "dead loathsomeness and disgrace of our day" (*"gràinealachd mharbh* [...] *masladh ar latha-ne"*)[93]? As T.E Lawrence wrote on WWI:

> "We could see that a new factor was needed in the East [...] No encouragement was given us by history to think that these qualities could be supplied ready-made from Europe. The efforts of the European Powers to keep a footing in the Asiatic Levant had been uniformly disastrous [...] Our successor and solution must be local"[94].

I spent ten days in Syria ten years ago, working with the Syrian Arab Red Crescent to strengthen their logistics capacity (since the start of the war in 2011, 22 SARC volunteers have been killed on duty). I travelled extensively around that fantastic country and was treated royally by my hosts, Samir and Hašim. Where are they now? The admirable activities of the heroic "White Helmets" civil defence volunteers in Syria are a ray of hope, not only for the immediate victims of the violence, but also because they allow a glimpse of the resources the Syrians have at their disposal to rebuild their country tomorrow. Damascus (liberated from the Turks on 1 October 1918 by an Arab army inspired by British officer T.E. Lawrence; when he left three days later, "the Syrians had their *de facto* government, which endured for two years, without foreign advice, in an occupied country wasted by war, and against the will of important elements among the Allies"[95]) is a marvel, with its Al Azem palace (once the Turkish *vezir*'s residence, and now converted into a museum), its magnificent mosques, such as the Umajad, its bathhouse (men only), its Hamidija bazaar that appears to have been the inspiration for Sarajevo or Mostar, its wonderful foods and fruit juices, roving coffee vendors and story-tellers in traditional dress, biblical landmarks, such as Straight Street, where a friend of mine, the late Ayman, used to live, and statue of Saladin on horseback strikingly reminiscent of the monument to his nemesis, Richard the Lionheart, in Westminster (Saladin was a Kurd from Tikrit, Saddam Hussein's home town, who became Sultan, and defeated the Crusaders in 1187). Then there is the pre-Roman city of Palmyra in the ever-present desert, and Homs with its multitude of *baklave* shops and Crusader fortress Crac des Chevaliers, described by T.E. Lawrence as the "finest castle in the world". Between Homs and Damascus there is a stretch of road known as the "magic road", where through an optical illusion (I think), stationary vehicles on terrain that appears to be flat start to move by themselves. I doubt anyone in Syria has time for such harmless pursuits at the moment. Half the population of Syria has left the country since the start of the war, and half the people still living in the country are IDPs. ICRC recently called the situation in Aleppo "devastating and alarming". The SARC and ICRC and the White Helmets continue to do sterling work supporting those worst affected by the crisis, but it is up to the politicians to put an end to the killing.

In conclusion, is the very idea of a Balkan powerhouse so dangerous, so abhorrent not so much to the general public, as to the guardians of our geopolitical vested interests and the established order, who purport to be the guardians of civilisation, that it is infinitely less acceptable than the reunited Germany? Does the ghost of Gavrilo Princip roam the capitals of the EU and NATO (and Moscow), stalk the corridors of power, and strike fear into their hearts? It would appear that the powers that be have decided that the Balkans are safer divided, indebted, bled white, and tenants in their own homes (if they are not in exile), dependent on the bounty and good grace of their elders and betters. Like *narkomani* ("heroin addicts").

Meanwhile, life goes on. *Biće bolje*[xi].

[xi] "Things can only get better". In October 2011, I attended the *Kestenijada* ("chestnut festival") in Pećigrad. Tetin came and picked me up in Velika Kladuša, from Jadra's house, where previously Seka and I had lived. On the way down through what had formerly been no-man's land, we passed Asfaltina, touting for business. As we approached Pećigrad, there were cars parked by the side of the road for a good few hundred metres, and pedestrians of all ages milling about everywhere. Off the side of the road, amid much smoke, Hamonja was roasting chestnuts to sell to the *meraklije* ("merrymakers"). He was the first NOZB soldier to have been wounded, in the hip, and I knew him from before Operation Storm. At the time he had walked with crutches and had fixators on his leg, but now he can walk unaided, albeit still with a pronounced limp. He was also in Kuplensko. In Pećigrad, we went to a crowded bar, with a calendar featuring Tito on the wall. Đedović was there, and Mirvet was to deliver a speech later on. After a few beers, some Romany *ćavorre* ("children") came into the bar, begging under the watchful eye of a lady who might have been their *dej* ("mother") or their *phen* ("sister"), who stayed outside. I addressed one of the children in Romany, and was rewarded with a Bosnian "Fuck your mother" for my pains. Tetin's mate Mario, from Split, a former merchant seaman, was also there. Outside, there were some pensioners dressed in Partisan uniforms with an accordion, singing Partisan songs. In a field below the opposite side of the road, a stage had been put up, and further down the field was another, improvised bar. We retired there, to better watch the show that had been laid on for the day's celebrations. There was much country dancing, music, and a few speeches. Tetin's daughter Sumaja was there, with his wife Mine and their son Senaid, as well as Mario's family. A good time was had by all: this time the people of West Bosnia could gather and celebrate their way of life without fear, on their home ground. It was as if there had never been a war.

"Those who dream by night in the dusty recesses of their minds wake in the day to find that it was vanity: but the dreamers of the day are dangerous men, for they may act their dream with open eyes, to make it possible."

T.E. Lawrence, Seven pillars of Wisdom

"It's not about how much meat you can eat, how many times a year you can go on holiday, or how many expensive items you can buy with your salary. It's about being a complete individual, with inner peace and along with it great responsibility. [...] In such circumstances a large dose of humanity is required, a dose of the sense of truth and justice, to avoid falling into routine and procedure, and ending up isolated from the people. This love for living humanity is a daily struggle and requires concrete acts that serve as an example and inspire."

"If I should die in some foreign field, my last thoughts will be for this people, and especially for you."

Che Guevara, Man and Socialism in Cuba/Farewell letter to Fidel Castro

---

[1] Maclean, 1949:327
[2] Kržišnik-Bukić, 1991:134-196
[3] Kržišnik-Bukić, 1991:202
[4] Kržišnik-Bukić, 1991:499-500
[5] Trkulja & Božić, 2008:161
[6] Maclean, 1949:328; Kržišnik-Bukić, 1991:275-410
[7] Trkulja & Božić, 2008:189
[8] Kržišnik-Bukić, 1991:555
[9] Kržišnik-Bukić, 1991:263
[10] Kržišnik-Bukić, 1991:275-410
[11] Kržišnik-Bukić, 1991:570
[12] Kržišnik-Bukić, 1991:239
[13] Kržišnik-Bukić, 1991:246
[14] Kržišnik-Bukić, 1991:382
[15] Kržišnik-Bukić, 1991:518
[16] Kržišnik-Bukić, 1991:512
[17] Kržišnik-Bukić, 1991:519-521
[18] Kržišnik-Bukić, 1991:268
[19] Chang & Halliday, 2005:436-442
[20] Tusell, 1997:255
[21] Kržišnik-Bukić, 1991:228, 246
[22] Kržišnik-Bukić, 1991:269
[23] Kržišnik-Bukić, 1991:530-538
[24] Kržišnik-Bukić, 1991:viii
[25] Kržišnik-Bukić, 1991:150
[26] West, 1942:242
[27] Erdélyi, 2016 :260-273
[28] Maclean, 1980:20
[29] Silber & Little, 1995:139

[30] Crnobrnja, 1994:223
[31] Baker, 2015:86-87
[32] Crnobrnja, 1994:5
[33] Dizdarević, 2000:426
[34] Dizdarević, 2000:42-43
[35] Britić
[36] Crnobrnja, 1994:56
[37] Maclean, 1980:14-46, 86-95
[38] ICRC
[39] Dizdarević, 2000:38, 52-53
[40] Dizdarević, 2000:53
[41] Dizdarević, 2000:57
[42] Crnobrnja, 1994:81
[43] Dizdarević, 2000:65
[44] Dizdarević, 2000:68
[45] Dizdarević, 2000:61
[46] Dizdarević, 2000:129, 137, 145-148; Crnobrnja, 1994:71-77; Maclean, 1980:103, 196
[47] Maclean, 1949:282
[48] Baker, 2015:21; Crnobrnja, 1994:84
[49] Montefiore, 2003:661; Waller, 1998:1
[50] Crnobrnja, 1994:258; Abdić, 2016:320
[51] Crnobrnja, 1994:255
[52] Owen, 1995:36
[53] Crnobrnja, 1994:45
[54] Crnobrnja, 1994:124
[55] Dizdarević, 2000:427
[56] Dizdarević, 2000:97
[57] Dizdarević, 2000:101
[58] Dizdarević, 2000:431
[59] Dizdarević, 2000:108,124
[60] Crnobrnja, 1994:87
[61] Dizdarević, 2000:424-425
[62] Crnobrnja, 1994:127
[63] Buckley & Cummings, 2001:13
[64] Buckley & Cummings, 2001:219
[65] Kolb, 2014:177-186
[66] Buckley & Cummings, 2001:228
[67] Courthiade, 2006:27
[68] The Wire
[69] Buckley & Cummings, 2001:241, 233
[70] Buckley & Cummings, 2001:235-237, 241, 245, 247
[71] Malcolm, 1994:136; Crnobrnja, 1994:43
[72] West, 1942:105-106; Crnobrnja, 1994:40
[73] Crnobrnja, 1994:138. 246; Buckley & Cummings, 2001:233
[74] Buckley & Cummings, 2001:235; Kržišnik-Bukić, 1996:56; BBC, 2003:part 4
[75] Van Selm et al, 2003:190
[76] Crnobrnja, 1994:245
[77] Maclean, 1980:122-123
[78] Kržišnik-Bukić, 1991:510
[79] Dizdarević, 2000:123-124
[80] Baker, 2015:97
[81] Facebook
[82] Dizdarević, 2000:433-435
[83] Crnobrnja, 1994:254
[84] West, 1942:535
[85] West, 1942:595-596
[86] West, 1942:578
[87] Crnobrnja, 1994:58
[88] West, 1942:611
[89] Maclean, 1980:90-91
[90] Dizdarević, 2000:161

[91] Baker, 2015:121
[92] Crnobrnja, 1994:255
[93] MacAulay, 1976:70-76
[94] Lawrence, 1997:39
[95] Lawrence, 1997:644-649

APPENDIX 1

Foreword by way of conclusion

If you ask me, being a refugee is a feeling of bitter hopelessness, of sweet desire for life, and naïve hope in a miracle. These feelings can only be fully understood by those few who have gone through that experience. And, of course, by John Farebrother.

Driven by some innate urge to selflessly help the helpless as they escape from persecution and death, blessed with goodness on his humanitarian mission, he has become the witness to hard and bloody times, like a passer-by lost in someone else's tragedy, which has somehow become his own. In the little refugee rooms and tents, in the fractured refugee camps, and in the hell of human tragedy and death, John was always welcomed with a smile, as a friend.

When in the summer of 1995, as a defeated and disarmed soldier with my back to the wall, isolated and without rights, exhausted by the uncertainty, and by the fear of being killed in front of my parents, John risked his life to save mine. His acts are sound proof that humanity and courage exist even in today's world.

We met just before the end of the Bosnian war in the spring of 1995. What brought John to our war, and what brought me at the age of 19 to be fighting in a war that I didn't really understand, is another story, but under those unhappy circumstances we met. Like so many other things in war, including death and the moments when we cheat death, our meeting was pure chance.

At that time, I was serving in the 2nd assault brigade of the NOZB, the rebel army of the autonomous region of West Bosnia. I found myself in dangerous company. My commanding officer was the former foreign legionnaire Milorad "Legija" Ulemek, who is now serving 40 years in prison as the mastermind of the assassination of the prime minister of Serbia, Zoran Đinđić[i1]. John had just arrived in Velika Kladuša, a small town in north-west Bosnia, stricken by war, and was working for the charity "Feed the Children". We were introduced by a mutual friend one day when I was on one-day leave from the front.

A few months later, at the beginning of August 1995, I met John again. This time my army had been completely routed, and for the second time, tens of thousands of the residents of the Bosnian Borders fled the onslaught of the ABiH, against whom we had fought. A long column of civilians and armed soldiers, of which I was one, crossed into Croatia and stopped about 20 km from the Bosnian border. That was the start of the Kuplensko refugee camp, one of countless refugee camps in the world that no-one wants to know about.

The humanitarian disaster in the camp deteriorated from one day to the next. The refugees were not given enough aid, but the starvation and exhaustion were not a chance occurrence: they were a method of pressurising the refugees into returning, to their homes under the control of an enemy army. In breach of the rules of war as prescribed by the Geneva Conventions, and of the Charter of the United Nations and the Universal Declaration of Human Rights, the Croatian army and police would enter the camp at night, separate men from their families, and hand them over to the regime that had driven them out.

---

[i] Legija notes in the conclusion to his memoirs that their "quality would have been greatly improved if I was not where I am today".

Like everyone else around me, I nervously counted the days, waiting for my turn to come. I would go to sleep at night in fear, and wake up in the morning in fear. And then one day when I was walking through the camp with the friend who had introduced me to John, I saw him again. I'll never forget that day. He was sleeping in his dust-covered white Toyota, parked under a stout oak that provided him with some shade that hot August. When we woke him up by tapping on the dirty window, overjoyed to see him, we asked him what he was doing there, because we thought he had been transferred to central Bosnia. John's answer changed our lives forever, and may even have saved us:

"I've come to save you", he said, half asleep, and happy to find us alive.

At that time, escaping from the camp was unthinkable. The Croatian army and police had tightened a noose around the camp, and some attempts to escape had ended in blood. In order to send a clear message to the rest, anyone caught trying to escape was beaten, and some were even shot in the arms and legs, and then deported to Bosnia, to the tender mercies of the people they had fled from.

We were determined to leave, which involved a great deal of risk, but for the five of us there was no hesitation. We were desperate. John's plan was for us to simply get in the car with him and drive out of the camp. However, three checkpoints full of soldiers had been set up at the entrances and exits to the camp, and we would have to go through them without being stopped. His idea was so crazy and dangerous, that we liked it immediately. There was nothing for it but to raise a glass of *rakija*, which was always available for special occasions. Finally, there was just one small outstanding detail that we had not fully understood.

"John, what if the army stop us at one of the checkpoints?", we asked him, expecting an answer that would reassure us he had a well thought-out plan that had a chance of success.

John first looked at us in silence, raised his glass of *rakija* and said, "In that case, we're all fucked".

In the infernal 35-degree heat, the soldiers in full battle dress weren't keen to leave their shade to stop Feed the Children's dust-covered Toyota. After three and a half years, the war was over for us.

After the former Yugoslavia, John has witnessed wars and natural disasters, and the suffering of refugees and IDPs, in the former Soviet Union, Africa, Central America and South-East Asia. His rich experience unquestionably qualifies him to address the subject of refugees and IDPs from his first-hand observations, but also to draw people's attention to the sad fact that refugees and IDPs are the innocent victims, not only of crazed authoritarian and totalitarian regimes and the geopolitics of the West, but also of the failings of the institutions responsible for providing aid and protection.

Today we are the witnesses to the greatest number of refugees and IDPs ever. There are currently around 70 million people forced to live away from their homes, among them around 25 million refugees. Today, around 10 million persons wander the earth without nationality, which by itself is an obstacle to the basic protection provided by the state: education, health, and freedom of movement, etc. Unfortunately, the situation is only getting worse bearing in mind that every day, 35 thousand people are forced to leave their homes because of armed conflicts or the fear of persecution.

Today's refugee and IDP tragedy is different from earlier such tragedies, because their struggle for survival, their search for a safe home and efforts to secure a happy childhood for their children are dogged by an unprecedented media campaign and a rise in the popularity of far-right fanatics in Europe. Even in the US, directly responsible for creating millions of refugees, they are viewed as a threat to national interests and security, and even as potential terrorists. The facts prove overwhelmingly that the fear of refugees is unfounded. Since the tragedy of 11 September 2001, almost one million refugees have gone to America, and yet so far, none of those refugees has been arrested for activities related to terrorism.

We, the citizens of the rich and arrogant West, have allowed our democratically elected leaders to embark on their criminal, geopolitical adventures, however and whenever they want, regardless of the damage caused, and with total impunity. The results are death, destruction and unprecedented human tragedy. The numbers of the dead, the wounded, the refugees and IDPs have become mere statistics.

Before anyone says we are not responsible for those people, those statistics, we should recall some facts. It is not true that we are free of responsibility for the tragedies that have struck Afghanistan, Iraq, Libya, Syria and Yemen. Directly or indirectly, we have destroyed those countries. It is not true that Islamic State and the crimes committed by its militants have nothing to do with the overthrow of the regimes in Iraq and Syria. It is not true that the countries of Western Europe and America are not directly responsible for creating regional instability in the Arab world. It is not true that we have a clear conscience.

The truth is that we have blood on our hands. And not just a little. The truth is that we have repeated the lies of our innocence so many times that we firmly believe them. The truth is that the fanatics of Islamic State fight with the most modern weapons of the US army. The truth is that they fund themselves by selling oil to Turkey and Israel. The truth is that schools and hospitals in Yemen are destroyed by planes and missiles bought from the West. The truth is that Islamic militants in Libya were armed by the West in order to overthrow Gaddafi, and now Al Qaeda ["the base"] is being armed in Syria. The truth is that we have abandoned innocent refugees to the tender mercies of organised criminals who every day send them on boats towards Europe, charging their whole life savings for a journey that many of them do not survive. The truth is that we are abandoning those refugees to drown in the deep waters of the Mediterranean when their boats capsize. The truth is that we will continue to do so.

The migration of refugees is an international problem, and it is the duty of all countries, their political and social institutions to secure the refugees' right to life. Today, when we are richer than ever before, when we can help far more, we watch refugees dying from hunger, treatable diseases, and in the dark waters of the Mediterranean. We watch and say that it isn't our problem.

I am fully aware how lucky I am that my refugee story had a happy ending. I am not the only one John saved, nor was John the only one who saved someone. I am one of the few refugees who was moved to a safe country and offered the chance to start again. According to UNHCR's official statistics, less than 1% of refugees are moved to safe countries. Can't we do better than that? Don't we want to do better than that? What about the millions of refugees crammed into mega refugee camps in Lebanon, Jordan and Turkey? The conditions in those camps are so bad that increasing numbers of people are returning to the hell on earth of war-stricken Syria. But we don't want to help.

John's book, in which he selflessly shares his rich life experiences, sends a very clear and simple message. Refugees are ordinary people who in the darkest moments of their lives have not forgotten humour and humanity, how to fight for their rights, for an opportunity to live. Refugees celebrate birthdays, fall in love and get married, and hide away when they cry; they have ambitions, and want to be something in life. This book will rightly shame many, who might ask themselves why they didn't do more when refugees from Bosnia needed help. But let's move on, forget Bosnia and give help to the people who need it today.

Help is urgently required. Some people will say that the current institutional framework is adequate to deal with the problems of refugees. No, it isn't. Even though there is practically no continent from where refugees do not come, and not a year goes by without a new wave of refugees, we continue to approach every new refugee crisis as an *ad hoc* accident. This has to change. Our attitude towards refugees and their problems has to change. There is nothing more painful than the moment when you pack your life into a small suitcase and leave your house, setting out on a one-way journey in the knowledge that you no longer have a home. Refugees leave their homes weeping not because they want to, but because they have to. Rather than being ashamed before them, we are afraid of them.

My and my friends' story had a happy ending. Today, more than 20 years since those events, Samir has a MA in political science and is a successful consultant in Denmark, Nero and Šeki have built careers in the US, and Denis after graduating from university is a civil servant in the UK. After obtaining a BA and a MA at London School of Economics, I have built a career in the financial sector in London. Just like the refugees who today set out on dangerous journeys and arrive in Europe by boat, we are ordinary people who experienced an extraordinary tragedy. We have managed to create a normal life for ourselves, although the scars of our trauma are engraved deep within us.

While you read John's book, ask yourself why our story with a happy ending is still a rarity 20 years later. Why it is that almost 99% of refugees are never resettled in peaceful countries, but are forced to live for years and in some cases for decades in refugee camps, dependent on the charity of others, and deprived of fundamental human rights. Ask yourself how you can help.

Dragan Karajić

3 September 2016

APPENDIX 2

Figures

Agrokomerc promotion, pre-war, available at
https://youtu.be/Axingu63NKEv

Proclamation of autonomous region of West Bosnia, September 1993, available at
https://youtu.be/z4M8i3h5Sn8

NOZB surrender negotiations in Pećigrad, July 1994
https://youtu.be/n-xaYBqCKZE

Arrival in Kuplensko, August 1995, available at
https://youtu.be/U3qVE8RlB3M

Facebook page: https://www.facebook.com/damnedbalkans/

Maps

APPENDIX 3

It is difficult, if not impossible, to do proper justice to poetry in translation. For that reason, the unpublished original poems used in the book are set below, to allow readers familiar with SH *to enjoy them to their full extent.*

Ulazi Srbin u slastičarnu i traži sladoled.
Pita ga Albanac, "Hoćeš li kuglu ili iz automata?"

DOBRI LJUDI OVOGA SVJETA

O dobri ljudi ovoga svjeta
Čujte vapaj pjesme moje
Pomozite nama ovdje
Sjetite se djece svoje

Zar da naša mala djeca
Ovih dana zimskih hladni
Gaze ovo ovdje blato
Idu bosi, goli, gladni

O kakvo je vaše srce
Od kamena il od leda
Pa zar može cijeli svjet
Ovu bjedu sad da gleda

Zar smatrate, kod naroda
Da to nije velki grijeh
Pa vratite našoj djeci
Vratite im vi osmjeh

Što šutite i gledate
Naše muke i probleme
Sjetite se vaše djece
Sjetite se sad je vrijeme

Jesul naša djeca kriva,
Što ostaše sad bez kuća
Sjetite se doma svoga
Al i našeg, al od pruća

Sjetite se svojih vila
Sjetite se svog balkona
Sjetite se naših kuća
Krovovi su od najlona

Sjetite se svoga jela
Što ručate – večerate
Zar moraju naša djeca
U Kupljenskom da se pate?

I da misle za doručak
Šta će majke da im spreme
Sjetite se naše djece
Sjetite se sad je vrijeme

Sad vas pitam ja gospodo
I molim vas sada sviju

Gdje će naša mala djeca
Svoje noge da ugriju.

Dok sjedite kraj TV-a
I gledate razne vijesti
Pitajte se dobri ljudi
Šta će naša djeca jesti.

Možda će ova pjesma
Imati nekog jeka
Zar ovo da nam se desi
Na kraju dvadesetog vijeka

I cijeli svijet gleda
Znateli to je grijeh
Jedino vi možete
Vratiti djeci osmjeh.

HUMANITARNE KATASTROFE

Ja se stvarno sam sebi divim
Kako uopšte mogu da živim
Sve mogu da pojim skoro do noći
Ono što dobijem humanitarne pomoći

Jednom sedmično humanitarna se dijeli
I hranom je ugrožen kamp cijeli.
I mnogi zbog hrane imaju brige
Zato što dobiju samo dvije ribe.

Recimo evo u četvrtak prošli
Kada su kamioni u kamp došli.
Dovezli pomoć navodno nama
Al teško se živi ovih dana.

Po jednom članu ribe dvije
Zadovoljan ovdje niko nije.
Šećera kilu ni govora o grahu
I pola kile mlijeka u prahu.

Uvijek je moja hrana suha
Ujutro dobijem pola kile kruha.
Za ručak pojedem ribe dvije
Jedino večera suha nije.

Kako će biti suha večera
Kad jedem samo vode i šećera.
Sutradan pojim po kile mlijeka
Sljedeći četvrtak stomak mi čeka.

Šta da vam kažem u pjesmi sad
Ovdje je stvarno velika glad.
Stomak mi nema nimalo mira
Jer nema brašna a ni krompira.

I stvarno ljudi izgledam jadan
U sedmici pet dana sam gladan.
Jedino eto tu je izuzetak
Samo četvrtak, a možda i petak.

Četvrtak ribe u petak mlijeko
A drugi četvrtak je daleko.
Sudbina je moja izgleda taka
Subota i nedjelja praznog stomaka.

Oslabio sam same kosti
Ponedjeljak i utorak ovdje se posti

I cijeli svijet sve to gleda
Bogami često posti se i srijeda.

Oh Bože dragi šta se to dešava
Kad niko našu sudbinu ne riješava.
Može li brašna kila jedna
Biti nama četiri tjedna.

Stvarno sa malo brašna tako
Ovdje nije živjeti lako.
Iako nije vrijeme Ramazana
Ovdje se posti svakog dana.

Nemamo hrane nema ni struje
Narod je jadan mora da psuje.
Da li to svijet baš tako želi
Kada nam malo pomoći dijeli?

LOKALNI CRVENI KRST

U Šatoru Crvenog krsta
Na šestom kvartu na mostu
Pruži se usluga svaka
Svakome našem gostu

Pročita se poruka lična
Još pruža usluga raznih
Kafa se posluži često
I da se poruka praznih

Rasim ko Rasim šef
Lokalnog Crvenog krsta
Pa nema budale veće
Od Skoplja pa do Trsta

I tako svaki dan
Tu svrati mnogo raje
Dugo bi trebalo tražiti
Budalu veću od Smaje

A ja sam sam u kampu
I kafu sebi pečem
Dali sam i ja budala
To neću sad da rečem

Stavimo sad na stranu
Te muke i dileme
Idemo sada dalje
Da vidimo sve probleme

Recimo vatra negori
Jer drvo samo tinja
Uvjek samo galame
Smajo Seka i Minja

Dežurni danas sam ja
A sutra možda i ti
U šatoru Crvenog krsta
Ludi smo izgleda svi

Onda kada ja uđem
I stanem pored zida
Hajde baci mi grah
Navali luda Aida

Fadila sjedi za stolom
I uvjek nešto piše

Na vratima što su pisali
Ćamila mora da zbriše

A ja je onda gledam
Čudna mi neka faca
Predi joj Smajo ime
Nije Fadila nek Maca

Husmira samo šuti
Nešto je previše tiha
Još jedna mjenja ime
A to je naša Mediha

Zlatan sjedi sa strane
Tačnije s desnog boka
Nije Mediha Mediha
Ona je sada koka

Onda Račinović Ajša
To mi je slabija strana
Uvjek mi nešto šuti
I muti ismihana

Ako sve nije vako
Dabogda haman umro
Ostali su Rurić i Velić
I snjima Kudić Zumro

Skroz mi se s uma sklonila
Družanova kuma bila
Mirna mirna simpatična
Feđinca Purić Džemila

Al ima još jedan problem
I još Curića nema
Posebni slučaj je ovdje
Ta Omanović Eka

Čudna je stvarno čudna
I samo zjeva i šuti
Mirvetom igra bele
I uvjek nešto muti

Slatka simpatična vesela
Odjednom joj neka muka
Na um joj tada padne
Holandija i Orčeva Luka

Nju muči jedan problem
To ona od nas krije

Znam da joj je stvarno teško
Zbog toga i suze lije

Ja problem njezin znam
To mi je kazalo vreme
Ali će ona uskoro
Riešiti svoje probleme

Irfo i Hasiba nastranu
Njih krasi jedno djelo
Svaku noć nas zovu
Il dođu nama na sjelo

I eto tako je to
U šatoru Crvenog krsta
Ludnice veće nema
Odavde pa do Trsta.

ROĐENDANSKA PJESMA

Skupismo se noćas ovdje ljudi sa svih strana
A došli smo mi večeras svi zbog rođendana
A na stolu mnogo jela a i raznih pića
Tu je bilo djevojaka a i par mladića

Kad smo pošli na rođendan Harisa smo zvali
Nije išo jer je imo jedan poso mali
Nema poklon on da dadne a nema ni pića
Morao je on da skokne malo do Vojnića

Dok Hasiba tu po stolu reda razno suđe
A na vrata policajac Omer tada uđe
Na vratima nako stoji i sviju nas gleda
Pozdravlja nas te nazdravlja i kod Irfe sjeda

A kraj Irfe Mirvet sjedi i pomalo drema
A Hasiba kraj šporeta i kafu priprema
Tad se čuje tu u sobi galama i vika
A Bajrić nas sviju redom tu u sobi slika

Dok nas slika sjaji mu se tu na glavi ćela
Dođe kafa ja pogleda al previše bjela
Šta je ovo ja se pitam znali od vas neko
Hasiba nam podvalila tu u kafu mlijeko

Na kauču Haris mali a kraj njega Eka
Glava ju je zabolila ali nema lijeka
Sjedi Tetin na kauču odmah pored Eke
A Džon se je navalio ljudi preko Seke

Gledam Eku pa mi žao što je glava boli
Tad mi naum pade onaj koga srce voli
Pa od muke pijem konjak da ublažim tugu
Vjeran hoću da joj budem i neželim drugu

Družan pije a do njega sjedi mala Minja
Ode Smajo do šatora dovede Džastina
A i Mirvet malo jede a malo i pije
Pa nazdravlja skupa samnom za nju što tu nije

Uđe Džastin i Hasibi rođendan čestita
A na stolu mnogo halve i sirnica pita
Tad je ljubi kraj Hasibe nako malo stade
Pa izvadi litru pića i Hasibi dade

Tad Hasiba uze litru i piće nam toči
U sviju se od konjaka zasvijetlile oči

I Dino je tu u sobi i nema drugara
Tad Hasibi Džastin reče pa sretno ti stara

A Inbrinca isto prešla ali Ibre nema
Ostao je on u sobi da malo odrema
Tad svi piju nazdravljaju a sa njima Ija
Pa počešmo da igramo asocijacija

Neko priča razne priče neko neku foru
Tad Omera neko zove onda na metrolu
Da izađe i pogleda kakvo li je stanje
A u šumi neko sječe one male grane

Tada ode pola društva a pola ga osta
Ja se napi jedva pređe preko onog mosta
A što piješ Tetin sine kad ti piće škodi
Nemaš nikog da te pjana takvog kući vodi.

KUPLJENSKO

Kupljensko, jedno malo selo,
Preko noći postalo je grad.
Nekda je malo tu ljudi bilo a
Mnogo, mnogo, mnogo ih je sad

Nije to grad ko svaki grad,
Jer nema zgrada, škola i kina,
To je grad užasa i bijede,
Mnogi ga nazvaše paklena dolina.

Ja gledam, ulicom prolaze ljudi,
Na licu vidim samo bol i tugu.
U našem gradu, jedna je ulica,
Koja je šest kilometara duga

U našem gradu nemamo struje,
Zato narod živi u mraku.
Sretan je onah ko ima kuću
Ili neku možda drvenu baraku.

Ja možda griješim što sad kažem,
Da nema škola, kina i zgrada.
Imamo čudne zgrade i škole,
A škola naša je obična cerada.

Imaju i ulice, al opet čudne,
Kvartova deset u tom je gradu.
Zima je stigla al drva nema
Pa drva moraju ljudi da kradu.

I svako jutro ovdje je čudno
Najviše majke nemaju mira,
Od čega djeci spremiti ručak,
Kad nema luka, graha i krompira.

U tom je gradu zabranjeno svakom,
Da dođe i vidi nekog svoga,
Pogledaj, svijete, malo taj grad,
Pogledaj bar u ime Boga.

Ponekad prođe vozilo neko,
Ali uglavnom prolaze stranci.
Porodica je puno u ovom gradu,
Al ima i onih koji su samci.

Mnogo je djece koja ulicom trče
Da dobiju možda od stranca čokoladu,

Čudno je ovdje, čudno baš sve,
Al ipak se živi u ovom gradu.

U gradu ima, a opet čudnih,
Štandova raznih i par kafića,
Možeš da kupiš sebi ponekad
Cigarete mesa i litru pića,

Ponekad naiđe i pjanac neji
I svi znamo da s razlogom pije,
Nijedan grad na ovom svijetu,
Koa naš grad, čudan nije.

U svakom su gradu obučeni ljudi,
Igraju se u toplom domu svom,
A ovdje ljudi bosi i goli
I opet se nekako čudno smiju.

I cijeli svijet to dobro zna,
I tako hladno na to sve gleda,
Al što nam ne daju voće i povrće,
Zašto bar mira nam ne da.

Kad je u pitanju naš čudni grad
Tada je svijet veoma škrt.
Ja to sve gledam i pitam sebe,
Je li to grad ili zoološki vrt.

Neki nas navlače majmuni da smo,
A neki ipak da smo mi ljudi.
I zato ovaj naš čudni grad
Sviju nas ovdje, baš sviju čudi.

Okolo grada ograde čudne,
Al to nije bodljikava žica,
Već čudna uniformisana lica,
Strah i jeza hvata nas sviju,

I gdje god kreneš, niz ukicu čudnu,
Rampa i policajac stoji,
Ali sa nama neće da zbori,
I zato je ovaj naš grad, baš čudan grad.

O svijete, svijete, pogledaj malo,
Gledaj malo baš čudni grad:
Sve što imamo u ovom gradu,
To je blato, bijeda i glad.

Imamo ponos i to je naše,
I osmijeh naš, to svijet nek vidi,

Ali zbog čudnog našeg grada
Ti cijeli svijete, stvarno se stidi.

Stidi se, svijete, bar djece naše,
Jer što će oni sutra da kažu.
Istinu tražite u ovom gradu
Pitajte njih oni ne lažu.

Istina je ovdje u ovom gradu
Od tebe, svijete, tražimo glas
O sudbini našoj ne pitaj nikog,
Dođite ovdje, pitajte nas.

Čudan, baš čudan ovo je grad
Kao da ga se svijet boji.
Dođite, slobodno pitajte nas
U ovom gradu istina stoji[2].

MOJA SOBA

U sobi sjedim sam
Sam i kafu pijem
Onda razmišljam malo
I sam se sebi smijem

Soba je 3 puta 3
I izgleda jako mala
Ja imam ležaj neki
A nemam svoga regala

Na vratima visi objesita košulja
Papuče u ćošku sobe
Dvije ormarice male
U njima nešto robe

Stolica jedna isto
Stoji tu pored vrata
U drugom ćošku sobe
Moje cipele od blata

Zatim visoka peć
I pored nje nešto drva
Na prozoru narezak stoji
I pored njega krušna mrva ?

I dalje kafu pijem
Cigaru za cigarom pušim
A pored peć ja neku
Mokru svoju robu sušim

Na dvije ormarice stoje
Upaljene dvije svijeće
Narezak riba i maza
Kraj vrata vreće za smeće

Džugumić jedan mali
I na ormariću špigla
Kanister za frišku vodu
I jedna staklena krigla

I tako soba je moja
Ja u njoj imam mira
Na prozoru visi bunda
Kraj maskirnoga šešira ?

I šećera imam svoga
To neću da krijem

Al' nemam nikog svog
Da sa njim kafu pijem

I onda se onako sjetim
Na stara prošla vremena
O Bože Bože dragi
Gdje mi je sada žena?

U drugom dijelu sobe
Brašno ulje i soli
Gdje mi je mala Maja
Za njom me duša boli

Teško je bez njih teško
Zato mi duša pati
Gdje su mi braća i sestre
Gdje mi je otac i mati?

Ali ja mislim da vidim svoje najmilije
Da će doći i to vrijeme
I da će dragi Bog
Riješiti moje probleme

KADA DOĐEM KOD DŽONA I SEKE

Kada dođem kod Džona i Seke
Uvjek čujem od njih svađe neke
Svađaju se ko ručak da pravi
Ko će vodu za kafu da stavi

Džon tad kaže mene boli glava
Seka reče da mora da spava
Onda Džonko da se ne obruži
Sam ustane i goste posluži

Tada vodu on za kafu stavi
Počne jadan i ručak da pravi
Al nemože Seka da ga gleda
Pa mu ona praviti ručak neda

Ko to pravi sada bitno nije
Važno mi je da se kafa pije
Gledam Džona sa njom sav je jadan
Al je važno da on nije gladan

I dok Seka sve za ručak meće
Narezaka Džon da jede neće
A artikli ovdje su nam skupi
Ode Džonko i mesa da kupi

Kad su skupa e Bog s njima brate
Kad su sami tad oboje pate
E tako je životami moga
Tad nemogu jedno bez drugoga

Eto tako Džon se Sekom muči
I Tetinog on engleski uči
Seka živac stalno nešto psuje
Eto tako u šatoru tu je

Razdvojeni kad su Boga mole
Da su skupa da se opet vole
Svađati se oni uvjek neće
Nek su skupa Bog im dao sreće

ZAGRLILA SEKA DŽONA

Zagrlila Seka Džona
Pa joj sada zvone zvona
O vidi je vrag te jebo
Otišla u sedmo nebo

Voleće ga sve do smrti
U naručju s njim se vrti
On je gornji ona dole
Vrag te jebo što se vole

Džon je stigo izdaleka
Jer ga stvarno voli Seka
Ali i on Seku voli
Boga dragog za nju moli

Gledaju se s puno žara
U njima se ljubav stvara
A srce im jako lupa
Presrećni su kad su skupa

Od srca im želim sreću
Malo tuge radost veću
Prava ljubav u njih toje
Pa neka ih nek se spoje

Nek se vole treba tako
Razumjet ih nije lako
Nek se vole dok su mladi
Bože dragi šta joj radi

A i Seka prava čigra
Pa po Džonu igru igra
Seka za njim stvarno žudi
Hoće za njim da poludi

Nek se vole neka neka
Pa polako malo Seka
Ko od vatre tako gori
Porodicu sebi stvori

Zagrljaji im se stežu
Polako se oni vežu
Bože dragi vidi vidi
Pa sa njih se i znoj cidi

Izvinite vi na šali
Što vam piše Tetin mali

Samo nek se Džon ne ljuti
I Seka će znam da šuti[3].

Sead "Tetin" Kajtazović, Paklena Dolina

---

[1] Ulemek, 2013:298
[2] Hirkić, 1998:284-286
[3] Kajtazović, 1996:9-16

ACKNOWLEDGEMENTS

Many thanks to Mike and Mrs Ivey for your hospitality, and for taking me to see *Schindler's List*; to Dr Vera Kržišnik-Bukić for allowing me to reproduce the first three chapters of her seminal work on the 1950 Peasants' Revolt; Eddie Duranović for filling in some gaps in my memory, and for high level information of which I was unaware re Kuplensko; Dragan Karajić for filling in the many gaps in my knowledge of modern Balkan history, for his political analysis of the war, and not least his inspiration; Adis Jugo for more historical and local knowledge, and for some flashbacks; Graham "Kiwi" Wootton for his technical knowledge, anecdotes, photographs and encouragement; Tony Conlay for background information to which I would otherwise not have access; Sead "Tetin" Kajtazović for filling in gaps in my memory; Julian Neale for his encyclopaedic technical expertise; Milan Gačić for more flashbacks; Gordon Bacon for filling in gaps; Mike "Canbat" Rarog for anecdotes before my time; Mirvet Beganović for filling in other details before my time; Justin Cockerell for details on the first days of Kuplensko; Dr Mladen Pupovac for political insight and moral support; Zuhdija "Hope" Miljković for cutting some Gordian knots; Asim Abdurahmanović for his cartographic skills; Paul Anticoni and Ros Armitage for providing historical data; Alessandra Morelli for a frank and open interview; Goran Boljanović for his initiation into Yugoslav smoking habits; Dr Skender Baca for personal recollections; Dr Curtis Doebbler for his insights into the workings of UNHCR and the Bosnian and Croatian governments; Zlatan Delić for political insights; Fikret "Babo" Abdić for an extensive interview; Thomas Farebrother and Adnan Kajtazović for graphics services; the hundreds of Yugoslavs who have gone out of their way to make me feel at home in their country, even in the most difficult of times; and last but not least, Seka Farebrother for a thousand and one gentle encouragements.

BIBLIOGRAPHY

Abdić, Fikret "Babo" (2016), *Od idola do ratnog zločinca i natrag*, Naklada Kvarner, Rijeka

Abdić, Muhamed (1992), *Kraini u Amanet*, Tiskara Rijeka, Rijeka

Aljazeera America, *Sex abuse scandals cast shadow over UN peacekeeping summit*, available at http://america.aljazeera.com/articles/2015/9/28/sex-abuse-scandals-cast-shadow-over-un-peacekeeping-summit.html [accessed 13 December 2015]

Ambrose, Stephen E (1975), *Crazy Horse and Custer*, Simon & Schuster, Sydney

Andrić, Ivo (1967), *Deca*, Mladost, Zagreb

Andrić, Ivo (1967), *Gospođica*, Prosveta, Belgrade

Andrić, Ivo (1962), *Na Drini Ćuprija*, Mladost, Zagreb

Andrić, Ivo (1967), *Nemirna Godina*, Prosveta, Belgrade

Andrić, Ivo (1967), *Prokleta Avlija*, Prosveta, Belgrade

Andrić, Ivo (1967), *Staze Lice Predeli*, Prosveta, Belgrade

Andrić, Ivo (1967), *Travnička Hronika*, Prosveta, Belgrade

Andrić, Ivo (1967), *Znakovi*, Prosveta, Belgrade

Arnold, Roberta (Ed) (2008), *Law Enforcement within the framework of Peace Support Operations*, Martinus Njihoff Publishers, Leiden

Avaz, *mr. Ibrahim Đedović – kandidat za člana predsjedništva BiH*, available at http://forum.avaz.ba/showthread.php?2783-mr-Ibrahim-%C4%90edovi%C4%87-kandidat-za-%C4%8Dlana-Predsjedni%C5%A1tva-BiH [accessed 17 July 2016]

Avaz, *Svjedok Šabić: Bilal Bosnić je uništio svaku kuću u koju je ušao*, available at http://www.avaz.ba/clanak/170432/svjedok-sabic-bilal-bosnic-je-unistio-svaku-kucu-u-koju-je-usao?url=clanak/170432/svjedok-sabic-bilal-bosnic-je-unistio-svaku-kucu-u-koju-je-usao [accessed 14 December 2015]

Bakker, Peter and Kzuchukov, Hristo (Eds) (2000), *What is the Romani language?*, University of Hertfordshire Press, Hatfield

B92 and Vreme Film, *Jedinica*, available at http://www.b92.net/specijal/jedinica/index.php [accessed 16 December 2015]

Baker, Catherine (2015), *The Yugoslav Wars of the 1990s*, Palgrave, London

525

Balkaninsight, *Croatia 'destroyed books by non-Croats in wartime'*, available at http://www.balkaninsight.com/en/article/belgrade-pays-tribute-to-destroyed-books [accessed 5 December 2016]

Balkaninsight, *Fascist slogan near Croatia concentration camp sparks anger*, available at http://www.balkaninsight.com/en/article/plaque-near-wwii-concentration-camp-scandalises-region-12-05-2016 [accessed 5 December 2016]

Bastabalkana, *Izlamska deklaracija*, available at http://www.bastabalkana.com/wp-content/uploads/2012/09/Islamska-Deklaracija-knjiga-o-islamizaciji-muslimana-Alija-Izetbegovic.pdf [accessed 19 October 2015]

BBC, *Smrt Jugoslavije,* available at http://tvprofil.net/show/3944501/smrt-jugoslavije [accessed 8 August 2017]

BBC News, *Bosnian candidate jailed for war crimes*, available at http://news.bbc.co.uk/1/hi/world/europe/2165007.stm [accessed 10 January 2016]

BBC News, *Bosnia-Herzegovina protests break out in violence*, available at http://www.bbc.co.uk/news/world-europe-26086857 [accessed 10 January 2016]

BBC News, *France's unwanted Roma*, available at http://www.bbc.co.uk/news/magazine-25419423 [accessed 14 December 2015]

BBC News, *Kosovo EU bribe faces independent enquiry*, available at http://www.bbc.co.uk/news/world-europe-29912404 [accessed 26 February 2016]

BBC News, *The Greek debt crisis story in numbers*, available at http://www.bbc.co.uk/news/world-europe-33407742 [accessed 24 July 2016]

BBC News, *Poland's former PM Tadeusz Mazowiecki dies aged 86*, available at http://www.bbc.co.uk/news/world-europe-24700801 [accessed 10 January 2016]

BBC News, *Red Cross marks battle anniversary*, available at http://news.bbc.co.uk/1/hi/world/europe/8121805.stm [accessed 10 January 2016]

BBC News, *What does the International Criminal Court do?*, available at http://www.bbc.co.uk/news/world-11809908 [accessed 8 March 2016]

BBC News, *Why is there a crisis in Calais?*, available at http://www.bbc.co.uk/news/uk-29074736 [accessed 13 December 2015]

Belišova, Jana (Ed) (2005), *Phurikane gilja*, Žudro Civic Association, Bratislava

Benedek, Wolfgang (Ed) (2012), *Human Rights in Bosnia and Herzegovina after Dayton*, Martinus Njihoff Publishers, Leiden

Bieber, Florian (2014) "Undermining democratic tradition: the case of the 1990 fouding elections in Bosnia and Herzegovina", *Southeast European and Black Sea Studies*, vol. 14, no. 4, pp. 548-555

Blic, *Ove stihove je Gavrilo Princip u zatvoru noktima urezao*, available at http://www.blic.rs/vesti/drustvo/ove-stihove-je-gavrilo-princip-u-zatvoru-noktima-urezao/qh3n6tc [accessed 23 December 2015]

Bosnienbloggen, *Aleksandar Vučić's amnesia*, available at https://bosnienbloggen.wordpress.com/2014/06/20/aleksandar-vucics-amnesia/ [accessed 23 December 2015]

Bosnjaci.net, *Presuda kojom se osuđuju Alija Izetbegović i njegovi prijatelji*, available at http://bosnjaci.net/prilog.php?pid=33707 [accessed 23 December 2015]

Britić, *Tito's titbits*, available at http://www.britic.co.uk/current_issue.php?article_id=46 [accessed 10 April 2016]

Brown, Dee (1991), *Bury my Heart at Wounded Knee*, Vintage, London

Buckley, Mary and Cummings, Sally N. (2001), *Kosovo Perceptions of War and its Aftermath*, Continuum, London

Ćano, Kasim (Ed) (1994), *Drmeljevo svjedok optužbe*, Odis – Radio-Televizija Bihać, Bihać

Centar za Mir, *Fiket Abdić County Court*, available at http://www.centar-za-mir.hr/uploads/Fikret_Abdic__County_Court_Karlovac__2002.pdf [accessed 8 January 2016]

Chang, Jung and Halliday, Jon (2005), *Mao the Unknown Story*, Jonathan Cape, London

Commission on Human Rights, *Situation of human rights in the territory of the former Yugoslavia*, available at http://www.nato.int/ifor/un/u960823a.htm [accessed 8 January 2016]

Commission on Human Rights, *Situation of human rights in the territory of the former Yugoslavia*, available at http://www.heritage.sense-agency.com/assets/Uploads/sg-1-05-tadeusz-report-may-en.pdf [accessed 8 January 2016]

Courthiade, Marcel et al (2006), *Sagesse et humour du people Rrom*, L'Harmatan, Paris

Crnobrnja, Mihailo (1994), *The Yugoslav Drama*, IB Tauris, London

Dizdarević, Raif (2000), *Od smrti Tita do smrti Jugoslavije*, Svjetlost, Sarajevo

Djurić, Rajko (1990), *Bi Kheresko Bi Limoresko*, L'Harmatan, Paris

Dnevni avaz, *Najopasnije bitke – Sarajevo i BiH 92-95*, available at http://forum.avaz.ba/showthread.php?99-Najopasnije-bitke-Sarajevo-i-BiH-92-95/page5 [accessed 23 August 2016]

DW.com, *Fikret Abdić "Babo" ponovo na slobodi*, available at http://www.dw.com/sr/fikret-abdi%C4%87-babo-ponovo-na-slobodi/a-15798775 [accessed 23 August 2016]

Erdélyi, Gabriella (Ed) (2016), *Armed Memory: agency and peasant revolts in central and southern Europe (1450-1700)*, Vandenhoek & Ruprecht, Göttingen

Executive Intelligence Review, *Mazowiecki resigns UN post*, available at http://www.larouchepub.com/eiw/public/1995/eirv22n32-19950811/eirv22n32-19950811_035-mazowiecki_resigns_un_post_blast.pdf [accessed 19 October 2015]

Executive Intelligence Review, *Yugoslavia's 1971 Crisis of Decentralisation*, available at http://www.larouchepub.com/eiw/public/1977/eirv04n48-19771129/eirv04n48-19771129_051-yugoslavias_1971_crisis_of_decen.pdf [accessed 19 October 2015]

Facebook, *Ognjen Daković*, available at https://www.facebook.com/profile.php?id=664102767 [accessed 17 November 2016]

Financial Times, *The Hague rules Netherlands liable for 300 Srebrnica deaths*, available at http://www.ft.com/cms/s/0/f8803366-0cd7-11e4-90fa-00144feabdc0.html#axzz42EaW99hn [accessed 7 March 2016]

Forsyth, Frederick (1969), *The Biafra Story*, Pen and Sword, Barnsley

Freshpress, *Dogovor u Karađorđevu*, available at http://freshpress.info/kolumne/dogovor-u-karadordevu-tudman-milosevic-htjeli-bosnjake-preseliti-u-tursku/ [accessed 17 November 2016]

Grahović, Šejla (2014), *While you played I ran*, Xlibris, United States of America

Grupa za direktnu zaštitu ljudskih prava, *Statement concerning the status of human rights in the Kuplensko camp near Vojnić*, available at https://groups.google.com/forum/#!topic/cl.europa.balkan/-6Oo-CLvU84 [accessed 8 January 2016]

Guardian, *Bosnia and Herzevogina: the world's most complicated system of government?*, available at http://www.theguardian.com/news/datablog/2014/oct/08/bosnia-herzegovina-elections-the-worlds-most-complicated-system-of-government [accessed 26 February 2016]

Guardian, *Cruel to be kind?*, available at
https://www.theguardian.com/world/2005/jun/24/g8.debtrelief [accessed 7 February 2016]

Guardian, *Dutch cabinet resigns over Srebrenica masacre*, available at
https://www.theguardian.com/world/2002/apr/17/warcrimes.andrewosborn [accessed 24 August 2016]

Guardian, *Ebola crisis brutally exposes failures of the aid system, says MSF*, available at
http://www.theguardian.com/global-development/2015/mar/23/ebola-crisis-response-aid-who-msf-report-sierra-leone-guinea [accessed 16 March 2016]

Guardian, *Fearful Serbs ready to flee an independent Kosovo*, available at
http://www.theguardian.com/world/2007/dec/02/balkans [accessed 12 January 2016]

Guardian, *Haitians launch new lawsuit against UN over thousands of cholera deaths*, available at
http://www.theguardian.com/world/2014/mar/11/haiti-cholera-un-deaths-lawsuit [accessed 20 February 2016]

Guardian, *How Britain and the US decided to abandon Srebrnica to its fate*, available at
http://www.theguardian.com/world/2015/jul/04/how-britain-and-us-abandoned-srebrenica-massacre-1995 [accessed 15 December 2015]

Guardian, *Lebanon: Blair's other Middle East mistake*, available at
https://www.theguardian.com/commentisfree/2010/sep/09/lebanon-blair-middle-east-mistake [accessed 15 December 2015]

Guardian, *One family's story of the terror inside Kosovo*, available at
https://www.theguardian.com/world/1999/jun/17/balkans8 [accessed 15 December 2015]

Guardian, *Surviving Serbia*, available at
http://www.theguardian.com/theobserver/2001/jun/24/life1.lifemagazine4 [accessed 15 May 2016]

Guardian, *The real reasons Bush went to war*, available at
http://www.theguardian.com/theobserver/2001/jun/24/life1.lifemagazine4 [accessed 15 May 2016]

Guevara, Ernesto Che (2014), *El socialismo y el hombre en Cuba*, Ocean Sur, New York

Helsinki Watch, *Report 1994 Bosnia-Herzegovina*, available at
https://www.hrw.org/reports/1994/WR94/Helsinki-04.htm [accessed 14 February 2016]

Hirkić, Ramo (2007), *Afera 87*, Tampeldo, Velika Kladuša

Hirkić, Ramo (1998), *Egzodus naroda zapadne Bosne II dio*, Klubovi zapadne Bosne u inostranstvu, Phoenix/Hamilton

Huffington Post, *Was Tito und Willy Brandt im April 1971 auf der Insel Brijuni tatsächlich vereinbarten*, available at http://www.ifrc.org/docs/appeals/RPTS96/CROAT1.PDF [accessed 14 February 2016]

Humanitarian Law Centre, *Compensation of damages for former detainees of Šljivovica and Mitrovo Polje camps*, available at http://www.hlc-rdc.org/?p=30399&lang=de [accessed 25 March 2016]

Humanitarian Outcomes, *Aid Worker Security Database*, available at https://aidworkersecurity.org/incidents/report/summary [accessed 29 June 2016]

Human Rights Watch (1999), *Aucun témoin ne doit survivre*, Editions Karthala, Paris

Human Rights Watch, *DR Congo: army, UN failed to stop massacre*, available at https://www.hrw.org/news/2014/07/02/dr-congo-army-un-failed-stop-massacre [accessed 13 December 2015]

Human Rights Watch, *Kosovo: poisoned by lead*, available at https://www.hrw.org/report/2009/06/23/kosovo-poisoned-lead/health-and-human-rights-crisis-mitrovicas-roma-camps [accessed 16 March 2016]

Human Rights Watch, *The fall of Srebrenica*, available at https://www.hrw.org/report/1995/10/15/fall-srebrenica-and-failure-un-peacekeeping/bosnia-and-herzegovina [accessed 16 March 2016]

ICRC, *Civilians bear the brunt of the changing nature of hostilities*, available at https://www.icrc.org/eng/resources/documents/interview/research-interview-240609.htm [accessed 6 January 2016]

ICRC, *Former Yugoslavia: Kuplensko: suffering at degree zero*, available at https://www.icrc.org/eng/resources/documents/misc/57jmng.htm [accessed 6 January 2016]

ICRC, *Wars without limits are wars without end*, available at https://www.icrc.org/en/document/wars-without-limits-are-wars-without-end [accessed 6 January 2016]

IFRC, *Emergency Assistance in Gašnici Camp, Croatia*, available at http://www.ifrc.org/docs/appeals/RPTS96/CROAT1.PDF [accessed 7 January 2016]

Independent, *British troops mete out rough justice to Serb snipers*, available at http://www.independent.co.uk/news/world/europe/british-troops-mete-out-rough-justice-to-serb-snipers-in-the-besieged-muslim-enclave-of-maglaj-1367943.html [accessed 30 March 2016]

Independent, *How Saddam Hussein's former military officers and spies are controlling Isis*, available at http://www.independent.co.uk/news/world/middle-east/how-saddam-husseins-former-military-officers-and-spies-are-controlling-isis-10156610.html [accessed 30 March 2016]

Independent, *Is life really worth living under king Babo?*, available at http://www.independent.co.uk/news/world/europe/is-life-really-worth-living-under-king-babo-its-all-gone-horribly-wrong-for-fikret-abdic-the-bosnian-1417047.html [accessed 30 March 2016]

Independent, *Margaret Thatcher's son Sir Mark*, available at http://www.independent.co.uk/news/people/margaret-thatchers-son-sir-mark-was-driven-by-greed-and-was-indulged-by-mother-new-biography-claims-a6679506.html [accessed 30 March 2016]

Independent, *Thatcher cancels visit*, available at http://www.independent.co.uk/news/thatches-cancels-visit-1456973.html [accessed 30 March 2016]

IndexHR, *Hrvatska odbila zahtjev BiH o procesuiranju bjegunca Jelavića*, available at http://www.index.hr/vijesti/clanak/hrvatska-odbila-zahtjev-bih-o-procesuiranju-bjegunca-jelavica-/944037.aspx [accessed 1 February 2017]

IndexHR, *Nestao prije 21 godina: Prosvjed u Mostaru zbog zataškavanja ubojstva general HVO-a Vlade Šantića*, available at http://www.index.hr/vijesti/clanak/nestao-prije-21-godinu-prosvjed-u-mostaru-zbog-zataskavanja-ubojstva-generala-hvoa-vlade-santica/879765.aspx [accessed 14 March 2016]

IndexHR, *Pročitajte Brijunske transkripte, glavni dokaz Haškog suda*, available at http://www.index.hr/vijesti/clanak/procitajte-brijunske-transkripte-glavni-dokaz-haskog-suda-/547318.aspx [accessed 15 December 2015]

International Journal of Peace Studies, *Economic Sanctions as a Foreign Policy Tool: the case of Yugoslavia*, available at http://www.gmu.edu/programs/icar/ijps/vol3_1/Delvic.htm [accessed 11 January 2016]

International Relations and Security Network, *Successful sanctions – Serbia and Montenegro 1992-1995*, available at http://www.isn.ethz.ch/Digital-Library/Articles/Special-Feature/Detail/?lng=en&id=154572&tabid=1453376834&contextid774=154572&contextid775=154574 [accessed 2 January 2016]

ITN Source, *Bosnia-Herzegovina: former enemies, Bosnian war veterans unite in protest over benefit cuts*, available at http://www.itnsource.com/shotlist/RTV/2012/03/20/RTV897112/?v=1 [accessed 10 January 2016]

Jerusalem Post, *Exposing Waldheim's Nazi past awakened Austrians*, available at http://www.jpost.com/Jewish-World/Jewish-Features/Exposing-Waldheims-Nazi-past-awakened-Austrians [accessed 3 May 2016]

Judah, Tim (2002), *Kosovo War and Revenge*, Yale University Press, New Haven

Jutarnji List, *Fikret Abdić Babo nako 17 godina i 34 dana vratio se u Kladušu*, available at http://www.jutarnji.hr/fikret-abdic-babo-nakon-17-godina-i-34-dana-dosao-u-kladusu--docekale-ga-tisuce-ljudi/1053401/ [accessed 22 February 2016]

Kajtazović, Sead "Tetin" (1996), *Paklena Dolina*, unpublished

Kenrick, Donald and Puxon, Grattan (1996), *Bibaxtale Berša*, Editorial Presencia Gitana, Madrid

Kolb, Robert (2014), *Advanced Introduction to International Humanitarian Law*, Edward Elgar Publishing Limited, Cheltenham

Kržišnik-Bukić, Vera (1996), *Bosanski Identitet*, Bosanska knjiga, Sarajevo

Kržišnik-Bukić, Vera (1991), *Cazinska Buna 1950*, Svjetlost, Sarajevo

Kržišnik-Bukić, Vera (1997), *Prilog Programu za Bosnu*, self published, Ljubljana

Lawrence, T.E. (1997), *Seven Pillars of Wisdom*, Wordsworth Editions, Ware

Le Carré, John (1963), *The Spy who came in from the Cold*, Planet Three Publishing Network Ltd, London

Le Monde Diplomatique, *Croatia's entry fee*, available at http://mondediplo.com/2013/07/09croatia [accessed 25 February 2016]

Lee, Ronald (2005), *Learn Romani*, University of Hertfordshire Press, Hatfield

LegalUN, *Rome statute of the International Criminal Court*, available at http://legal.un.org/icc/statute/99_corr/2.htm [accessed 13 August 2016]

Lieven, Anatol (1998), *Chechnya Tombstone of Russia Power*, Yale University Press, London

Los Angeles Times, *Serbian spy's trial lifts cloak on his CIA alliance*, available at http://articles.latimes.com/2009/mar/01/world/fg-serbia-spy-cia1 [accessed 13 August 2016]

MacAulay, Donald (1976), *Nua-Bhardachd Ghàidhlig*, Cannongate Classics, Edinburgh

Maclean, Fitzroy (1949), *Eastern Approaches*, Jonathan Cape, London

Maclean, Fitzroy (1980), *Josip Broz Tito*, Mladost, Zagreb

Malcolm, Noel (1994), *Bosnia, A Short History*, Macmillan, London

Malcolm, Noel (1998), *Kosovo, A Short History*, Macmillan, London

Malcolm, Noel (1996) "David Owen and his Balkan Bungling", *Bosnia Report*, no. 14, p. 5

Mark Curtis, *A covert war in Bosnia*, available at http://markcurtis.info/2016/10/11/a-covert-war-in-bosnia/ [accessed 23 February 2016]

Médecins Sans Frontières (2015), *MSF and the war in the former Yugoslavia*, MSF Speaks Out, Australia

Médecins Sans Frontières, *Syria: Our bombs are smarter than yours*, available at http://www.msf.org/article/syria-%E2%80%9Cour-bombs-are-smarter-yours%E2%80%9D [accessed 23 February 2016]

Médecins Sans Frontières (2014), *Violence against Kosovar Albanians, NATO's intervention 1998-1999*, MSF Speaks Out, Australia

Miljković, Zuhdija "Hope" (2014), *Krug smrti 1992-1995*, Grafis d.o.o., Velika Kladuša

Montefiore, Simon Sebag (2003), *Stalin, the Court of the Red Tsar*, Phoenix, London

Naša Stranka, *Kurtović: na mjestu sukoba osmanske i bosanske vojske*, available at http://www.nasastranka.ba/kurtovic-na-mjestu-sukoba-osmanske-i-bosanske-vojske-sda-slavi-pobjedu-osmanske-vojske/ [accessed 17 March 2016]

Nekrasov, Andrei and Konskaya, Olga, *Rebellion: the Litvinenko Case,* available at http://www.imdb.com/title/tt1038914/ [accessed 3 August 2017]

New York Times, *Alija Izetbegović, Muslim who led Bosnia, dies at 78*, available at http://www.nytimes.com/2003/10/20/world/alija-izetbegovic-muslim-who-led-bosnia-dies-at-78.html?pagewanted=all [accessed 6 January 2016]

New York Times, *Bosnia's elite force: Fed, Fit, Muslims*, available at http://www.nytimes.com/1995/06/16/world/bosnia-s-elite-force-fed-fit-muslim.html [accessed 17 February 2016]

New York Times, *New horror for Sarajevo*, available at http://www.nytimes.com/1993/10/31/world/new-horror-for-sarajevo-muslims-killing-muslims.html?pagewanted=all [accessed 17 February 2016]

Nezavisne novine, *Ko je Bilal Bosnić, vođa vehabija u BiH?*, available at http://www.nezavisne.com/novosti/hronika/Ko-je-Bilal-Bosnic-vodja-vehabija-u-BiH/261130 [accessed 14 December 2015]

Nezavisne novine, *Napadnut Dujo Šantić, sin nestalog generala HVO-a*, available at http://www.nezavisne.com/novosti/hronika/Napadnut-Dujo-Santic-sin-nestalog-generala-HVO-a/359267 [accessed 5 April 2016]

Orbus, *Tajna četverostrukog ubistva 20. jula 1993.g.*, available at http://www.orbus.be/aktua/2012/aktua3337.htm [accessed 5 April 2016]

Orwell, George (1949), *1984*, Penguin Books, London

Orwell, George (1986), *Burmese Days*, Penguin Books, London

Orwell, George (1962), *Homage to Catalonia*, Penguin Books, Harmondsworth

OSCE, *OSCE mission in Kosovo factsheet 2016*, available at http://www.osce.org/kosovo/143996 [accessed 5 April 2016]

Chronology of War, *Abdićevi policajci pucali u narod*, available at http://abunodisceomnes.wellcomecollection.org/wp-content/uploads/2015/03/Chronology-of-War-3-October-1993-Oslobodjenje-Press-Clippings-Source-Media-Center-15.pdf [accessed 5 April 2016]

O'Shea, Brendan (1998), *Crisis at Bihać*, Sutton Publishing Limited, Stroud

Otvorene Oči/Balkan Peace Team, *Special Report: February 3 1996*, available at http://www.peacebrigades.org/archive/bpt/bpt96-02.html [accessed 7 January 2016]

Owen, David (1995), *Balkan Odyssey*, Victor Gollanz, London

Perica, Vjekoslav (2002), *Balkan Idols*, Oxford University Press, Oxford

Pakenham, Thomas (1991), *The Scramble for Africa*, Avon Books, New York

PSE, *Absolute and overall poverty*, available at http://www.poverty.ac.uk/definitions-poverty/absolute-and-overall-poverty [accessed 16 March 2016]

Rieff, David (1995), *Slaughterhouse: Bosnia and the Failure of the West*, Touchstone, New York

Roberts, Andrew (2014), *Napoleon the Great*, Penguin Books, UK

Reuters, *In first census since war, Bosnia's "Others" threaten ethnic order*, available at http://www.reuters.com/article/us-bosnia-census-idUSBRE98Q0DT20130927 [accessed 2 July 2016]

Reuters, *Sarajevo gunman commits suicide after killing two soldiers*, available at http://www.reuters.com/article/us-bosnia-attacks-idUSKCN0T735520151119 [accessed 16 March 2016]

Sandler, Todd and Hartley, Keith (Eds) (2007), *Handbook of Defense Economics Volume 2*, North-Holland, Amsterdam

Savić, Svenka (2000), *Rromnja trajo purane Rromnjango ande Vojvodina*, Futura Publikacije, Novi Sad

Selimović, Meša (2005), *Magla i mjesečina*, Biblioteka Dani, Sarajevo

Selimović, Meša (2006), *Tišine*, Book-Marso, Belgrade

Selimović, Meša (1999), *Tvrđava*, Sarajevo-Publishing, Sarajevo

Silber, Laura and Little, Allan (1995), *The Death of Yugoslavia*, Penguin, London

Sky News, *Serb war crimes suspect refuses Hague return*, available at http://news.sky.com/story/1657384/serb-war-crimes-suspect-refuses-hague-return [accessed 16 March 2016]

Slobodan Praljak, *278*, available at http://www.slobodanpraljak.com/materijali/RATNI%20DOKUMENTI/IZBJEGLIC E%20IZ%20BIH%20U%20HRVATSKOJ/A-Dokumentacija/278.pdf [accessed 11 January 2016]

Slobodan Praljak, *326*, available at http://www.slobodanpraljak.com/materijali/RATNI%20DOKUMENTI/IZBJEGLIC E%20IZ%20BIH%20U%20HRVATSKOJ/A-Dokumentacija/326.pdf [accessed 7 September January 2016]

Sv-Luka.org, *Destruction of Christian churches and monasteries in Kosovo and Metohija*, available at http://www.sv-luka.org/Kosovo2000Part1.pdf [accessed 7 September January 2016]

Solženicin, Aleksandar (2009), *Arhipelag GULAG, 1918-1956*, Izdateljstvo Astrelj, Moscow

Somerset Maugham, W. (1953), *The Selected Novels, vol. II*, William Heineman Ltd, Melbourne

Spectator, *How the battle lines were drawn*, available at http://www.spectator.co.uk/2003/06/how-the-battle-lies-were-drawn/ [accessed 16 March 2016]

Stević, Rajko (Ed) (1995), *Ključ rješenja BiH krize*, Saniteks, Velika Kladuša

Telegraph, *Tito's top secret bunker in Bosnia*, available at http://www.telegraph.co.uk/news/picturegalleries/worldnews/11258143/Titos-top-secret-bunker-in-Bosnia-is-a-time-capsule-back-to-1950s-Yugoslavia.html [accessed 14 February 2016]

The Australian, *In his own words: memorable Mandela quotes*, available at http://www.theaustralian.com.au/in-depth/nelson-mandela/in-his-own-words-memorable-mandela-quotes/story-fn7qgt20-1226776864615 [accessed 17 July 2016]

The Wire, *If Albania took George W. Bush's watch, it also gave him a statue*, available at http://www.thewire.com/global/2011/07/george-w-bush-gains-statue-albanian-town-where-his-watch-disappeared/39701/ [accessed 17 March 2016]

Theremustbejustice, *Erdogan fulfilling his neo-Ottoman dream*, available at https://theremustbejustice.wordpress.com/2015/10/19/erdogan-fulfilling-his-neoottoman-dream-through-bosnia/ [accessed 23 December 2015]

Thomspon, Mark (1999), *Forging War*, University of Luton Press, Luton

Times of Israel, *Croatian president poses with pro-Nazi regime symbol*, available at http://www.timesofisrael.com/croatian-president-poses-with-pro-nazi-regime-symbol/ [accessed 28 November 2016]

Tolj, Ivan (Ed) (1996), *Domovinski Odgoj*, Ministarstvo Obrane Republike Hrvatske Politička Uprava, Zagreb

Trkulja, Petar and Božić, Borivoje (2008), *Crnaja oteta od zaborava*, Caligraph, Belgrade

Tusell, Javier (1996), *La Dictadura de Franco*, Ediciones Altaya S.A., Barcelona

Ulemek, Milorad (2016), *Babo*, MFK/MCF, Belgrade

Ulemek, Milorad (2013), *Staze Poraza*, Dinex export-import, Belgrade

UNHCR, *Lessons learned from the Rwanda and Burundi emergencies*, available at http://www.unhcr.org/3ae6bcfc4.html [accessed 17 January 2016]

UN security council, *Further Report on the situation of human rights in Croatia pursuant to security council resolution 1019 (1995)*, available at http://www.nato.int/ifor/un/u960823a.htm [accessed 7 January 2016]

UN security council, *Further Report on the situation of human rights in Croatia pursuant to security council resolution 1019 (1995)*, available at http://www.un.org/Docs/s1996109.htm [accessed 7 January 2016]

UN Economic and Social Council, *Report submitted by Ms Elizabeth Rehn*, available at https://www1.umn.edu/humanrts/commission/country52/63-yugos.htm [accessed 18 January 2016]

UN Economic and Social Council, *Eighth periodic report on the situation of human rights in the territory of the former Yugoslavia*, available at https://documents-dds-ny.un.org/doc/UNDOC/GEN/G94/133/86/PDF/G9413386.pdf?OpenElement [accessed 30 March 2016]

UN Economic and Social Council, *Final periodic report on the situation of human rights in the territory of the former Yugoslavia*, available at https://www1.umn.edu/humanrts/commission/country52/9-yug.htm [accessed 30 March 2016]

UN Economic and Social Council, *Tenth periodic report on the situation of human rights in the territory of the former Yugoslavia*, http://hrlibrary.umn.edu/commission/country51/57.htm [accessed 30 March 2016]

Van Selm, Joanne *et al* (Eds) (2003), *The Refugee Convention at Fifty*, Lexington Books, Lanham

Večernji List, *Balkanski lideri i državnici – svi proijeklom iz BiH*, available at http://www.vecernji.ba/balkanski-lideri-i-drzavnici-svi-porijeklom-iz-bih-1108856 [accessed 26 August 2016]

Večernji List, *Povukli film jer za zločin na Dvoru tereti HV*, available at http://www.vecernji.hr/hrvatska/povukli-film-15-minuta-masakr-u-dvoru-jer-za-zlocin-tereti-hrvatsku-vojsku-1065012 [accessed 3 April 2016]

Waller, Douglas (1998) "Mission Impossible", *Time,* vol. 151 no. 26, 6 July 1998

West, Rebecca (1942), *Black Lamb and Grey Falcon*, Macmillan, London

Wikileaks, *Deputy PM Tells A/S Shattuck GOC plans to repatriate Abdic Muslims*, available at https://wikileaks.org/plusd/cables/95ZAGREB3839_a.html [accessed 8 January 2016]

Wikipedia, *European Migrant Crisis*, available at https://en.wikipedia.org/wiki/European_migrant_crisis [accessed 29 January 2016]

Wikipedia, *Geography of Kosovo*, available at https://en.wikipedia.org/wiki/Geography_of_Kosovo [accessed 1 April 2016]

Zakon.hr, *Ustav Republike Hrvatske*, available at https://www.zakon.hr/z/94/Ustav-Republike-Hrvatske [accessed 6 November 2016]

ZapadnaBosna, *Podizanje optužnice protiv Dudakovića sve izvjesnija!*, available at https://zapadnabosna.info/2016/11/06/podizanje-optuznice-protiv-dudakovica-sve-izvjesnija/ [accessed 6 November 2016]

Zona Sumraka, *Opseda me duh pokojnog Maršala*, available at http://www.zonasumraka.net/opseda-me-duh-pokojnog-marsala-i-kaze-novi-tito-ce-se-pojaviti-do-kraja-godine-u-bosni-i-ujedinice-jugoslovenske-narode/ [accessed 12 July 2016]

Printed in Great Britain
by Amazon